FEDERAL CORPORATE TAXATION

SEVENTH EDITION

By

HOWARD E. ABRAMS
Professor of Law
Emory University

RICHARD L. DOERNBERG
Professor Emeritus
Emory University

DON A. LEATHERMAN
Professor of Law
University of Tennessee

CONCEPTS AND INSIGHTS SERIES ®

FOUNDATION PRESS

© 1987, 1990, 1995, 1998, 2002, 2008 FOUNDATION PRESS
© 2013 by LEG, Inc. d/b/a West Academic Publishing

610 Opperman Drive
St. Paul, MN 55123
1-800-313-9378

Printed in the United States of America

ISBN: 978–1–60930–052–4

Mat #41181365

PREFACE

This book is aimed at students taking a course in corporate taxation. We hope it will serve to aid and to enrich students' understanding of what is unquestionably dense and difficult statutory material. Because the focus of the book is on corporation taxation, little attention is paid to those topics normally covered in an individual tax course. Accordingly, the tax consequences of day-to-day corporate operations (e.g., what constitutes income, what is deductible under § 162, depreciation methods) are not emphasized.

As the tax system in general and the corporate tax provisions specifically reach greater heights (or depths) of complexity, it becomes more important than ever to understand the framework of the system—the big picture. Failure to do so will condemn a student to a purgatory of isolated rules, seemingly unconnected to one another. Even with a framework, the intricacies can be overwhelming. This book is purposely noncomprehensive: it is not a treatise. Our goal is to find and contemplate the forest rather than each tree. On the other hand, if we avoid all the trees, we would not know much about the forest.

We have tried to look at corporate tax through a variety of perspectives. Where appropriate, historical and economic analyses are offered. But much of what follows is a search for an internal logic and consistency in the corporate tax system itself: given the goals of a corporate tax structure, how do the rules implement those goals. The internal logic, or lack thereof, is what many students find appealing about the study of tax. In order to keep the book manageable in length, there are places where we can do no more than introduce intriguing ideas tangential to the subject at hand.

This book takes a "cradle-to-grave" approach to corporate taxation. We believe that this presentation is easiest for students. We also have no doubt that other approaches are equally worthwhile. With that in mind, we have tried to make each chapter stand alone so that the chapters can be read out of order. For example, Chapter 1 dealing with some policy questions will perhaps make more sense if it is read at the end of the book. Chapter 2 considers the formation or birth of a corporation—§ 351 and related provisions. Chapter 3 then looks at a collection of issues relating to the operation of a corporation once formed. Matters such as tax rates, the minimum tax, capital structure and the corporation as an entity are discussed. Chapters 4 through 7 deal with nonliquidating distributions: dividends, redemptions, stock dividends, and preferred stock bailouts. In Chapter 8, liquidation of a corporation is the subject. Chapters 9 through 11 focus on corporate acquisitions. Chapter 9 addresses taxable acquisitions, while Chapter 10 considers tax-free reorganizations. In Chapter 11, the carryover of tax attributes in both taxable and nontaxable corporate acquisitions is explored. The final two chapters are concerned with subjects that are covered in some basis corporate tax courses but not in others. Chapter 12 explains the corporate penalty provisions while Chapter 13–15 dissect the intricacies of subchapter S.

While this is not a casebook, leading cases are discussed and cited where they are helpful to the discussion. Throughout the book, we have liberally cited to the Code and regulations. We believe that it is the ability to read and understand the Code that will make the study of corporate taxation a joyous occasion. Indeed, it is probably wise to show your ambidextrous talent by reading this book simultaneously with the Code.

In short, we hope that this primer will help students solve or at least understand some of the wondrous mysteries of corporate taxation. Many of you were hooked on tax by your individual tax course. We hope to sink the hook deeper.

This book is current through February 28, 2013.

HOWARD E. ABRAMS
DON A. LEATHERMAN

February 2013

TABLE OF CONTENTS

FEDERAL CORPORATE TAXATION

SEVENTH EDITION

Chapter 1

THE CORPORATE DOUBLE TAX

1.01 Introduction and History

We have had a corporate income tax continuously since 1909, longer than we have had a personal income tax. Before enactment of the sixteenth amendment in 1913, the Supreme Court upheld the 1909 corporate tax as a valid excise tax imposed on businesses exercising the privilege of operating in corporate form.[1] With the passage of the sixteenth amendment, the constitutional foundation of the corporate income tax became secure whether characterized as an excise tax or as an income tax.

Most rules of corporate taxation are found in Subchapter C.[2] The subchapter's basic premise is that a corporation should be a taxpayer distinct from its shareholders. Form this premise follows the central feature of corporate taxation: the double tax on corporate profits. The first tax on corporate profits is imposed at the corporate level when profits are earned by a corporation. The second tax is imposed at the shareholder level when these profits are distributed by the corporation to its shareholders. Because the distributing corporation cannot deduct amounts distributed as dividends, the over-all effect of this system of taxation is to impose a double tax on distributed corporate profits.

Early on, the Supreme Court dealt the double tax a body blow. It considered whether a corporation recognized gain when it distributed appreciated property to a shareholder. Although the government argued that the corporation should recognize gain on the distribution as if the property had been sold, the Court concluded that no gain or loss was recognized at the corporate-level.

---

[1] *Flint v. Stone Tracy Co.*, 220 U.S. 107 (1911). In *Pollock v. Farmers' Loan & Trust Co.*, 158 U.S. 601 (1895), the Supreme Court invalidated the federal personal income tax as a direct tax requiring apportionment under article 1, clause 9 of the Constitution. As part of that early decision the Court also invalidated a corporate income tax too intertwined with the personal income tax to stand on its own.

[2] Sections 301 through 386 comprise subchapter C (corporate distributions and adjustments) of Chapter 1 (normal taxes and surtaxes) of subtitle A (income taxes) of title 26 [the Internal Revenue Code] of the United States Code. Note that the Internal Revenue Code is divided into a number of "subtitles," each subtitle into "chapters," each chapter into "subchapters," and each subchapter into "parts." Thus, the study of the code is something like the study of living organisms, with species replaced by parts, genus replaced by subchapters, and so on.

This rule, known as the *General Utilities* doctrine,[3] opened the door to avoidance of the corporate-level tax, allowing corporations to distribute appreciated assets in anticipation of sale. The *General Utilities* doctrine and the congressional attempts to circumscribe its potential for abuse influenced much of the development of subchapter C.

Beginning in 1969, Congress began to erode the *General Utilities* doctrine, with its substantial repeal made part of the Tax Reform Act of 1986. Much of subchapter C has changed as a result, including not only the taxation of distributions but also the taxation of asset sales before liquidating distributions and the taxation of purchases of stock of one corporation by a second corporation. Critics of the *General Utilities* doctrine long argued that its repeal would simplify the Code. In theory they probably are right, but you will have to decide for yourself whether the congressional treatment of the repeal brought simplicity or new complexity.

Historically, distributed corporate profits were taxed as ordinary income to the shareholders. However, gain from the sale of corporate stock always has been treated as capital gain. Because the increase in value of corporate stock often reflects corporate profits that have not been distributed,[4] a shareholder wishing to obtain his share of the corporation's profits while avoiding ordinary income could sell his stock before the corporation declared a dividend. In fact, in many circumstances the shareholder could sell his stock back to the issuing corporation and still qualify for capital gains treatment.[5] This relative favoritism of undistributed corporate profits taxed as capital gain as compared with distributed profits taxed as ordinary income has motivated many a taxpayer to avoid dividends in favor of other, less direct ways of obtaining corporate earnings.[6]

You may be surprised to discover that you already know many of the rules governing the taxation of corporations. Corporations determine their gross income like other taxpayers. See § 61. Thus, rents, royalties and interest are taxable to corporations just as to non-corporate taxpayers, as are gains from the sale or exchange of property. Similarly, corporations may deduct their ordinary and necessary business expenses under § 162, their interest payments

---

[3] See Section 4.04 *infra*.

[4] Stock appreciation can result from market revaluation of the corporation's future prospects, from realized but undistributed corporate profits, and from unrealized appreciation in corporate assets.

[5] See Chapter 5 *infra*.

[6] Since 2003, however, "qualified" dividends paid to individuals have been taxed at the same rate as long-term capital gain. *See* § 1(h)(11).

under § 163, and their losses under § 165. The concern of subchapter C—and the concern of this book—is not on the various rules applicable to corporate and non-corporate taxpayers alike but rather on those rules applicable uniquely to corporations and their shareholders. For the most part, these rules concern the transactions between a corporation and its shareholders.

1.02 Revenue Effects

The corporate tax raises substantial revenue, in round figures about $228 billion per year,[7] or a little more than 22 percent of the revenue raised by the individual income tax. Relatively few corporate returns are filed, though, with individual returns numbering about 143 million per year as compared with about 1.8 million corporate returns.[8] The highest corporate tax rate is 35 percent.[9]

There is a second sense in which we have more than one corporate income tax, for there is the regular income tax and the alternative minimum tax. Discussed more fully elsewhere,[10] the alternative minimum tax is intended to ensure that profitable companies pay some federal tax even if they structure their investments to exploit every tax incentive in the Code. While not a substantial revenue raiser, the alternative minimum tax may respond to a widespread concern that wealthy taxpayers and large corporations are able to avoid paying their fair share of the federal tax burden.

1.03 The Incidence of the Corporate Tax

Because the corporate tax raises, both absolutely and relatively, a substantial amount of revenue, it is reasonable to ask who ends up paying the corporate income tax. By "paying the tax" we do not mean who "tenders payment to the taxing authority" but rather who bears the economic burden of the tax, who is worse off by reason of that particular tax having to be paid.

---

[7] These figures are for taxable years ending in 2008. Note that over $200 billion of that tax was paid by corporations filing consolidated returns. Data on the number of returns filed, the amount of taxes paid, and a host of other tax-related information is publicly available from the Internal Revenue Service on its web page (http://www.irs.gov) and is published on the Statistics of Income Bulletin.

[8] This number excludes returns for S corporations, regulated investment companies, and real estate investment trusts.

[9] §11(b)(1)(D) (ignoring the surtax in the final flush language of §11(b)(1); *see* Section 3.01 *infra.*

[10] See Section 3.01 *infra.*

To see the difference between the nominal payor of a tax and the party bearing the burden of the tax, consider the sales tax imposed under state law on most purchases of tangible goods. Suppose a hot dog vendor at an amusement park sells delectable hot dogs for $1.00 apiece and charges no sales tax. One day, the vendor is told that he must remit four cents per dog to the state. If he changes his sign to read: "Hot Dogs: $1.00, tax included," and if you buy one dog, who ends up paying the tax?

Phrased differently, have you paid $0.96 for the hot dog plus $0.04 in tax, or did you pay $1.00 for the hot dog and the vendor paid the tax? To begin to answer this question, you must ask another: If no sales tax had been imposed, how much would you have paid for the hot dog? If the answer is $1.00, you have not paid the tax because, *tax or no tax*, you would be out the full $1.00.[11] Rather, it seems to be the vendor who has paid the tax because, *but for the tax*, he would have the full $1.00 to keep.

On the other hand, suppose the vendor changes his sign to read: "Hot Dogs: $1.00, plus tax." If you now purchase a hot dog, it is you and not the vendor who bears the burden of the tax because it is you who is worse off because of the tax.[12]

Return to the first example where the hot dog costs $1.00 including tax, and assume that you paid no part of the tax. Does that mean that the full burden of the tax landed squarely on the shoulders of the vendor? Not necessarily, because the vendor may have offset the tax by cutting his employee's pay or reducing the amount paid to the supplier of the hot dogs, buns, or condiments. In other words, the vendor may have passed the tax on to his employee or suppliers, who would have borne and thus effectively paid the tax.

Where a tax ultimately lands is referred to as the "incidence" of the tax. As the above example demonstrates, the incidence of a tax may be hard to discover and is dependent on the business relations among large numbers of people. In the example, it is dependent on the price customers are willing to pay for hot dogs, on the wages that the vendor's employee is willing to accept, on the profit margins of the vendor and his suppliers, and probably on a variety of other items such as the effect of the tax on the cotton candy distributor and other competitors of the hot dog vendor. Indeed, because

---

[11] This analysis assumes that the vendor has not changed the size or quality of the hot dog, reduced the number of available condiments, limited the availability of napkins, or in any other way reduced the value of his product.

[12] Perhaps the most likely response by the vendor to the tax is to change the price of his dogs to 99 cents plus tax, in which case only part of the tax is shifted to consumers.

the soft drink vendor may suffer if fewer hot dogs are sold, some of the burden of the tax may, indirectly, be felt by vendors not in competition with the one on whom the tax nominally is laid.

In general, the incidence of a tax nominally paid by one person will be divided in some proportion between the nominal payor and the persons with whom he deals.[13] In particular, the incidence of the tax need not (and usually will not) fall on any one person but may be shared in seemingly arbitrary ways. The customer might in effect bear one cent of the tax, the vendor one-half of one cent, and the remainder by the condiment supplier. Or the incidence might be entirely different depending on the ways in which the various economic actors in this little play adjust their relationships to account for the tax.[14]

Where is the incidence of the corporate tax? One thing that can be said without qualification is that *no* part of the corporate tax is borne by corporations: corporations do not bear taxes, only people do. A corporation is simply a nexus of contracts between individuals—shareholders, creditors, suppliers, customers, employees, etc. To be sure, it may be that the corporation's treasury is depleted because of a certain tax, and for that reason the equity owners of the corporation may be worse off by reason of the tax. In such a case, the incidence of the tax is on the corporation's shareholders (or perhaps its creditors), not on the corporation. On the other hand, it could be that a tax nominally paid by the corporation is shifted from the equity owners to the corporation's employees or suppliers. If so, we say that the tax has been shifted "backward." Conversely, the corporation may raise its price to cover the tax, in which case we say that the tax has been shifted "forward" to the corporation's customers.[15]

Can we determine empirically how the corporate tax is shifted around? The answer, as of now, is no—the task is simply beyond our means. Studies have been conducted and have suggested where the incidence might lie, but unfortunately these studies often con-

---

[13] See J. Pechman, Who Paid the Taxes, 1966–85, at 24–31 (1985); Harberger, *The Incidence of the Corporation Income Tax,* 70 J.Pol. Econ. 215 (1962).

[14] Economists use the term "elasticity" to describe the extent to which a change in price or other factor affects economic behavior. With the proper definitions, the concept of "elasticity" can be quantified in such a way that predictions can be made regarding, for example, the incidence of a tax.

[15] More accurately, raising the price of its product will not shift the tax fully forward unless the quantity of goods sold by the corporation does not change despite the price increase. Since quantity demanded usually falls as price rises, the price increase will fail to fully offset the tax, leaving some of it to be borne by the corporation's investors or shifted backward to its employees.

flict and even the best can only suggest possible answers.[16] It may be that someday the economists will have a good answer to this question, but that day is not yet here.

In trying to determine the incidence of the corporate tax, it is helpful to break down the problem into two smaller problems. First, who bears a tax immediately after it is imposed and before most individuals and companies can modify their behavior to account for the tax? That is, who bears the tax *in the short run*? Second, who bears the tax after sufficient time has passed to allow for adjustments to the tax; that is, who bears the tax *in the long run*?

It may seem as if only the long run is relevant to the corporate tax because the corporate tax has been around a long time. Although it is true that we have had some corporate tax since 1909, we have had the current form of that tax only a short while: the corporate tax, like the individual tax, is changed by Congress almost annually in ways great and small.[17]

The various changes that Congress makes affect the incidence of the corporate tax. The short run effects of these changes can be substantial, substantial enough at times to warrant special transition rules intended to mitigate the costs of adjusting to the tax changes.[18] To frame the appropriate *transition rules*, one must predict short-run effects of legislation.

The short-run effect of increasing the corporate income tax should be to reduce the wealth of equity owners of corporations. If corporations are engaging in activities that maximize their profitability prior to the tax increase, the effect of the increase will be to lower the corporations' profits. Those holding residual interests in the corporations should be the first to suffer as a result.

Over the long-run, corporations will change their behavior in ways that minimize the effect of the tax increase on corporate profitability, including sometimes by shifting profits to lower-tax

---

[16] See generally Jensen & Miller, *Corporate Tax Burden on Labor: Theory and Empirical Evidence*, 131 Tax Notes 1083 (June 6, 2011); J. Pechman, Federal Tax Policy 135–40 (4th ed. 1983); Klein, *The Incidence of the Corporation Income Tax: A Lawyer's View of a Problem in Economics*, 1965 Wis.L.Rev. 576.

[17] See Doernberg & McChesney, *On the Accelerating Rate and Decreasing Durability of Tax Reform*, 71 Minn.L.Rev. 913 (1987).

[18] See generally Graetz, *Legal Transitions: The Case for Retroactivity in Income Tax Revision*, 126 U.Pa.L.Rev. 47 (1977); Shachar, *From Income to Consumption: Criteria for Rules of Transition*, 97 Harv.L.Rev. 1581 (1984); Abrams, *Rethinking Tax Transitions: A Reply to Dr. Shachar*, 98 Harv.L.Rev. 1809 (1985); Kaplow, *An Economic Analysis of Legal Transitions*, 99 Harv.L.Rev. 509 (1986).

jurisdictions. Investors also will change their behavior, investing in corporations that best adapt to the new economic climate or investing in non-corporate enterprises. As investment capital is redeployed away from the corporate sector, average returns from corporate and non-corporate investments should tend to equalize. Thus, the burden of the corporate tax may be shifted to all investment capital, corporate and non-corporate alike.

Under some circumstances, investors may reduce the aggregate amount invested in all business enterprises, with a concomitant increase in personal consumption. Thus, the corporate tax may have a negative impact on the aggregate amount of savings in this country. Because of the variety of these possible long-run responses, estimation of long-run effects is considerably more complex than estimation of the short-run effects. All we can know for sure is that people—not corporations—pay the corporate income tax.

1.04 Integrating the Corporate and Individual Income Taxes

Having seen that no one knows—or probably can know—which taxpayers actually bear the corporate income tax, what can we say about the legitimacy of the tax itself? It is of course within congressional power to levy a corporate tax, but does it make sense to do so?

The federal income tax primarily raises revenue—revenue used to pay for the federal government's various expenditures. The incidence of the income taxes accordingly determines in large measure the way in which the cost of government is divided. Reasonable people can differ over how that cost should be allocated.[19] Some argue that the cost of government should be spread among taxpayers in proportion to income, taxing all economic receipts at a single, flat rate. Others argue that taxpayers with substantial disposable income have a greater ability to pay and so should be taxed more heavily; that is, they argue in favor of a progressive income tax.

Can the corporate income tax satisfy anyone's notion of fairness? It may be that the corporate income tax is borne by the very wealthy, thereby satisfying at least those in favor of a "soak the rich" philosophy of taxation. It also could be that it falls primarily on consumers of corporate goods—that is, it falls on everyone—and so is reasonably consistent with flat rate taxation. The problem is, of course, that no one knows for sure and so no one can be satisfied.

---

[19] Reasonable people also can differ over the ideal level of government expenditure, but the allocation issue exists for any level of government expenditure.

Additional arguments can and have been raised against the corporate income tax. As we shall see, the tax encourages corporations to raise capital as debt rather than equity, arguably causing undue loan defaults and corporate bankruptcies. Also, to the extent that the corporate tax is not shifted forward or backward, it is borne by shareholders of profitable corporations, disproportionately by shareholders of the most profitable ones. If so, it will have the unfortunate effect of making inefficient producers competitive with their more efficient rivals to the detriment of consumers generally.

Why does Congress not eschew corporate taxation entirely, taxing only individuals?[20] Congress can levy the individual income tax using flat rates, progressive rates, or any other way it desires.[21] By using an increased individual income tax in lieu of a corporate tax, the tax burden can be targeted more accurately. Does this suggest that the corporate tax is a low-cost tax from the legislator's perspective: revenue can be raised without particular taxpayers knowing—and complaining—that they are paying the tax?

If Congress wanted to eliminate the corporate income tax, what should it do? The answer, it turns out, is more difficult than first meets the eye, at least if the individual income tax rates are progressive. Suppose for example that Congress repealed the corporate income tax, making all corporations completely tax-exempt.

Taxpayer B wants to invest $100 in a taxable bond paying 8 percent per year for 20 years. If B purchases this bond directly, he will receive $8.00 of income for 20 years. If B is in the 28-percent bracket, his after-tax annual return will be 5.76 percent. Assuming that B can reinvest his after-tax returns in some other investment paying 8 percent per year, B will have $306.50 after 20 years.

On the other hand, suppose that B invests $100 in a corporation, and the corporation then purchases the bond. Assuming that the corporation receives $8.00 per year on the bond, and assuming also that the corporation can reinvest the bond interest in some other investment paying 8 percent per year, the corporation will have $466.10 after 20 years.[22] If that amount is distributed to B, he then will be taxed on a gain of $366.10, producing a tax liability of

---

[20] See generally Joshua Mishkin, *The State of Integration in a Partial Integration State*, 59 Tax Law. 1047 (2006).

[21] Of course, if the corporate tax is eliminated, the individual income tax (or some other tax) must be increased to raise the same aggregate revenue.

[22] Of that amount, $366.10 will be interest and $100.00 will be B's initial principal.

$102.51.[23] After paying his federal income taxes, B will be left with a total of $363.59.

How is it that B ends up with substantially more ($363.59 compared to $306.50) by having the corporation to make the investment? By using the corporation, B has avoided the periodic imposition of tax on the bond interest, instead paying a tax only when that interest income is removed from corporate solution. In this example, B has managed to defer taxes on year one's interest for 19 years, on year two's interest for 18 years, and so on. The total value of that deferral for B ends up worth $57.09, or more than half the amount of B's original investment.

As this example shows, simply abolishing the corporate-level income tax without making additional changes to the individual income tax would give taxpayers a significant opportunity to lower their effective tax if they could afford to keep profits in corporate solution. Indeed, given the basis rule of § 1014 (which provides a fair market value basis for property, including stock, passing through the estate of a decedent), a taxpayer who invested in corporate form and held the stock until death would avoid all taxation of gain earned by the corporation. To eliminate those deferral possibilities, corporate profits must be taxed annually.

To tax corporate profits annually without imposing a double tax, one might impose only a corporate-level tax on corporate profits. That is, the corporate-level tax would be retained but the shareholder-level tax on distributed corporate profits would be eliminated. Done in this manner, the corporate-level tax serves as a withholding tax on the income of the shareholders. This corporate income tax, coupled with the elimination of the shareholder income tax on distributed profits, seemingly would eliminate the double tax without creating deferral opportunities.

For example, suppose that X Corp. is wholly owned by individual B. If X has profits of $100 and those profits are taxed immediately to X at B's tax rate, the tax imposed on X is a complete substitute for an immediate tax on B. Thus, if B's tax rate is 28 percent, X will pay $28 in taxes and will have $72 to distribute. If that entire amount is distributed tax-free to B, it is just as if B were distributed the full $100 and then B were taxed on that amount.

While coupling a corporate-level tax with tax-free receipt of dividends by shareholder will at times eliminate the double tax, under some circumstances the double tax will remain. Consider the

---

[23] B's stock basis equals $100 so that his gain under § 1001(a) will be $366.10. At a tax rate of 28%, B's tax liability is $102.51.

case of X Corp. formed by individual B with cash of $100. The incorporation is tax-free to both X and B,[24] and B takes a basis in the X Corp. stock of $100.

Assume that X invests the $100 in some asset that appreciates during the first year to $150. Assuming that X retains the asset, no tax will yet be due because unrealized gains are not taxable to corporations just as they are not taxable to individuals. B's stock should now be worth $150 because it represents the entire ownership of a corporation with assets of $150.

What if B now sells his stock for $150? B will have a taxable gain under § 1001 equal to the excess of the amount realized, or $150, over B's adjusted basis in his stock, or $100. Thus, B is taxed on the sale on the appreciation of the asset held by X. Of course, if X now sells its asset for fair market value of $150, X also will recognize a gain of $50. Thus, both individual B and X Corp. end up taxed on the appreciation of corporate assets. The double tax remains![25]

It remains because we eliminated the double tax on *distributed* corporate profits but left intact the shareholder-level tax on *undistributed* profits, a tax incurred whenever a shareholder sells appreciated stock. If we are to eliminate all vestiges of the shareholder-level tax, we must provide not only that dividends can be received tax-free but also that gains from the sale or exchange of stock will be ignored.

Will this change eliminate the double tax without creating new problems? To see that it does not, we need to step back at bit and view the problem from a broader perspective. Ignoring for the moment all problems of valuation, the corporate tax could be eliminated by requiring shareholders to include corporate profits on their individual returns as earned at the corporate level whether distributed or not.

Suppose that this complete integration of the corporate and individual taxes were enacted when all income was subject to a flat tax, say of 28 percent. Consider the case of X Corp. having 3 equal shareholders. If X has $300,000 of taxable income, each shareholder

---

[24] See §§ 351(a) (shareholder's taxation), 1032 (corporation's taxation) and 358 (shareholder's basis in stock received). See generally Chapter 2 *infra.*

[25] This problem would be avoided if the gain recognized by B increased X's adjusted basis in its assets. Compare § 743(b) applying such an approach to partnerships and the sale of partnership interests. The basis adjustment provided by § 743(b) is elective in the partnership setting, and when elected it introduces substantial complexities into the partnership's tax computations (such as recomputing depreciation schedules).

would report $100,000 of tax on his individual return, increasing his tax liability by $28,000.

As we have seen, the government could obtain the same revenue without imputing the corporation's profits to its shareholders by simply taxing the corporation itself at the shareholders' rate. Thus, the corporation would pay a tax of $84,000, precisely equal to the sum paid by all three shareholders under the imputation scheme. Of course, the shareholders would pay no further taxes when the profits were distributed because they were already taxed (implicitly) when the profits were earned. A corporate-level tax operates as a proxy for a shareholder-level tax so long as the corporation's tax rate equals that of the shareholders.

Unfortunately, there is no single tax rate for shareholders. If we tax corporate profits at the highest individual rate, then we are implicitly over-taxing those shareholders whose individual incomes (including their share of corporate profits) would put them in some lower bracket. In particular, corporations owned fully or in part by tax-exempt organizations will be dramatically over-taxed (at least on passive income), because the proper corporate-level tax allocable to such shareholders is zero.

If we tax corporations at some lower rate, then we offer a windfall to corporations (and through them to their investors) having shareholders in the highest bracket. In other words, complete integration of the corporate and individual income taxes cannot be achieved in a system having multiple tax brackets without imputing corporate profits to shareholders.

Is such imputation feasible? Possibly—it is done for subchapter S corporations and partnerships, even for partnerships with hundreds of partners.[26] However, except as to the simplest partnerships in which every partner has a fixed share of all items of income and loss, allocating the partnership tax items among partners having varying interests in the partnership (as common and preferred shareholders have varying interests in their corporation) is complicated.[27]

---

[26] Several European nations including Germany, France and the United Kingdom employ imputation systems where shareholders have received a tax credit for taxes paid at the corporate level. Cf. Department of the Treasury, *Integration of the Individual and Corporate Tax Systems* (Jan. 1992) (in which Treasury recommended a comprehensive business tax system under which all business income would be taxed and the business owners would receive a credit for the business tax).

[27] For an idea of this complexity, see Regs. § 1.704–1(b).

Alternatively, we might tax shareholders on the annual change in value of their shares.[28] This approach taxes shareholders on their share of corporate profits and on their share of unrealized appreciation in corporate assets, since both recognized profits and unrealized asset appreciation should increase share value.

Consider the case of corporations traded over a major securities exchange. We could require each shareholder to value his stock at the beginning and at the end of the year. The difference between those two values, plus all amounts distributed to the shareholder during the year as dividends, would constitute the shareholder's allocable portion of the corporation's realized and unrealized income (or loss).

Unfortunately, for many corporations this system cannot be easily implemented. There is no active market for the stock of most closely-held corporations, eliminating annual valuation as a serious possibility. In addition, annual taxation of stock value changes effectively repeals the realization doctrine for corporate securities. Unless a move were made to eliminate the realization doctrine generally, eliminating it only with respect to stocks raises troubling questions of tax equity as the financial markets respond to such a dramatic change.

In recognition of these and other difficulties,[29] some tax theoreticians have argued in favor of *dividend relief* rather than complete integration. Under this proposal, a corporate tax is imposed but with a deduction provided for dividend distributions.[30] The effect is to tax undistributed corporate profits at the corporate rate while taxing distributed profits at the shareholders' ordinary income tax rates.

The charts that follow compare both complete integration and dividend relief with the classical, double tax system. The comparison assumes that $1,000 is invested in a corporation for 10 years, and that the corporation earns 10 percent per year on its capital. In Chart 1–1, it is assumed that the corporate profits are retained by the corporation for the entire 10 years and then distributed in com-

---

[28] See Joseph Bankman, *A Market-Value Based Corporate Income Tax Approach*, 68 Tax Notes 1347 (Sept. 11, 1995) (advocating such an approach).

[29] Another problem that must be faced in trying to integrate the individual and corporate income taxes is that the character of corporate-level income and deductions must be preserved. This issue includes the distinction between ordinary income and capital gains but expands well beyond it. For a partial list of the items posing this characterization problem, see §§ 702(a) (partnerships), 1366(b) (S corporations).

[30] Deductibility provides an incentive for corporations to distribute earnings, something many corporate managers may oppose.

plete liquidation of the corporation. In Chart 1–2, it is assumed that the profits are distributed annually and that the shareholder earns 10 percent on his reinvested dividends. Chart 1–3 repeats the comparison of Chart 1–2 with debt replacing equity as the shareholder's investment under the classical, double tax system. In all cases it is assumed that the corporate tax rate is 35 percent, that the individual tax rate is 40 percent on ordinary income, 20 percent on capital gains and dividends, and that the corporation liquidates after 10 years.[31]

Chart 1–1
Full Retention

	After-Tax Return to Shareholder[32]	Annual Return
No Taxes Imposed	$1,594	10.0%
Complete Integration	791	6.0%
Dividend Relief	702	5.5%
Classical Double Tax	702	5.5%

Chart 1–2
Full Distribution With Equity

	After-Tax Return to Shareholder	Annual Return
No Taxes Imposed	$1,594	10.0%
Complete Integration	791	6.0%
Dividend Relief	791	6.0%
Classical Double Tax	685	5.4%

Chart 1–3
Full Distribution With Debt

	After-Tax Return to Shareholder	Annual Return
No Taxes Imposed	$1,594	10.0%
Complete Integration	791	6.0%
Dividend Relief	791	6.0%
Classical Double Tax	791	6.0%

---

[31] We additionally assume that the corporation and the shareholder each receive a 10% annual return on investments. Note that the maximum individual tax rate is currently 39.6% and, disregarding § 1411, the maximum individual rate on long-term capital gains and qualified dividend income is 20%. Note as well in computing the return in a complete integration regime, dividends are not taxed, while dividends are taxed at the ordinary income tax rate in the dividend relief regime.

[32] As of the end of year 10, excluding the initial investment of $1,000.

What can we learn from these charts? First and not surprisingly, under a system of complete integration, the taxpayer's after-tax return equals 6.0 percent, his pre-tax return of 10 percent less his taxes of 40 percent.[33] Thus, he is taxed just as if the investment had been made individually and not through his corporation.

Dividend relief produces the same result as complete integration only when the corporation distributes its profits annually.[34] This result makes sense because dividend relief system taxes the shareholders on distributed corporate profits and taxes the corporation on undistributed profits. Accordingly, if there are no undistributed corporate profits, dividend relief eliminates the corporate tax as fully as does complete integration.

Chart 1–3 illustrates that the corporate interest deduction under current law goes a long way in the direction of dividend relief. Because interest payments are deductible to the corporation while dividend distributions are not, corporations can reduce their tax liability by raising debt capital in preference to equity capital. In certain instances, the Commissioner has asserted that corporate investments labeled debt by the corporation and its investors should be treated as equity. This issue, the debt/equity issue, is explored more fully in Chapter 3.

The consequences under a classical double tax system depend not only on whether the corporation retains or distributes its profits (see line 4 in Charts 1–1 and 1–2) but also on the interplay between the corporate tax rate on ordinary income, the individual tax rate on ordinary dividend income, and the individual tax rate on capital gain. When all corporate profits are retained until final liquidation, the investment's annual return of 10% is taxed each year at the corporate rate of 35% and then in year ten at the individual capital gain rate of 20% because the corporate profits are then distributed to the shareholder in complete liquidation of the corporate venture. Thus, the corporation will have $1877.14 after 10 years,[35] and that amount will be distributed to the shareholder, producing a taxable gain of $877.14.[36] This yields a tax liability of $175.43,[37] leaving the shareholder with an after-tax profit of $701.71.

---

[33] See the second line of each Chart.

[34] Compare lines two and three of Chart 1–1 with lines two and three of Chart 1–2.

[35] The corporation has an after-tax return on its investments of 6.5%, and $1000 compounded at 6.5% for 10 years equals $1877.14.

[36] The amount distributed to the shareholder will be $1,877.14, and the shareholder's adjusted basis in the stock surrendered equals $1,000, leaving a taxable gain of $877.14.

If the corporation distributes its after-tax profits annually, the shareholder will receive $65.00 from the corporation each year, and that dividend distribution will be subject to the shareholder's individual tax rate on qualified dividends of 20%, leaving only $52 for the shareholder to spend or invest.[38] We assume that the shareholder invests the after-tax distributions in some non-corporate vehicle paying 10% per year, so the shareholder receives an after-tax return from this non-corporate investment of 6.0% per year, (*i.e.*, the 10% investment return minus the shareholder's 40% tax on ordinary income). Thus, after 10 years, the shareholder will have received 10 dividends in the after-tax amount of $52.00 each as well as compounded interest on those reinvested dividends. While the distributed corporate profits are subject each year to a double tax at an aggregate 48% rate,[39] the compounded earnings on the dividends are taxed only at the individual tax rate on ordinary income of 40%.[40] Accordingly, the shareholder's total tax burden will be somewhere between 40% and 48%, and in fact it turns out to be 46%. In other words, because the shareholder's investment over the 10 years is partially made in corporate form and partially made individually, the return on the shareholder's initial investment is determined by a blending of the tax burdens imposed on corporate and non-corporate investments. With the assumptions underlying Chart 1–2, that blended rate is 46%.

Let us reconsider the classical double tax system with full retention of profits as compared with full distribution of profits, but this time we will assume that the individual tax rate on ordinary income and the individual tax rate on capital gains equals the corporate tax rate of 35%. Under this new assumption, we get the following results:

Chart 1–4
Classical Corporate Double Tax

	After-Tax Return to Shareholder	Annual Return
Full Retention	$570	4.6%
Full Distribution With Equity	570	4.6%

---

[37] The taxable gain of $877.14 is taxed at the capital gain rate of 20%, yielding a tax liability of $175.43.

[38] That $52.00 amount equals the $65.00 distribution minus a $13.00 tax (20% of $65.00).

[39] The corporate tax burden of 35% coupled with an individual tax burden of 20% produces a total tax burden of 48%.

[40] Note that the highest nominal individual tax rate currently is 39.6%.

At first blush, Chart 1–4 may seem counter-intuitive: annual distributions trigger the shareholder-level tax each year while corporate retention postpones that tax until liquidation. Why is there no benefit from this tax deferral?

If a corporation earns $65 after taxes and distributes it as a dividend, a shareholder-level tax will be imposed on that $65. If the corporation reinvests the $65 instead of distributing it, the corporation will have $69.23 to distribute one year later. If the $69.23 is then distributed, the shareholder-level tax will have been postponed but its eventual imposition will be on a greater amount. So long as the annual corporate tax rate equals the annual individual tax rate and the tax rate on dividend distributions equals the tax rate on liquidating (i.e., capital gain) distributions, the greater tax on the distribution will offset any benefit of deferring the individual tax.[41]

Historically, the tax rate imposed on dividend distributions was significantly higher than the rate imposed on long-term capital gain.[42] When that was true, there was a significant bias in favor of corporate retention of earnings to avoid the high rate of tax imposed on dividend distributions. Alternatively, taxpayer mechanisms were created (sometimes successful, sometimes not) to bail-out corporate earnings as capital gain. As we will see, much of the complexity in Subchapter C arose from congressional attempts to distinguish proper capital gain distributions from inappropriate bail-outs. With the tax rate on most dividend distributions now set equal to the rate applicable to long-term capital gain, that struggle (though not all of the complexity) has disappeared.

For a brief time about a quarter century ago, the corporate tax rate exceeded the individual tax rate, and the maximum individual rate imposed on capital gains as well as on dividend distributions equaled the maximum individual (ordinary) tax rate of 28%. In Chart 1–5, we reconsider the facts of Chart 1–4 but assume that the corporate tax rate is 34% while the individual tax rate imposed on

---

[41] See generally Warren, *The Timing of Taxes*, 39 Nat'l Tax J. 499 (1986). For those with an arithmetic bent, the equality is explained by the distributive principle.

[42] For example, assume that the corporate tax rate is 35%, the individual tax rate on ordinary income and dividend distributions is 35%, while the individual tax rate on capital gains is just 20%. If the corporation retained its earnings for the entire 10 years and distributed them in complete liquidation, the individual would enjoy capital gains on the distribution and net $702 (see line 4 of Chart 1-1). However, if the corporation distributed its profits annually, the individual would net just $570 (see line 2 of Chart 1-4).

ordinary income and capital gains is 28%.[43] Making these assumptions, we get the following results:

Chart 1–5
Classical Corporate Double Tax

	After-Tax Return to Shareholder	Annual Return
Full Retention	$644	5.1%
Full Distribution With Equity	663	5.2%

Now, the shareholder is slightly better off with annual distributions, because the shareholder can earn a greater after-tax return on investments than the corporation. Although the discounted value of the shareholder-level tax is the same whether corporate profits are distributed annually or after 10 years, the total tax paid on the earnings is determined by both the shareholder-level tax and by the corporate-level tax. If annual profits are distributed, the shareholder will invest them on the investment earnings at the individual tax rate of 28 percent. On the other hand, if the corporation retains its profits, it will invest them and be taxed on those earnings at its tax rate of 34 percent.

Thus, the slight preference appearing in Charts 1–5 for annual distributions reflects the slightly higher tax rate applicable to corporate reinvested profits as compared with shareholder reinvested profits.[44] When the individual and corporate tax rates are equal, the shareholder is indifferent between annual distributions and complete corporate retention of profits. When individual rates are higher than corporate rates, there is an incentive for corporations to accumulate profits rather than to distribute them.

---

[43] These rates were enacted by the Tax Reform Act of 1986 and lasted about one year.

[44] If the difference between the corporate and individual tax rates were greater, then the incentive to distribute profits annually also would be greater. See generally Warren, *The Relation and Integration of the Individual and Corporate Income Taxes*, 94 Harv.L.Rev. 717 (1981).

Chapter 2

FORMING A CORPORATION

2.01 Introduction

If a taxpayer exchanges property for other property, the taxpayer generally must recognize any realized gain or loss on the exchange. § 1001(c). For example, if T exchanges undeveloped real estate with a $5,000 basis for a fishing boat with a $20,000 fair market value, T recognizes his $15,000 realized gain ($20,000 amount realized minus $5,000 basis). T's result is no different than if he had sold the land for $20,000 and used the cash to purchase the boat.

The case for recognition is weakened if the exchange does not substantially alter the nature of T's investment. For instance, suppose that T continues as an owner of undeveloped real estate by exchanging the real estate for other undeveloped real estate worth $20,000. While T has a $15,000 realized gain, § 1001(c) and § 1031 may provide that T does not recognize the realized gain, since the properties surrendered and received in exchange are like-kind.[1] If T's gain is not recognized, § 1031(d) provides that T takes a $5,000 basis in the property received, preserving the realized but not recognized gain for any later disposition.[2]

Section 1031 reflects a congressional policy that taxing an exchange is inappropriate where a taxpayer maintains a sufficient continuity of investment after the exchange, but § 1031 does not apply to every exchange that preserves that continuity. For example, it does not apply to T's exchange of the land for all of the stock of newly created X Corp,[3] even though T's continuity of investment is stronger than if he received other real estate in exchange: T continues to own exactly the same real estate, albeit indirectly through his 100-percent ownership of the X stock.

Since 1921, however, Congress has provided that this kind of property-for-stock exchange is not a taxable event, but it has never been the case that all transfers of property to a corporation are tax-

---

[1] Among other requirements under § 1031, the property exchanged and received must be held for use in a trade or business or for investment.

[2] It is as if T has continued an investment in the same property, and under our tax system, the mere appreciation in value of property is not a taxable event.

[3] See also § 1031(a)(2)(B) (providing that § 1031 does not apply to any exchange of stock).

free. For example, a taxpayer who transfers appreciated property to a corporation in which she owns no stock in exchange for cash no longer has a continuity of investment in the property transferred and will recognize any realized gain.

The essence of § 351 and related provisions is to ascertain whether a transferor has a continuing relationship with the property transferred to a corporation sufficient to justify non-recognition treatment or whether the transferor has severed the relationship with the transferred property, justifying recognition.

2.02 An Overview of § 351

(a) Qualification.

Section 351 is not elective. If it applies, a taxpayer defers recognition of gain or loss. Section 351 applies only if the taxpayer-transferor: (1) transfers property to a corporation; (2) receives stock in exchange; and (3) along with other transferors, if any, controls the corporation immediately after the exchange. Note that § 351 can apply both to the formation of a new corporation and to a transfer to an existing corporation (with the latter sometimes referred to as a "midstream" transfer).

Each of the three major requirements of § 351 is intended to ensure a continuity of investment. First, § 351 requires the transfer of property and not the provision of services. If a person provides services to a corporation for its stock, the person has compensation income. See § 351(d)(1). Congress is unwilling to allow non-recognition when a taxpayer converts human capital into corporate capital—the change in form of investment is too great.

Second, the transferor must receive stock of the transferee-corporation, a requirement intended to ensure that the transferor maintains a sufficient connection to the property transferred. Suppose T and three other joint owners of appreciated real estate transfer the property to newly formed X Corp. T receives cash while the other transferors receive X stock. For T, non-recognition is unavailable since T merely sold the property. If T had instead received stock, § 351 would have provided non-recognition for T and the others, each of whom would continue to own the property indirectly through ownership of X stock, benefitting from any appreciation in value of the property (or suffering from any decline in value).

What happens if T transfers the property in exchange for an X Corp. financial instrument, like a debt instrument, rather than stock? Some debt instruments, such as long-term debt, arguably provide continuity similar to stock. For example, a forty-year bond may link the transferor to the property transferred in much the same way as stock. Indeed, for financially troubled corporations, debt ownership may provide greater ownership rights in the corporation's assets than stock. On the other hand, if T were to receive a three-year debt instrument bearing appropriate interest in exchange for the transfer of property, it is as if T sold the property on the installment method, almost like a sale for cash.

Section 351 adopts a bright-line rule: stock is qualified property while debt is not. The section used to distinguish between long-term debts (securities) and short-term debts (notes), providing non-recognition treatment for receipt of the former and sales treatment for receipt of the latter. This distinction proved troublesome as the line between securities and notes was not easily drawn, and Congress adopted the bright-line rule.[4]

Finally, the transferors must control the corporation immediately after the exchange, a requirement that also implements the continuity concept. Just because a person exchanges property for stock, the exchange does not guarantee that the person will possess a sufficient continuity in the property transferred. For instance, if T and the other transferors transfer their jointly owned real estate to Microsoft in exchange for a small amount of Microsoft stock, the transferors' relationship to the real estate is far more attenuated than if they had transferred the property to a newly formed, closely held corporation. The transfers to Microsoft will be taxable exchanges, because the transferors will not control Microsoft immediately after the exchange.

Transferors control a corporation only if they own at least 80 percent of the total combined voting power of all classes of the corporation's voting stock and at least 80 percent of the total number of each class of the corporation's non-voting stock. § 368(c); Rev. Rul. 59-259.[5] These 80-percent tests offer some certainty, avoiding a painstaking factual analysis of what constitutes control in many situations, but they still offer less than complete certainty. Section 351 may apply by considering the property transferred by several persons, and it may not be clear when various property transfers should be considered together as part of the same "transaction." For example, if two transfers are made to X Corp. within six months,

---

[4] Unfortunately, astute tax planners blurred even this line by creating financial instruments that were nominally equity but lacked any significant long-term relationship to the corporation. Congress responded in § 351(g) by defining a class of "nonqualified preferred stock" that is for some purposes treated as stock and for others as less than debt.

[5] 1959-2 C.B. 115.

are the 80-percent tests applied after each transfer or are the two transfers combined and the 80-percent tests applied only once?

Consider one final point on the basics of § 351. Suppose a dozen independent business people transfer their separate and unrelated businesses to a newly-formed corporation, each receiving stock equal in value to the assets exchanged. Notice that the nature of each business person's economic interest has changed dramatically, but § 351 can still apply. Diversification of business assets achieved through § 351 is not prohibited.[6]

(b) Tax Consequences.

If § 351 applies to a person's transfer of property to a corporation, the person may recognize gain but not loss. § 351(a) and (b). Sections 351 and 357 determine the extent to which the transferor recognizes gain. The transferor's basis in the stock and other property received from the corporation is determined under § 358.[7] With adjustments, the basis of the property surrendered becomes the basis of the property received.

Under § 1032 the transferee-corporation recognizes no gain or loss when it acquires property for its stock. It determines its basis in the property received under § 362. With adjustments, the transferee-corporation carries over the transferor's basis, although generally the corporation's aggregate basis in property received from a transferor cannot exceed the property's aggregate value. § 362(e). Under § 1223(2), the corporation "tacks" the holding period of property received from a transferor.

To illustrate how these provisions work, suppose that B owns a building with a $25,000 basis and $70,000 fair market value and C owns undeveloped real estate with a $50,000 basis and a $30,000 fair market value.[8] Together they form X Corp. in exchange for their assets with B and C receiving X stock worth $70,000 and $30,000, respectively. Because B and C transfer property to a corporation (X Corp.) solely for X stock and own all X stock (and therefore control it) immediately after the exchange, § 351 applies to the exchange.[9]

---

[6] But see § 351(e)(1) which addresses so-called swap funds. Investors holding undiversified appreciated securities cannot take advantage of § 351 to diversify by forming a holding company with other similarly situated investors.

[7] Further, because the transferor takes an exchanged basis in the stock received in the exchange, she includes the holding period for property surrendered in the exchange (*i.e.*, the holding period "tacks") to the extent the property surrendered was a capital asset or § 1231 asset. § 1223(1).

[8] Assume that B, C, and X Corp. are all domestic taxpayers.

[9] Note that B and C may be individuals, corporations, partnerships, trusts, or estates. § 7701(a)(1).

Under § 351(a), neither B nor C recognizes gain or loss. As a "price" of B's non-recognition, he takes a $25,000 basis in the X stock, preserving his $45,000 pre-contribution built-in gain in the building. § 358(a), a gain that B may recognize when he sells the stock. As a "consolation," C takes a $50,000 basis in her X stock, preserving her $20,000 pre-contribution built-in loss in the real estate, a loss that she may recognize if she sells the stock.[10]

Because B and C each take an exchanged basis in their stock, each "tacks" the holding period of the assets surrendered to the holding period of the stock received (assuming those assets were capital or § 1231 assets in his or her hands at the time of the exchange). § 1223(1). For example, if B held the building as a capital asset, he would tack his holding period for the building on to his holding period for the stock. Then, if he actually held the building for 9 months and sells the stock after holding it for more than three months, he will be treated as having held the stock for more than a year and will recognize long-term capital gain or loss on its sale (assuming he held the stock as a capital asset).

X Corp. acquires the assets from B and C for its stock, recognizing no gain or loss under § 1032. It succeeds to B's $25,000 basis in the building under § 362(a) but takes a $30,000 basis in the real estate under § 362(e)(2).[11] X Corp. tacks on the holding period of B for the building and C for the real estate, whether or not the assets were capital or § 1231 assets in the hands of the transferors. § 1223(2).

Note that the § 351 transfer duplicates B's built-in gain in the building. If B sells his stock for $70,000, he will recognize a $45,000 gain, and if X Corp. sells the building for $70,000, it also will recognize a $45,000 gain.[12] Thus, the same gain may be taxed twice, once at the corporate level and a second time at the shareholder level.[13] Although the double tax is a central feature of the corporate tax system, it is aimed at post-incorporation earnings or gain. Why

---

[10] This conclusion assumes that C and X Corp. do not make the election described in § 362(e)(2)(C) to eliminate B's built-in loss in the stock but preserve the built-in loss in the real estate in X Corp.'s hands.

[11] X Corp. computes its basis in the real estate by starting with C's basis ($50,000) and reducing it by $20,000, the built-in loss that X Corp. would have had in the property if it had determined its basis in the real estate under § 362(a). § 362(e)(2)(A). *See also* Prop. Treas. Reg. § 1.362-4(b)(1). This conclusion assumes that X Corp. and C do not make the election under § 362(e)(2)(C).

[12] Similarly, if X Corp. sells the asset and distributes the proceeds, there will be a double tax. See the discussion of § 301 in Chapter 4 *infra*.

[13] Note that a shareholder may avoid a double tax on pre-incorporation appreciation through a pre-incorporation sale of the asset.

should there be a potential double tax on pre-incorporation appreciation?

Could Congress avoid this double tax by giving B, the transferor, a step up in basis? If B received a $70,000 basis in the stock received, B could cash in on the building's appreciation with no immediate tax consequences by selling the stock for $70,000. At some point in the future if X Corp. sold the building for $70,000, the tax on the pre-incorporation appreciation would be paid by X Corp. In short, B could convert the asset to cash without immediate tax consequences.

Suppose instead that X Corp. took the building with a basis of $70,000 while B acquired a $25,000 basis in the X Corp. stock received. Now if X Corp. sells the property, it could convert the $45,000 of unrealized appreciation into cash without recognizing gain. At some point in the future, if B sells the X Corp. stock, the pre-incorporation gain may be recognized.

Both of these approaches may suffer from the problem of deferral. While both approaches preserve a single tax on the pre-incorporation appreciation, by strategic selling of the stock or of the asset the shareholder or the corporation could turn that appreciation into cash without immediate tax consequences. Perhaps Congress should design a system whereby gain is recognized on whichever is sold first—the stock or the building— with a step up in basis for the asset not sold? Cf. § 705 and § 743 (for such partnership adjustments). Would such a system present undue administrative hurdles? In any event, § 358 and § 362(a) duplicate the gain at the shareholder and corporate levels

An additional problem with assigning a fair market value basis to the stock or to the contributed assets is that there is no easy way to determine the value of such assets: the transaction does not provide a valuation, and the parties do not have incentives to get the value right. While this is not an insurmountable hurdle (we generally tax parties who exchange one property for another even though such an exchange does not provide a market valuation and each of the parties has an incentive to minimize the reported value), it does provide another, practical reason why Congress might want to give both the shareholder and the corporation a carry-over basis on the transaction.

In sharp contrast, § 358 and § 362 do not duplicate built-in loss. Consider C's transfer of the real estate. If C and X Corp. do not make a § 362(e)(2)(C) election, C takes a $50,000 basis in her X stock, while X Corp. takes a $30,000 basis in the real estate. § 358(a); § 362(e)(2)(A). If they make the election, C takes a $30,000 basis in the X stock, while X Corp. takes a $50,000 basis in the real estate. § 362(a) and (e)(2)(C)(i). Thus, because of § 362(e)(2), if C immediately sells her stock and X Corp. immediately sells the undeveloped real estate, each for $30,000, one will recognize a $20,000 loss, but the other will recognize neither gain or loss. In other words, § 362(e)(2) prevents C and X Corp. from duplicating C's built-in loss in the real estate through the § 351 transfer.

Can the disparate treatment of gain and loss be justified? Perhaps Congress was concerned that the shareholder and corporation would recognize duplicate losses more often than duplicate gains. Whether or not disparate treatment can be justified, however, it is the rule. And for those still troubled by these inconsistent rules, note that it is the taxpayer who chooses to incorporate assets, so while the basis rules are in a sense a one-way street, it is the taxpayer who elects whether or not to drive.

2.03 Qualification

With the basics of § 351 in mind, consider the three major requirements for non-recognition treatment: A person must transfer property to a corporation; the transferor must receive the corporation's stock in exchange; and the transferor, together with others transferring property in the same transaction, must control the corporation immediately after the exchange.

(a) Property Requirement.

For § 351 to apply to a person, the person must transfer property to a corporation in exchange for the corporation's stock. For this purpose, "persons" include not only individuals ("natural persons") but also trusts, estates, partnerships, associations, companies, and corporations. § 7701(a)(1) (defining "person"); Regs. § 1.351-1(a)(1) (repeating that definition).

Surprisingly, neither the Code nor the Regulations define the term "property" for purposes of § 351, leading to two types of disputes. First, a taxpayer may create an asset through her own effort, and the Service may assert that the taxpayer created the asset on behalf of the corporation and therefore provided services to the corporation. Second, the taxpayer may transfer less than all of the taxpayer's interest in an asset to a corporation, and the Service may argue that the taxpayer has not transferred "property" in an exchange to which § 351 applies.[14]

---

[14] The Service has concluded that money qualifies as property for the purposes of § 351. See Rev. Rul. 69–357, 1969–1 C.B. 101.

To the extent that a person provides services for stock, § 351 does not apply and the person typically recognizes compensation income. § 351(d). This restriction applies to stock received for past, present or future services and prevents the conversion of ordinary compensation income into capital gain when the service-provider sells the stock received. Although § 351 prevents this limited conversion, it does not more broadly prevent the conversion of ordinary income into capital gain: one need not transfer a capital asset in order to satisfy the property requirement of § 351. For example, the transferor of appreciated inventory who receives stock in a § 351 transaction might be able to sell the stock and report a capital gain, and if the property is not inventory in the hands of the corporation, it, too, might get capital gain treatment upon a sale.

Another possible explanation for the property requirement is that the philosophy of § 351 does not countenance nonrecognition for a change in form from human to financial capital. Yet, suppose a cash basis transferor holds accounts receivable after performing services for a third party prior to incorporation. Will a transfer of receivables satisfy the property requirement of § 351? In *Hempt Bros., Inc. v. United States*,[15] the court ruled that accounts receivable did constitute property for purposes of § 351.[16]

Suppose a transferor agrees to perform services for the transferee and transfers that promise in exchange for stock. Alternatively, suppose that the transferor has already performed services for the corporation for which he receives an account receivable. The transferor then exchanges the account receivable for stock of the corporation.[17] Will any of these transactions allow a transferor to sidestep the property requirement of § 351? Transactions like these will almost certainly be viewed with

---

[15] 490 F.2d 1172 (3d Cir.1974). See also *United States v. Frazell*, 335 F.2d 487 (5th Cir.1964). There the taxpayer, a geologist, investigated certain oil and gas properties to be acquired by a joint venture. Before any interest in the joint venture was transferred to him, a corporation was formed and part of the stock was given to the taxpayer. It was not clear whether the taxpayer acquired an interest in the joint venture which was then exchanged for stock or whether he acquired stock directly in exchange for services performed. The court found that either the taxpayer was taxable on transferring services for an interest in the joint venture or he was taxable on transferring services in exchange for stock in the corporation. See also *Mark IV Pictures, Inc. v. Commissioner*, 969 F.2d 669 (8th Cir.1992), for a collection of cases on the property vs. services issue.

[16] Consider the assignment of income implications at Section 2.08(b) *infra*.

[17] Similar transactions might include the promise to perform services for another transferor which is then exchanged for stock or the actual performance of services for another shareholder in exchange for an account receivable which is then exchanged for stock.

skepticism by the Service, which may characterize the supposed property transfer, in substance, as a transfer of services.[18]

Nowhere is the line between services and property fuzzier than in cases involving intellectual property. It is clear that a person's rights in patents, patent applications, trademarks, tradenames and goodwill constitute property under § 351. Less clear is the status of "know-how." That umbrella term encompasses inventions, unpatented or unpatentable secret processes or secret formulae and technical information and skills. In Rev. Rul. 64–56,[19] the Service concluded that property included "secret information as to a device, process, formula etc., in the general nature of a patentable invention," but that the status of other "know-how" would be determined on a case-by case basis.[20] Although the Service did not explain its discomfort with "know-how," it emphasized that the transferor often provided technical assistance to the transferee, a service that may create the "know-how," and that should escape the protection of § 351.

Note that § 351 requires that the property be "transferred" to the corporation. Ordinarily, the "transfer" requirement is straightforward. However, in the case of certain intangibles, the transfer requirement can pose a problem. Suppose the owner of a patent or trademark grants a license to a corporation for the right to exploit the property and receives stock in exchange. The owner might have assigned the property outright, but instead preferred to retain certain controls over its utilization and the right to recover the property in the event of the transferee's bankruptcy or misappropriation. For example, the transferor may want to retain a veto over any sublicensing agreements or the right to terminate the license if the transferee fails to utilize the property rights effectively.

The Service has taken the position that in order to qualify under § 351, the transfer must amount to a sale or exchange within the meaning of § 1222.[21] However, in *E. I. Du Pont de Nemours & Co. v. United States*,[22] the court held that the sale or exchange re-

---

[18] See, e.g., *James v. Commissioner*, 53 T.C. 63 (1969) (contract promising to perform services not property for purpose of § 351).

[19] 1964–1 C.B. (Part 1) 133. See also Rev. Rul. 71–564, 1971–2 C.B. 179.

[20] The Service's focus on a nexus to a "patentable invention" may be out of step with judicial decisions emphasizing secrecy and the right of the holder to protect against unauthorized disclosure. See, e.g., *Commercial Solvents Corp. v. Commissioner*, 42 T.C. 455 (1964).

[21] See, e.g., Rev. Rul. 69–156, 1969–1 C.B. 101; Rev. Rul. 71–564, 1971–2 C.B. 179.

[22] 471 F.2d 1211 (Ct.Cl.1973).

quirement of § 1222 is not embodied in § 351. Accordingly, a nonexclusive, royalty-free license exchanged for stock was a "transfer" within the meaning of § 351 because the license was irrevocable and perpetual.

The transfer requirement is inextricably related to the property requirement. If too many strings are retained by the transferor, the Service may well argue that there has been no transfer and that if there was a transfer, the bundle of licensed rights does not amount to property for purposes of § 351.

(b) "Stock" Requirement.

For § 351 to apply to a person's transfer of property to a corporation, the person must receive the corporation's stock, in whole or in part, in exchange. Although § 351(a) suggests that stock must be the sole consideration, § 351(b) allows stock and other property ("boot") to be received in the exchange.

The term "stock" is not defined in the Code and is defined in the Regulations only by exclusion. The term "stock" includes common and preferred stock, whether voting or nonvoting, but excludes stock rights, options, warrants or other rights to purchase stock at a fixed price.[23] Perhaps these potential equity investments do not currently evidence a sufficient continuity of investment to justify nonrecognition under § 351.[24]

Courts have been more lenient towards contingent stock than stock rights. Suppose a transferor transfers property to X Corp. in exchange for X stock and a certificate for additional X shares to be issued later, contingent on valuation of the transferor's property. The Tax Court in *Hamrick v. Commissioner,*[25] distinguished contingent stock from stock rights and the like because with the former no additional payment was required from the transferor, a distinction

---

[23] Regs. § 1.351–1(a)(1) (excluding stock rights, and warrants). This regulation may have originated from *Helvering v. Southwest Consolidated Corp.,* 315 U.S. 194 (1942), holding that warrants were not voting stock within the meaning of a reorganization provision.

Although stock includes nonqualified preferred stock, as defined in § 351(g), if a person receives nonqualified preferred stock as part of a § 351 exchange, the person takes that stock into account as other property in determining her consequences under § 351.

[24] But what if a transfer satisfies the control requirement under § 368(c) without taking stock rights into account? Why then should those instruments be treated in the same manner as cash or other boot? Cf. Regs. § 1.354-1(e) (treating stock rights as qualified property in certain cases involving reorganizations).

[25] 43 T.C. 21 (1964). See also *Carlberg v. United States,* 281 F.2d 507 (8th Cir.1960).

that is less than satisfying.[26] For purposes of the stock continuity requirement, the focus should be on the nature of what is *received*. Whether additional payments by a shareholder are required seems irrelevant. Nevertheless, whatever the policy merits, stock rights and similar instruments are not treated as stock for purposes of § 351.

Could § 351 apply to a person's transfer, even when a person actually receives no stock in exchange? For example, if B transfers property to X Corp., his wholly owned corporation, and receives no X stock, is X stock "deemed" issued to B for purposes of § 351? The answer is yes. Under the "meaningless gesture" doctrine, stock is deemed issued if, with or without the issuance, the rights of the corporation's shareholders would be the same.[27] In this example, whether or not B receives X stock, he is entitled to all distributions from X and exercises 100 percent of the vote. Thus, B's rights in the X stock would be unchanged by an issuance of stock, and he is deemed to receive X stock in exchange for the property transferred to X Corp.

Could this doctrine also apply if someone else received a new class of non-voting preferred stock as part of the same transaction? To answer that question, you must examine the characteristics of the issued stock and understand the differences between common and preferred stock. A corporation's common stock is a residual interest in the entity, which means that its holders are paid last but in a potentially unlimited amount. In contrast, holders of preferred stock are typically paid both dividends and liquidating distributions before holders of common stock. Further, their return is often limited to a fixed dividend rate and fixed amount on liquidation, regardless of the success of the venture. Thus, common shareholders take a larger risk (because they are paid last) for a bigger potential gain (because their return is unlimited)

Suppose, in the example above, that B and C transferred property to X Corp., the corporation that B wholly owned before the transfer. As part of the transfer, B received no X stock, while C re-

---

[26] Perhaps, Congress concluded that stock options were not qualified consideration in a § 351 exchange to prevent transferors from selectively recognizing loss while deferring gain. A transferor could defer gain by transferring appreciated property for qualified stock in the § 351 exchange. If stock options were qualified consideration, a transferor could recognize loss as follows: She could receive a stock option from the corporation without gain or loss recognition and, in a separate step, exercise the option using built-in loss property, recognizing that built-in loss. § 1001(c). However, because stock options are not qualified consideration in a § 351 exchange, the transferor could recognize gain in the first step, impeding selective loss recognition.

[27] See *Peracchi v. Commissioner*, 143 F.3d 487 (9th Cir. 1998).

ceived non-voting preferred stock that was limited and preferred as to dividends and liquidating distributions. Whether or not B received X common stock, he would enjoy 100 percent of the voting rights on X stock and all distributions from X Corp. after any preferred distributions to B. Thus, the meaningless gesture doctrine should apply, and B should be deemed to receive X common stock.[28]

Finally, what if a taxpayer transfers property to a corporation in a transaction otherwise described in section 351 but the property is encumbered by a liability equal to or in excess of the value of the contributed property? If the corporation assumes the liability, then arguably no portion of the property has been exchanged for stock, because no net value has been transferred to the corporation. Proposed regulations now adopt this analysis. *See* Prop. Reg. § 1.351-1(a)(1)(iii) (proposed March 10, 2005).

(c) Transferor Group and Control.

Finally, for § 351 to apply, the transferor and any others who transfer property in the same exchange must control the corporation immediately after the exchange. This requirement raises several questions: (i) what is control, (ii) which persons transfer property in the same exchange, and (iii) who owns stock "immediately after the exchange?"

(i) Control. Section 368(c) defines control as "stock possessing at least 80 percent of the total combined voting power of [the corporation's voting stock] and at least 80 percent of the total number of shares of all other classes of stock of the corporation." Rev. Rul. 59-259[29] "clarifies" § 368(c), concluding that the second 80-percent test applies separately to *each* class of nonvoting stock. With this clarification, a person or persons control a corporation if they own stock of the corporation possessing at least 80 percent of its total voting power plus at least 80 percent of *each* class of nonvoting stock.[30]

If the control test were applied literally (*i.e.,* without the clarification), it may make § 351 functionally elective, contrary to Con-

---

[28] If, however, C were issued X *common* stock, the meaningless gesture doctrine should not apply, because B's relative interest in any dividends and liquidating distributions would change if he were issued X stock.

[29] 1959-2 C.B. 115.

[30] Suppose after a purported § 351 transaction, the transferors own 95 percent of the voting stock, 75 percent of the class A nonvoting preferred stock and 95 percent of the class B nonvoting preferred stock, for an overall 88 percent interest in the total preferred stock and a 91 percent interest by fair market value of all of the stock. Do the transferors have control? In Rev.Rul. 59–259, 1959–2 C.B. 115, the Service ruled that while classes of voting stock can be combined in applying the 80 percent test, *each* class of nonvoting stock must satisfy the 80-percent test.

gressional intent. The literal test considers the aggregate number of nonvoting shares, a number that can be manipulated without changing the relative rights of the shareholders, as the following example illustrates:

Suppose that B owns 80 percent of the only class of voting stock of X Corp., C owns the remaining 20 percent of the X voting stock and all 100 shares of the only class of X nonvoting common stock. B will transfer property to X Corp. and receive a new class of X nonvoting common stock. The new class will entitle B to receive exactly 10 percent of any dividends and liquidating distributions paid by X Corp., something that will be true whether B receives 100 shares or 900 shares of that stock. Thus, B would satisfy the literal control test if he receives 900 shares of the new class of X stock, but not if he receives just 100 shares.[31] Because B's rights in X Corp. are the same whether he receives 100 or 900 shares, he could functionally elect to meet (or fail) the control test if it were literally applied. Note that with the clarification provided by Rev. Rul. 59-259, B would fail the test, regardless of the number of shares of the new class of stock he received, because he owns none of the class of nonvoting X stock that C owns.

Accordingly, as clarified, the control test avoids that functional election. It is also objective, looking to voting power (for the voting shares) and the number of shares of each class of nonvoting stock, all amounts that may be simply and objectively determined. Thus, the test avoids stock valuation, a sometimes uncertain task.[32]

Still, the 80 percent tests are somewhat arbitrary in at least two respects. First, consider the 80 percent figure itself. Why not 67 percent or 85 percent? Second, because those tests may apply to a group of transferors, they do not assure a significant continuity for any one transferor. For example, if 1,000 transferors form a corporation and each receives the same amount of stock for the same amount of property transferred, § 351 is available even though each shareholder holds a 0.1 percent interest in the corporation.[33]

---

[31] If B received 900 shares of the new class of X stock, he would control X Corp. under the literal test, because he would own 80 percent of the only class of X voting stock and 90 percent of the total number of shares of the X nonvoting stock (900/1,000). If, however, he received only 100 shares of that stock, he would not control X Corp under that test, because he would own only 50 percent of the X nonvoting stock (100/200).

[32] The valuation of a share will depend on its attributes, which may include the right to vote, dividend rights and preferences, and liquidation rights and preferences. Particularly for closely held corporations, a share's value may be difficult to determine with precision.

[33] Note that it may be difficult to corral multiple investors to achieve this type of broad diversification, except perhaps in one situation: The in-

Note that a person need not acquire stock that constitutes control for § 351 to apply. Suppose that X Corp. was formed several years ago by B and C with B receiving 60 percent and C receiving 40 percent of the only class of X stock. B now transfers sufficient additional property to give him 20 percentage points more of X stock—B now holds 80 percent and C 20 percent. Even though B has increased his stock interest by only 20 percentage points, he controls X Corp. after the transaction within the meaning of § 368(c).

Finally, under § 351(g)(2), certain "disqualified" preferred stock is taxed as other property rather than as stock. Despite that special treatment, "disqualified" preferred stock is treated as stock in applying the control test. Thus, this disqualified preferred stock is something of a chameleon, looking like stock for purposes of control but like boot for purposes of recognition of gain (or loss).

(ii) The "Transferor" Group. Section 351 may apply if a person or persons transfer property to a corporation, and it may apply even if those persons do not make simultaneous exchanges. The regulations state that persons are considered together (*i.e.*, as a transferor group) in applying § 351 if their rights "have been previously defined and the execution of the agreement proceeds with an expedition consistent with orderly procedure." Regs. § 1.351-1(a)(1).

For example, suppose that B and C agree to transfer property to X Corp., receiving only X stock in return. B and C transfer assets worth $70,000 and $30,000, respectively, for 70 percent and 30 percent of X Corp. common stock. Even if the transfers do not occur simultaneously (but assuming that they occur with all due speed), B and C should be members of a transferor group because, before the first transfer, they defined the assets to be transferred and the X stock to be received.

Suppose that D later transfers enough property to X Corp. to give her 50 percent of the X stock outstanding.[34] By herself, D would not satisfy the control requirement and would not qualify for nonrecognition under § 351. Aware that transferors have to control the corporation immediately after the exchange but do not have to acquire control in the exchange, D induces B to purchase one additional share of X stock for $1 as an accommodation to D. Together D

---

vestors, each owning stock or securities, band together to form an investment company. Section 351(e)(1) denies the non-recognition of § 351 to this attempted diversification.

[34] B's interest is reduced to 35 percent and C's to 15 percent.

and B now control at least 80 percent (actually 85 percent plus one share) of the outstanding X stock.

Do D and B form a transferor group? The regulations answer this question in the negative by treating B as if he did *not* transfer property (*i.e.*, as an "accommodation transferor"). Under Regs. § 1.351–1(a)(1)(ii), an accommodation transferor is a person (i) who in form transfers property and receives stock "which is of relatively small value" compared with stock already owned (or to be received for services) and (ii) whose primary purpose for the transfer is to qualify others under § 351.[35] B is an accommodation transferor because the stock that he received (worth $1) has a relatively small value compared with the X stock that he already owned (worth $70,000) and he purchased the stock to qualify D under § 351. As an accommodation transferor, B is not treated as transferring property to X Corp. and therefore cannot be a member of a transferor group with D. As a result, because D does not control X Corp. by herself, § 351 does not apply to her exchange, and she recognizes any gain (or loss) on the exchange.

In Rev. Proc. 77–37,[36] the Service stated that for purposes of obtaining an advanced ruling, property will *not* be considered "of relatively small value" if it equals at least 10% of the value of stock already owned by the transferor (or to be received for services). In the example above, if B contributes enough property to acquire an additional $7,000 of X stock, he and D should be on safe ground.[37]

Although accommodation transfers typically involve existing corporations, an accommodation transfer may be made when a corporation is formed if the accommodation transferor receives some stock for services. First consider a case that does not involve an accommodation transfer. Suppose that B and C form X Corp. as equal shareholders with B contributing property with a $10,000 basis and $40,000 fair market value and C contributing $40,000 of services. Not only will C be taxable on the fair market value of the stock received for her services but B will not qualify under § 351 since the transferors of *property* do not satisfy the control requirement of § 368(c) (B holds only a 50 percent interest).[38]

---

[35] See also *Kamborian v. Commissioner,* 56 T.C. 847 (1971), aff'd, 469 F.2d 219 (1st Cir.1972) (upholding the regulation and also concluding that stock received that was worth about 0.84% of the stock already owned by the transferor had a relatively small value).

[36] 1977–2 C.B. 568.

[37] Remember that Rev. Proc. 77–37 only represents the Service's ruling position; it does not mean the Service will challenge all transactions failing its standards or that such challenges, if made, will hold up in court.

[38] See *James v. Commissioner*, 53 T.C. 63 (1969).

Could C become a transferor of property by also acquiring one share of stock for $1? Assuming (as seems almost certain) that C acquires the stock to qualify B under § 351, the answer would be no, because C would be an accommodation transferor. Her X stock acquired for the cash (worth $1) would have a relatively small value compared with the stock to be acquired for services (worth $40,000). Note that if C contributes enough property to be considered a transferor of property, she will still be taxable on the fair market value of the stock received for the services performed. However, B may now qualify for non-recognition under § 351 since the transferors of property satisfy the control requirement under § 368(c).[39]

(iii) "Immediately After the Exchange." Control" is determined by comparing the stock owned by the transferor group with all outstanding stock, both measured "immediately after the exchange." The outstanding stock includes not only stock issued to members of the transferor group in the exchange but also any stock issued to a person providing services to the corporation as part of the same transaction. But exactly when should the 80 percent tests under § 368(c) be applied? This question arises in two contexts: where a transferor disposes of stock received shortly after the purported § 351 exchange and where the transferee-corporation issues additional stock shortly after a purported § 351 exchange.

Suppose that B and C form X Corp. by each contributing appreciated property ($10,000 basis and $40,000 fair market value) in exchange for X stock in an attempted § 351 transaction. Shortly after the exchange, B sells her X stock to D for $40,000. Section 351 applies to the transfers only if B and C controlled X Corp. immediately after the exchange. If control is measured before B's sale to D, B and C control X Corp., owning all of its stock, and § 351 applies to their exchanges. If, however, control is measured after the sale, § 351 does not apply, because the transferors (B and C) own only 50 percent of the X Corp. stock (the stock C retains) and do not control X Corp.[40]

C and X Corp. also have vital interests in whether § 351 applies. If § 351 applies, C defers his $30,000 gain but X Corp. takes

---

[39] If a transferor of services and property qualifies as a transferor of property, *all* of that transferor's stock can be counted for purposes of the 80-percent tests—not just the stock received for property transferred.

[40] Section 351 is unavailable since D, the other X shareholder, is not a transferor of property to X Corp. If, instead, D had purchased stock directly from X Corp. while C contributed property, the exchange would qualify under § 351. X Corp. could then have purchased the property from B. Throughout subchapter C it is often the case that choosing the correct form is paramount. But cf. Regs. § 1.368–1(e)(i) (disposition of stock to persons not related to issuing corporation after a reorganization does not break continuity of interest).

transferred bases of $10,000 in each asset. If it does not apply, C recognizes his $30,000 gain, while X takes cost bases of $40,000 in each asset. B also may care whether § 351 applies to the transaction even though she will recognize $30,000 of gain in either case (*i.e.*, on the sale if § 351 applies or on the exchange if it does not), because the timing of the gain and its character may differ.[41]

Similarly, suppose that B and C make their transfers to X Corp., but that shortly after the transaction, X Corp. issues additional stock (enough stock to constitute a 1/3 equity interest) to D for services performed. In any case, D will have taxable compensation income equal to the fair market value of stock received, but the fate of B and C will depend upon how D's transaction is treated. If it is deemed to be separate, B and C will satisfy the control requirement. On the other hand, if D's transaction is combined with that of B and C's, B and C will fail the control requirement and must recognize any gain on their exchange with X Corp.[42]

Having set out the stakes, focus now on the resolution of the problem. In deciding whether to combine multiple transactions (e.g., an exchange followed by a sale or an exchange followed by a second exchange), courts have articulated a variety of tests. Perhaps the most widely used test is the "mutual interdependence"[43] test set out in *American Bantam Car Co. v. Commissioner*:[44] "Were the steps so interdependent that the legal relations created by one transaction would have been fruitless without a completion of the series?" In that case, the court determined that transferors who received common stock for their manufacturing assets qualified under § 351 even though five days later the transferors agreed to pay more than 20 percent of their common stock to underwriters for their services in selling the corporation's preferred stock to investors. The court found that the loss of control was not an integral part of the § 351 transaction.

---

[41] If § 351 does not apply B would have recognized the entire $30,000 gain on the transfer and would have taken a cost basis in the X stock under § 1012, thereby recognizing no further gain on its sale.

[42] A similar issue would arise if D instead acquired C's X stock by purchase and the exchange and purchase were combined, so that D, rather than C, was treated as owning X stock "immediately after the exchange." Note that if the two steps were combined, § 351 might still apply if, as part of the same transaction, D transferred property to X Corp. in exchange for X stock. But see Rev. Rul. 79-194, 1979-1 C.B. 145 (concluding that a purchaser was excluded from the transferor group as an accommodation transferor (*i.e.*, the stock acquired in exchange for property had too small a value when compared with the stock purchased as part of the overall transaction)).

[43] One wonders what "non-mutual interdependence" might be.

[44] 11 T.C. 397 (1948), aff'd per curiam, 177 F.2d 513 (3d Cir.1949).

Certainly, the absence of a preexisting binding commitment was helpful to the taxpayer in *American Bantam Car.* If there is a binding agreement, transactions will be stepped together; if there is not a binding agreement, transactions may be stepped together.[45] Aside from the presence or absence of a binding agreement, the amount of time between the transactions is probably the most important aspect—in general, the closer the transactions are in time, the more likely they will be combined.[46]

The Service has recognized that not all post-incorporation transfers of stock run afoul of the goals underlying § 351. In Rev. Rul. 2003-51,[47] the Service explained that a pre-arranged transfer of stock in a second § 351 transaction will not preclude satisfaction of the control requirement of a prior § 351 transaction because the tax-free transfer of stock, being a mere change in form of ownership, "is not necessarily inconsistent with the purposes of section 351." A similar conclusion was reached in Rev. Rul. 84-111[48] in which a partnership converted to corporate form by transferring its assets to a corporation and then distributing the stock received in complete liquidation of the partnership.

In noncommercial settings, it is also less likely that a purported § 351 exchange followed by the transferor's gift will be stepped together to deny § 351 treatment to the transferor. If B and C form X Corp. in exchange for X stock, and B makes a gift of her stock to her daughter shortly after the exchange § 351 treatment will probably be available.[49]

---

[45] See *McDonald's Restaurants of Ill., Inc. v. Commissioner,* 688 F.2d 520 (7th Cir.1982). But see *Intermountain Lumber Co. v. Commissioner,* 65 T.C. 1025 (1976) (concluding that a subsequent stock sale was stepped with a property transfer, because the transferor had relinquished his legal right to retain the shares sold, also suggesting in *dicta* that if the transferor had "no restrictions upon [his] freedom of action" to retain those shares, the property transfer and sale would not have been stepped together).

[46] But compare *Commissioner v. Ashland Oil & Refining Co.,* 99 F.2d 588 (6th Cir.1938) (steps that were six years apart were integrated) with *Henricksen v. Braicks,* 137 F.2d 632 (9th Cir.1943) (steps that were one-half hour apart were treated separately). In the special statutory rule of § 351(c), corporate transferors can distribute the stock received in a § 351 transaction to their shareholders without violating the control requirement.

[47] 2003-1 C.B. 938.

[48] 1984-2 C.B. 88.

[49] Compare *Wilgard Realty Co. v. Commissioner,* 127 F.2d 514 (2d Cir.1942) (§ 351 applicable since no obligation to make gift) with *Fahs v. Florida Machine & Foundry Co.,* 168 F.2d 957 (5th Cir.1948) (direct issuance of shares to donee precluded § 351).

2.04　Tax Consequences—Shareholders

This section considers the tax consequences to a property transferor of a § 351 exchange, considering the gain or loss, if any, recognized by transferor and her basis and holding period in any property received in the exchange.

(a) Recognized Gain or Loss.

(i) In general. Under § 1001(a), a person realizes gain or loss on the exchange of property, in whole or in part, for stock of a corporation. Under § 1001(c), the person recognizes that gain or loss, except as the Code provides. Section 351 provides one exception.

If § 351 applies to a person's exchange of property for stock of the transferee corporation, the person recognizes no gain or loss if she receives *solely* transferee stock in the exchange. § 351(a). If the person receives other property ("boot") in addition to transferee stock, she still recognizes no loss but recognizes any realized gain up to the boot's fair market value.[50] Thus, if § 351 applies to a person's exchange, the person recognizes no loss and recognizes gain equal to the smaller of (i) any realized gain and (ii) the fair market value of any boot received in the exchange.

For example, suppose that T transfers an asset with a $6,000 adjusted basis and $20,000 fair market value to X Corp. in exchange for $15,000 of X stock and $5,000 of cash in a transaction that qualifies under § 351. T realizes a $14,000 gain ($20,000 amount realized minus $6,000 adjusted basis), recognizing a $5,000 gain, the smaller of $5,000 (the boot's value) and $14,000 (the realized gain). Although T may prefer to treat the cash as a return of T's original $6,000 investment in the property, § 351(b) requires recognition of gain before basis can be recovered.

The gain's character is determined by the nature of the property transferred. In the example above, T's $5,000 recognized gain would be ordinary if he transferred inventory or capital gain if he transferred investment real estate. If T transferred machinery used in a trade or business, the recognized gain would be § 1231 gain, except to the extent recaptured as ordinary income under § 1245.

---

[50] § 351(b). The term "boot" presumably originates from the fact that the transferor receives stock and other property "to boot." Where does the expression "to boot" come from? Under Anglo–Saxon law, a freeman who injured another would redeem himself with the king by paying the "wite," or fine. Having avoided execution, he would then be required to pay an additional amount, the "bot," as compensation to the injured party. The "bot" was thus further payment, and "to boot" came to mean "in addition" or "additionally." See F. Pollock & F. Maitland, The History of English Law 45 (2d ed. 1968).

Note that if a transferor does not recognize gain on a § 351 transaction, no gain is recaptured under § 1245 or § 1250. § 1245(b)(3); § 1250(d)(3).

In the example above, suppose T transfers property with a basis of $25,000 and a fair market value of $20,000 in exchange for $15,000 of X stock and $5,000 of cash. The boot does not trigger recognition of gain since there is no realized gain on the transaction. Although T realized a loss on the exchange, he does not recognize that loss. § 351(b)(2). Instead, he treats the $5,000 cash received as a return of his original investment in the property.

(ii) Nonqualified preferred stock. Under § 351(g), "nonqualified preferred stock" is treated as boot, although it still counts as stock for purposes of the control test. Nonqualified preferred stock has the following characteristics:

First, that stock must be preferred and limited as to dividends, and it cannot participate in corporate growth to any significant extent. § 351(g)(3)(A) (adding that to participate in growth to any significant extent, there must be "a real and meaningful likelihood of the shareholder actually participating in the earnings and growth of the corporation" beyond any limited and preferred distributions). Thus, stock is not preferred and limited if it can be converted into common stock. This definition of "preferred" stock is more restrictive than that used for § 305 and § 306.[51]

Further, nonqualified preferred stock must have certain features that make it more like straight debt than common stock on the debt/equity continuum. It must either have (a) a dividend rate tied to interest rates, commodity prices, or the like, or (b) one of the following three redemption features:

>(i) The shareholder may require the issuer to redeem the stock;

>(ii) The issuer must redeem the stock; or

>(iii) The issuer may redeem the stock, and the redemption is, as of the issue date, more likely than not to occur.

§ 351(g)(2)(A) (also adding corresponding rules for purchases by persons related to the issuer under § 267(b) or § 707). However, the-

---

[51] See Chapters 6–7 *infra*. Note that taxpayers can avoid the application of § 351(g) by using stock that is either not preferred (*i.e.*, that does not stand ahead of common stock as to the payment of dividends) or not limited (*i.e.*, that participates to some significant extent in the growth of the company).

se redemption provisions are relevant only if they may be exercised within 20 years of the stock's issuance and the redemption is not subject to a contingency which makes the likelihood of redemption remote. § 351(g)(2)(B). In addition, there are special rules that except certain redemptions related to death, disability, or change of employment status. § 351(g)(2)(C).

Nonqualified preferred stock is treated as boot in determining a transferor's recognized gain or loss, but it is treated as stock in determining the transferor group and control immediately after the exchange. For example, suppose that three equal transferors, A, B, and C, form X Corp., contributing property in exchange for X stock. A and B each receive X common stock and C receives X nonqualified preferred stock. A, B, and C are members of a transferor group, each transferring property for X stock, and they control X immediately after the exchange, owning all outstanding X stock. Thus, § 351 applies to the exchange. A and B recognize no gain or loss, receiving solely X stock in the exchange. § 351(a). C receives solely nonqualified preferred stock, which she treats as boot in applying § 351 (and § 1001). Because C is treated as receiving solely boot, § 351 defers none of C's realized gain or loss (measured by the difference between the value of that stock and the adjusted basis of the property transferred by C). Unless another exception to recognition applies, C recognizes her realized gain or loss. § 1001(c). But see § 267.

If C had received X common stock in addition to the X nonqualified stock, she would have treated the nonqualified stock as boot for purposes of § 351(b). Then, she would have recognized any realized gain up to the value of the X nonqualified stock received but would not have recognized any realized loss.

(iii) Debt instruments. Under current law, if a transferor exchanges property for a combination of transferee-corporation stock and debt instruments in a § 351 exchange, the debt instruments will be treated as boot under § 351(b). However, under § 453, the transferor may be able to report gain on the debt instruments under the installment method.[52] Note that under § 453(a)(2)(B), gain from inventory exchanged for a note must be recognized immediately. Further, under § 453(d) a transferor may elect out of installment reporting, an election that may make sense if the transferor has an expiring loss carryover.

---

[52] Prop. Regs. § 1.453–1(f)(3)(ii). Even though nonqualified preferred stock has characteristics similar to debt, no statutory provision permits a transferor who receives such disqualified preferred stock to use installment reporting to defer the recognition of gain. Thus, such stock is actually taxed more harshly than actual corporate debt.

For example, suppose that T transfers an asset with a $10,000 basis and $40,000 fair market value to X Corp. in a § 351 exchange, receiving X stock worth $20,000 and an X debt instrument bearing appropriate interest with a $20,000 principal amount and value. Assume that § 453 applies to the exchange. As discussed in more detail below, T's $10,000 basis in the asset transferred is allocated to the X stock received, so that T's basis in the debt instrument is $0. When X Corp. satisfies the debt instrument, T will recognize a $20,000 gain (reduced by any gain previously recaptured as depreciation recapture). The character of that gain will be determined by looking to the character of the asset transferred in the § 351 transaction. Note that if the asset transferred is subject to depreciation recapture, T must recognize any depreciation recapture as ordinary income in the year of the § 351 transaction, even though no cash is received at that time.[53]

(b) Assumption of Liabilities.

(i) In general. When a buyer assumes a seller's liability, the seller's amount realized includes the amount of the assumed liability. *See* § 1001(b). In effect, the seller is treated as receiving property with a dollar value equal to the liability amount.

Should the result be comparable if the transferee-corporation assumes a transferor's liability as part of a § 351 exchange? Suppose that T transfers an asset with a $40,000 basis and $50,000 fair market value to X Corp. in a § 351 exchange for X stock worth $40,000 and X Corp.'s assumption of T's $10,000 liability secured by the property. After the transaction, T holds $40,000 of X stock and X Corp. holds the transferred asset and, by assuming the liability, is obligated to pay $10,000 to T's lender.[54] Should X Corp.'s assumption of T's liability be treated just as if T had received boot equal to the liability amount?

In *United States v. Hendler,*[55] the Supreme Court concluded that an assumption of the transferor's liability was boot under somewhat parallel reorganization sections, boot that would trigger recognition of gain to the transferor under § 351(b). Having won the battle, Treasury soon realized it might lose the war. One consequence of boot treatment for a transferor is that the transferee-corporation is entitled to increase its basis in the property received under § 362(a), thereby increasing depreciation

---

[53] § 453(i). See also § 1245(b)(3) (limiting depreciation recapture in a § 351 exchange to the gain recognized under § 351(b)); § 1250(d)(3) (providing a corresponding rule).

[54] For tax purposes, T is deemed to be relieved of the obligation even if T remains secondarily liable on the note. § 357(d)(1)(A).

[55] 303 U.S. 564 (1938).

deductions and decreasing gain (or increasing loss) on the eventual sale of the property. While the statute of limitations may have run on many pre-*Hendler* transferors of encumbered property, the transferee-corporations were eager to utilize any basis increase.[56] The Service hastened to overturn its victory, an effort that culminated in Congress enacting § 357.

Under the general rule of § 357(a), if the transferee corporation assumes a liability in a § 351 exchange, the assumption is not treated as the payment of boot. Thus, the transferor generally does not recognize gain in a § 351 exchange merely because the transferee corporation assumes the transferor's liability. That result makes sense, for example, if the transferor incurred the liability to acquire the transferred property. Then, the transferor did not cash out any gain on the transferred property through the transferee's liability assumption.

The result seems troubling, however, if a transferor's assumed liabilities exceed the aggregate basis of the transferred property, because the transferor then either cashed out a portion of the gain (*e.g.*, by borrowing against appreciation) or enjoyed a tax benefit (*e.g.*, depreciation deductions) that should be recaptured on the transfer. Section 357(c)(1) responds to that concern, providing that a transferor generally recognizes gain to the extent that the assumed liabilities exceed the aggregate adjusted basis of *all* property transferred by the transferor.[57]

Consider again that example above. When X Corp. assumes T's $10,000 liability, a liability T incurred to acquire the property that he transferred to X Corp, T recognizes no gain or loss under § 351 and § 357. The liability is not treated as boot for purposes of § 351. § 357(a). Further, because the amount of the liability assumed ($10,000) does not exceed T's basis in the transferred property ($40,000), T recognizes no gain under § 357(c)(1) (although as discussed below, T's basis in the X stock will be reduced by $10,000 to account for the liability). If, instead, T's basis in the transferred

---

[56] See the mitigation provisions of § § 1311–1314 which now might prevent the Treasury from such a one-sided fate. Note that the *Hendler* "problem" was a one-time event due to the statute of limitations. In general, taxing a shareholder on transferred liabilities while giving the corporation a stepped up basis causes no problems for the Treasury and accelerates the collection of revenues.

[57] Section 357(c) applies even where the transferor remains personally liable on the liabilities assumed by the transferee-corporation. § 357(d)(1)(A). See *Smith v. Commissioner,* 84 T.C. 889 (1985). This result is consistent with the treatment of the transferor when the transferee satisfies the liability. There will be no gain to the transferor even though *Old Colony Trust Co. v. Commissioner,* 279 U.S. 716 (1929), might suggest there should be if another person discharges a personal liability of the transferor.

property had been only $6,000, T would have recognized a $4,000 gain under § 357(c)(1), the excess of the liability assumed ($10,000) over the aggregate basis of T's transferred property ($6,000).[58]

Sometimes, however, the basis-first rule of § 357(c)(1) seems either too generous or too harsh. It seems too generous, for example, if T makes the following choice: Instead of receiving $10,000 of cash in the § 351 exchange, T incurs a $10,000 liability in anticipation of the exchange and X Corp. assumes the liability, transferring X stock worth $40,000 to T in exchange for property with a $40,000 basis and $50,000 value. If § 357(c)(1) applies, T recognizes no gain, because T's basis in the transferred property ($40,000) exceeds the liability assumed ($10,000). If T had instead received boot, he would have recognized a $10,000 gain (the smaller of the $10,000 realized gain and the $10,000 boot).

The concern raised by this example may be addressed by § 357(b). Under § 357(b), a transferor treats the assumption of *all* liabilities by the corporate transferee as the payment of boot for purposes of § 351(b) if the transferor's principal purpose with respect to the assumption of *any* transferor liability was to avoid federal income tax on the exchange or was not a "bona fide business purpose."[59]

To understand the reach of § 357(b), assume that in the preceding example T incurred the liability assumed by X Corp. immediately before the § 351 exchange and used the money for personal purposes. Under these facts, T likely must treat the $10,000 assumption as boot under § 357(b) and recognizes a $10,000 gain. In general, however, § 357(b) should not reach liabilities incurred in the ordinary course of business such as mortgages placed on business property, trade obligations, and business bank loans. But note that if the tax-avoidance motive exists with respect to *any* assumed liability, *all* liabilities are treated as boot under § 357(b).[60] This harsh and seemingly unwarranted treatment may sometimes have discouraged courts from finding the necessary tax avoidance motive.

Thus, § 357(b) addresses some circumstances when § 357(c)(1) seems too generous. But in other instances, § 357(c)(1) seems too

---

[58] Thus, § 357(c)(1) is a regime in which basis is recovered before gain is recognized, a "basis first" rule. In contrast, under § 351(b), a transferor recognizes gain up to the boot received, a "gain first" rule.

[59] See *Thompson v. Campbell*, 353 F.2d 787 (5th Cir. 1965) (considering a mortgage placed on property on the eve of incorporation). Under § 357(c)(2)(A), § 357(b) takes precedence over § 357(c) where the two conflict.

[60] Regs. § 1.357–1(c).

harsh. If, for example, a transferor recognizes gain merely because the corporate transferee assumes a liability that would have resulted in a deduction if paid by the transferor, the net effect of the assumption should be zero (imputed income offset by imputed deduction). Such a liability may include, for example, an account payable of a cash-basis taxpayer.

Congress addressed such liabilities in § 357(c)(3), which provides that a liability is disregarded in applying § 357(c)(1) if it would have given rise to a deduction if paid by the transferor. In Rev. Rul. 95-74, 1995-2 C.B. 36, the Service expanded § 357(c)(3) liabilities to include ones that would have created or increased basis if paid by the transferor. Cf. § 357(c)(3)(B) (providing that § 357(c)(3) liabilities do not include any liability that *when incurred* resulted in the creation of, or increase in, basis).

For example, assume that T transfers property with a $0 basis to X Corp. in a § 351 exchange, and X Corp. transfers X stock worth $35,000 to T and assumes T's $5,000 account payable, a liability that T could have deducted if he had paid it. Because the liability is described in § 357(c)(3), it is disregarded in applying § 357(c)(1) (and § 351).[61] Thus, T is treated as receiving solely X stock in the exchange and recognizes none of his $40,000 realized gain.[62]

But does this result make sense? The transaction could be treated as if (i) X Corp. borrowed $5,000 from T's creditor (obligating itself for repayment), (ii) X Corp. distributed the $5,000 along with $35,000 of X stock in exchange for T's property, and (iii) T used the $5,000 to pay T's obligation to the creditor. Viewed in this way, T would recognize a $5,000 gain (the smaller of the $5,000 of boot distributed and the $40,000 realized gain) and have an offsetting $5,000 deduction for the payment of the account payable. Section 357(c)(3) achieves a similar result by disregarding deductible liabilities for purposes of § 357(c)(1), so that no gain is recognized under that provision.[63]

---

[61] Even prior to the enactment of § 357(c)(3), courts achieved the same results through some creative reasoning. See, e.g., *Bongiovanni v. Commissioner,* 470 F.2d 921 (2d Cir.1972) (account payable not a liability for purposes of § 357); *Thatcher v. Commissioner,* 533 F.2d 1114 (9th Cir.1976) (constructive deduction permitted under § 357(c)); *Focht v. Commissioner,* 68 T.C. 223 (1977) (following *Bongiovanni*).

[62] Note that liabilities assumed are included in computing the amount realized under § 1001, whether the liabilities are described in § 357(b), § 357(c)(3), or otherwise.

[63] Note that if the underlying property is a capital asset, T's gain would be capital gain, perhaps taxed at a preferential rate. Thus, the "wash" treatment of § 357(c)(3) may deny the transferor the benefit of enjoying capital gain, taxed at a preferential tax rate, and an ordinary deduction that offsets income taxed at a higher rate.

For purposes of consistency, one would expect that X Corp. would not get a deduction when it paid T's creditor. In essence, X Corp. made a capital expenditure when it acquired the property from T by assuming the account payable, and its payment of the assumed liability is akin to payment of loan principal. Nevertheless, in Rev. Rul. 80–198,[64] the Service ruled that the transferee-corporation can take the deduction. While it might be easy to dismiss this result as another manifestation of the corporate double tax system, there is no apparent reason why a pre-incorporation account payable ought to be deducted twice—once implicitly by the transferor and once explicitly by the transferee.[65]

(ii) Avoiding gain under § 357(c)(1). As a review, if a transferee-corporation assumes a transferor's liabilities in a § 351 exchange, the liabilities are taken into account in computing the transferor's gain, if any, realized on the exchange. For purposes of § 351(b), however, assumed liabilities are treated as boot only if they are described in § 357(b) or to the extent they are described in § 357(c)(1). Further, for purposes of § 357(c)(1), the only assumed liabilities taken into account are those other than § 357(b) and § 357(c)(3) liabilities.

Under § 357(c)(1), a transferor recognizes gain to the extent those liabilities assumed exceed the aggregate adjusted basis of all assets transferred by the transferor in the § 351 exchange.[66] Suppose that T incorporates his sole proprietorship in a § 351 exchange, transferring his business assets with a combined $40,000 basis and a $100,000 fair market value to X Corp. for X stock worth $45,000 and X Corp.'s assumption of T's liabilities totaling $55,000. If the liabilities are not described in § 357(b) or (c)(3), then under § 357(c)(1) T recognizes a $15,000 gain.[67]

T could readily avoid that gain in two ways: (1) T could have X Corp. assume only $40,000 of his liabilities or (2) he could contribute additional cash or property with an aggregate $15,000 basis. In either case, T would recognize no gain on the transfer under § 357(c)(1) because the amount of T's liabilities assumed would not

---

[64] 1980–2 C.B. 113; see also Rev. Rul. 95–74, 1995–2 C.B 75.

[65] If the transferee corporation may deduct assumed account payables, is it also taxable on transferred account receivables when payment on those receivables is collected? See Hempt Bros. v. United States, 490 F.2d 1172 (3d Cir. 1974) (assignment of income doctrine not applicable).

[66] § 357(c)(1); Regs. § 1.357–2(a).

[67] If the liabilities were described in § 357(b), T would recognize a $55,000 gain under § 351(b) (the smaller of T's $60,000 realized gain and the $55,000 liabilities assumed, which would be treated as boot received). If the liabilities were described in § 357(c)(3), T would recognize no gain (or loss), because the liabilities would not be treated as boot for purposes of § 351(b) and would be disregarded for purposes of § 357(c)(1).

exceed the aggregate adjusted bases of all property transferred by T.

Would T also avoid that gain by transferring his written "promise" to pay X Corp. $15,000? He would if he is treated as having a $15,000 basis in his own note as the court concluded in *Peracchi v. Commissioner*.[68] In that case, the court found that the note was *bona fide* debt, in part because it bore interest at an appropriate rate and the transferor was creditworthy. The court concluded that the transferor's basis in his own note equaled its face value, because there was a realistic possibility that the transferee-corporation's creditors would enforce the note. Because the transferor had a basis in the transferred note, he avoided gain under § 357(c).[69]

The Service, however, continues to believe that a transferor has a $0 basis in her note, possibly because when the transferor is the sole shareholder of the transferee-corporation (as in *Peracchi*), she may essentially choose whether the corporation will enforce the note, at least if the corporation can pay its debts without relying on the note. In any event, a transferor may readily avoid gain under § 357(c)(1) and that "zero-basis" issue either by transferring additional property to the transferee-corporation or by reducing the amount of liabilities assumed by that corporation.

(iii) Assuming a Liability. For purposes of § 357, a corporate-transferee "assumes" a transferor liability even when the transferor remains legally responsible for the liability (*e.g.,* a recourse liability where the transferor remains secondarily liable).[70] However, if it is expected that the transferor ultimately will satisfy the liability, the liability is not considered to be "assumed" for purposes of § 357(c). For purposes of § 357, even a nonrecourse liability can be "assumed."[71] However, if the nonrecourse liability that encumbers transferred property also encumbers other property and it is expected that the transferor rather than the transferee will satisfy part or all of the liability, the amount of the nonrecourse liability "assumed" for purposes of § 357 cannot exceed the fair market value of the property transferred.

If encumbered property is transferred to a corporation and the encumbrance is *not* treated as "assumed" by the corporation under

---

[68] 143 F.3d 487 (9th Cir.1998).

[69] See also *Lessinger v. Commissioner,* 872 F.2d 519 (2d Cir.1989) (where the court reached the same conclusion (*i.e.,* no gain under § 357(c)) but on different grounds). Cf. *Alderman v. Commissioner,* 55 T.C. 662 (1971) (concluding that a taxpayer has no basis in her note).

[70] § 357(d)(1).

[71] § 357(d)(1)(B).

§ 357(d), the corporation still may pay off some or all of the encumbrance to increase its equity in the property. While the statute does not directly speak to the tax consequences of such a payment, it seems clear that the transaction ought to be taxed as a deemed distribution from the corporation to the shareholder followed by a payment by the shareholder to the creditor. As discussed in Chapter 4, such a deemed distribution often will result in dividend income to the shareholder without any increase in the shareholder's stock basis. In such circumstances, gain recognition under § 357(b) or (c)(1) ultimately might prove more favorable than deferring the gain by avoiding a corporate "assumption" of the encumbrance.

(iv) A Curious Case of Double Counting. Suppose that B owns Blackacre with an adjusted basis and fair market value of $1,000 and wants to buy Whiteacre for $1,000, funded entirely by seller financing. B might offer both Blackacre and Whiteacre as security for the seller's loan. For example, B might acquire Whiteacre for nothing down but sign a nonrecourse note for $1,000 secured by both properties.

If, in a § 351 exchange, B now contributes both properties to a newly formed corporation in exchange for its stock, B recognizes no gain or loss and takes a $1,000 basis in the stock received ($2,000 aggregate basis of property transferred minus $1,000 liability assumed). § 351(a); § 357(a); § 358(a)(1) and (d)(1). But if B transfers each parcel to a separate, newly formed corporation, B still recognizes no gain or loss but arguably takes a $0 basis in each corporation's stock ($1,000 aggregate basis of property transferred minus $1,000 liability assumed): because the liability encumbers each asset, it appears to reduce B's stock basis in each § 351 exchange. Yet, this plainly counts the liability twice. B can avoid this double counting by having the two corporations agree that one of the corporations will satisfy the debt (as long as that corporation is also expected to satisfy the debt). See § 357(d)(2)(A).

(c) Basis and Holding Period.

(i) In general. Section 351 defers gain or loss, rather than eliminating it, and § 358(a) achieves this deferral by preserving a transferor's realized but not recognized gain or loss in the basis of the qualified stock received in the exchange (*i.e.*, the stock of the transferee corporation received without the recognition of gain or loss). That basis generally equals the following:

(a) The aggregate basis of the transferor's property surrendered in the exchange, plus

(b) The transferor's gain, if any, recognized under § 351(b) and § 357(c)(1) as part of the exchange, minus

(c) The value of any boot received by the transferor in the exchange, minus

(d) The amount of the transferor's liabilities (other than § 357(c)(3) liabilities) assumed by the transferee-corporation in the exchange.[72]

A transferor takes a basis in any boot received equal to its fair market value.[73]

Further, the transferor may determine her holding period for qualified stock received in the exchange by including ("tacking" on) the holding period of property surrendered in the exchange. Under § 1223(1), a person's holding period of property received in an exchange includes the holding period for property surrendered in the exchange (*i.e.*, the holding period "tacks") if—

(a) The person takes an exchanged basis in the property received (*i.e.*, her basis in that property is determined by looking to the basis of the property surrendered); and

(b) The property surrendered was a capital asset or § 1231 asset.[74]

Because a transferor takes an exchanged basis in qualified stock received in a § 351 transaction, her holding period for the qualified stock received includes the holding period (or periods) for the property surrendered in the exchange to the extent the surrendered property was a capital asset or a § 1231 asset.[75]

The holding period may matter, because it can affect whether the transferor recognizes long- or short-term capital gain or loss on a later disposition of the qualified stock. Cf. § 1222(3) and (4) (providing that long-term capital gain or loss arises on the sale or

---

[72] § 358(a)(1) and (d). Note that § 358(a) requires a reduction for the value of boot received, and for this purpose, § 358(d) treats the assumption of a transferor's liabilities, other than § 357(c)(3) liabilities, as money received by the transferor.

Section 358(h) and § 362(e)(2)(C) provide possible exceptions to this general basis rule. Section 358(h) is discussed at section 2.04(c) *infra*, and § 362(e)(2)(C) is discussed at section 2.05(b) *infra*.

[73] § 358(a)(2). For this purpose, boot would include nonqualified preferred stock.

[74] See § 7701(a)(44) (defining "exchanged basis property").

[75] The transferor's holding period for any boot received begins on the date of receipt.

exchange of a capital asset held for more than one year). Recall that an individual's long-term capital gain may be taxed at preferential rates. See § 1(h).

Note as well that because a transferor cannot tack the holding period of an ordinary-income asset surrendered in the exchange, § 1223(1) prevents the transferor from quickly converting ordinary income to long-term capital gain through a § 351 exchange. Instead, if the transferor receives qualified stock for an ordinary-income asset, she will recognize long-term capital gain on a sale of that stock only if she has actually held the stock for more than one year.

Suppose that T transfers property to X Corp. with a $21,000 basis and a $30,000 fair market value in exchange for $30,000 of X stock in a § 351 transaction. Under § 351(a), T recognizes none of his $9,000 realized gain. Under § 358, T's basis in the X stock is $21,000 (*i.e.*, his basis in the property surrendered), preserving that $9,000 gain.

If T receives boot in addition to X stock, T recognizes his realized gain up to the value of the boot received, and the boot and gain are taken into account in determining T's basis in the X stock. For example, assume that in a § 351 exchange T transfers property with a $21,000 basis to X Corp. but receives X stock worth $24,000 and $6,000 of boot in return. T recognizes $6,000 of his $9,000 realized gain. § 351(b). His X stock basis again equals $21,000 computed as follows: $21,000, the basis of the property transferred by T, plus $6,000, his recognized gain, minus $6,000, the value of the boot received.[76] Again, T's basis in the X stock preserves his realized but not recognized gain ($3,000 in this case). His basis in the boot received equals its fair market value ($6,000). § 358(a)(2).

What happens in the preceding example if the boot is an X debt instrument with a $6,000 principal amount and value and T takes his recognized gain into account under the installment method? T's basis in the X stock still equals $21,000 ($21,000, his basis in the property, plus $6,000, the gain to be recognized, minus $6,000, the fair market value of the boot received).[77] Thus, T's X stock preserves the realized but not recognized $3,000 gain. The remaining $6,000 of gain is preserved by giving the $6,000 debt instrument a $0 basis,

---

[76] § 358(a)(1). T's basis in the X stock equals his basis in the transferred property, because his recognized gain exactly offsets the value of the boot that he received. As subsequent examples illustrate, that equality will not occur if the value of the boot received exceeds recognized gain or, in some cases, when liabilities are assumed.

[77] Notice that basis is increased by the $6,000 of gain even though the gain on the note will not be recognized until payment is made. Prop. Reg. § 1.453–1(f)(3)(ii).

the difference between T's basis in the transferred property ($21,000) and the amount allocated to the qualifying stock ($21,000).[78] Note that boot is typically given a basis equal to its value because it is taxable on receipt. If the installment method applies, however, debt instruments are not taxable on receipt and, therefore, are allocated only that basis left over after determining the basis of the qualifying stock under § 358(a).

Suppose, instead, that T receives $18,000 of X stock and $12,000 of boot in the exchange. T recognizes a $9,000 gain (the smaller of his $9,000 realized gain and the $12,000 boot received). He takes a $12,000 basis in the boot and an $18,000 basis in the X stock (equal to $21,000, the basis of the property transferred by T, plus $9,000, his recognized gain, minus $12,000, the value of the boot received). Thus, his basis in the X stock equals its value, a result that makes sense, because T recognized all of his realized gain on the exchange.[79]

If X Corp. assumes T's liabilities, T may recognize gain and the assumption may affect T's basis in the X stock. Assume that in a § 351 exchange T again transfers property with a $21,000 basis but receives only $24,000 of X stock and X assumes a $6,000 T liability. If the liability is described in § 357(b), the results are the same to T as if T had received $6,000 of boot. Thus, T recognizes a $6,000 gain and takes a $21,000 basis in the X stock.

If the liability is described in § 357(c)(3), the liability assumption is not treated as boot for purposes of § 351(b), is disregarded in applying § 357(c)(1), and is disregarded in applying § 358. Thus, the results are the same as if T received no boot in the exchange, and T recognizes none of his realized gain and takes a $21,000 basis in the X stock.[80]

If the liability is described in neither § 357(b) nor § 357(c)(3), the liability will not be treated as boot for purposes of § 351(b), but will be taken into account for purposes of § 357(c)(1) and § 358. Because the liability ($6,000) does not exceed T's basis in the transferred property ($21,000), T recognizes no gain under § 357(c)(1).

---

[78] Prop. Regs. § 1.453–1(f)(3)(ii).

[79] If the boot is an X debt instrument and the installment method applies, all of T's $9,000 of gain is preserved through his basis in the debt instrument, which equals $3,000, the difference between T's basis in the transferred property ($21,000) and the amount allocated to his X stock ($18,000). Prop. Regs. § 1.453–1(f)(3)(ii).

[80] Because T's X stock is worth $24,000, his $21,000 basis in that stock defers $3,000 of gain, equal to T's $9,000 realized but not recognized gain minus $6,000, the deduction or basis that would have resulted if T had paid the liability before the transfer.

His basis in the X stock is $15,000 (equal to $21,000, the basis of the property transferred by T minus $6,000, the amount of the liability assumed). Because the X stock is worth $24,000, T's basis preserves his realized but not recognized $9,000 gain.

Note that if in any of the examples above, T received multiple classes of X stock, he would allocate his aggregate basis for that stock, among the classes in proportion to their relative fair market values.[81] For example, assume that in a § 351 exchange, T transfers property with a $21,000 basis in exchange for $20,000 of X common stock and $10,000 of X preferred stock. Under § 351(a), T recognizes none of his $9,000 realized gain, and under § 358, his aggregate basis in the X stock is $21,000. He allocates $14,000 of that amount ($20,000/$30,000 times $21,000) to the common stock and $7,000 ($10,000/$30,000 times $21,000) to the preferred stock.

Finally, if in any of the examples above, the property T transferred in the exchange was a capital or § 1231 asset in his hands, he tacks the holding period of that property on to the holding period for his X stock. Otherwise, his holding period for the stock begins on the date of the exchange.

(d) Multiple Asset Transfers.

When a person transfers more than one asset to a corporation in a § 351 exchange, several additional questions arise, including the following: (i) Can the basis of a transferred asset be specifically allocated to a portion of any qualified stock received in the exchange; (ii) how does the transferor determine her holding periods in the qualified stock received; and (iii) if boot is received, how is the boot to be allocated among the transferred assets and taken into account?

First, if a person transfers multiple assets to a corporation in a § 351 exchange, the person cannot designate that a particular asset is exchanged for specific shares.[82] Instead, an allocable portion of each asset is deemed transferred for each share of qualified stock received in the exchange, with the allocation made in proportion to the fair market values of the transferred assets.

Suppose that T owns two assets each worth $1,000, Asset 1 with a $1,000 basis and Asset 2 with a $200 basis. In a § 351 exchange, T transfers the assets to X Corp. in exchange for 100 shares

---

[81] Regs. § 1.358–2(b)(2).

[82] Cf. Regs. § 1.358-2(a)(2) (for a different rule for reorganization exchanges under § 354 and § 356). See also Prop. Regs. § 1.358-2(g)(2) (allowing the basis of stock transferred to the transferee to be tacked if no liabilities are assumed by the corporate transferee in the exchange).

of X common stock and 100 shares of X preferred stock, and each block of stock is worth $1,000. If T plans to sell the X preferred stock shortly after the exchange, he may prefer to designate that he received the preferred stock for Asset 1, the high-basis asset, so that the preferred stock took a $1,000 basis. In Rev. Rul. 85–164,[83] however, the Service concluded that a portion of each asset transferred is exchanged for each share of qualified stock received. As a corollary, it concluded that the aggregate basis of the assets transferred is allocated among classes of stock received in proportion to the fair market values of each class. Thus, in the example, the common and preferred stock each have an aggregate basis of $600 (one-half of $1,000 plus one-half $200), and each share of stock has an aggregate basis of $6 ($600/100).

Second, because a portion of each asset is deemed transferred for each share of qualified stock received in the exchange, a share may have a split holding period (and split basis) to reflect the assets transferred. In the example above, assume Asset 1 was a capital asset that T had held for more than one year while Asset 2 was inventory. Under § 1223(1), T can tack his holding period for Asset 1, a capital asset, but not for Asset 2, the inventory. Thus, an X share has a holding period of more than one year, to the extent received in exchange for Asset 1, but a holding period that begins on the date of the exchange, to the extent received in exchange for Asset 2. Because T received an undivided one-half interest in each X share in exchange for each asset, an undivided one-half interest in each X share has a holding period of more than one year (and a basis of $5), and an undivided one-half interest has a holding period that begins on the date of the exchange (and a basis of $1). As a result, the sale of each share can result in both long-term and short-term capital gain.

Finally, if a person transfers multiple assets and receives boot in a § 351 exchange, the person determines realized and recognized gain or loss separately for each transferred asset. In making this determination, the total consideration and boot received is allocated among the transferred assets in proportion to their fair market values.[84]

Suppose that in a § 351 exchange, T transfers Assets 1, 2, and 3 to X Corp. in exchange for X stock worth $100,000 and $40,000 in

---

[83] 1985–2 C.B. 117 (noting that a specific designation cannot be made even if the property is transferred at separate times if the transfers are as part of one integrated transaction).

[84] Rev. Rul. 68-55, 1968-1 C.B. 140 (also providing that § 351(b) applied separately to each transferred asset). See also Prop. Regs. § 1.351-2(b) (providing for the allocation of boot among the transferred assets in proportion to their fair market values).

cash. Asset 1 had a $20,000 basis and $35,000 value, Asset 2 a $10,000 basis and $35,000 value, and Asset 3 an $80,000 basis and $70,000 value. In allocating the total consideration and boot, T is treated as receiving one-fourth of each amount ($35,000/$140,000) for Asset 1 as well as for Asset 2 and one-half of each amount ($70,000/$140,000) for Asset 3. Thus, T receives total consideration of $35,000 for each of Assets 1 and 2 (one-fourth of $140,000) and $70,000 for Asset 3 (one-half of $140,000), realizing a $15,000 gain on Asset 1, a $25,000 gain on Asset 2, and a $10,000 loss on Asset 3. Further, T receives boot of $10,000 on each of Assets 1 and 2 (one-fourth of $40,000) and $20,000 on Asset 3 (one-half of $40,000).

Under § 351(b)(1), a transferor recognizes realized gain up to value of the boot received, while under § 351(b)(2), she recognizes none of her realized loss. Because the value of the boot that T received for each of Assets 1 and 2 ($10,000) was less than her realized gain on the asset, she recognized a $10,000 gain on the transfer of each asset. § 351(b)(1). Because Asset 3 is a loss asset, she recognized no loss on her transfer of that asset. § 351(b)(2). In total, T recognizes a $20,000 gain. Thus, her aggregate basis in the X stock equals $90,000 ($110,000, the aggregate basis of the transferred assets, plus $20,000, the recognized gain, minus $40,000, the value of the boot received).[85]

---

[85] Note that this proportionate allocation scheme for boot may not make sense if, as part of a § 351 exchange, the transferee corporation also assumes transferor liabilities. Boot is accounted for under a gain-first regime, while liabilities are accounted for under a basis-first regime. Consequently, if boot is allocated among the transferred assets based on their relative values but without considering liabilities assumed, the same basis may be claimed twice, once to account for boot and a second time to account for liabilities.

For example, assume that T transfers two assets, Assets 1 and 2, to X Corp. in a § 351 exchange. Asset 1 had a $10 basis and $10 value, while Asset 2 had a $10 basis and $90 value. In the exchange, T receives X stock worth $70 and $10 cash and X Corp. assumes a $20 liability of T's, a liability not described in § 357(b) or § 357(c)(3). Under § 357(c)(1), T recognizes no gain on X Corp.'s assumption of the liability, because the amount of the liability assumed ($20) does not exceed the aggregate basis of the assets transferred (also $20).

If T determines his gain under § 351(b) by allocating the boot among the transferred assets in proportion to their values, however, T eliminates $1 of gain. In the proportionate boot allocation, $1 would be allocated to Asset 1 and $9 to Asset 2, and under § 351(b), T would recognize no gain on Asset 1 and a $9 gain on Asset 2. If § 358(a)(1) were applied literally, T's basis in the X stock would be a negative $1 ($20 aggregate basis of assets transferred, plus $9 of gain recognized, minus $10 of boot received, minus $20 of liabilities assumed). Because an asset cannot have a negative basis, T's basis in the X stock would be $0, thereby eliminating $1 of gain. See Priv. Let. Rul. 2008-45-14 (Nov. 7, 2008) (appearing to bless the proportionate allocation scheme in a comparable case).

(e) § 358(h)—An Anti-Abuse Rule.

Suppose, in a § 351 exchange, that T transfers property with a basis and fair market value of $20,000 in exchange for X stock with a fair market value of $1,000 and X Corp.'s assumption of T's $19,000 deductible expense (*e.g.,* a liability for deferred compensation or environmental remediation). T recognizes no gain, because he has no realized gain. At first glance, because § 351 applies to the exchange and the liability is described in § 357(c)(3), it appears that T receives stock with a $20,000 basis and a $1,000 fair market value. § 358(d)(2) (not treating § 357(c)(3) liabilities as money received in applying § 358(a)). If so, T could sell the stock and report a $19,000 loss and X Corp. might also be able to take a $19,000 deduction under § 162 if it pays the liability. However, § 358(h) generally requires T to reduce his basis in the X stock by the amount of any § 357(c)(3) liability (or more precisely any liability that does not reduce basis under § 358(d)(1)).[86] In the example, T's basis in the X stock would be $20,000 minus $19,000 or $1,000. That is, T cannot create a loss on the X stock by having X Corp. assume the liability. Note, however, that § 358(h) does not apply (and so the transferor's stock basis is not reduced) if the trade or business with which the liability is associated is transferred to X Corp. § 358(h)(2)(A) See also Regs. § 1.358-5(a).

Section 358(h) may also apply to the assumption of contingent liabilities, which historically were disregarded much like § 357(c)(3) liabilities. A series of famous tax shelters involved the assumption of contingent liabilities and taxpayers relied on § 351 and its associated basis provisions to create stock with an adjusted basis far in excess of value, stock that when sold would produce an immediate capital loss.

Consider the following case: X Corp. forms SubCo by transferring unimproved real estate having adjusted basis and value of $100 million but subject to environmental clean-up obligations of approximately the same amount. Thus, the stock of SubCo received by X Corp. has little or no value. However, if the environmental clean-up costs are ignored either because they are too contingent to be taken into account or because they would be deductible by X Corp. when paid, X Corp. will take a basis in the SubCo stock of $100 million unreduced by the liability. If the SubCo stock is then sold by X Corp., X Corp. will be entitled to claim an immediate capital loss of the full $100 million less the little it receives for the stock.[87] Arguably, SubCo. might also deduct the environmental

---

[86] Note, however, that the stock's basis is not reduced below its value.

[87] See, e.g., *Coltec v. United States*, 434 F.3d 1340 (Fed. Cir. 2006).

clean-up costs when paid, essentially duplicating the loss.[88] Section 358(h) also responds to these types of transactions, generally eliminating X Corp.'s loss (to the extent tied to the liability). And even if the liability is not deductible by SubCo when paid, the transaction in the absence of § 358(h) would still represent acceleration of the deduction to X Corp.

2.05 Tax Consequences—The Corporate Transferee

(a) In General.

When a corporation acquires property for its stock, it should not recognize gain or loss. Its stock has no intrinsic value to the corporation: the stock's value, if any, is a function of what the corporation receives for it. For example, suppose a corporation exchanges its stock for $10,000 of cash. Taxing the corporation on the $10,000 received makes little sense. No asset has increased in value, no services have been performed, and no productive activity of any kind has taken place.

Section 1032 confirms that a corporation recognizes no gain or loss on the receipt of property (including cash) in exchange for its stock (or stock rights).[89] Under general principles, a corporation also recognizes no gain or loss when it acquires property for cash, its debt, or the assumption of the transferor's liabilities. However, if a transferee corporation transfers boot in the § 351 exchange, it may recognize gain, but not loss. § 351(f) (adopting the principles of § 311).[90] It recognizes gain on its use of appreciated non-cash property, equal to the excess of the property's fair market value over its adjusted basis.

Section 358 gives the transferor an exchanged basis in the qualified stock received, preserving any unrecognized gain. Section

---

[88] But see Rev. Rul. 80-198, 1980-2 C.B. 113 (allowing the deduction but noting that the transaction did not have a tax avoidance purpose); Rev. Rul. 95-74, 1995-2 C.B. 36 (warning that the transferee-corporation may be unable to deduct the payment of an assumed "deductible" liability, particularly in a case involving tax avoidance).

[89] Note that § 1032 applies to the corporation even if § 351 does not apply to the shareholder. For example, if a taxpayer sells property to a corporation in exchange for the corporation's stock in a transaction not governed by § 351, § 1032 still gives non-recognition treatment to the corporation. Further, while § 1032 shields the corporation from recognition of gain (or loss) on an exchange of stock for property, Regs. § 1.1032–1(a) offers the same protection when stock is issued for services. Not only is gain not recognized, but a transferee-corporation issuing stock for services can take a deduction equal to the fair market value of the stock if payment in cash would be an ordinary and necessary business expense. Rev.Rul. 62–217, 1962–2 C.B. 59, modified by Rev.Rul. 74–503, 1974–2 C.B. 117.

[90] See the discussion of § 311 at Section 8.02 *infra*.

362(a) preserves the same gain in the basis that the transferee corporation takes in the transferred property. When the transferee corporation receives property in a § 351 exchange, § 362(a) generally provides that the transferor's basis for the transferred property "carries over" to the corporation. If the corporation receives multiple assets, the transferor's basis in each transferred asset "carries over" to the corporation.[91]

More precisely, the transferee corporation generally takes a basis in the property transferred equal to the transferor's basis plus any gain recognized by the transferor under § 351(b) and § 357(c)(1). § 362(a).[92] If more than one asset is transferred, it is not altogether clear how this gain is allocated among the transferred assets, but under the apparent Service approach and consistent with Rev. Rul. 68-55, any gain recognized by a transferor on an asset should be allocated to that asset under § 362 by the corporation.

Because a transferee-corporation determines its basis in transferred property with reference to the transferor's basis, the corporation tacks the transferor's holding period for the property. § 1223(2).

By way of illustration, suppose that in a § 351 exchange, T transfers Assets 1, 2, and 3 to X Corp. in exchange for X stock worth $100,000 and $40,000 in cash. Asset 1 had a $20,000 basis and $35,000 value, Asset 2 a $10,000 basis and $35,000 value, and Asset 3 an $80,000 basis and $70,000 value. T recognizes a $10,000 gain on each of Assets 1 and 2. Under § 1032(a) and general principles, X Corp. recognizes no gain or loss on its acquisition of T's assets in exchange for X stock and cash. Under § 362(a), X Corp. takes a basis in each transferred asset equal to T's basis plus T's gain recognized on the asset, or a $30,000 basis in Asset 1, a $20,000 basis in Asset 2, and an $80,000 basis in Asset 2. Because X Corp. takes a transferred basis in each transferred asset, it tacks T's holding period for each asset. § 1223(2).

The results to X Corp. generally would be the same if X Corp. transferred non-cash property to T rather than $40,000 in cash, except that X Corp. could recognize gain. For example, if X Corp. transferred an asset with a $15,000 basis and $40,000 value to T (and neither § 1031 nor another non-recognition section applied), X Corp. would recognize a $25,000 gain, the excess of the asset's value over its basis. § 351(f). If the asset instead had a $48,000 basis,

---

[91] See *P.A. Birren & Son v. Commissioner*, 116 F.2d 718 (7th Cir. 1940).

[92] This basis increase may be limited if the transferor recognizes gain as the result of the transferee assuming a liability. See § 362(d), discussed in section 2.05(d) *infra*.

however, X Corp. would not recognize a loss, and because T would take a fair market value basis in the asset (§ 358(a)(2)), the $8,000 built-in loss in the asset would simply disappear. And be sure to note that the gain recognized by X does not affect X's basis in the assets received in the exchange.

(b) Section 362(e)—Limiting Duplicate Loss.

The general basis rule under § 362(a) is limited by § 362(e) to ensure that a contribution of property under § 351 generally does not create an aggregate built-in loss to the corporate transferee. Under § 362(e)(2), a corporation cannot take an aggregate basis in property contributed by a transferor in excess of the property's aggregate fair market value. This provision applies on a transferor-by-transferor basis to all § 351 transactions, including those in which the transferor is subject to U.S. taxation, but it disregards any transferred property to which § 362(e)(1) applies.[93]

Section 362(e)(2) applies if the transferee's aggregate basis in the applicable property received *from a transferor* would exceed (under § 362(a)) the property's aggregate value. § 362(e)(2)(A). Under § 362(e)(2)(B), that aggregate basis is reduced to the property's aggregate value, and this basis reduction is allocated among the transferred built-in loss property in proportion to their built-in losses. For this purpose, property has a built-in loss to the extent its adjusted basis exceeds its value immediately before the transfer.

Instead of reducing the corporate transferee's basis in the transferred property, the transferor can instead apply the basis reduction to decrease her basis in the corporation's stock received in the exchange. § 362(e)(2)(C)(i). Both the transferor and transferee corporation must elect to have this alternative rule apply. § 362(e)(2)(C)(ii). Thus, the effect of § 362(e)(2) is to preserve the aggregate built-in loss at the shareholder or corporate level, but not at both.

Consider the following example: In a § 351 exchange, T forms, X Corp., contributing Assets 1, 2, and 3 to X Corp. solely in exchange for X stock. Each asset has a $1,000 value, and at the time

---

[93] Section 362(e)(1) may apply to an inbound cross-border incorporation of loss property; that is, to the transfer to a domestic corporation by a person not subject to U.S. taxation. For § 362(e)(1) to apply to a transfer of property, two requirements must be met: First, the property must be section 362(e)(1)(B) property. Second, before taking § 362(e) into account, the transferee's aggregate basis in the section 362(e)(1)(B) property received in the transaction must exceed the property's aggregate value (*i.e.*, it would have a net built-in loss). Prop. Regs. § 1.362-4(b)(3). Section 362(e)(1)(B) property is any piece of transferred property that is not subject to federal income tax in the transferor's hands immediately before the transfer but is subject to such tax in the transferee's hands immediately after the transfer.

of the contribution, Assets 1, 2, and 3 have adjusted bases, respectively, of $800, $1,200, and $1,200. Assume that none of the assets is section 362(e)(1)(B) property.

Under § 351(a), T recognizes no gain or loss on the exchange and under § 358(a)(1), assuming no § 362(e)(2)(C) election is made, T takes an aggregate $3,200 basis in the X stock (*i.e.*, the sum of the bases of Assets 1, 2, and 3). Under § 1032, X Corp. recognizes no gain or loss on its acquisition of the assets for its stock. Under § 362(a), it would take a transferred basis in each asset, or $800 for Asset 1, $1,200 for each of Assets 2 and 3, or $3,200 in total.

Because that aggregate basis amount ($3,200) exceeds the aggregate value of the transferred assets ($3,000), § 362(e)(2) applies and X Corp. must reduce the § 362(a) basis amounts by that excess of $200. The basis reduction is allocated between the two built-in loss assets, Assets 2 and 3, in proportion to their built-in losses. Thus, $100 of the reduction ($200/$400 times $200) is allocated to each of Assets 2 and 3, and X Corp.'s basis in each of those assets is $1,100 (*i.e.*, $1,200 basis under § 362(a) minus $100).

If T and X Corp. make the election under § 362(e)(2)(C) to reduce T's basis in the X stock, T takes a $3,000 basis in the X stock ($3,200, the § 358 basis amount, minus $200, the basis reduction). X Corp. would then determine its basis in the assets under § 362(a), so that its basis in each of Assets 2 and 3 would be $1,200.

Note that § 362(e)(2) may apply to a transfer of assets even if the transferor's aggregate basis in the assets does not exceed their aggregate value but the transferor recognizes gain in the § 351 exchange. Consider the previous example, but assume that Asset 2 has a $1,000 basis and T receives $2,700 of X stock and $300 of cash in the exchange. Although T's aggregate basis in the assets equals their aggregate value (both $3,000), § 362(e)(2) applies to the exchange.

Under § 351(b), T allocates $100 of the boot to each transferred asset and recognizes a $100 gain on his transfer of Asset 1 (*i.e.*, the smaller of the $100 boot received and his $200 realized gain on the asset). T recognizes no gain on the other asset transfers, because none is realized. Under § 362(a), X Corp. would take a $900 basis in Asset 1 ($800 basis to T plus $100 recognized gain), a $1,000 basis in Asset 2, and a $1,200 basis in Asset 3, or an aggregate $3,100 basis.

Because that aggregate basis amount ($3,100) exceeds the aggregate value of the transferred assets ($3,000), § 362(e)(2) applies and, assuming no § 362(e)(2)(C) election is made, X Corp. must reduce the § 362(a) basis amounts by that excess of $100. This basis reduction is allocated to the sole built-in loss asset, Asset 3, and X Corp. reduces its basis in that asset by $100 to $1,100, taking a carryover basis under § 362(a) in the other assets.

(c) Section 362(d)—Limiting "Free" Loss Creation.

Suppose that T transfers property with a $7,000 basis and $30,000 fair market value to X Corp. in a § 351 exchange and the property is subject to a $60,000 nonrecourse liability secured only by the transferred property.[94] If the liability is not described in § 357(b) or § 357(c)(3), T recognizes a gain of $53,000 under § 357(c)(1), the excess of the $60,000 liability over the $7,000 basis. Without more, under § 362(a), X Corp. would take a $60,000 basis in the transferred property, T's $7,000 basis plus T's $53,000 recognized gain. Perhaps those results are acceptable if T is taxable on the $53,000 gain, but suppose that she is not either because she is a nonresident of the United States or is otherwise tax-exempt on the transfer. Now X Corp. enjoys an inflated basis at no cost to T.

Section 362(d) addresses that potential problem, sometimes limiting the corporate transferee's basis increase for gain recognized because of a liability assumption. First, under § 362(d)(1), the transferee cannot increase its basis in a transferred asset above its fair market value because of such gain.[95] Thus, in the example above, X Corp.'s basis in the transferred property would be limited to $30,000.

Second, under § 362(d)(2), the corporate transferee's basis increase may be limited if (i) a transferor recognizes gain on the assumption of a nonrecourse liability that is secured by assets not transferred to the transferee and (ii) no person is subject to tax on that gain. If those requirements are met, the transferee determines its basis in the transferred property by calculating the transferor's gain as if the transferee assumed only a ratable portion of the liability, a portion based on the relative fair market values of all assets subject to the liability.

Suppose in the preceding example, that T was not subject to tax on any gain recognized under § 357(c)(1) and that the assumed liability was secured by property with a $120,000 fair market value,

---

[94] Note that under proposed regulations, § 351 would not apply to a transfer if the fair market value of the property transferred by a transferor does not exceed the transferor's liabilities assumed in the transfer. See Prop. Regs. § 1.351-1(a)(1)(iii)(A) (providing in that case that "[s]tock will not be treated as issued for property").

[95] In the case of a nonrecourse liability in excess of the fair market value, the transferee would walk away from the property if confronted with a payment obligation.

only $30,000 of which was transferred in the § 351 exchange. Thus, § 362(d)(2) could limit X Corp.'s basis increase. To calculate that basis increase, X Corp. would be treated as assuming a ratable portion of the liability, determined by comparing the relative values of the transferred and non-transferred property subject to the liability. The transferred property constitutes one-fourth by value ($30,000/$120,000) of all property subject to the liability. Thus, to compute X Corp.'s basis increase under § 362(a) (but not T's gain under § 357(c)(1)), X Corp. would be deemed to assume one-fourth or $15,000 of the liability and T would be deemed to recognize only an $8,000 gain ($15,000 liability assumed minus $7,000 basis). As a result, X Corp. would take a $15,000 basis in the transferred asset, equal to T's $7,000 basis plus the $8,000 gain deemed recognized.[96]

(d) Parent Stock Paid to a Subsidiary Employee.

Suppose that Parent Corp. owns all stock of Sub Corp., and E, a Sub employee, wants to acquire equity in the venture. Parent Corp. might be reluctant to allow E to receive a direct interest in Sub Corp., but Parent Corp. might transfer some of its own stock to E as part of E's compensation. Since E does not work directly for Parent Corp., how should this transaction be taxed?

Under Regs. § 1.83–6(d), this transaction is treated as if Parent Corp. contributed its own stock to Sub Corp., which then transferred the stock to E. Because Parent Corp. owns all Sub stock, the first step of this two-step transaction is treated as a contribution of capital by Parent Corp. to Sub Corp. (or a § 351 exchange under the meaningless gesture doctrine). Consequently, the transaction is tax-free to both corporations, and under § 362(a), Sub Corp. would take a transferred basis in the Parent Corp. stock deemed contributed to its capital. But what is that basis?

Under Regs. § 1.1032–3, Sub Corp. takes a fair market value basis in the contributed Parent Corp. stock, just as if Parent Corp. contributed cash equal to the stock's value to Sub Corp. and Sub Corp. then used the cash to purchase the stock. The regulations adopt this circular cash approach only when the stock of Parent Corp. (or its stock option) is transferred by Sub Corp. in a taxable transaction *immediately after* receiving it.[97] Thus, because Sub

---

[96] The liability amount considered assumed under § 357(d)(2) could in some cases be less than the amount determined under § 362(d)(2). Thus, if § 362(d)(2) is interpreted literally, it could actually provide a basis benefit to the corporate transferee, a curious result for a rule born to combat abuse.

[97] In addition for Regs. § 1.1032-3 to apply, Sub Corp. must acquire the Parent Corp. stock directly or indirectly from Parent Corp. in a transaction to which § 362(a) or § 723 applies (but for Regs. § 1.1032-3), E cannot take a substituted basis in the stock, and the stock cannot be exchanged for Parent Corp. stock. Those requirements are met, because Sub. Corp. acquires

Corp. is treated as transferring the Parent Corp. stock to E immediately after receiving it, Sub Corp. recognizes no gain or loss on the
second step of the transaction.[98] If, though, such stock had actually
been contributed by Parent Corp. to Sub Corp. and then transferred
from Sub Corp. to E after some delay, the Service may argue that
Sub Corp. would take a zero basis in that stock and recognize gain
on the transfer to E. See, e.g., Rev. Rul. 74–503, 1974–2 C.B. 117,
revoked in part by Rev. Rul. 2006-2 2006-1 C.B. 261. But cf. Rev.
Rul. 80-76, 1980-1 C.B. 15 (concluding that when the parent corporation's majority shareholder transferred parent stock to a subsidiary employee, the employee had compensation income, the subsidiary was entitled to a corresponding deduction under § 162, and the
subsidiary recognized no gain or loss on the transfer of parent
stock).

(e) A Note on Installment Sales.

Under § 362(a), the transferee corporation generally takes a
basis in property received from a transferor in a § 351 exchange
equal to the transferor's basis plus any gain recognized by her on
the exchange. If a transferor receives transferee debt instruments
and the installment method under § 453 applies, she defers gain
until the debt instruments are satisfied. Prop. Regs. § 1.453–
1(f)(3)(ii). The transferee corporation correspondingly defers its
basis increase to account for that gain. As the transferor recognizes
gain under the installment method, the transferee increases its
basis in the transferred assets. *Id.*

2.06 The Relationship of Section 351 to Other Provisions and Legal Doctrines

Having focused on the components of § 351, we now step back
to view the non-recognition provision in a broader context. The alternative to non-recognition under § 351 is recognition under
§ 1001(c). While non-recognition often is a superior alternative for a
taxpayer, that is not always the case. For example, a transferor
might have a realized loss that she would prefer to recognize or a
transferor with an expiring net operating loss carryover may wish
to recognize gain to use the loss and secure a higher basis for the
transferee-corporation.

---

the Parent Corp. directly from Parent Corp. in a transaction to which
§ 362(a) would apply (but for Regs. § 1.1032-3) and E acquires the stock for
services, taking a cost basis in the stock.

[98] Assuming that payment to E for services rendered is an ordinary
and necessary expenditure if made by Sub Corp., the transfer of Parent
Corp. stock to E will give rise to a deduction to Sub Corp.

While § 351 nominally is not an elective provision, its requirements offer taxpayers the flexibility to avoid nonrecognition treatment when desirable (*i.e.*, to "bust" the § 351 transaction). For example, a transferor with property whose basis exceeds its fair market value might attempt to divorce her transfer from those of other transferors seeking nonrecognition. If successful, the nonrecognition-seeking transferors will control the corporation after their exchange thereby qualifying under § 351 while the loss-seeking transferor will fail the control test after her exchange thereby recognizing her loss.

The ability to sell property to oneself or to a related party to recognize a loss is circumscribed by § 267. This provision is intended to prevent taxpayers from recognizing built-in losses while retaining control over the property through a related party. An individual is considered related to a corporation only if the individual owns more than 50 percent in value of the corporation, actually and constructively. Thus, a taxpayer may recognize loss while still maintaining a modicum of control.

(a) Section 351 vs. Sale.

Often the owner of appreciated real estate slated for development would prefer to recognize the gain while the property is investment property rather than waiting until it is converted to property held for sale to customers. By so doing, an owner may be able to lock in some of the gain at favorable capital gains rates instead of recognizing all of the gain at ordinary income rates. Section 267 does not preclude a taxpayer from recognizing gain on a transfer to a controlled corporation. Even when there is no capital gains rate preference, because of the restrictions on deducting capital losses, there still may be an advantage in generating capital gain rather than ordinary income since capital losses can be deducted to the extent of capital gain.[99]

Suppose B owns investment real estate with a $100,000 basis and $300,000 fair market value. B intends to develop and subdivide the property into single family dwellings that will have an aggregate fair market value of $600,000 upon completion.[100] If B develops and then sells the property, B will recognize $500,000 of ordinary income. B would prefer to recognize $200,000 of the gain as capital gain, but current law does not permit such bifurcation.

Suppose that B transfers the undeveloped real estate to X Corp., a previously formed corporation wholly owned by B. In ex-

---

[99] § 1211.

[100] For purposes of the example, ignore the costs of development.

change B receives five-year notes bearing appropriate interest with a fair market value of $300,000. B would like to treat the transaction as a sale, reporting $200,000 of capital gain on the installment method as the notes are paid off. X Corp., the purchaser, would take a $300,000 cost basis under § 1012 and following development and sale would report $300,000 of ordinary income. The economic effect of a sale to a wholly owned corporation is as if B had sold the property to himself. But for tax purposes, the treatment is quite different.

Section 1239 in some circumstances recharacterizes what would otherwise be capital gain as ordinary income on a sale between related parties. However, the application of § 1239 is restricted to property that would be subject to depreciation in the hands of the purchaser. Here, since the transferee-corporation would hold the purchased property as inventory, the transferor would escape recharacterization of any recognized gain.

Under these circumstances, the Service has several weapons in its arsenal to recharacterize the transaction. It might argue that the financial instruments received by the transferor constitute stock in the corporation. Particularly if the corporation is thinly capitalized, the Service might argue that the transferor's likelihood of payment is inextricably tied to the performance of the transferee and therefore there is sufficient continuity to bring the transfer within § 351. Under this recharacterization, the transferee would take the transferor's basis under § 362. Alternatively, the Service might argue that the financial instruments received by the transferor should be ignored because payment is so speculative. Under this rationale, the transfer of property would be treated as a nontaxable contribution to capital, and the transferee would take the transferor's basis under § 362(a).

In *Burr Oaks Corp. v. Commissioner*,[101] three individuals transferred land to a controlled corporation, receiving in exchange three notes bearing interest of 6 percent, due in two years. Each note had a face amount of $110,000. The taxpayer claimed that the transaction was a sale, but both the Tax Court and the Court of Appeals ruled that the transaction was a contribution to the corporation in exchange for preferred stock. Since the corporation was capitalized with only $4,500, the purported debt was more than 80 times that amount. The courts found that the payment of the transferors was dependent on an undercapitalized corporation with uncertain prospects, depending on the success of the corporation. The finding that the transaction was not a sale meant that the

---

[101] 365 F.2d 24 (7th Cir.1966).

corporation took a carryover basis under § 362 rather than a cost basis under § 1012.[102]

When an attempted sale is recharacterized by the Service as a contribution to capital, what are the consequences to the transferor and to the corporate transferee? When a shareholder makes a contribution to capital, the shareholder recognizes no gain or loss and must increase his or her stock basis by the basis of the property contributed. Regs. § 1.118–1. Under § 118, the corporation recognizes no gain or loss and generally receives a carryover basis in the property. § 362(a). When the corporation makes payments on the "notes," the purported interest may be a dividend that may be ordinary income to the shareholder. See § 301. Retiring the "debt" may create ordinary income due to a failed redemption. See Chapter 5 *infra*.

(b) Assignment of Income.

A shareholder may be able to report gain on her sale to a wholly owned corporation, because the corporation is respected as a taxpayer separate from the shareholder. That separate treatment also causes problems in the judicially developed assignment of income area. Recall that if a transferor transfers an account receivable to a corporation in exchange for stock, the transferor recognizes no gain if the requirements of § 351(a) are met. The transferee-corporation will take the transferor's basis in the accounts receivable. § 362(a). However, even though § 351 applies, that section does not determine who will be taxed when the account receivable is paid off.

In *Lucas v. Earl,*[103] Mr. Earl attempted to shift his income from future services to his spouse, but the Supreme Court held that the assignment of future income did not shift the income to the assignee for federal tax purposes. The Supreme Court in *Helvering v. Eubank*[104] extended the rationale of *Lucas v. Earl* to previously earned income. There, a taxpayer assigned the right to receive insurance commissions which he had earned from work in previous years. In *Commissioner v. P.G. Lake, Inc.*[105] involving an exchange rather than a gratuitous transfer, the taxpayer assigned an oil payment right to a creditor to discharge a debt. Viewing the oil payment right as a right to receive future income, the Supreme Court held that the consideration received by the taxpayer was taxable as or-

---

[102] See also *Aqualane Shores, Inc. v. Commissioner,* 269 F.2d 116 (5th Cir.1959).

[103] 281 U.S. 111 (1930).

[104] 311 U.S. 122 (1940).

[105] 356 U.S. 260 (1958).

dinary income rather than capital gain since it was a substitute for future ordinary income.

Taking these cases together, one might conclude that if a taxpayer transfers an accounts receivable to a wholly owned corporation in a § 351 exchange, she should be taxed on the ordinary income when the account receivable is paid off. In many ways, a § 351 transfer is treated as a gratuitous transfer since gain normally is not recognized and the transferee-corporation carries over the transferor's basis. If so, *Lucas v. Earl* and *Eubank* suggest that the transferor ought to be taxed on collection. If viewed as a nongratuitous transfer, the transaction might be governed by *P.G. Lake.* Nevertheless, in *Hempt Bros., Inc. v. United States,*[106] the court held that Congress intended for § 351 to facilitate the incorporation of ongoing businesses and that to apply assignment of income principles would frustrate such incorporations.

It is worthwhile noting that favoring § 351 over the assignment of income doctrine does not necessarily mean a shifting of income. Indeed, the transferor and the transferee-corporation both take the basis that the transferor has in the receivables,[107] preserving the possibility of a double tax—a tax on the transferee-corporation when the receivables are paid off *and* a tax on the transferor if and when her stock is sold or a tax on the transferor upon distribution of the receivable proceeds. Conversely, when a taxpayer transfers deductible accounts payables to a corporation as part of a § 351 transaction, the Service has permitted the transferee-corporation to deduct the payables[108] even though the effect of § § 357(c)(3) and 358(d)(2) is to give the transferor-shareholder an equivalent deduction.[109]

(c) Business Purpose.

Before concluding that § 351 is all powerful, overriding entrenched judicial doctrines, note that in *Hempt Bros.,* the transferors were incorporating an ongoing business for an uncontested business purpose. Where § 351 is employed for a nonbusiness purpose, the non-recognition provision will often be ignored or give way to other principles. In general, neither the Service nor the courts consider tax avoidance standing alone or as a major motivation for the transaction as a "business purpose." The ubiquitous "business

---

[106] 490 F.2d 1172 (3d Cir.1974).

[107] Section 358 (transferor) and § 362 (transferee-corporation).

[108] Rev. Rul. 95–74, 1995–2 C.B. 36 (warning that the transferee-corporation may be unable to deduct the payment of an assumed "deductible" liability, particularly in a case involving tax avoidance).

[109] See p. 43–44 *supra.*

purpose" doctrine rears its head in a variety of contexts. For example, a transferor who forms a corporation under § 351 solely for the purpose of collecting the transferor's accounts receivable will be taxed when the transferee-corporation collects the payment.[110] Similarly the formation of a corporation solely for the purpose of qualifying a subsequent exchange of stock for non-recognition under the reorganization provisions will be disregarded where a direct exchange of assets for stock would have been a taxable event. If a transferor transfers appreciated property to a corporation which then sells the property and distributes the proceeds, the purported § 351 transfer may not apply and the transferor may be treated as having sold the property directly.[111]

(d) Tax Benefit Rule.

The tax benefit rule creates another tension between the non-recognition principles of § 351 and the judicially developed conservation of income principles. Under that rule, a taxpayer who derives a tax benefit (e.g., a deduction) in one year must recover that deduction in income in a subsequent year if some event inconsistent with the earlier deduction (e.g., a recovery of the deducted item) occurs. Suppose that B, an accrual-basis transferor, holds $10,000 in accounts receivable. B has taken the $10,000 into income, but has deducted $4,000 of the receivables as an uncollectible bad debt.[112] If B forms a corporation in a transaction governed by § 351, must B report gain to the extent of the previous deduction?

In *Nash v. United States,*[113] the Supreme Court held that § 351 was not inconsistent with the tax benefit rule since the transferor received stock equal to the net value of the assets transferred—in the example above, $6,000 of stock. The holding in *Nash* does not preclude application of the tax benefit rule if the transferor in the example above received $10,000 of stock since receipt of property equal to the face value of the receivables would be inconsistent with the earlier deduction.[114] Note also that the basis taken by both the transferor and the transferee-corporation will be $6,000 reflecting the bad debt deduction. If and when the transferee-corporation collects the full $10,000 face value of the receivable, it will be taxed on $4,000, and the transferor faces the possibility of a $4,000 tax upon disposition of his stock.

---

[110] See, e.g., *Brown v. Commissioner,* 115 F.2d 337 (2d Cir.1940).

[111] See e.g., *Estate of Kluener v. Commissioner,* 154 F.3d 630 (6th Cir.1998).

[112] See § 166(a).

[113] 398 U.S. 1 (1970).

[114] See, e.g., *Hillsboro Nat. Bank v. Commissioner,* 460 U.S. 370 (1983), for a discussion of the tax benefit rule.

Chapter 3

THE CORPORATION AS A
TAXABLE ENTITY

3.01 Corporate Tax Rates and Base

The corporate tax rate schedule[1] is a funny creature, progressive for some corporations, regressive for others, and flat for most. For corporations with taxable income of $100,000 or less, the rates are progressive, with brackets of 15 percent (on taxable income up to $50,000), 25 percent (on taxable income between $50,000 and $75,000), and 34 percent (on taxable income in excess of $75,000). There is a 35-percent bracket for corporate taxable income in excess of $10 million. What little graduation there is disappears for corporations with taxable income in excess of $18,333,333. These corporations are taxed at a flat 35-percent rate, because Congress wanted to restrict the benefits of lower rates to smaller businesses.

The graduation is eliminated in a convoluted manner through two surtaxes. First, an additional 5-percent tax is imposed on a corporation's taxable income in excess of $100,000, with a maximum additional tax of $11,750, which occurs at $335,000 of taxable income. Note that $11,750 equals the difference between taxing the first $75,000 of taxable income at a flat 34 percent ($25,500) and taxing it at the graduated rates ($13,750). Because of the 5-percent surtax, the benefits of reduced rates gradually disappear as a corporation's income increases from $100,000 to $335,000, and income within that range is taxed at a 39 percent rate (*i.e.*, the 34-percent nominal rate plus the 5-percent surtax). Second, a surtax phases out the 34-percent bracket for corporate taxpayers with taxable income exceeding $15 million. Those corporations pay an additional 3-percent tax on taxable income between $15 million and $18,333,333 (for a maximum additional tax of $100,000). Accordingly, for taxpayers with taxable income in excess of $15 million and less than $18,333,333, the marginal tax rate is 38 percent. Taxpayers with taxable income exceeding $18,333,333 are taxed at a flat 35-percent rate.

What little graduation exists in corporate tax rates is denied to "qualified" personal service corporations. § 11(b). Such corporations are "qualified" to be treated more harshly than other corporations by paying taxes at a flat 35-percent tax rate. A corporation is a

---

[1] See § 11.

qualified personal service corporation if it meets a function and an ownership test. § 448(d). Under the function test, substantially all of the activities of the corporation must involve the performance of services in the fields of health, law, engineering, architecture, accounting, actuarial science, performing arts or consulting. Under the ownership test, substantially all of the stock (by value) of the corporation must be held directly or indirectly by employees performing those services, by retired employees who performed those services in the past, by their estates, or by persons who hold stock in the corporation by reason of the death of such an employee or retired employee within the past two years.

Congress both giveth to and taketh away from qualified personal service corporations. While such corporations are subject to a flat 35-percent rate, they are entitled to use the cash-basis method of accounting.[2] There does not appear to be a well founded policy reason that justifies treating personal service corporations differently from manufacturing or sales corporations. Moreover, it is not always apparent whether a corporation constitutes a qualified personal service corporation. For example, a corporation that engages in financial planning is a qualified personal services corporation if the corporation is paid for its advice regardless of outcome. On the other hand, if payment is based on trade orders executed, the corporation is not a qualified personal service corporation.[3]

The graduated income tax rate structure may lure a high-income individual to use the corporate form to shelter income from the top individual rates. This incentive is enhanced by the preferential rates typically imposed on the individual's sale of stock or her receipt of dividends. Currently for individuals, the top tax rate applicable to most long-term capital gains and qualified dividends is 20 percent, while the top rate for ordinary income is 39.6 percent. For corporations, capital gains, whether long- or short-term, are taxed at the same rate as ordinary income.[4] Capital losses of corporations are also treated differently than those of individual

---

[2] Section 448 prohibits the use of cash method accounting by C corporations other than qualified personal service corporations, farming businesses, and corporations with no more than $5,000,000 of average annual gross receipts over the preceding three taxable years. § 448(a)(1) (for the general rule); *id.* at (b) and (c) (for the exceptions).

[3] Regs. § 1.448–1T(e)(4)(iv).

[4] Note that § 1201 provides for an alternative tax on net capital gains in lieu of the § 11 tax if the § 1201 tax is less. The § 1201 tax is the sum of (1) the § 11 tax on the corporation's taxable income minus net capital gains and (2) 35% of the net capital gains. Section § 1201 takes effect if the tax rate under § 11, disregarding the 3% and 5% surtaxes, exceeds 35%. Because that rate does not exceed 35%, the alternate tax on net capital gains does not apply, and those gains are taxed at § 11 rates.

taxpayers. A corporation can deduct capital losses only to the extent of capital gains.[5] Further, unlike individuals who can carry forward capital losses indefinitely, corporations generally can only carry losses back three years (perhaps resulting in a tax refund) and forward five years, if necessary. A loss unused in the current year is first carried back and then carried forward chronologically until the entire loss is used to offset income or the carryforward period expires.

Because corporate distributions historically were taxed to the recipient shareholders at ordinary income rates, while gains from the disposition of stock were taxed as capital gain, the capital gains preference historically has encouraged shareholders to eschew dividends and similar distributions in favor of corporate retention of capital. Alternatively, taxpayers and their advisors divined innumerable strategies to cause corporate distributions to be taxed as capital gain. At least for the time being, however, that calculus has changed, as "qualified dividend income" received by an individual is taxed at a rate no greater than 20 percent, the same rate as long-term capital gain.[6] Note that qualified dividend income is still ordinary income, not long-term capital gain, and therefore generally cannot be offset by capital loss.

The corporate tax is applied to taxable income. Unlike an individual, a corporation has no adjusted gross income from which deductions are taken to determine taxable income. Instead, a corporation computes its taxable income by subtracting all deductions directly from gross income. Deductions allowed to corporations differ from those available to individuals in several ways. For example, corporations have no standard deduction, personal exemption deduction, or personal deductions under §§ 211–223 (including items such as medical expenses and alimony). Section 162 does allow corporations to deduct expenses incurred for the production of income even if the income is not derived in a trade or business. Corporations are also allowed to deduct charitable contributions, but only up to 10 percent of taxable income. § 170(b)(2).

---

[5] § 1211(a). Other taxpayers can use capital losses to offset up to $3,000 of ordinary income. § 1211(b).

[6] § 1(h)(11). Qualified dividend income is a dividend paid on stock of a domestic or certain foreign corporations that meets the following added requirement: The shareholder must hold the stock for at least 61 days during the 121-day period that begins 60 days before the ex-dividend date (for common stock) or for at least 91 days during the 181-day period that begins 90 days before the ex-dividend date (for preferred stock). §1(h)(11)(iii) and §246(c). The ex-dividend date is the first date that the stock trades without the dividend.

Once a corporation's taxable income is determined, corporate tax liability may be offset by tax credits which offset corporate tax liability dollar-for-dollar. While the foreign tax credit (§ 27 and § 901) often is the most significant for a corporation, credits are also available for research (§ 41), targeted job expenditures (§ 51), and rehabilitation and energy expenditures (§§ 46–48).

Companion to the regular corporate income tax is the corporate alternative minimum tax. Perhaps in response to television and newspaper stories focusing on wealthy taxpayers paying little or no income tax, Congress acted to limit the advantages that a taxpayer can obtain from the various tax incentive provisions appearing throughout the Code. Under § 55(a), a taxpayer pays the excess, if any, of its minimum tax liability over its regular tax liability. In effect, the taxpayer's total federal income tax liability equals the *greater of* its regular tax liability or its minimum tax liability.

The corporate minimum tax equals 20 percent of a corporation's "alternative minimum taxable income" (or "AMTI") less an exemption amount.[7] The exemption amount equals $40,000, reduced (but not below zero) by one-quarter of the corporation's AMTI above $150,000. § 55(d)(3). Thus the exemption amount is zero for a corporation with AMTI equal to at least $310,000.

AMTI is intended to better reflect a corporation's economic income than is the regular taxable income as defined under § 61. AMTI is defined in § 55 as regular taxable income increased (or decreased) by specified tax preferences and other adjustments. Many of the adjustments made to taxable income to arrive at AMTI modify the *timing* of corporate deductions, rather than their *amount*. § 56–§ 58.

For example, under § 168 the cost of depreciable residential real estate used in a trade or business is recovered ratably over 27.5 years, while for the AMTI, the recovery period is lengthened to 40 years. Thus, for a piece of residential real estate costing $275,000, the" regular" cost recovery deduction is $10,000 ($275,000/27.5) each year, while the annual "AMTI" deduction is just $6,875 ($275,000/40).[8] Then, for the first 27.5 years: taxable income is increased by $3,125 each year in computing AMTI. But what about years 28 through 40? For those years, there is no cost recovery deduction to compute regular taxable income but there should still be

---

[7] § 55(b)(1)(B) and (d)(2). This tax is also reduced by the alternative minimum tax foreign tax credit for the year. § 55(b)(1)(B)(ii).

[8] In these computations, it is assumed that all property is purchased on the first day of the taxable year and the mid-month convention of § 168(d)(2) is ignored.

a cost recovery deduction of $6,875 for the AMTI. That is, taxable income should be adjusted *downward* in the latter years to arrive at AMTI.

While such a downward adjustment to a corporation's AMTI is permitted,[9] it may produce no tax benefit to the corporation. Recall that a corporation's effective tax liability is the greater of the regular tax or the alternative minimum tax. In the first 27.5 years, the depreciation adjustment may cause a tax increase by increasing the AMTI over taxable income. Unfortunately, the subsequent reduction of AMTI in years 28 through 40 may produce no tax benefit because the corporation will still be required to pay its regular tax liability, a tax liability no longer reflecting any cost recovery deduction.[10]

However, some relief may be offered by the alternative minimum tax credit, which is a credit against the taxpayer's *regular* tax liability. § 53. This credit reflects that, at least in part, AMTI is intended to defer, not eliminate, certain deductions (like cost recovery deductions). It is computed by taking into account deferral preferences (not those that result in permanent exclusion of certain income for regular tax purposes). The credit may allow the taxpayer to offset the regular tax liability for a taxable year with a portion of prior year's alternative minimum tax liability. The credit can be used in any year to the extent that the taxpayer's regular tax liability exceeds its minimum tax liability. § 53(c). The credit can be carried forward indefinitely. See § 53(b).

Even with tax preferences added back to taxable income to form alternative minimum taxable income, Congress was concerned that some highly profitable corporations might still pay insufficient taxes. This problem might arise because some transactions might increase a corporation's "earnings and profits" but not taxable income. For example, tax-exempt interest increases earnings and profits but not taxable income. To deal with these situations, a corporation with earnings in excess of alternative minimum taxable income must include a portion of such excess in alternative minimum taxable income. § 56(g).

Corporate AMTI includes three-quarters of a corporation's "adjusted current earnings" over AMTI (determined without this addi-

---

[9] See § 56(a).

[10] Of course, because of other possible adjustments to AMTI, the different tax rates applicable to taxable income and to AMTI, and the exemption amount applicable only to the minimum tax, it is impossible to know in advance the over-all effect of such timing problems on a corporation's tax liability.

tion).[11] Adjusted current earnings consist of AMTI less the alternative net operating loss deduction and less adjustments intended to better reflect the economic picture of the corporation. For example, accelerated depreciation deductions are replaced by straight-line deductions. In addition, amounts not otherwise taken into account in computing AMTI but affecting a corporation's earnings and profits account contribute to the "adjusted current earnings" stew.

Note that AMTI is computed using an "alternative" net operating loss, because "regular" net operating losses may reflect the tax preferences that the alternative minimum tax is trying to address. § 56(a)(4). Thus, the alternative net operating loss is determined by adding to taxable income any tax preferences or adjustments. § 56(d)(2). In addition, the alternative tax net operating loss deduction cannot exceed 90 percent of AMTI. §56(d)(1)(A)(i)(II). Suppose that for the year in question a taxpayer has $10 million of AMTI and an alternative net operating loss of $11 million. The net operating loss reduces AMTI to $1 million, giving rise to $200,000 of AMT liability. The taxpayer may then carry forward $2 million of AMT net operating loss.

3.02 Associations Taxable as Corporations

Both the regular corporate tax of § 11 and the alternative minimum tax of § 55 are imposed on "corporations." Under § 7701(a)(3), the term "corporation" includes "associations, joint-stock companies, and insurance companies" but it does not include "partnerships." For several decades regulations tried to distinguish entities taxable as partnerships from associations taxable as corporations by reference to certain supposed "corporate characteristics" such as continuity of life, centralization of management, limited liability; and free transferability of interests. Reg. § 301.7701–2(a)(1) (repealed 1996) While these regulations were not by their terms elective, taxpayers usually could choose the desired business classification for their unincorporated business organizations (*i.e.*, to be taxed as partnerships or corporations) by manipulating relatively insignificant aspects of the organization. Regulations, often referred to as the "check-the-box" regulations, now make the election explicit, eliminating the formalities of the old regime and their attendant costs.

The switch to the "check-the-box" regulations could be tied to two events—(1) the rise of limited liability companies and (2) special tax treatment for publicly traded corporations. First, in the late 1980s and early 1990s, most states enacted statutes permitting businesses to organize as limited liability companies, entities that

---

[11] See § 56(g).

have all the non-tax characteristics of corporations (including limited liability for all investors) while technically not being corporations. The organizer of a limited liability company files articles of organization and an operating agreement instead of articles of incorporation and corporate by-laws, investors contribute cash or other property to the limited liability company and receive membership certificates instead of shares, and these investors are called "members" instead of "shareholders." Somewhat surprisingly, courts and the Service were willing to treat such corporate look-alikes as unincorporated entities, and so limited liability companies could then qualify for taxation as partnerships by manipulating their various "corporate characteristics."

As the use of limited liability companies spotlighted weaknesses in the old association regulations, Congress enacted § 7704 providing that publicly-traded partnerships (including limited liability companies and similar business organizations otherwise taxable as partnerships) would be taxed as corporations. Thus, two factors—the increasing failure of the meaningless "corporate characteristics" in the association regulations and the more objective standard imposed by § 7704—ultimately convinced the Treasury to replace the old association regulations with the "check-the-box" regulations, an explicitly elective regime for distinguishing entities taxable as partnerships from associations taxable as corporations. Note that because the statutory term "partnership" explicitly excludes all corporations, the regulations continue to provide that incorporated entities may not be taxed as partnerships.

Under Reg. § 301.7701–2(b)(1)–(8) (excluding (2)), a variety of business organizations are denied elective classification and must instead be taxed as corporations. These entities include all incorporated entities, heavily regulated entities such as insurance companies and banks, entities wholly owned by a state or municipality, and a variety of foreign business entities traditionally treated as corporations under domestic and foreign laws. All other business organizations are classified as "eligible" entities, see Reg. § 301.7701–3(a), and such organizations can elect to be taxed as a partnerships or as a corporations, with the default rule generally favoring partnership treatment. See Reg. § 301.7701–3(b)(1)(i). However, if an eligible entity has a single owner and does not elect to be taxed as a corporation, the entity is disregarded for federal income tax purposes and treated as a division if its owner is a corporation or a partnership or as a sole proprietorship if its owner is an individual. Reg. § 301.7701–3(b)(1)(ii). Thereafter, the entity need only file a new election if it is changing its status. Reg. § 301.7701–3(c)(1)(i). An eligible entity may change its election at any time, but once such a change is made, a subsequent change may not be made for 60 months. Reg. § 301.7701–3(c)(1)(iv).

Some foreign business organizations are not eligible entities. See Reg. § 301.7701–2(b)(8). For example, a Naamloze Vennootschap (NV) formed in the Netherlands is always taxable as a corporation. Reg. § 301.7701–2(b)(8)(i). If in response to our current elective classification regime the Netherlands creates a new form of business organization (say, a NNV) with all the attributes of an NV but with a new name, will such an entity be eligible for elective classification or will the Treasury amend its list of ineligible foreign entities? If we have truly moved to elective classification, then presumably foreign governments will be able to exploit elective classification by creating their own versions of limited liability companies.

In fact, invariably there is a corporate form in every country that can be treated as a corporation for foreign purposes and as a flow-through entity for U.S. tax purposes (*i.e.,* a hybrid entity). The ability of a U.S. business to structure its foreign operations in this manner opens up a Pandora's box of opportunities. For example, suppose that USCO has an entity in High Tax Land and an entity in Low Tax Land. Both entities are transparent for U.S. tax purposes but corporations for foreign tax purposes. An "interest payment" from High Tax Entity to Low Tax Entity will decrease overall foreign taxes and is completely ignored for U.S. purposes (*i.e.,* USCO is paying interest to itself).[12] Similar opportunities exist when a foreign entity is treated as transparent for foreign tax purposes but as a corporation for U.S. tax purposes (*i.e.,* a reverse hybrid). Consider USCO which wholly owns an entity in country X that is treated as a transparent entity for country X purposes but as a corporation for U.S. purposes. When the entity earns income, country X may not tax it because the tax authorities think the income is earned in the U.S. while the U.S. may not tax it because the Service thinks the income is earned by a country X corporation.

In § 7704(a), Congress provided that certain publicly traded partnerships will be taxed as corporations. For this purpose, a "publicly traded partnership" is one whose partnership interests are (1) traded on an established securities market or (2) are readily traded on a secondary market. § 7704(b). This provision was enacted as part of the Revenue Act of 1987 in response to the growth of "master limited partnerships," huge entities having thousands of partners and assets worth tens (or hundreds) of millions of dollars.

---

[12] If the entities were corporations for U.S. tax purposes, the interest received by Low Tax Entity might be subject to U.S. taxation even if not distributed. See § 951.

Note, though, that if the income of a partnership consists of 90% or more of investment income as defined in § 7704(d), the partnership will avoid the clutches of § 7704(a). The legislative history of this provision explains that no corporate-level tax need be imposed because a corporate-level tax was imposed on the underlying income-producing investment. The definition of "qualifying income" in § 7704(d), however, imposes no requirement that the passive-type income come from a corporate taxpayer.

3.03 Ignoring the Corporation: Dummy Corporations

Under certain circumstances, taxpayers will use the corporate form but try to avoid the corporate income tax by ignoring their own corporation. In some of these cases, the taxpayers simply ask the courts to pierce the corporate veil and attribute the corporation's income to its shareholders, arguing that the corporation should not be respected for tax purposes. In other cases, the taxpayers argue that income nominally earned by the corporation should be taxed to some other taxpayer because the corporation was acting as an agent.

The first argument—that the corporate form should be ignored—rarely succeeds. In *Moline Properties v. Commissioner,*[13] the Supreme Court held that a corporation engaging in any business activity will be treated as a taxpayer distinct from its shareholders, reasoning that the taxpayer, having sought the advantages of incorporation, must live with the disadvantages as well. On the other hand, if it is the Commissioner who seeks to challenge the bona fides of the corporation, the challenge may be more successful. In those circumstances, the Commissioner should be free to make the traditional "substance over form" argument because the Commissioner did not choose the taxpayer's form.

Hard-pressed to avoid the corporate income tax by piercing the corporate veil after *Moline,* taxpayers often argue that their corporations are dummies not properly taxable on income nominally received. For example, in *Commissioner v. Bollinger,*[14] individual taxpayers formed a corporation to hold title to land on which the taxpayers constructed apartment complexes. The corporate structure was used to acquire bank financing while avoiding Kentucky's usury law, which at the time limited the annual interest rate for noncorporate borrowers. Because lenders were willing to loan money only at higher rates, they required the nominal debtor and record

---

[13] 319 U.S. 436 (1943).
[14] 485 U.S. 340 (1988).

title holder of mortgaged property to be a corporate nominee of the true owner and borrower.

The loan documents referred to the corporate borrower as the "corporate nominee" of Bollinger. Moreover, Bollinger and the corporation entered into an agreement specifying in detail the agency relationship, with Bollinger assuming full responsibility for the property and agreeing to hold the corporation harmless from any liability it might sustain as his agent and nominee. In fact, Bollinger acted as general contractor for the construction and hired a resident manager for the operation of the completed project.

While Bollinger reported all income and losses generated by the corporate activities on his individual tax return, the Commissioner argued that the income and losses should be reported by the corporation. According to the Service, because the corporation held title to the real estate, its transactions could not be directly reported by its shareholders under the *Moline* doctrine.

The taxpayers argued that the corporation was acting as their *agent*. Just as a Sears clerk is not taxable on profits he rings up for Sears, so, too, the taxpayers argued, should the corporation not include the income and losses from their real estate project. In *National Carbide Corp. v. Commissioner,*[15] the Supreme Court indicated that, under some circumstances, a corporation could be the true, nontaxable agent for its shareholders. In its *National Carbide* opinion, the Supreme Court set forth six factors that determine whether a corporation should be treated as such an agent.

> (1) Whether the corporation operates in the name and for the account of the principal; (2) whether the corporation binds the principal by its actions; (3) whether the corporation transmits money received to the principal; and (4) whether receipt of income is attributable to the services of employees of the principal and to assets belonging to the principal; . . . (5) If the corporation is a true agent, its relations with its principal must not be dependent upon the fact that it is owned by the principal, if such is the case. (6) Its business purpose must be the carrying on of the normal duties of an agent.[16]

The Service argued that the taxpayer failed to satisfy the fifth factor because the corporation's actions were wholly dependent on its being controlled by the taxpayers, its shareholders. For a controlled corporation to satisfy the fifth *National Carbide* test, according to the Service, the relationship between the corporation and its

---

[15] 336 U.S. 422 (1949).

[16] *Id.* at 437.

shareholders must reflect an arm's length agreement between principal and agent. Paying nothing to the corporation for its services as agent was inconsistent with an arm's length agreement.

The Supreme Court ruled that the fifth *National Carbide* factor serves only as a generalized statement of the concern that the separate-entity doctrine of *Moline* not be subverted. The Court in siding with the taxpayer reasoned that an agency relationship is established if a writing memorializes the principal-agency relationship, the corporation indeed functions as an agent, and the corporation is held out as an agent and not the principal in all third party dealings.

The issue wrestled with by the courts in *Bollinger* is a difficult one in part because it arises in such counter-intuitive settings. Ignoring the corporation in these cases is natural—what is surprising is that they should be recognized under state usury law. Tax law has matured to the point where form usually will be disregarded in favor of substance. Somehow, state usury laws seem not to have been developed that far. After all, what is the difference between individual liability and corporate liability when the corporation has no assets and the shareholders individually guarantee the debt?

In many areas of the tax law, taxpayers are forced to take the bad as well as the good implications of a form they have adopted. The *Moline* doctrine discussed above is one such example. To the extent that taxpayers win cases like *Bollinger,* their victories may be explained, at least in part, with judges' discomfort with state or local laws, such as the usury statute in *Bollinger,* drawing seemingly arbitrary distinctions, distinctions which can have substantial legal impact far beyond the jurisdiction of the enacting legislatures. On the other hand, perhaps these judges ought to be more concerned with the need for certainty in applying the tax laws, forcing taxpayers to accept the tax consequences of the organizational form selected.

3.04 Ignoring the Corporation: Reallocation of Income and Related Issues

The previous section considered ways in which taxpayers seek to attribute corporate income away from the corporation and to other taxpayers. Sometimes a taxpayer may wish to attribute income *to* a corporation. For example, suppose that a taxpayer earns a salary of $400,000 per year. If the taxpayer can cause his wholly owned corporation to report $50,000 of that salary, he can reduce the rate of tax on this $50,000 from his 39.6-percent rate to the corporation's

15-percent rate.[17] In those circumstances, it is the Commissioner who wants to reallocate income, and there are a variety of statutory and common law weapons available to him. Somewhat surprisingly, the common law assignment of income doctrine is, in general, not part of the Commissioner's arsenal.[18]

A leading case is *Rubin v. Commissioner.*[19] In that case, Richard Rubin was the majority shareholder of Park International, Inc. ("Park Corp."). Park Corp. was formed exclusively to provide management services to Dorman Mills, Inc., a corporation owned by an unrelated third-party (although Rubin voted the third-party's stock and had an option to acquire it). All the management services were in fact performed by Rubin as Park Corp.'s employee, and Rubin was paid a salary for these services provided on behalf of Park Corp.

Because of Rubin's management abilities, Dorman Mills turned a substantial profit, one-quarter of which was paid to Park Corp. as the price of its management services. At issue in the case was whether the payments from Dorman Mills to Park Corp. were taxable to Park Corp. or to Rubin. In arguing that they should be taxed to Rubin, the Commissioner argued that the assignment of income doctrine of *Lucas v. Earl*[20] demanded that earned income be taxed to the earner.

The Circuit Court was unwilling to apply the rule of *Earl,* saying that the case—

> reveal[s] a tension between competing policies of the tax law. On the one side is the principle of a graduated income tax rate, which is undercut when individuals are permitted to split their income with others or to spread it over several years. . . . Opposing this is the policy of recognizing the corporation as a tax-

---

[17] This rate of 15 percent assumes that the corporation has no other taxable income. Note that if the corporation distributes the after-tax income of $42,500 (*i.e.,* 85% of $50,000), the distribution, at least currently, likely results in qualified dividend income also taxed at a 15% rate (assuming that the shareholder has in total no more than $400,000 of taxable income). § 1(h)(11). Thus, the taxpayer would net $36,125 (*i.e.,* 85% of $42,500), or $3,625 more than if the corporation had not been interposed (*i.e.,* the difference between $36,125 and $32,500, which is 65% of $50,000).

[18] If the assignment of income doctrine could be applied in a case like *Bollinger,* discussed in the preceding section, would it have been appropriate to assign an amount equal to a reasonable agency fee from Bollinger to the corporation, tax the assigned amount to the corporation as income, and then treat the corporation as distributing the after-tax amount as a dividend to Bollinger, who would be taxed on the dividend?

[19] 429 F.2d 650 (2d Cir.1970).

[20] 281 U.S. 111 (1930).

able entity distinct from its shareholders in all but extreme cases.[21]

While the Court in fact held only that broad, common law doctrines should not be used when more narrow statutory provisions are available,[22] the case has come to stand for the proposition that the assignment of income doctrine cannot be used to reallocate income from a corporation to its shareholder-employee. This reading of *Rubin*—supported by the quotation above—is unfortunate because there is no reason why the assignment of income doctrine cannot be applied with full vigor in the corporate context.

The *Rubin* court saw a conflict between the assignment of income doctrine and the principle that corporations should generally be recognized as distinct taxpayers. If such a conflict existed, surely it also would be present in the non-corporate context because individuals, at least as much as corporations, are respected as distinct taxpayers. Was the Supreme Court in *Lucas v. Earl* holding that Mrs. Earl was not a legitimate or recognizable taxpayer? Of course not.

In *Rubin,* the taxpayer worked for a Park Corp. as an employee loaned to Dorman Mills. Dorman Mills paid Park Corp. for the services provided, and the taxpayer received a salary in his capacity as employee of Park Corp. Under the court's holding, Park Corp. was taxable on what it received less what it paid to the taxpayer as salary. Suppose that the taxpayer had accepted a salary of $1.00. Is it not clear that what should have been paid—and taxed—to the employee as salary will now be taxed to the corporation?

Why should such income-shifting be countenanced? Suppose that Park Corp. was not a corporation but rather was the taxpayer's sister. Could the taxpayer have circumvented the doctrine of *Lucas v. Earl* simply by signing an employment contract with his sister? If not, why should such a technique work as between the taxpayer and his corporation?

Would application of the assignment of income doctrine to corporations and their employee/shareholders vitiate the corporate income tax? Mrs. Earl, for example, could earn her own income and be taxable on it. A corporation, of course, cannot physically earn anything.

---

[21] 429 F.2d at 652.

[22] The court remanded the case for reconsideration under § 482, a provision discussed *infra.*

Consider General Motors Corp. It builds cars and makes a profit on them. Is this corporate profit nothing but income of GM workers improperly assigned to the corporation? Surely not, because the GM workers are paid fair market value for their labor. The profit that GM makes on its cars equals the sale price of the cars over the fair market cost of production. That profit is a return on GM's capital, for when consumers buy a GM car, they receive not only the workers' labor but also part of the value of the GM plant and equipment. The corporation's profit represents a return on this capital as well as on the capital invested in producing a favorable business reputation, in maintaining that reputation (e.g., advertising), and in a host of other benefits sold to the consumers as part of their cars.

The Tax Court in *Rubin*[23] had agreed with the Commissioner that the assignment of income doctrine could be used to reallocate income from a corporation to its shareholder-employee. Despite its reversal in *Rubin,* the Tax Court maintained that position in *Foglesong v. Commissioner.*[24] The Tax Court was again reversed,[25] however, and in *Keller v. Commissioner,*[26] the Tax Court followed the circuit courts and rejected its prior position.

In *Keller,* the Tax Court did not reject application of the assignment of income doctrine entirely, but rather limited it to the case of a corporation failing to satisfy the *Moline* test of viability.[27] This limitation of the doctrine by the Tax Court reflects a complete misunderstanding of the assignment of income doctrine.

The assignment of income doctrine determines which of two taxpayers must report certain income. In the case of a corporation failing the *Moline* test, the corporation is ignored entirely for tax purposes so that all corporate income is taxable directly to its shareholder. In such circumstances, there is no room for—or need of—the assignment of income doctrine because there is only one taxpayer (the shareholder) to whom the income can be allocated. The assignment of income doctrine, in other words, cannot be applied in the one case to which the Tax Court purported to limit it.

---

[23] 51 T.C. 251 (1968), rev'd, 429 F.2d 650 (2d Cir.1970).

[24] T.C. Memo. 1976–294, rev'd, 621 F.2d 865 (7th Cir.1980).

[25] *Foglesong v. Commissioner,* 621 F.2d 865 (7th Cir.1980).

[26] 77 T.C. 1014 (1981).

[27] *Moline Properties v. Commissioner,* 319 U.S. 436 (1943), discussed in Section 3.03 *supra.*

Each reported case makes it even less likely that this area of the law will ever be straightened out.[28]

In *Rubin,* the circuit court remanded the case for reconsideration under § 482. That section empowers the Commissioner to reallocate income, deductions, credits and other tax items among related taxpayers to more clearly reflect income. Suppose that B owns two corporations, X and Y. X has sustained substantial losses in prior years, giving it a net operating loss ("NOL") carryforward. Y, on the other hand, has been profitable. If X and Y jointly manufacture and sell some product, B will prefer that most of the income be taxed to X so that it can be sheltered by the NOL carryforward. However, if B fails to allocate the joint profit in a manner properly reflecting Y's contribution to the venture, the Commissioner will reallocate some of the income to Y and away from X under § 482.

Although the Commissioner has broad discretion under § 482, it is discretion only to reallocate tax items. Thus, § 482 cannot be used to deny deductions or credits. In addition, the reallocation under § 482 is limited to commonly owned or controlled "organizations, trades or businesses."

It is this last limitation that makes the application of § 482 to the facts of *Rubin* and similar cases so problematic. Recall that the taxpayer in *Rubin* worked for Park Corp., and the issue was whether payments received for the taxpayer's services were properly taxed to Park Corp. or to the taxpayer. Surely Park Corp. was one organization controlled by the taxpayer, but what was the second? In order for § 482 to apply to *Rubin,* presumably the "business" of being an employee must be considered as the second business controlled by the taxpayer.

Section 482 may be susceptible to such a reading,[29] but even so, problems remain. Because the only activity engaged in by Park Corp. was that of employing the taxpayer to perform services on its behalf, was there any business in the case *other than* that engaged in by the taxpayer in his individual capacity? At least one court has held that § 482 cannot be applied in similar circumstances.[30]

---

[28] See, e.g., *Johnson v. Commissioner,* 78 T.C. 882 (1982) (income from personal services taxed to employee rather than corporation only because payor would not agree to arrangement).

[29] See Regs. § 1.482–1(a)(1).

[30] *Foglesong v. Commissioner,* 691 F.2d 848 (7th Cir.1982) (providing that § 482 cannot apply when individual works exclusively for his corporation; only one business present). *But see* Rev. Rul. 88–38, 1988–1 C.B. 246 (providing that § 482 can apply to allocate income between a corporation and its shareholder-employee).

Consider the case of K Corp., a personal service corporation owned entirely by Dr. K. The corporation becomes a partner in a medical partnership in which each partner is required to perform medical services for the partnership in exchange for a share of partnership profits. Because K Corp. cannot perform such services directly, it hires Dr. K as its sole employee to perform the services.[31]

Assume that K Corp. will receive one-fourth of the partnership's profits, anticipated to be about $100,000. Assume also that Dr. K's salary from K Corp. is set at a fixed amount of $60,000 cash plus pension and other fringe benefits costing the corporation $20,000. If a court is willing to apply the assignment of income doctrine or § 482 to Dr. K and his corporation, how much (if any) of the corporation's income should be reallocated to Dr. K?

Under both the assignment of income doctrine and § 482, income should be reallocated between the corporation and its shareholder/employee only if the salary is less than that which would be paid in an arm's-length agreement. One is tempted to say that all of K Corp.'s income should be allocated to Dr K., but that may not be true for at least two reasons. First, although the cost of the fringe benefits may be $20,000, their worth to Dr. K may be substantially more. For example, if the corporation provides Dr. K with a medical expense reimbursement plan, the cost of the plan to the corporation will be less than its value to Dr. K because of the tax-preferred status given to such plans.[32] Indeed, any fringe benefit given to Dr. K which represents a tax expenditure ought to be worth more than it costs, with the excess being the amount of the tax expenditure captured by Dr. K and his corporation. Thus, it may be the case that Dr. K's total compensation has an after-tax value to Dr. K in excess of the income generated by his services. If so, no reallocation of income is appropriate.

In addition, even if the value of the fringe benefit package does not fully offset the reduction in salary that Dr. K has accepted by working for his corporation, Dr. K enjoys an additional benefit from the arrangement that may have some value. Dr. K's salary is a guaranteed $60,000 (plus fringe benefits) independent of the partnership's profits. Even if the corporation's partnership share is less than $60,000, Dr. K must be paid his full salary. This freedom from uncertainty may be worth something. If so, its value ought to be added to Dr. K's compensation package to determine if he has sold his services for less than they are worth.

---

[31] This example is based on the facts of *Keller,* discussed *supra.*

[32] Medical reimbursements described in § 105(b) are deductible to the employer/payor although excludible by the employee/recipient.

However, this freedom from uncertainty is worthless and should not be taken into account if it is illusory. For example, suppose that the corporation is capitalized with only $100. It is clear that the corporation will be unable to meet its salary obligation to Dr. K unless its partnership share is sufficient, and so Dr. K's compensation is as dependent on the partnership's profits as it would be if he worked directly for the partnership. In this case, Dr. K's arrangement really offers no risk avoidance.

On the other hand, if the corporation has substantial assets, then its promise of $80,000 (or more) in salary and other compensation may be worth more than an uncertain draw from the partnership. In this case, any partnership profits retained by the corporation reflect a return on its capital, since only by having capital available was it able to ensure Dr. K his full compensation arrangement.

Section 482 has implications well beyond that of personal service corporations. The regulations under § 482 list several situations in which § 482 may be applicable including: (1) below-market loans between related enterprises; (2) performances of services by one business enterprise on behalf of a related one for less than market compensation; and (3) intercompany sales at less than fair market value.[33] In each case, § 482 will be used by the Commissioner if the effect of the transaction is to shift income from a high-bracket taxpayer to a related, low-bracket one.

The most important use of § 482 is in the international arena—often referred to as the transfer pricing issue. In many cases U.S. corporations subject to U.S. taxation have an incentive to shift income to a related foreign corporation which may not be subject to U.S. taxation and is often subject to little foreign taxation. For example, suppose a U.S. corporation with a foreign subsidiary in a low-tax jurisdiction manufactures thermostats at a cost of $100 which it sells to the foreign subsidiary, and the subsidiary resells the thermostats to unrelated purchasers in the subsidiary's jurisdiction at a price of $500. If the U.S. parent charges the subsidiary $140 for the thermostats, it will have $40 subject to U.S. taxation. The $360 gain the subsidiary realizes on the resale is typically not subject to U.S. taxation. Often the Service in this type of situation will attempt to reallocate some of the subsidiary's income to the U.S. parent., arguing that the transfer price between parent and subsidiary is not an arm's length price and should be adjusted upwards.

---

[33] Regs. § 1.482–2(a) through (e).

A similar issue arises if a foreign corporation sells goods to a related U.S. corporation at a relatively high price. Suppose, for example, that a foreign corporation manufactures automobiles at a cost of $4,000 per automobile, it sells the automobiles to its U.S. subsidiary, and the subsidiary resells the automobiles to unrelated purchasers at a cost of $15,000 per automobile. If the foreign parent corporation charges a transfer price of $12,000 to its U.S. subsidiary, most of the profit would in form be enjoyed by the foreign parent, which typically will not be subject to taxation in the United States. The Service often will argue that the transfer price between parent and subsidiary is not an arm's length price and should be adjusted downwards.

Section 482 applies to commonly controlled enterprises, even those whose common control is only "indirect." The use of the term "indirect" suggests that some set of rules should be used to attribute ownership—stock or otherwise—from one taxpayer to related taxpayers. Although the Code has several such attribution rules,[34] § 482 fails to incorporate any of them. Despite the lack of explicit incorporating language, the Courts have been willing to look to these attribution rules in making determinations under § 482.[35]

The Commissioner has statutory weapons beyond § 482 in his arsenal. Under § 269, the Commissioner may disallow any deductions, credits or other corporate tax benefits when the principal purpose for forming or acquiring control of a corporation is tax avoidance. This section has been used, for example, to disallow a corporate net operating loss carryover following a change of corporate control.[36]

The Service also tried to use § 269 to limit access to certain tax-favored pension benefits. Before the Tax Equity and Fiscal Responsibility Act of 1982, the tax-favored pension benefits available to employees of corporations far exceeded those available to self-employed individuals. In response, some highly-compensated professionals such as doctors and lawyers formed professional service corporations to act as their employers principally to take advantage of the greater pension opportunities. The Commissioner challenged these arrangements under § 269, arguing that the professional service corporations were formed for tax avoidance.

It was conceded that the corporations were formed to obtain a tax *advantage,* but does that mean that they were formed for tax

---

[34] See §§ 267(b), 318(a).

[35] E.g., *Hall v. Commissioner,* 294 F.2d 82 (5th Cir.1961) (using the rules of § 318).

[36] Section 382 now addresses this issue.

avoidance? Tax-favored pension plans, like all other tax expenditures, represent an implicit congressional subsidy of an activity determined by Congress to be desirable. The whole point of enacting tax expenditures is to create incentives for taxpayers to change their behavior. How can it be wrong to follow those incentives? For example, although it is hard to explain why Congress might have wanted to encourage incorporations by professionals to obtain pension plans not available to the self-employed, the Tax Court nevertheless reached that conclusion in *Achiro v. Commissioner.*[37]

What role should § 269 play? Statutes cannot be drafted with absolute precision, and sometimes a taxpayer may fit himself within the terms of a provision without fulfilling its spirit. Presumably § 269 speaks to such incidents. That is, § 269 should apply only when it fairly can be said that a taxpayer formed or acquired control of a corporation to obtain a tax advantage not intended by Congress to be available to one in the taxpayer's position. Read this way, though, is § 269 necessary?

Related to §§ 482 and 269 is § 269A. Under § 269A, the Commissioner may reallocate income from a professional service corporation to its shareholder/employee. In its remedial feature, then, § 269A is like § 482. However, application of § 269A is triggered by a tax avoidance motive, just like § 269. This peculiar marriage of the two sections is attributable to congressional dissatisfaction with the victories of taxpayers like Mr. Foglesong and Dr. Keller in the courts. According to the legislative history of § 269A, the reach of § 269A should extend to "corporation[s] serv[ing] no meaningful purpose other than to secure tax benefits which would not otherwise be available."

3.05 The Passive Loss Limitations

Enacted as part of the Tax Reform Act of 1986, § 469 seeks to ensure that deductions from passive investments (typically through limited partnership) not be used to offset unrelated income such as salary and income from portfolio investments. Although the reach of § 469 extends well beyond the corporate tax and corporate taxpayers, one should not forget that many corporations are subject to its provisions. For those who have not been introduced to § 469, the following is a brief description of its interplay with corporations.

To curtail investments made solely or primarily for tax advantages, Congress enacted the passive loss rules of § 469. These rules limit a taxpayer's ability to use deductions and credits from

---

[37] 77 T.C. 881 (1981). Substantial equalization of employee and nonemployee pension plans under recent tax acts has repudiated this holding of *Achiro.*

passive activities to offset active income such as income from a trade or business or from services and portfolio income such as interest and dividends. Passive losses and credits disallowed in the current year are suspended and treated as deductions or credits in subsequent years available to offset passive income in those years. In addition, suspended passive losses can offset any income in the year in which the taxpayer disposes of his entire interest in the passive activity.[38]

In general, an activity is "passive" if it involves the conduct of a trade or business in which the taxpayer does not materially participate. Material participation in this context means participation on a regular, continuous and substantial basis.[39] By definition, the ownership of a limited partnership interest is passive as is generally any rental activity. However, the rental of real estate is subject to special rules which, in effect, allow up to $25,000 of excess net real estate deductions to offset non-passive income if the taxpayer "actively" participates in the real estate activity.[40] If a closely held corporation derives more than 50 percent of its income from real property trades or businesses[41] in which the corporation materially participates, then the rental activities are not considered passive. § 469(c)(7).

Although the passive loss rules do not, in general, apply to corporate taxpayers, they do apply to personal service corporations, closely held C corporations, and to shareholders of S corporations.[42]

---

[38] See § 469(b), (g).

[39] § 469(h)(1). To materially participate, one or more of the shareholders together having at least a 50-percent interest (by value) in the corporation each must spend more than 500 hours on the activity (§ 469(h)(4)) or meet one of the other tests under the regulations. Regs. § 1.469–1T(g),–5T. In addition, a corporation other than a personal services corporation materially participates in its business for a taxable year if the following requirements are met:

(i) During the entire year, the corporation has at least one full-time management employee in the business;

(ii) During the entire year, the corporation has at least three full-time employees in the business, none of whom owned more than 5 percent of the corporation's stock; and

(iii) For the year, the corporation's deductions under §§162 and 404 related to the business exceed 15 percent of its gross income from the business.

§ 469(h)(4)(B); § 465(c)(7)(C).

[40] See § 469(i). (providing, however, that this benefit phases out for a taxpayer with adjusted gross income exceeding $100,000, being fully phased out once that income amount reaches $150,000).

[41] A real property trade or business is any real property development, construction, acquisition, conversion, rental, operation, management, leasing, or brokerage trade or business. § 469(c)(7)(C).

42 See § 469(a)(2). Broadly speaking, a "closely held C corporation" is a corporation taxed under the rules of subchapter C (and not under the rules

For example, a personal service corporation that also rents computer equipment may not offset any of its personal service income by its excess rental losses stemming from depreciation, interest deductions, and the like. A personal service corporation includes any corporation no matter how large if employees of the corporation own at least 10 percent of the corporation's stock and the principal activity of the corporation is the performance of services by employee/shareholders.[43]

Material participation for a personal service corporation subject to § 469 is achieved if one or more shareholders owning 50 percent or more of the corporation's stock materially participate in the activity. For a closely held C corporation, a further requirement is added to ensure that the corporation engages in at least one active business.[44]

Note that closely held C corporations (other than personal service corporations) may offset active income with passive loss deductions and credits. § 469(e)(2). This offset does not completely eliminate the passive loss restriction to such corporations, because passive losses still cannot offset portfolio income. Nevertheless, the ability to shelter active business income offers a substantial benefit to taxpayers who need to operate a closely held business in corporate form. If the corporation conducts a passive activity that produces excess deductions (*e.g.,* depreciation), those deductions can offset taxable income from the corporation's business.

3.06 A Corporation's Capital Structure

A corporation needs capital to begin or expand its business, and to raise needed capital, a corporation must offer prospective investors a return on their investment. This promised return might take the form of periodic payments of a sum certain (interest payments), periodic returns of net profits (dividends), or some combination of the two. The return also might be in the form of accumulated earnings that can be realized by the sale of stock.[45] The investor also will expect to recover his principal at some point down the road, either at a specified time in the future (retirement of debt instruments or of callable stock) or on final liquidation of the corporation.

---

of Subchapter S) that has more than 50 percent of its stock held by 5 or fewer shareholders. See § 469(j)(1); § 465(a)(1)(B); § 542(a)(2).

[43] See § 469(j)(2).

[44] See § 469(h)(4)(B); § 465(c)(7)(C).

[45] It is the ultimate distribution of these earnings that makes a purchaser of stock willing to pay a price that reflects prior undistributed profits.

The classic equity interest in a corporate enterprise is a share of common stock. The owner of such a share is entitled to participate in the earnings of the corporation, but payments with respect to such stock are made only after all persons with more preferred interests in the corporation (e.g., holders of debt instruments and preferred stock) have received their due. Such an interest in the corporation is called a *residual* interest because it comes after all other interests. Note, though, that the residual interest in a corporation is also unlimited: whatever profits have not been paid to creditors and preferred shareholders are available for distribution to the common shareholders.

The interest in a corporation at the opposite end of the spectrum is a corporate note. The holder of such a note typically receives a fixed return on his investment for a limited period, followed by a return of capital. Thus, the investment in the corporation is both *limited* and *preferred:* limited in the sense that the return will not increase even if the corporation's profits climb and preferred in the sense that payments made on corporate debt must be paid before dividends may be declared on corporate stock. In particular, if a corporation has insufficient funds with which to pay both interest on its debts and a dividend, the interest must be paid and the dividend deferred.

You should not think of equity and debt as qualitatively different but rather as the two extremes on a continuous spectrum. All investments in a corporate enterprise are made with an expectation of profit and with the recognition of risk. Common stock and notes simply offer different *returns* subject to differing amounts of *risks.*

Looking first at relative *returns* on investment, we have seen that returns can be either unlimited or fixed. Some instruments can have elements of both: for example, a class of stock could share ratably in corporate profits subject to a minimum return of 6 percent per year. Convertible bonds are another example of such hybrid instruments, because they guarantee the fixed return of a bond but offer the opportunity through conversion of an unlimited return as stock. Also the return on a debt instrument can be tied to the performance of the corporation, sometimes referred to as an "equity kicker."

Similarly, the *risk* associated with an interest in a corporation can be large, small, or somewhere in between. For example, the risk associated with common stock of a corporation is always greater than that associated with the corporation's debt. If a corporation has sufficient assets to meet the claims of its creditors, any excess may be distributed to shareholders. But if there are insufficient assets, the creditors will take everything and the shareholders will receive nothing.

If a corporation has two or more classes of stock, it may provide that the claims of one class come before those of another. The preferred stock (*i.e.*, the stock with the preferred claim) will have a lower risk than the non-preferred common stock but will have a greater risk than corporate debt. So, too, the corporation may have subordinated debt, the holders of which take a greater risk than the holders of unsubordinated debt but less than that of shareholders. And, of course, the holders of one corporation's equity may be subject to less risk than the holders of another corporation's debt.

Although the risks and returns of preferred stock blend into that of unsubordinated debt on our spectrum, the Code treats debt and equity very differently. The most important tax distinction between debt and equity is that periodic payments on debt—called interest—can be deducted by the corporation while the equivalent payments on equity—dividends—cannot be. From the "corporation's perspective"[46] and all other things being equal, the corporation is better off raising needed capital in the form of debt rather than equity.

How about from the holder's perspective? For non-corporate taxpayers, most dividends now are taxed at the same rate as most long term capital gain, at a rate no greater than 20 percent,[47] while interest payments are subject to the usual ordinary rates up to a maximum rate of 39.6 percent. On the back end, the retirement of corporate debt qualifies for exchange treatment[48] while the retirement of stock may qualify for exchange treatment or may result in ordinary dividend income.[49] Thus, individual taxpayers have two reasons for preferring debt to equity: their individual tax position *may* be improved and the corporation's tax position *will* be improved. Do not forget that any taxpayer having a stake in the

---

[46] There is of course no "corporate" perspective, only the perspectives of its investors, employees, suppliers and customers. Nevertheless, we sometimes refer to the "corporation's perspective" as short-hand for the perspective of one who wishes to maximize the corporation's net worth.

[47] § 1(h)(11).

[48] § 1271(a)(1).

[49] Because dividends for non-corporate taxpayers are now generally taxed at the same rate as long-term capital gains, the difference between exchange and dividend treatment is less significant than it used to be. One significant difference remains, however. The taxpayer enjoys full basis recovery in an exchange, but may recover no basis if the stock retirement does not qualify for exchange treatment. Compare § 1001 with § 301(c)(1). See also § 301(c)(2) and (3).

corporation profits when the corporation profits,[50] and taxpayers having residual (i.e., unlimited) interests may profit even more.

For corporate taxpayers, the analysis is altered because of the dividends-received deduction of § 243. Under that section, a corporate shareholder can deduct an amount equal to all (*e.g.,* dividends from a wholly owned subsidiary) or a portion of any dividends, reducing the effective rate of taxation on dividends. Interest payments, on the other hand, are taxed at the usual rates without reduction. Thus, the corporate taxpayer may be better off owning stock rather than debt.

However, consider the case of X Corp, a corporation with two shareholders, individual B and corporation C. These shareholders agree to invest additional funds in their corporation in proportion to their current ownership interests. Should they receive in return debt or equity?

Assume that B owns 40 percent, and C 60 percent, of X Corp. Whether B and C make debt or equity investments, B will continue to have a claim to 40 percent of X Corp.'s profits and assets. Similarly, C will continue to have a claim to 60 percent of X Corp.'s profits and assets. By investing in debt, B and C increase X Corp.'s after-tax profits, and that profit redounds directly to their benefit.

In this situation, the corporate shareholder as well as the noncorporate shareholder benefits from debt more than from equity, because interest payments may be deductible but distributions on stock are not. Assume that the infusion of capital will produce additional pre-tax profits to X Corp. of $100 and that this $100 represents a reasonable return on the shareholders' new investment. If the shareholders invested in additional equity, the $100 of pre-tax profit results in $65 of after-tax profit.[51] Of that amount, $26 (40 percent of $65) will be distributed to B and $39 (60 percent of $65) will distributed to C. C will be entitled to deduct 80 percent of the dividend received, leaving only $7.80 to be taxed. If C is in the 35-percent bracket, it will pay a tax of $2.73, giving C an after-tax return of $36.27 ($39.00 less $2.73). If B is treated as receiving qualified dividend income and taxed at a 20-percent rate, B will pay a $5.20 tax, giving her an after-tax return of $20.80 ($26 less $5.20)

---

[50] It may seem as though those persons having limited interests in the corporation (such as bondholders) are indifferent to the corporation's tax liability. However, the lower a corporation's tax liability, the more likely it is that the corporation will be able to meet its debt and equity obligations in the future. Thus, debt as well as equity holders profit as a result of a reduction in the corporation's tax liability.

[51] Assume that X Corp. is in the 35-percent tax bracket.

On the other hand, if B and C loaned money to X Corp., the deductibility of interest would permit the corporation to distribute the entire $100 after taxes. Of that amount, $60 would go to C and $40 to B. Because interest received is fully taxable, C would pay a tax of $21, giving it an after-tax return of $39 ($60 less $21). Further, assuming that B is taxed at a 39.6-percent rate, she would pay a tax of $15.84, giving her an after-tax return of $24.16 ($40 less $15.84). Thus, both B and C are better off if they invest in debt rather than equity.

Why is debt more favorable even though a dividend recipient may be favorably taxed under § 1(h)(11) (for non-corporate shareholders) or under § 243 (for corporate shareholders)? The usual "cost" of investing in debt is that one's return is fixed. Although a corporation may deduct interest payments on debt, reducing its taxes, that reduction for the most part benefits the equity owners. Thus, if the X Corp.'s current equity owners make pro rata debt investments, they enjoy the tax-reduction benefit in their capacity as shareholders. In essence, the debt holders make more profits for the equity owners, so that if the debt owners *are* the equity owners, they create more profits for themselves.

In the example above, investment as equity subjects the profits to full taxation at the corporate (X Corp.) level and at least some taxation at the shareholder level (20 percent for C and 100 percent for B but at a reduced rate). In contrast, investment as debt avoids all corporate-level tax, so that the over-all tax inclusion is only 100 percent.

It should not be surprising, then, that the Commissioner sometimes seeks to characterize as equity what taxpayers assert is debt. Because there is really no bright-line rule to distinguish the two, courts are often hard-pressed to resolve such a dispute. Resolve it they must, though, because as we've seen the tax consequences of debt and equity are quite different.

In deciding whether a corporate interest should be classified as debt or equity, the courts consider a large number of factors, the most important of which usually is the ratio of debt to equity. While no ratio is necessarily too high or low enough, if a corporation has a high ratio of debt to equity, the risk associated with the corporation's debt becomes very high, high because the corporation may not have sufficient assets to meet the needs of the debt holders. Consequently, the debt holders, in effect, become holders of residual interests. High risk, of course, is usually associated with the unlimited but subordinated return of equity.

A second important factor is the proportion in which the nominal debt is held by shareholders. As shown above, if the shareholders own the corporation's debt in the same proportion as they own the stock, the debt gives them all the benefits associated with debt without the loss of residual interest. On the other hand, if corporate debt and stock ownership is substantially disproportionate (e.g., one 50-percent shareholder invests an additional $1,000 in corporate debt while the other 50-percent shareholder invests in stock), the debt holder will reduce his residual return as well as his risk by investing in debt rather than in equity.

Other factors considered by the courts include whether the formalities associated with debt (such as the execution of a promissory note) have been observed, whether interest obligations were met by the corporation, and whether the purported loans were made during the corporation's formative stage and used to acquire "essential" corporate assets.[52] These other factors, especially the last, are hard to justify. For example, why must a corporation purchase its first assets with equity capital rather than with debt capital? Would a court recharacterize an early loan as an equity investment if made by a non-shareholder commercial lender?

A particular area of difficulty in the debt/equity calculus is the treatment of a guarantee. Often a commercial lender will require a shareholder guarantee in order to make a loan to a corporation. In some cases, the Service may regard the loan as being made to the guaranteeing shareholder. If a shareholder/guarantor is treated for tax purposes as the true borrower under a third-party loan to a controlled corporation, the following is generally the result: (1) the guarantor is deemed to have received the funds directly under a loan from the lender; (2) the guarantor is treated as having contributed the funds to the underlying corporation as a capital contribution; (3) any interest or principal payments made by the controlled corporation to the third-party lender are treated as dividend distributions to the guarantor (subject to the existence of earnings and profits); and (4) the guarantor is treated as having made potentially deductible interest payments to the lender.

The leading case in the area is *Plantation Patterns, Inc. v. Commissioner.*[53] In that case an individual, Mr. Jemison, and his wife established New Plantations to acquire the assets of an existing business from Old Plantations, a corporation owned by unrelated persons. Mr. Jemison contributed $5,000 of capital to New Plantations, and New Plantations then received an advance of $150,000 from an unrelated third party in exchange for its non-guaranteed,

---

[52] See *Bauer v. Commissioner,* 748 F.2d 1365 (9th Cir.1984).

[53] 462 F.2d 712 (5th Cir.1972).

subordinated note. New Plantations then acquired the business of Old Plantations in exchange for cash and a combination of interest bearing and non-interest bearing notes. The interest bearing notes were payable over ten annual installments and were guaranteed by Mr. Jemison and Mr. Jemison's wholly owned investment company. New Plantations claimed deductions for interest payments made on the guaranteed debt. The Commissioner challenged this treatment on the basis that the guarantees were the "real undergirding" for the debt and that Mr. Jemison should be treated as the true borrower under the loans for federal income tax purposes. The Commissioner argued that, as a result of the guarantees, Mr. Jemison should be treated as having made a direct contribution of capital to New Plantation in the principal amount of the debt and that the subsequent payments made by New Plantations on the debt should be treated as dividends paid by New Plantations to Mr. Jemison. The Tax Court held for the Commissioner and was affirmed on appeal by the Fifth Circuit on the basis that the corporation was "thinly capitalized."

Unhappy with the judicial uncertainty in this area, Congress enacted § 385 as part of the Tax Reform Act of 1969. This section instructs the Treasury to issue regulations distinguishing corporate debt from equity. While several sets of regulations have been proposed under § 385, none have survived public criticism. Treasury's inability to promulgate regulations implementing § 382 for more than 40 years strongly suggests that such a distinction cannot practically be made. Because both debt and equity investments in a corporation reflect ownership interests, albeit with different rates of return and associated risks, drawing a line between the two probably cannot be done in a way that will receive widespread support. How then should debt be distinguished from equity? "No answer is what the wrong question begets. . . ."[54]

In any case, Congress has taken piecemeal steps to prevent perceived misuse of the interest deduction by corporations. In some cases the Service has been "whipsawed" by inconsistent treatment of instruments by the issuer and holders. A corporate issuer may prefer to designate an instrument as debt so that it can deduct the interest. However, a holder of that instrument may prefer to treat it as stock to benefit from a dividends-received deduction under § 243 (for a corporate holder) or a favorable tax rate under § 1(h)(11) (for a non-corporate holder). Under § 385(c)(1) the issuer's characterization is binding on the holder.

Section 385 has been amended to allow the Service to bifurcate the treatment of "hybrid securities"—debt instruments with both

---

[54] A. Bickel, The Least Dangerous Branch 103 (1962).

equity and debt characteristics—so that part of the return on the investment is treated as interest and part as a nondeductible equity distribution.[55] For example, debt instruments that provide for a fixed return (e.g., 6 percent of the face value) as well as an "equity kicker" (e.g., 2 percent of the corporation's profits) may be bifurcated so that the fixed return is treated as deductible interest while the contingent return is treated as an equity distribution.

Congress has applied the bifurcation technique as well with regard to certain high yield discount obligations issued by corporations. § 163(i). The "disqualified portion" of such instruments is not deductible and even the remaining deductible portion of the original issue discount is only deductible upon payment rather than as the interest accrues, as is normally the case. The details of this provision are not as important as its general philosophy.

Suppose that X Corp. issues a debt instrument which has an issue price of $100 and matures in six years, at which time the lender receives $300. No periodic interest payments are required, and the yield to maturity is 20 percent. If at the time the instrument is issued, the applicable federal rate is 9 percent, a portion of the original issue discount which X Corp. would normally deduct each year will be disallowed. The disallowed amount equals (i) the original issue discount, multiplied by (i) the "disqualified yield" and divided by (iii) the yield to maturity. The disqualified yield is the portion of the yield that exceeds the applicable federal rate plus six percentage points. Thus, in this case, the disqualified yield is 5 percent, the 20-percent yield to maturity minus 15 percent (the applicable federal rate (9 percent) plus the 6 percentage points). Since the original issue discount in the first year is $20, the disallowed amount for that year is $5 (($20 times 5 percent (the disqualified yield) divided by 20 percent (the yield to maturity)).

Even when treatment of an investment return as interest is questionable, normally there is a maximum loss of one level of taxation. That is, the corporation's deduction may wipe out a corporate level tax on the earnings generated by the borrowed funds, but the lender will be taxed on the receipt of the interest. A potentially more serious problem arises where two levels of taxation are avoided by characterizing certain payments as interest rather than equity distributions. This occurs when the recipient of the purported

---

[55] Hybrid securities often have the following characteristics: (1) ownership solely by shareholders and in the proportion to the stock held; (2) transferability permitted only if accompanied by stock transfer; (3) lengthy or no fixed maturity dates; (4) interest payments that are discretionary or linked to corporate income; (5) payment of interest and/or principal subordinate to general creditor claims; and (6) issuance to a current shareholder for no new consideration.

interest is tax-exempt. For example, a private foundation that owns stock in a corporation or a foreign taxpayer who is not subject to U.S. taxation because of an applicable income tax treaty can strip away the earnings of a corporation that would otherwise be subject to one and maybe two levels of taxation.

To deal with this "earnings stripping" problem, Congress has enacted a provision that denies a deduction for "disqualified interest" paid to (or guaranteed by) a related party exempt from U.S. tax on such interest payments. § 163(j). The related party requirement is designed to distinguish bona fide loans from independent parties from intercorporate loans undertaken to generate interest deductions. A taxpayer cannot avoid the reach of § 163(j) by borrowing from a bank if a tax-exempt related party guarantees the loan. For example, § 163(j) may apply to a U.S. subsidiary that borrows from a bank if a foreign parent corporation guarantees the loan.

There are additional requirements before an interest deduction will be disallowed. Because Congress was concerned with equity masquerading as debt, the deductibility of interest paid to tax-exempt, related parties hinges on whether the ratio of debt to equity of the paying corporation exceeds 1.5 to 1, as measured on certain specified days of the year. In addition, interest deductions will be disallowed only if the interest is deemed to be excess interest, as determined under a formula measuring the relationship of the interest expense to taxable income with certain adjustments.

Given the complexity and ad hoc nature of these provisions designed to distinguish debt from equity, perhaps Congress should provide that debt and equity be treated equivalently, using the current treatment of debt or equity as the model. For example, dividends as well as interest payments could be deductible by the corporation. This change would equalize the taxation of debt and equity, although it would do so by, in effect, abolishing the corporate tax.

An alternate approach is to tax all corporate investments as equity is treated under current law; that is, do not permit corporations to deduct interest paid. This would equalize the treatment of corporate debt and equity without eliminating the corporate double tax. In fact, denying the interest deduction would substantially increase the efficacy of the corporate income tax by increasing its base. If such an implicit raising of the effective corporate tax rate is thought to be inappropriate by Congress, an offsetting downward adjustment to the nominal rates could be made.

Chapter 4

CASH AND PROPERTY DISTRIBUTIONS

4.01 Introduction

A corporation generally determines income and deductions in much the same ways as an individual. A corporation may retain its earnings or distribute them to its shareholders, and much of what follows in this and subsequent chapters focuses on the different ways shareholders can obtain corporate earnings, including, most directly, through distributions.

Many, but not all, corporate distributions are "dividends" for federal income tax purposes, included in gross income under § 61(a)(7). Suppose that B forms X Corp., contributing $1,000 in exchange for all X Corp. stock. In year 1, X Corp. has no income, gain or loss, but makes a $200 distribution to B. Should B be taxed on the distribution? B has experienced no accession to wealth. Nor has B realized a previously unrealized gain. Before the distribution, B owned X Corp. stock with a $1,000 basis and $1,000 fair market value. § 358. After the distribution, B owns $200 in cash and stock with a fair market value of $800. B has simply received a return of her original investment and should not be taxed on the distribution, but B's stock basis in X Corp. should be reduced by $200, from $1,000 to $800.

Suppose instead that in year 1 X Corp. earned $200, which it distributed to B. First, X Corp. would be taxed on its earnings.[1] What about B? B would like to claim that the distribution comes from B's original $1,000 contribution. If so, the distribution would reduce B's basis in her X stock from $1,000 to $800. B would hold $200 in cash and stock with an $800 basis and $1,000 fair market value, treatment that would defer B's tax on the $200 earned by X Corp. On the other hand, one could argue that the distribution represents the earnings of X Corp. in year 1 and should be taxable to B.

Note that the distribution itself does not increase B's wealth. Just before the distribution, B holds X Corp. stock with a $1,200 fair market. Just after the distribution, she holds $200 of cash and stock with a $1,000 fair market value. Although B has "converted"

---

[1] The quantitative effect of corporate taxes on amounts distributed or available for distribution is ignored throughout this chapter.

stock to cash, her "undeniable accession to wealth"[2] occurred as X Corp. earned the $200. The question, simply put, is should B continue to defer her tax until she sells the X stock or is the cash distribution a significant enough event to justify taxing the previously accrued accession to wealth.

Both ways of treating distributions draw strength from other areas of tax law. For example, under the open transaction doctrine of *Burnet v. Logan,*[3] a taxpayer can recover basis first if the amount realized cannot readily be determined. Arguably, it is impossible to determine how much will be distributed during the life of the corporation. Following *Burnet v. Logan,* shareholders should be allowed to recover their investment before reporting gain. On the other hand, where a taxpayer holds property, periodic returns are taxed under the general principles of *Commissioner v. Glenshaw Glass Co.*[4] Thus, rent is fully taxable to a holder of real estate and interest is fully taxable to a holder of a debt instrument.

The arguments supporting either treatment give way to a web of statutory provisions. Section 301 addresses distributions of "property," as defined by § 317(a), with an assist from § 316, which defines dividends. Note that § 317(a) defines property mostly by negation, specifying that property excludes a corporation's own stock (or stock rights).[5] It does state that property includes cash, securities, and (somewhat unhelpfully) other property.

Section 301(a) applies only when a corporation distributes property *with respect to its stock:* that is, distributions to shareholders in their capacity as shareholders. Other distributions such as salaries or interest payments on debt obligations are not addressed by § 301(a). If a corporation makes a distribution with respect to its stock, the amount of the distribution is computed in accordance with § 301(b). That amount equals the cash and the fair market value of other property distributed, reduced (but not below zero) by the corporate liabilities assumed by the shareholder in connection with the distribution.[6] Note that the shareholder takes a basis in any distributed property equal to its fair market value. § 301(d). For example, if X Corp. distributes land with a $100 fair market value to B and B assumes a $40 X liability in connection with the

---

[2] *Commissioner v. Glenshaw Glass Co.*, 348 U.S. 426 (1955).

[3] 283 U.S. 404 (1931).

[4] *Commissioner v. Glenshaw Glass Co.*, 348 U.S. 426 (1955).

[5] Stock distributions are treated separately under § 305. See Chapter 6 *infra.*

[6] To the extent the shareholder assumes a corporate liability, the shareholder acquires the distributed property because of that assumption, not in her capacity as a shareholder.

distribution, the amount of the distribution is $60 (*i.e.*, $100 gross value of the land minus the $40 liability) but B's basis in the land is $100, its fair market value.

Once a shareholder determines the amount of a distribution, its treatment is described in § 301(c)—a three-tiered provision. The shareholder treats that amount first as a dividend, then as a recovery of stock basis, and finally as gain from the sale or exchange of stock. Section 301(c)(1) states that the amount treated as a dividend is included in gross income, referring to § 316 for the definition of a dividend. Section 316(a) provides that distributions out of specified "earnings and profits" are treated as dividends. Earnings and profits help distinguish a distribution of income earned by the corporation from a distribution of a shareholder's contribution to the capital of the corporation. Despite the importance of the phrase "earnings and profits," no comprehensive definition appears in the Code.

If the amount distributed is not treated in full as a dividend, it is next treated under § 301(c)(2) as a nontaxable return of the shareholder's investment in the corporation. Accordingly, that portion reduces the basis of the shareholder's stock. If the shareholder fully recovers that basis. any remaining amount is treated as gain from the sale or exchange of property (*i.e.*, stock), generally producing capital gain for the shareholder. § 301(c)(3).

Note that distributions taxed under both (c)(1) and (c)(3) are includible in the shareholder's income but the (c)(1) component is includible as a "dividend" while the (c)(3) component is includible as gain. Historically, "dividend" income was taxable at ordinary rates, but since 2003 most dividends (called "qualified" dividends) have been taxed to individuals at the same rate as long-term capital gain; that is, at no more than 20 percent. See § 1(h)(11). Note, however, that qualified dividends are *not* capital gain. In particular, dividend income is includible without any offset for basis and generally cannot be offset by capital loss. Note that this special rule does not apply to a corporate shareholder, but the corporate shareholder may benefit from a dividends received deduction.

Qualified dividend income is a dividend paid on stock of a domestic or certain foreign corporations that meets the following added requirement: The shareholder must hold the stock for at least 61 days during the 121-day period that begins 60 days before the ex-dividend date (for common stock) or for at least 91 days during the 181-day period that begins 90 days before the ex-dividend date (for preferred stock). §1(h)(11)(iii) and §246(c). The ex-dividend date is the first date that the stock trades without the dividend. Note that qualified dividend income does not include any amount that the shareholder takes into account as "investment income" for purposes of the investment interest limitation in § 163(d). § 1(h)(11)(D)(i).

Section 301 and the other provisions briefly sketched above address the treatment of shareholders. A distribution may also trigger tax consequences for the distributing corporation. Should a distributing corporation recognize gain or loss? Historically, the corporation recognized neither gain nor loss on a distribution. Loss non-recognition is still the rule, but now a corporation recognizes gain when it distributes appreciated property, computing the gain as if it sold that property to the distributee shareholder for its fair market value. § 311(b). Because a corporation does not recognize loss when it distributes built-in loss property but the shareholder takes a fair market value basis in that property, any built-in loss in distributed property simply disappears.

Note that the distributions addressed in this chapter are not the only type of distributions made by corporations. Distributions *of* stock are addressed by § 305. Distributions *in exchange for* a shareholder's stock (called "redemptions") are addressed by § 302. Liquidating distributions are described in § 331–§ 338. Finally, distributions in connection with a reorganization are discussed in § 354–§ 368. In Chapter 2, we looked at distributions in connection with the formation of a corporation. We explore the remaining distributions in subsequent chapters.

4.02 Earnings and Profits

While the term "earnings and profits" is not defined in the Code, the concept plays an integral role in characterizing distributions. The backbone of our corporate taxation system is that corporate earnings are taxed twice—once when earned at the corporate level and once again when distributed to shareholders. The earnings and profits account helps to measure whether a distribution originates from corporate earnings or from other sources.

At the outset it is important to note that the earnings and profits concept is not synonymous with "earned surplus" "retained earnings" or any other financial reporting or accounting concept of corporate earnings. For example, a nontaxable, pro rata distribution of common stock by a corporation decreases earned surplus but has no effect on earnings and profits. Otherwise a corporation could sweep away its entire earnings and profits account by making such distributions. Through this simple device, a corporation could subsequently distribute cash or other property without tax to its shareholders.

Similarly, the term "dividend" may not mean the same thing for income tax and state law purposes. For example, a distribution may be a dividend under § 316(a) even though under state law the distribution impairs capital.[7] Conversely, a dividend under state law may not be a dividend under § 316(a).

Put aside for the moment how the earnings and profits account is calculated and consider how the account works.[8] Suppose B forms X Corp. by exchanging $50,000 for all of X Corp.'s stock in a transaction that falls under § 351. B takes a $50,000 basis in the stock. § 358. In year 1, X Corp. is profitable, increasing its earnings and profits account from $0 to $20,000. Suppose X Corp. makes a $20,000 distribution at the end of year 1. Under § 301(c)(1), B must include in ordinary income that part of the distribution that is a dividend. Under § 316(a), since X Corp. has current earnings and profits of $20,000, the entire distribution is a dividend.[9]

Suppose instead that X Corp. has operating losses in year 1 which produce negative earnings and profits of $20,000. In year 2, X Corp. has $20,000 of earnings and profits. If X Corp. makes a $20,000 distribution at the end of year 2, B will still have a $20,000 dividend even though X Corp. has no overall (or aggregate) earnings and profits. Section 316(a)(2) employs a "nimble dividend" rule whereby distributions will be taxable to shareholders as ordinary dividend income, regardless of any accumulated earnings and profits deficit, if there are current earnings and profits for the distribution year.[10] If there is more than one distribution during the year, the current earning and profits are prorated among the distributions for purposes of determining if a distribution is a dividend.[11]

---

[7] See, e.g., *United States v. Lesoine,* 203 F.2d 123 (9th Cir.1953) (claim of right doctrine requires dividends be taxed in year of receipt even if distribution was illegal under state law).

[8] For a good presentation of how the earnings and profits account works, see Rev. Rul. 74–164, 1974–1 C.B. 74.

[9] Note that corporate-level taxes would actually decrease the earnings and profits account below $20,000. See note 1 *supra.*

[10] Interestingly, the rule originated in 1936 as a pro-taxpayer relief measure from the since-repealed undistributed profits tax. Taxpayers were able to reduce their undistributed profits only by making dividend distributions and the predecessor to § 316(a)(2) facilitated the characterization of distributions as dividends.

[11] If total distributions exceed current earnings and profits, each distribution shares in current earnings and profits in the proportion that the distribution bears to the total distributions for the year. See Regs. § 1.316-2(b). However, if a corporation has multiple classes of stock and one class enjoys a dividend preference, distributions on the stock with the dividend preference absorb current earnings and profits first. Rev. Rul. 69-440, 1969-2 C.B. 46.

Accumulated earnings and profits are allocated to distributions on a first-come, first-served basis.[12]

Thus, current earnings and profits are decreased at the end of the year in which a distribution was made, while accumulated earnings and profits essentially are reduced as distributions are made. Regs. § 1.316-2(b). To the extent that a corporation has both accumulated and current earnings and profits, distributions are deemed to come first from the current earnings and profits. § 316. Section 312(a)(1) requires that the earnings and profits account is decreased by the amount of any cash distributed. Note that earnings and profits cannot be decreased below zero by a distribution. How then can there be an earnings and profits deficit? A corporation which has an operating deficit may have an earnings and profits deficit.

Suppose X Corp. has $20,000 of earnings and profits in year 1, and on the last day of year 1, B sells her stock to C. C receives a $20,000 distribution from X Corp. after the purchase and before X Corp. has any additional earnings. At first glance, it may seem somehow unfair that C will have ordinary income when the corporation earned that income while B was a shareholder. From C's perspective, the distribution is merely a return of part of C's investment in X Corp. However, the rules of § 301(c)(1) and § 316 are unremitting. Since X Corp. has earnings and profits, C must report a dividend.

The Supreme Court in *United States v. Phellis*[13] long ago explained why this "miracle of income without gain" is not as troublesome as it may seem.[14] Suppose that B owns 1 share of X Corp. stock with a fair market value of $100 and an adjusted basis of $60. In one month, X Corp. will distribute $10 per share as a dividend, reducing each share's value to $90. If B wants to sell his share prior to the dividend, what price will the share fetch? Assume that income is taxed at a flat rate of 30 percent.

A prospective purchaser will know that with the share comes a tax liability of $3.00 tied to the impending dividend. Accordingly, B should receive the current value of the share *less the anticipated tax liability.* B will bear the burden of the tax not by actually paying it but rather by receiving a reduced sales price. The purchaser, on the other hand, will actually pay the tax but will not bear its burden.

---

[12] Regs. § 1.316–2(b), (c).

[13] 257 U.S. 156, 171–172 (1921).

[14] The phrase comes from Powell, *Income from Corporate Dividends,* 35 Harv. L. Rev. 363 (1922).

Of course, this example depends on two assumptions. First, it was assumed that the seller and purchaser knew when the corporation would make a distribution and the amount thereof. More realistically, the seller and purchaser can only estimate this information, and to the extent they err, the tax burden may be shifted from the seller to the purchaser.

In addition, it was assumed that the seller and purchaser were taxed at the same rate. This often will not be true. If their tax rates differ, the failure to tax corporate profits to those taxpayers who are shareholders when the profits are earned may result in reduced (or increased) income to the Treasury.

To compute a corporation's earnings and profits, many start with taxable income. A corporation's taxable income and its current earnings and profits will typically not coincide since the earnings and profits account is intended to measure what the corporation has available for distribution (*i.e.*, its change in economic value) while taxable income reflects a number of preferences and incentives. Three types of adjustments are necessary to convert taxable income into earnings and profits.[15] First, some items that are excluded from taxable income are included in the earnings and profits account because they represent an accretion to the corporation which can be distributed without impairing the corporation's original capital. For example, a corporation's interest income on obligations excluded from gross income under § 103 is nevertheless available for distribution to shareholders and, therefore, increases the corporation's earnings and profits account.

In computing taxable income a corporation can sometimes defer recognition in a manner that may not reflect the corporation's ability to make distributions without impairing its capital. For example, a corporation might sell property under the installment method of § 453, thereby including as taxable income for the year of sale only the proceeds received (minus some allocated basis). From an economic standpoint, though, the corporation has earned the present value of all expected payments regardless of when they are actually paid. Indeed, the notes themselves are available for distribution. Consequently, for purposes of computing earnings and profits, the entire gain is included in earnings and profits to reflect this dividend paying capacity.

The second category of adjustments are for those items that are deductible in computing taxable income but are not deductible in computing earnings and profits. Some of these are "artificial" deductions that require no outlay and therefore do not deplete what is

---

[15] See Regs. § 1.312–6.

available for distribution. For example, while a corporation may take a dividends-received deduction under § 243 for purposes of computing taxable income, the full amount of the dividend received is available for distribution. A corporation must therefore add the § 243 deduction to taxable income in computing earnings and profits. Similarly net operating losses under § 172 and capital loss carrybacks under § 1212 do not reduce earnings and profits since these are accounting conventions. The actual losses reduce earnings and profits in the year they occurred, reflecting the decline in the corporation's value in the loss year. To reduce earnings and profits again would be double counting.

Congress has shown signs of mild schizophrenia in its treatment of depreciation for taxable income and earnings and profits purposes.[16] Under § 168, corporations (and other taxpayers) can depreciate property rapidly and often in an accelerated manner. Yet for purposes of computing earnings and profits, accelerated depreciation is not permitted and even the straight-line depreciation must be computed over longer time periods. § 312(k). Presumably these differences stem from a congressional belief that the deductions permitted under § 168 are more generous than economic depreciation—perhaps to encourage investment—and therefore understate a corporation's true economic income and accordingly a corporation's ability to make distributions.

The third category of adjustments is the converse of the second category. Some items that cannot be deducted in computing taxable income are deductible in determining earnings and profits. While various policy reasons may preclude deduction of these items for taxable income purposes, these items do represent economic costs that deplete what is available for distribution. For example, expenses that are not deductible on policy grounds (e.g., fines and kickbacks) under § 162(c), (f) or (g) can be subtracted in computing earnings and profits. Similarly, unreasonable compensation and nondeductible expenses under § 265 (e.g., interest incurred to produce tax-exempt income) are subtracted in the earnings and profits calculation. Dividends paid in previous years also are subtracted in determining earnings and profits as are federal income taxes.

To see how the three types of adjustments work, consider the following problem where X Corp. is an accrual-basis taxpayer taxed at a flat 30-percent rate and has the following income and expenses:

---

[16] For computation of the corporate minimum tax, depreciation is treated in the same manner as it is for computation of earnings and profits. See Section 3.01 *supra*.

	Income
Gross income from business	$30,000
Dividend income (dividends-received deduction under § 243 = $14,000)	20,000
Interest on municipal bonds	8,000
Long-term capital gain	6,000
	$64,000

	Expenses
Wages, rent, supplies, etc.	$17,000
Fines and kickbacks	5,000
Depreciation (§ 312(k) recapture amount = $6,000)	9,000
Capital losses	7,000
	$38,000

To compute current earnings and profits, we start with X Corp.'s taxable income. X Corp. has gross income of $56,000 ($30,000 from operations, plus $20,000 of dividend income, plus $6,000 of long-term capital gain). Its deductible expenses total $46,000 ($17,000 of deductible expenses under § 162 plus $9,000 of depreciation deductions, plus $6,000 of capital losses,[17] plus the $14,000 dividends-received deduction). Thus, its taxable income equals $10,000 ($56,000 of gross income minus $46,000 of deductions). As a 30-percent taxpayer, X Corp. therefore incurs a $3,000 tax.

This $10,000 amount is adjusted in three steps to determine X Corp.'s earnings and profits. First, it is increased for items excluded from taxable income that nevertheless reflect an accretion to the corporation, or, in our case, the $8,000 of tax-exempt interest income. Next, the $18,000 subtotal is increased by items that are deductible in computing taxable income, but do not reflect a corresponding decline in the corporation's value, such as the $14,000 dividends-received deduction and the excess depreciation of $6,000,[18] bringing the subtotal to $38,000. Finally, this subtotal is reduced by nondeductible items that reflect an economic cost to the corporation. In this example, those items include the $5,000 in fines and kickbacks, the $1,000 excess capital loss over the capital gain

---

[17] Capital losses are permitted only to the extent of a corporation's capital gain. See §§ 165(f) and 1211.

[18] Note that for earnings and profits purposes not only must straight-line depreciation be used, but the time periods are increased. §§ 312(k) and 168(g)(2).

and the $3,000 of accrued tax liability.[19] With that $9,000 reduction, X Corp.'s earnings and profits for the year would be $29,000.

Considering all of the complexity involved in the earnings and profits concept, might it not be better to eliminate it?[20] This could be done by taxing the shareholder on all distributions rather than distinguishing distributions of earnings from distributions of invested capital.

For example, suppose B forms X Corp. by exchanging $10,000 for all of the X Corp. stock. In year 1, X Corp. has no earnings and profits, but distributes $2,000. Under current law, the $2,000 would not be a dividend under § 301(c)(1) and would reduce B's stock basis from $10,000 to $8,000. § 301(c)(2). Without the earnings and profits concept, B would report the $2,000 as a dividend. B would then hold the X Corp. stock with a basis of $10,000 and a fair market value of $8,000. When B disposes of the stock through sale or liquidation, the $2,000 loss deduction would offset the earlier inclusion.[21] B, who started off with $10,000, ends up with $10,000— $2,000 on the distribution and $8,000 on the sale. From a tax standpoint, B has a $2,000 inclusion and a $2,000 deduction.

Whatever appeal this treatment might have, it is time to reconsider a question raised at the outset of this chapter—why are distributions taxed at all? Suppose in the previous example, X Corp. produces $2,000 of earnings in year 1. On the last day of the year, B holds the X Corp. stock with a $10,000 basis and $12,000 fair market value. B will not be taxed on the appreciation in the stock until it is realized. If X Corp. makes a distribution on the last day of year 1, B will hold $2,000 in cash and the X Corp. stock with a basis and fair market value of $10,000, or total assets of $12,000. By itself, the distribution does not increase the shareholder's overall wealth: With or without the distribution, the shareholder holds assets worth $12,000. However, the distribution changes the nature of the shareholder's assets. Under our tax system, we tax B on the distribution because we consider it to be the appropriate time to tax the unrealized gain that occurred earlier. This policy is a manifestation

---

[19] Regs. § 1.312–6(a) provides that the method of accounting used to compute taxable income should also be used to compute earnings and profits. X Corp. as an accrual basis taxpayer can accrue the federal income taxes to be paid.

[20] See Colby, Blackburn & Trier, Elimination of Earnings and Profits from the Internal Revenue Code, 39 Tax Lawyer 285 (1986).

[21] This somewhat simplistic analysis ignores the time value of money problem—the tax cost of the inclusion may precede by several years the tax savings from the deduction. Also unless the limitations on the deductibility of capital gains are revised, the capital loss deduction may not fully offset the ordinary income inclusion, even ignoring differences in timing. §§ 165(f), 1211 and 1212.

of the realization doctrine—that the cash or other property received by the shareholder cannot be offset by the corresponding decrease in the value of the shareholder's stock.

4.03 Relief from Dividends

By now it is clear that Congress has legislated a system whereby corporate earnings are generally taxed twice—once at the corporate level and once at the shareholder level. For example suppose B owns all of the stock of X Corp. and is taxed at a 20-percent rate. If X Corp. earns $100 and is taxed at a 35-percent rate, it must pay a tax of $35. When B receives the $65 distribution, B will pay an additional $13,00 in income tax, leaving $52.00 for B out of the original $100.[22]

Suppose instead that X Corp. operates its business through a wholly owned subsidiary Y Corp. Now Y Corp. earns $100, pays $35 in taxes and distributes $65 to X Corp. If X Corp. is taxed on receipt of the dividend, it will pay $22.75 to the government and distribute the remaining $42.25 to B who must pay an additional $8.45 in federal income tax. The result is that out of the original $100 earned, B ends up with $33.80. If more corporate layers of tax are interposed, B will end up with less.

One must ask whether the tax results should vary depending on the number of corporate entities involved. There was only one productive activity—the earning of $100 by performing services or selling goods. With enough corporate entities interposed, the taxes could almost completely whittle away the $100.

Because of this cascading tax problem, the Code makes a special allowance for dividends received by corporate shareholders. Section 243 provides for a deduction equal to a specified percentage of dividends received by a corporation from a domestic corporation, a percentage that depends primarily on the degree of ownership.[23] Broadly speaking, if the corporate shareholder is affiliated with the distributing corporation, it is entitled to a 100-percent dividends

---

[22] This example assumes that X Corp. has sufficient earnings and profits so that the distribution would be a dividend under §§ 301(c)(1) and 316 and that both X Corp. and B are taxed at a flat rate on the additional $100 of income.

[23] The provision does not generally extend to dividends from foreign corporations since they are not subject to U.S. taxes. But see § 245 providing a dividends received deduction for certain foreign corporations subject to U.S. taxation. A distribution from a foreign corporation not subject to U.S. taxation to a U.S. corporate shareholder does not qualify for the § 243 dividends received deduction, but may entitle the receiving corporation to a foreign tax credit for foreign income taxes imposed on the income that made the dividend possible. *See* §§ 901 and 902.

received deduction ("DRD").[24] If the corporate shareholder is not entitled to a 100-percent DRD but owns at least 20 percent (by vote and value) of the distributing corporation's stock, it is entitled to an 80-percent DRD. § 243(c) (disregarding § 1504(a)(4) stock in making the 20-percent determination). Otherwise, it is entitled to a 70-percent DRD.[25] Thus, at the current 35-percent corporate rate, the maximum tax rate on dividends received by a corporation is 10.5 percent—*i.e.*, the highest corporate rate of 35 percent imposed on 30 percent of the distribution includible in taxable income for a less than 20-percent shareholder.

The DRD offers corporations several arbitrage opportunities with both leveraged and non-leveraged acquisitions, opportunities that Congress has addressed under § 246A and § 1059. Suppose that stock of Y Corp. regularly pays dividends of $6.00 per year on its common stock selling for $100 per share, a 6-percent return. If X Corp. can borrow funds at 8-percent interest, it would not, absent tax considerations, purchase the stock of Y Corp, because it does not make sense to borrow at 8 percent to earn a 6-percent return. But suppose that X Corp., in the 35-percent tax bracket, borrows $100 to buy one share of Y Corp. stock. The after-tax cost of borrowing $100 at 8 percent is $5.20 because of the interest deduction (*i.e.*, $8.00 minus $2.80, which is 35 percent of $8.00). The after-tax return on the $6.00 dividend is $5.58, assuming an 80-percent DRD, resulting in a $.42 tax on the $1.20 that enters taxable income. With tax considerations, the investment becomes profitable, producing a $5.58 return at a cost of $5.20.

---

[24] More precisely, it is entitled to a 100% DRD to the extent the following two requirements are met:

     (i) The shareholder and distributing corporations are members of the same affiliated group at the close of the distribution date; and

     (ii) The dividend is paid out of earnings and profits that arose in a year on each day of which those corporations were affiliated (or the distributing corporation is a § 936 corporation),

§ 243(a)(3) (allowing a 100-percent DRD for a qualifying dividend); § 243(b)(1) (defining qualifying dividends); § 243(b)(2) (looking to § 1504(a) to define an affiliated group but including life insurance companies and § 936 corporations). For example, two corporations are affiliated if one owns 80% or more of the stock of the second (by vote and value). That 80% determination is made by disregarding § 1504(a)(4) stock (*i.e.*, non-voting, non-convertible preferred stock that neither participates in corporate growth to any significant extent nor has an unreasonable redemption or liquidation premium).

[25] § 243(a)(1). Note that a DRD is not allowed for any dividend paid on stock if that stock was held for 45 days or less during the 91-day period that begins 45 days before the ex-dividend date. § 246(c)(1). See also *id.* at (c)(2) (for a further limitation on certain dividends on preferred stock); *id.* at (b) (unless the distributing corporation has a net operating loss, limiting the 70% or 80% DRD to a percentage of the distributing corporation's taxable income, as computed with some modifications).

You may recall that in § 265 Congress prohibits a deduction for interest incurred to produce tax-exempt income. For a corporate shareholder, dividend income, to the extent of the DRD, is tantamount to tax-exempt income. In § 246A, Congress has chosen to limit the *de facto* tax-exemption (*i.e.*, the DRD) rather than the interest deduction. A 70-percent or 80-percent DRD otherwise permitted under § 243 is reduced by a percentage related to the amount of debt used to purchase the stock. Thus, if a taxpayer purchases stock with some cash and some debt such that the "average indebtedness percentage" is 50 percent, then the § 243 deduction will be cut in half. § 246A(a) and (d).[26] Section 246A requires the Service to try to trace what proceeds were used to make the purchase and, not surprisingly, tracing creates administrative headaches.

Even when a corporation does not use debt to acquire another corporation's stock, the DRD offers arbitrage possibilities. Suppose that X Corp. purchases all Y Corp. stock for $1,000 and shortly thereafter receives a $200 dividend. Immediately before the distribution, Y Corp. is worth $1,000; after the distribution, it is worth just $800. If X Corp. now sells the Y Corp. stock for $800 but still retains a $1,000 basis in that stock, X Corp. will recognize a $200 capital loss.[27] Overall, but for any tax benefit, X Corp. broke even, starting with $1,000 and ending up with the same amount—$200 from the distribution and $800 from the sale. However for tax purposes, X Corp. may be entitled to an 80-percent DRD, thereby reducing its taxable income to $40.[28] At the same time, X Corp. might use the $200 loss deduction under § 165 to offset a full $200 of income. In short, for no net investment, X Corp. would produce a net $160 deduction. Assuming a 35-percent tax rate, X Corp. would profit by $56 (35 percent of $160), the tax savings from the net $160 deduction.

---

[26] Section 246A applies to "portfolio stock" only. Stock typically will be considered portfolio stock if the corporate shareholder owns less than 50 percent of the total voting power or value of the subsidiary stock. § 246A(c)(2) (also providing that stock is not portfolio stock if the corporate shareholder owns at least 20 percent of the total voting power and value of the subsidiary stock and the 50-percent test is collectively met by five or fewer corporate shareholders). Where there is at least 50-percent ownership, perhaps it suggests that the parent is interested in more than the subsidiary's dividends—the corporations are likely to be part of a multicorporate structure.

[27] The character of the loss as short- or long-term depends on X Corp.'s holding period for the Y Corp. stock.

[28] Even though X Corp. and Y Corp. would be affiliated, it is likely that the dividend will not be paid out of earnings and profits for a year each day of which the two corporations were affiliated. Thus, the dividend would not be a qualifying dividend eligible for the 100% DRD. See § 243(b).

Section 1059 now mandates a reduction of basis for corporate shareholders on the receipt of "extraordinary dividends" if the stock on which the dividends are paid has not been held for more than two years before the dividend announcement date.[29] In the example above, X Corp. would reduce its basis in the Y Corp. stock by $160—the amount excluded under § 243—from $1,000 to $840. When X Corp. sells the Y Corp. stock, it would realize and recognize a $40 loss, matching its $40 of net dividend income and accurately reflecting that X Corp. broke even in the deal.[30]

But is it clear that § 1059 should cause a basis reduction in this case? Suppose, in the example above, that X Corp. purchased the Y Corp. stock from W Corp. for $1,000. W Corp. had formed Y Corp. by contributing $800 in exchange for all of the Y Corp. stock. After its formation, Y Corp. had earned $200 on which it was taxed. When W Corp. sells the Y Corp. stock to X Corp., W Corp. is taxable on $200—a second corporate-level tax.[31] If X Corp. is allowed a $200 loss deduction when it sells the Y Corp. stock, after receiving the nontaxable dividend from Y Corp., the deduction will, in the aggregate, offset one of the corporate-level taxes, thereby preserving a single-level corporate tax. Of course there will be a second level of tax when the corporate earnings are ultimately distributed to individual shareholders.

Note that if the Y Corp. stock is originally held by W, an individual, it would be inappropriate to allow X Corp. a deduction on the sale of the Y Corp. stock following the dividend from Y Corp. That is because the Y Corp. earnings were taxed once when earned and once again at the individual-shareholder level when W sold the appreciated stock to X Corp. No deduction is needed by X Corp. on the sale of the Y Corp. stock because there has only been a single level of corporate tax. By mandating a reduction in X Corp.'s basis in the Y Corp. stock in this situation, § 1059 preserves two levels of tax—one at the corporate level and one at the shareholder level.

---

[29] For common stock, dividends during any 85-day period that equal or exceed 10% of a taxpayer's stock basis (5% for preferred stock) generally are considered "extraordinary dividends." § 1059(c) (adding that dividends in a year exceeding 20% of the taxpayer's stock basis are extraordinary). Dividends with respect to certain preferred stock are subject to § 1059 regardless of the stock's holding period, § 1059(f), as are certain redemptions taxable as dividends, see § 1059(e)(1)(A).

[30] If the amount of the extraordinary dividend excluded under § 243 exceeds the corporate shareholder's adjusted basis in the stock on which the dividend was declared, that excess amount is taxable gain when the dividend is received. § 1059(a)(2).

[31] Note, however, that if W Corp. is a foreign corporation, it may pay no federal income tax on that gain.

Perhaps because it is administratively difficult to determine from whom X Corp. purchased the Y Corp. stock (*i.e.*, from an individual or a domestic or foreign corporate seller), it may be a reasonable accommodation for § 1059 to automatically reduce X Corp.'s basis in the Y Corp. stock if the dividend is "extraordinary" (but not otherwise).[32] This result is not unreasonable even if X Corp. purchased the Y Corp. stock from W Corp., a corporate seller. After all, W Corp. could prevent two levels of corporate tax by causing Y Corp. to distribute a dividend before the sale of the Y Corp. stock to X Corp. If § 243 would have rendered the dividend nontaxable to W Corp., then W Corp. would have sold the Y Corp. stock to X Corp. for $800. In the aggregate, there would have been one level of corporate tax—the tax imposed on Y Corp. when it earned the $200.[33]

Section 1059 can apply to any transaction taxed as a dividend including distributions in redemption of stock, see § 302(d), as well as redemptions through related corporations, see § 304(a). If a sale of stock in one corporation (called the issuing corporation) to another corporation (called the acquiring corporation) is taxed as a distribution under § 304(a)(1), the sale is recast as (1) a transfer of the stock sold for stock of the acquiring corporation (2) which is then redeemed by the acquiring corporation in a transaction described in § 302(d). If the shareholder engaging in this § 304 transaction is itself a corporation (call it the "selling" corporation), then the effect of this hypothetical stock acquisition and redemption is to ensure that if the selling corporation excludes more than its basis in the shares sold by reason of the § 243 DRD, that excess will be taxable immediately as gain under § 1059(a)(2).

For example, assume Parent Corp. owns all the outstanding stock of Brother Corp. with an adjusted basis of $5,000 as well as all the outstanding stock of Sister Corp. with an adjusted basis of

---

[32] To eliminate all possibility of a triple tax on corporate earnings, the corporate and individual taxes would have to be integrated completely with respect to corporate taxpayers. Recall from Chapter 1 how difficult such integration can be.

[33] In lieu of Y Corp. distributing $200 to W Corp., W Corp. and X Corp. could have joined in making a § 338(h)(10) election. As one consequence of the election (see section 9.03 below), W Corp. would be treated as receiving the sales proceeds in liquidation of Y Corp. and would recognize none of its realized $200 gain under § 332.

Regardless of whether W is a corporation or an individual, to the extent that the distribution from Y Corp. is not out of its earnings and profits, it is appropriate for X Corp. to reduce its basis. Suppose that W had formed Y Corp. by exchanging $1,000 for all of the Y Corp. stock which was then sold to X Corp. which then caused Y Corp. to make a $200 distribution. The distribution is a nontaxable return of capital to X Corp. which then reduces its basis in the Y Corp. stock to $800. If X Corp. then sells the Y Corp. stock for $800, no gain or loss is recognized on the sale. In the aggregate, there is no corporate gain or loss because there have been no corporate earnings.

$50,000, and assume that the fair market value of each subsidiary corporation equals $50,000. If Parent Corp. sells the stock of Brother Corp. to Sister Corp. for cash of $50,000, this transaction is a redemption by related corporations as described in § 304(a)(1), and because Parent Corp. retains complete control of Brother Corp. after the transaction, it is taxable as a distribution pursuant to § 304(a)(1).

Suppose that the combined earnings and profits of Brother and Sister exceed $50,000, so that the entire distribution is taxed as a dividend. See § 304(b)(2); § 301(c)(1). If the distribution is treated as an extraordinary distribution, Parent Corp. is deemed to contribute its stock of Brother Corp. to Sister Corp. for Sister Corp. stock which is then redeemed and taxed as a dividend. The Sister Corp. stock hypothetically received by Parent has a substituted basis of only $5,000 under § 358(a)(1), so that the subsequent hypothetical $50,000 redemption produces not only a $50,000 dividend and a $50,000 dividends-received deduction but also a taxable gain of $45,000 under § 1059(a)(2). Note in particular that Parent Corp. was unable to offset that gain with its pre-existing basis in the stock of Sister Corp. that it actually owns.[34]

4.04 Treatment of the Distributing Corporation

Suppose X Corp. holds an asset with a $100 basis and a $500 fair market value. If X Corp. sells the asset and distributes the proceeds, X Corp. will be taxed on the $400 gain and the shareholders would be taxed on the $500 distribution as a dividend (assuming X Corp. had sufficient earnings and profits)

If, instead, X Corp. distributed the property to its shareholders who then sold the asset, should the tax consequences differ? The shareholders will still be taxable on a $500 dividend distribution under § 301(b), but there would be no further shareholder-level tax on the sale since the shareholders take a fair market value basis in the assets received. See § 301(d) discussed in more detail *infra*. Unless there is a corporate-level tax on the distribution, however, the tax system would seem to reward this form of the transaction.

Under either form of the transaction, the shareholders end up with the cash from the sale and a purchaser ends up with the asset. To the extent that the chosen form is dictated by non-tax considerations (*e.g.*, easier transfer of title), it makes no sense to have economically identical situations be treated differently for tax purposes. Thus, if a taxpayer has latitude in choosing the form of a

---

[34] Note, however, that § 1059 generally does not apply to a qualifying dividend (*i.e.*, qualifying for a 100% DRD). § 1059(e)(2).

transaction, a tax system is wasteful and inefficient if it causes taxpayers to invest resources (*e.g.*, money or time) in a nonproductive search to determine the best form for tax purposes of economically equivalent transactions.[35]

In 1935, the Supreme Court decided *General Utilities & Operating Co. v. Helvering*,[36] a case that shaped corporate taxation for more than 50 years. In that case, the corporate taxpayer contemplated a sale of stock in another corporation. Realizing that a sale by the corporation followed by a distribution of the proceeds would result in corporate-level and shareholder-level taxes, the corporation distributed the appreciated stock to its shareholders who reported a shareholder-level dividend. Under the predecessor of § 301(d), the shareholders took a fair market value basis in the distributed stock and reported no further gain when they sold the stock to the purchaser at fair market value.

Before the Board of Tax Appeals (the predecessor to the Tax Court), the Commissioner argued that the taxpayer should be taxed on the distribution since it had declared a dividend of $1 million and satisfied that obligation through a distribution of appreciated property. The trial court rejected that argument because in fact the corporation declared a dividend of the stock and not a dividend of cash. On appeal, the Commissioner added a second argument—that the sale should be attributed to the corporation rather than to the shareholders.

While this second argument convinced the circuit court, the Supreme Court held that the argument was raised too late. In its Supreme Court brief, the Commissioner raised a third argument— that a distribution of appreciated property constituted a "sale or other disposition" under § 1001, thereby triggering a corporate-level tax, an argument that the Supreme Court may have ignored. Whether this argument was ignored because it was raised belatedly or rejected on the merits is not clear. What is clear is that the latter interpretation gave rise to the *General Utilities* doctrine—a distributing corporation recognized no gain or loss on a distribution of property with respect to a shareholder's stock. The doctrine was codified in § 311(a).

Beginning in 1969, Congress began eroding the doctrine, essentially sounding its death knell in the Tax Reform Act of 1986. Section 311(a) still provides for non-recognition of gain or loss on a

---

[35] There may be equity problems as well since it is the wealthy that have better access to informed tax advice and some may have no choice but to use the less favorable form.

[36] 296 U.S. 200 (1935).

distribution with respect to stock, but § 311(b) provides a substantial exception. It now requires a distributing corporation to recognize gain on a distribution of property (other than the distributing corporation's own obligation) where the property's fair market value exceeds its adjusted basis. The gain is recognized as if the property had been sold to the distributee shareholders at fair market value.

The reach of § 311(b) is quite broad. A distributing corporation must recognize not only post-incorporation appreciation but pre-incorporation appreciation as well. Suppose that C forms X Corp. in a § 351 transaction by transferring property including one parcel with a $300 basis and $1,000 fair market value in exchange for all of the X Corp. stock. Before X Corp. earns any income, the corporation distributes the property to C. Under § 311(b), X Corp. is treated as having sold the asset to C for $1,000, recognizing a $700 gain. That gain will be capital or ordinary, depending upon the nature of the underlying property, and will be taxed to X Corp., and will increase its earnings and profits account. Consequently, C will have a shareholder-level tax on the distribution as well.

Note that these two levels of taxation stem from appreciation that occurred prior to the incorporation of X Corp. Could Congress have written a provision that distinguished between pre-and post-incorporation gain? Curiously, Congress did make similar distinctions involving liquidating distributions of property whose basis at the time of incorporation exceeded its fair market value. It is not clear why such distinctions are reserved for liquidating distributions and for property with a built-in loss rather than built-in gain.

The repeal of *General Utilities* embodied in § 311(b) does not apply to the distribution of property whose basis exceeds its fair market value—built-in loss property. Suppose that X Corp. (with ample earnings and profits) holds property with a $1,000 basis and $300 fair market value. Assume further that the decrease in the asset's value occurred while it was held by the corporation. If X Corp. sells the property and distributes the proceeds, the corporation will recognize a $700 loss and the shareholders will be taxed on the distribution as a dividend to the extent of X Corp.'s earnings and profits. If instead X Corp. distributes the property to its shareholders who then sell it, the shareholders will be treated in the same manner, but the corporation will recognize no loss. Moreover, because the shareholders take the distributed property with a basis equal to fair market value or $300, the $700 built-in loss is not preserved when the shareholders sell the property for $300; that loss simply disappears.[37]

Why should Congress countenance a difference in form when loss property is involved while eliminating form considerations when gain property is involved? Perhaps Congress was concerned that shareholders could exploit the realization doctrine by causing a corporation to distribute loss property but not gain property, thereby triggering loss recognition while keeping the gain unrealized. If that is the problem, the solution does not seem to fit.

It is always in a taxpayer's power to exploit the realization doctrine by selling loss property rather than gain property. This power gave rise to the enactment of §§ 165(f), 1211 and 1212 which limit the amount of loss immediately available from the sale of capital assets. Generally, capital losses can only be used to offset capital gains plus (for non-corporate taxpayers) up to $3,000 of ordinary income. If these provisions are deemed inadequate, perhaps Congress should somehow limit the deduction of losses that do not arise from the sale of capital assets, but it should limit such losses on sales as well as distributions.

Not surprisingly, Congress *has* enacted provisions that further curtail the exploitation of the realization doctrine. Suppose a taxpayer sells loss property under circumstances where the capital loss limitations are ineffective. Perhaps the taxpayer has sufficient capital gains from other transactions so that the loss would not be limited by § 1211. Or perhaps the asset sold would not give rise to a capital loss. If the property is sold in a manner that permits the taxpayer to control the property after sale, Congress has deemed that recognition of the loss is inappropriate. In effect the continued taxpayer control means that the loss has not truly been realized.

Section 267 prohibits the deduction of losses resulting from the sale or exchange between related parties. This section disallows a loss where the transferor and transferee are related and the transferor may be deemed to retain control of the asset.[38] A corporation and a more than 50 percent (by value) shareholder either through direct or indirect stock ownership are considered related for purpos-

---

[37] Note that § 311 applies on an asset-by-asset basis, not in the aggregate, so that if a corporation distributes both built-in gain and loss assets, the loss cannot offset the gain. Suppose that X Corp. distributes two assets to a shareholder, each worth $1,000 but with $500 and $1,500 bases. Under § 311(b), X Corp. recognizes its $500 gain on the built-in gain asset, but under § 311(a), it does not recognize its $500 loss on the built-in loss asset.

[38] In substance, § 267 is a kin of § 1091, the "wash sale" provision, where a person's loss on stock or securities is deferred in certain cases when the person acquires (or has acquired) a substantially identical asset.

es of § 267. If X Corp. sells property with a $1,000 basis and $300 fair market value to a shareholder, C, who owns more than 50 percent (by value) of X Corp. stock, X Corp. is not allowed a loss on the sale. A similar result follows if C is a 5-percent shareholder as long as more than 45 percent of the remaining stock is held by someone related to C within the meaning of § 267(b) (such as C's son). If X Corp. and C are not related, however, § 267 would not disallow the deduction on the sale to C.

In light of § 267, why doesn't § 311(b) allow a loss on a distribution of loss property to a shareholder subject only to the rules of § 267? In fact, the language of § 311(b) treats the distributed property as if it had been sold to a shareholder at fair market value. It would have been easy enough to subject the deemed sale to § 267. If the distribution were to a more than 50-percent shareholder, then no loss would be allowed to the distributing corporation. On the other hand, if the distribution were to a 50-percent or less shareholder, a loss would be allowed.

There are some peculiar side effects that arise because § 267 applies to actual sales but not to deemed sales under § 311(b). On a sale governed by § 267, a purchaser takes a cost basis under § 1012. But if the purchaser later sells the property at a gain, he may offset that gain with the loss that was disallowed to the original seller. § 267(d). If X Corp. sells property with a $1,000 basis and $300 fair market value to C, its only shareholder, X Corp. will recognize no loss pursuant to § 267, and C's basis is $300. If C later sells the asset to D for $1,000, however, C can offset the gain with the loss disallowed to X Corp.

Even though § 311(b) disallows losses, there is no provision that preserves the loss. If X Corp. distributes property with a $1,000 basis and $300 fair market value to C, X Corp. is unable to deduct the loss. C's basis in the property is its fair market value or $300. § 301(d). If C subsequently sells the asset for $1,000, C will recognize a $700 gain, a gain that cannot be offset by the previously disallowed loss.

To avoid that disappearing loss, a distributing corporations may try to sidestep the application of § 311(b). Suppose X Corp. owns property with a $1,000 basis and $300 fair market value. If X Corp. declares a dividend of that property, it will not be allowed a $700 loss on a distribution. § 311(a). Suppose instead that X Corp. declares a cash dividend of $300 but then satisfies the cash dividend with a distribution of the loss property. Can X Corp. now deduct the $700 loss (subject to § 267) since it has used property to satisfy a pecuniary obligation?[39] Note that this position is precisely what the Service argued in *General Utilities*—only in that case the distributed property had appreciated prior to the distribution.

Similar techniques may be employed when the property distributed is appreciated. Suppose X Corp. distributes property with a $300 basis and $1,000 fair market value to its shareholders with respect to their stock. Under § 311(b) X Corp. must recognize the $700 gain in the year of distribution as if the property were sold at its fair market value. Suppose instead that X Corp. sells the property to its shareholder in exchange for a note bearing appropriate interest. If the sale is respected, X Corp. would be entitled to defer the $700 gain pursuant to the installment provisions of § 453 while the shareholder would not have to treat the property as a dividend distribution.

If the shareholder ultimately honors the note, it is appropriate that the treatment of X Corp. and the shareholder should differ from distribution treatment, because there has been an exchange and not merely a distribution. But what if the shareholder ultimately defaults on the note? In that case, the shareholder ends up in essentially the same position as if the property had been distributed, except that by casting the transaction as a sale, X Corp. has avoided recognition of gain and the shareholder has avoided dividend treatment.

It is true that some correction will occur upon the discharge of indebtedness, but the parties have enjoyed the benefits of deferral and the correction is incomplete. Presumably, the shareholder will have discharge of indebtedness income of $1,000 under § 61(a)(12) which is in effect a deferred recognition of what would have been a dividend if the property had been distributed. On the discharge, X Corp. would seem to be entitled to a bad debt deduction under § 166 equal to the basis in the note, or $300. Stated differently, X Corp. not only avoids the recognition of gain but is entitled to a loss deduction when the note is discharged. Of course these and other attempts to circumvent the reach of § 311(b) will be closely scrutinized. The Service will press to recharacterize such transactions as distributions falling within the confines of § 311(b).[40]

---

[39] See *Kenan v. Commissioner,* 114 F.2d 217 (2d Cir.1940) (satisfaction of a cash legacy with appreciated stock treated as a sale or disposition).

[40] The Service may argue that the issuance and cancellation of the note should be disregarded, so that the purported sale of property by the corporation to the shareholder was properly treated as a dividend distribution subject to § 301 and § 311(b). Alternatively, the Service may respect the note's issuance but assert that the corporation should be treated as distributing the note as a dividend. Then, the shareholder would have dividend

Aside from the recognition or non-recognition of gain or loss on the distribution of property, § 311 raises some other unanswered questions relating to the treatment of liabilities associated with a distribution. Suppose X Corp. distributes property with a $300 basis and $1,000 fair market value. The property is subject to a $200 mortgage. Section 311(b) treats the distribution as if X Corp. had sold the property for $1,000, its fair market value. Of course, a purchaser would not pay $1,000 but instead would pay $800 because of the $200 liability encumbering the property. However under *Crane v. Commissioner,*[41] the amount realized would include the encumbering liability and would therefore equal the $1,000 fair market value measure used in § 311(b).

Suppose instead that the property is subject to a $1,300 liability. X Corp. is treated as having sold the property for its fair market value, but under § 311(b)(2), the fair market value is considered to be the amount of the liability or $1,300. This rule codifies the treatment mandated by *Crane* and *Commissioner v. Tufts,*[42] that the amount realized includes indebtedness even if it exceeds the fair market value of the property.

But conceptually there is an alternative way of characterizing the situation where a corporation distributes property subject to a liability in excess of the property's fair market value.[43] Taking the example above, it is as if the shareholder makes a contribution to the corporation's capital of $300 which the corporation uses to pay off the $300 excess liability. Viewed in this manner, the distribution by the corporation would produce a $700 gain to the distributing corporation, rather than a $1,000 gain. Of course the shareholder has not actually contributed $300 to the corporation but in effect has contributed a promise to discharge the $300 excess liability.[44] Conceptually, such a promise might be equated to an actual cash contribution.

As indicated above, the formulation under § 311(b) is an inexact way of providing that a distributing corporation be treated as if

---

income, while the corporation would recognize gain under § 311(b) and have no deduction.

[41] 331 U.S. 1 (1947).

[42] 461 U.S. 300 (1983).

[43] Crane, *Toward A Theory of the Corporate Tax Base: The Effect of A Corporate Distribution of Encumbered Property to Shareholders,* 44 Tax L. Rev. 113 (1988). Note that at least if the liability is a recourse liability, the corporation seems to have simply made a sale and not a distribution.

[44] This characterization may be inappropriate if the liability is nonrecourse because a shareholder would not normally advance funds to pay off a liability in excess of the encumbered property's value if there was no personal liability.

it sold the appreciated asset to the shareholder followed by a distribution of the proceeds. The formulation might cause a problem where the liability encumbering the property is a deductible one. Suppose X Corp. distributes an asset with a $300 basis and $1,000 fair market value, secured by accounts payable in the amount of $200. Under § 311(b), it appears as if the distributing corporation must recognize a $700 gain since the corporation is treated as if it had sold the property for the $1,000 fair market value. Of course if a purchaser were to pay $1,000 for the property, it would be conditioned on the corporation removing the encumbrance. If the distributing corporation were deemed to pay off the account payable, it would have a $700 gain on the sale, but would have a $200 deduction.[45] If the distributing corporation is not permitted to deduct the $200 on the deemed § 311(b) sale, the deduction would seem to be lost since the acquiring shareholders would not be entitled to take a deduction when the accounts payable were paid.[46]

It is not clear how the regulations or the courts will deal with the distribution of deductible liabilities. But prior to the enactment of § 357(c)(3), courts demonstrated great ingenuity in overcoming § 357(c)(1) on the transfer by a shareholder to a corporation of accounts payable. For a discussion of this issue, see Section 2.06(b) *supra.*

4.05 Effect of Property Distributions on Earnings and Profits

Section 4.02 *supra* considers the treatment of a corporate distribution, treatment that depends on available earnings and profits. Recall that a corporation's earnings and profits are increased for its income items and reduced for its losses, deductions, and distributions. Thus, a distribution may affect the amount of earnings and profits available for subsequent distributions.

Conceptually, it makes sense that the earnings and profits account is decreased for distributions, because distributions reduce a corporation's value. If the corporation distributes all of its earnings, the earnings and profits account should be $0. Sensibly, § 312(a)(1) provides that earnings and profits are decreased by the amount of money distributed.

But what happens to earnings and profits if a corporation distributes property whose basis differs from its fair market value? A

---

[45] For a discussion of this issue see *Commercial Security Bank v. Commissioner,* 77 T.C. 145 (1981) (allowing a comparable deduction in a liquidation context).

[46] See, e.g., *Hyde v. Commissioner,* 64 T.C. 300, 306 (1975).

corporation distributing appreciated property must recognize gain as if it sold the asset for its fair market value. § 311(b). Suppose that X Corp. distributes property with a $5,000 basis and $14,000 fair market value to its shareholders. On the distribution, X Corp. must recognize a $9,000 gain (the excess of that value over basis). The gain enters X Corp.'s taxable income. It also increases its earnings and profits to measure the distribution's tax consequences to the shareholders. Following the distribution, the earnings and profits account should be decreased to reflect the distribution. Under § 312(a)(3) and (b)(2), earnings and profits are decreased by the *fair market value* of the property distributed. Because the appreciation was recognized for tax purposes by X Corp., it is appropriate to decrease earnings and profits by not only the distributed asset's basis ($5,000) but also the recognized appreciation ($9,000), which together sum to the fair market value.

Notice that § 312(a)(3) and (b)(2) work by indirection. Section 312(a)(3) decreases earnings and profits by the "adjusted basis" of the property distributed while § 312(b)(2) defines "adjusted basis" to mean "fair market value" in the case of a distribution of appreciated property. You might ask why Congress did not directly amend § 312(a)(3) to decrease earnings and profits by the fair market value of property distributed. To answer that question, we must consider the treatment of distributed loss property, that is, property whose basis exceeds fair market value immediately before the distribution.

Suppose X Corp. distributes property with a $14,000 basis and $5,000 fair market value. Under § 311(a), X Corp. cannot deduct the unrealized loss on the distribution. But if X Corp. could recognize the $9,000 loss, that loss would decrease taxable income and consequently the earnings and profits account. It would also be appropriate to decrease earnings and profits by the fair market value of the property as a result of the distribution itself. Thus, the total reduction of earnings and profits should be $14,000—$9,000 from the loss deduction and $5,000 from the distribution itself.

But where the loss is not recognized to the distributing corporation, earnings and profits still should be reduced by $14,000, that is by the adjusted basis of distributed property. That reduction reflects that $14,000 of corporate earnings were used to acquire the property and have now been distributed to the shareholders. In summary, therefore, a corporation increases its earnings and profits by any gain recognized on an asset's distribution, and it reduces its earnings and profits (after the shareholders account for the distribution) by the greater of the asset's adjusted basis or fair market value immediately before the distribution. These determinations are made on an asset-by-asset basis.

To illustrate the operation of § 311 and § 312, suppose X Corp. with no earnings and profits distributes an asset with a $0 basis and $2,000 fair market value to its shareholders. On the distribution X Corp. recognizes a $2,000 gain under § 311(b). The gain increases X Corp.'s earnings and profits before measuring the tax consequences to the shareholders. Under § 301(c)(1), the shareholders will treat the entire distribution as a dividend, because there are sufficient earnings and profits (ignoring the effect of corporate taxes paid on the distribution) to cover the full distribution. Following the distribution, X Corp.'s earnings and profits will be reduced from $2,000 to $0 under § 312(a)(3) and (b)(2), since X Corp.'s earnings were fully distributed. Note that the reduction for the distribution occurs only after determining the tax treatment of the shareholders.

Suppose X Corp., with $50,000 of earnings and profits, distributes its own debt obligation with a face value of $50,000. The note bears no interest and matures in 20 years. The distribution of the note does not trigger a tax to X Corp. on the distribution because of an express exception provided in § 311(b). As discussed in more detail in the following section, the shareholders will be taxed on the fair market value of the distributed obligations. At a 10-percent discount rate, the obligation has a present value of merely $7,432.

While individual shareholders include the present value as a dividend (to the extent of earnings and profits), how should X Corp. adjust its earnings and profits account? Prior to the Deficit Reduction Act of 1984, a distributing corporation was permitted to reduce its earnings and profits by the full face value of the obligation (or, in the example, by $50,000). The effect of this Congressional largesse was to allow a corporation to wipe out its earnings and profits account at a small tax cost to its shareholders when the corporation issued a debt obligation with original issue discount.

This technique paved the way for future nontaxable distributions under § 301(c)(2). In the example above, X Corp. would have reduced its earnings and profits account to $0 by distributing a debt obligation that produced only $7,432 of dividend income to the shareholders. Section 312(a)(2) now provides that earnings and profits are decreased by the issue price of the debt obligation, not its face amount. Thus, in the example, X Corp. would reduce its earnings and profits by $7,432, matching the dividend income to the shareholders. Each subsequent year, the corporation can reduce its taxable income, and accordingly its earnings and profits, by the portion of the original issue discount that the shareholders must report as income. § 163(e).

4.06 Treatment of Shareholders—Property Distributions

Although the treatment of a shareholder receiving a property distribution has been alluded to earlier, a full discussion has been deferred to this point, because the distribution may increase the distributing corporation's earnings and profits, making dividend treatment more likely for the shareholders. Recall that a shareholder treats the amount distributed first as a dividend, then as a recovery of stock basis, and finally as gain from the sale or exchange of stock. § 301(c).

How is the amount distributed measured if a corporation distributes non-cash property or the shareholder assumes a liability in connection with the distribution? Suppose that X Corp. distributes property with a $4,000 basis and $10,000 fair market value to shareholders. The amount distributed is $10,000, because § 301(b) provides that amount distributed equals the property's fair market value. Suppose, in addition, that the property is subject to a $3,000 mortgage. Under § 301(b)(2), the amount distributed is reduced (but not below zero) by the liability assumed (or taken subject to). Thus, the amount distributed is $7,000 ($10,000, equal to the value of the distributed property, minus $3,000, for the liability).[47]

The basis rule for distributed property is found in § 301(d). Not surprisingly, shareholders take a fair market value basis in the property. Notice that assuming or taking subject to a liability has no effect on the basis of the distributed property. This result too should not be surprising. Section 301(d) simply confirms the *Crane*[48] doctrine that basis includes assumed or "subject to" indebtedness.

4.07 Constructive Dividends

Dividend treatment may be undesirable to a corporation and its shareholders After all, a corporation is taxed when it earns income, and a dividend distribution will result in a second tax at the shareholder level while the distributing corporation receives no deduction. Tax planners have conjured a plethora of imaginative ways to disguise a dividend distribution as some sort of non-dividend distribution.

Notwithstanding the variety of techniques, the attempts to disguise seem to fall under one of three prototypes. First, the

---

[47] The shareholders acquire $3,000 worth of the property for the liability and only the remaining portion of the property ($7,000 worth) is distributed on their stock.

[48] *Crane v. Commissioner*, 331 U.S. 1 (1947).

distribution might be disguised as a deductible expense even though the receipt by the shareholder would be taxable. This prototype eliminates the corporate-level tax by providing a deduction that will offset the corporate inclusion of the earnings which were distributed. The second prototype is a distribution which is excludable from income by shareholders while the distributing corporation receives no deduction. This prototype eliminates the shareholder-level tax rather than the corporate-level tax. To the extent that corporate tax rates exceed individual tax rates, this prototype may be less advantageous than the former. But note that both are preferable to dividend treatment. There is also a third prototype—the best of all worlds from the taxpayer's point of view—which is a corporate distribution that generates a deduction and yet is excluded from the shareholder's income.[49]

Perhaps the most common illustration of the first prototype is in the compensation area. Reasonable compensation, unlike dividends, are deductible by a distributing corporation. See § 162. From the shareholder's perspective, both dividends and compensation produce ordinary income, (historically taxed at the same rate). Because shareholders generally will benefit to the extent the corporation has a lighter tax burden, the tax system provides an incentive for corporations to characterize distributions as deductible reasonable compensation. Determining whether a distribution should be treated as a nondeductible dividend or deductible compensation calls for uncertain and sometimes artificial distinctions. Those distinctions would assume less importance in a world where corporate earnings were taxed only once at shareholder rates.

But until that world arrives, taxpayers, the Service and courts must wrestle with the dividend/compensation distinction. The mere fact that a shareholder-employee receives a large salary—say $5 million—will not necessarily mean that part or all of the purported compensation will be treated as a dividend distribution. It must be determined whether the shareholder-employee has performed services commensurate with the payment. This determination is made by looking at payments to other employees, payments to other similarly situated employees in comparable companies, what services the employee actually performed for the corporation, and how those services affected the corporation's performance.[50]

---

[49] It is difficult to disguise dividends in this manner, but compensation frequently can be disguised. For example, if a corporation rents a car for an employee's use, the corporation may deduct the rental payments under § 162 while the employee may attempt to exclude the value of the rental car from income as a "working condition" fringe benefit under § 132.

[50] See, e.g., *Elliotts, Inc. v. Commissioner,* 716 F.2d 1241 (9th Cir.1983).

One might think that the free market will assure that a corporation pays reasonable compensation. If a corporation pays unreasonable compensation, it may be disciplined by the market, disadvantaged by its higher costs of production. Or perhaps shareholders will object to the unreasonable levels of compensation paid to certain shareholder-employees that might deplete the amount otherwise available for distribution to all shareholders.

The market may fail to police reasonable compensation, however, for at least two reasons. First, there may be high transaction costs that make it difficult or costly for shareholders to prevent some level of over-compensation to shareholder-employees. For example, the costs of bringing a lawsuit against the corporation can be significant. Second, while the market may in fact dictate a level of return for both employees and shareholders, in the case of a shareholder-employee, the market is indifferent about how that return is allocated.[51] Whether the payments are considered to be dividends or compensation will not be determined by the market so long as the shareholder-employee's overall return is commensurate with the level of investment and services rendered. Predictably, it is the closely held corporation where most or all of the shareholders are employees where purported compensation is most susceptible to be characterized as a dividend distribution.

In addition to gauging the level and value of services rendered, the Service and the courts may also look to the history of dividends paid by the corporation. In general, it is probably true that if the corporation has a history of dividend distributions that reflect a "reasonable" rate of return on investment, amounts denominated as compensation are more likely to pass muster. Conversely, if a corporation has never paid dividends, the level of compensation will be more closely scrutinized.

In at least one case, a court recharacterized purported compensation as a dividend even where the compensation was found to be reasonable. The court found that no dividends had ever been declared and that a 15-percent return on shareholders' investment was appropriate.[52] If the court found the payments for services and other factors of production to be reasonable, it is not clear what justification there is for recharacterizing some of those payments as dividends. It just might be that after meeting its obligations the

---

[51] More accurately, the market will value those corporations that minimize taxes more favorably than those corporations that do not. Thus, the market may encourage an over-allocation to compensation.

[52] *Charles McCandless Tile Service v. United States,* 422 F.2d 1336 (Ct.Cl.1970). But see *Laure v. Commissioner,* 70 T.C. 1087 (1978), and Rev. Rul. 79–8, 1979–1 C.B. 92, rejecting the automatic dividend rule.

corporation had no earnings left for the residuary claimants—the shareholders.

As a variation on the first prototype, a controlling shareholder may cause a corporation to pay excessive compensation to a relative of the shareholder—a child, for example—who might do some work for the corporation. The excessive compensation will be treated as a distribution to the shareholder, who then will be deemed to make a gift to her child. There will be no deduction for the excess compensation and, assuming sufficient earnings and profits, the shareholder will have dividend income.

The second prototype for disguised dividends covers those transactions where the corporation receives no deduction, but the shareholder has no income inclusion. Distributions disguised as corporate loans serve as a good illustration. Suppose that X Corp. has just earned $50,000 on which it was taxed. Its shareholder, B, would like to get the $50,000 out of the corporation and into her hands. If X Corp. makes a distribution, B will have a dividend under § 301(c)(1) and § 61(a)(7), since X Corp. has earnings and profits, and X Corp. receives no deduction for the distribution.

Suppose instead that X Corp. "loans" B $50,000. If the transaction is respected as a loan, X Corp. still receives no deduction,[53] but now B has no income inclusion. While it is true that in the loan situation B has an obligation to repay X Corp., until repayment is made B has tax-free use of the funds. Moreover, if repayment is never made, then it is only in the year that the indebtedness is discharged (not the year the loan is made) that B will have ordinary income under *United States v. Kirby Lumber Co.* (or perhaps a dividend distribution).[54]

This corporate-loan scheme raises two issues. First, the Service or the courts must determine whether the transfer of funds is in fact a loan. If it is a loan, the second issue is whether the loan bears an appropriate level of interest. Note that if the transfer of funds is not in fact a loan, there is no need to resolve the second issue.

In resolving the first issue, the Service and the courts first look to see whether the transaction on its face seems to be a loan— whether transfer of funds satisfies the formal indicia of a loan often found with third-party borrowings, including whether there is a written loan agreement, whether an adequate interest rate is pro-

---

[53] While a distribution will reduce X Corp.'s earnings and profits under § 312(a), a loan will not.

[54] 284 U.S. 1 (1931). The corporation may then be entitled to a bad debt deduction under § 166.

vided, whether the note is secured, whether a repayment schedule is provided, and whether any repayments have been made. The purported loan is then viewed in a broader context by looking at factors such as whether any previous loans between the corporation and shareholder have been repaid. The corporation's dividend history may also be important. If a corporation has been successful but has made few or no distributions to shareholders, it is more likely that a purported loan will be closely scrutinized.

Finally, if the corporation loans funds in proportion to shareholders' equity interests, that proportionality may negatively influence the loan/dividend determination. For example, suppose X Corp., with ample earnings and profits, has ten shareholders, each holding 10 percent of the outstanding stock. If X Corp. purports to make equal loans to each shareholder, it is likely the Service will characterize its transfer of funds as dividend distributions, rather than capital contributions, with any subsequent interest payments by shareholders treated as contributions to the corporation's capital.

A corporate loan to a shareholder may be respected for federal income tax purposes but still result in distributions to the shareholder. Suppose that X Corp. makes a $50,000 loan to its shareholder B that is respected for federal income tax purposes but the loan makes no provision for interest.[55] Even though the loan is respected for tax purposes, B still receives an economic benefit, the interest-free use of X Corp.'s money. More generally, the personal but below-market use of corporate property (*e.g.*, the corporate hunting lodge) by a shareholder will often give rise to a "constructive" distribution to the shareholder.[56]

Constructive distributions are mandated by § 7872 when a corporation makes a below-market interest loan to a shareholder. If the loan is payable on demand, § 7872 recharacterizes the transaction as though shareholder pays a market rate of interest.[57] In the example from the preceding paragraph, suppose that the loan is a demand loan and the applicable market rate of interest is 10 percent. B will be treated each year as paying $5,125 in interest to X

---

[55] While the lack of interest may be one factor that suggests a loan is not a loan, it is not determinative. The concept of a no-interest loan is not an oxymoron.

[56] In fact, the free or below-market use represents the actual transfer of an economic benefit from the corporation to the shareholder but the transfer, imprecisely, is termed a "constructive" distribution.

[57] The market rate of interest is determined by looking at certain specified federal rates. See § 7872(f)(2).

Corp.[58] In fact, B makes no such payment. To complete the recharacterization, X Corp. is treated as though it not only loaned $50,000 but also made a distribution of $5,125. B is treated as having received the $5,125 distribution which she turns around and pays back to X Corp. in the form of interest. The $5,125 distribution and the $5,125 interest payment are deemed to occur each year the loan is outstanding.[59]

Note that for a demand loan, the deemed distribution is matched by a deemed interest payment. Historically, taxpayers offset the income from the distribution with the interest deduction.[60] However, under § 7872 the offsetting deduction is not automatic. For example, if the taxpayer uses the borrowed proceeds to purchase tax-exempt securities, § 265 will not allow the shareholder to deduct the deemed interest payment. Similarly if the shareholder uses the borrowed funds for personal purposes, § 163(h) generally does not permit a deduction. If a deduction is not permitted, the shareholder who receives a below-market interest loan may have dividend income without an offset.[61]

A related transaction that purports to generate neither a deduction nor income inclusion is a loan between related corporations. Suppose that all of the stock of X Corp. and Y Corp. are owned by B

---

[58] Section 7872 uses semiannual compounding. Accordingly, a 10-percent rate of interest is equivalent to 10.25 percent ($1.05^2 - 1$) when compounded semiannually.

[59] If the loan is a term loan (that is, a loan made for a stated period rather than a loan payable on demand), the timing of the deemed distribution and deemed interest repayment differs. Suppose that X Corp. loans B $50,000 to be repaid in five years but without interest. In the year the loan is made, B is deemed to receive a loan of $30,695.66, assuming a 10-percent interest rate compounded semiannually. B is also deemed to receive a distribution of $19,304.34, the difference between the deemed loan amount and the amount B actually received. § 7872(b)(1) (providing that the amount distributed equals the amount loaned over the present value of all loan payments). At the end of year 1, B would be deemed to pay interest on the $30,695.66 loan of $3,146.31 (10.25 percent × $30,695.66). § 7872)b)(2) (treating the loan as having original issue discount). In year 2 there would be no deemed distribution but B would have a deemed interest payment of $3,468.80 (10.25 percent × ($30,695.66 + $3,146.31)). *Id.* Overall, B will receive a deemed distribution of $19,304.34 and will be deemed to pay the same amount in interest, but the distribution is all in year 1 while the deemed payments occur in each of the 5 years. The large inclusion in year 1 is appropriate since B could put aside the $30,695.66 which by the end of 5 years would grow to $50,000—the amount necessary to repay the loan—at a 10.25 percent interest rate. Meanwhile the excess $19,304.34 can be spent without using it to repay the loan.

[60] See *Dean v. Commissioner,* 35 T.C. 1083 (1961) (no taxable income since deemed interest deduction offsets deemed income).

[61] Dividend treatment assumes the distributing corporation has adequate earnings and profits. The corporation that makes the below-market interest loan will have no deduction for its deemed distribution and will have income for its deemed receipt of the interest payment.

and that X Corp. lends $300,000 to Y Corp. If the Service cannot find a business reason for the loan and if the loan formalities are not observed (*e.g.*, executed loan agreement, repayment schedule), it might recharacterize the transaction as though X Corp. had made a $300,000 distribution to B who in turn will be deemed to make a $300,000 contribution to the capital of Y Corp. Viewed in this manner, the transaction will produce a dividend for B, assuming sufficient X Corp. earnings and profits.[62] However, if X Corp. had a valid business purpose for the loan, then treatment as a constructive dividend may not be appropriate.[63]

It is not only loans that fall into the second prototype. Suppose X Corp. owns an asset (*e.g.*, an apartment, yacht, car) which it leases to B, a shareholder, for $5,000 a year. Just as a below-market interest loan can be a disguised dividend, so too can a bargain purchase or lease. If the fair market value for leasing the asset is $7,000 a year, B will be deemed to have received a $2,000 distribution. Conversely, suppose B leases an asset to his corporation for $7,000 a year. If the fair market rental value of the asset is only $5,000 a year, B will be treated as receiving a $2,000 distribution.

The third prototype—a corporate deduction with no shareholder inclusion—might arise where the corporation makes a payment on behalf of a shareholder, claiming it to be for the benefit of the corporation. Suppose X Corp. pays for a trip to Bermuda for several prospective investors or lenders including B, a controlling shareholder. X Corp. might seek to deduct the expense under § 162, arguing that the trip significantly benefits the corporation. At the same time, B might argue that the benefit to the corporation exceeds any incidental personal benefit, thereby justifying an exclusion from income. We need more facts to resolve the issue. If in fact the trip to Bermuda was filled with conferences, presentations, and other tedious events, arguably the transaction could produce a corporate deduction with no inclusion. On the other hand, if the trip were filled with snorkeling, deep sea fishing, and festive parties, dividend recharacterization may be appropriate.

If the transaction is recharacterized as a distribution with respect to B's stock, then B will have a dividend if X Corp. has sufficient earnings and profits. Note that if the transaction is recharacterized not only would B have a dividend but also X Corp.

---

[62] See, e.g., *Stinnett's Pontiac Serv., Inc. v. Commissioner,* 730 F.2d 634 (11th Cir.1984). When a transaction is recharacterized in this manner, it is not at all clear what tax treatment occurs if Y Corp. should in fact make interest payments or repay the loan. It is certainly not inconceivable that the Service may recharacterize those payments also as disguised dividends to B—this time from Y Corp.

[63] See *Rapid Electric Co. v. Commissioner,* 61 T.C. 232 (1973).

would lose its deduction. It is as though X Corp. made a cash distribution to B equal to the fair market value of B's Bermuda trip and B then used the cash to purchase the trip.

Note that in any of these disguised dividend situations, whether the deemed distribution will be treated as a dividend depends on the earnings and profits of the distributing corporation.[64] If the distributing corporation has no earnings and profits, the deemed distribution will first offset the shareholder's stock basis and, once basis is exhausted, will typically produce a capital gain. § 301(c)(2) and (c)(3).

In *Truesdell v. Commissioner*,[65] the sole shareholder of two corporations diverted income earned by the corporations to himself. Neither the taxpayer nor his corporations reported the income on their returns. The Service argued that the full amount of the diverted funds was taxable to Truesdell as ordinary income without regard to the earnings and profits of the corporations. The Tax Court rejected the Service's position, holding that Truesdell was taxable on the constructive dividend only to the extent of the corporations' earnings and profits. Because the corporations did not have sufficient earnings and profits to cover the entire amount of the distribution, only a portion of the diverted funds was taxable. Note, however, that the Service neglected to assess additional income to the corporations. Had it done so, the corporations would have owed additional tax and the increase in the taxable income of the corporations would have increased earnings and profits, thereby making the constructive distributions to Truesdell fully taxable as a dividend.

4.08 Dividends and Corporate Shareholders

The last few pages were devoted to transactions in which taxpayers were attempting to disguise dividend payments as other transactions. The disguise can be played out in reverse when a corporate shareholder is involved. Suppose that X Corp. owns all of the Y Corp. stock with a $500,000 basis and $2 million fair market value. If X Corp. sells the stock outright for its value, it recognizes a $1.5 million gain. Suppose instead that X Corp. causes Y Corp. to distribute $1.5 million to X Corp. Assume that Y Corp. has sufficient earnings and profits to give X Corp. dividend treatment, that the distribution is not an extraordinary dividend under § 1059, and that under § 243 X Corp. can deduct 80 percent[66] of the $1.5 million

---

[64] *DiZenzo v. Commissioner,* 348 F.2d 122 (2d Cir.1965).

[65] 89 T.C. 1280 (1987).

[66] § 243(a)(1) and (c). To the extent that the requirements of § 243(b) were met, X Corp. would be entitled to a 100-percent deduction. See section 4.03 *supra* (discussing the dividends-received deduction).

dividend or $1.2 million. Of course X Corp. will be taxed on $300,000 but will have no gain when it sells the Y Corp. stock (now worth $500,000 after the distribution), since X Corp. can offset the amount realized with its $500,000 basis.

Whether a corporate shareholder will succeed in converting sales proceeds into dividends may depend on events surrounding the distribution. For example, if the purchaser were to infuse Y Corp. with $1.5 million in cash shortly after completing the purchase of the stock from X Corp., the Service might ignore the distribution from Y Corp. and treat X Corp. as though it realized $2 million on the sale.

Timing of the dividend declaration may dictate the outcome in these cases. In *Waterman Steamship Corp. v. Commissioner*,[67] the Fifth Circuit reversed the Tax Court and held that the distribution of a note was not treated as dividend when the dividend was declared after the negotiations began with the purchaser and the stock purchaser provided the cash to the purchased corporation to pay off the note. Thus, the purported dividend was treated as part of the purchase price of the stock, ineligible for the dividends received deduction.

However, the Tax Court in *Litton Industries, Inc. v. Commissioner*[68] respected the dividend distribution, in part because it was declared before negotiations for the prospective sale began. In *Litton Industries*, before selling the stock of its Stouffer subsidiary to Nestle, Litton arranged for Stouffer to declare a $30 million dividend in the form of a debt instrument. Litton, an accrual-basis taxpayer, reported the dividend income for tax purposes and took a fair market value basis in the note.[69] It also claimed an 85-percent (now 80-percent) dividends-received deduction. When Nestle purchased the Stouffer stock, it presumably paid $30 million less for the stock than it would have paid if Stouffer did not have a $30 million liability. Nestle also paid $30 million to satisfy the debt instrument. Litton reported no gain on the payment of the debt instrument with a $30 million basis and $30 million less gain on the sale of the stock than it would have reported if no dividend had been declared.

In ruling for Litton, the Tax Court distinguished *Waterman Steamship* because the *Waterman Steamship* dividend was declared after negotiations for the stock sale commenced. The Tax Court noted that the dividend in *Litton Industries* was declared two weeks

---

[67] 430 F.2d 1185 (5th Cir.1970).

[68] 89 T.C. 1086 (1987).

[69] Regs. § 1.301–1(h)(2)(i).

before Litton announced that Stouffer was for sale. Consequently, the court concluded, the declaration of the dividend and the sale of the Stouffer stock were not interdependent.

Conceptually, it seems a little too facile to distinguish *Waterman Steamship* and *Litton Industries* based solely on whether the dividend declaration precedes or follows negotiations for a stock sale.[70] In any case, *Litton Industries* provides a blueprint for using a dividend to reduce overall gain on the sale by a parent corporation of the stock of its subsidiary.

Of course, a distribution cannot be a dividend unless the distributing corporation has sufficient earnings and profits. Thus, when a corporation has corporate shareholders and plans to make a distribution, the corporation may try to increase its earnings and profits, thereby increasing the dividend income to its corporate shareholders. One technique that a corporation may employ is an installment sale: Its earnings and profits will be increased immediately by the full installment gain but its gain recognition may be deferred under the installment method.[71] Thus, an installment sale may pave the way for dividend treatment (and a dividends-received deduction) on a subsequent distribution, but § 301(e) may impede that favorable result.

Under § 301(e), adjustments to earnings and profits otherwise mandated by § 312(k) and (n) are generally disregarded in determining the taxable income (and adjusted basis) of any "20 percent corporate shareholder."[72] As a consequence, § 301(e) may reduce the earnings and profits that such a shareholder takes into account in applying § 301(c) to a distribution.[73] That reduction, in turn, makes it more likely that the distribution will reduce the shareholder's

---

[70] *Litton* presented the more compelling case, not only because of the dividend declaration's timing but also because the dividend represented less than 29% of the subsidiary's net equity (as opposed to about 80% in *Waterman Steamship*) and the subsidiary could have borrowed funds to pay off the distributed note. It was unclear whether the subsidiary in *Waterman Steamship* had that borrowing capacity.

[71] Under § 312(n), certain items deferred from currently taxable income are included for purposes of computing earnings and profits. Installments sale gains are one such item. See also § 453 (for installment reporting).

[72] A "20 percent corporate shareholder" is a corporation, entitled to a dividends-received deduction, that owns, directly or indirectly, 20 percent of the total voting power or value (excluding nonvoting preferred stock) of the distributing corporation.

[73] Note, however, that § 301(e) does not affect the amount by which the distributing corporation reduces, or the corporate shareholder increases, its earnings and profits to account for the distribution. Further, § 301(e) may produce a favorable result if the corporate shareholder would not otherwise be entitled to a dividends received deduction on any dividend.

basis in its stock, resulting in increased capital gain (or decreased capital loss) on a later sale of the shareholder's stock. For example, if the distribution to Litton was not a dividend but was treated as a return of basis, Litton would have recognized the same gain as if the distribution had not taken place. That is, Nestle would pay less because of the distribution but Litton's basis would be decreased by precisely the amount of the distribution.

4.09 "Fast Pay" or "Stepped-Down Preferred" Stock

Tax advisers can be a clever lot. Many devote much of their professional lives to parsing complex code provisions in an effort to create tax savings that may never have been intended. Recharacterizing transactions to create constructive distributions is one method of dealing with this phenomenon. In the transaction described below, the taxpayer was attempting to shift taxable income to a taxpayer who was not subject to tax while not affecting the economic positions of the participants.

In the basic fast-pay transaction, a U.S. corporate sponsor (the "sponsor") forms a closely held real estate investment trust (called a REIT)[74] with accommodating tax-exempt investors. (The "exempt participants" might be foreign investors not subject to U.S. taxation.) The REIT, generally treated as a corporation but with the ability to deduct dividends, issues common stock to the sponsor and fast-pay stock to the exempt participants. The fast-pay stock is structured to have an above-market dividend rate for a fixed period of time, after which the dividend rate "steps down" to a *de minimis* rate. In addition, after the step-down, the arrangement generally gives the sponsor (or the REIT) the right to redeem the fast-pay stock for its then-fair market value, a small fraction of its issue price. As an economic matter, the fast-pay stock performs much like self-amortizing debt: to the exempt participants, the high periodic dividend payments represent in part distributions of income and in part returns of capital.

For federal income tax purposes, by contrast, before remedial legislation was enacted, the periodic dividend payments on the fast-pay stock were entirely deductible distributions of income by the REIT. This mischaracterization of the dividends (entirely as income when economically a portion represented a return of capital) effectively allowed the REIT to overallocate its taxable income to the exempt participants. This overallocation resulted in a corresponding underallocation to the taxable sponsor. If the sponsor eventually

---

[74] A REIT is a statutory entity that generally invests in real property or mortgages. See § 857.

sold its interest in the REIT, the underallocation would allow the sponsor to defer its economic income from the transaction to the time of the sale and convert the income's character from ordinary to capital gain. If the sponsor liquidated the REIT in a tax-free parent-subsidiary liquidation, the sponsor's economic income from the transaction would permanently escape tax.

The following hypothetical example illustrates the intended tax benefits of the transaction: A U.S. corporation forms a REIT by contributing $1,000 in exchange for substantially all of its common stock. At the same time, a tax-indifferent party contributes $1,000 in exchange for fast-pay stock that has a stated dividend rate of 14 percent. The REIT invests its $2,000 in a 10–year, 7 percent, balloon payment mortgage. The mortgage provides for 10 annual payments of $140 (7 percent times $2,000) and a single payment of its $2,000 principal at the end of the ten year term. The fast-pay stock provides for annual dividend distributions of $140 (14 percent times $1,000) for ten years. After the initial 10–year period, the dividend rate on the fast-pay stock steps down to 1 percent per year. At that time, the REIT has the ability to redeem the fast-pay stock for its then-fair market value of, say, $100. If the fast-pay stock is redeemed, the U.S. corporation that owns the corporation can then liquidate the REIT in a tax-free manner.

The U.S. corporation expects that it will realize a predictable economic benefit over the anticipated 10–year term of the transaction without ever incurring any tax liability for that benefit. In particular, the U.S. corporation anticipates that the dividends-paid deduction on the fast-pay stock will eliminate the REIT's income for the initial 10–year period. Immediately after this period, the U.S. corporation anticipates that the fast-pay stock will be redeemed for $100 and that the REIT will then be liquidated in a tax-free manner. Upon the liquidation, the U.S. corporation will succeed to the $1,900 cash on hand ($2,000 cash on hand less the $100 payment to redeem the fast-pay stock) without incurring a tax. Thus, the U.S. taxpayer will have realized a $900 economic benefit ($1,900 amount received less $1,000 initial investment) over the 10–year term of the transaction without ever incurring a tax on it.[75]

In response to fast-pay transactions, the IRS has issued regulations that treat the fast-pay stock as if the stock were a security

---

[75] In effect, the exempt participants would share their tax exemption with the U.S. corporate sponsor. Assuming that the exempt participants and the sponsor each earn a before-tax return of 7% and that the sponsor is taxed at a 35% rate (and therefore earns a 4.55% after-tax return), each party comes out ahead on a present-value basis (disregarding transaction costs) if the exempt participants receive somewhere between $32.85 and $447.03 in the stock redemption.

issued by the sponsor, instead of the REIT.[76] Consistent with this recharacterization, the regulations treat the fast-pay distributions as if they were made by the REIT to the sponsor and then by the sponsor to the exempt participants. The payments from the sponsor to the exempt participants would only be deductible to the extent they constituted interest. Repayments of principal would not be deductible. This recharacterization ensures that the sponsor is taxed on its economic income from the transaction.[77] In effect, the fast pay stock rules treat the sponsor as receiving a constructive distribution.

---

[76] *See* Regs. § 1.7701(*l*)–0 *et seq.* The "security" may be treated as debt or stock depending on its characteristics.

[77] In the example, the sponsor would be taxable on $140 each year, but each $140 payment to the exempt participants would in most cases be partly interest and partly a return of the loan principal. Only the interest portion would be potentially deductible.

Chapter 5

REDEMPTIONS

5.01 Introduction

A "redemption" (more precisely, a "distribution in redemption of stock") is the purchase by a corporation of some of its own stock. § 317(b). How should a redemption be taxed to the corporation and to the selling shareholder? On the one hand, a redemption might be treated as any other distribution made with respect to a shareholder's stock, producing ordinary income, recovery of basis, and capital gain to the distributee shareholder depending on the corporation's earnings and profits account and on the shareholder's stock basis. See § 301. Consistent with this approach, the distributing corporation would recognize gain but not loss on the distribution. See § 311(b). On the other hand, a redemption could be treated like any other purchase and sale of a capital asset, giving the selling shareholder exclusively recovery of basis and capital gain, independent of the corporation's earnings and profits account. Were this characterization followed at the corporate level, gain or loss could be recognized on the exchange.

Consider a corporation with a single shareholder that redeems some of the shareholder's stock. The redemption is just like any other distribution. Before and after the redemption, the shareholder owns all of the corporation's stock, is entitled to all distributions on the stock, and enjoys all voting rights on the stock. As you may suspect, that redemption is treated like a § 301 distribution. In contrast, if a small shareholder of a large corporation has all of her stock redeemed, that redemption is treated as a sale (at least if she is related to none of the other shareholders).

The shareholder-level taxation of redemptions is governed by § 302, and this section incorporates both approaches.[1] Under § 302, redemptions resembling a sale of stock to a third party qualify for exchange treatment, while those redemptions more closely resembling dividend distributions follow the general distribution rules of § 301. The rules of § 302 distinguish among types of redemptions by generally considering the effect of the redemption on the distributee shareholder's interest in the corporation. Exchange treatment offers to the shareholder whose stock is redeemed the recovery of basis implicit in the definition of gain: only the excess amount realized

---

[1] The corporate level taxation of redemptions is discussed at Section 5.04 *infra*.

over the shareholder's basis is taxable to the shareholder (generally as capital gain).

For example, suppose that individual B owns 100 outstanding shares of X Corp. with adjusted basis of $70 per share and fair market value of $100 per share and that X redeems 10 of B's shares for $1,000 (their fair market value). If the redemption is accounted for under the distribution rules of § 301, B has dividend income of $1,000 (assuming sufficient earnings and profits). In contrast, if the redemption is treated as an exchange, B has $300 of capital gain ($1,000 amount realized minus $700 basis). Thus, dividend treatment results in ordinary dividend income,[2] while exchange treatment results in basis recovery and typically capital gain (or loss). With most dividends now taxable at the same rate as long-term capital gain,[3] a shareholder owning stock with a very low basis may be practically indifferent to the distinction between exchange and distribution treatment. Conversely, a shareholder with high share basis generally will prefer exchange treatment. In fact, with a sufficiently high stock basis exchange treatment can generate a taxable loss while distribution treatment can at best be tax-free.

The possibility of exchange treatment becomes even more significant in the case of inherited stock because of the fair market value basis given to property at death by § 1014. Thus, if B in the example above dies and devises his shares to children C and D, each child will take a $100 basis in each share. If the corporation then redeems all of C's stock, distribution treatment produces income up to $100 per share while exchange treatment results in no gain or loss. As this example demonstrates, qualifying for exchange treatment can mean, for the devisee of stock, the difference between taxation on the entire amount distributed and no taxation at all.

Section 302 is structured as follows. Exchange treatment is given to the recipient shareholder under § 302(a) if and only if[4] the redemption qualifies under one of the provisions of § 302(b). Thus, one *obtains* the benefit of § 302(a) by *qualifying* under § 302(b). A redemption that fails to qualify under § 302(b) is subjected to the distribution rules of § 301 pursuant to § 302(d). Thus, subsections (a) and (d) are the taxing provisions while subsection (b) contains the qualifying rules.

---

[2] To the extent the distribution exceeds available earnings and profits, the shareholder reduces basis and then recognizes gain, typically, capital gain. § 301(c)(2) and (3).

[3] Although qualified dividend income is taxed at the same rate as long-term capital gain (*see* § 1(h)(11)), it is not capital gain. For example, capital loss generally cannot offset qualified dividend income.

[4] See also § 303 (exchange treatment for certain redemptions used to pay death taxes).

Subsection (b)(1) gives (shareholder-level) exchange treatment to redemptions "not essentially equivalent to a dividend." Until enactment of the 1954 Code, only this ambiguous language distinguished qualifying from non-qualifying redemptions. As you might expect, substantial litigation and transactional uncertainty resulted.[5] Congress responded by creating the safe harbor provisions now found in § 302(b)(2)–(4),[6] provisions giving exchange treatment to redemptions based upon objective criteria. These rules are explored in detail in Section 5.02 below. Section 302(b)(1) now is a residuary provision, a last resort for taxpayers who fail to navigate into the safe harbors of § 302(b)(2)–(4).

In focusing on the effect of a redemption on the recipient shareholder's stock interest in the distributing corporation, Congress recognized that stock owned by a relative of the recipient shareholder might appropriately be imputed to the recipient shareholder. For example, if B and C are equal co-owners of X Corp., the redemption by X of all of B's stock has a substantial effect on B's control of the corporation if B and C are strangers but perhaps only a nominal effect if B and C are husband and wife. Accordingly, Congress provided in § 302(c) that a set of *attribution rules* are applied to determine qualification under § 302(b), attribution rules that are exceedingly complex and that apply with varying degrees of rigor. These rules also impute stock ownership from (and to) entities (corporations, partnerships, estate and trusts) and to (and from) their equitable owners.

For example, with two exceptions[7] the redemption of stock from a sole shareholder is taxed like a current distribution rather than as an exchange.[8] On the other hand, the redemption of all the stock held by one taxpayer will, in general, qualify for exchange treatment.[9] Suppose that X Corp. has two shareholders, individual B and Y Corp. If B has no relationship to Y, then the redemption of all of B's X stock by X will qualify as an exchange. On the other hand, if B owns all of the Y stock as well as half of the X stock, the redemption by X of B's stock will be treated as a distribution: Y's ownership of stock of X will be imputed to B and B will therefore be deemed to be the sole shareholder of X both before and after the distribution.[10]

---

[5] See, e.g., B. Bittker & J. Eustice, Federal Income Taxation of Corporations and Shareholders ¶ 9.01 (7th ed. 2000).

[6] The safe harbor provision for partial liquidations in § 302(b)(4) was, until 1982, in § 346.

[7] The two exceptions are redemptions constituting partial liquidations, see § 302(b)(4), and redemptions to pay death taxes, see § 303.

[8] *United States v. Davis,* 397 U.S. 301 (1970).

[9] See § 302(b)(3) discussed at Section 5.02(a) *infra.*

[10] See § 318(a)(2)(C).

Section 304 takes these attribution rules one step further, treating the purchase of one corporation's stock by a second corporation as a redemption if the two corporations have sufficient commonality of ownership. The attribution rules are discussed in Section 5.02 below, while discussion of § 304 is deferred until Section 5.07.

As a final introductory note, redemptions often occur in the context of larger transactions. For example, a sale of a corporation often is structured as the part sale, part redemption of a controlling shareholder's stock. As a second example, employment agreements of key corporate employees sometimes provide that the employee's stock must be redeemed if the employment relationship is terminated. These and similar transactions are discussed in Section 5.05 below.

5.02 Redemptions Taxed as Exchanges

If a redemption is taxed as an exchange, the redeemed shareholder is treated as selling or exchanging his stock for the redemption proceeds. § 302(a). Thus, under § 1001, the shareholder recognizes gain or loss (likely capital gain or loss), equal to the difference between the value of the redemption proceeds (*i.e.*, the amount realized) and his basis in the redeemed stock. A redemption is taxed as an exchange if it is described in § 302(b) or § 303.

(a) Complete Terminations.

Consider the case of a shareholder whose entire stock interest in the corporation is redeemed. Because the shareholder completely terminates his interest in the corporation, the redemption's effect is identical to a sale of his shares to a third party, and Congress has recognized that such a redemption presents a compelling case for exchange treatment to the shareholder. Under § 302(b)(3), a redemption is treated as an exchange if the redemption "is in complete redemption of all the stock of the corporation owned by the shareholder."

As indicated above, to make this and other determinations under § 302(b), the attribution rules of § 318 apply. Section 302(c)(1) expressly incorporates those rules, rules that attribute stock between family members, between business entities and their beneficial owners, and between corporations and owners of options to purchase shares of the corporation's stock.[11] While a general discussion of the § 318 attribution rules can be deferred, there is a

---

[11] Note that the attribution rules of § 318 apply only if expressly made applicable. § 318(a) (introductory language).

special relationship between the family attribution rules of § 318(a)(1) and the complete termination safe harbor of § 302(b)(3).

In general, a shareholder wishing to qualify under the complete termination safe harbor of § 302(b)(3) must have neither actual nor constructive ownership of stock of the redeeming corporation after the redemption. In the case of closely held corporations, this burden might be difficult (if not impossible) to meet because, under § 318(a)(1), any stock owned by the shareholder's spouse, children, grandchildren and parents will be imputed to the shareholder. In particular, this safe harbor would be essentially unavailable for parents wishing to pass control of the family corporation to the younger generation by means of a redemption.

For example, suppose X Corp. is owned by Father and Daughter. If X redeemed all of Father's stock, in the absence of a remedial provision Father would not have completely terminated his interest in the corporation within the meaning of § 302(b)(3). Rather, he would be deemed to continue to own a stock interest because Daughter's stock would be attributed to him.[12] Thus, although his actual stock ownership of X would be reduced to zero, his constructive stock ownership would be 100 percent.

However, Congress has provided relief through the so-called waiver attribution rule, under which a shareholder seeking to qualify under § 302(b)(3) may elect to waive the family attribution rules in limited circumstances. The terms of this waiver are set forth in § 302(c)(2), but before examining that section in detail, it is worthwhile to recognize precisely what the waiver does and does not cover. First, it applies only to the *family* attribution rules of § 318(a)(1): the entity and stock option attribution rules of § 318(a)(2)–(4) continue to apply. Second, this waiver applies only to determinations under § 302(b)(3), the complete termination safe harbor; it does not apply to the general rule of § 302(b)(1) nor to the other safe harbors in § 302(b)(2) and § 302(b)(4).

If the waiver attribution rule applies, it will allow a shareholder to obtain exchange treatment under § 302(b)(3) even if the shareholder's spouse, child or grandchild (for example) continues to own stock of the corporation after the redemption. Thus, this waiver makes the complete termination safe harbor a viable possibility for shareholders of closely held corporations.

The waiver attribution rule is subject to several limitations to prevent abuse. First, the rule generally does not apply if the shareholder acquired any of his stock within 10 years of the redemption

---

[12] See § 318(a)(1)(A)(ii).

from a family member (as defined by § 318(a)(1)) or transferred any of his stock to a family member within the same period. § 302(c)(2)(B). This limitation prevents the following obvious abuse of the complete termination safe harbor. Individual B owns all the stock of X Corp. B gives half of his stock to his spouse, and B's stock (or his spouse's stock) is redeemed one week later. But for § 302(c)(2)(B), this redemption would fall within the complete termination safe harbor as long as B (or his spouse) filed the § 302(c)(2) waiver form. In either case, the tax avoidance potential is clear—cloaking a dividend distribution as an exchange—and Congress reasonably has excluded such transactions from the reach of § 302(b)(3) unless the taxpayer can establish an absence of a tax avoidance motive for the initial transfer.[13]

Second, immediately after the redemption, the redeemed shareholder cannot have an interest in the corporation other than as a creditor. § 302(c)(2)(A)(i).[14] Third, the redeemed shareholder cannot acquire such an interest in the redeeming corporation (other than by bequest or inheritance) within 10 years after the redemption. § 302(c)(2)(A)(ii).

Finally, a shareholder must file a statement with his return for the redemption year, representing that (i) he has not acquired such an interest in the corporation (other than by bequest or inheritance) since the distribution and (ii) if he acquires such an interest within 10 years after the redemption, he will notify the Service within 30 days after the acquisition. Regs. § 1.302-4(a). To put some teeth in the notification requirement, the statute of limitations is kept open until at least one year after the notification occurs. Thus, the Commissioner can reopen the redemption year to assert a deficiency if the redemption fails as a complete termination under § 302(b)(3) once the redeemed shareholder has failed to meet the third requirement of the waiver attribution rule.

---

[13] Transfers often are treated as lacking a principal tax-avoidance purpose if the transfer is from parent to child and intended to encourage the child's interest in the business. *See, e.g.,* Rev. Rul. 56-584, 1956-2 C.B. 179, Rev. Rul. 77-293, 1977-2 C.B. 91, Rev. Rul. 77-455, 1977-2 C.B. 93, Rev. Rul. 79-67, 1979-1 C.B. 128, and Rev. Rul. 85-19, 1985-1 C.B. 94.

[14] Thus, among other things, the redeemed shareholder cannot be an officer, director, or employee of the corporation. *Id.*

Section 302(c)(2)(A)(i) has at least three possible rationales. First, it assures that the redeemed shareholder does not retain a financial stake in the success of the enterprise (*i.e.,* a proprietary or equity interest). Second, it may prevent the corporation from disguising a non-deductible distribution on stock as a deductible payment. Finally, it may prevent the redeemed shareholder from, in substance, receiving payments for the stock over time but recognizing relatively more gain as the later payments are received. *Cf.* § 453 (requiring gain to be taken into account proportionately as payments received).

Not surprisingly, substantial litigation has centered on the second requirement, in particular on what constitutes a prohibited "interest in the corporation." The statute prohibits any "interest in a corporation (including an interest as officer, director, or employee), other than an interest as a creditor." § 302(c)(2)(A)(i). The regulations offer little guidance in this area, saying only that "a person will be considered to be a creditor only if the rights of such person with respect to the corporation are not necessarily greater or broader in scope than necessary for the enforcement of his claim. Such claim must not in any sense be proprietary and must not be subordinate to the claims of general creditors."[15] This regulation is seeking to distinguish the claim of a *creditor* from that of an *equity owner.* Accordingly, all the problems plaguing the debt/equity issues in other contexts[16] can reappear here.

In *Lynch v. Commissioner,*[17] the Tax Court held that a taxpayer did not run afoul of this regulation even though he permitted the corporation to subordinate his debt to that of a note acquired after the redemption. In addition, the Service has ruled that a taxpayer can obtain the benefit of the § 302(c)(2) waiver despite retaining his interest as lessor of the corporation's office building.[18] Presumably the "creditor" exception in § 302(c)(2)(A) was intended to permit exchange treatment to retiring shareholders even if they were the continuing beneficiaries of a company pension plan. The Tax Court's opinion in *Lynch* and the Service ruling indicate how far "creditor" can be stretched.[19]

The Code specifically provides that a § 302(c)(2) waiver is invalid if the shareholder retains or acquires an interest in the corporation as "officer, director, or employee." See § 302(c)(2)(A)(i)–(ii). Further, it is clear that a waiver will be invalid if such an interest is retained by the shareholder solely as a result of ignorance of the law.[20] However, it has been held that § 302(c)(2)(A) does not prohibit retention of an interest as an officer or director if the shareholder performs no duties, receives no compensation, and exercises no influence over the affairs of the corporation,[21] and in a surprising opinion, the Tax Court held that continuing to work for the corporation as an independent contractor is not a tainted interest akin to

---

[15] Regs. § 1.302–4(d).

[16] See Section 3.06 *supra.*

[17] 83 T.C. 597 (1984), rev'd, 801 F.2d 1176 (9th Cir.1986).

[18] Rev. Rul. 77–467, 1977–2 C.B. 92.

[19] *Lynch* was reversed on other grounds and the proper treatment of a subordinated note expressly was left undecided. 801 F.2d 1176 (9th Cir.1986).

[20] *Seda v. Commissioner,* 82 T.C. 484 (1984).

[21] *Lewis v. Commissioner,* 47 T.C. 129 (1966).

the explicitly forbidden interest of being an employee.[22] This dubious distinction was reversed, however, on the entirely sensible theory that Congress intended to impose a bright-line test in § 302(c)(2)(A). Whether the Tax Court's precarious reliance on the distinction between "employee" and "independent contractor" can ever gain traction remains to be seen.[23]

While the § 302(c) waiver limits application only of the *family* portion of the attribution rules, the waiver itself can be made by entities as well as by individuals.[24] Because entities have no spouses, children or other family members, the ability to waive the family attribution rules is important to entities only because, under § 318(a)(5), the attribution rules can be used to form *chains* of attribution between individuals and entities.

For example, suppose that Father's estate owns shares in X Corp., and assume that the only beneficiary of Father's estate is Mother. If X Corp. redeems all of the estate's shares, the estate will fail to qualify for exchange treatment under § 302(b)(3) if Mother owns any stock of X. To be sure, the estate can file for a waiver of the family attribution rules, but because Mother's stock is imputed to the estate under one of the entity attribution rules, the waiver will not prevent attribution from Mother to the estate. Thus, the redemption will not work a complete termination of the estate's interest in the corporation, so § 302(b)(3) will not apply.

Suppose, however, that Mother owns no stock of X Corp. but that Son does. If the estate is unable to file a § 302(c) waiver, the redemption of all of its stock once again will fail to qualify under the complete termination provision of § 302(b)(3), because Son's stock will be imputed to Mother under the family attribution rules[25] and that constructive ownership will be imputed to the estate under the entity attribution rules.[26] If the estate can file a § 302(c) waiver, though, the chain of attribution will be broken at the link from Son to Mother, so that the estate will have no actual or constructive ownership of X Corp. after the redemption and § 302(b)(3) will apply.

---

[22] *Lynch v. Commissioner*, 83 T.C. 597 (1984), rev'd, 801 F.2d 1176 (9th Cir.1986).

[23] See also *Cerone v. Commissioner*, 87 T.C. 1 (1986), in which the Tax Court reasoned that a former shareholder performing services for the corporation will fail § 302(c)(2)(A) only if the individual has a significant financial stake in the corporation or continues to control the corporation.

[24] See § 302(c)(2)(C).

[25] See § 318(a)(1)(A)(ii).

[26] See §§ 318(a)(3)(A), 318(a)(5).

While individual shareholders ordinarily will prefer redemptions to qualify for exchange treatment, corporate shareholders often prefer distribution treatment because of the dividends received deduction of § 243. The safe harbor provisions of § 302(b) are not elective, thus encouraging corporate shareholders to structure redemptions to fall *outside* the terms of § 302(b). Can a corporate shareholder structure a complete termination as a series of partial redemptions to avoid exchange treatment on all of the redemptions other than the last? In *Bleily & Collishaw v. Commissioner*,[27] such a series of redemptions was telescoped into a single redemption taxable as an exchange under § 302(b)(3). Cf. § 302(b)(2)(D) (providing express authority to collapse a series of redemptions made pursuant to a plan in applying § 302(b)(2)).

If a redemption fails to qualify for exchange treatment, it is treated as a corporate distribution subject to the general distribution rules of § 301. Ordinarily, § 301 can be applied to failed redemptions without difficulty: the basis of the shares redeemed flows into the shareholder's remaining stock,[28] and the amount distributed is taxed as a dividend to the extent of the corporation's earnings and profits.

However, consider the case of a shareholder whose stock is completely redeemed but whose constructive ownership does not decrease to zero (because, for example, a relative continues to own stock of the corporation and a valid § 302(c) waiver is not, or cannot be, filed). For example, suppose that individual B and corporation C each owns half the stock (50 shares) of X Corp. with adjusted basis of $10 per share and fair market value of $100 per share. Suppose further than B is the sole shareholder of C. If X redeems all the stock owned by B for fair market value of $5,000, that amount will be taxed under the distribution rules of § 301 because C's shares will be attributed to B. Assuming that all of the distribution is taxed as a dividend, what happens to the shareholder's basis in the redeemed shares? Does that basis simply disappear? In *Levin v. Commissioner*,[29] the court ruled that the shareholder's basis is transferred to the shares held by the related shareholder whose stock was imputed to the distributee-shareholder, a result consistent with the current regulatory approach.[30]

---

[27] 72 T.C. 751 (1979), aff'd without opinion, 647 F.2d 169 (9th Cir.1981).

[28] Regs. § 1.302–2(c).

[29] 385 F.2d 521 (2d Cir.1967).

[30] Regs. § 1.302-2(c), *Ex. (2)* (providing that when a husband and wife owned all stock of a corporation, which redeemed the husband's stock, the remaining basis in the husband's stock was added to the wife's basis in her stock). Note that proposed regulations would change that result by giving

(b) Substantially Disproportionate Redemptions.

If a redemption reduces a shareholder's interest significantly but not completely, exchange treatment may be obtained if the redemption qualifies under § 302(b)(2). Such a redemption must satisfy a three-part test: (1) The redeemed shareholder must own less than 50 percent of the voting power of the corporation immediately after the redemption; (2) the shareholder's voting power after the redemption must be less than 80 percent of his pre-redemption voting power;[31] and (3) the shareholder's percentage ownership of common stock of the corporation after the redemption also must be less than 80 percent of his pre-redemption ownership.[32]

As an example of the computational aspects of § 302(b)(2), consider individual A, who owns 90 of the 300 outstanding shares of X Corp, a corporation with only one class of stock outstanding. X redeems 20 of A's shares, leaving 280 shares outstanding. Does A qualify for exchange treatment under § 302(b)(2)?

After the redemption, A owns 70 of 280 outstanding shares, or 25 percent.[33] Thus, A's post-redemption stock constitutes less than 50 percent of the total X voting power, and part (1) of the three-part test is satisfied. Before the redemption, A owned 90 of 300 shares, or 30 percent of the total X voting power. Since 80 percent of 30 percent is 24 percent, A's post-redemption voting percentage of X is *not* less than 80 percent of his pre-redemption voting percentage, so A fails the second test. (A also fails the third test because his ownership of common stock also decreases from 30 percent to 25 percent while a decrease below 24 percent is required.) Note that tests two and three require a computation of A's pre-and post-redemption ownership of X Corp.: it is *not* sufficient to determine whether 20 percent of A's stock has been redeemed.

---

the shareholder a deferred loss, a loss that he would take into account on the first day that he would qualify under § 302(b)(1), (2), or (3) if the stock ownership at the end of that day had been in place immediately after the redemption. *See* Prop. Regs. § 1.302-5(a)(3) and (b)(4)(i); *cf. id.* at (b)(4)(ii) (for special rules for corporate shareholders).

[31] Although the statute refers to "voting stock," this reference has been interpreted to mean "voting power." *See* Rev. Rul. 81-41, 1981-1 C.B. 121.

[32] *See* Rev. Rul. 87-88, 1987-2 C.B. 81 (concluding that when the corporation has more than one class of common stock outstanding, the percentage of common stock owned before and after the redemption is determined by looking to the aggregate value of the common stock owned, not the value of each class of common stock owned).

[33] Even if the redeemed stock is held as treasury stock, it is not counted as outstanding stock. Stated more prosaically, the redemption reduces not only the numerator of the fraction, but also the denominator.

Compare the tax treatment to A if the corporation had redeemed 50 of his 90 shares. In that case, A's post-redemption ownership of the corporation would be 40 of 250 shares, or 16%. A would thus have dropped below 80 percent of his former ownership percentage (because 80 percent of 30 percent is 24 percent) and would qualify for exchange treatment, meeting each of the three tests in § 302(b)(2).

As a final note, these § 302(b)(2) computations must take into account the attribution rules of § 318, and there is no waiver available under § 302(b)(2) corresponding to that available under § 302(b)(3). Accordingly, a shareholder's actual and constructive ownership always must be considered under § 302(b)(2). It is thus time for a thorough examination of the attribution rules.

(c) The Attribution Rules.

The attribution rules of § 318 consist of *family attribution rules*, § 318(a)(1), *attribution-from-entity rules*, § 318(a)(2), and *attribution-to-entity rules*, § 318(a)(3). In addition, there is the *stock option rule* of § 318(a)(4) and a series of *operating rules* in § 318(a)(5). It is the operating rules that permit the other rules to be chained together to attribute stock between shareholders whose relationship can be quite distant.[34]

We already have been exposed to the family attribution rules in the discussion of complete terminations under § 302(b)(3). While those rules are perhaps the most natural set, they hold their own surprises. For example, while there is attribution from grandchild to grandparent, there is no attribution in the other direction.[35] Thus, the redemption of stock held by grandchildren is unaffected by the stock holdings of grandparents and more distant relatives.

In addition, there is no attribution between siblings. However, there is attribution between parents and children, meaning that if the family attribution rule could be applied repeatedly, stock could be attributed from brother to parent to sister, thereby attributing stock between siblings at least when one of their parents is alive. However, by virtue of the anti-sidewise operating rule of § 318(a)(5)(B), such chains are not allowed. The familial relations warranting attribution are set forth in § 318(a)(1), and the anti-

---

[34] For example, if F and S are father and son, S is a 75% shareholder in X Corp., and X is a 25% partner in the P partnership, stock of any unrelated corporation owned by F will be imputed to P via the following chain: (1) F to S under § 318(a)(1)(A)(ii); (2) S to X under § 318(a)(3)(C); and (3) X to P under § 318(a)(3)(A).

[35] Congress apparently believed that a grandparent may exercise control over a grandchild's stock, but not the other way around.

sidewise rule prohibits enlarging that class: it provides that stock imputed to a taxpayer under the family attribution rules may not then be re-attributed under the family attribution rules. For example, the congressional failure to impute stock from grandparents to grandchildren cannot be circumvented by attributing the grandparents' stock to the parent and then reattributing it to the grandchildren. Of course, any stock *actually* owned by the parents will be imputed to their children under a single operation of the family attribution rules (and thus not implicating the anti-sidewise operating rule).

Attribution from trusts, estates, partnerships and corporations to the beneficial owners of such entities is pro rata according to percentage ownership in the entity. Thus, a one-quarter partner will be deemed to own one-quarter of any stock owned by the partnership. Of course, describing a partner's interest in a partnership by reference to a single percentage is impossible in many of today's complex partnerships, but the attribution rules assume that it can be done. In the case of trusts, ownership is determined by reference to actuarial interests, except that stock owned by grantor trusts is deemed to be owned by their grantors.

Attribution from corporations to their shareholders is based on the fair market value of each shareholder's stock interest as compared with the total value of all of the corporation's outstanding shares. That rule recognizes that a corporation may have multiple classes of stock outstanding. However, Congress specifically provided that there is no attribution from a corporation to any shareholder owning, actually and constructively, less than 50 percent by value of the corporation's outstanding stock. Thus, attribution from corporations to their shareholders is limited to closely held corporations and their majority shareholders.

There also is attribution *to* entities from their beneficial owners, but it is a much simpler rule: all stock owned by partners, trust and estate beneficiaries and shareholders is attributed to their entities without regard to percentage ownership. The only limitations on this rule are (1) there is no attribution to a trust estate from any beneficiary having a contingent interest with a maximum actuarial value of five percent or less of the trust corpus, and (2) there is no attribution to a corporation from any shareholder owning, actually and constructively, less than 50 percent by value of the corporation's outstanding stock. Once again, attribution between corporations and their shareholders effectively is limited to closely held corporations and their majority shareholders.

Just as chains between family members is limited by the anti-sidewise operating rule, there is a limitation imposed on chains linked by the entity attribution rules. Congress did not provide for attribution from, for example, one partner to another, and the operating rule of § 318(a)(5)(C) prohibits circumvention of that rule; it provides that stock ownership imputed to an entity from a beneficial owner may not then be attributed out of the entity to another beneficial owner.

Do these operating rules eliminate all possibilities of constructing chains of attribution? Certainly not. For example, if X Corp. stock is owned by the ABC partnership, that ownership will be imputed to partner A based upon his ownership interest in ABC. That constructive ownership can then be imputed to W, A's wife. If W is a beneficiary of the T Trust, the constructive ownership will be reattributed to T. And on it goes.

The last operating rule is the stock option rule. That rule provides that any person having an option to acquire stock of a corporation is to be treated as owning the option stock. This rule often can be used by taxpayers to their advantage because it increases the total number of shares outstanding, thereby implicitly reducing the ownership interests of all shareholders other than the optionee. For example, granting an option to one shareholder while redeeming some of the shares held by a second shareholder will make it easier for the second shareholder to qualify under the disproportionate redemption rule of § 302(b)(2).[36] Note that this option rule may also be used, particularly by corporate shareholders, to avoid § 302(b).

(d) Redemptions Not Essentially Equivalent to a Dividend.

A redemption that is neither a complete termination under § 302(b)(3) nor substantially disproportionate under § 302(b)(2) still can be taxed as an exchange at the shareholder level if, considering all the facts and circumstances, the redemption "is not essentially equivalent to a dividend." § 302(b)(1). The Supreme Court in *United States v. Davis*[37] interpreted § 302(b)(1) narrowly, concluding that a redemption qualified under that provision only if the redemption resulted in a "meaningful reduction" in the distributee shareholder's stock ownership of the distributing corporation.

---

[36] See, e.g., *Henry T. Patterson Trust v. United States,* 729 F.2d 1089 (6th Cir.1984), in the context of a § 302(b)(1) redemption.

[37] 397 U.S. 301 (1970).

In *Davis*, the corporation was required to increase its working capital by $25,000 to qualify for a Reconstruction Finance Corporation loan. The taxpayer, then a major shareholder of the corporation, purchased 1,000 shares of $25 par value preferred stock, with the understanding that the preferred stock would be redeemed once the loan was repaid. By the time of the debt's repayment, the taxpayer and his family were the corporation's only shareholders. As agreed, the corporation redeemed the preferred stock for $25 per share (or $25,000 in total), and the taxpayer reported the transaction as a tax-free return of basis.

The Supreme Court held that the redemption was taxable to the taxpayer as a distribution, not an exchange, and because the corporation had adequate earnings and profits, the redemption proceeds were includible as a dividend in full. In making that determination under § 302(b)(1), the Court held that the attribution rules of § 318(a) are fully applicable, meaning that the taxpayer's actual and constructive ownership of the corporation both before and after the redemption was 100 percent. Therefore, "this case viewed most simply involves a sole stockholder who causes part of his shares to be redeemed by the corporation. We conclude that such a redemption is always 'essentially equivalent to a dividend' within the meaning of that phrase in § 302(b)(1) . . . ." In particular, the Supreme Court held that any corporate-level motivation for the redemption transaction was irrelevant to the determination under § 302(b)(1).[38]

The *Davis* case once again illustrates the extreme difference in treatment of corporate debt and equity. Had the shareholder contributed the additional funds in exchange for a debt instrument of the corporation, the issue confronted by the *Davis* court could not have arisen because the retirement of corporate debt, unless recharacterized as equity, always qualifies for exchange treatment. Corporate equity, on the other hand, must on occasion be tested by the rules of § 302.

Since the *Davis* case, § 302(b)(1) has played a decidedly modest role. The legislative history of § 302(b)(1) indicates that it was intended to cover redemptions of minority holdings of preferred, non-voting stock.[39] However, § 302(b)(1) is not expressly so limited, so that any time a redemption works a reduction in a shareholder's percentage interest in the corporation, the claim can be raised that

---

[38] *See also* Rev. Rul. 81-289, 1981-2 82 (following *Davis* where a minority shareholder owned the same percentage of stock (and therefore had no reduction in relative economic interest) before and after the redemption).

[39] *See, e.g.*, Rev. Rul. 77-426, 1977-2 C.B. 87 (concluding that a redemption qualified under § 302(b)(1) when the redeemed shareholder owned only non-voting, non-convertible preferred stock).

the reduction was "meaningful." For example, in *Henry T. Patterson Trust v. United States*,[40] it was held that a reduction from 80 percent to 60 percent was "meaningful," and the court in that case indicated that a reduction from 97 percent to 93 percent also could be "meaningful." Did the court in this case confuse "meaningful" and "non-zero"?[41]

Courts and the Service have looked not only to the change in percentage ownership but to other factors, particularly the extent of voting control, to determine whether a reduction is meaningful. For example, in *Wright v. United States*,[42] the court held that a reduction from 85 percent to 61.7 percent was meaningful because state law imposed a two-thirds voting requirement on certain corporate actions. On the other hand, in Rev. Rul. 78–401[43] the Service ruled that a reduction from 90 percent to 60 percent was not meaningful because no corporate action requiring a two-thirds vote was anticipated.[44]

One issue that has plagued the courts is whether family hostility can mitigate application of the attribution rules. For example, suppose Father and Daughter each own 40 of 100 of the outstanding shares of X Corp. If 20 of Father's shares are redeemed, can the redemption qualify under § 302(b)(1)?

---

[40] 729 F.2d 1089 (6th Cir.1984).

[41] *Cf.* Rev. Rul. 72-569, 1972-2 C.B. 203 (concluding that a reduction from 90% to 85% was not meaningful).

[42] 482 F.2d 600 (8th Cir.1973).

[43] 1978–2 C.B. 127.

[44] Although the scope of § 302(b)(1) is not clear, the Service has ruled that a redemption qualified under § 302(b)(1) when the redeemed shareholder exercised control over the corporation before the redemption but significantly reduced that control because of the redemption. *See* Rev. Rul. 75-502, 1975-2 C.B. 111 (reduction from 57% to 50% meaningful when a single, unrelated individual owned the remaining stock after the redemption); Rev. Rul. 76-364, 1976-2 C.B. 91 (reduction meaningful when the redeemed shareholder lost the ability to join with any one of three other shareholders to control the corporation). *Cf.* Rev. Rul. 85-106, 1985-2 C.B. 116 (redemption of non-voting preferred stock not qualified under § 302(b)(1), because the shareholder could control the corporation both before and after the redemption by joining with two other shareholders); Rev. Rul. 77-218, 1977-1 C.B. 218 (reduction in interest from 60% to 55% not meaningful). Further, the Service has concluded that a redemption qualified under § 302(b)(1) in the following cases when the redeemed shareholder reduced his relative economic interest and exercised no control over the corporation both before and after the redemption: Rev. Rul. 76-385, 1976-2 C.B. 92 (shareholder's percentage interest in a large publicly traded corporation reduced from .0001118% to. 0001018%); Rev. Rul. 75-512, 1975-2 C.B. 112 (minority shareholder exercised no control over the corporation); Rev. Rul. 56-183, 1956-1 C.B. 161 (shareholder's interest reduced from 11% to 9% and remaining stock owned by unrelated shareholders).

Father's actual ownership of the corporation before the redemption was 40 of 100 shares, or 40 percent. After the redemption, Father's actual ownership drops to 20 of 80 shares, or 25 percent. Although Father's actual ownership drops substantially as a result of the redemption, his constructive ownership barely changes, however.[45]

Prior to the redemption, Father's actual plus constructive ownership was 80 of 100 shares, or 80 percent. After the redemption, Father's actual plus constructive ownership is 60 of 80 shares, or 75 percent. Ordinarily, such a minor reduction in percentage ownership would fail to qualify under § 302(b)(1). However, if Father can prove that great antagonism has come between himself and his daughter, should the § 302(b) determination be based on the effect of the redemption on Father's actual ownership of the corporation?

Both the Tax Court[46] and the Fifth Circuit Court of Appeals[47] have said in dicta that such family hostility should be irrelevant to application of § 302(b)(1), but Judge Tannenwald of the Tax Court has argued strongly that the issue merits further consideration.[48] At least one court has affirmatively entertained the suggestion that family hostility *can* mitigate application of the attribution rules to § 302(b)(1) determinations.[49] Should the courts ignore family hostility under § 302(b)(1) to avoid costly factual determinations in favor of applying an easy, bright-line test? Perhaps not. After all, the "not essentially equivalent to a dividend" rule of § 302(b)(1) is not a bright-line under the best of circumstances.[50]

(e) Partial Liquidations.

A redemption qualifying as a "partial liquidation" within the meaning of § 302(b)(4) is taxed to the distributee, non-corporate shareholders as an exchange under § 302(a). Partial liquidations are defined in § 302(e), which makes clear (see § 302(e)(1)(A)), in contradistinction to the shareholder-level inquiry under § 302(b)(1)–(3), that we look to a redemption's *corporate-level* effects to deter-

---

[45] The drop in *actual* ownership would qualify under § 302(b)(2) were there no attribution.

[46] *David Metzger Trust v. Commissioner,* 76 T.C. 42 (1981), aff'd, 693 F.2d 459 (5th Cir.1982).

[47] *David Metzger Trust v. Commissioner,* 693 F.2d 459 (5th Cir.1982).

[48] *David Metzger Trust v. Commissioner,* 76 T.C. 42, 80–84 (1981) (Tannenwald, J., concurring), aff'd, 693 F.2d 459 (5th Cir.1982).

[49] *Haft Trust v. Commissioner,* 510 F.2d 43 (1st Cir.1975).

[50] *But see* Rev. Rul. 80-26, 1980-1 C.B. 66 (concluding that family hostility is irrelevant in applying § 302(b)(1)). If family hostility were taken into account to in measuring control, should control also be measured by considering stock owned by unrelated close friends (or a paramour)?

mine whether it is a partial liquidation. Note as well that to qualify under § 302(e)(1)(B), the distribution must occur no later than the year following the year in which the plan of partial liquidation was adopted.

The taxation of partial liquidations dates back at least to 1935 and passed through old § 346 on its way to its present form in § 302(b)(4).[51] In essence, a partial liquidation is a *corporate contraction* in which a distinct part of the corporation's business is discontinued and the assets (or the proceeds from a sale of those assets) are distributed to the corporation's shareholders. Because qualification under § 302(b)(4) is made at the corporate level, shareholder-level aspects of the distribution (including, for example, that the distribution is made pro rata) are irrelevant.[52]

Shareholder-level exchange treatment of partial redemptions can be justified by analogy to shareholder-level taxation of complete liquidations. In general, a shareholder receiving corporate assets as part of a complete liquidation of the corporation will receive exchange treatment on the distribution. Thus, if multiple businesses are each conducted in distinct corporations, one of the businesses can be discontinued and liquidated in a non-dividend transaction. Exchange treatment for partial liquidations gives the same tax advantage to those taxpayers conducting multiple businesses in the form of distinct divisions within a single corporation.

Any distribution "not essentially equivalent to a dividend" (determined at the corporate level) will meet the statutory definition of a partial liquidation in § 302(e)(1)(A). In the well-known case of *Imler v. Commissioner*,[53] a fire destroyed the top two floors of the corporation's seven-story factory. Rather than rebuilding, the corporation scaled down its business operations and distributed the insurance proceeds and some of its working capital in what was held to be a partial liquidation. In an attempt to inject more certainty into this area of the law, Congress has added an alternative set of objective criteria also defining a partial liquidation. Under § 302(e)(2), any redemption meeting the cessation of business test and the continuing business test of § 302(e)(2)(A) and (B) automatically will be treated as being not essentially equivalent to a dividend at the corporate-level. Consistent with the underlying policy of § 302(b)(4) giving exchange treatment to redemptions analogous to complete liquidations, these tests ensure that the redemption is at-

---

[51] Because the wording of old § 346 is continued in current § 302(b)(4), the regulations promulgated under § 346 should continue their validity.

[52] See § 302(e)(4).

[53] 11 T.C. 836 (1948).

tributable to a genuine corporate cessation of a business and not to the mere reduction in scope of a continuing business.

The cessation of business test requires only that the redemption be attributable to the distributing corporation ceasing to conduct a "qualified" trade or business, and the continuing business test requires the distributing corporation to be engaged in a "qualified" trade or business immediately after the redemption. In each case a "qualified" trade or business is one that has been actively conducted (by the distributing corporation or otherwise) for at least five years and, if the distributing corporation acquired the business during the five-year period, that the acquisition was entirely tax-free.

These requirements ensure that a corporation cannot invest accumulated earnings in property that the shareholders are willing to hold as individuals and then distribute the newly acquired property in a transaction qualifying for exchange treatment to the shareholders. In addition, the "active" trade or business requirement prevents the partial liquidation provision from being used to bail out passive corporate investments.

It has been held that a distribution of less than the entire proceeds from the sale of an active trade or business cannot qualify as a partial liquidation.[54] Could, however, a distribution of more than the proceeds from the sale of one active business qualify for partial liquidation treatment? For example, suppose X Corp., which actively conducts two businesses, sells one. X Corp. then distributes not only the sale proceeds but also the accumulated earnings attributable to the business sold. Such a distribution should qualify as a partial liquidation because, going back to the theory underlying § 302(b)(4), the distribution is akin to the complete termination of a single corporate entity. On the other hand, if X Corp. also distributes some of the accumulated earnings of the second business, giving full exchange treatment to the liquidation will work an end run around the dividend distribution rules of § 301. Presumably the Service will bifurcate the distribution into a partial liquidation component and a dividend component. The same problem can arise if the earnings from one business are invested in a second business prior to a partial liquidation of the second

---

[54] *Gordon v. Commissioner,* 424 F.2d 378 (2d Cir.1970); see also Rev.Rul. 67–299, 1967–2 C.B. 138, in which the Service ruled that a transaction failed to qualify for partial liquidation treatment when the proceeds from the sale of one active business were temporarily invested in a second trade or business prior to distribution.

business, and the Service has indicated that it will see through such a charade.[55]

The partial liquidation provisions have much in common with divisive reorganizations. Under § 355, a corporation actively conducting two trades or businesses can place one into a subsidiary and then distribute all of the subsidiary's stock, thereby splitting up the corporation's business activity into two corporate entities. Because that transaction is entirely tax-free under § 355 (and § 361), such a reorganization will be preferred to a partial liquidation by most taxpayers. However, if the corporation's shareholders wish to terminate one of the two businesses or conduct it outside of the corporate form, the divisive reorganization route becomes unavailable and favorable taxation will be found only in the partial liquidation format.[56]

Since 1982, a redemption distribution to a corporate shareholder cannot qualify under § 302(b)(4).[57] However, because of § 1059(e), the corporation takes into account the non-taxed portion of any dividend received first by reducing its basis in the stock of the redeeming corporation and, to the extent that non-taxed portion exceeds basis, recognizes gain from the sale or exchange of stock.[58]

Because the shareholder-level effect of a redemption is irrelevant in the case of a partial liquidation, a partial liquidation could occur without the tendering of any shares by any shareholder. Indeed, in the case of a pro rata partial liquidation, pro rata stock exchange would be a needless formality (i.e., a meaningless gesture). The legislative history of § 302(b)(4) indicates that such stockless partial liquidations should qualify for exchange treatment at the shareholder-level,[59] a result verified by the Service.[60] In such case, a

---

[55] See Rev. Rul. 59–400, 1959–2 C.B. 114, in the context of a § 355 distribution.

[56] Divisive reorganizations under § 355 are discussed at Section 10.04 *infra*.

[57] This limitation can be traced to a congressional concern that selective use of partial liquidations, coupled with the consolidated return provisions and the *General Utilities* doctrine, allowed acquiring corporations to step-up the basis in the assets held by acquired corporations without the imposition of any corporate level tax. The demise of *General Utilities* eliminates this problem, but the limitation to non-corporate shareholders in § 302(b)(4)(A) remains.

[58] § 1059(a). If the shareholder and redeeming corporation are not members of the same consolidated group, the non-taxed portion of the dividend generally equals the corporate shareholder's dividends received deduction for the dividend. *See id.* at (b).

[59] H.Rept. No. 760, 97th Cong., 2d Sess. 530 (1982); see *Fowler Hosiery Co. v. Commissioner,* 301 F.2d 394 (7th Cir.1962).

[60] See Rev. Rul. 90–13, 1990–1 C.B. 65 (treating the surrender of stock as a meaningless gesture).

shareholder computes gain or loss as if he exchanged stock with a value equal to the redemption proceeds.[61]

(f) Redemptions to Pay Death Taxes.

In general, § 303 gives exchange treatment to redemptions from estates in which more than 35 percent of the estate's net value consists of the stock of a single corporation. In addition, stock of two or more corporations can be combined (i.e., treated as stock of a single corporation for purposes of § 303) if the value of the stock of each corporation is at least 20 percent of the value of the corporation. When § 303 applies, its benefits are limited in amount to the taxes and expenses incurred by the estate.

The motivation behind § 303 is a congressional concern that the burden of death taxes could force some taxpayers to liquidate their holdings of stock in family corporations. In light of the attribution rules applicable to determinations under § 302(b), redemptions of such stock might fail to qualify for exchange treatment under § 302(a). Accordingly, the shareholders may sell the stock to a third party to obtain exchange treatment, even though, in the absence of tax considerations, they would prefer to continue to run the family business themselves. Note, though, that the benefit of § 303 is available only to stock actually owned by the estate and does not include, for example, stock includible in the estate under § 2035. See Rev. Rul. 87–76, 1984–1 C.B. 91. However, in that revenue ruling the Service allowed that stock to contribute to the 35% threshold required by § 303, thereby allowing stock actually owned by the estate to qualify under § 303. Note also that the attribution rules of § 318 cannot be used to satisfy the 35-percent test of § 303 because § 303 does not expressly reference § 318.[62]

Should a provision like § 303 be in the Code? No special provision is made for other needy redemptions, such as redemptions to pay for medical expenses. Further, no showing must be made under § 303 that the estate lacked sufficient liquid assets to meet its liabilities. Recall that when combined with § 1014, exchange treatment under § 303 means that an estate will pay no taxes on the redemption of its stock. At least in some cases, § 303 cannot be justified, because it will do nothing more than provide an opportunity to bail-out earnings and profits of a corporation without shareholder-level taxation.

---

[61] Rev. Rul. 77-245, 1977-2 C.B. 105.

[62] *Estate of Byrd v. Commissioner*, 388 F.2d 223 (5th Cir.1967).

5.03　Redemptions Taxed as Distributions

If a redemption fails to qualify for exchange treatment under § 302(a) or § 303, the amount distributed is subject to the distribution rules of § 301. As you will recall, those rules treat the amount distributed as dividend income to the extent of the distributing corporation's earnings and profits, then as a return of basis, and finally as gain from an exchange.

If the entire amount distributed in redemption is taxed as a dividend, the shareholder will enjoy no recovery of basis on the redemption. Accordingly, his basis in the shares turned in flows into his remaining stock of the corporation, and it will be recovered when those shares are sold or exchanged.

For example, suppose that Father and Daughter each owns 40 of the 100 outstanding shares of X Corp. with adjusted basis of $10 per share and fair market value of $100 per share. If X redeems 20 of Father's shares for $2,000 (their fair market value), Father's actual plus constructive interest drops from 80 percent (80 of 100 shares) to 75 percent (60 of 80 shares). Assuming that this reduction is not "meaningful," Father will be taxed on the distribution of $2,000 under § 301. If X has sufficient earnings and profits, Father will recognize the full amount as ordinary income. Father's basis in the shares redeemed will flow into his remaining shares, leaving Father with actual ownership of 20 shares with an adjusted basis of $20 per share.

This rule works in most cases, but what if the shareholder has no more shares in the corporation? Usually, this problem will not arise because the shareholder will qualify for exchange treatment under the complete termination safe harbor of § 302(b)(3). However, if a related party owns stock in the corporation, the shareholder may not qualify for the complete termination safe harbor, and so distribution treatment is a possibility.

Reconsider the example above, but assume that all 40 of Father's shares are redeemed in one transaction. Father's actual and constructive ownership will fall as a result of the redemption from 80 percent (80 of 100 shares) to 67 percent (40 of 60 shares). If Father fails to file a valid waiver under § 302(c)(2),[63] the redemption will be taxed under the distribution rules of § 301 unless the reduction from 80 percent to 67 percent is considered "meaningful." Assuming that Father is taxed on a dividend equal to

---

[63] Father might fail to file a valid § 302(c)(2) waiver out of ignorance of the law or because he remains as an officer, director or employee of the corporation and for that reason is statutorily incapable of filing the waiver.

the full $4,000, what happens to Father's basis in the shares redeemed?

One case has held that the shareholder's basis flows into the basis of the stock held by the related party, a result consistent with the regulations.[64] That is, Father's basis is transferred to Daughter. While no alternative readily presents itself, one cannot help but wonder if this rule might not, in some extreme cases, be counter to the shareholder's desires. For example, might not the shareholder be given the right to simply eliminate the basis rather than transfer it to the related party? After all, but for the related party (and the attribution rules), the taxpayer would have obtained exchange treatment on the redemption.

If this was the rule, the shareholder might entice the related party to pay for the windfall basis. Do not assume that all parties "related" under § 318(a) necessarily share love and affection or that they regard themselves as having common interests and goals. Indeed, family hostility sometimes might cause a shareholder to prefer a lost basis over a transfer of basis simply out of spite. Should the Code preclude such a choice? Recall that the basis in the shareholder's stock presumably reflects an investment by the shareholder, an investment the shareholder in most circumstances can transfer or not transfer, in his absolute discretion.[65]

An additional question arises when a redemption fails to qualify as an exchange and related parties own stock of the corporation. If the distributing corporation lacks sufficient earnings and profits to cover the distribution, the amount distributed is applied first to offset basis. Since an amount not offsetting basis is treated as taxable gain, it is to the shareholder's advantage to maximize the basis offset. Is the stock basis of the related party available to the shareholder for a recovery of basis?

Reconsider the Father/Daughter example above, but assume that the corporation has only $3,000 of accumulated and current earnings and profits. Father will have ordinary dividend income of $3,000, and the remaining $1,000 can be treated as a recovery of

---

[64] *Levin v. Commissioner,* 385 F.2d 521 (2d Cir.1967); Regs. § 1.302-2(c), *Ex. (2)* (providing that when a husband and wife owned all stock of a corporation, which redeemed the husband's stock, the remaining basis in the husband's stock was added to the wife's basis in her stock)

[65] Proposed regulations offer a different approach. Instead of shifting the unused basis, the redeemed shareholder has a deferred loss equal to that basis amount, a loss that he would take into account on the first day that he would qualify under § 302(b)(1), (2), or (3) if the stock ownership at the end of that day had been in place immediately after the redemption. *See* Prop. Regs. § 1.302-5(a)(3) and (b)(4)(i); *cf. id.* at (b)(4)(ii) (for special rules for corporate shareholders).

basis. Unfortunately, Father's basis in his shares was only $400, leaving $600 to be taxed as capital gain. Can Father argue that this additional $600 be offset against Daughter's $400 stock basis before producing recognized gain, gain in this case of only $200? Currently, the rule is no, although allowing the shareholder to steal basis from the related party in this way seems a logical companion of the basis transfer rule discussed above. Particularly if it was the related party's stock ownership that caused the redemption to be taxed as a distribution, would it be so unfair to allow the shareholder to steal a little basis in this way to avoid the recognition of gain?

5.04 Corporate–Level Taxation of Redemptions

A distribution in redemption of stock can have two distinct sets of tax consequences for the distributing corporation. First, because a redemption is simply one kind of corporate distribution, if the distributing corporation uses appreciated property in a redemption, it will recognize gain as if it sold the appreciated property for its fair market value. § 311(b) (requiring gain recognition for nonliquidating corporate distributions generally). Cf. § 311(a) (providing that no loss is recognized on a distribution of a built-in loss asset). If the corporation recognizes gain under § 311(b) on the distribution, it increases its earnings and profits account.

Second, because of the redemption, the corporation reduces its earnings and profits, if any. For a current distribution, the distributing corporation reduces its earnings and profits under § 312(a), usually by the fair market value of the property distributed. The same rule applies to a redemption treated as a distribution. In contrast, if a redemption is taxed to the distributee as an exchange, some part of the amount distributed might properly be treated as a distribution of the corporation's paid-in capital. If so, then this portion of the distribution ought not be charged against the corporation's earnings and profits account. In fact, § 312(n)(7) expressly limits the reduction of earnings and profits in just this way.

Under § 312(n)(7), if the distribution in redemption of stock is taxed to the distributee as an exchange, the distributing corporation limits its reduction in its earnings and profits to "an amount which is not in excess of the ratable share of the earnings and profits of [the] corporation . . . attributable to the stock so redeemed." In some cases, this limitation is easy to apply and understand. For example, suppose that X Corp. has cash of $1,000,000, and assume that X has only 1,000 shares of stock outstanding, all being part of a single class of common stock. Each share is worth $1,000, and if the corporation redeems 100 shares in a transaction taxed as an exchange under § 302(a), the distributee should receive 10 percent of the corporation, or $100,000.

If X Corp.'s earnings and profits account stands at $400,000, then that account should be reduced by $40,000 (10 percent of $400,000) to $360,000. That is, of the $100,000 amount distributed, $40,000 is treated as a distribution of earnings and profits and $60,000 as a return of paid-in capital. Note that X Corp.'s paid-in capital should total $600,000 prior to the redemption because the corporation has $1,000,000 in cash, only $400,000 of which is attributable to earnings and profits.

The problem becomes more difficult if X Corp. owns appreciated property. Suppose X Corp., while still worth $1,000,000, has cash of $200,000 and Blackacre with adjusted basis of $450,000 and fair market value of $800,000. Because the appreciation in Blackacre is as yet unrealized, the corporation's earnings and profits plus its paid-in capital should total only $650,000: the appreciation in Blackacre will contribute to the corporation's earnings and profits only upon disposition of Blackacre. If the corporation has earnings and profits of $400,000, then its paid-in capital should equal $250,000. How should a distribution of $100,000 in redemption of 100 shares affect the corporation's earnings and profits, assuming that the redemption is taxed as an exchange to the distributee?

Ten percent of $400,000, or $40,000, is properly allocable to the redeemed shares from the earnings and profits account. Similarly, 10 percent of $250,000, or $25,000, is properly allocable to the corporation's paid-in capital. But what of the remaining $35,000? Conceptually, this amount is properly allocable to the unrealized appreciation in Blackacre. State law will not permit the corporation to reduce its paid-in capital account by this amount, leading the Tax Court to conclude that reduction of the earnings and profits account was appropriate. See *Anderson v. Commissioner*.[66] However, Congress enacted what is now § 312(n)(7), overruling *Anderson* by limiting the earnings and profits reduction in this example to $40,000.

The rule of § 312(n)(7) ensures that a distribution in redemption of stock will not reduce the earnings and profits account for gain not yet in the earnings and profits account. However, because the rule of § 312(n)(7) *eliminates* rather than *delays* the proper earnings and profits reduction, a discontinuity will be created once Blackacre is sold and its gain recognized.

After Blackacre is sold by the corporation for $800,000, the corporation's earnings and profits will increase to $710,000.[67] At that

---

[66] 67 T.C. 522 (1976), aff'd per curiam, 583 F.2d 953 (7th Cir.1978).

[67] The pre-redemption amount of $400,000 less the redemption charge of $40,000 plus the $350,000 gain recognized on the sale of Blackacre produces earnings and profits of $710,000.

time, the paid-in capital will equal $225,000.[68] Note that the sum of the earnings and profits account and the paid-in capital account equals $935,000 although the company is worth but $900,000. This extra $35,000 is the gain in Blackacre properly allocable to the shares redeemed prior to the recognition of gain on Blackacre, the same $35,000 that was not charged to any corporate account at the time of the redemption. Although there are only $675,000 of earnings in the corporation, its earnings and profits show $710,000.

Under § 312(n)(7), the proper charge to the corporate earnings and profits account turns on the earnings and profits properly allocable to the shares redeemed. If common stock is redeemed, this allocation can be determined by reference to the share's proportionate interest in a hypothetical liquidating distribution. On the other hand, if preferred stock is redeemed, presumably no charge to the earnings and profits account is appropriate because, in general, preferred stock entitles the holder only to a return of capital on liquidation. Of course, if dividends on the preferred stock are in arrears at the time of the distribution, the redemption amount should include the dividend arrearages and the corporate earnings and profits account should be reduced in the same amount.

One further corporate-level question arises in connection with redemptions, and that is the proper tax treatment of redemption expenses. Consider, for example, the case of a large, publicly held corporation that avoids a hostile take-over by redeeming all of its stock owned by a "corporate raider." The corporation may incur substantial legal and accounting fees in connection with the redemption, expenses that seem to fall within the reach of § 162(a). However, § 162(k) denies a deduction for all expenses incurred in connection with the redemption of its stock. The legislative history of § 162(k) indicates that the phrase "in connection with the redemption" should be construed broadly. Further, the committee reports list legal fees, accounting fees, appraisal fees, and premiums paid for the stock itself (i.e., greenmail) as items specifically disallowed under § 162(k).

Section 162(k) does not limit the deduction of an interest expense incurred on funds used by a corporation to reacquire its own stock.[69] Suppose, though, that X Corp. pays an investment banker $100,000 to guarantee that a loan of $1,000,000 will be available if that amount is needed to redeem some shareholder's stock. Assum-

---

[68] Paid-in capital of $250,000 minus $25,000 distributed in the prior redemption.

[69] § 162(k)(2)(A)(i). Note, however, that the carryback of a net operating loss, to the extent attributable to that interest may be limited. *See* § 172(b)(1)(E) and (h) (limiting the carryback of corporate equity reduction interest losses).

ing the loan eventually is made and the redemption occurs, what is the proper tax treatment of the loan guarantee fee of $100,000 paid to the investment banker? The fee does not seem to fall within the definition of "interest" as that term is used in § 163 and § 162(k)(2)(A)(i). However, because such a guarantee fee presumably is "properly allocable to indebtedness" and because the fee should be recoverable over the term of the loan, the fee will be deductible despite the general rule of § 162(k)(1) because of § 162(k)(2)(A)(ii).

Note that § 162(k) does not say how amounts paid by a corporation in connection with a redemption should be treated other than that no deduction should be allowed. Can such amounts be capitalized by the corporation and recovered when it liquidates or sells its business? It long has been the case that an amount paid to a shareholder by a corporation in exchange for the corporation's stock (that is, the actual amount used by the corporation to effect the redemption) can be neither deducted nor capitalized.[70] But what of other corporate expenditures falling within § 312(k) such as legal and accounting fees? Can these be capitalized by the corporation. The legislative history of § 162(k) describes such corporate expenditures as nonamortizable capital expenses. Recall that § 197 now generally permits the amortization of intangibles over 15 years. Can a redemption premium be characterized as payment for an intangible? Does *INDOPCO* have any relevance to resolution of the matter?[71]

5.05 Redemptions Related to Other Transactions

In a corporate acquisition called a "bootstrap" acquisition, part of the consideration used to acquire the target corporation consists of assets of the target corporation. If that transaction seems like a snake swallowing its tail, consider the case of T Corp. owning the assets of an active business worth $600,000 as well as cash and other liquid assets worth $400,000. All of the T stock is owned by individual B, and B has an aggregate basis of $700,000 in his T stock. X Corp. would like to acquire the business run by T, but X has no special interest in T's liquid assets, and X will pay only $600,000 for

---

[70] But see *Five Star Mfg. Co. v. Commissioner*, 355 F.2d 724 (5th Cir.1966), an opinion which has engendered substantial criticism and which was expressly overruled by enactment of § 162(k).

[71] Congress deliberately excluded the expenses at issue in *INDOPCO* from amortization under § 197, see § 197(e)(8), but that exclusion should not apply to redemption premiums because a redemption is a taxable transaction. However, to the extent that a redemption premium or related expense is treated as part of the price paid for by the corporation for its own stock, arguably § 197 will not apply by reason of § 197(e)(1)(A), although that provision does not seem to have been written with treasury stock in mind.

the active business assets of T. To ensure that no corporate tax is incurred on the transaction, X insists on buying the stock of T rather than directly acquiring the active business assets.

If X can raise the full $1,000,000 value of the T stock, a direct stock purchase is possible and may be the best way to structure the transaction. But it might be the case that X has only $600,000 available to fund the acquisition. Because that is enough to purchase T's active business assets, as long as the liquid assets are removed before the sale, the sale can proceed without X needing to secure additional funds. Most simply, T could distribute $400,000 to B before X acquires the T stock.

Historically, this structure was tax-disadvantaged. Although a direct sale of the shares without a prior distribution would give B a full basis recovery and $300,000 of capital gain, the pre-sale distribution would be taxable to B under § 301 as ordinary dividend income if X had adequate earnings and profits. When dividend income could not qualify for a preferential rate of taxation (that is, prior to 2004), B had $400,000 of ordinary dividend income taxable at ordinary income rates on the distribution and a $100,000 of capital loss ($700,000 basis minus $600,000 amount realized) on the stock sale.[72] A distribution to B in redemption of some of his stock would prove no better, because the redemption of stock held by a sole shareholder always is essentially equivalent to a dividend within the meaning of § 302(a) under Davis.[73] Such a redemption also could not qualify for exchange treatment as a partial liquidation because a partial liquidation requires a distribution attributable to an active trade or business rather than liquid assets representing accumulated earnings and profits.

B could, of course, get exchange treatment by selling all of the T stock for $1,000,000, but that would require X to raise $400,000 more than the value of the assets it seeks to acquire and possibly more than X can obtain. To satisfy X without compromising B's tax result, the acquisition could be structured as a part sale/part redemption, with B selling 60 percent of his stock to X while simultaneously causing T to redeem the remaining 40 percent with its liquid assets. X Corp. would end up owning all T stock with a $600,000 basis, T would retain only its active business assets (worth

---

[72] Even today this structure is disadvantageous, even though the dividend income may be taxed at the same rate as long-term capital gain, because it would produce a capital loss that could not be used to offset the dividend income.

[73] See Section 5.02(c) *supra*.

$600,000), while B would qualify for exchange treatment on the full $1,000,000 received, recognizing an overall $300,000 gain.[74]

Of course, B will only obtain exchange treatment on the redemption if he falls within § 302(b)(1)-(4), most likely § 302(b)(3) (complete termination of interest). The various intricacies of § 302(b)(3), including application of the constructive attribution rules, waiver of the family attribution rules, and the like, must be reconsidered in this context. If B does not completely terminate his interest in T, he still may qualify for exchange treatment under the other provisions of § 302(b). In particular, the Service has ruled that the sale and redemption can be linked so as to satisfy the requirements of § 302(b)(2),[75] the substantially disproportionate redemption safe harbor.

If T Corp. is owned by a corporation rather than by an individual, the analysis always has been and continues to be different. In those circumstances, the seller will seek to convert taxable gain on the sale into effectively tax-exempt dividend income by causing T to distribute its liquid assets as a dividend prior to the sale. Because of the dividends-received deduction of § 243, this will reduce the taxable gain by up to $400,000.[76] Not surprisingly, the Service may argue in those cases that the dividend should be taxed as if made to the buyer (X Corp.) who then uses it as part of the consideration for the acquisition.[77]

For a corporate seller, it arguably makes sense to amend the Code to favor non-taxation. The rules of subchapter C are premised on the double taxation of corporate profits, once when earned at the corporate level and a second time when distributed to shareholders. When tiers of corporations are formed, intercorporate distributions

---

[74] See *Zenz v. Quinlivan,* 213 F.2d 914 (6th Cir.1954). In tax jargon one refers to B as having been "zenzed" out. The Service has ruled that the redemption may precede the sale in a *Zenz* transaction as long as the redemption and sale are "clearly part of an overall plan." See Rev. Rul. 75–447, 1975–2 C.B. 113. Note that if a sale follows a redemption and the *Zenz* doctrine applies, § 302(b) is applied by taking into account stock ownership before the redemption and after the sale.

[75] Rev. Rul. 75–447, 1975–2 C.B. 113. The *Zenz* doctrine should also apply, where appropriate, to determine qualification under § 302(b)(1). *See* Priv. Let. Rul. 2009-12-006 (Mar. 20, 2009). *See also McDonald v. Commissioner,* 52 T.C. 82 (1969).

[76] The corporate parent of a wholly owned subsidiary may be entitled to a 100% deduction for dividends received from the subsidiary. § 243(a)(3).

[77] See *Waterman Steamship Corp. v. Commissioner,* 430 F.2d 1185 (5th Cir.1970); *Basic, Inc. v. United States,* 549 F.2d 740 (Ct.Cl.1977); *Dynamics Corp. of America v. United States,* 449 F.2d 402 (Ct.Cl.1971). *Cf. Litton Indus. v. Commissioner,* 89 T.C. 1086 (1987) *(acq. in result)* (pre-sale distribution respected as a dividend; distribution announced before sales negotiations began).

should be tax-free to avoid a triple (or greater) tax: corporate profits should be taxed only when earned and then when removed from corporate solution, not at every rung of the corporate ladder. Indeed, this is precisely the role that § 243 plays today.[78]

While intercorporate dividends effectively are excluded from the tax base of the recipient corporation, the same is not true for gain from the sale of corporate shares by a corporate shareholder. That gain, though, reflects either corporate profit earned by the subsidiary corporation but not yet distributed or appreciation in the subsidiary's assets. Such profit either was or will be subjected to the corporate tax when earned. Particularly when the gain reflects corporate profits already earned, some may propose that it should pass through all corporate tiers unscathed by further taxation for the same reason that intercorporate distributions do: the second level of taxation should be imposed only when the profit is removed from corporate solution.[79]

That proposed treatment was not adopted by the drafters of subchapter C, who failed to take a comprehensive view of corporate profits attributable to the business activity of another corporation. Instead, subchapter C may result not only in a potential triple tax of corporate profits but also possible phantom loss. Suppose P Corp. purchases all the stock of Sub Corp. for $1,000,000. The assets of Sub consist exclusively of cash, and assume that Sub, when purchased, has earnings and profits of the full $1,000,000. If P causes Sub to distribute all but $100,000 of its cash, P will receive $900,000 but pay tax on only $180,000 of that amount because of the 80% dividends-received deduction of § 243.[80] P can then sell the stock of Sub for its fair market value of $100,000 and realize a taxable loss of $900,000. No economic loss has been sustained by P or by Sub, but if P is allowed and utilizes its loss deduction on the sale, it enjoys a net tax loss of $720,000, equal to the dividends received

---

[78] That less than 100% of intercorporate dividends are excluded in many situations under § 243 is better explained by revenue needs of the government than by tax policy.

[79] In its broadest form, this proposed treatment not only reduces the overall tax burden but also defers corporate-level tax from when the appreciated stock is sold by a top-or middle-tier corporation until when the bottom-tier corporation earns the income. If the proposed treatment is this broad, it may require anti-abuse rules to prevent a corporation from incorporating appreciated assets, selling the stock of the newly formed corporation, and escaping gain. It also presumably would not apply unless the bottom-tier corporation was fully subject to U.S. taxation.

[80] § 243(a)(1) and (c). The 100% dividends received deduction would not apply, because the earnings and profits arose before P and Sub were affiliated. *See* § 243(b)(1)(B)(i).

deduction. Congress has in piecemeal fashion tried to attack these phantom losses.[81]

Why has Congress limited relief from the corporate triple tax to intercorporate dividends, and even then complete relief is limited to dividends paid between members of an affiliated group?[82] Why has Congress not generally provided that no gain or loss is recognized by a corporation on the receipt of an intercorporate distribution or on the disposition of stock? In part, the explanation may be a case of cognitive dissonance: it is easy to see the potential for a triple tax in the case of intercorporate dividends, less easy in the case of gain or loss from the casual sale of shares in unrelated corporations, especially given the paradigm upon which subchapter C is based that each corporation is a separate taxpayer distinct from its (corporate or noncorporate) shareholders. It may also be that Congress is concerned that if the seller is not taxed on the gain, it may never be taxed. Whatever the reason, the effect is clear: corporate shareholders should eschew recognizing gain on the disposition of stock in favor of receipt of intercorporate distributions.

Redemptions can play a substantial role not only in the sale of a corporation but also in the retention of corporate control. Suppose that X Corp. is owned equally by unrelated individuals A and B. If A and B come to a parting of the ways, one can buy the stock of the other. If, instead, they have the corporation redeem all the stock of one of the two shareholders, they accomplish their goal while removing substantial assets from corporate solution without triggering the recognition of any ordinary income (at least at the shareholder level). However, case law has developed a trap for the unwary if a redemption is used when a shareholder has the primary and unconditional obligation to buy the redeemed stock.

Suppose X Corp. is owned 95 percent by Owner and 5 percent by Employee. Owner and Employee have agreed that Employee must sell his stock back to Owner if he ever terminates his employment with X Corp. One day Employee quits, tendering his shares to Owner for purchase at fair market value.

At this point, it may occur to Owner that he should have X Corp. redeem Employee's shares. By restructuring the transaction in this way, Owner effectively obtains the funds to purchase Employee's shares from the corporation but, he hopes, he can avoid div-

---

[81] See Section 4.03 *supra* discussing § 246A and § 1059.

[82] The American Law Institute adopted a set of proposals aimed at simplifying the corporate income tax. In those proposals, the ALI, although adopting a slightly broader perspective in this context, also has limited its proposal to the case of controlled corporations.

idend income. However, the Service may argue that by redeeming the shares, X Corp. has made a constructive distribution to Owner, taxable (if X Corp. has adequate earnings and profits) as a dividend. If Owner in fact had a primary and unconditional obligation to purchase Employee's shares, the Service will win on this issue.[83]

Note that the stakes at issue are high: if the transaction is characterized as a dividend to Owner followed by a purchase from Employee, Owner will recognize dividend income equal to the fair market value of Employee's shares (assuming adequate earnings and profits). If the transaction is simply treated as a redemption, Owner will recognize no income whatsoever. In either event, Employee should qualify for exchange treatment on the disposition (and if the transaction is characterized as a redemption, exchange treatment should be available under the complete termination provision of § 302(b)(3)). What should Owner have done?

Owner should have provided initially that when Employee terminated his employment with X Corp., Owner would purchase Employee's stock *or would have the shares acquired by some other person or entity*. That is, Owner should have preserved the redemption possibility *ab initio*. If Owner had, the redemption would not be recharacterized and he would not have to recognize any dividend income.[84] If this seems like a formalistic distinction, it is. Yet, so long as redemptions have no adverse tax consequences on shareholders not participating in the redemption, such lines must be drawn.

If Owner has an unconditional obligation to purchase the shares owned by Employee, and if those shares are instead redeemed by the corporation, the transaction will be taxed as if the redemption proceeds were distributed by the corporation to Owner and then used by Owner to purchase the shares owned by Employee. But since those shares in fact end up in the corporate treasury, to close the circle we must treat Owner as if he contributed the shares to the corporation after purchasing them from Employee. This sequence should suggest an alternate characterization of the transaction: We could treat Owner as purchasing the shares from Employee and then treat the corporation as redeeming those shares

---

[83] *Sullivan v. United States,* 363 F.2d 724 (8th Cir.1966); *Wall v. United States,* 164 F.2d 462 (4th Cir.1947); Rev. Rul. 69-608, 1969-2 C.B. 43 (concluding that one shareholder received a constructive distribution when a corporation redeemed a second shareholder's stock and the first shareholder had a primary and unconditional obligation to purchase the redeemed stock when the redemption occurred).

[84] *Holsey v. Commissioner,* 258 F.2d 865 (3d Cir.1958); *Fox v. Harrison,* 145 F.2d 521 (7th Cir.1944); *Niederkrome v. Commissioner,* 266 F.2d 238 (9th Cir.1958).

from Owner. While this alternate characterization is unlikely to change the tax consequences to Owner—the redemption of shares from a sole shareholder generally will be taxed as a distribution under § 301 pursuant to the Supreme Court's decision in the *Davis* case[85]—it will offer Owner the opportunity to argue for exchange treatment under § 302(b)(4) if the transaction includes a corporate contraction.[86]

The same issue can arise in the context of divorce. For example, H and W might each own stock in X Corp. Incident to divorce and pursuant to the decree, H might be obligated to purchase any stock of X Corp. owned by W. If instead X Corp. redeems that stock, should the transaction be taxed as if (1) W transferred the stock to H under § 1041 and then (2) the stock was redeemed by X Corp from H? Courts have applied differing standards in this context, with the result that in one case the redemption was not taxed to *either* spouse.[87] To prevent future whipsaws, the regulations now generally provide that the same analysis applicable outside of the divorce context be applied within it.[88] As a result, the transaction should be treated as a stock transfer from W to H only if H had an unconditional obligation to acquire the stock directly. However, such an unconditional obligation will be ignored if so provided in a divorce decree, separation instrument, or written agreement between the spouses (or ex-spouses).[89] Similarly, a redemption of stock held by one spouse (or ex-spouse) will be imputed to the other

---

[85] See Section 5.02 *supra*.

[86] Moreover, if Owner was not the sole X shareholder after the redemption, the alternative better fits the economic substance of the transaction. Suppose, for example, that Owner, Employee, and Minority own X stock and that X Corp. redeems Employee's stock when Owner has a primary and unconditional obligation to purchase that stock.

As the transaction is apparently characterized, X Corp. is deemed to make a distribution to Owner, then Owner is deemed to buy Employee's X stock, and finally Owner is deemed to contribute that stock to X Corp. In fact, however, X Corp. may be legally prohibited from making a distribution only to Owner and, an economically rational Minority would object to such distribution because it would hurt her stock's value. Further, Owner would be unlikely to contribute property to the corporation without receiving additional X stock in return. Thus, the apparent characterization does not conform to a transaction that is likely to actually occur.

Under the alternative characterization, Owner would be deemed to purchase Employee's stock, which X Corp. would redeem. Assuming that the amount paid for the stock equals its value, it is easy to see a transaction actually occurring along those lines. X Corp. could redeem that stock without affecting the value of Minority's X stock and Owner should willingly accept the redemption payment. Thus, the alternative characterization of the transaction better conforms to its economic substance.

[87] *Arnes v. United States*, 981 F.2d 456 (9th Cir.1992) (transferor spouse); *Arnes v. Commissioner*, 102 T.C. 522 (1994) (transferee spouse).

[88] Regs. § 1.1041–2(a) and (b).

[89] Regs. § 1.1041-2(c)(1).

spouse if such a decree, instrument, or written agreement so provides.[90] Thus, the parties largely can control whether the form of the transaction will be respected or ignored, but in all events the parties must treat the transaction consistently.[91]

5.06 Redemptions for More or Less Than Fair Market Value

(a) Redemption Premiums.

There are a variety of reasons why a corporation might pay more than fair market value for stock it redeems from a shareholder. One possibility easy to forget is that, because the fair market value of nonreadily traded stock often is difficult to determine, a price that after the fact appears to include a redemption premium might before the fact have seemed to be a fair market value price. To the extent a corporation pays no more than fair market value for stock it redeems, certainly it would be improper to allow the corporation to deduct or capitalize the expenditure: in measuring a corporation's profit or loss, amounts paid in redemption of stock should be irrelevant, a result now codified in § 162(k).

A redemption premium might also represent a disguised dividend or similar payment. For example, suppose a minority shareholder complains that dividends are declared too infrequently. A troublesome shareholder might be removed and a lawsuit avoided by purchasing the shares of this minority shareholder at some premium over fair market value. Yet, treating the redemption premium as part of the amount realized to the shareholder would convert what seemingly should be ordinary income into capital gain. Presumably courts will have little difficulty in recharacterizing the transaction as a redemption for fair market value coupled with a dividend or other payment.

Similarly, suppose a corporation redeems the shares held by an employee/shareholder, and as part of the transaction the employee/shareholder gives the corporation a covenant not to compete. Amounts received for a covenant not to compete are ordinary income, and an individual should not be able to transmute such ordinary income into capital gain simply by combining the covenant with a stock transfer. Once again courts should have no difficulty in characterizing the transaction as a redemption coupled with the purchase of a covenant not to compete.

---

[90] Regs. § 1.1041-2(c)(2).

[91] Regs. § 1.1041-2(c)(3).

Now consider these transactions from the perspective of the redeeming corporation. If removal of a troublesome minority shareholder allows the corporation to conduct its affairs more easily or more cheaply, should the corporation be permitted to deduct the redemption premium? While, intuitively, the answer might seem to be yes, that possibility is foreclosed by application of § 162(k).

And what is the proper corporate-level treatment of the redemption premium paid in exchange for a covenant not to compete? Note that § 162(k) provides that no deduction is allowable for such expenditures, but it does not speak to the possible capitalization of such amounts. Indeed, the legislative history repeatedly speaks of expenditures captured by § 162(k) as being nonamortizable capital expenditures. If, though, corporate expenditures falling within the ambit of § 162(k) can be capitalized, the reach of § 162(k) is small. After all, few expenditures described in § 162(k) would otherwise be deductible, especially in light of *INDOPCO*. Further, § 197 now permits the cost of many intangibles to be recovered over 15 years. To the extent that a redemption premium can be characterized as made to improve business rather than as a cost of acquiring stock, § 197 may be applicable.

The legislative history of § 162(k) further makes clear that payments otherwise deductible will not be rendered nondeductible merely because they are paid simultaneously with a redemption. For example, payment by a corporation to a retiring employee for accrued vacation time will be deductible as compensation under § 162(a) even if accompanied by a redemption of the retiring employee's stock in the corporation.

Consider in this vein the proper tax treatment of greenmail: that is, a redemption premium paid to a substantial minority shareholder threatening a potential hostile takeover. Such a payment might represent an attempt by entrenched management to retain its position, or it might be a cost incurred to find a more profitable corporate suitor. How should the redeeming corporation treat such a payment? The possible deduction of greenmail payments was the major impetus for enactment of what is now § 162(k). In this context consider also a corporate payment made in exchange for a standstill agreement (i.e., an agreement by a shareholder not to acquire additional shares of the corporation). The legislative history of § 162(k) specifically identifies payments made for standstill agreements as falling within the reach of § 162(k). Note that the no-deduction rule of § 162(k) also applies to appraisal fees, accountants' fees, lawyers' fees, and similar costs incurred in connection with a redemption.

(b) Stock Surrenders.

Shareholders sometimes accept less than fair market value for stock turned in to the corporation. For example, in *Schleppy v. Commissioner*,[92] a dispute arose between the holder of $1,000,000 of corporate convertible securities and the issuing corporation. In settlement, it was agreed to lower the conversion ratio from $7 to $5 per share, in effect allowing the securities holder to acquire 57,142 additional shares on conversion. Two major shareholders of the corporation, owning in aggregate just over 70 percent (810,500 of 1,155,833 shares) of the corporation's outstanding stock, turned in 57,142 shares to the corporation. The shareholders claimed losses on the transaction equal to their bases in the shares turned in.

Is such a loss appropriate? The only effect of the stock surrender is to rearrange shareholder interests in the corporation: the surrendering shareholders' interests decline in favor of the nonsurrendering shareholders (including the holder of convertible securities). Precisely the same effect could have been obtained by paying a stock dividend to the nontendering shareholders, a transaction never thought to produce a loss to nonrecipient shareholders. In *Schleppy*, the court disallowed the deduction on the ground that the stock surrender was made to protect the tendering shareholders' remaining stock, and so no gain or loss from the transaction is appropriate until the remaining stock is sold or exchanged.[93]

In *Commissioner v. Fink*,[94] a struggling, closely held corporation was told by its lender to acquire $900,000 of new capital, $700,000 of equity and $200,000 of subordinated debt. The corporation decided to raise the new equity by issuing 700,000 shares of $1 par preferred stock convertible into 1,400,000 shares of common stock. Two major shareholders of the corporation surrendered just under 13 percent of the corporation's outstanding common shares so that, prior to the issuance of the new preferred stock, there would be less than 1,400,000 shares of common stock outstanding. Thus, a purchaser of all of the new convertible preferred stock could be assured of obtaining control of the corporation.

The circuit court allowed the taxpayers in *Fink* to deduct their bases in the surrendered stock, except to the extent that the surrender increased the value of the taxpayers' remaining shares. The court was not bothered that the surrendering shareholders then purchased the newly issued convertible preferred stock, thus

---

[92] 601 F.2d 196 (5th Cir.1979).

[93] Accord, *Frantz v. Commissioner*, 83 T.C. 162 (1984), aff'd, 784 F.2d 119 (2d Cir.1986).

[94] 483 U.S. 89 (1987), rev'g 789 F.2d 427 (6th Cir.1986).

obviating the need to offer control of the corporation to an outside purchaser. In addition, the court did not seek from the taxpayers an explanation why the stock surrender was necessary at all: majority control of the corporation could have been given to any purchaser of the convertible preferred stock without a stock surrender simply by increasing the conversion ratio. The court wrote that "[t]he purpose of the stock surrender was to improve [the corporation's] financial position, to preserve its business, and to increase the attractiveness of the corporation to outside investors." Yet, a non-pro rata surrender of stock does not change the financial structure of the corporation at all—it merely rearranges the relative interests of the current shareholders.

The Supreme Court reversed the decision in Fink and disallowed the deduction. Following the reasoning of the Circuit Court in *Schleppy*, the Supreme Court held that the taxpayers' non-pro rata stock surrender was made to enhance the value of their remaining shares and thus was nondeductible under § 263. In addition, the Court said that the stock surrender was akin to a shareholder's forgiveness of a corporate debt and so should be nondeductible as a contribution to capital.

Taking these explanations in order, is it true that a non-pro rata stock surrender is made to enhance the value of the surrendering shareholder's remaining shares? If the stock surrender does not increase the overall worth of the corporation in the eyes of outside investors, the only effect of the surrender is to rearrange relative shareholder interests in the corporation. And while it is true that the value of the surrendering shareholder's remaining shares will increase, that increase will never offset the value lost to the surrendering shareholder by reason of the surrender. For example, suppose that X Corp. has 120 shares of stock outstanding, with 100 shares owned by individual P and the remaining 20 shares owned by individual Q. Further, assume that the corporation is worth $120,000, so that each share is worth $1,000.

If P surrenders 20 shares to the corporation, the number of outstanding shares will drop from 120 to 100. Because the value of the corporation remains at $120,000, the per share value increases to $1,200. Accordingly, P's interest in the corporation drops from $100,000 (100 shares at $1,000 each) to $96,000 (80 shares at $1,200) each. The net loss to P occurs because the value in the surrendered shares inures, after the surrender, in part to Q, the remaining shareholder. That is, P loses the full value of the surrendered shares by reason of the transaction but regains only a part of it through his non-surrendered shares of the corporation. The remaining value of the surrendered shares is transferred to the other shareholder. Here, that remaining value is $4,000 (*i.e.*, 20 percent of the surrendered stock's value).

Why then would a shareholder make a non-pro rata stock surrender? In *Fink*, the taxpayers argued that the surrender was intended to increase the net value of the corporation. The Supreme Court accepted this explanation as the basis for its holding that the stock surrender was non-deductible under § 263, an outlay made to increase the value of the shareholder's total investment in the corporation. A similar argument was made and accepted in *Schleppy*.

Yet, a stock surrender should have no appreciable effect on the value of the corporation. The surrender does not change the assets available to the corporation for investment or other productive use nor change its obligations to creditors and other investors.[95] Simply changing the number of common shares outstanding, whether decreasing the number by a stock surrender or increasing it by a stock split, should not affect the market value of the on-going corporate enterprise.

The second reason offered by the Supreme Court for its holding in Fink was that the stock surrender should be treated as a contribution to the capital of the corporation. This reasoning, also found in the Circuit Court's opinion in *Schleppy*, is even more troubling. The Supreme Court likened a stock surrender to a shareholder forgiveness of corporate debt, but the flaw in this reasoning is that the surrender of common stock adds nothing to the capital of the corporation while the debt forgiveness does. When a true capital contribution is made to a corporation, whether of cash, property, or forgiven indebtedness, the net value of the corporation increases. No such increase results from a stock surrender because no assets are added to the corporate treasury and no obligations upon it are removed. This point was not lost on Justice Scalia, who observed in concurrence: "I do not believe that the Finks' surrender of their shares was, or even closely resembles, a shareholder contribution to corporate capital."[96]

So how should a non-pro rata stock surrender be treated under the Internal Revenue Code? One approach would be to treat the transaction as a redemption in which the redemption price is $0 per share. Under this reasoning the surrendering shareholder would recognize a loss only if the effect on the shareholder's interest in the

---

[95] The surrender of preferred stock may increase the value of the corporation vis-a-vis holders of the corporation's common stock because such a surrender reduces the corporation's obligation to make distributions on preferred ahead of distributions on the common.

[96] See also the discussion in *Tilford v. Commissioner*, 705 F.2d 828 (6th Cir.1983), discussed below.

corporation was significant as judged by the tests of § 302(b). A second approach would be to treat the transaction as a stock dividend to all non-surrendering shareholders. From this perspective there would be no income or loss recognized to any shareholder unless the surrendering shareholder received some form of compensation, in which case the non-surrendering shareholders would be taxable under § 305(b)(2) and the surrendering shareholder would be taxable on the additional compensation. Indeed, now that the Supreme Court has held in *Fink* that the surrendering shareholder will not recognize a loss on the transaction, presumably shareholders will refuse to make non-pro rata surrenders unless some form of compensation is offered. While both the redemption and stock dividend recharacterizations of the stock surrender have advantages, no true solution to the problem will be found until Congress provides a unified treatment of all rearrangements of shareholder interests. Until that time, the form of a rearrangement—whether as redemption, stock dividend, or stock surrender—will be important in determining its tax consequences.

Non-pro rata stock surrenders can arise in other settings. Consider the case of a sole shareholder who transfers stock of his corporation to a corporate employee as an inducement for the employee to remain with the corporation. Should the transferor be entitled to a deduction on account of the transfer? To bring the issue into clearer focus, assume that A owns all 100 outstanding shares of X Corp. with adjusted basis and fair market value of $9.50 per share. E agrees to perform $50 worth of services for the corporation in exchange for some of A's shares. How many shares should A transfer to E?

Before the transaction, the corporation is worth $950. After the transaction, the corporation should be worth $1,000, its prior value plus the value of the services performed by E. Since there are 100 shares outstanding, each share is now worth $10.00. Accordingly, E should be entitled to receive 5 shares for his services.

Should A be entitled to deduct his basis in the shares transferred to E?[97] Regulations disallow such a deduction,[98] treating the transaction as if A contributed the shares back to the corporation as a contribution to its capital, followed by a distribution of the shares

---

[97] A more aggressive taxpayer in A's position might argue for a deduction equal to the fair market value of the shares transferred with no recognized gain, but that result cannot be correct: since any appreciation in the shares is as yet unrealized, it cannot be deducted. Perhaps, though, the shareholder should argue for an ordinary deduction equal to the value of the transferred shares and a capital gain equal to the appreciation in those shares.

[98] Regs. § 1.83–6(d).

by the corporation to E. Under this analysis, A is not entitled to a deduction for the shares transferred but rather adds his basis in those shares to the shares that he retained.[99]

This analysis and the regulation in question were upheld in *Tilford v. Commissioner.*[100] While the result seems correct, the analysis is open to question: in what sense is the transfer to a corporation of its own stock a "contribution to its capital"? No assets were put into corporate solution by A nor were any assets received by X Corp. Accordingly, it is hard to find any capital contribution.

The transaction is better viewed in two steps: (1) the contribution of shares by A, and (2) the distribution of those shares by X to E. Since A was the sole shareholder at the time of the contribution, the contribution had no effect other than a formal reduction in the number of shares held by A: both before the contribution and immediately after, A was the sole shareholder of X Corp. This first step, then, is like a recapitalization, and A's aggregate basis in his X stock should be the same before and after the transaction.

Step 2, the distribution of stock to E, should not produce a loss deduction to A for several reasons. First, no economic loss has been sustained by A or X Corp. As to X Corp., it exchanged stock worth $50 for services worth $50. As to A, he began as the 100 percent shareholder of a corporation worth $950 and ended up as a 95 percent shareholder of a corporation worth $1000—A's position has not changed in any substantial way.

Note that the transaction could have been structured without the transfer by A. X Corp. could have issued 5 shares[101] (newly issued or treasury) directly to E. Had this been done, A would have made no transfer and would have no argument for a loss deduction.

5.07 Redemptions Through Related Corporations

The rules of § 302 ensure that a redemption will not produce exchange treatment to the shareholder unless the transaction produces a meaningful reduction in the shareholder's interest in the corporation. Similar rules do not, in general, apply to a sale of shares to another shareholder, even though the sale may have an insignificant effect on the selling shareholder's relation to the corpo-

---

[99] X may be entitled to a deduction, however. *See* § 83(h).

[100] 705 F.2d 828 (6th Cir.1983).

[101] Actually X Corp. would have to issue 5.263 shares to E because E should end up with 5% of the company, and if 5 new shares are issued to E, there will be 105 shares outstanding. If 5.263 shares are issued, E will own 5.263 of the 105.263 shares outstanding, or 5% of the total outstanding shares.

ration. Indeed, if the purchaser is related to the selling shareholder, application of the attribution rules might suggest that the sale has no effect at all. Nonetheless, the selling shareholder generally will be entitled to exchange treatment on the disposition, limited only if the sale produces a loss.[102]

For the most part, exchange treatment on a sale of shares presents no abuse because the transaction removes no funds from corporate solution. Even if the purchaser is a related party, no bailout of earnings and profits has occurred because no assets have been distributed.[103] However, if the purchaser is itself a corporation, the sale *does* result in a corporate distribution (by the purchaser) and the potential for a bailout occurs.[104]

For example, suppose individual T owns all the stock of X Corp. and all the stock of Y Corp. A redemption by X or Y of any stock will produce distribution treatment to T under the *Davis* rule absent a partial liquidation or qualification under § 303. However, if T simply sells some of his X stock to Y, T seemingly can avoid § 302 without relinquishing any effective control of X. Indeed, if after the purchase a dividend is paid to Y on its X shares, T will have obtained exchange treatment without regard for § 302 even though the purchase price ultimately will have been paid by X itself.[105]

Section 304 speaks to this and similar transactions in which a sale of stock of one corporation is made to a second corporation. Consistent with the abuse to which it speaks, § 304 recharacterizes the transaction as a redemption to which the rules of § 302 apply. See § 304(a). Thus, a sale covered by § 304 will not necessarily produce distribution treatment to the taxpayer. Rather, distribution or exchange treatment will turn on the effect (if any) of the transaction on the taxpayer's relationship with the corporation whose stock nominally is being sold.[106]

---

[102] See § 267.

[103] Under some circumstances, the sale could set the stage for a subsequent redemption and bailout. See the discussion at Chapter 7 *infra*.

[104] A "bailout" of corporate earnings refers to a transaction in which such earnings are removed from corporate solution as capital gain rather than as dividend income under circumstances in which exchange treatment is inappropriate. For more on bailouts, see Chapter 7.

[105] Note that § 243 will allow Y to deduct most or all of the distribution from income.

[106] If a transaction described in § 304 is taxed as a distribution, the transferor is treated as receiving stock from the acquiring corporation which is then immediately redeemed, and this redemption is then taxed under § 301. This peculiar hypothetical redemption (which only arises if the transaction has *already* been determined to be taxable as a distribution, and so the redemption rules of § 302(b) are not implicated) is important if the transferor is itself a corporation; in such circumstances, this hypothet-

Section 304 applies in both the brother/sister and parent/subsidiary contexts. The example above illustrates the brother/sister context, because X and Y, both controlled by the taxpayer T, form a pair of sibling corporations. In the parent/subsidiary context, the taxpayer controls P Corp. which in turn controls S Corp. A sale of P stock by T to S will be captured by § 304 and subjected to the redemption rules of § 302.

The touchstone of a § 304 transaction is the sale of stock of one corporation to another, where the seller controls both corporations. Note that "control" for § 304 is defined in § 304(c) to mean ownership of 50 percent of the total voting power or 50 percent of the total value of all stock of the corporation. In computing control under § 304(c), the attribution rules of § 318 are used, § 304(c)(3), and the entity rules of § 318(a)(2)-(3) are expanded, applying to 5% or greater shareholders, rather than 50% or greater shareholders. See § 304(c)(3)(B). Note that stock acquired in the transaction is counted in determining whether the shareholder is in control of the transferee (i.e., "acquiring") corporation. § 304(c)(2)(A).

The corporation whose stock is being sold in the § 304 transaction is called the "issuing corporation," while the corporation purchasing the stock is called the "acquiring corporation." For example, suppose that individual B owns 50 of 100 shares of X Corp. and all 100 shares of Y Corp. If B sells 10 shares of X to Y, X is the "issuing corporation" and Y is the "acquiring corporation."

Under § 304(a), the rules of § 302(b) are applied to the taxpayer's ownership interest in the *issuing* corporation. See § 304(b)(1). Note that, because of the attribution rules, some or all of the taxpayer's stock sold to the acquiring corporation will be attributed back to the taxpayer under § 318(a)(2)(C). In the X/Y example above, the rules of § 302 will be applied to B's ownership in X Corp. In this example, B has constructive ownership of 50 percent of X Corp. both before and after the transaction. The following rule can be generalized from this example: if the taxpayer owns 100 percent of the stock of the *acquiring* corporation, the sale will work no change in the taxpayer's constructive ownership of the issuing corporation.

To determine whether the § 304 sale qualifies for exchange treatment, one must compare the taxpayer's pre-sale ownership of the issuing corporation with his post-sale ownership interest in that

---

ical redemption affects the transferor's tax treatment because the transaction will be taxed as a extraordinary dividend under § 1059. See § 1059(e)(1)(A).

corporation. In making this comparison, the rules of § 302(b) apply. A taxpayer might qualify for exchange treatment under the substantially disproportionate safe harbor of § 302(b)(2) or under the general rule of § 302(b)(1). Indeed, if the transaction is coupled with a contraction of the *acquiring* corporation's business, the taxpayer may qualify under the partial liquidation provision of § 302(b)(4).[107]

In the X/Y example, the sale by B of 10 shares of X to Y has no effect on B's constructive ownership of X because of the attribution rules. Thus, under the *Davis* case,[108] B cannot qualify for exchange treatment unless the transaction qualifies as a partial liquidation. Suppose, though, that B sells 10 shares of *Y stock to X.*

Before the transaction, B has complete ownership of Y. After the transaction, B's actual ownership drops to 90 percent. However, because B is a 50-percent shareholder of X Corp., half of X's stock in Y must be attributed to B.[109] Thus, B's total actual and constructive ownership is 95 of 100 shares, or 95 percent. Such a reduction is extraordinarily unlikely to qualify as "meaningful" under § 302(b)(1), thus denying exchange treatment to B on the exchange. If, however, B had transferred all of his stock of Y to X, his total constructive ownership would have dropped from 100 percent to 50 percent, a reduction that might be "meaningful."

One question that often arises is whether the complete termination provision of § 302(b)(3) can be useful in a § 304 transaction? Suppose that Father owns all the stock of P Corp. and that Son owns all the stock of Q Corp. If Father sells all of his P stock to Q, how should he be taxed?

This transaction falls within the reach of § 304(a)(1) because Father has constructive ownership of both corporations. Can Father file a § 302(c)(2) waiver and thereby avoid application of the family attribution rules in making the § 302(b)(3) determination? Since such a waiver is permitted in the context of a true redemption, surely Father should not be worse off by reason of selling his stock to a related corporation. Yet, it is unclear if such a waiver is permitted in the context of § 304. See the introductory clause in § 302(c)(2)(A) (applying to a distribution described in § 302(b)(3)).

---

[107] *Blaschka v. United States,* 393 F.2d 983 (Ct.Cl.1968).

[108] See Section 5.02(c) *supra.*

[109] See § 318(a)(2)(C). In applying these attribution rules in the context of § 304, attribution from a corporation to a shareholder is required whenever the shareholder owns 5% or more of the corporation's stock. See § 304(c)(3)(B)(i). The same is true for attribution from a shareholder to the corporation. See § 302(c)(3)(B)(ii).

If a taxpayer qualifies for exchange treatment on the § 304 sale, gain or loss will be recognized under § 1001(a) subject to the loss limitation of § 267. However, if distribution treatment is mandated because the taxpayer fails to qualify under the tests of § 302(b), dividend treatment will be accorded up to the earnings and profits of *both* corporations. See § 304(b)(2).

For example, if B is the sole shareholder of X Corp. and Y Corp., the sale by B of X stock to Y will be covered by § 304. Further, because of the attribution rules, the sale will work no change in B's ownership of X, the issuing corporation. Accordingly, B will be taxed on the amount received from Y under the distribution rules of § 301 (assuming that the § 302(b)(4) does not apply). Under § 304(a)(1), B and Y are treated as if B transferred the X stock to Y in a § 351(a) transfer. Thus, subject to § 362(e), B's basis in the X shares sold will flow into his Y stock and Y will succeed to B's basis in the X shares. See § 358(a); § 362(a).[110]

Section 304 applies only to sales of stock to related corporations, where a "sale" means the exchange of stock for "property." The definition of "property" in § 317(a) is applicable to § 304, and thus "property" under § 304 does not include stock of the acquiring corporation. Accordingly, the transfer of Brother Corp. stock to Sister Corp. will not fall within § 304 if all that is received in exchange is stock of Sister. In particular, a bootless incorporation under § 351 cannot fall within § 304.[111]

But what of a § 351 incorporation in which boot is received by the transferor/taxpayer? Suppose for example that stock of Brother Corp. is transferred to Sister Corp. in exchange for stock of Sister and $10,000 of cash. If the transferor meets the 80 percent control tests of § 368(c) with respect to Sister, this transaction meets the definition of an incorporation taxable under § 351(b). Under that provision, the gain (up to $10,000) on the exchange would be taxable, possibly as capital gain.

However, if the transferor also meets the 50-percent control test of § 304(c) with respect to Brother Corp., § 304(a)(1) also seems to apply. (The 50-percent control test also must be met with respect to Sister, but if the 80-percent test of § 368(c) has been met, so has the 50-percent test of § 304(c) *a fortiori*.) In this case, must the

---

[110] In the parent/subsidiary context, the basis consequences are less clear. Presumably the basis will flow into the shareholder's remaining stock of the issuing corporation (i.e., into his remaining stock of the parent).

[111] See also the discussion of *Bhada v. Commissioner,* 89 T.C. 959 (1987), *aff'd sub nom. Caamano v. Commissioner,* 879 F.2d 156 (5th Cir.1989), discussed at Section 10.04(d) *infra,* for the acquisition by a subsidiary corporation of stock of its parent in exchange for its own stock.

transferor run the hurdles of § 302(b) via § 304 to obtain exchange treatment, or does § 351(b) provide it automatically?

This question, once a thorny one for the courts, has been resolved by statute. Under § 304(b)(3), the rules of § 351(b) must give way to those of § 304. Thus, taxation of the boot will turn on the application of § 304 and § 302(b). Of course, § 351 applies to the receipt of the Sister stock because § 304 can only apply to "property."

Consider the following example. B owns all 100 shares of X Corp. with adjusted basis of $10 per share and fair market value of $30 per share. B also owns 50 of the 70 outstanding shares of the only class of Y Corp. stock with adjusted basis of $1 per share and the other 20 shares are owned by an unrelated taxpayer. B transfers all his shares of X to Y in exchange for 30 treasury shares of Y as well as $1,200 of cash. Assume that the treasury shares are worth a total of $1,800.

In effect, B has received Y stock for 60 percent of his X shares and cash for 40 percent. As to the 60 percent, the transaction is described in § 351 because B is in "control" of Y immediately after the transaction (because 80 of 100 shares constitutes "control"). Section 304 cannot apply to this part of the exchange because B receives only stock of Y and that stock is not considered property for purposes of § 304. Thus, no gain or loss is recognized and B's basis in the shares received in the transaction is $600.[112]

As to the other 40 percent of the transaction, B has exchanged stock of X for property. This transaction meets all the tests of § 304, so that B will be taxed on the $1,200 received as dividend income unless § 302, applied to B's interest in X, gives exchange treatment. B's interest in X drops from 100 percent (all actual ownership) to 80 percent (all constructive). If this reduction is not "meaningful" enough to qualify under § 302(b)(1), the $1,200 will be taxed under the distribution rules of § 301.

The examples so far have all involved brother/sister transactions implicating § 304(a)(1). Recall that § 304 also can apply to distributions by a subsidiary corporation in exchange for stock of its parent. § 304(a)(2). Unfortunately, the application of § 304 to parent/subsidiary transactions is problematic.

Before looking at the difficult aspects of the parent/subsidiary application of § 304, note that at least one aspect of § 304 is appreciably simpler here than in the brother/sister context. Recall that

---

[112] Sixty shares with a basis of $10 per share, carried over to the Y stock received under § 358(a).

for § 304(a)(1) to apply to a brother/sister pair, the taxpayer must "control" both corporations. In the parent/subsidiary case, though, § 304(a)(2) requires only that the parent corporation control the subsidiary, where control continues to mean direct or indirect ownership of at least 50 percent (by vote or by value) of the stock of the controlled corporation. Accordingly, § 304(a)(2) can apply even if the shareholder's ownership interest in the parent corporation is small.

That aspect of the statute aside, the problem becomes much more difficult. For example, assume that individual J owns all 100 outstanding shares of P Corp. and that P owns all 100 shares of S Corp. If J sells 60 of his P shares to S in exchange for property, is the sale taxed under § 304(a)(2) as an exchange or as a distribution? Exchange treatment will permit J to recover his basis in the shares transferred before reporting any gain. Distribution treatment, on the other hand, will cause J to report the entire consideration received as ordinary income, subject only to the limitation that there must be sufficient earnings and profits in the two companies to cover that amount. See § 304(b)(2).

Under § 304(a)(2), exchange or distribution treatment to J will turn on application of the redemption rules of § 302 to the transaction. From § 304(b)(1) we know that it is J's change in ownership interest of the issuing corporation (*i.e.*, P Corp.) that must be examined. Prior to the transaction, J owns 100 percent of P Corp. After the transaction, J has actual ownership of 40 of the 100 outstanding shares. Can the remaining shares be imputed to J under the attribution rules of § 318(a)? A technical reading of that section permits the attribution from S to P under § 318(a)(2)(C) and then from P to J under a second application of § 318(a)(2)(C). However, two challenges can be mounted to this application of § 318(a)(2). First, the second link in the chain (from P to J) will impute to J only a proportion of the 60 shares depending on J's (direct or indirect) percentage ownership of P. But what is J's percentage ownership of P? That is the precise question we are trying to answer, thus showing that the application of the attribution rules in this context is circular. Note that this problem in the application of the § 318 attribution rules occurs only because P owns stock of S and S owns stock of P at the same time.

In addition, the attribution of shares owned by S Corp. to J through P requires the attribution from P Corp. of its own stock. We do not attribute P stock actually owned by P (i.e., treasury shares) to its shareholder. Is it appropriate to attribute P stock owned only constructively by P to its shareholders?

One approach is to treat the P Corp. shares acquired by S on the transaction as no longer outstanding. Indeed, state law presumably would prohibit S from voting the shares. Should we then treat J as having 100% actual ownership of P Corp. because his 40 shares are the only P Corp. shares properly considered outstanding? While this approach is a reasonable one, Congress should clarify the application of the § 318(a) attribution in the context of a parent/subsidiary transaction described in § 302(a)(2).[113] Of course, if J is deemed to own 100 percent of P Corp. after the transaction, the proceeds of the sale received from S Corp. will be taxed as a distribution.

---

[113] See generally Land, Strange Loops and Tangled Hierarchies, 49 Tax L. Rev. 53 (1993).

Chapter 6

STOCK DIVIDENDS

6.01 Overview and History

Before considering the taxation of stock dividends, it is worthwhile to reconsider the taxation of cash and property dividends.[1] Recall that a "dividend" is a distribution by a corporation made to a shareholder with respect to the shareholder's stock, taxable as ordinary income.[2] Why is it that cash dividends, for example, are includible by the recipient as income?

At first blush, cash dividends seem to be "undeniable accessions to wealth, clearly realized, . . . over which the taxpayers have complete dominion."[3] Yet, upon closer inspection we see that such dividends are *not* accessions to wealth, because cash dividends, or at least pro rata cash dividends, reduce *pro tanto* the value of the corporate stock held by the shareholders. More generally, no pro rata distribution of corporate assets increases the wealth of the shareholders but only transmutes part of the value of their shares into the form of distributed property.

Why then are dividends includible in gross income? The answer to that question touches on both the realization doctrine and the double taxation of corporate profits. For better or worse, Congress has decided that corporations should be treated as taxable entities distinct from their shareholders. As a consequence, corporate profits are subjected to a double tax, once to the earning corporation and a second time to the corporation's shareholders. In theory, both layers of taxation could be imposed as corporate profits are earned at the corporate level, with the shareholders taxed in some manner akin to that of partners and S corporation shareholders. Congress has always provided as to C corporations, however, that the shareholder-level taxation is imposed only when the corporate profits are distributed as dividends.

Imposition of the shareholder-level tax on only *distributed* corporate profits follows from the principle that corporations and their shareholders are distinct taxpayers. Undistributed corporate profits increase shareholder wealth by increasing the value of the corpora-

---

[1] See Chapter 4 *supra*.

[2] Throughout this discussion it is assumed that the distributing corporation has sufficient earnings and profits to cover any distribution.

[3] *Commissioner v. Glenshaw Glass Co.*, 348 U.S. 426, 431 (1955).

tion's shares. Under the realization doctrine, the mere increase in value of an asset is not taxable until that increase is converted into some new form, usually by sale or exchange. Accordingly, while corporate profits can be taxed to the corporation as earned, the realization doctrine protects the shareholders from taxation until such profits are converted into some form other than an increase in stock value.[4]

With this in mind, how should stock dividends be taxed? Consider first the case of a corporation having only a single class of common stock outstanding, and assume that the stock dividend consists of additional shares of the same class of stock distributed to the shareholders in proportion to their predividend stock ownership. Should such a distribution be taxable to the shareholders?

The distribution does not increase the wealth of the distributees, but of course no pro rata distribution does. The form of each shareholder's wealth undergoes a change: the number of shares held increases although the aggregate value of those shares does not. This change in form is particularly minimal: each shareholder's wealth remains in the form of corporate stock. Before and after the distribution, each shareholder has the same relative voting power, rights to current distributions, and rights to liquidating distributions.

Note as well that this common on common stock dividend does not remove any assets from corporate solution. Whatever corporate profits have been earned, therefore, still can be taxed when distributed even if the stock dividend goes untaxed. Since imposition of a tax liability other than when funds are generated to pay the tax is difficult to administer, taxation of a pro rata common on common stock dividend seems inappropriate.

Perhaps for these reasons, Congress does not now seek to tax common on common stock dividends. But once it did, as part of the Revenue Act of 1916. In *Eisner v. Macomber*,[5] the Supreme Court held that common on common stock dividends were constitutionally immune from federal income taxation. Justices Holmes and Brandeis dissented in *Macomber,* Holmes on the ground that the purpose

---

[4] Note that the value of the property distributed to any particular shareholder will, in general, bear no relationship to the corporate profits earned since that shareholder acquired his stock. However, the price paid for shares of a corporation should reflect not only the value of the corporation but also the potential tax liability to be incurred by the purchaser. In fact, though, because corporate earnings often have been bailed out of corporate solution at less than ordinary rates, the value of corporate shares traded on the market probably reflects little discounting for potential taxes owed.

[5] 252 U.S. 189 (1920).

of the Sixteenth Amendment was to "get rid of nice questions" as to what could be taxed. Justice Brandeis wrote a lengthy dissent, arguing that stock dividends were sufficiently akin to cash dividends to preclude a *constitutional* line between the two. History seems to have borne out Justice Brandeis: it is practicality rather than constitutional mandate that precludes the taxation of common on common stock dividends.[6]

The taxation of stock dividends is covered by § 305. Subsection (a) states the general rule that "gross income does not include the amount of any distribution of the stock of a corporation made by such corporation to its shareholders with respect to its stock." Exceptions in subsection (b) practically swallow the general rule, though, limiting its application to little more than pro rata stock dividends made with respect to common stock.

6.02 The General Rule of § 305(a)

The general rule of nontaxability under § 305(a) only applies to distributions made with respect to a shareholder's stock. It does not apply, for example, to a distribution of stock to an employee as compensation or to a lender in discharge of a debt. Such stock distributions are taxable under other provisions of the Code.[7] In addition, § 305 does not apply to the distribution by one corporation of stock in a second corporation.[8] On the other hand, § 305 *does* apply to distributions of stock rights as well as to stock itself.[9]

Stock received tax-free under § 305(a) is treated as a continuation of the recipient's old stock. Accordingly, the recipient's old basis in the old shares is divided among the old and new shares in proportion to relative fair market values. § 307(a); Regs. § 1.307–1(a).[10]

---

[6] See, e.g., Surrey, *The Supreme Court and the Federal Income Tax: Some Implications of Recent Decisions,* 35 Ill.L.Rev. 779 (1941). See also § 951 et seq. taxing shareholders of controlled foreign corporations on unrealized "subpart F" income.

[7] See, e.g., § 83 (distribution of stock in exchange for services).

[8] Distributions of "property" (as defined in § 317(a) to include stock of any corporation other than the distributing corporation) are covered by § 301.

[9] Section 305(d).

[10] For a distribution of stock rights qualifying for nonrecognition under § 305(a), as a general rule, the recipient's basis for the old shares is divided among the old shares and stock rights in proportion to their relative fair market values. However, under a de minimis rule in § 307(b), which applies if the distributed stock rights have a fair market value less than 15% of the value of the shareholder's stock, the shareholder takes a zero basis in those rights, unless he elects to apply the allocation rule described in the preceding sentence. To prevent manipulation, if basis is allocated to distributed stock rights but those rights lapse, no loss to the shareholder is allowed. Rather, the basis of the lapsed rights flows back to the shareholder's stock. Regs. § 1.307–1(a).

The close connection between the old and new shares is recognized in § 1223(4), which provides that a taxpayer's holding period of the old shares is tacked onto the holding period of the new shares. Of course, because stock distributions described in § 305(a) result in no taxation to the recipients, such distributions do not reduce the earnings and profits account of the distributing corporation. § 312(d)(1)(B).

For example, suppose that individual B owns all outstanding 100 shares of X Corp. with adjusted basis of $20 per share. If X pays a one-for-one stock dividend (that is, distributes one share of stock for every share outstanding), B will own 200 shares after the transaction. Because such a stock dividend is tax-free to B under § 305(a), B allocates his pre-dividend stock basis among his old and new shares, leaving him with a stock basis of $10 per share after the distribution.

6.03 Exceptions to the General Rule Under § 305(b)

Despite the broad language used in the nonrecognition provision § 305(a), its application is quite narrow. Under § 305(b), many distributions of stock (and of stock rights) are treated as distributions of property subject to the usual distribution rules in § 301. Since nonrecognition under § 305(a) is appropriate only when the stock distribution does not substantially alter the form of the recipient's investment in the distributing corporation, the rules in § 305(b) tax most stock distributions that rearrange the relative interests of the shareholders in the distributing corporation. In addition, stock distributions appropriately considered to be property distributions followed by a reinvestment of the distributed property also are removed from the protection of § 305(a) by the rules of § 305(b). Note, though, that a stock distribution falling within § 305(b) is not automatically taxable to the recipient as dividend income. Rather, such stock distributions are simply subject to the usual rules covering corporate distributions in § 301, rules which can produce dividend income, tax-free recovery of basis, and capital gain. See § 301(c).[11]

Section 305(b)(1) covers stock distributions in which any shareholder could have elected to receive money or other property in lieu of stock. Of course, shareholders electing to receive cash or

---

[11] In the case of a stock dividend taxable under § 305(b) and § 301, the distributing corporation does not have income on the distribution because the corporation could have sold the stock tax-free under § 1032 and then distributed the cash. Because the corporation is treated as making a property distribution, its earnings and profits account will be reduced (but not below zero) by the fair market value of the distributed stock. See § 312(a) (applying to distributions of property); § 305(b) (treating a distribution of stock described in § 305(b) as a property distribution).

other property will not be taxed under § 305: such shareholders will be subject to the rules of § 301 by the express terms of that section. The reach of § 305(b)(1) is thus limited to shareholders electing to receive their distribution in stock and to shareholders having no choice but forced to receive stock *if* any other shareholder had the opportunity to receive cash or other property. As to each group, the distribution will be taxed as if the distribution had been in cash, followed by a purchase of additional stock with the cash received.

As one example, suppose that X Corp. declares a dividend payable in cash of $10 or 1 share of $10 par value preferred stock. Those X Corp. shareholders electing to receive cash will be taxed directly under § 301. Those shareholders electing to receive the stock also will be taxed under § 301 by virtue of § 305(b)(1). This example shows that the rule of § 305(b)(1) can be justified at least in part by reference to the *constructive receipt* doctrine: because the shareholders had the freedom to elect between cash and stock, shareholders electing to receive stock are taxed as if they received the cash and used it to purchase additional stock.

As a second example, suppose that X Corp., having only one class of common stock outstanding, declares a one-for-one stock dividend. However, the terms of the dividend provide that any shareholder holding 4 or more shares may elect to receive a $50 bond in lieu of the dividend stock. Once again all shareholders will be taxed under § 301, those receiving the bond without implicating § 305 and those receiving stock by virtue of § 305(b)(1). Note that even shareholders holding fewer than 4 shares of the corporation will be taxed under § 301 via § 305(b)(1) even though they had no choice as to the form of the dividend.[12]

An election to receive stock in lieu of cash or other property will trigger application of § 305(b)(1) whether made before or after the stock distribution. In addition, an indirect election to receive stock rather than cash or other property will suffice. For example, suppose X Corp. has two classes of common stock outstanding, identical in all respects except that dividends on one class must be paid in cash while dividends on the other class must be paid in stock. A taxpayer who purchases shares receiving stock dividends rather than cash dividends has elected to receive stock dividends in lieu of cash within the meaning of § 305(b)(1),[13] and so subsequent stock distributions will be taxed under the rules of § 301.

Compare the case of two related corporations jointly engaged in a single productive activity. One of the two corporations pays its

---

[12] See Regs. § 1.305–2(a)(5).

[13] See Regs. § 1.305–2(a)(4).

dividends in cash while the other pays in stock. Although the decision to buy the stock of one of these two corporations rather than the other is in effect a decision to receive dividends in cash or stock, § 305(b)(1) does not capture such an implicit election: the language of § 305(b)(1) will not support its application *among* corporations.

Corporations sometimes offer dividend reinvestment plans to their shareholders. Such a plan might provide that shareholders can elect to receive 105 percent of the value of declared cash dividends in the form additional stock. Shareholders electing to participate in such a plan will be taxed on the fair market value of the stock received by virtue of § 305(b)(1).[14]

Suppose a corporation declares a stock dividend and then offers to redeem the dividend shares of any shareholder wishing to tender them. Of course, the tendering shareholders will be taxed under one theory or another, but should this sequence of events constitute the equivalent of a dividend optionally paid in stock or in property within the meaning of § 305(b)(1) so that those shareholders who keep the dividend stock should be taxed? In *Frontier Savings Association v. Commissioner,*[15] the Tax Court refused to apply § 305(b)(1) in such circumstances even though the distributing corporation habitually offered to redeem its shares.

The rule in § 305(b)(2) for disproportionate distributions is the cornerstone of § 305(b). This rule captures stock distributions increasing the recipients' interest in the distributing corporation, but only if some other shareholder receives a distribution of cash or other property. Thus, the rule of § 305(b)(2) embodies two distinct tests: the increased interest test and the companion distribution test.

The increased interest test will be satisfied by an increased claim to the assets or the earnings and profits of the distributing corporation. Consider the case of X Corp. having two classes of stock outstanding, class A common and $100 par class B 10-percent cumulative preferred. A distribution of class B shares to the holders of the common or holders of the preferred will satisfy the increased interest test. Since the holders of class B shares are entitled to 10-percent dividends each year, receipt of class B shares increases any recipient's interest in the earnings and profits of the corporation. In addition, because the holders of class B shares are entitled to $100 in liquidation per share, receipt of class B shares increases a recipient's interests in the assets of the corporation.

---

[14] See, e.g., Rev. Rul. 78–375, 1978–2 C.B. 130.

[15] 87 T.C. 665 (1986), aff'd, 854 F.2d 1001 (7th Cir.1988).

A distribution of class A shares, on the other hand, will not necessarily satisfy the increased interest test. Consider a distribution of class A shares only to holders of class A shares. Since common stock has only a residual interest in dividends and on liquidation, the additional shares of the class A stock do not give a recipient an increased interest in the earnings and profits or in the assets of the corporation. Accordingly, the increased interest test is not satisfied by this distribution. But if the common stock is distributed to holders of preferred stock, the increased interest test will be satisfied because a recipient will hold not only a preferred interest but a residuary interest in the corporation as well.

The companion distribution requirement of § 305(b)(2) usually will be met for any stock distribution satisfying the increased interest test because those shareholders not receiving stock of the corporation ought to receive something else of value in exchange for a reduction in their ownership of the corporation. A dividend of cash or other property will of course satisfy the companion distribution requirement, and so will less obvious corporate distributions such as excess salary payments constituting disguised dividends. Indeed, any payment to a shareholder not participating in the stock distribution will qualify as the companion distribution so long as the payment is made to the shareholder in his capacity as shareholder.[16] While cash or other property distributed as part of a plan to give some shareholders an increased interest in the corporation obviously will qualify as the companion distribution, so too will a distribution of cash or other property *not* made pursuant to such a plan if made within 36 months of the stock dividend.[17]

Suppose a distribution of stock satisfying the increased interest test of § 305(b)(2) is closely followed or preceded by a corporate distribution in redemption of some of the corporation's shares held by taxpayers *not* receiving any of the dividend stock. Since a redemption of stock technically is a distribution of property with respect to stock, will this redemption distribution satisfy the companion distribution test of § 305(b)(2)? One might expect that it would, at least if the redemption is essentially equivalent to a dividend within the meaning of § 302(d) and therefore taxed as a distribution under the rules of § 301. Nonetheless, the regulations under § 305 provide that a distribution of property in redemption of stock will not satisfy the companion distribution requirement of § 305(b)(2) unless the

---

[16] Regs. § 1.305–3(b)(3).
[17] See Regs. § 1.305–3(b)(4).

redemption is part of a periodic plan to increase the proportionate interests of some of the shareholders.[18]

The regulations excuse from § 305(b)(2) one common situation that technically falls within the statute's terms. A stock dividend will not be covered by § 305(b)(2) simply because cash in lieu of fractional shares is distributed by the corporation. To be sure, the effect of such a distribution is to increase ever so slightly the interests of those shareholders entitled to receive integer numbers of shares at the expense of those receiving cash in lieu of fractional shares. Furthermore, the cash paid in lieu of the fractional shares seems to satisfy the companion distribution requirement. Nevertheless, such distributions will escape § 305(b)(2) "[p]rovided the purpose of the distribution of cash is to save the corporation the trouble, expense, and inconvenience of issuing and transferring fractional shares."[19]

Note that the companion distribution requirement of § 305(b)(2) causes one taxpayer (who receives a stock dividend having a disproportionate impact) to have his taxation turn on events happening to another taxpayer (any shareholder receiving a companion distribution). Why *should* the tax consequences of a stock dividend to one shareholder be influenced by the distributions to another? Congress apparently has been satisfied that there is an answer to this question, because several of the other provisions of § 305(b) echo § 305(b)(2).[20]

For example, the disproportionate distribution rule of § 305(b)(2) is extended in § 305(b)(3) to include distributions of common stock to some common shareholders and preferred stock to other common shareholders. Such stock distributions satisfy the increased interest test of § 305(b)(2) as to both the common and preferred shareholders but they fail the companion distribution test imposed by that subsection since the definition of "property" applicable to § 305 excludes stock of the distributing corporation.[21] The rule of § 305(b)(3) overcomes this deficiency in the definition of "property," at least in the specific context of disproportionate distributions of stock to common shareholders.

---

[18] See Regs. § 1.305–3(b)(3) (not applying § 302(b)(2) to an "isolated" redemption to which § 301 applies); Rev. Rul. 78–60, 1978–1 C.B. 81 (for an example of a periodic plan).

[19] Regs. § 1.305–3(c)(1).

[20] The target shareholder's non-recognition in an acquisitive reorganization also may depend on the consideration received by other target shareholders, because non-recognition requires continuity of shareholder interest. See Section 10.02 *infra*.

[21] Section 317(a).

Any stock distribution on preferred stock will alter the preferred shareholders' investment in the corporation, either by increasing the shareholders' preferred claim to earnings and profits as well as liquidation proceeds (if preferred stock is distributed) or by adding residual rights to the shareholders' preferred claims (if common stock is distributed). For this reason, § 305(b)(4) makes taxable any stock distribution made with respect to (that is, any stock distribution *on*) preferred stock.[22]

Consider the distribution of preferred on common as well as preferred on preferred. Depending on the values of the common and preferred shares as well as on the terms of the distribution, it may be the case that no shareholder's interest in the corporation is changed *as measured by fair market value of the stock held*. Why then are the shareholders taxed?[23] Because the focus of § 305(b), like that of most nonrecognition provisions, is not on a change in *value* but on a change in *form*. After all, if an equal-value exchange were always the proper occasion for nonrecognition, no arms'-length exchange would be taxable!

The last provision of § 305(b), that contained in § 305(b)(5) applicable to distributions of convertible preferred stock, is quite peculiar. It provides that distributions of convertible preferred stock are taxable unless the distribution does not have the result described in § 305(b)(2), the disproportionate distribution provision. The situations intended to be covered by this provision, as identified in the regulations,[24] involve the distribution of convertible preferred stock in which the right to convert is limited to a short time and the price of the common stock into which the preferred is convertible is greater than that of preferred stock lacking the convertibility feature. Because the convertibility premium must be exploited quickly if at all, those shareholders wishing to hold additional convertible stock will exercise their conversion rights and those not wishing to convert will sell their preferred shares immediately. In effect, some shareholders will end up with additional common stock and others with cash, the situation covered by § 305(b)(2).

---

[22] See also § 305(e) (accounting for the discount on "stripped" preferred stock (*i.e.*, the excess of the stock's redemption price over its purchase price) like original issue discount on a bond).

[23] The shareholders receiving preferred on preferred are taxed under § 305(b)(4). The shareholders receiving preferred on common are taxed under § 302(b)(2) because the stock dividend gives them an increased interest in the corporation and the preferred stock distributed to the preferred shareholders, because it is taxed under § 305(b), qualifies as a companion distribution of "property." See the flush language in § 305(b) preceding subsection (1).

[24] See Regs. § 1.305–6(b) (example 2).

Section 305(b)(5) does not cover all distributions of convertible preferred stock but only those having a disproportionate effect on the recipients' interests in corporate earnings and profits or assets. Such an effect will obtain only if some but not all of the distributed stock is converted. Consistent with the legislative history of § 305(b)(5), the regulations provide that such an effect will not be presumed if the conversion right can be exercised over many years and the dividend rate is consistent with market factors.[25]

The peculiar aspect of § 305(b)(5) is that it seemingly fails to address another situation to which it quite easily might speak. If any convertible preferred stock is distributed by a corporation (whether or not there is a convertibility premium), some shareholders may retain the stock while others may convert it into common stock. The effect of the distribution, in other words, may approximate that of a distribution composed in part of preferred stock and in part of common stock. That effect would be described in § 302(b)(2) and thus the distribution would be captured by § 305(b)(5) except that neither common stock nor convertible preferred stock is "property" within the meaning of § 305. Thus, the companion distribution requirement of § 305(b)(2) is not met. To close this loophole, § 305(b)(5) should cover distributions of convertible preferred stock having the effect described in § 305(b)(2) *or in § 305(b)(3)*.[26]

6.04 Deemed Distributions Under § 305(c)

Many transactions not involving an actual distribution of stock nevertheless can have the effect of a stock dividend. Consider X Corp. having 300 shares outstanding, 150 owned by B and 150 owned by C. Assume that each share is worth $100 because X Corp. has assets worth $30,000.

If X distributes cash of $5,000 to B and 75 shares to C, the distribution will be taxable to both shareholders: B will be taxed under § 301 directly while C will be taxed under the same section pursuant to § 305(b)(2). After the transaction, B will own 150 of the 375 (40 percent) outstanding shares of X Corp., each share having a value of $66.67, or $10,000 in the aggregate.[27] C, on the other hand, will own the remaining 225 shares (60 percent), having an aggregate value of $15,000. Accordingly, the value of the distributed

---

[25] Regs. § 1.305–6(a)(2).

[26] Note that distributions of convertible preferred stock to holders of preferred stock need not be covered by § 305(b)(5) because such distributions already are covered by the general rule of § 305(b)(4) applicable to all stock distributions on preferred stock.

[27] After the distribution, X Corp. has assets worth $25,000.

shares is $5,000 (75 shares at $66.67 per share), and C will be taxed on that amount under the rules of § 301.[28]

The same effect can be obtained by replacing the two distributions with a single redemption by X of 50 of B's shares. If that is done, B will receive the same $5,000 (50 shares at $100 per share), and B's ownership in X will drop to 100 of 250 shares outstanding, or 40 percent. C's percentage ownership of X will increase to 60 percent (150 of 250 shares outstanding). Each share will continue to be worth $100, making the aggregate value of C's stock $15,000, just as in the case of the two distributions considered above. Should C, who is totally passive in this case, be taxed under § 305(b)(2)?

To ensure that this transaction and others having the same effect as a stock dividend do not offer a potential for abuse, § 305(c) provides that, under regulations promulgated by the Secretary of the Treasury, certain transactions having the effect of a stock distribution are to be subjected to the rules of § 305. These transactions include the change in conversion ratio of stock, a change in stock redemption price, a difference between stock issue and redemption price, and a redemption taxed to the recipient shareholder under § 301. While the thrust of § 305(c)—that transactions having the effect of a stock dividend should be taxed like a stock dividend—makes sense, its arbitrary lines and mechanical application undercut its coherence.

For example, the statute recharacterizes as stock distributions only those redemptions failing to qualify for the exchange treatment of § 302(a). Yet, it is precisely those redemptions qualifying for exchange treatment that work the greatest rearrangement of shareholder interests. Nothing leaps to mind that would explain why highly disproportionate stock distributions should trigger § 305 (and result in ordinary dividend income) while redemptions having the same effect do not (and typically result in capital gain or loss). The best that can be offered in defense of this rule is that the companion distribution requirement of § 305(b)(2) is not met when the redemption is taxed as a sale or exchange.[29]

A change in conversion ratio also can trigger application of § 305(c). However, not all changes in the conversion ratio of pre-

---

[28] Note that C is taxed on the fair market value of the shares distributed to him without any offset for the decrease in value of his remaining shares. That decrease under § 305(b) remains unrealized until disposition by C of his shares.

[29] That is, a redemption taxed as an exchange should not be treated as a distribution with respect to stock, just as the sale of property to a corporation for cash is not a "distribution with respect to stock" if the corporation pays no more than fair market value.

ferred stock are proper candidates for § 305(c). Consider X Corp. having 2 classes of stock outstanding, 100 shares of class A common and 100 shares of class B preferred convertible one-for-one into class A stock. If the class A stock splits (or if a stock dividend payable in shares of class A stock is declared on the class A shares), then the conversion rights of the class B shares must be adjusted to avoid dilution of the class B shares. For example, if the class A shares split one-for-one, then the conversion ratio of the class B shares must be increased from one-to-one to two-to-one. Such an increase to avoid dilution is explicitly permitted by statute without taxation.[30]

Reconsider the example above, but assume that the class B shareholders do not benefit from an antidilution provision increasing their conversion ratio in the case of stock splits or dividends. Suppose X Corp. declares a stock dividend on the class A shares payable with one share of additional class A stock for each share of class A stock held. In addition, to prevent dilution of the class B shareholders' interests, they too receive a stock dividend, payable in one share of class A stock for each share of class B stock held. Is such an antidilution distribution protected from taxation? No—the only antidilution provision sanctioned by the Code is an increase in conversion ratio. The stock dividend declared on the class B shares, even though having the effect of avoiding a disproportionate impact by the stock dividend declared on the class A, is simply a stock distribution made with respect to preferred stock and thus taxable according to the rule of § 305(b)(4).[31] Of course, if the conversion ratio of the class B shares had been adjusted and then half of the shares converted, the same result would have been obtained without taxation to the class B shareholders (except they would have had less preferred stock).

6.05 Poison Pills

When corporate takeovers became common in the 1980s, antitakeover practices blossomed. And these practices continue today. One such practice is the "poison pill," by which the corporation ensures that a hostile takeover will be too expensive to pursue. For example, the corporation might provide that each shareholder can purchase additional shares of the corporation at a 50% discount if an outsider acquires 20% or more of the company's stock or announces its intention to mount a tender offer without the approval of the corporation's board of directors. Until such a triggering event, the rights to buy discounted stock cannot be separated from the actual shares and can be redeemed by the corporation for a nominal

---

[30] Section 305(b)(4). See also Regs. § 1.302-7(b)(1).
[31] Rev. Rul. 83–42, 1983–1 C.B. 76.

amount. Once triggered, though, the discounted stock rights can be sold and are not subject to redemption.

Should the adoption of such a poison pill be treated as a distribution of stock rights to current shareholders of the corporation? In Rev.Rul. 90–11,[32] the Service ruled that the adoption of a similar poison pill is not subject to taxation under § 305. Unfortunately, the ruling provides no analysis whatsoever in support of its conclusion that the adoption of the pill "does not constitute a distribution of stock or property by [the corporation] to its shareholders, an exchange of property or stock (either taxable or nontaxable), or any other event giving rise to the realization of gross income by any taxpayer." The only hint of any justification for this very broad ruling was the assumed fact that "[a]t the time [the corporation] adopted the [poison pill], the likelihood that the [shareholders' rights] would, at any time, be exercised was both remote and speculative."

Despite the lack of a conceptual underpinning, it is hard to fault Rev.Rul. 90–11. If the adoption of the poison pill were treated as a distribution subject to § 305, the rights would have to be valued if there were a companion distribution of cash or other property to some shareholders. How would these rights be valued given their highly contingent nature? Indeed, given that adoption of a poison pill is intended to stave off hostile takeovers—and if there are no hostile takeovers, exercise of the poison pill stock rights will never be triggered—do the rights have any significant current value? The revenue ruling explicitly did not consider the tax consequences of the exercise or transfer of the poison pill stock rights following a triggering event, but because such rights are created to inhibit all triggering events, the tax implications of this remote possibility are of little concern to most corporate lawyers.

---

[32] 1990–1 C.B. 10.

Chapter 7

TAINTED STOCK

7.01 The Preferred Stock Bailout

It may seem as if the exceptions in § 305(b) swallow the general rule of nonrecognition in § 305(a). To be sure, a host of stock dividends will be taxable under § 305(b). On the other hand, many stock dividends will be tax-free, at least those made on common stock. Indeed, a pro rata distribution of common stock on common stock will always be tax-free under § 305(a), while a pro rata distribution of preferred stock on common stock will be tax-free in the absence of a companion distribution of cash or property to other shareholders.

The rule allowing a tax-free, pro-rata distribution of preferred stock to common shareholders created what is known as the "preferred stock bailout." Consider the case of X Corp. having 100 shares of appreciated common stock outstanding. X Corp. has earnings and profits of $10,000 that the shareholders would like to remove from corporate solution as capital gain. Declaration of a cash dividend will not work, nor will a pro rata stock redemption. If the shareholders are unwilling to dissolve the corporation, it seems that the shareholders must recognize dividend income (without any basis recovery) according to the rules of § 301.

Suppose, though, that the corporation declares a stock dividend payable in one share of a newly created class of $100 par preferred stock for each share of common stock outstanding. Such a distribution will be tax-free under § 305(a). If the shareholders then sell the preferred stock, they will recognize capital gain on the sale, thereby accomplishing their goal. Of course, the $10,000 has not been removed from corporate solution, but that is done easily enough. The purchaser, having a cost (fair market value) basis in the preferred stock under § 1012, simply has it redeemed, a transaction taxed as an exchange under § 302(a) and (b)(3) and producing no gain.[1]

In one sense, a taxpayer always can bail out corporate earnings and profits as capital gain by the simple expedient of selling some or all of his stock. However, if common stock is sold, the taxpayer may lose some or all of his interest in the future profits of the corpo-

---

[1] An alternate form of the preferred stock bailout is for preferred stock to be distributed tax-free under § 305(a), followed by a redemption of the preferred stock under circumstances qualifying for exchange treatment under § 302(a) because of § 302(b)(1).

ration. The virtue of the *preferred* stock bailout is that earnings and profits can be bailed out by a taxpayer without reducing the taxpayer's interest in corporate growth. Further, if the preferred stock is nonvoting, the bailout will not even reduce the taxpayer's control of the corporation.

The linchpins of the preferred stock bailout are (1) a tax-free distribution of stock and (2) capital gain on the disposition of the stock so obtained. Congress could have substantially eliminated these bailouts by restricting the nonrecognition rule of § 305(a); that is, impose an immediate tax liability on any distribution of preferred stock. Such an approach, though, works an unnecessary hardship on shareholders receiving distributions of preferred stock that are not the first step of a bailout. Accordingly, Congress has attempted to eliminate preferred stock bailouts by hitting its other link, the capital gain on disposition of the dividend stock. In § 306, Congress has provided that much (but not all) of the preferred stock distributed by a corporation, if received tax-free by the shareholders under § 305(a), will produce dividend income if subsequently disposed of in a manner constituting a bailout.[2]

7.02 Definition of § 306 Stock

Stock subject to the disabilities of § 306—tainted stock, as it usually is called—is defined in § 306(c). Any stock other than common stock distributed by a corporation is § 306 stock if received by the taxpayer tax-free under § 305(a). The definition of § 306 stock also includes stock (other than common stock) received in a tax-free reorganization if receipt of the stock had the effect of a stock dividend. Stock exchanged for § 306 stock also will be § 306 stock if received in an exchanged or transferred basis transaction (such as in a § 351 transaction). Thus, § 306 stock does not include stock acquired in a taxable transaction (taking a cost basis under § 1012) or stock acquired from a decedent (taking a basis determined under § 1014).

Because a § 306 taint will not, in general, attach to common stock, the definition of "common" stock plays an important role in § 306. Nevertheless, neither that section nor the regulations promulgated under it define common stock. Recall, though, that the distinction between common and preferred stock was important in the related context of § 305. For purposes of § 305, preferred stock is

---

[2] If the § 306 stock is redeemed, the rules of § 301 will apply directly by reason of § 306(a)(2). If the § 306 stock is disposed of other than by redemption, the amount realized generally will be taxed as dividend income by reason of §§ 306(a)(1)(A) and 306(a)(1)(D).

stock which, in relation to other classes of stock outstanding, enjoys certain limited rights and privileges . . . but does not participate in corporate growth to any significant extent. The distinguishing feature of "preferred stock" . . . is not its privileged position as such, but that such privileged position is limited. . . .[3]

This definition of preferred stock responds to the abuse presented by preferred stock bailouts. Shareholders of a corporation always can obtain the earnings and profits of their corporation at capital gains rate by selling their stock—that is the essence of the rule that treats a corporation as an entity distinct from its shareholders and which considers stock to be a capital asset regardless of corporate-level activity. The abuse of the preferred stock bailout is that shareholders will bail out the corporation's earnings and profits without recognizing ordinary income *and* without reducing their interests in corporate growth.[4] In a number of revenue rulings, the Service has adopted this view of the preferred stock bailout abuse, holding that common stock for purposes of § 306 is any stock, whether voting or not, that participates without substantial restriction in corporate growth.[5]

Consistent with limiting application of § 306 to preferred stock bailouts, Congress provided an exception to the § 306 taint for distributions of stock made by a corporation without earnings and profits.[6] Since such a corporation could have distributed cash or property without producing dividend income to its shareholders, the distribution of stock works no end run around the dividend rules of § 301. However, this rule permitted sophisticated taxpayers to avoid the reach of § 306 by using a pair of related corporations.

Consider individual A who owns all the stock of X Corp., a corporation with substantial earnings and profits. A creates Y Corp., exchanging the stock of X Corp. for common and preferred stock of Y. Is the Y preferred tainted under § 306? If not, sale of the Y preferred will work a preferred stock bailout of the earnings and profits of X Corp.

---

[3] Regs. § 1.305–5(a).

[4] A question of timing arises in the preferred-stock bailout: exactly when does the bailout occur? From the shareholders' perspective, it occurs once the dividend stock is sold because at that moment they possess the cash equal to the corporation's accumulated earnings and profits. However, nothing yet has been distributed out of corporate solution: the bailout is not completed until the dividend stock is redeemed.

[5] Rev. Rul. 81–91, 1981–1 C.B. 123; Rev. Rul. 76–387, 1976–2 C.B. 96.

[6] Section 306(c)(2).

Observe that newly formed Y Corp. has no earnings and profits.[7] Thus, it would seem as if the Y preferred would not be § 306 stock. However, Congress recognized the abuse in this situation and provided that preferred stock received in a § 351 exchange is tainted under § 306 if, had money been distributed in lieu of the preferred stock, the taxpayer would have had dividend income to any extent.[8] To appreciate the implications of this rule, one must recall the operation of § 304.

Section 304 recharacterizes as a redemption the sale of one corporation's stock to a second, related corporation. If the transferor receives stock of the second corporation in addition to cash or property, then § 304 applies only to the cash and property.[9] This hypothetical redemption is then taxed under the rules of § 302.

The interplay of § 306 and § 304 is as follows. If our taxpayer—A—exchanges his X stock for common and preferred Y stock, *then to determine the § 306 taint on the Y preferred,* we ask how the exchange would have been taxed under § 304 had cash been used instead of the preferred stock. If any of the cash would have been taxed to A as a dividend, then the Y preferred is tainted under § 306.

In order for there to be dividend income under § 304, the redemption must fail to qualify for exchange treatment under § 302(b)(1)-(4) *and* there must be earnings and profits available to cover some or all of the distribution. Because A owns all of the stock of Y, A will fail to qualify for exchange treatment under § 302(b). Further, under the rule of § 304(b)(2), the earnings and profits of both X and Y are available to cover the distribution. In the case of A's exchange of X stock for Y stock, the Y preferred stock appropriately will be tainted under § 306.

The following problem, although technical, is worth studying closely both because it illustrates the relationship of § 306 to § 304 and because it reviews the mechanics of § 304 and § 302. X Corp. has 100 shares of stock outstanding, 80 owned by individual A and 20 by individual B. A and C, an unrelated individual, form Y Corp. A contributes his stock of X Corp. to Y in exchange for 60 shares of Y common stock and 600 shares of Y $10 par-value preferred stock. C contributes cash to Y in exchange for 40 shares of Y common stock as well as 400 shares of Y $10 par-value Y preferred stock.

---

[7] This conclusion assumes that X Corp. was not the common parent of a consolidated group before Y Corp.'s formation. Cf. Regs. § 1.1502-33(f)(1).

[8] Section 306(c)(3).

[9] As this example illustrates, there can be an over-lap of § 304 and § 351, resolved in favor of § 304. See § 304(b)(3).

Assume that the Y Corp. preferred stock is worth par and that X Corp. has earnings and profits of $5,000. Is the Y preferred stock tainted under § 306 in the hands of A?

The transfer by A is wholly within the confines of § 351. However, if A had received cash in lieu of the Y preferred stock, the taxation of that cash would have been determined under § 304. If in these circumstances the application of § 304 would produce dividend income to A, then the Y preferred stock *is* tainted under § 306.

Under § 304, A's stock interest in X Corp. must be tested under the rules of § 302. Prior to the formation of Y, A owned 80 percent of X. After the formation of Y, A had no direct ownership of X Corp. but A has an indirect ownership (under the constructive ownership rules of § 318) of 60 percent of 80 percent, or 48 percent. A will fail to qualify for exchange treatment under § 302 (in this case, that is, the preferred stock of Y will be tainted under § 306) unless A meets one of the tests in § 302(b)(1)–(4).

Under § 302(b)(2), a redemption will qualify for exchange treatment if the redemption (or hypothetical redemption under § 304) reduces the taxpayer's ownership interest below 50 percent *and* leaves the taxpayer with less than 80 percent of his pre-redemption percentage ownership. In this case, the hypothetical redemption reduced A's interest to 48 percent, and that is both less than 50 percent and less than 80 percent of his former percentage interest (since 80 percent of his prior 80 percent interest is 64 percent). Accordingly, A falls within the safe harbor of § 302(b)(2) and his preferred stock is not tainted under § 306.

7.03 Disposition of § 306 Stock

A taxable disposition of § 306 stock will, in general, produce dividend income to the transferor. If § 306 stock is redeemed, the amount realized on the redemption is treated as a distribution subject to the rules of § 301. Thus, if the corporation has adequate earnings and profits at the time of the redemption, the entire amount distributed can be taxed to the shareholder as a dividend.

If § 306 stock is sold, a more complex rule applies. The selling shareholder has ordinary income on the sale equal to the lesser of (1) the amount realized on the sale and (2) the stock's ratable share of the amount that would have been a dividend had the corporation distributed cash instead of the § 306 stock in the first place. Thus, the earnings and profits of the corporation at the time of disposition are relevant only if § 306 stock is redeemed; if § 306 stock is sold or exchanged, the earnings and profits of the corporation are relevant only as of the time of distribution of the § 306 stock.[10] In addition, in the case of a sale or exchange of § 306 stock, the selling shareholder recognizes gain from the sale of stock to the extent that the amount realized exceeds (i) the stock's share of the corporation's earnings and profits plus (ii) the stock's adjusted basis. § 306(a)(1)(B). Any ordinary income arising from these rules is treated as dividend income for purposes of § 1(h)(11). § 306(a)(1)(D). *See also* § 1(h)(11) (providing that qualified dividends are taxed at the rate applicable to long-term capital gain).

For example, suppose that B is the sole shareholder of X Corp. On January 1 of year 1, X distributes 100 shares of preferred stock to B in a distribution that is tax-free under § 305(a). The fair market value of the preferred shares is $10 per share, and assume that B's basis in the preferred shares becomes $3 per share under § 307(a). Assume further that X has accumulated earnings and profits of $600 at the time of the distribution and that X has no current earnings and profits for the entire taxable year.

The preferred stock is tainted by virtue of § 306(c)(1)(A). Suppose that B sells her preferred stock one year later on January 1 of year 2 for its then fair market value of $11 per share. B is taxed under § 306(a)(1), producing ordinary income of $600 and capital gain of $200.

These amounts are computed as follows. B's amount realized on the sale is $1,100. Under § 306(a)(1)(A), that entire amount constitutes ordinary income to B except to the extent that the "ratable share" limitation in § 306(a)(1)(A) applies.

The limitation ensures that the dividend income on disposition does not exceed the amount of ordinary income that B would have recognized had she received cash instead of the preferred shares back in year 1. Since the corporation had earnings and profits of $600 for year 1, a cash distribution of $1,100 in 2007 would have produced dividend income to B of $600. Since 100 shares of preferred stock were distributed, each preferred share has a "ratable share" of that dividend in the amount of $6. Thus, under the "ratable share" limitation of § 306(a)(1)(A), B's ordinary income is limited to $6 per share, or $600 total.

The remainder of the amount realized—$500—is first treated as a recovery of basis and then as taxable gain.[11] Since B's basis in

---

[10] Of course, if the distributing corporation has no earnings and profits at the time of distribution of the stock, it is not § 306 stock and the rules of § 306 will not apply to it. § 306(c)(2).

[11] See § 306(a)(1)(B).

the preferred stock was $3 per share (or $300 total), B has $200 of taxable gain. Note that the corporation's earnings and profits at the time of sale are irrelevant in this example.

However, suppose that B's preferred stock is redeemed rather than sold. Now, taxation is determined under § 306(a)(2), and the tax consequences likely differ because that provision provides the blanket rule that the entire amount realized is taxed as a distribution under § 301.

Does this mean that the entire $1,100 amount distributed is taxed as dividend income without any recovery of basis? Not necessarily, because § 301 limits the amount of ordinary income to the earnings and profits of the corporation. Note, however, that this limitation is determined by reference to the earnings and profits as of the end of the year in which the distribution takes place and *not* as of the end of the prior year. Thus, if X's earnings and profits account has decreased, the amount of ordinary income to B will be less than $600. On the other hand, if the earnings and profits account has risen, the amount of ordinary income will be greater. Indeed, if the corporation's earnings and profits equals or exceeds $1,100, X will be required to recognized the entire amount distributed as ordinary income.[12]

Section 306 contains a number of exceptions to its draconian rules. First, disposition of § 306 stock as part of the complete liquidation of a corporation is not covered by § 306. Since the earnings and profits of a corporation are bailed out at capital gains rates in a complete liquidation, there is no reason to treat the disposition of the § 306 stock in this manner as an abusive bailout. Second, the sale or exchange of § 306 stock will not be subject to the § 306 rules if the disposition terminates the shareholder's entire interest in the corporation (after applying the constructive ownership rules of § 318(a)). Once again, because earnings and profits can be bailed out at capital gains rates by selling one's stock in the corporation, completely terminating one's interest in a corporation is not an abusive bailout. Similarly, disposition of § 306 stock in a redemption will not be taxed as ordinary income if the redemption qualifies for exchange treatment as a complete termination of the shareholder's interest in the corporation or as part of a partial liquidation (*i.e.*, it qualifies under § 302(b)(3) or (b)(4)).

---

[12] Section 306(a) produces the following rules of thumb: (1) if the corporation's earnings and profits are low in the year of disposition, redeem; (2) if the corporation's earnings and profits are low in the year of distribution, sell; (3) if the corporation's earnings and profits are low in both years, you can't go wrong; and (4) if the corporation's earnings and profits are high in both years, hold on to the stock until you die. As noted above, death cleanses the § 306 taint.

Suppose taxpayer T owns 200 shares of stock in X Corp., 100 shares of common stock as well as 100 shares of § 306 stock. We know that disposition of the 100 common shares will permit T to avoid the § 306 taint on disposition of the § 306 stock.[13] Can T avoid half of the § 306 taint by selling half of his common shares? This issue was raised but not settled in *Fireoved v. United States.*[14]

In *Fireoved,* the taxpayer began as one of three equal owners of a corporation. Before some of his § 306 stock was redeemed, the taxpayer and one of the other owners sold some of their common stock to the third owner, leaving the taxpayer and the other selling shareholder each with a 25 1/3 percent ownership of the corporation's common stock. However, because the corporate by-laws required at least a 76-percent vote to make substantial changes, this reduction in the taxpayer's voting interest was irrelevant; in fact, the affirmative vote of all three shareholders was necessary both before and after the stock sale.

The court indicated that partial disposition by the taxpayer of his common stock should not remove a proportionate part of the § 306 taint on his preferred stock. However, the court felt that it could avoid that issue in general because, on the facts of the case before it, the partial disposition of the common stock had no effect on the taxpayer's voting control of the corporation and so should have no effect on the § 306 taint. The court's analysis of this issue was unfortunately thin.

Recall that common stock for purposes of § 306 is any stock participating without substantial restrictions in corporate growth. Only non-common stock is tainted under § 306[15] because only that stock presents the bailout abuse. As made clear in Rev. Rul. 76–387, the preferred stock bailout abuse arises whenever a shareholder is able to obtain corporate earnings and profits as capital gain without a concomitant reduction in the shareholder's interest in the future growth of the corporation. Reduction of the shareholder's voting interest in the corporation, if any, should not be relevant. Accordingly, the court's focus in *Fireoved* on the lack of reduction in voting control seems misplaced.

While the language of § 306 does not easily support the conclusion that a partial disposition of common stock should reduce

---

[13] See § 306(b)(1)(A).

[14] 462 F.2d 1281 (3d Cir.1972).

[15] Common stock can be tainted under § 306 if it is received in exchange for § 306 stock in a substituted basis transaction (such as a § 351 exchange). See § 306(c)(1)(C).

a proportionate part of the § 306 taint,[16] such a rule is consistent with the rationale of § 306 (as can be determined from examination of the statute itself). That is, a taxpayer can "bail-out" all corporate earnings by giving up all interest in future growth of the corporation. Similarly, a taxpayer should be able to bail-out *part* of the corporate earnings by giving up *an equivalent part* of his interest in the future growth of the corporation.

There are exceptions to the application of § 306 for certain transactions "not in avoidance" of Federal income taxes,[17] and these exceptions may protect (in part) taxpayers disposing of their § 306 stock subsequent to a partial disposition of their common stock. The first exceptions applies if a taxpayer establishes that the distribution and disposition of the § 306 stock were not in pursuance of a plan having one of its principal purposes the avoidance of Federal income tax. The second exception applies regardless of the motivation behind the distribution of the § 306 stock if, "in the case of a prior or simultaneous disposition (or redemption) of the stock with respect to which the section 306 stock disposed of (or redeemed) was issued," the taxpayer establishes that the disposition of the § 306 stock was not for tax avoidance. § 306(b)(4)(B). It is this second exception that was at the heart of the taxpayer's argument in *Fireoved.*[18]

Under what circumstances should it be held that a distribution or disposition of § 306 stock did not have tax avoidance as one of its principal purposes? In *Fireoved,* the court held that a distribution of preferred stock has a tax avoidance motive even if made for a business purpose of the distributing corporation if a taxable dividend could have achieved the equivalent result. Apparently, not adopting the most expensive route possible is tax avoidance. In Revenue Ruling 80–33,[19] the Service ruled that the distribution of preferred stock had as one of its principal purposes the avoidance of

---

[16] Under § 306(b)(1), the sale or exchange of § 306 stock will not be subject to the § 306 rules if the transferee is unrelated to the transferor and the transfer "terminates the *entire* interest of the [transferor] in the corporation." (emphasis added.)

[17] Section 306(b)(4).

[18] These exceptions by their terms apply only if a taxpayer "establishe[s] to the satisfaction of the Secretary [of the Treasury]" that the transactions lack a tax avoidance motive. Can a taxpayer seek to obtain the benefit of either of these exceptions in court if a prior administrative determination was not sought? This issue was raised but not decided in *Fireoved.* If the failure to seek an administrative ruling on this issue forecloses judicial review, then presumably a taxpayer cannot report a transaction as falling within one of these two exceptions absent an administrative review, even if the taxpayer believes in good faith that one of the exceptions should apply.

[19] 1980–1 C.B. 69.

Federal income tax because a taxable dividend of corporate debt could have accomplished the same business objective.

Chapter 8

LIQUIDATIONS

8.01 Introduction

When a corporation is formed, a shareholder typically recognizes no gain or loss.[1] If the shareholder has realized but not recognized gain, the corporation preserves the gain by taking a transferred basis in the transferred assets and the shareholder also preserves the gain by taking an exchanged basis in the corporation's stock. § 362(a); § 358(a). For example, if B forms X Corp. by transferring an asset with an $8,000 basis and $15,000 fair market value to the corporation in exchange for all of its stock, B will not be taxed on the exchange. § 351. B will take an $8,000 basis in the stock, and X Corp. will take an $8,000 basis in the property. § 358; § 362.

If B were to liquidate X Corp. when X Corp.'s basis in the asset was $5,000, the asset had a $15,000 fair market value, and B's stock basis was $8,000, one might expect similar nonrecognition treatment. That is, neither X Corp. nor B would recognize gain and B would succeed to X Corp.'s basis in the assets of $5,000. But nonrecognition typically is not the order of the day for liquidations. Instead, a complete liquidation usually is a recognition event to both the distributing corporation and its shareholders. The distributing corporation recognizes gain (or generally loss) as if the distributed property were sold to the distributee shareholder at fair market value. In the example, X Corp. would recognize a $10,000 gain ($15,000 amount realized minus $5,000 basis). The shareholders must recognize gain or loss on the difference between the fair market value of the property received on the distribution and the shareholder's stock basis. In the example, B would recognize a $7,000 gain ($15,000 amount realized minus $8,000 basis).

Notice that in general there is nonrecognition treatment for incorporations under § 351 and recognition treatment for liquidations. One reason for the difference may be that there is a continuity of investment when an unincorporated business incorporates, a continuity that is often lacking in a liquidation. An incorporation usually signifies the continuation of a business in corporate form. A corporate liquidation, on the other hand, often signifies the discontinuation of the business with the assets sold or converted to personal use.

---

[1] This conclusion assumes the absence of boot.

But of course that is not always the case. It may be that incorporated assets were used for some other purpose prior to incorporation or that following a liquidation the shareholders will continue the business. Congress, however, has chosen to draw a bright line, giving nonrecognition to corporate formations while generally denying nonrecognition treatment to "disincorporations."

A liquidation presents the last opportunity to tax shareholders on any earnings and profits that the corporation has accumulated. But that reason does not explain why a shareholder will be taxed on a corporation's unrealized appreciation—particularly, as in the example, where the appreciation occurred before incorporation. Additionally the taxation of the shareholders in a liquidation is independent of the corporation's earnings and profits account.

In any event, a liquidation is typically treated as if the shareholders had sold their stock to the corporation in exchange for the corporation's assets. The liquidating corporation recognizes gain (or generally loss) as if it had sold the distributed assets to the shareholders at fair market value. § 336. Each shareholder recognizes gain (or loss) on the difference between the adjusted basis of the shareholder's stock and the amount realized. § 331; § 1001. Finally, each shareholder takes a fair market value basis in the assets received on liquidation. § 334(a).

There is an alternative liquidation pattern that applies to the liquidation of a subsidiary into its parent corporation. See § 332. Because the subsidiary's assets remain in corporate form, the likelihood of business continuity is greater here than where individuals liquidate a corporation. When a parent liquidates its subsidiary, it has merely simplified the corporate structure. Accordingly, § 332 postpones the parent-corporation's recognition, requiring the parent to step into the liquidating subsidiary's tax shoes. The parent receives the liquidated assets with the subsidiary's basis. In the example, assume that B is a corporation and that the corporate asset has a $5,000 basis. Upon a liquidation qualifying under § 332, B Corp. would recognize no gain, but it would take a $5,000 basis in the asset received from X Corp. § 334(b)(1). Note that B's $8,000 basis in the X Corp. stock does not play a role in this liquidation. In this liquidation pattern, the liquidating corporation generally recognizes no gain or loss. § 337.

These liquidation provisions apply to "complete liquidations." A corporation completely liquidates if it makes "a series of distributions in redemption of all of [its] stock . . . pursuant to a plan."[2] To

---

[2] Section 346(a). That definition, however, does not pinpoint when a liquidation begins, although the regulations offer some useful guidance. See

liquidate, a corporation need not dissolve under state law nor adopt a formal plan of liquidation. Note that there is no requirement that assets be converted to cash—an in-kind distribution will qualify. Furthermore, there is no specific time frame during which a liquidation must be completed: A corporation might distribute its assets over a period of time and meanwhile continue some corporate activity. The longer the liquidating process and the more active the liquidating corporation, however, the more likely it is that the Service will treat a distribution not as part of the liquidation but rather as a distribution taxable under § 301.[3]

In some cases, a liquidation may occur even when no assets are transferred. Suppose that USCO wholly owns an entity which it has treated as a corporation for U.S. tax purposes.[4] If USCO "checks-the-box" to now treat the entity as a disregarded entity for U.S. tax purposes, the check-the-box election is treated as if USCO liquidated the entity even though nothing has changed, other than filing a form with the Service. Typically, the check-the-box election with respect to a foreign entity will be ignored for foreign tax purposes which continues to regard the entity as a corporation. An entity that is treated one way in a foreign jurisdiction (here, as a corporation) and a different way for U.S. tax purposes (here, as a disregarded entity) is referred to as a "hybrid" entity.

8.02 Section 331 Liquidations

(a) Treatment of the Shareholders.

Section 331(a) treats a shareholder as having exchanged stock for the amount received in liquidation. If the shareholder held the exchanged stock as a capital asset, he recognizes capital gain or loss, measured by difference between the amount realized and the shareholder's adjusted basis in the stock. § 1001; § 1222. If a shareholder had acquired stock in the liquidating corporation on different dates or at different prices, he measures the gain or loss separately for each block.[5] The distributing corporation's earnings and profits account, so vital in determining the tax consequences of nonliquidating distributions, generally does not affect the taxation

---

Regs. § 1.332–2(c) (providing that the status of liquidation exists when the corporation has adopted a plan of liquidation and ceased to be a going concern, and its remaining activities are merely for the purpose of winding up its affairs).

[3] Many tax lawyers use the three-year time period described in § 332 as a guide.

[4] Regs. § 301.7701–3.

[5] Regs. § 1.331–1(e).

of shareholders in a liquidating distribution. But see § 316(b)(2) (for a special election for a liquidating personal holding company).

Suppose X Corp., with an earnings and profits account of $6,000, has $5,000 of cash and an asset with a $3,000 basis and $8,000 fair market value.[6] Individual B holds all of the X Corp. stock with a $2,000 basis and $13,000 fair market value. If X Corp. liquidates, B will recognize an $11,000 gain, the difference between the $13,000 amount realized and the $2,000 stock basis. § 1001. Assuming B is not a dealer in stock, the gain will be a capital gain despite the earnings and profits account. § 331; § 1222.

Since B is treated as having exchanged X Corp. stock for X Corp.'s assets, B will take a fair market value basis in the non-cash assets received—in the example above, the basis will be $8,000 in those assets. § 334(a). Often this is referred to as a step-up in basis, but if an asset has declined in value, its basis in the hands of the shareholder will be stepped-down.

Suppose in the example above that the assets were subject to a $4,000 liability. The amount realized by B for his X stock must be reduced to reflect the liability to which the property is subject or which the shareholder assumes.[7] Consequently, B has a $7,000 gain on the liquidation ($9,000 amount realized for the stock minus the $2,000 stock basis). B's basis in the non-cash assets is still $8,000, their fair market value. Sometimes shareholders may inherit liabilities that are disputed (*e.g.*, if the $4,000 liability represented a claim for patent infringement). If a liability cannot be valued, it will not be taken into account in reducing the amount realized.

Often the assets themselves may be difficult to value even where there are no disputed liabilities. Suppose X Corp.'s assets consisted of a contractual claim on a percentage of some other corporation's future profits. If the claim cannot be valued on liquidation, the shareholder's gain will remain open until valuation is possible.[8] However, the Service requires valuation except in rare and extraordinary circumstances.[9]

Suppose that a corporation sells its assets on the installment method prior to making a liquidating distribution of the installment

---

[6] Recall that the earnings and profits account is just that—an account. For example, it is not synonymous with cash on hand (e.g., corporate earnings might be reinvested in the corporation which would deplete cash available for distribution but not the earnings and profits account).

[7] Essentially, B acquires $4,000 worth of the X assets because of the liability.

[8] See *Burnet v. Logan*, 283 U.S. 404 (1931).

[9] See Regs. § 1.1001–1(a); see also § 453(j)(2).

Why the difference? Perhaps the answer lies in the finality of a liquidating distribution. A full repeal of *General Utilities* would permit any distributing corporation to recognize a loss on the distribution of property with a basis exceeding fair market value. That principle should be the starting point. On a nonliquidating distribution, the distributing corporation may "cherry pick" the assets to be distributed. Thus, it may choose to distribute "loss" property to recognize loss, while retaining "gain" property and deferring gain. In contrast, in a liquidating distribution, the distributing corporation distributes all of its property—any "gain" property as well as any "loss" property.

(ii) Loss disallowance rules. Even with a liquidating distribution, Congress has been concerned that taxpayers could exploit the loss allowance by artificially creating corporate-level losses. Congress addressed that concern in § 336(d)(1) and (2), a response that seems too broad, however, following the enactment of § 362(e)(2). Consider the following example to illustrate why Congress may have enacted § 336(d)(1) and (2) and why § 362(e)(2) makes those sections sometimes unnecessary:

Suppose that B owns all the stock of X Corp., whose assets have a $90,000 basis and $120,000 fair market value. Assume B's X stock basis is also $90,000. B also holds a piece of property with a $130,000 basis and $80,000 fair market value. If X Corp. liquidated, it would recognize a $30,000 gain under § 336(a), and B would recognize a $30,000 gain under § 331.[16]

Suppose instead that B exchanges the loss property for additional X Corp. stock in a transaction that qualifies under § 351. (A contribution to capital will achieve the same result.) If § 362(e)(2) does not apply to that transaction, B's $50,000 built-in loss in the transferred asset is duplicated in B's basis in the X Corp. stock and X Corp.'s basis in the asset: Under § 358, B's basis in the X stock increases to $220,000, and X Corp.'s total basis in the assets increases to $220,000 under § 362. Now when X Corp. liquidates, it is treated as if it sold the property to its shareholder in the aggregate for $200,000, its fair market value. Assuming that § 336(d)(1) and (2) do not apply, X Corp. recognizes an overall $20,000 loss under § 336. Further, B recognizes a $20,000 loss under § 331.[17] Those losses allow both X Corp. and B to offset other taxable income. Note that B's basis in the loss property after the liquidation is $80,000, its fair market value under § 334(a). But B will gladly surrender a

---

[16] X Corp. and B each would have an amount realized of $120,000 and aggregate basis of $90,000.

[17] X Corp. and B each have an aggregate basis of $220,000 and amount realized of $200,000.

higher basis in exchange for a double loss deduction—once by X Corp. and once by B.

Section 336(d)(1) and (2) target that double-loss deduction, but so does § 362(e)(2). If § 362(e)(2) applies to the § 351 transaction in the example above, under the general rule of § 362(e)(2)(A),[18] X Corp. takes an $80,000 basis in the transferred asset and B takes a $220,000 basis in the X stock. Then, on the liquidation, X recognizes an overall $30,000 gain, while B recognizes a $20,000 loss. If X Corp. and B instead make the election provided in § 362(e)(2)(C), X Corp. takes a $130,000 basis in the transferred asset and B takes a $170,000 basis in the X stock. Then, on the liquidation (assuming that § 336(d)(1) and (2) do not apply), X recognizes an overall $20,000 loss, while B recognizes a $30,000 gain. Thus, in either case, § 362(e)(2) eliminates the double loss, preserving the loss either at the shareholder or corporate level, but not both.

Despite § 362(e)(2), § 336(d)(1) and (2) remain in the Code and may apply to the example above. Under § 336(d)(1), the liquidating corporation cannot recognize a loss on a distribution to a "related person" if the distribution is not pro rata or if the distributed property is "disqualified property." A "related person" is defined by reference to § 267.[19] Under § 336(d)(1)(B), "disqualified property" is property acquired by the liquidating corporation in a transaction to which § 351 applied (or as a capital contribution) within five years of the distribution date.

Stated differently, § 336(d)(1) applies if (i) the liquidating corporation and a distributee shareholder are related persons, (ii) the liquidating corporation distributes loss property to the shareholder, and (iii) the loss property is disqualified property or it is not distributed pro rata among the shareholders. If § 336(d)(1) applies, the liquidating corporation does not recognize loss on its distribution of the loss property to the related person.[20] For example, assume that

---

[18] Under the general rule of § 362(e)(2), a corporate transferee cannot take an aggregate basis in property contributed by a transferor in excess of the property's aggregate fair market value. The transferor's basis equals the amount determined under § 358. Instead of applying that general rule, the transferor and corporate transferee may together elect to have the corporate transferee determine its basis in the transferred property under § 362(a), while the transferor reduces his basis in the corporate transferee's stock received in the exchange. § 362(e)(2)(C)(i). The effect of § 362(e)(2) is to preserve the aggregate built-in loss at the shareholder or corporate level, but not at both. See section 2.05(b) *supra* for a fuller discussion of § 362(e)(2).

[19] Accordingly, a liquidating distribution of loss property to a shareholder who directly or indirectly owns more than 50 percent of the liquidating corporation's stock would fall under this loss prevention rule.

[20] Section § 267 addresses the same problem and Congress may have opted to treat a liquidating distribution as if the property had been sold to

X Corp. liquidates, making a non-pro rata distribution of loss property to B, who is a related person. Under § 336(d)(1), X Corp. would not recognize its loss on the distribution of the loss property to B. However, B should be entitled to recognize any loss on the liquidation under § 331 and § 1001.

Note that the "disqualified property" rule, like § 362(e)(2), is an "anti-stuffing" provision that targets the creation of duplicate loss at the shareholder and corporate levels. However, the two rules may operate in concert to reach an untoward (and likely unintended) result. Consider again the example above where B contributes property with a $50,000 built-in loss to X Corp. Also assume that B and X Corp. are related, they make the § 362(e)(2)(C) election, and the contributed loss asset is disqualified property. Then, § 336(d)(1) literally applies to X Corp. when it distributes the loss asset in liquidation. If it applies, X Corp. does not recognize its $50,000 loss on the asset, so that both B and X Corp. recognize an overall $30,000 gain on the liquidation. Thus, § 336(d)(1) and § 362(e)(2) may operate in tandem to eliminate not only the duplicate loss but any loss associated with the loss asset.

Notice as well that even if the property declines in value while held by the liquidating corporation, no loss is permitted. Suppose B owns all the stock of X Corp. In year 4, B contributes to X Corp. additional property with a $20,000 basis and a $60,000 fair market value. In year 7, B decides to liquidate X Corp. At the time of the liquidating distribution, the property still has a $20,000 basis, but it has declined in value to $5,000. Section 336(d)(1)(B) appears to preclude X Corp. from recognizing any loss under § 336(a). Perhaps future regulations will soften the provisions in obvious non-abuse cases and will better coordinate § 362(e)(2) and § 336(d).

---

the shareholders and allow § 267 to operate where it will. To employ this solution, Congress would need to modify the second sentence of § 267(a)(1) so that § 267(a)(1) applies to the liquidating corporation. Currently, that sentence specifically denies the application of § 267(a)(1) to the liquidating corporation (and distributee) in a liquidation context. In the example above, if § 267 applied to the liquidating corporation (but not the distributee), it would deny the loss to the liquidating corporation on the deemed sale under § 336(a) since B is a related party under § 267(b)(2).

Congress may have chosen to add § 336(d)(1), rather than amend § 267, because the loss disallowance rule of § 267(a)(1) does not apply in one critical case—when the liquidating corporation and shareholder are members of a controlled group. See § 267(f). Instead of the loss being disallowed, it is deferred, taken into account under the principles of the consolidated return regulations (*e.g.*, immediately before the shareholder leaves the controlled group). See § 267(f)(2); Regs. § 1.267(f)-1(c)(1) (applying the principles of the matching and acceleration rules for intercompany transactions under Regs. § 1.1502-13).

Section 336(d)(1)(B) also applies if the basis of property is determined by reference to the basis of property acquired in the described transaction. Thus, if a liquidating corporation acquires property in a § 351 transaction three years before a liquidation, it cannot avoid the impact of § 336(d)(1)(B) by exchanging the acquired property for like-kind property under § 1031 sometime later but before the liquidation, because the basis of property acquired in a § 1031 transaction is determined by looking to the basis of the property exchanged. § 1031(d).

Suppose that a controlling shareholder of X Corp. transfers property to Y Corp., a newly formed corporation, in a transaction that qualifies under § 351. Two years after the transfer, Y Corp. is merged tax-free into X Corp. in a transaction described in § 368(a)(1)(A).[21] One year later, X Corp. liquidates. Does § 336(d)(1)(B) apply? Note that X Corp. did not acquire property under § 351 nor did it acquire property whose basis is determined by reference to property acquired by the liquidating corporation in a § 351 transaction.

Could § 336(d)(1) be avoided through with proper planning? First consider the application of the "non-pro rata" rule (§ 336(d)(1)(A)(i)), under which a liquidating corporation cannot recognize a loss on a non-pro rata distribution of property to a related party.

Suppose, that X Corp. has two shareholders B, a 75-percent shareholder (and therefore a related person) and C, a 25-percent shareholder. It also has two assets, $4,000 cash and a loss asset with a $40,000 basis and $12,000 value. If X Corp. liquidates, distributing the loss asset to B and the cash to C, it cannot recognize its $28,000 loss on the loss asset, because it makes a non-pro rata distribution of the asset to B, a related person.

Suppose instead that X Corp. makes pro rata distributions of the assets to B and C, distributing $3,000 and a three-quarter's interest in the loss asset to B and $1,000 and a one-quarter interest in that asset to C. Assuming that the loss asset is not disqualified property, X Corp. would be able to deduct the $28,000 loss on the liquidation.[22]

Now suppose that following the pro rata distribution B agrees to purchase C's interest in the loss asset for $3,000. If C sells his

---

[21] See Chapter 10 *infra.*

[22] Note that whether the distribution is non pro rata or pro rata will have no effect on the taxation of the shareholders. Either way, B will have an amount realized of $12,000 while C's amount realized is $4,000.

one-quarter interest for $3,000, C recognizes no gain or loss, since C took a fair market value ($3,000) basis in the asset upon liquidation under § 334(a). B would use the cash received on the liquidation to make the purchase. After the liquidation and purchase, B would hold the former loss property with a $12,000 basis, and C would hold $4,000 of cash. The only difference between this pattern of a pro rata liquidation followed by a sale and non pro rata liquidation is that if the liquidation and sale are respected for tax purposes, X Corp. will be allowed a loss on the distribution. Otherwise that loss is precluded.

Whether the transactions will be respected would turn on the particular circumstances surrounding the transactions. If there was a preconceived and binding plan for B to purchase C's one-quarter interest in after the transaction, then the Service will successfully recharacterize the liquidation as a non pro rata distribution. On the other hand, if C was under no obligation to sell that interest to B following the liquidation, the transactions should probably stand for tax purposes.[23]

Could a liquidating corporation avoid § 336(d)(1) by selling its loss property before the liquidation and thereby ensure recognition of the loss? As might be expected, this route is sometimes discovered only after a liquidation has been set in motion. For example, a shareholder, in anticipation of the liquidation, may agree to sell the distributed property once the liquidation is completed. However, upon realizing that the distributed property has a loss in the hands of the distributing corporation that will be eliminated by operation of § 336(d)(1), the sale may be restructured as a sale by the corporation with the sale proceeds distributed to the shareholder. Will a last-minute conversion of a liquidation-followed-by-sale into a sale-followed-by-liquidation be respected?

This issue implicates the Court Holding doctrine, named after *Commissioner v. Court Holding Co.*[24] In *Court Holding Co.*, the taxpayer's only asset was an apartment building. All the stock of the corporation was owned by Minnie Miller and her husband. The corporation negotiated to sell the apartment to the lessees of the property, reaching an oral agreement as to the terms and conditions of sale. When the parties met to reduce the terms to writing, the corporation's attorney informed the purchaser that the sale could not be consummated because a large tax would be imposed on the seller. The next day, the corporation liquidated with the Millers surrendering their stock for the deed to the building. Three days

---

[23] See, e.g., *American Bantam Car Co. v. Commissioner,* 11 T.C. 397 (1948), aff'd per curiam, 177 F.2d 513 (3d Cir.1949).

[24] 324 U.S. 331 (1945).

later, the sale was completed as previously agreed, but this time with the Millers selling the property. Under the law then in effect (that is, before the repeal of the *General Utilities* doctrine), this reordering, if respected, eliminated the corporate-level tax.

The Tax Court ruled that the sale had to be attributed to the corporation with the result that the corporation had a gain on the sale and the Millers were taxed on the liquidation in accordance with the rules of § 331 and § 1001. While the Court of Appeals reversed, the Supreme Court supported the Tax Court, holding that the steps of the transaction must be viewed as a whole and that the Millers could not serve as a conduit for a sale by the corporation.

On the other hand, in *United States v. Cumberland Public Service*,[25] the Supreme Court refused to recharacterize a transaction. There, shareholders first attempted to sell their stock, but the buyer refused to purchase it.[26] However, the buyer and the shareholders agreed that following the liquidation of the corporation, the shareholders would sell the assets to the purchaser. The Supreme Court upheld the lower court's factual finding that the sale of assets was made by the shareholders. Compared with *Court Holding Co.*, in *Cumberland Public Service* the plan for liquidation was adopted earlier in the negotiating process and the sale was not negotiated on behalf of the corporation.

The results in *Court Holding Co.* and *Cumberland Public Service* put a premium on good tax advice, since choosing the wrong form of the transaction could be costly. And while the *Court Holding* doctrine no longer arises in the specific context at issue in these two cases, the more general characterization issue and its resolution remain mainstays of corporate taxation. Thus, if a liquidating corporation distributes loss property described in § 336(d)(1), the loss is gone forever. But if that same property is sold by the corporation before the liquidation, the loss will be recognized (unless another disallowance rule applies). How far along can a liquidation be before it is too late to negotiate a sale of the corporation's loss assets? For such a fact-specific inquiry, no clear line can be drawn.

Another loss disallowance rule that applies in connection with a liquidation is § 336(d)(2). This rule does not focus on the relationship between the liquidating corporation and its shareholders. Instead the rule can apply to liquidating distributions to any shareholders (related or not) and to sales in connection with

---

[25] 338 U.S. 451 (1950).

[26] Perhaps the buyer did not want to assume any undisclosed liabilities.

a liquidation if the distributed or sold property was acquired by the corporation for the purpose of recognizing loss.

Like § 336(d)(1), § 336(d)(2) restricts a liquidating corporation's loss and is also an "anti-stuffing" rule aimed at preventing double deductions. The rule is triggered by a distribution, *sale, or exchange* of property that had been acquired in a § 351 transaction (or as a contribution to capital) if the following additional condition is met: The property's acquisition was "part of a plan a principal purpose of which was to recognize loss by the liquidating corporation with respect to such property in connection with the liquidation."[27] Property acquired by the liquidating corporation "after the date two years before the date a corporation adopts a plan of liquidation" is presumed to have been acquired with that principal purpose. § 336(d)(2)(B)(ii).[28]

Suppose the § 351 transaction occurs six months before a plan of liquidation is adopted, but the acquisition was not motivated by a loss recognition purpose. For example, a shareholder might contribute loss property that the liquidating corporation will use in its trade or business. Under these circumstances, the Secretary is given authority to enact regulations that will exempt this and other non-abuse transfers occurring within the 2–year period. Although no regulations have been published to date, the legislative history suggests that regulations should exempt non-abuse transfers occurring within the two-year period. It gives as examples of non-abuse transfers contributions of property to be used in the corporation's trade or business or contributions of property during the first two years of a corporation's existence

---

[27] Section 336(d)(2)(B)(i). Note again that § 336(d)(2) applies to a sale or exchange. Thus, a liquidating corporation's loss on its sale of a loss asset in connection with its liquidation may be disallowed in two ways. First, it may be directly disallowed under § 336(d)(2). Second, the sale by the loss corporation and its distribution of the sales proceeds to its shareholders may be recharacterized under the *Court Holding* doctrine as a distribution of the asset to the shareholders and their sale of that asset. Under the recharacterization, the liquidating corporation's loss on the distribution may be disallowed under § 336(d)(1).

[28] Note that the two-year rule of § 336(d)(2)(B) looks to the date of adoption of a plan of liquidation, not the date of the liquidating distribution like the five-year rule of § 336(d)(1)(B). Thus, if a corporation acquires property and then adopts a plan of liquidation within two years, the acquisition is considered to be part of a plan to recognize a loss even if the actual liquidation takes place more than two years after acquiring the property. For example, if property is acquired by X Corp. on January 1 of Year 1, X Corp. adopts a plan of liquidation on December 31 of Year 2, and X Corp. liquidates on July 15 of Year 3, § 336(d)(2) may apply even though more than two years elapsed between the acquisition of the property and the actual distribution.

Suppose, however, that the § 351 exchange occurs more than two years before a plan of liquidation is adopted but it has a loss-recognition motive. The conference report states that "[the provision disallowing a loss] will apply only in the most rare and unusual cases under such circumstances."[29]

If § 336(d)(2) applies, the liquidating corporation is not automatically denied the entire loss deduction relating to offending property. Instead, for purposes of determining loss, the basis of the property is decreased by the excess of the asset's basis on the date of contribution over its fair market value at that time.[30] Suppose that one year prior to adoption of a plan of liquidation, X Corp. acquires, in a § 351 transaction, property that has a $40,000 basis and $25,000 fair market value. The property continues to decline in value, and on the date of the liquidating distribution it has a fair market value of just $18,000. Section 336(d)(2) will not prevent X Corp. from recognizing a loss of $7,000—the decline that occurred while X Corp. held the property.

It is interesting to note that in § 336(d)(2)(A) Congress evidences the ability to draft a provision that precludes a liquidating corporation from deducting pre-incorporation losses. One must ask why Congress didn't draft § 336(d)(1) and § 311, the later dealing with nonliquidating distributions, to preclude recognition only of pre-incorporation gains that are unrealized when the corporation acquires the property.

As a final note, Congress is concerned not only with duplicate loss but also with the avoidance of corporate-level gain. Because that avoidance may circumvent the repeal of the General Utilities doctrine, Congress authorized Treasury to issue regulations where necessary.[31] For example, suppose that a corporation qualified to become a real estate investment trust (a REIT)[32] in what would normally be a nontaxable event. After

---

[29] H.R. Rep. No. 841, 99th Cong., 2d Sess. (1986).

[30] § 336(d)(2)(A). As a result, this loss disallowance rule should now play a minor role since § 362(e)(2) now generally precludes using a § 351 transaction to create a corporate built-in loss. Section 336(d)(2) may still apply in limited circumstances, because § 362(e)(2) may still allow a corporation to take a basis in a contributed asset greater than its value. First, the general rule of § 362(e)(2) only requires that the aggregate basis of assets contributed by a shareholder equal their aggregate value. Thus, some contributed assets may have built-in gain, while others have built-in loss. Second, if the election is made under § 362(e)(2)(C), the transferee corporation will acquire built-in loss assets. In either case, § 336(d)(2) may then apply to the contributed built-in loss assets.

[31] Section 337(d).

[32] A REIT is a special kind of corporation that has a variety of requirements, including the type of property held (generally real estate).

becoming a REIT, the corporation could sell appreciated assets and distribute the proceeds with only a tax at the shareholder level.[33] Pursuant to § 337(d), regulations have been issued to prevent the elimination of a corporate-level gain on the appreciated property.[34] In this case, the corporation would be deemed to sell the asset, resulting in gain to the corporation and a stepped-up basis in the hands of the REIT.[35]

(c) The Corporate Triple Tax.

While our corporate tax system generally seeks to tax corporate earnings twice—once when earned and once when distributed. Congress has taken steps to minimize the imposition of triple, quadruple or more taxes on corporate earnings: Section 243 was enacted to provide a dividends received deduction for dividends received by a corporation.[36]

However, the repeal of the *General Utilities* doctrine increased the potential for a corporate triple tax in the context of a liquidation. Suppose B owns all of the stock of X Corp., a holding company, whose only asset is all of the stock of Y Corp. C, an unrelated individual, wants to acquire all of Y Corp.'s assets. Assume that all of the stock and assets have appreciated in value. There are a variety of ways that the parties can complete the transaction. Suppose, improvidently, that C buys the Y Corp. stock from X Corp. and then both B and C liquidate their wholly owned corporations. C, who will take a cost basis in the purchased stock under § 1012, will realize and recognize no gain or loss on the liquidation of Y Corp., but Y Corp. will recognize gain under § 336. X Corp. already recognized gain on the sale of the Y Corp. stock to C. When B liquidates X Corp., B will recognize gain under § 331 and § 001.

The result is a triple tax on the unrealized gain inherent in Y Corp.'s assets. Y Corp. recognizes gain on its liquidation, X Corp., whose Y stock was appreciated because of the unrealized gain in the underlying Y assets, recognizes that gain on the stock sale to C, and B, whose X stock has appreciated to reflect the appreciated Y stock held by X Corp., recognizes gain on the liquidation of X Corp.

Suppose the transaction is structured in a different manner. Y Corp. sells its assets directly to C. Y Corp. and then X Corp. liquidate. On the asset sale, Y Corp. would recognize gain. When Y

---

[33] While generally treated as a corporation, a REIT can generally deduct dividends it pays, thereby functioning as a flow-through entity.

[34] Regs. §§ 1.337(d)–6 and –7.

[35] No recognition and no basis adjustment occurs for loss property—property the basis of which exceeds the fair market value.

[36] See discussion at Section 4.03 *supra.*

Corp. liquidates into its parent, X Corp., X Corp. would not recognize gain.[37] Finally, on the liquidation of X Corp., B would recognize gain. If the parties proceed in this manner, there will only be a double tax on the unrealized appreciation in Y Corp.'s assets—a tax to Y Corp. and a tax to B.

Regardless of which method is used, C ends up with the assets of Y Corp. with a fair market value basis[38] and B ends up with the sale proceeds. To allow the tax consequences to differ the form raises the transaction costs, since the parties must spend more on tax advice in order to insure that they have used the best form. Moreover, a triple tax would place a high cost on operating a business in corporate form.

Congress addressed the problem by enacting § 336(e) which authorizes the Treasury to promulgate regulations that will treat a sale of stock as if the underlying assets were sold.[39] In the example above, X Corp.'s gain on the sale of stock would be the difference between amount realized for the Y Corp. stock and the adjusted basis of the Y Corp. assets. The Y Corp. assets would then take a fair market value whether or not C liquidated Y Corp. No other gain or loss would be recognized on the sale of the Y Corp. stock by X Corp. B would recognize gain on the liquidation of X Corp. under §§ 331 and 1001. This treatment which reduces the triple tax to a double tax is available if a corporation meets substantial ownership tests under § 1504(a)(2).[40] Where the ownership tests are not met, it is likely that the Court Holding Co. doctrine may play a role in determining who sold what to whom and when. Where § 336(e) does not apply, the triple tax problem endures.[41]

8.03 Subsidiary Liquidations

(a) Shareholder Treatment.

Section 332 provides that a parent corporation recognizes no gain or loss when it liquidates a subsidiary. Congress decided in 1935 that taxing that liquidation was inappropriate because it resulted in a simplified corporate structure. Since the shareholder-parent corporation

---

[37] See the discussion of subsidiary liquidations that follows.

[38] A fair market value basis results under § 334(a) if the first method is used and under § 1012 if the assets are purchased directly.

[39] See Prop. Regs. § 1.336-1 through § 1.336-5 (which would implement § 336(e).

[40] Section 1504(a)(2) imposes two 80 percent tests—one for voting control and one for total value of outstanding stock.

[41] See also § 338 (for an election to treat certain stock purchases like asset purchases where the purchasers are corporations). Section 338 is discussed in Section 9.03 *infra*.

also recognizes no gain or loss on the liquidation, it would also be inappropriate to step up (or step down) the subsidiary's asset bases. Instead, the parent succeeds to the subsidiary's asset bases. § 334(b)(1). The parent also inherits the holding periods of the subsidiary's assets. § 1223(2). In effect for tax purposes, the parent steps into the shoes of the subsidiary.[42]

Viewed together, § 332 and § 334(b)(1) remove any unrealized gain or loss in the parent's stock from consideration for tax purposes. Consider the following two situations:

	Situation 1	Situation 2
Parent's stock basis	$15,000	$15,000
Subsidiary's asset basis	7,000	24,000
Value of subsidiary's asset	9,000	18,000

In each situation, the parent owns all subsidiary stock, the subsidiary has no liabilities, and the subsidiary liquidates in a liquidation to which § 332 applies.

In situation 1, the parent has a potential $6,000 loss in its subsidiary stock. However, the parent will not recognize that loss and will take a $7,000 basis in the former subsidiary asset. Thus, the parent's built-in loss in its subsidiary stock disappears, and if the parent later sells the asset for $9,000, it will recognize a $2,000 gain.

In situation 2, the parent has a potential $9,000 gain in its subsidiary stock. The parent will recognize no gain on the liquidation and will take a $24,000 basis in the former subsidiary asset. Thus, the parent's built-in gain in its subsidiary stock disappears, and if the parent later sells the asset for $18,000, it will recognize a $6,000 loss.

The American Law Institute has suggested a method to eliminate the discontinuities illustrated by situations 1 and 2.[43] When a parent-corporation forms a subsidiary under § 351, generally the basis of the subsidiary's stock in the hands of the parent is the same as the basis of the assets in the hand of the subsidiary. See § 358(a); § 362(a). But cf. § 362(e). Under the ALI proposal the parent's stock basis would be continuously adjusted to equal to the subsidiary's

---

[42] If, as part of the liquidation, the parent corporation receives property in satisfaction of a debt owed by the subsidiary to the parent, the parent will recognize gain or less, measured by the difference between its amount realized for the debt and its basis in the debt. Regs. § 1.332-7.

[43] American Law Institute, Federal Income Project—Subchapter C 60–61 (1982) (the "ALI proposal").

net asset basis (i.e., its gross asset basis less its liabilities). Accordingly the gain or loss on the sale or exchange of the stock in the subsidiary would always equal the gain or loss on the sale of the subsidiary assets. On the liquidation of a subsidiary, no gain or loss would be recognized by the parent which would then step into the subsidiary's shoes with respect to the basis in the subsidiary's assets. Unfortunately, nothing like this proposal has ever been enacted (or seriously considered) by Congress.[44]

If § 332 applies to a liquidation, the non-recognition offered by § 332 does not apply to every corporate shareholder, however. Instead, it applies only to the corporate shareholder meeting the ownership requirement of § 332(b). The tax consequences for every other shareholder are governed by § 331 and § 334(a).

For example, suppose that X Corp., owned by B and C Corp., has assets with a $60,000 basis and $100,000 fair market value. B, an individual, owns X stock with a $6,000 basis and $20,000 fair market value. C Corp. owns X stock with a $30,000 basis and $80,000 fair market value. Assume that X Corp. has only one class of stock. If X Corp. liquidates and makes a pro rata distribution, B recognizes a $14,000 capital gain under § 331 and § 1001 and takes a $20,000 fair market value basis in the assets received under § 334(a). If § 332 applied to C Corp., it recognizes no gain on the liquidation and takes a $48,000 carryover basis in distributed assets under § 334(b)(1).[45]

For § 332 to apply, ownership, distribution, and timing requirements must be met. More specifically—

> (i) A corporate shareholder (called the "parent") must own an affiliated interest in the liquidating corporation (the "subsidiary") at all times from adoption of the plan of liquidation until receipt of the final liquidating distribution.[46]

---

[44] To implement something like the ALI proposal, Congress would need to consider how to account for a subsidiary with minority shareholders, how to allocate basis among multiple classes of subsidiary stock, and how to account for a subsidiary with liabilities exceeding its aggregate asset basis. These issues, among others, make implementing such a proposal more complicated than it may appear at first blush. For an example of how similar issues have been addressed, consider Regs. § 1.1502-19 and Regs. § 1.1502-32, discussed in Section 11.07 *infra*.

[45] C Corp. receives 80 percent of X Corp.'s assets and 80 percent of X Corp.'s $60,000 basis in those assets.

[46] Section 332(b)(1). An affiliated interest is stock that comprises at least 80% of the total voting power of the corporation's stock and at least 80% of its total value. § 1504(a)(2). For this purpose, stock is disregarded if it is limited and preferred as to dividends, non-voting, and non-convertible and if it does not participate in corporate growth to any significant extent.

(ii) The liquidating distributions must be in complete cancellation or redemption of all subsidiary stock.[47]

(iii) The liquidating distributions must occur within one taxable year or by the end of the third taxable year that follows the taxable year in which the first liquidating distribution occurs.[48]

While § 332, in form, is a mandatory provision, the ownership test may offer a *de facto* means to escape (or fall into) the provision's coverage, if desired. If a corporate parent's stock basis in a subsidiary exceeds the stock's fair market value, the parent may prefer immediate loss recognition available under § 331 and § 1001 to nonrecognition under § 332. In some circumstances, the parent may be able to sell enough stock to fall under one of the 80-percent ownership thresholds. Since § 332 does not invoke the attribution rules, the purchaser can even be a related party, so long as the price paid reflects fair market value. Since there is no intent test, a motive to avoid the coverage of § 332 should not defeat this effort.[49] Conversely, a parent corporation that fails to meet the ownership test may avail itself of § 332 by acquiring sufficient stock before the plan of liquidation is adopted.[50] It is less certain, however, whether the parent can meet the 80-percent ownership thresholds by having the subsidiary redeem stock of minority shareholders, particularly

---

§ 1504(a)(4) (adding that the stock must not have redemption or liquidation rights in excess of issue price, except for a reasonable redemption or liquidation premium).

Note that the Code refers to the parent variously as the "corporate distributee" (§ 334(b)(2)) and the "80-percent distributee" (§ 337(c)).

[47] Section 332(b)(2) and (3). In other words, for a liquidation to be described in § 332, the subsidiary must make a distribution on *each* of its shares. Thus, an insolvent subsidiary cannot liquidate under § 332, because its shareholders would receive no amount for their subsidiary stock. Further, if a liquidating subsidiary has both common and preferred stock outstanding but, because of insufficient assets, makes a distribution only on its preferred stock, § 332 cannot apply to the liquidation. *Commissioner v. Spaulding Bakeries, Inc.*, 252 F.2d 693 (2d Cir. 1958). Note, however, that the "Spaulding Bakeries" type of liquidation may qualify as a tax-free reorganization under § 368(a)(1)(A) or (C). See Chapter 10 *infra*.

[48] Section 332(b)(2) and (3). Generally if there is a shareholders' resolution authorizing a liquidation that does not specify a time period, the liquidating distribution must be completed within the taxable year. With a "three-year" liquidation, the plan of liquidation must state that it will be completed within that period and the parent may have to post a bond to assure completion. *See* § 1.332-4(a)(3).

[49] See, e.g., *Granite Trust Co. v. United* States, 238 F.2d 670 (1st Cir. 1956); *Commissioner v. Day & Zimmermann, Inc.*, 151 F.2d 517 (3d Cir.1945). But see *Associated Wholesale Grocers, Inc. v. United States*, 927 F.2d 1517 (10th Cir.1991) (transaction structured to avoid § 332 recharacterized as § 332 liquidation).

[50] Rev. Rul. 75-521, 1975-2 C.B. 120.

if the redemption anticipates the adoption of a formal plan of liquidation.[51]

(b) Treatment of the Subsidiary.

The tax-free contraction of a parent-subsidiary structure would be thwarted if the liquidating subsidiary's gain (or loss) were recognized under § 336. Thus, as a companion to § 332, § 337 generally provides that the subsidiary recognizes no gain or loss on a distribution to the parent (*i.e.*, the corporate shareholder meeting the ownership test of § 332(b)(1)).

The combination of §§ 337, 332 and 334(b)(1) means that the unrealized gain (or loss) in the subsidiary assets will be preserved when the assets are received by the parent. Suppose Y Corp. is wholly owned by X Corp. Y Corp. holds assets with a $10,000 basis and $16,000 fair market value. X Corp. has a $7,000 basis in its Y Corp. stock. If Y Corp. is liquidated, neither X Corp. nor Y Corp. recognizes gain, and X Corp. holds the Y Corp. assets with a basis of $10,000. If and when X Corp. sells or distributes the property the $6,000 unrealized gain may be recognized.

Where the parent is tax-exempt, nonrecognition under § 337 could be the equivalent of a permanent exclusion. For that reason, § 337(b)(2)(A) contains an exception to the general nonrecognition of § 337(a).[52] Similarly, if the parent is a foreign corporation beyond the jurisdiction of the federal tax system, the liquidating subsidiary will be taxed on the distribution of its appreciated assets that are being removed from U.S. taxing jurisdiction.[53] Conversely, if a U.S. parent liquidates a foreign subsidiary, the U.S. parent is subject to tax on the foreign subsidiary's earnings and profits.[54] Otherwise, the earnings and profits might never be subject to U.S. taxation at the corporate level. Note that this treatment applies if the foreign

---

[51] Compare *George L. Riggs, Inc. v. Commissioner*, 64 T.C. 474 (1975) (looking to the adoption of a formal plan of liquidation in applying the ownership test and treating a redemption as a pre-liquidation event, when the redemption occurred before a formal plan was adopted) with Rev. Rul. 70-106, 1970-1 C.B. 70 (concluding on indistinguishable facts that an informal plan of liquidation had been adopted before the redemption occurred, so that the ownership test was not met).

[52] If the property distributed will be used in an unrelated trade or business of the tax-exempt organization, there is an exception to the exception. Unrealized appreciation will not be recognized by the liquidating corporation since the parent corporation will be taxed on a sale of the property. §§ 511 and 512.

[53] § 367(e)(2).

[54] § 367(b). Note that the liquidation of a foreign subsidiary by a U.S. parent cannot be used to import loss property into the U.S. because the parent will take a fair market value basis in such loss property under § 334(b)(1)(B).

subsidiary makes a check-the-box election to be treated as a disregarded entity.

If a liquidating subsidiary is owned by both a parent and minority shareholders, the tax consequences to the subsidiary will be determined under both § 337 and § 336. Suppose Y Corp.'s sole class of stock is 80 percent owned by X Corp. and 20 percent owned by B, an individual. Suppose that Y Corp. owns assets, some with unrealized gain and some with unrealized losses. If Y Corp. liquidates, it will not recognize gain or loss on the distribution to X Corp. What about its distribution to B? Curiously, while § 336 applies to the portion of the liquidating distribution made to B, it does not apply entirely. Under § 336(d)(3), Y Corp. cannot recognize any loss on the distribution of loss property to B.

Perhaps Congress worried (if Congress worries) that a liquidating corporation would take advantage of § 336 and § 337 by distributing a disproportionate amount of the loss property to shareholders other than the parent while distributing a disproportionate amount of gain property to the parent. Such manipulation would allow the liquidating corporation to recognize loss while avoiding the recognition of gain. It is not clear that this result is inappropriate manipulation if in fact only the loss property is removed from corporate solution. Moreover, § 336(d)(3) denies a loss to the liquidating corporation even in the event of a pro rata distribution where there is no manipulation.

More likely, Congress elected to treat the distribution to the minority shareholder as a non-liquidating distribution viewed at the corporate level. Recall that § 311 denies a loss deduction to the distributing corporation for a distribution of loss property. Because nonrecognition in the context of a parent-subsidiary liquidation is justified by the continuation of the subsidiary's business in a simplified corporate structure, it may make sense to treat the distribution to non-corporate shareholders as non-liquidating distributions incidental to, and a part of, the larger non-liquidating distribution—in effect, the distribution to the minority shareholder is treated as a distribution in redemption under § 311.

One final aspect of § 337 deserves comment. Normally when a taxpayer transfers appreciated property in satisfaction of a debt, gain (or loss) is recognized.[55] However where the transfer occurs in connection with a subsidiary liquidation and the parent is the creditor, it is often difficult to trace whether appreciated property is transferred to a parent to extinguish its debt or in liquidation of its subsidiary stock. As a result, § 337(b)(1) provides for the subsidi-

---

[55] See, e.g., *United States v. Davis,* 370 U.S. 65 (1962).

ary's nonrecognition of gain or loss on its transfer of property to extinguish a debt in connection with the liquidation. Under § 334(b)(2), the parent takes the subsidiary's basis in the transferred asset.

What if the indebtedness of the subsidiary exceeds the value of the subsidiary's assets; that is, what if the subsidiary is insolvent at the time of the liquidation? Regulations have long provided that in such circumstances § 332 does not apply to the transaction (and so § 337 does not apply as well) because there is no "property distributed in complete liquidation" within the meaning of § 332(a).[56] As a result, the transaction is fully taxable to both parties (with the parent corporation generally entitled to a worthless security deduction under § 165(g)).[57] If the parent wishes to make the transaction tax-free, can it contribute assets immediately prior to the liquidation of the subsidiary so that the subsidiary is then solvent? Under familiar step-transactions principles, such a pre-liquidation infusion of value will be ignored.[58]

(c) Carryover of Tax Attributes.

When a parent liquidates a subsidiary, nonrecognition may be deemed appropriate because the corporate structure is being simplified. Generally, the tax system is indifferent as to whether a corporation conducts a business directly or through a subsidiary. The price paid for nonrecognition on a liquidation is the carryover of the subsidiary's basis in its assets under § 334(b). Consistent with this treatment, § 381(a) provides that the subsidiary's tax attributes also flow to the parent. Those tax attributes include net operating losses, the earnings and profits account, and capital loss carryovers. § 381(b).

However, any time that one taxpayer acquires tax attributes of another taxpayer, the transaction will be closely scrutinized. In general, the Code frowns on trafficking in tax attributes where the transaction is not motivated by non-tax, business reasons. Sections 269 and 382 serve as a check on the carryover of tax attributes under § 381.[59]

---

[56] Regs. § 1.332-2(b).

[57] Rev. Rul. 2003-125, 2003-2 C.B. 1243.

[58] Rev. Rul. 68-602, 1968-2 C.B. 135.

[59] See Chapter 11 *infra*.

Chapter 9

TAXABLE ACQUISITIONS

Suppose that X Corp. holds non-cash assets with a $150,000 basis and $450,000 fair market value, along with $105,000 in cash. X Corp. is wholly owned by S, an individual, who has a $200,000 basis in the X stock. B wants to buy the X Corp. stock or assets for cash. Assume that the X assets constitute a trade or business. The acquisition could be structured as follows:

(1) As an asset purchase, where—

(a) X Corp. sells its assets, remains in existence, and reinvests the net sales proceeds,

(b) X Corp. sells its assets to B and then liquidates, or

(c) X Corp. liquidates and S sells the former X assets to B;

(2) As a stock purchase, where S sells the X stock to B and either B—

(a) liquidates X Corp. and operates the X business directly, or

(b) continues to operate the X business through X Corp.[1]

Each of these transactions is taxable. For example, if B buys the X assets from X Corp., X Corp. will recognize gain or loss on the sale of its assets. § 1001. B's bases in the X assets will be determined under § 1060.[2] If X then liquidates, S will recognize gain or loss under § 331 and § 1001. Further, none of X's tax attributes

---

[1] B could also use an acquisition vehicle to acquire the X stock or assets. For example, B could form a new entity (*e.g.*, a corporation or limited liability company) and X Corp. could merge into that entity. For federal income tax purposes, the merger should be treated as if the following two steps occurred: First, X Corp. transferred its assets to the entity in exchange the cash received by S and the assumption of its liabilities. Second, X Corp. liquidated, distributing the cash to S. See Rev. Rul. 69-6, 1969-1 C.B. 104.

[2] If X Corp. merges into a newly formed entity, the results depend on whether, for federal income tax purposes, the entity is treated as a corporation or disregarded entity. If it is disregarded, B will be treated as if B acquired the X assets directly, with the results noted in the text. If the entity is treated as a corporation, that corporation will be treated as acquiring the X assets and take a basis in the assets determined under § 1060.

(*e.g.*, its net operating loss carryovers or earnings and profits account) will survive the transaction.

If, instead, X Corp. liquidates and S then sells the former X assets to B, both X Corp. and S will recognize gain or loss on the liquidation. § 331(a); § 336(a). None of X's tax attributes (*e.g.*, its net operating loss carryovers or earnings and profits account) will survive the liquidation. S will take a fair market value basis in the former X assets (§ 334(a)), and therefore will recognize no gain or loss on his sale of those assets to B. B's bases in those assets will be determined under § 1060.

If B acquires or is treated as acquiring X stock for cash, S will recognize gain or loss, measured by the difference between the cash received and his X stock basis. § 1001. B will take a cost basis in the X stock acquired. § 1012. Unless a § 338 election is made for the stock purchase, X Corp. will recognize no gain or loss when its stock is acquired and will retain its historic tax attributes (including historic asset bases).[3]

A § 338 election can be made only if B is a corporation and acquires the X stock in a qualified stock purchase. If a § 338 election is made for a stock purchase, that purchase is treated in certain ways as an asset purchase. In this case if the election is made, X Corp. will be deemed to sell its assets, but S will be treated as selling his S stock.[4]

Assuming that B and S are economically rational and sophisticated with equal bargaining positions, they should price and structure the X acquisition to maximize S's after-tax consideration and minimize B's cost. They would consider the present and future expenses relating to each structure, including tax costs. Would it not then make sense to try to structure the transaction to avoid all tax costs?

---

[3] If X Corp. then liquidates, the tax consequences depend on whether or not B is a corporation. If it is and the liquidation qualifies under § 332, neither X Corp. nor B will recognize gain or loss, B will take a transferred basis in the X assets, and important X attributes will flow to S. § 332(a); § 334(a); § 337(a); § 381. If the liquidation does not qualify under § 332, X Corp. and B will recognize gain or loss on the liquidation, the X tax attributes will not survive, and B will take fair market value bases in the X assets. § 331(a); § 334(a); § 337(a).

[4] If S were a corporation, S could join with B to make a special election under § 338(h)(10). Under that election, X Corp. would still be treated as selling its assets but S would be treated as receiving the sales proceeds in liquidation of X Corp. § 338(h)(10); § 1.338(h)(10)-1(c); *id.* at (d)(4). If the liquidation qualified under § 332, S would recognize no gain or loss on its deemed receipt of liquidation proceeds and will succeed to important X tax attributes. § 332(a); § 381.

Tax costs may be avoided (or, more precisely, deferred) in their entirety if the transaction is structured as a nontaxable reorganization. (Those reorganizations are discussed in Chapter 10.) For example, if B is a corporation, B may be able to acquire the stock or assets of X Corp. without B, S, or X Corp. recognizing gain or loss. Given nontaxable alternatives, why would taxpayers ever choose a taxable structure? There are several possible reasons. First, to qualify for a nontaxable reorganization, a transaction must meet stringent requirements. Often, a those requirements cannot be met or can be met only at an unacceptable cost. Second, a taxable transaction may, in fact, be cheaper than a nontaxable one. In a taxable transaction, gain *or loss* may be recognized, and if the transaction produces loss, it may also produce a tax benefit (a tax reduction or refund). That benefit may make the taxable (or, more precisely, recognition) alternative the preferable choice.

9.01 Asset Purchases

Consider again the example that began this chapter. If B buys the non-cash assets from X Corp. for $450,000, X Corp. recognizes a $300,000 gain on the sale. If X Corp. is taxed at a 35-percent rate, the tax is $105,000, which X Corp. pays with its available cash. When X Corp. liquidates, S is taxed on $250,000 of gain under § 331 and § 1001. If S if taxed at a 20-percent rate, S pays a $50,000 tax and ends up with $400,000. B takes a cost basis in the assets of $450,000. § 1012.[5] The same treatment occurs if X Corp. merges into B Corp. with the X Corp. shareholder (B) receiving cash—a taxable merger.

Instead of selling its assets, if X Corp. liquidates and S sells the assets to B, the tax consequences would be the same as in the previous example. On liquidation, X Corp. would recognize a gain of $300,000 under § 336, using the cash to discharge the tax liability. S would be taxed on $250,000 of gain—the difference between the 450,000 fair market value of the X Corp. assets and S's $200,000 basis in the X Corp. stock. Under § 334(a), S would take a fair mar-

---

[5] Suppose that X Corp. had sold its assets to B on the installment method. Upon liquidation X Corp. would have to recognize all deferred gain. § 453B(a). Further, S generally would have to immediately take into account the fair market value of the note in determining his gain or loss and would have a basis in the note equal to its fair market value. However, if the installment obligation arose from a sale or exchange of the X assets after the adoption of the plan of liquidation and the liquidation was completed within 12 months, S could take his gain on the installment note into account as the note was paid. §453(h)(1)(A). See also *id.* at (h)(1)(B) (providing that if the installment obligation arose from the sale of inventory, installment reporting is available to shareholders only if substantially all the inventory was sold in bulk to a single purchaser); *id.* at (g) (providing that installment reporting is not available for sales of depreciable property between related persons).

ket value basis in X Corp.'s assets, and upon sale to B, S would recognize no gain or loss. B would take a cost basis in the former X assets.

In both patterns there are two levels of taxation—a corporate-level tax on X Corp. and a shareholder-level tax on S. Further, B takes a fair market value basis in the acquired assets. As explained below, the stock sale may avoid a corporate-level tax, but that avoidance comes at a "cost"—X Corp. retains its historic asset bases.

In the asset sale, both the seller and buyer have an interest in how the purchase price is allocated among the various assets sold. For the seller, the amount of gain or loss and its character as ordinary or capital are determined asset-by-asset.[6] For the buyer, the allocation of the purchase price determines the basis of each acquired asset, including inventory, goodwill, each depreciable asset, and each non-depreciable asset.

Historically, the parties to a sale often had adverse interests in allocating the purchase price among assets. Sellers wanted to allocate as much of the purchase price as possible to assets yielding tax-favored capital gain, such as land and goodwill. In contrast, buyers benefitted from allocating as much as possible to inventory, depreciable property (e.g., buildings, equipment) and amortizable intangibles (e.g., a covenant not to compete), because that allocation reduced the net ordinary income that the buyer would recognize in the future. Because of these adverse interests, the Service typically respected negotiated purchase agreements that specifically allocated the purchase price to each asset sold. Both buyer and seller were bound by the agreement unless mistake, undue influence, fraud or distress were shown.[7]

However, agreements often contain no specific allocation of purchase price. In these situations, the seller and buyer historically have often taken inconsistent positions, whipsawing the government. For example, a buyer may try to allocate a portion of the purchase price to a covenant not to compete which was amortizable over the life of the covenant (but produced ordinary income to the seller) while the seller would try to allocate that portion of the purchase price to goodwill, which resulted in capital gain to the seller (but historically was not amortizable by the buyer). Also, if there was no, or little, differential between the rate of tax on capital gain and ordinary income or if the seller was tax-indifferent (*e.g.*, because of significant loss carryovers), the buyer and seller may not

---

[6] Williams v. McGowan, 152 F.2d 570 (2d. Cir. 1945).

[7] See, e.g., *Commissioner v. Danielson*, 378 F.2d 771 (3d Cir.1967).

have adverse interests, and the seller might accede to the buyer's favorable allocation scheme, to the detriment of the fisc.

Those concerns were addressed by § 1060, which requires a specific method of allocation to be followed by both the seller and buyer for any "applicable asset acquisition." An "applicable asset acquisition" is any transfer (direct or indirect) of assets that constitute a trade or business and with respect to which the transferee's basis in the purchased assets is determined wholly by the consideration paid for the assets (i.e., cost basis). § 1060(c). Assets constitute a trade or business if, among other things, goodwill or going concern value could attach to the assets under any circumstances. Regs. § 1.1060-1(b)(2)(i)(B).

Under the regulations, the purchase price is allocated among the transferred assets using a residual, seven-tier allocation method described in Regs §1.338-6(b). See Regs. §1.1060-1 (cross-referencing Regs. § 1.338-6). The consideration is first reduced by the amount of Class I assets. The remainder is then allocated, in order, among Class II assets, then Class III assets, then Class IV assets, then Class V assets, and then Class VI assets, to the extent of, and in proportion to, the fair market value of the assets in each class. Any residual is allocated to Class VII assets.[8]

The seven classes of assets are as follows: Class I comprises cash, bank deposits, and similar assets. Class II covers certificates of deposits, U.S. government securities, and readily marketable stock or securities. Class III includes accounts receivable, mortgages, and credit card receivables which arise in the ordinary course of business. Class IV applies to stock in trade or inventory of a taxpayer. Class VI assets include all § 197 intangibles except goodwill and going concern value, which make up Class VII. Class V is reserved for all other assets.

Some of the allocation disputes under § 1060 may be lessened by the enactment of § 197. Generally, § 197 requires 15–year, straight-line amortization for all purchased intangibles. Among the assets covered by § 197 are: goodwill and going concern value; workforce in place; customer lists and other customer-based intangibles; favorable contracts with suppliers and other supplier-based intangibles; business books and records and any other information base; patents, copyrights, formulas, processes, know-how, designs and similar items; computer software; franchises, trademarks and trade

---

[8] Thus, if the consideration to be allocated exceeds the aggregate value of all assets other than Class VII assets, each asset other than a Class VII asset is allocated an amount equal to its fair market value. Anything left over (*i.e.*, the residual) is allocated to Class VII assets.

names; licenses, permits and other governmental rights; and covenants not to compete.

Some assets are specifically excluded from § 197 including
the following: off-the-shelf intangibles (e.g., computer software sold
in stores); interests in tangible property leases (e.g., a lease
premium); interests in debt obligations; certain intangibles
requiring contingent payments (e.g., payments for a franchise based
on productivity); financial interests; interests in land; and some fees
for professional services (e.g., *INDOPCO*-type expenses).[9] Some
intangibles, including patents, copyrights and covenants not to
compete are covered by § 197 only when there is a related
acquisition of the assets (or in some cases the stock) of a business.

9.02 Stock Purchases

Suppose that instead of B buying X assets from X Corp or S, B
buys the X stock from S for $450,000.[10] On the sale, S recognizes a
$250,000 gain, pays a $50,000 tax (20 percent of $250,000) and ends
up with $400,000 of cash. Notice that B has acquired X stock, and
unlike with the asset purchase and liquidation described above, B's
stock purchase results in only a shareholder-level tax, not both a
shareholder-level and corporate-level tax. But also notice that B has
acquired (indirectly through X Corp.) assets (other than the cash)
that still have a $150,000 basis and reflect $300,000 of built-in gain.
In the asset purchase, B acquires the X assets with a $450,000 basis
and no built-in gain.

If X Corp. had many shareholders, it may be both overly costly
and impracticable for B to negotiate separately with each X shareholder to buy the X stock. If most X shareholders were willing to sell
their X stock to B, B could form an entity (*e.g.*, a corporation or limited liability company) to merge into X Corp. Through the merger, B
would acquire all X stock by operation of law, with the following
significant advantages: B could avoid the cost and hassle of separate negotiations with shareholders and could also force the transfer of X shares by those who might otherwise retain their shares or
hold out for a higher price. For federal income tax purposes, the

---

[9] *INDOPCO, Inc. v. Commissioner*, 503 U.S. 79 (1992).

[10] Although X Corp. has assets worth $555,000, if B anticipates that X
Corp. will soon either sell its assets or liquidate (thereby recognizing a
gain), B will discount the price by the anticipated tax ($105,000 or 35% of
$300,000) on that gain. Thus, B's purchase price for the X stock will be the
same as for a direct purchase of the X assets. If, however, B does not antici-
pate either the asset sale or liquidation, B may be willing to pay up to
$555,000 for the X stock. The actual purchase price will depend on the de-
mand for the X stock, among other factors.

merger would be treated just like a direct stock purchase.[11] Thus, if the X shareholders receive cash, they would be treated as selling their X stock for that cash and recognize gain or loss. § 1001. Further, X Corp. would not recognize gain or loss and would retain its historic asset bases and other tax attributes.[12]

Now suppose that the purchaser, B, is an individual. If B wants to step up the basis of the X assets to $450,000, B can do so, but only if a corporate-level tax is paid. If, after buying S's X Corp. stock, B liquidates X Corp., under § 336, X Corp. recognizes a $300,000 gain on the liquidation, incurring a tax liability of $105,000 (35 percent of $300,000), which can be paid with X Corp.'s cash. B realizes and recognizes no gain on the liquidation under § 331 and § 1001 because B's stock basis in the X stock is $450,000, equal to the fair market value of the distributed assets. B's basis in those assets is $450,000. § 334(a).

Obtaining a higher basis in X Corp.'s assets may be benefit B. If the assets are depreciable, the depreciation deductions in the aggregate will be larger (although the recovery periods may lengthen). Even if the assets are not depreciable, B will have less gain or a larger loss deduction if the assets are later sold. But B can acquire a stepped-up basis in the X Corp. assets only if X Corp. recognizes a corporate-level gain on the liquidation. Typically, that gain will result in an immediate tax, and a prudent taxpayer will not trade immediate taxation for future tax benefits (e.g., larger depreciation deductions), unless those future benefits have a present value exceeding the immediate tax cost. That equation may favor B, however, if X Corp. has a net operating loss carryover. Then, a liquidation might provide a higher asset basis at no (or a reduced) immediate tax cost. Also, if X Corp.'s assets have bases that exceed fair market value, its liquidation may allow X Corp. an immediate loss (and tax benefit) that B may gladly trade for a lower fair market value basis in the assets received in the liquidation.

---

[11] See Rev, Rul. 90-95, 1990-2 C.B. 67 (concluding that when a buyer formed a corporation to merge into a target corporation, for federal income tax purposes, the buyer was treated as acquiring target stock and the formation and merger of the new corporation were disregarded under the step-transaction doctrine).

[12] If B is a corporation and forms a subsidiary to merge into X Corp. and the X shareholders receive cash, that transaction would be a taxable "reverse subsidiary merger." Nontaxable reverse subsidiary mergers are addressed *infra* in Section 10.02(e).

9.03 Section 338 Elections

(a) Overview.

If B, a corporation (B Corp.), merely purchases the X Corp. stock from S and retains that stock, the tax consequences are the same as if B were an individual. In either case, X Corp. recognizes no gain and retains its $150,000 aggregate, non-cash asset basis, and the buyer (B) takes a cost basis in the X stock. If B is an individual and chooses to liquidate X Corp., X Corp. recognizes gain and B takes stepped-up bases in the X assets. § 331; § 336. In contrast, if B is a corporation and liquidates X Corp., X Corp. recognizes no gain and B Corp. inherits X Corp.'s historic asset bases, rather than taking stepped-up bases in the assets. § 337; § 332; § 334(b). B Corp. can obtain stepped-up bases in the X Corp. assets by purchasing them directly, but can B Corp. somehow obtain stepped-up bases if it purchases S's X Corp. stock?

Because of § 338, it can. Under § 338, B Corp. may make an election that allows X Corp. to take stepped-up bases in its assets, but at the cost of X Corp.'s recognizing the gain inherent in its assets (and incurring a tax on that gain). Thus, from a tax standpoint (but not necessarily a non-tax business standpoint), B Corp. is more likely to be indifferent whether it purchases the X assets or stock.

A corporation may make a § 338 election for its acquisition of target corporation stock if, within a 12-month period, it purchases an affiliated interest in that stock. An affiliated interest in target stock is at least 80 percent of the voting power and value of that stock (disregarding non-voting, non-convertible, preferred stock that is limited as dividends). See § 1504(a)(2).

A § 338 election affects the target and, depending on its form, the target shareholders. The target shareholders are *not* affected if a "regular" § 338 election is made; those shareholders recognize gain or loss on their stock sale under § 1001, just as if no election were made. Their tax consequences may be affected, however, if a special election is made under § 338(h)(10), an election available only in limited circumstances. With the § 338(h)(10) election, the selling target shareholders are generally treated as receiving their consideration in liquidation of the target. Thus, if the purchasing corporation acquires the target stock from one corporate shareholder, with a § 338(h)(10) election, the shareholder recognizes no gain or loss on its receipt of the sales proceeds. See § 332.

With either the regular § 338 or § 338(h)(10) election, the target corporation is deemed to do the following for federal income tax purposes: First, it is deemed to make a taxable sale of its assets.

Next, the target, treated as a newly formed subsidiary of the purchasing corporation, is deemed to purchase those assets. Note, however, that for non-tax purposes, the purchaser simply acquires target stock, and the target does not sell or purchase its assets.

In the example above, if B Corp. purchases all X Corp. stock and makes a § 338 election, X Corp. is first deemed to sell all of its assets. Next, X. Corp. is treated as a newly formed subsidiary of B Corp. for federal income tax purposes and is deemed to purchase those assets. In other words, X Corp. sells the assets to itself. As a result of this circular fiction, X Corp. recognizes a $300,000 gain and takes a $450,000 basis in its non-cash assets.

As the example illustrates, under § 338, a purchasing corporation secures a cost basis in the target corporation's assets without liquidating the target. If the purchaser then liquidates the target, § 332, § 334, and § 337 apply to the liquidation, and the purchaser inherits the target corporation's asset bases, bases that were stepped up because of the deemed asset sale. Thus, § 338 makes the form of an acquisition (stock or asset purchase) more tax neutral for the purchasing corporation.

Note that § 338 cannot apply if an individual purchases the target stock, a result that more likely is an oversight than a deliberate policy choice. Unless Congress changes § 338, however, an individual purchaser of target stock can secure a cost basis in target assets only by liquidating the target.

The regular § 338 election had more importance before the repeal of the *General Utilities* doctrine. Before the repeal, it was possible under § 338 to obtain a fair market value basis with limited corporate-level gain recognition. Since the repeal, corporate-level gain is fully recognized on the deemed sale, and the § 338(h)(10) election has assumed the greater prominence.

It often makes sense to make a § 338(h)(10) election (if it is available). Suppose, in the example above, that S Corp. owns all X Corp. stock with a $150,000 basis. If B Corp. buys the X Corp. stock for $450,000 and no § 338 election is made for the purchase, S Corp. recognizes a $300,000 gain, but X Corp. recognizes no gain and retains its $150,000 aggregate asset basis. If, however, a § 338(h)(10) election is made, S Corp. recognizes none of its realized gain, while X Corp. recognizes a $300,000 gain and takes a $450,000 aggregate basis in its non-cash assets. Thus, in this example, a § 338(h)(10) election produces the same corporate-level gain as without a § 338 election, but with the added benefit of a $300,000 step-up in X Corp.'s aggregate asset basis.

Typically, however, if a § 338(h)(10) election cannot be made, it is better to forego a regular § 338 election. In the example above, if the regular election is made, X Corp. gets a stepped-up basis in its assets only if it recognizes its $300,000 gain and S Corp. also recognizes a $300,000 gain on B's X stock sale. Generally, B Corp. will not make that § 338 election, even though X will step up its asset bases, since it will result in an added level of gain. It is likely that the present-value tax cost of that gain will exceed the present value of the tax benefits generated by the basis step-up.

In some situations, though, a regular § 338 election may still make sense. Suppose, that X Corp. has a $150,000 basis in its non-cash assets worth $450,000 but also has a net operating loss carryforward (NOL) of $300,000. If B Corp. makes a regular § 338 election, X Corp.'s $300,000 gain will be fully offset by its NOL, and X Corp. will take a $450,000 basis in its assets on its deemed purchase. The higher basis may allow larger depreciation deductions, thereby decreasing X Corp.'s taxable income (or it may decrease gain or increase deductible loss on a sale of the assets). But even if X Corp. has such an NOL, a § 338 election may not be advisable: B Corp. may be able to use X Corp.'s NOL after B Corp. liquidates X Corp., or perhaps X Corp. can use its own NOL against future earnings. See § 381; § 382. If X Corp.'s NOL is about to expire, however, a § 338 election may provide a net present-value tax benefit.

A regular § 338 election may also be advantageous if X Corp. has an aggregate built-in loss in its assets. Then, the deemed sale produces a loss that can be carried back and produce an immediate tax refund.

Finally, a regular § 338 election may be useful when B Corp. purchases a foreign target corporation with appreciated assets. The gain on the deemed § 338 sale is not usually taxable in the United States (or abroad) and the stepped-up basis on the deemed purchase may result in lower U.S. taxation on any eventual distribution from the target to B Corp. The higher asset basis may in turn result in greater depreciation deductions, lower earnings and profits, and therefore a smaller dividend upon eventual distribution.

(b) Qualified Stock Purchases.

To make a §338 election, the purchasing corporation must acquire an affiliated interest in the target corporation by "purchase" over a 12-month period. §338(d)(3). "Purchase," as defined in §338(h)(3), generally includes all acquisitions other than those in which the purchasing corporation carries over the transferor's basis or acquires the target stock in an acquisitive or divisive reorganization. For example, acquisitions by gift or in a §351 transaction do not qualify. In addition, a "purchase" generally does not include an acquisition from a related party. §338(h)(3)(A)(iii). But see *id*. at (h)(3)(C) (for an exception).

The affiliated target stock interest must be acquired by purchase within a twelve-month acquisition period that begins with the date of the first acquisition by purchase. See §338(h)(1). That purchase of stock is a "qualified stock purchase," commonly called a "QSP." § 338(d)(3). Further, the date on which that affiliated interest is first acquired is the "acquisition date." §338(h)(2).

(c) Election.

Either the regular §338 or §338(h)(10) election may be made any time before the fifteenth day of the ninth month following the month that includes the acquisition date. § 338(g)(1). Either election is irrevocable. See §338(g)(3). The regular election is made exclusively by the purchasing corporation. Regs. §1.338-2(d).

A §338(h)(10) election, however, must be made jointly by the purchasing corporation and target shareholders. Regs. §1.338(h)(10)-1(c)(3). Note that a §338(h)(10) election can be made only if the purchasing corporation acquires target stock from—

(i) A consolidated group that includes the target corporation on the acquisition date as a subsidiary;

(ii) A domestic corporation that owns an affiliated interest in the target corporation on the acquisition date; or

(iii) S corporation shareholders, but the target corporation must have been an S corporation immediately before the acquisition date.

See Regs. §1.338(h)(10)-1(b) and (c).

(d) Consequences to the Target.

(i) In general. With a regular § 338 election, any gain (or loss) recognized by the target corporation on its deemed asset sale cannot be offset by losses (or gains) of affiliates in either the selling or purchasing groups. §338(h)(9). But see Regs. §1.338-10(a)(1) and (4) (providing that a deemed sale return may combine all "deemed sale" gains and losses of targets that belonged to the same consolidated group and were acquired by the purchasing corporation on the same acquisition date). However, if a §338(h)(10) election is made for a target that was a subsidiary of a selling consolidated group, the target's gain (or loss) from the deemed sale can be offset by (or offset)

other group members' losses (or gains). See Regs. §1.338(h)(10)-1(d)(7).

(ii) Computing the Target's Aggregate Gain or Loss on its Deemed Asset Sale. Whether a regular § 338 election or § 338(h)(10) election is made, the target corporation is deemed to sell its assets at the close of the acquisition date, recognizing gain or loss. A new subsidiary of the purchasing corporation is deemed to purchase those assets at the beginning of the next day.

In the aggregate, the target assets are deemed sold for the "aggregate deemed sales price" (ADSP). Regs. §1.338-4. There are two major components of ADSP: (i) the amount paid by the purchasing corporation for the target stock in the qualified stock purchase and (ii) the target liabilities. If the purchasing corporation purchases less than all target stock (but still the requisite affiliated interest), the amount paid for the stock is proportionately increased (*i.e.,* "grossed up") to reflect what the payment would have been if all target stock had been purchased.[13]

Return to our example, in which X Corp. holds $105,000 cash plus non-cash assets with a $150,000 basis and $450,000 fair market value. If B Corp. acquires all the stock of X Corp. for $450,000 and makes a regular § 338 election, X Corp. recognizes a $300,000 gain and its basis in its non-cash assets becomes $450,000.[14] Suppose B Corp. purchases 80 percent of the X Corp. stock for $360,000. If the election is made, X Corp. is still deemed to receive $450,000 in

---

[13] See Regs. §1.338-4(c)(1). More precisely, if the purchasing corporation acquires all target stock in the qualified stock purchase, the ADSP equals (i) the amount realized by the target shareholders, minus (ii) the shareholder's selling costs, plus (iii) target liabilities (including any tax liability on the deemed sale that the target bears). Regs. § 1.338-4(b) and (c). The target's liabilities are determined at the beginning of the day after the acquisition date. Regs. § 1.338-4(b)(2)(i). If less than all target stock is acquired in the qualified stock purchase, the amount realized by the selling shareholders is "grossed up." Regs. § 1.338-4(c)(1).

[14] This example assumes that X Corp. pays tax at a 35% rate and will bear the tax liability on the deemed sale. Then, the ADSP equals $555,000, the amount realized by the target shareholders ($450,000) plus the target liabilities (*i.e.,* the tax on the deemed sale, which in this case is $105,000). The ADSP is first allocated to the X Corp.'s cash of $105,000, leaving $450,000 to be allocated to the non-cash assets. Thus, those assets are deemed sold for $450,000, producing a $300,000 gain ($450,000 amount realized minus $150,000 basis) and a $105,000 tax (35% of $300,000).

With a regular § 338 election, unless the target shareholders assume the tax on the deemed sale, that tax becomes a target liability included in the ADSP. However, because the amount of the tax depends on the ADSP, which in turn depends on the tax, the computations of the tax and ADSP are interrelated. In many cases, their computations can be made only by trial and error.

the deemed sale of the non-cash assets and thus will still recognize a $300,000 gain.[15]

(iii) Computing the Target's Aggregate Asset Basis after the Deemed Asset Sale. Turning from the deemed sale to the deemed purchase, we find even more complexity. The rules contained in §338(a)(2) and (b) determine the basis that the target takes in its assets following the deemed purchase. The rules specially deal with two phenomena: First, a purchasing corporation may not purchase all target stock, but the target will still be deemed to sell and purchase all of its assets; second, the purchasing corporation may hold "nonrecently purchased stock." That stock is all target stock held by the purchasing corporation on the acquisition date that was not acquired in the qualified stock purchase.[16] All other target stock then held by the purchasing corporation is "recently purchased stock." §338(b)(6)(A).

Section 338(b) accounts for those two different types of target stock in computing "adjusted grossed-up basis" (AGUB), an amount that equals the aggregate basis of the target's assets immediately following the deemed purchase. Regs. §1.338(b)-5. AGUB equals the sum of (i) the purchasing corporation's basis in recently purchased, plus (ii) its basis in non-recently purchased target stock, plus (iii) target liabilities.[17] If the purchasing corporation holds less than all target stock on the acquisition date, its basis in its recently purchased stock is proportionately increased ("grossed up") for the AGUB computation to reflect what the basis would have been if the purchasing corporation had purchased all remaining target stock that it did not hold. §338(b)(4).

In our example, there is no nonrecently purchased stock, because B Corp. acquired all X stock by purchase during the acquisition period. If B Corp. paid $450,000 for that stock, §338(b)(1)(A) and (b)(4) provide that X Corp.'s aggregate basis in its non-cash assets following the deemed purchase is $450,000, the same basis as if B Corp. had purchased the assets directly.[18] If B Corp. acquires 80

---

[15] The ADSP again equals $555,000. The $360,000 amount realized by the target shareholders is grossed up ($360,000/.8) to $450,000. That amount is added to the target liabilities (*i.e.*, the $105,000 tax on the deemed sale) to total $555,000.

[16] §336(b)(6)(B). Thus, non-recently purchased stock is target stock held by the purchasing corporation on the acquisition date that was either (i) acquired before the acquisition period began or (ii) acquired during the acquisition period but not acquired by purchase.

[17] Regs. § 1.338-5(b)(1). Those amounts are determined at the beginning of the day after the acquisition date.

[18] The AGUB equals $555,000, $450,000 (for B Corp.'s basis in the X stock) plus $105,000 (for the tax on the deemed sale). That amount is first

percent of the X Corp. stock for $360,000, the new basis of the X Corp. assets is still $450,000.[19] Note that the new basis of the X Corp. non-cash assets is the same whether B Corp. purchases 80 or 100 percent of the X stock, because in either case X Corp. will recognize a $300,000 gain and incur a $105,000 tax.

The complexity worsens when nonrecently purchased stock is introduced, since it must be excluded from the gross-up calculation. Suppose in our example that B Corp. acquires 80 percent of X Corp. stock for $360,000 during the acquisition period and that B Corp. held an additional 8 percent of the X Corp. stock (acquired before the acquisition period began) with a $20,000 basis and $36,000 fair market value on the acquisition date. The remaining 12 percent of the stock continues to be held by unrelated persons. If B Corp. makes a regular §338 election, X Corp.'s basis in its assets will equal $434,000, reflecting the $16,000 built-in gain on the nonrecently purchased X Corp. stock.[20]

In the previous example, however, B Corp. can elect to fully step up the basis of the target's assets to $450,000 by recognizing gain on the nonrecently purchased stock (i.e., the 8-percent holding). In the example, the gain would be the difference between the $20,000 basis and the $36,000 deemed sales price under §338(b)(3).[21] The effect of this election is to increase the basis for the

---

reduced by the amount of X Corp.'s cash ($105,000), leaving $450,000 to be allocated to the X non-cash assets.

[19] In this case, B Corp.'s basis in the X stock is grossed up to account the 20% of the X stock that B Corp. did not acquire. The grossed-up basis equals $450,000, which is $360,000 (B Corp.'s basis in the X Corp. stock), multiplied by 100% (the percentage of X stock other than nonrecently purchased stock), divided by 80% (the percentage of X stock that is recently purchased stock). Regs. § 1.338-5(c). Thus, the AGUB equals $555,000, which is $450,000 (the gross-up basis in B Corp.'s recently purchased stock) plus $105,000 (the X liabilities). That amount is first reduced by the amount of X Corp.'s cash ($105,000), leaving $450,000 to be allocated to the X non-cash assets.

[20] In this case, B Corp.'s basis in the X stock is grossed up to account for the 12% of the X stock that B Corp. did not acquire. The grossed up basis equals $414,000, which is $360,000 (B Corp.'s basis in the recently purchased X Corp. stock), multiplied by 92% (the percentage of X stock other than nonrecently purchased stock), divided by 80% (the percentage of X stock that is recently purchased stock). Regs. § 1.338-5(c). Thus, the AGUB equals $539,000, which is $414,000 (the gross-up basis in B Corp.'s recently purchased stock), plus $20,000 (B Corp.'s basis in its nonrecently purchased stock), plus $105,000 (the X liabilities). That amount is first reduced by the amount of X Corp.'s cash ($105,000), leaving $434,000 to be allocated to the X non-cash assets.

[21] This amount equals $414,000 (the grossed-up basis of B Corp.'s recently purchased stock) times 8% (its percentage of target stock which is nonrecently purchased stock) divided by 92% (the percentage of target stock other than nonrecently purchased stock) See also Regs. § 1.338-5(d)(3).

non-recently purchased stock to $36,000, which, when added to the $414,000 grossed-up basis, provides a full $450,000 basis. To achieve this additional corporate-level step-up, the shareholder (*i.e.*, B Corp.) must recognize a $16,000 gain.

Note that losses are not recognized if a gain recognition election is made for non-recently purchased stock. Regs. §1.338-5(d)(3)(iii). Note as well, that if a §338(h)(10) election is made, a gain recognition election is deemed made for any non-recently purchased stock. Regs. §1.338(h)(10)-1(d)(1).

(iv) Adjustments for Liabilities. The preceding examples were unusual in one respect—X Corp., the target, had no stated liabilities. Suppose in our example that X Corp.'s assets have a $450,000 fair market value but are subject to a $100,000 of stated liabilities. Further assume that B Corp. purchases all the X Corp. stock for $350,000 (*i.e.*, X Corp.'s net value). If B Corp. makes a regular §338 election, X Corp. still recognizes a $300,000 gain on the deemed asset sale and takes a $450,000 basis in its non-cash assets. Regs. §1.338-4(d)

Assume again that X Corp. pays tax at a 35% rate and will bear the tax liability on the deemed sale. Then, the ADSP equals $555,000, the amount realized by the target shareholders ($350,000) plus the target liabilities of $205,000 (*i.e.*, the $100,000 stated liability plus the tax on the deemed sale, which in this case is $105,000). The ADSP is first allocated to the X Corp.'s cash of $105,000, leaving $450,000 to be allocated to the non-cash assets. Thus, those assets are deemed sold for $450,000, producing a $300,000 gain ($450,000 amount realized minus $150,000 basis) and a $105,000 tax (35% of $300,000).

The AGUB also equals $555,000, $350,000 (for B Corp.'s basis in the X stock) plus target liabilities of $205,000 (the $100,000 stated liability plus the tax on the deemed sale of $105,000). That amount is first reduced by the amount of X Corp.'s cash ($105,000), leaving $450,000 to be allocated to the X non-cash assets.

Note that the ADSP and AGUB both take into account stated and unstated target liabilities, including the tax on the deemed sale if borne by the target. Regs. §1.338-5(e). A buyer should take the tax liability arising on the deemed asset sale into account in pricing the target stock, treating it like any other target liability.

(v) Contingent liabilities. Even disregarding selling costs, the aggregate deemed sales price (ADSP) on the target's sale to itself may not initially equal the adjusted grossed-up basis (AGUB) on the deemed purchase. For example, there may be some contingent lia-

bilities that are taken into account in determining gain but cannot be immediately reflected in the purchaser's basis. General tax principles determine when liabilities are taken into account to determine a target's gain and its subsequent basis on the deemed sale. Regs. §1.338-5. Some contingent liabilities that may not initially be reflected in the AGUB may later be reflected when an adjustment is appropriate under general tax principles. Regs. §1.338-5(b)(2)(ii).

(vi) Allocating of the ADSP and AGUB among Target Assets. In the example above, if X Corp. holds only one non-cash asset, the allocation of the amount realized and basis (*i.e.*, the ADSP and AGUB) on a deemed §338 sale by X Corp. to itself is straightforward. If X Corp. holds more than one non-cash asset (including intangible assets such as goodwill), those amounts must be allocated among the assets. In general, the regulations require that the seven-tier residual method be used. Regs. §1.338-6(b). This is the same method of allocation mandated by §1060 on asset sales. See pages 231–232.

Note that there are special rules to allocate the AGUB if the purchasing corporation holds appreciated non-recently purchased target stock but does not make a gain recognition election. Regs. §1.338-6(c)(3).

Suppose that B Corp. purchases the stock of X Corp. from X's shareholder S. The X stock has a $200,000 basis and $600,000 fair market value. B Corp. pays $900,000 for the stock plus S's covenant not to compete for five years. Under § 197, B Corp. must amortize the amount paid for the covenant not to compete over the statutory 15–year period rather than the 5–year period of the covenant itself. If P Corp. makes a § 338 election, any amount of the purchase price allocated to goodwill or other intangibles will be amortizable over a 15–year period under § 197.

(e) Consequences to the Purchasing Corporation and Target Shareholders.

A § 338 election generally does not affect how a purchasing corporation determines its tax consequences for its target stock acquisition. In other words, it generally determines its gain or loss and its basis in the target stock in the same way as if a § 338 election had not been made. See, e.g., § 1012; § 358. However, if a gain recognition election is made (or deemed made), the purchasing corporation recognizes gain but not loss on its nonrecently purchased target stock, and it takes a basis in that stock tied to the average cost of its recently purchased target stock. Regs. § 1.338-5(d)(3) (noting that "if [the] target has a single class of outstanding stock, the purchasing corporation's basis in each share of nonrecently purchased target stock after the gain recognition election equals the average price per share of [its] recently purchased target stock").

Generally, a § 338 election also does not affect a target shareholder's tax consequences. Thus, the target shareholder generally recognizes gain or loss on the target stock sold or exchanged in the qualified stock purchase. § 1001. Further, to the extent a target shareholder retains his target stock, nothing happens.

Special rules apply to certain target shareholders when a § 338(h)(10) election is made, however. That election may be made only if the target was a subsidiary of a consolidated group on the acquisition date or an S corporation immediately before the acquisition date or if a domestic corporation (called a "selling affiliate") owned an affiliated interest in the target on the acquisition date. Regs. § 1.338(h)(10)-1(c)(1); *id.* at (b). Recall that the acquisition date is the first day on which a purchasing corporation has made a qualified stock purchase of target stock. § 338(h)(2).

If a § 338(h)(10) election is made, the special rules apply to target shareholders other than "minority" shareholders. For this purpose, minority shareholders are target shareholders other than members of the selling consolidated group, the selling affiliate, or S corporation shareholders. Regs. § 1.338(h)(10)-1(d)(6)(i). Just as with a regular § 338 election, a minority shareholder recognizes gain or loss on his sale or exchange of target stock included in the qualified stock purchase. *Id.* at (d)(6)(ii). Further, to the extent a minority shareholder retains target stock, nothing happens. *Id.* at (d)(6)(iii).

A non-minority target shareholder (*i.e.*, a member of the selling consolidated group, the selling affiliate, or an S corporation shareholder) is not treated as if it sold the target stock. That shareholder is instead treated as if it received proceeds of the deemed asset sale in complete liquidation of the target. Regs. § 1.338(h)(10)-1(d)(5)(i). For a member of the selling consolidated group or the selling affiliate, § 332 typically applies to the deemed liquidation, and the shareholder recognizes no gain or loss. *Id.*

For an S corporation shareholder, § 331 typically applies to the deemed liquidation, so that the shareholder recognizes gain or loss (including on target stock actually retained by the shareholder). *Id.* Note that the shareholder computes that gain or loss after adjusting his stock bases to account for the target's gain or loss recognized in its deemed asset sale under § 338. *Id. See also* § 1367(a) (for the stock basis adjustments).

If a non-minority shareholder retains target stock, the shareholder is treated as acquiring that stock for its fair market value on the day after the acquisition date. *Id.* at (d)(5)(ii) (also providing that the fair market value of all target stock equals the grossed-up amount realized on the sale to the purchasing corporation of the recently purchased target stock). Thus, the holding period for that stock begins on that day. *Id.*

The following example illustrates some differences between a regular § 338 election and a § 338(h)(10) election. Suppose that Target Corp. holds assets with an aggregate $400,000 basis and $1.5 million fair market value. Target Corp. is owned by Parent Corp. which has a $200,000 basis in the Target stock. Buyer Corp. wants to acquire Target stock or assets but to step up the basis of the Target assets. To achieve those results, Buyer Corp. could buy the Target assets for $1.5 million and the Target could liquidate or Buyer Corp. could buy the Target stock for $1.5 million and a regular or § 338(h)(10) election could be made for the stock purchase.[22]

If Buyer Corp. bought the Target assets from Target Corp. for $1.5 million, Target Corp. would recognize a $1,100,000 gain. Buyer Corp. would take an aggregate $1.5 million (*i.e.*, stepped-up basis). basis in the acquired assets. § 1012; § 1060. When Target Corp. liquidated, neither Target Corp. nor Parent Corp. would recognize gain or loss, because Parent Corp. owned all Target stock. § 332; § 337. Thus, the asset sale and liquidation would result in one level of corporate tax.

Now suppose that Parent Corp. sells the stock of Target Corp. to Buyer Corp. for $1,500,000. If Buyer Corp. and Parent Corp. join in filing a § 338(h)(10) election, Target Corp. would be deemed to sell its assets for $1.5 million, recognizing a $1,100,000 gain.[23] Further, Target Corp. would take an aggregate $1.5 million basis in its assets. See Regs. § 1.338-5. Finally, the Target Corp. would be deemed to liquidate, and on the deemed liquidation, Parent Corp. would recognize no gain or loss. § 332. Thus, the tax consequences of § 338(h)(10) alternative are in relevant respects identical to the direct asset purchase and liquidation.

The regular § 338 election alternative, however, is less favorable. If Buyer made that election for its Target stock purchase,

---

[22] For convenience, assume that Parent Corp. assumes any tax on Target Corp.'s deemed or actual asset sale.

[23] If Parent Corp. and Target Corp. were members of a consolidated group, the group would report the deemed sale gain on its consolidated return. See Regs. § 338(h)(10)-1(d)(4)(i). Because of that consolidated reporting, that deemed sale gain may be offset by losses of other members of the consolidated group. See Regs. § 1.1502-11; Regs. § 1.1502-12.

Target Corp. again would be deemed to sell its assets for $1.5 million, recognizing a $1,100,000 gain. Further, Target Corp. would still take an aggregate $1.5 million basis in its assets. See Regs. § 1.338-5. However, Parent Corp. would be treated as selling its stock, rather than as receiving a liquidating distribution from Target Corp. On that sale, Parent would recognize a substantial gain.[24] Thus, the regular § 338 election results in two levels of corporate tax., not just one like the other alternatives.

(f) Consistency Requirements and Deemed Elections.

Sections 338(e) and (f) present purchasing corporations with an all-or-nothing choice regarding §338. If a §338 election is made, it applies not only to the target corporation but also to any "target affiliates" (§338(g)(6)) whose stock is purchased during the "consistency" period. §338(f). The consistency period is the period that spans a year before the acquisition period begins, the 12-month acquisition period (up to the acquisition date), and a one-year period following the acquisition date. §338(h)(4).

If a purchasing corporation makes a §338 election with respect to a qualified stock purchase of a target corporation, § 338(f) deems a §338 election to be made for any qualified stock purchase of a target affiliate within the consistency period. However, the regulations "interpreting" this rule all but eliminate this deemed election. Regs. §1.338-8(a)(6).

The statute also literally provides that if a purchasing corporation does not make a §338 election, it will be deemed to have made an election if during the consistency period it acquires any asset of the target or a target affiliate. §338(e). This deemed election prevents a purchasing corporation from stepping up the basis of desired assets by purchasing them directly while preserving the basis of other assets (and perhaps avoiding gain) by not electing §338. The regulations, however, take a completely different approach.

Instead of deeming a §338 election, the regulations sometimes require the purchasing corporation (or an affiliate) to take a carryover basis in assets acquired from the target (or a lower-tier affiliate). Further despite the literal language of §338(e), the regulations no longer permit the Service to impose a deemed §338 election. Moreover, §338(e) generally only applies when the target is a subsidiary in a consolidated group. Regs. §1.338-8(a).

---

[24] Parent's gain would equal $1.3 million reduced by the tax liability that it assumed arising from Target's deemed asset sale.

For example, suppose that T Corp. holds two assets: undeveloped land with a $50,000 basis and $200,000 fair market value, and a building with a $150,000 basis and $400,000 fair market value. T Corp. is owned by S Corp., which has a $350,000 basis in its T stock. B Corp. wants to acquire the T stock and to step up the basis of the building (to increase the depreciation deductions) but not that of the undeveloped land. Suppose that B Corp. buys the building for $400,000 directly from T Corp., which reinvests the sales proceeds. Sometime later but during the consistency period, B Corp. buys the T Corp. stock from S Corp. for $600,000. Under Regs. §1.338-8(d), if S Corp. and T Corp. had joined in filing consolidated returns, B Corp. takes a $150,000 carryover basis in the building.

On the asset sale, T Corp. recognizes a $250,000 gain ($400,000 amount realized minus $150,000 basis). Because S Corp. and T Corp. joined in filing consolidated returns, S Corp increases its basis in its T stock by the amount of that gain, from $350,000 to $600,000. Regs. § 1.1502-32(b)(2)(i). Thus, on its sale of the T stock for $600,000, S Corp. recognizes no gain or loss. If the consistency rules did not apply to B Corp.'s purchase of the building, B Corp. could then take a stepped-up basis in the building at no real tax cost to the S consolidated group.[25] The consistency rules prevent that result by requiring B Corp. to take a $150,000 basis in the purchased building.

Arguably, this approach is completely inconsistent with the statutory language in § 338 and might therefore be invalid,[26] but who will raise the issue? Note that the rule adopted by the regulations is favorable to B Corp. because it is not saddled with an unwanted § 338 election.

(g) Qualified Stock Purchases and the Step-Transaction Doctrine.

Although § 338 was enacted in 1982, it can trace its origins to a judicial rule developed shortly before 1954. The judicial rule applied when, as part of a plan, a corporation purchased all target stock and then liquidated the target. If form were followed, the target shareholders would be treated as selling their stock to the buyer and the buyer would be treated as liquidating the target in a separate step, taking transferred or carryover bases in the target assets.[27] The Tax

---

[25] If T Corp. had not sold the building but S Corp. had simply sold the T stock, S Corp. would have recognized a $250,000 gain on that sale ($600,000 amount realized minus $350,000 basis). Thus, with or without the building's sale, the S consolidated group recognized a $250,000 gain.

[26] But see § 338(e)(2)(D).

[27] This transferred basis rule has been in effect since 1936. See § 112(b)(6) and § 113(a)(15) of the Revenue Act of 1936, Pub. L. No. 74-740,

Court followed form for the target shareholders but not for the buyer.[28] It treated the buyer as acquiring the target's assets directly, so that its bases in target assets reflected its cost for the target stock. This application of the step-transaction doctrine is commonly called the *Kimbell-Diamond* doctrine.

Congress codified this doctrine in 1954, enacting § 334(b)(2), which in 1982 it replaced with § 338. Through § 338, a purchasing corporation could elect to treat a target stock purchase like a stock or asset purchase, whether or not it liquidated the target. To preserve that election, Congress recognized that the stock purchase and any subsequent liquidation had to be treated as independent steps for federal income tax purposes.[29]

In other words, in enacting § 338, Congress repealed the *Kimbell-Diamond* doctrine. Thus, if a purchasing corporation makes a qualified stock purchase of a target corporation and liquidates the target as part of the same plan, the target is treated as selling its assets only if a § 338 election is made. If the election is not made, the target is not treated as selling its assets and typically the purchasing corporation takes a carryover basis in the target assets. § 334(b).

The repeal left at least one question unanswered, however. Despite the repeal, should the step-transaction continue to apply to determine whether the purchasing corporation has made a qualified stock purchase? The Service has concluded that the answer is yes; the step-transaction doctrine applies.

For example, suppose that X Corp. has one class of stock outstanding and that B Corp. acquires the X Corp. stock in exchange for 70 percent B voting stock and 30 percent cash. As part of the same plan, B Corp. then liquidates X Corp. Standing alone, the stock acquisition would be a qualified stock purchase. If, however, the step-transaction doctrine applied, assume that the stock acqui-

---

49 Stat. 1679-80, 1684-85 (1936) (providing for complete non-recognition and transferred bases). Currently, those rules are found in § 332 and § 334(b)(1).

[28] See *Dallas Downtown Development Co. v. Commissioner*, 12 T.C. 114 (1949), *acq.* 1950-1 C.B. 2 (for the shareholders' treatment).; *Kimbell-Diamond Milling Co. v. Commissioner*, 14 T.C. 74, *aff'd per curium*, 187 F.2d 718 (5th Cir.), *cert. denied*, 342 U.S. 827 (1951) (for the buyer's treatment).

[29] H.R. Conf. Rep. No. 760, 97th Cong., 2d Sess. 536 (1982) (providing that § 338 was "intended to replace any nonstatutory treatment of a stock purchase as an asset purchase under the *Kimbell-Diamond* doctrine"); Rev. Rul. 90-95, 1990-2 C.B. 67 (concluding based on the legislative history that a stock purchase of a target and its subsequent, planned liquidation were treated as independent steps).

sition and liquidation would be characterized as a § 368 reorganization and the stock acquisition would not be a qualified stock purchase.[30]

In Rev. Rul. 2001-46, the Service concluded in a similar case that the step-transaction doctrine applied, because its application did not violate the policy behind § 338.[31] It reasoned that § 338 was intended to be the sole method to treat a stock purchase like a taxable asset purchase, quoting legislative history to that effect. Because the transaction, as stepped together, was treated as a reorganization, the target (X Corp. in our example) did not recognize gain or loss nor were its asset bases stepped up. See § 361(b); § 362(b). In other words, the transaction was not treated like a taxable asset acquisition, and applying the step-transaction doctrine did not circumvent § 338. Thus, the Service concluded, the step-transaction doctrine should apply in that case to determine whether the stock acquisition was a qualified stock purchase.[32]

In Rev. Rul. 2008-25, the Service concluded that the step-transaction doctrine also applies to the converse case.[33] Suppose that X Corp. has one class of stock outstanding, that B Corp. acquires the X Corp. stock in exchange for 90 percent B voting stock and 10 percent cash, and that as part of the same plan, B Corp. liquidates X Corp. Assume, however, that, standing alone, the stock acquisition would *not* be a qualified stock purchase, but if the step-transaction doctrine applied, it would be.

The Service concluded that the step-transaction doctrine applied only to characterize the stock acquisition as a qualified stock purchase, not to characterize the transaction as a whole.[34] The

---

[30] If the transaction were characterized as a reorganization, § 354 or § 356 would apply to the exchange by X shareholders of their X stock for B stock, and the X stock so exchanged would not be acquired by purchase. See § 338(h)(3)(A)(ii). Thus, the stock acquisition could not be a qualified stock purchase, because no more than 30% of the X stock (or far less than an affiliated interest) would be acquired by purchase.

[31] Rev. Rul. 2001-46, 2001-2 C.B. 321.

[32] By regulation, however, the step-transaction doctrine does not apply to a stock acquisition and planned liquidation if (i) the stock acquisition would be a qualified stock purchase if it were treated as a separate step and (ii) a § 338(h)(10) election is made. Regs. § 1.338(h)(10)-1(c)(2). Note that although the § 338(h)(10) election may affect the tax consequences of minority shareholders, they may have no say in whether the election is made. If it is made, the transaction may be taxable to them; if it is not made, it may be tax-free.

[33] Rev. Rul. 2008-25, 2008-21 I.R.B. 986.

[34] See Rev. Rul. 67-274, 1967-1 C.B. 141 (applying the step-transaction doctrine to characterize a transaction as an acquisitive § 368 reorganization). Note that in certain cases Regs. § 1.368-2(k) shuts off the step-transaction doctrine, but that regulatory provision did not apply to this

broader application of the doctrine would have been inconsistent with the policy behind § 338, allowing a stock acquisition to be treated like a taxable asset purchase without a § 338 election. Thus, under the step-transaction doctrine, the stock acquisition was treated as a qualified stock purchase, but that doctrine did not more broadly apply to treat the stock acquisition and liquidation together like an asset purchase. Instead, the stock acquisition and liquidation were treated as separate steps, with the stock acquisition being taxable and the liquidation tax-free under § 332 and § 337.

9.04 Expenses in Connection with an Acquisition

In *INDOPCO, Inc. v. Commissioner*[35] the Supreme Court concluded that expenses for investment banking, legal fees, etc. incurred during a friendly merger were not ordinary and necessary business expenses and, therefore, not deductible under § 162(a). Instead, the expenses had to be capitalized.[36] *INDOPCO* recognized two categories of acquisition expenses which must be capitalized because they produce long-term benefits: (i) benefits generated by the resources of the acquiring company; and (ii) benefits obtained by a target on becoming a wholly owned subsidiary instead of a publicly held corporation (e.g., avoiding extensive disclosure requirements).

INDOPCO addressed the deductibility of expenses incurred in a friendly takeover. Do the same rules apply to a hostile takeover? Regulations, which in some ways limit the reach of *INDOPCO*, now provide that a taxpayer must capitalize an amount paid to "facilitate" a transaction. Regs. § 1.263(a)-5(a). This rule may allow some expenses of fighting a hostile takeover to be deducted, rather than capitalized. See Regs. § 1.263-5(l), *Ex. 11*. If expenses are incurred primarily to protect rather than to acquire property, a deduction may be appropriate. For example, expenses incurred by a corporation to defend itself in a proxy contest are deductible.[37] Costs associated with specific defensive strategies, such as negotiating with a "white knight," counter-tender offers, poison pill plans, and corporate charter amendments, however, are generally nondeductible capital expenditures if the plans are implemented. If the plans are abandoned, a loss deduction should be permitted under § 165(a).[38] The full scope of *INDOPCO* is being

---

case because the target distributed its assets in complete liquidation. See Regs. § 1.368-2(k)(1)(i)(B)(1).

[35] 503 U.S. 79 (1992).

[36] Under § 197(e)(8), these expenses are not subject to amortization.

[37] See e.g., Rev. Rul. 67–1, 1967–1 C.B. 28. But see, e.g., Regs. § 1.212–1(k) (expenses to defend title to property must be capitalized).

[38] See *Lychuk v. Commissioner*, 116 T.C. 374 (2001).

worked out in Service rulings and court decisions. For example, in *Wells Fargo & Co. v. Commissioner*,[39] the court allowed a deduction for officers' salaries and a portion of legal and investigatory expenses incurred in connection with an acquisition.

9.05 Corporate Acquisitions and the Use of Debt

An acquiring corporation may choose to finance the acquisition of a target corporation in several ways including: (i) debt; (ii) its own retained earnings; (iii) or new equity contributed by investors.

(a) Stock Acquisitions out of Retained Earnings.

If a purchaser uses retained earnings to acquire a target corporation, there are no tax consequences to the shareholders of the purchaser. Shareholders of the target recognize gain or loss on the sale of their shares. Earnings of the target corporation which are distributed as dividends to a purchasing corporation after the acquisition should not result in federal income tax liability if the purchasing corporation and target are members of the same consolidated group. See Regs. § 1.1502-13(f)(2).

(b) Debt Financed Stock Acquisitions and Leveraged Buyouts.

A purchasing corporation which finances a buyout with debt may use either its own assets or the assets of the target corporation as collateral. When the target's assets are used as collateral, the transaction is often called a "leveraged buyout." In a leveraged buyout, the target corporation may pay the debt obligation out of its cash flow, or the purchasing corporation may sell assets of the target and use to the sales proceeds to retire the debt. Depending on the degree of leverage and security involved, the debt can range from investment grade to "junk" bonds.

A leveraged buyout is a taxable transaction for the shareholders of the target corporation. Target shareholders recognize gain or loss on the sale or exchange of their shares. At the corporate level, the target corporation does not recognize gain or loss (unless a § 338 election is made). An important consequence of the leveraged buyout is that some of the equity of the target corporation is replaced with debt. As a result, corporate income formerly paid to shareholders as nondeductible dividends is transmuted into deductible interest paid to creditors. Consequently, after a leveraged buyout a corporation may have little taxable income or may claim losses which after a loss carryback may result

---

[39] 224 F.3d 874 (8th Cir.2000).

in a refund of taxes paid in prior years.[40] Note, however, that creditors are taxable on any interest received. Still, the effect of a leveraged buyout is a reduction of the target's taxable income and a redistribution of income from its equity holders to debt holders.

Consider the following example: X Corp. with 99,000 shares of stock outstanding and no debt, has $750,000 annual income and pays tax at a 34-percent rate. Thus, X Corp.'s federal income tax is $255,000 ($750,000 times .34), leaving $495,000 of after-tax income or earnings of $5 per share. Assume that X Corp.'s stock trades at $40 per share (or 8 times earnings per share). X Corp. is acquired in a leveraged buyout in which the acquirors pay $60 per share of stock, or 50 percent more than the price at which the stock has been trading on the market, for a total price of $5.94 million. The X shareholders recognize gain or loss on the sale of their shares.

The acquirors put up $440,000 of their own funds and raise the remaining $5.5 million of the purchase price by issuing notes paying 12-percent interest to be secured by the X assets. The annual income of X Corp. after the leveraged buyout is unchanged.

The distribution of the operating income of X Corp. before and after the leveraged buyout is as follows:

	Before	*After*
X Corp. shareholders	$495,000	$0
Bondholders	0	660,000
Acquirors	0	59,400
Corporate income taxes	255,000	30,600
Total operating income	$750,000	$750,000

The leveraged buyout has redistributed the income stream of X Corp. Before the buyout, the X Corp. shareholders receive the after-tax profit of $495,000; they receive nothing after the buyout. Before the buyout, neither the acquirors nor bondholders received any payment. Afterwards, the acquirors receive the after-tax profit of $59,400. The bondholders receive interest of 12 percent on $5.5 million, or $660,000. Thus, after the leveraged buyout, the equity and debt investors receive one third more than the entire amount of X Corp.'s after-tax income before the buyout, even though the operating income of X Corp. is the same before and after the buyout.

How did the buyout increase the return to investors? The key is that X's taxable income Corp. has been reduced from $750,000 to $90,000 ($750,000 minus $660,000), because most of the income of

---

[40] But see the discussion of CERTs below.

the company is paid out to investors as deductible interest rather than non-deductible dividends. X's federal income taxes are thereby reduced from $255,000 to $30,600. Acquirors make an after-tax profit of $59,400 (pre-tax profit of $90,000 reduced by Federal income tax of $30,600), a 13.5 percent return on their $440,000 equity investment. The income tax reduction of $224,400 exactly pays for the increased returns to investors (bondholders and shareholders) as a result of the leveraged buyout. Depending on whether the increased investor returns are paid to taxable shareholders or holders of debt, there may be an increase in investor-level Federal income taxes paid.

The engine that drives this example is the assumption that the X Corp. stock initially sells for $40 per share and can be redeemed for $60 per share. Is this a realistic assumption? The example assumes that X Corp.'s pre-tax borrowing cost is 12 percent; presumably its rate of return on investment would be higher than 12 percent. Even assuming that the rate of return on investment is 12 percent, X Corp.'s assets should be worth $6,250,000 ($750,000/.12) to produce the assumed annual pre-tax profit of $750,000. Yet, the market seems to value the corporation at only $3,960,000 (99,000 shares x $40 per share).

Why might the market value of X Corp. be so much below its asset value? There may be a host of reasons. Perhaps the expected cost of a corporate-level tax is one reason. Also, stock may be undervalued because of information failure in the market place or perhaps the assets are not efficiently deployed and transactions costs prevent a more efficient deployment.

In any case, the example not surprisingly shows that if you can borrow at 12 percent to make an investment (i.e. X Corp. stock) which provides a return of almost 19 percent ($750,000 income ÷ (99,000 shares x $40 per share)), it's a good deal.

Notice that in this example the government receives less in taxes when debt is used. The example assumes that the benefits of this tax reduction are shared by the shareholders and the debt holders. However, as noted in Section 1.03 *supra,* the reduction in taxes might also inure to employees, suppliers, customers, and others. Regardless of who benefits from the tax reduction, tax liability (at least at the corporate level) is lowered through the use of debt.

(c) Risks of Excessive Corporate Debt.

Corporations with high debt ratios must devote large portions of their income to meet interest payments. If the corporation's income decreases or its costs increase, then the corporation may be forced to sell assets, reduce its workforce, and delay or cut back capital expenditures and expansion. If such actions cannot provide sufficient income to meet interest obligations, then the corporation may be forced into bankruptcy, resulting in significant transaction costs.

In the late 1960s, Congress became concerned about the extensive use of debt in corporate acquisitions, and enacted § 279 to discourage leveraged buyouts. Section 279 disallows an interest deduction to an acquiring corporation on specified "corporate acquisition indebtedness." Corporate acquisition indebtedness is a debt obligation issued by an acquiring corporation to purchase a specified amount of stock or assets (i.e. two thirds of the value of the noncash trade or business assets) of another corporation if (1) the obligation is subordinated to trade creditors or unsecured creditors; (2) the obligation is convertible into stock of the issuing corporation (or part of an investment unit); and (3) the ratio of debt to equity exceeds 2:1 or the projected earnings of the acquiring corporation do not exceed three times the interest paid or incurred with respect to the obligation.

Section 279 does not apply if any one of the requirements is absent. If all requirements are met, then § 279 denies an interest deduction in excess of $5 million paid on such corporate acquisition indebtedness. For example, at a 7-percent interest rate, a corporation could have more than $70 million of debt outstanding without triggering § 279.

After the stock market slump of 1987, Congress again acted to curb the use of debt in corporate acquisitions. An interest deduction may be denied to issuers of any "applicable high yield discount obligation." Such obligations usually have an issue price that is significantly lower than their redemption price. The spread between the issue and redemption prices is the original issue discount (OID). Normally, an OID bond issuer accrues and deducts the spread over the life of the bond even though payment is not made until maturity. § 1272; § 1273. A "payment in kind" (PIK) bond is a related instrument in which payments are made in the form of debt or stock of the issuer instead of cash. High yield and PIK bonds are attractive to issuers because they provide deductions before any cash outlay is made.

Section 163(e)(5) divides the OID amount on these bonds between interest that is deductible only when paid and a disqualified portion of interest for which no deduction is allowed, but which may qualify for a dividends received deduction for corporate lenders. The result is a compromise between treating the instrument as debt and treating it as equity. An "applicable high yield discount obligation" is an instrument with: (1) a maturity date of more than five years, (2) a yield at maturity that is at least 5 percentage points higher than a designated federal rate, and (3) a "significant original issue discount." § 163(i).

Congress was also concerned with the perceived abuse of using tax refunds to finance leveraged buyouts. Often tax refunds were generated by the acquiring corporation's carrying back its net operating losses (NOLs). § 172. With debt-financed acquisitions, interest deductions often generated the NOLs that provided the refund. Section 172(h) limits the carryback of NOLs if the losses are created by interest deductions attributable to a "corporate equity reduction transaction" (CERT). A CERT is a "major stock acquisition" or an "excess distribution." A "major stock acquisition" is a planned acquisition by a corporation of at least 50 percent of the voting power or value of stock in another corporation. § 172(h)(3)(B). An "excess distribution" is an unusually large distribution relative to the distributing corporation's distribution history or net worth. § 172(h)(3)(C). When the CERT limitation applies, interest attributable to the CERT (which can occur up to two years after the CERT) cannot be carried back to a year before the CERT.[41]

Congress has enacted a variety of other provisions—not necessarily related to debt-financed acquisitions—that were enacted to curtail perceived corporate acquisition abuses. For example, § 162(k) denies a deduction for any amount paid or incurred by a corporation to redeem its own stock.[42] This provision is aimed at "greenmail" payments made by a corporation to a potential corporate "raider" to repurchase the "raider's" stock. Furthermore § 5881 imposes an excise tax of 50 percent on any gain or other income realized by the greenmail recipient.[43]

Section 280G disallows deductions for certain "golden parachute" payments designed to soften the landing of management replaced by new owners in the event of a takeover or other specified event. Some have argued that "golden parachutes" are helpful to shareholders because it allows management to evaluate takeover offers free of financial concerns. Section 280G disallows a deduction

---

[41] A de minimis rule provides that the limitation applies only if the interest expense in question at least equals $1 million. § 172(h)(2)(D).

[42] See Chapter 5 *supra* for a discussion of redemptions. Even before the enactment of § 162(k), it was highly doubtful that such payments were deductible.

[43] "Greenmail" is defined as consideration paid by a corporation in redemption of its stock held for less than two years if the holder threatened a public tender offer, unless the redemption is pursuant to an offer made on the same terms to all shareholders. § 5881(b).

for payments to a "disqualified individual" (i.e., officer, shareholder, or other highly compensated individual), if the payment is contingent on a change of ownership or control and the payment exceeds three times the taxpayer's annual average compensation for the five-year period preceding the change of control. A companion provision, § 4999, imposes an excise tax equal to 20 percent of any excess parachute payment. See § 280G(b) (defining excess parachute payments).

Section 382, discussed in more detail in Chapter 11, does not attempt to increase the direct cost of corporate acquisitions. Instead, this provision limits the ability of acquiring corporations to use net operating losses of the acquired corporation to offset future income, thereby decreasing the attraction of some corporate takeovers.

Chapter 10

REORGANIZATIONS

10.01 Introduction

The subject of corporate reorganizations is hard to define. In its narrowest sense, corporate reorganizations include only those tax-free transactions described in § 368(a)(1), i.e., the so-called A (described in § 368(a)(1)(A)) through G (described in § 368(a)(1)(G)) reorganizations. More broadly, however, the term encompasses all corporate rearrangements by which the assets of a corporation are transferred to a new corporate entity or are retained by the corporation but controlled by new shareholders.

We adopt the broader interpretation of the term "reorganization" here not only because most tax lawyers use it that way (allowing them to speak of tax-free reorganizations without redundancy as well as of taxable reorganizations without contradiction), but also because it is pedagogically better: the statutory reorganizations constitute some but not nearly all the ways of rearranging corporate structures. Sometimes meeting the requirements of § 368(a)(1) will be easily accomplished and will provide the most favorable results. In such cases, the corporate rearrangement will be accomplished by means of a "corporate reorganization" in its narrowest sense. Often, though, meeting the dictates of § 368(a)(1) will be difficult, expensive, or impossible, and in those cases other methods will have to be adopted. In addition, it may well be the case that the tax treatment provided by the reorganization provisions (once again in the narrow sense) may not be what the taxpayer desires, and then a plan must be adopted which deliberately runs afoul of the § 368(a)(1) definitions.

You are already familiar with a number of corporate rearrangements. The bulk sale of a corporation's assets followed by a liquidating distribution of the proceeds is a corporate rearrangement, generally taxable at both the shareholder and corporate levels.[1] The sale of all the stock of a corporation accomplishes much the same result but is only partially taxable: a shareholder-level tax is imposed on the sale but corporate-level tax may be avoided. Indeed, you are also familiar with a fully tax-free corporate rearrangement: the liquidation by a parent of its wholly owned subsidiary.

---

[1] See Chapters 8 and 9 *supra*.

The reorganizations defined in § 368(a)(1) are, in tax effect, most similar to the liquidation of a wholly owned subsidiary because the § 368(a)(1) reorganizations can be tax-free at both the corporate and shareholder levels. The operative shareholder-level provision is § 354(a)(1), providing (with some limitations) for the tax-free exchange of stock or securities of one corporation for stock or securities of another corporation if both corporations are "parties" to a reorganization. The operative corporate-level provision is in § 361, providing in a complicated way (and with some exceptions) for tax-free treatment to the transferor corporation in a statutory reorganization. The transactions covered by these sections, the statutory reorganizations, are set out in § 368(a)(1) (though modified by other parts of § 368). Note that § 368 is a definitional section only: nowhere in § 368 are the tax implications of a reorganization mentioned. The importance of § 368 is that many other sections (e.g., §§ 354 and 361) are triggered by transactions meeting the definitions contained in § 368.

Most broadly, reorganizations can be divided into four groups: (1) amalgamating reorganizations in which two or more corporations are combined into a single corporate structure; (2) divisive reorganizations in which a single corporation is divided into two or more companies; (3) single-party reorganizations in which one corporation undergoes a substantial change in financial structure or modifies its place of incorporation or other similar corporate characteristic; and (4) bankruptcy reorganizations in which a distressed corporation seeks to improve its financial position. In terms of § 368, the amalgamating reorganizations consist of the types A through C as well as some D's; the divisive reorganizations include the remainder of the D's as well as transactions described in § 355 though not falling within the definitions of § 368(a)(1); the single-party reorganizations are the types E and F; and the bankruptcy reorganization is the type G.[2]

The one unifying aspect of the statutory reorganizations is that of *continuity of interest*. The various definitions in § 368 seek to provide tax-free treatment to corporate rearrangements in which the shareholders continue their investment in modified form. The rationale for tax-free treatment of such reorganizations is the same as that for § 351 incorporations: not enough is changed by the transaction to warrant an immediate imposition of tax. You will have to decide for yourself whether you think the lines drawn in § 368 properly distinguish mere changes in form not warranting taxation from sales and other rearrangements that are fully taxable.

---

[2] We consider only the tax (and not bankruptcy) aspects of bankruptcy reorganizations.

With few exceptions, the Code provisions specially applicable to the statutory reorganizations do not distinguish among the various types described in § 368(a)(1). Accordingly, it is customary to investigate the various definitions as a group and then consider the tax implications common to all. Before beginning that investigation, recall what we have already learned about the statutory reorganizations: if the detailed provisions of § 368(a)(1) are met, taxation may be avoided at both corporate and shareholder levels.

10.02 Amalgamating Reorganizations: Definitions

For a transaction to be treated as an amalgamating reorganization (or, as its generally referred to, an acquisitive reorganization), it must meet not only the statutory definition of a reorganization under § 368(a) but generally also certain judicial requirements: A reorganization must have a continuity of interest, continuity of business enterprise, and valid business purpose.[3]

Those judicial requirements help assure that a reorganization meets both the express language and the spirit of the statutory provisions. This willingness to look beyond the confines of the Code for the definition of a reorganization remains with us today, in both the case law and in the regulations, as is clearly stated in Regs. § 1.368–1(b):

> In order to exclude transactions not intended to be included, the specifications of the reorganization provisions of the law are precise. Both the terms of the specifications and their underlying assumptions and purposes must be satisfied in order to entitle the taxpayer to the benefit of the exception from the general rule. Accordingly, ... an ordinary dividend is to be treated as an ordinary dividend, and a sale is nevertheless to be treated as a sale even though the mechanics of a reorganization have been set up.

In this section, we first consider the judicial requirements for amalgamating reorganizations and then their statutory requirements.

(a) Judicial Requirements.

(i) Continuity of interest. A merger or other corporate combination qualifies as a §368(a) reorganization only if it has continuity of

---

[3] Courts have felt free to engraft their conception of what a reorganization should be onto the statute, a statute already complex and detailed. Judicial activism in tax is hardly limited to the reorganization arena, but it does seem to be the case that reorganizations have sparked more than their share of judicial creativity.

interest. This standard is met if "a substantial part of the value of the proprietary interest in the target corporation [is] preserved in the reorganization." §1.368-1(e)(1). Thus, the target shareholders must have a continuing, entrepreneurial interest in the combined venture.[4]

This standard raises at least three questions: (i) What type of consideration preserves the target shareholder's proprietary interest; (ii) how much qualifying consideration is needed for a transaction to be a reorganization; and (iii) how do sales or redemptions before or after the reorganization affect continuity? The first question was answered in a series of Supreme Court cases the 1930s and 1940s, as the Court developed the "continuity of interest" doctrine.

Continuity-preserving Consideration. Some corporate combinations may be little more than outright sales of corporate assets evidencing no continuity of investment, and the courts have struggled to separate corporate rearrangements deserving tax deferral from sales and similar transactions habitually taxed in full. In those circumstances what is at stake is often whether the transaction will be tax-free at the corporate-level.

For example, suppose that X Corp. merges into Y Corp., with the shareholders of X Corp. exchanging their X Corp. stock for cash and preferred stock of Y. Suppose further that for each X share turned in, a shareholder receives $90 cash and one share of Y preferred stock worth $10. While the transaction is structured as a merger, the transaction cashes out all but 10 percent of the X shareholders' investments. Long ago, the Supreme Court held that such a transaction could not qualify as a statutory "reorganization" despite meeting the literal language of § 368(a)(1) (or of its ancestors), because it lacked continuity of interest.

The Court introduced this continuity requirement in *Pinellas Ice & Cold Storage Co. v. Commissioner*, 287 U.S. 462 (1933). In that case, the seller corporations, in exchange for their assets, received cash plus well-secured promissory notes payable in less than four months. The Supreme Court concluded that the transaction constituted a taxable sale rather than a tax-free reorganization, stating: "Certainly, we think that to be within the [definition of a reorganization] the seller must acquire an interest in the affairs of

---

[4] More precisely, the holders of the target's proprietary interests must have a significant continuing interest in the combined venture. Sometimes, a target's creditors are treated as the holders of proprietary interests in the target, and their receipt of qualifying consideration may help satisfy the continuity of interest requirement. See Regs. § 1.368-1(e)(6) (treating target creditors as holders of target proprietary interests when the target is insolvent or in bankruptcy).

the purchasing company more definite than that incident to owner-ship of its short-term purchase-money notes." 287 U.S. at 470.

Two years later, in *Helvering v. Minnesota Tea Co.*, 296 U.S. 378 (1935), the Court upheld the tax-free status of a transfer by a corporation of substantially all of its assets for voting trust certifi-cates (worth about $540,000) representing 18,000 shares of common stock of another corporation as well as about $425,000 in cash. The 18,000 shares represented about 7½ percent of the outstanding stock of the transferee, a publicly held corporation. Because of this substantial reduction in the transferor's control over the transferred assets, the Board of Tax Appeals had denied reorganization treat-ment to the transaction. In coming to the opposite conclusion, the Supreme Court restated the rule of *Pinellas* and then wrote:

> True it is that the relationship of the taxpayer to the assets conveyed was substantially changed, but this is not inhibited by the statute. Also, a large part of the consideration was cash. This, we think, is permissible so long as the taxpayer received an interest in the affairs of the transferee which represented a material part of the value of the transferred assets.

296 U.S. at 386. Thus, the Court measured continuity by looking to the percentage of acquiror stock received in the exchange, not the percentage of acquiror stock held after the exchange.

Minnesota Tea failed to answer what constituted an "interest in the affairs of the transferee" or how much of such an interest was a "material part" of the value transferred. The second of these ques-tions is addressed in the next subsection. The first question was answered in large part by *John A. Nelson & Co. v. Helvering*, 296 U.S. 374 (1935), and *LeTulle v. Scofield*, 308 U.S. 415 (1940).

In *LeTulle*, all the assets of a corporation were conveyed for $50,000 in cash plus $750,000 in bonds of the transferee payable serially over 11 years. The Supreme Court characterized the trans-action as a sale, holding that "[w]here the consideration is wholly in the transferee's bonds, or part cash and part such bonds, we think it cannot be said that the transferor retains any proprietary interest in the enterprise." 308 U.S. at 420-421. In *John A. Nelson & Co.*, however, the Court upheld the tax-free reorganization treatment of a transfer by a corporation of substantially all of its assets for $2 million plus nonvoting preferred stock of the transferee worth about $1.25 million. The preferred stock was redeemable as well as non-voting, but the Court concluded that the statute did not require par-ticipation by the transferor shareholders in the transferee's man-agement.

The line of cases from *Pinellas* through *Nelson* stands for the proposition that for a transaction to qualify as a "reorganization," the target shareholders must receive some stock (a "material part") of the acquiror in the exchange. Thus, the continuity of interest requirement may be met if the target shareholders exchange target voting common stock for acquiror non-voting, preferred stock. The requirement cannot be met, however, if the target shareholders receive no stock, even if they receive a long-term debt interest.

Note that the continuity of interest doctrine applies to the consideration that the target shareholders receive in the aggregate, and not to what a shareholder receives individually. For example, if 75 percent of the consideration in a merger is stock of the surviving corporation, continuity of interest exists even if the stock received constitutes a small percentage of the acquiror stock or if one particular shareholder receives only cash or debt.[5] Of course, the recipient of cash may not avoid taxation on the exchange—as we shall see, cash or other boot received as part of a reorganization can give rise to gain (or sometimes loss) recognition. What it does mean is that all the parties to the transaction will be taxed under those provisions that apply to a § 368 "reorganization."

Although measuring continuity by looking to the transaction as a whole may be favorable, it is not always so. Suppose that the stock of X Corp. is owned equally by 10 individuals. X Corp. merges into Y Corp. under applicable state law, nine of the X shareholders receive solely cash, while one receives solely Y stock. Then, the continuity of interest requirement will not be met, and no shareholder will obtain the benefit of the reorganization provisions, even the X shareholder who receives solely Y stock in the transaction.[6] Thus, a shareholder's taxation in these circumstances may turn in part on the consideration received by other participants in the transaction.

Which corporation's stock preserves continuity in an acquisitive reorganization? Generally, the stock that preserves continuity is issued by the corporation that acquires the target stock or assets. See Regs. §1.368-1(b). In certain situations, however, the Code allows stock of a corporation that controls the acquiror to preserve continuity. See §368(a)(1)(B) (parenthetical language); §368(a)(1)(C) (parenthetical language); §368(a)(2)(D) and (E). For convenience in the discussion below and depending on the context, stock that preserves continuity is called "qualified acquiror stock" and the corporation that issues that stock is termed the "issuing corporation."

---

[5] See Rev. Rul. 66–224, 1966–2 C.B. 114.

[6] *Kass v. Commissioner,* 60 T.C. 218 (1973), aff'd without opinion, 491 F.2d 749 (3d Cir.1974).

As an aside, note how the continuity of interest doctrine, despite springing from well-founded concerns, has taken some peculiar turns. Consider *Roebling v. Commissioner,*[7] which concluded that the doctrine was not satisfied when target shareholders received no acquiror stock, even though the shareholders maintained essentially the same interest in the target assets. In *Roebling*, a corporation had leased its assets to a second corporation pursuant to a 900-year lease with rent set at $480,000 per year. The lessor corporation merged into the lessee, and the shareholders of the lessor received 100-year bonds of the surviving corporation paying interest of $480,000 per year. The court concluded that this transaction did not qualify as a tax-free reorganization because the shareholders of the lessor failed to acquire a "proprietary" interest in the continuing venture. Rather than asking whether the relationship of these shareholders to the transferred assets became too tenuous or remote (and surely it did not, as no real change was effected by the transaction), the court in *Roebling* applied an arbitrary rule (no stock consideration means no proprietary interest) to tax the transaction.

Thus, *Roebling* concluded that the continuity of interest requirement focused on what is received, an approach arguably inconsistent with the Supreme Court's reasoning in *Paulsen v. Commissioner.*[8] In *Paulsen*, two savings and loan associations merged; the target had issued "guaranty stock" to its owners, while the acquiring association was a federally-chartered mutual association with no stock of any kind. The target shareholders exchanged their guaranty stock for passbook accounts and certificates of deposit in the acquiror, which represented the exclusive ownership interests in the acquiror and gave the holders the right to vote on association matters and participate in liquidating distributions.

The Service had already ruled that a merger of two mutual savings and loan associations could constitute a tax-free reorganization,[9] concluding that the depositor interests received were proprietary interests. Although those interests in both the revenue ruling and *Paulsen* had a strong debt flavor, it was impossible to separate their debt and equity components. Thus, the taxpayer argued, the target shareholders exchanged their target stock solely for acquiror equity interests, and the continuity requirement was met.

Even though the target shareholders received as much of a proprietary interest in the acquiror as was possible, the Supreme Court concluded that the continuity requirement had not been met.

[7] 143 F.2d 810 (3d Cir.1944).
[8] 469 U.S. 131 (1985).
[9] Rev. Rul. 69–3, 1969–1 C.B. 103.

Although its reasoning is not altogether clear, the Court appeared to separate the debt and equity aspects of the depositor interests. If those two aspects can indeed be separated, the *Paulsen* decision is unremarkable—the equity aspects are relatively insubstantial and do not contribute substantially to the fair market value of the interests. Accordingly, it would not be unreasonable to hold that receipt of the passbook accounts and certificates of deposit cannot satisfy the continuity of interest requirement, because the equity aspect of the consideration was not substantial.

Amount of qualifying consideration. Target shareholders, in the aggregate, must receive a "substantial" amount of qualified acquiror stock for the continuity of interest test to be satisfied. Judicial and administrative guidance provides no bright-line standard for the minimum amount of qualified acquiror stock that target shareholders must receive in the transaction, however.

Historically, the Service ruled that a prospective corporate combination met the continuity requirement only if the taxpayer represented the following: The former target shareholders would receive qualified acquiror stock "equal in value, *as of the effective date of the reorganization*, to at least *50 percent* of the value of all of the formerly outstanding [target] stock . . . as of the same date." Rev. Proc. 77-37 (§3.02), 1977-2 C.B. 568 (emphasis added). Practitioners argued that the 50-percent threshold should be lowered to reflect current business practice. They also argued that qualified acquiror stock should be valued when the acquisition agreement became binding, at least if the target shareholders' rights in the qualified acquiror stock became fixed on that date.

Regs. §1.368-1(e)(2) addresses both concerns. The regulation clarifies that the continuity of interest requirement could be met if the target shareholders received qualified acquiror stock that in the aggregate comprised *40 percent* of the total consideration. See Regs. §1.368-1(e)(2)(v) (example 1) (concluding that 40-percent continuity is sufficient). *Cf. id.* (example 11) (concluding that 28.57-percent continuity is not sufficient).

Further, the regulation provides that if the contract to effect the potential reorganization has fixed consideration, continuity is measured on the last business day before the date the contract becomes binding. *Id.* at (e)(2)(i). A contract has fixed consideration if it provides the number of shares of each class of qualified acquiror stock and any other property (identified by value or specific description) to be exchanged for *all* target stock or for *each share* of target stock. *Id.* at (e)(2)(iii)(A). There are special rules to deal with modifications of the contract and with contingent consideration. Note that if the agreement does not provide for fixed consideration, continuity is measured as of the acquisition's effective date.

Pre- and post-reorganization continuity. The cases and regulations considered above did not address the impact of pre-reorganization sales of target stock or post-reorganization sales of qualified acquiror stock, two issues that confused the courts for many years. The confusion was caused because courts and the Service sometimes focused on the consideration received by historic target shareholders. With that focus, continuity of interest could be threatened when those target shareholders sold their target stock before, or their qualified acquiror stock after, the potential reorganization. See *McDonald's v. Commissioner*, 688 F.2d 520 (7th Cir. 1982), rev'g 76 T.C. 972 (1981).

With that focus, those shareholder sales could jeopardize a reorganization's tax-free status, leading to several pernicious effects. First, if the reorganization was not tax-free, the target corporation and those target shareholders retaining their acquiror stock could unexpectedly recognize gain, although the acquiror would take a cost basis in the acquired assets. Further, that focus may make it difficult to determine the tax consequences of a potential reorganization with substantial certainty until well after the transaction, if even then. Finally, that focus may whipsaw the government. That is, the acquiror may treat the transaction as a taxable transaction, claiming a stepped-up basis in the acquired (perhaps depreciable) assets,[10] while some shareholders (especially those who retain their acquiror stock) may treat the transaction as a tax-free reorganization, claiming non-recognition on their receipt of the acquiror stock.[11]

Regs. §1.368-1(e)(1) now avoids those concerns, shifting the focus to the consideration furnished by the acquiring corporation. Under the regulation's general rule, pre- or post-reorganization sales of stock for disqualified consideration are disregarded in measuring continuity of interest.

For example, suppose that A is a shareholder of T Corp. T Corp. merges into P Corp. with A receiving P stock in exchange for A's T Corp. stock. Immediately after the merger, A sells the P Corp. stock to B, a purchaser unrelated to P Corp.[12] Note that there is suf-

---

[10] Target shareholders who realize loss on the reorganization exchange may also claim recognition treatment.

[11] Even those shareholders who immediately sell their stock received in the reorganization may benefit if installment reporting is available on the sale.

[12] There is also continuity of interest if A sells the T Corp. stock to B immediately before the merger pursuant to a prearranged sale and B ex-

ficient continuity of interest even where A's sale of the P Corp. stock is prearranged before the merger.[13]

This general rule has two exceptions. First, sales of target or qualified acquiror stock in connection with the potential reorganization are taken into account if made directly or indirectly to the issuing corporation or a related corporation. Regs. §1.368-1(e)(1)(i). Broadly speaking, a corporation is related to the issuing corporation if, immediately before or after the relevant stock acquisition, it is (i) a direct or indirect 50-percent subsidiary of the issuing corporation or (ii) a member of the same affiliated group (determined without regard to §1504(b)). Regs. §1.368-1(e)(4).

Second, if a target shareholder receives a distribution (including a redemption distribution) before the reorganization, the distribution is disregarded unless §356 applies to the distribution (or would if the shareholder had received qualified acquiror stock in the reorganization). Reg. §1.368-1(e)(1)(i). An example suggests that §356 does not apply to such a distribution unless it is funded by the issuing corporation. Regs. §1.368-1(e)(7) (example 9).

For example, consider the merger of a target into an acquiring corporation in which the target shareholders receive exclusively acquiror stock but, as part of the same plan, the acquiring corporation redeems most or all of that stock for cash. In substance, the acquiror has paid mostly cash in the merger, and the regulations properly adopt that view. Regs. §1.368-1(e)(7) (example 4(i)). The result is the same if the acquiror acquires the target stock for cash immediately before the merger. Regs. §1.368-1(e)(7) (example 4(ii)).

Nor can an acquiror avoid that result by having a related corporation make the stock purchase. Suppose that T Corp. merges into B Corp., the T Corp. shareholders receive solely B stock in the merger, but, as part of the same plan, S Corp. purchases that B stock for cash. If B Corp. and S Corp. have a common parent, P Corp. (so that they are members of an affiliated group), the T

---

changes the T Corp. stock for the P Corp. stock as part of the merger. Regs. § 1.368–1(e)(8) (examples 1 and 3).

[13] The continuity of interest regulations on their face only apply to reorganizations, but should the reasoning also apply to corporate formations as well? Suppose that A forms X Corp. in a purported § 351 transaction and immediately after the formation, A sells half of the X Corp. stock to B. In *Intermountain Lumber Co. v. Commissioner,* 65 T.C. 1025 (1976), the court ruled that § 351 did not apply because of the prearranged sale to B who was not a "transferor." Has the result in *Intermountain (i.e.,* § 351 not applicable) been effectively eviscerated by the continuity of interest regulations? To date, the continuity of interest regulations have not been expanded beyond the realm of reorganizations.

shareholders will be deemed to receive solely cash in the merger, and the merger will lack of continuity of interest. See Regs. §1.368-1(e)(7) (example 4(iii)).

The rationale for the related party exception may be that because of the dividends-received deduction and other intercorporate benefits, it is not difficult for cash to find its way from B Corp. to S Corp. and then ultimately to the former target shareholders. Rather than actually tracing funds, the regulations conclusively assume that any purchase by a related corporation is funded by the acquiror. Note that if S were an individual and owned 80 percent of the B stock, a former target shareholder's sale of B stock to S would be disregarded in testing continuity of interest.[14]

(ii) Continuity of Business Enterprise. The continuity of interest doctrine is not the only non-statutory gloss on the definition of a reorganization. The Service long argued that the surviving corporation must continue the business of the transferor corporation if a reorganization is to be tax-free, a requirement intended to help assure that the reorganization affects a mere change in form of a corporate enterprise. However, the courts were unwilling to adopt the Service's view,[15] and the regulations now include only a reduced form of this *continuity of business enterprise* requirement.

The regulations now formally require that an acquisitive reorganization satisfy a continuity of business enterprise requirement. That requirement is satisfied if the issuing corporation either continues a significant historic business of the target or uses a significant portion of the target's historic assets in a business. Regs. §1.368-1(d)(1). See also id. at (d)(3)(iii) (defining significance based on the facts and circumstances); id. at (d)(5) (examples 1 and 9-11). See also Regs. §1.368-1(d)(3)(iii) (apparently concluding that if the issuing corporation owns at least one-third of the historic target assets, it will be treated as owning a "significant" portion of those assets).

For this purpose, the issuing corporation is treated as owning the assets of, and conducting the businesses of, each member of its qualified group. Id. at (d)(4)(i). Its qualified group includes (i) the issuing corporation, (ii) any corporation that the issuing corporation controls,[16] and (iii) any other corporation that qualified group

---

[14] The dividends-received deduction under § 243 is not available to individual shareholders.

[15] See e.g., *Bentsen v. Phinney,* 199 F.Supp. 363 (S.D.Tex.1961).

[16] One corporation controls another corporation, for this purpose, if it owns at least 80 percent of the voting power of the other corporation and also owns at least 80 percent of each class of the other corporation's non-voting stock. §368(c); Rev. Rul. 59-259, 1959-1 C.B. 115.

members together control.[17] Additional rules attribute partnership assets or businesses in certain cases to the issuing corporation.[18] See id. at (d)(4)(iii)(B) and (D).

As an example, this continuity requirement is met if target has three businesses of equal value, sells two of them, and then merges into an acquiring corporation. *Id*. at (d)(5) (example 1). It is also met if the acquiring corporation transfers the target assets to five members of its qualified group, because the group as a whole retains all target assets. *Id*. at (d)(5) (example 7). However, the requirement is not met when all target assets are sold in connection with the purported reorganization and the historic target business is discontinued. See *id*. at (d)(5) (examples 4 and 5). See also *id*. at (d)(2)(iii) (providing that a target's historic business is not one that it enters into as part of the plan of reorganization).

Nothing in the regulations requires that the *acquiring* corporation continue its own historic business or use its own historic assets in any capacity. Rev. Rul. 81-25, 1981 C.B. 65. Thus, the continuity of business enterprise requirement may be one of the facts that, taxpayers consider in choosing which corporation is the target and which is the acquiror. For example, if X Corp. and Y Corp. merge, the decision about whether X Corp. or Y Corp. survives may turn on whether the parties plan to dispose of the X or Y business assets. The decision may also be affected by which corporation has more goodwill associated with its name or whether either corporation owns an asset (such as a favorable long-term lease) that is difficult to transfer.

(iii) Business Purpose. The doctrines of continuity of interest and continuity of business enterprise were developed by the courts to deny tax-free reorganization status to transactions that closely resembled sales. Similarly, the business purpose doctrine was developed early on to deny tax-free status to transactions that meet

---

[17] Regs. §1.368-1(d)(4)(ii). For this purpose, a qualified group is treated as owning any stock owned by a partnership if the group owns partnership interests "meeting requirements equivalent to section 368(c)." Regs. § 1.368-1(d)(4)(iii)(D) (adding that any partnership interests owned by such a "controlled" partnership are treated as owned by the qualified group).

[18] A partner in a partnership is treated as owning target business assets used in a partnership business in accordance with its partnership interest. Regs. § 1.368-1(d)(4)(iii)(A). In addition, the issuing corporation is treated as conducting the business of the partnership if either—

(i) Members of the qualified group, in the aggregate, own a partnership interest representing a significant interest in the partnership business, or

(ii) One or more members of the qualified group actively and substantially manage the partnership as a partner.

Regs. § 1.368-1(d)(4)(iii)(B).

all the formal requirements of a "reorganization" but lack a valid non-tax business purpose. See, e.g., *Gregory v. Helvering*, 293 U.S. 465 (1935) (concluding that a transaction was taxable even though it met the literal requirements for a tax-free reorganization, labeling the transaction an "elaborate and devious form of conveyance masquerading as a corporate reorganization, and nothing else"). Under the business purpose doctrine, a transaction is likely be challenged if it serves no purpose other than tax avoidance.

Note that the business purpose doctrine has gained new prominence because of the statutory enactment of the economic substance doctrine. Under § 7701(o), for any transaction where the economic substance doctrine is relevant, the transaction is treated as having economic substance only if—

(i) It changes in a meaningful way (apart from Federal income tax effects) the taxpayer's economic position; and

(ii) The taxpayer has a substantial non-Federal income tax purpose for entering the transaction.

§ 7701(o)(5)(A). In other words, if the transaction lacks a meaningful profit motive or a substantial non-tax business purpose, its tax benefits may not be allowable. Section 7701(o) resolves a dispute that raged in the courts about whether economic substance required both a profit motive and non-tax business purpose, following the government's view that both are required.

In addition, as an adjunct to § 7701(o), Congress added substantial penalties for a transaction that fails economic substance. It is then subject to a tax penalty of 20- or 40-percent on the portion of the underpayment of tax attributable to that failure. § 6662(a) (providing for the 20-percent penalty); *id.* at (i) (increasing the penalty to 40 percent for any non-disclosed economic substance transaction). Most concerning for many, these are strict liability penalties; there is no reasonable cause exception.[19]

Despite the enactment of § 7701(o), there remain many unanswered questions about the economic substance doctrine. Those questions include when the doctrine is "relevant" to a transaction; when a transaction promises a "meaningful" change in a taxpayer's economic position; over what period of time that change should be measured; when a non-tax purpose is substantial; and so on. The government has announced that it will not address these or similar

---

[19] §6664(d)(2). Although the government pushed for a statutory enactment of the economic substance doctrine, its enactment may not help the government in the long run, because courts may be inclined to narrow the doctrine's focus to avoid imposing the strict liability penalties.

questions through regulations nor will it publish a list of transactions (sometimes called an "angels" list) that, it believes, will typically satisfy the doctrine. Thus, it appears that these questions will be answered over time by the courts on a case-by-case basis.

However, transactions that met the economic substance doctrine before the enactment of § 7701(o) should continue to do so after its enactment. § 7701(o)(5)(C) (providing that the determination of whether the economic substance doctrine is relevant to a transaction is made as if § 7701(o) had never been enacted). Thus, even though a reorganization may provide tax benefits to its participants, those benefits are ones intended by the Code, and a reorganization typically should not be subject to challenge under the doctrine merely because of those benefits.

(b) Statutory Requirements.

(i) "A" Reorganizations. The statutory terms of the A reorganization are beguilingly simple, seemingly applicable to all mergers and consolidations effected pursuant to federal, state or other local law. However, the courts and the regulations have long recognized that a merger or consolidation should be limited to transactions in which two or more corporations combine. Regs. § 1.368–2(b)(1)(ii). A transaction dividing one corporation into two does not become a tax-free "merger" simply because an accommodating legislature puts the word "merger" in the title of the statute. Regs. § 1.368–2(b)(1)(iv) (example 1).

Specifically, a transfer of assets by one corporation to another corporation meets the statutory requirements for an A reorganization if the transfer is effected under a statute or statutes necessary to effect the merger or consolidation and, as a result, the following two events occur simultaneously:

> (i) All target assets (other than those distributed in the transaction) and all target liabilities (other than those satisfied or discharged in the transaction) become assets and liabilities of a corporation; and

> (ii) The target ceases its separate legal existence.

Regs. §1.368-2(b)(1)(ii). An A reorganization may involve domestic corporations, foreign corporations, or a mix of domestic and foreign corporations.

Note that a target corporation and disregarded entity may combine in an A reorganization. That combination meets the statutory definition of an A reorganization if the target ceases to exist and simultaneously a corporation (*i.e.*, the direct or indirect sole owner of the disregarded entity) is deemed to succeed to the target's assets and liabilities. Regs. §1.368-2(b)(1)(i)(C) and (ii)(A); id. at (b)(1)(iii) (example 2). For federal income tax purposes, the assets held by a disregarded entity are treated as directly held by its owner. See, e.g., Regs. § 301.7701–2(c)(2)(i).

Disregarded entities include an unincorporated domestic entity (such as limited liability company) with a single owner, as long as it does not elect to be taxed as corporation. Regs. § 301-7701-3(b)(1)(ii). See also *id.* at 3(b)(2)(i) (providing that a foreign entity is treated as an association taxed as a corporation (and thus not a disregarded entity) if all of its members have limited liability). They also include certain wholly owned subsidiaries of S corporations (called "Q–Subs").

Suppose that X Corp. owns all membership interests in X1 LLC, a disregarded entity, and Y Corp. owns all membership interests in Y1 LLC, also a disregarded entity. There are a variety of ways in which X Corp., Y Corp., and their two disregarded entities might try to combine in a merger.

Suppose first that X Corp. merges into Y Corp., and by operation of law, X's assets and liabilities become Y's assets and liabilities and simultaneously X Corp. ceases to exist. Because Y Corp. succeeds to all X assets, including all membership interests in X1 LLC, X1 LLC remains a disregarded entity and Y Corp. is also treated as acquiring all assets held by X1 LLC. Thus, the existence for state law purposes of the two disregarded entities will not affect the application of § 368(a)(1)(A): under state law, X will disappear and Y will end up owning both X1 LLC and Y1 LLC, while for federal tax purposes Y will survive and be deemed to own directly the assets of X1 LLC and Y1 LLC.

What if X Corp. merges into Y1 LLC under state law? For federal income tax purposes, Y1 LLC's existence as a separate entity is disregarded, so this transaction may meet the statutory requirements of an A reorganization, just like a direct merger of X Corp. into Y Corp. The regulations confirm that result. Regs. § 1.368–2(b)(1)(iv) (example 2). Contrast this transaction with the state-law merger of X1 LLC into Y Corp. That transaction does not meet the statutory definition for an A reorganization, because X Corp. survives the merger and is treated as transferring only a portion of its assets to Y Corp., the portion held by X1 LLC but treated for federal income tax purposes as owned directly by X Corp. before the merger. Regs. § 1.368–2(b)(1)(iv) (example 5). For similar reasons, the merger of X1 LLC into Y1 LLC would also not qualify as an A reorganization.

(ii) "B" Reorganizations. A B reorganization is a stock acquisition that results in the target corporation becoming a subsidiary of the acquiring corporation. For example, suppose that X Corp. is owned by B and C. If Y Corp. exchanges its voting stock for the X stock held by B and C, the transaction will meet the statutory requirements of a B reorganization. Note that after the transaction B and C are shareholders of Y Corp., which in turn owns all X stock.

A B reorganization has three statutory requirements. First, the acquiring corporation must acquire stock of the target corporation. Second, its sole consideration must be either its voting stock or the voting stock of its parent, (*i.e.*, the corporation that controls the acquiror). The voting stock may be common, preferred, or a combination of the two, but voting stock of both the acquiring corporation and its parent cannot be used. See Regs. § 1.368-2(c). Thus, unless there are prohibited pre- or post-reorganization stock sales or redemptions, the continuity of interest doctrine must be satisfied in a B reorganization, because solely stock is used.

Third, the acquiring corporation must control the target (but not necessarily wholly own it) immediately after the acquisition. That is, acquiring corporation must own at least 80 percent of the total combined voting power of target stock plus at least 80 percent of the total number of shares of each other class of target stock. § 368(c); Rev. Rul. 59-259, 1959-1 C.B. 115. Note that the acquiror need not acquire an amount of target stock in the reorganization that constitutes control; it only needs to control the target immediately after the acquisition.

A variety of different transactions can fit the B reorganization pattern. For example, if a corporation uses solely its voting stock to acquire control of an unrelated corporation, the acquisition satisfies the statutory requirements of a B reorganization: The corporation has acquired stock of a target corporation, its sole consideration was its voting stock, and it controls the target immediately after the acquisition. Note that this acquisition meets those statutory requirements even if the acquiring corporation acquires less than all target stock, as long as it acquires control.

As a second illustration, suppose that a parent corporation already controls a subsidiary corporation (and has done so for many years) but a few other shareholders own subsidiary stock. If the parent exchanges its voting stock for the subsidiary stock held by the minority shareholders, the exchange meets the statutory definition for a B reorganization: The parent has acquired subsidiary stock solely for its voting stock and controls the subsidiary immediately after the acquisition. Thus, emphasizing a point noted above, to qualify as a B reorganization, the parent need not acquire an amount of subsidiary stock that constitutes control.

Suppose in the previous example that the parent owned only half of the subsidiary stock (and did not control the subsidiary). The parent could still acquire subsidiary stock in a B reorganization, as long as it used qualifying consideration (*e.g.*, its voting stock) and it controlled the corporation immediately after the acquisition.

This last form of the B reorganization is called a "creeping" B, because control of the target corporation is obtained in a series of transactions. In *Chapman v. Commissioner,*[20] the acquiring corporation purchased approximately 8 percent of the target corporation's stock for cash.[21] The acquiring corporation then exchanged its voting stock for the remaining stock of the target corporation, and at issue was whether this latter step constituted a tax-free B reorganization, even though the acquiring corporation acquired some target stock for cash as part of the overall plan.

The circuit court conceded that the statute permitted creeping B reorganizations but held that the transaction failed the "solely in exchange for voting stock" requirement of the B reorganization. The taxpayer in *Chapman* argued that the statute required voting stock be used only to acquire control of the target corporation. Since no more than 80 percent of the target's stock need be held by the acquiring corporation after the transaction, the taxpayer argued that any method of obtaining additional stock was consistent with the requirements of the B reorganization. The court rejected this interpretation of the statute, however, holding instead that however much stock of the target was acquired in the transaction, the *total* consideration furnished by the acquiring corporation had to be its voting stock or voting stock of its parent.[22]

The "solely for voting stock" requirement of the B reorganization can have an impact in other settings. For example, suppose

---

[20] 618 F.2d 856 (1st Cir.1980).

[21] Before the reorganization, the acquiring corporation sold this stock to a third party. The terms of this sale were such that the Service could persuasively argue that it was a sham, and for the summary judgment motion at issue in *Chapman,* the court assumed that the acquiring corporation did not sell that stock.

[22] The court also held that stock of the target acquired in a prior, unrelated transaction (not the 8-percent purchased and sold prior to the transaction) was irrelevant to the reorganization issue. That is, "old and cold" stock need not have been acquired solely for voting stock. But in *Chapman* the 8 percent stock interest was assumed not to be "old and cold," and the cash paid for it spoiled the B reorganization.

that the shareholders of the target company would like the acquiring corporation to pay their reorganization expenses (such as fees for lawyers and accountants). If the transaction is to qualify as a B reorganization, these shareholders' expenses cannot be paid by the acquiring corporation. Similarly, if a target shareholder has pledged his stock as security for a debt, the acquiring corporation may not pay off that debt.

On the other hand, cash can be paid in lieu of issuing fractional shares in a B reorganization without running afoul of the "solely for voting stock" requirement.[23] Further, that requirement may be met if cash is paid to dissenting target shareholders, as long as the target corporation makes that payment and the acquiring corporation does not directly or indirectly reimburse the target.[24]

Additionally, the acquiring corporation can use cash or other property in connection with a B reorganization as consideration for anything *other than* stock of the target. Thus, the acquiring corporation may purchase bonds of the target for cash, or it may exchange its own bonds for them. This use of non-voting stock consideration will not disqualify the reorganization for the simple reason that exchanges not involving the target's stock are not part of the definition of the reorganization, regardless of the consideration used.

Suppose that the acquiring corporation has adopted an anti-takeover poison pill, so that its shares contain the right to purchase additional shares at a discount upon the occurrence of some triggering event such as the acquisition of 20 percent of the company stock by an outside investor. Is the B reorganization invalidated automatically because the poison pill stock rights constitute non-stock consideration? In the context of § 305, the Service has ruled that the adoption of a poison pill does not constitute the distribution of stock or of property. Should the poison pill rights also be ignored for tax purposes in this context? In several private letter rulings, the Service ignored poison pill contingent stock rights, thereby implicitly ruling that they do not constitute impermissible other property.[25]

The terms of § 368(a)(1)(B) permit use of voting stock of the acquiring corporation *or* of a corporation "in control of" the acquiring corporation. When stock of the acquiring corporation's parent is used, the transaction often is called a "parenthetical" or triangular

---

[23] Rev. Rul. 66–365, 1966–2 C.B. 116.

[24] Rev. Rul. 68-285, 1968-1 C.B. 147.

[25] See Priv. Ltr. Rul. 9120006 (May 17, 1991); Priv. Ltr. Rul. 8808081 (Dec. 3, 1987). See also Rev. Rul. 75-237, 1975-1 C.B. 116; Rev. Rul. 73-205, 1973-1 C.B. 188.

B reorganization. In a parenthetical B reorganization, shareholders of the target become doubly removed from the target's assets. While the Supreme Court initially held that such transactions could not be tax-free reorganizations,[26] Congress has repudiated that position in the parenthetical language of § 368(a)(1)(B) as well as in a variety of other provisions.[27]

In a B reorganization, stock of the acquiring corporation *or* of the acquiring corporation's parent may be used, but not both.[28] This limitation is intended to ensure that a shareholder of the target corporation cannot cash out part of his investment without losing a proportionate part of his interest in the transferred assets. For example, suppose that A Corp. acquired all the stock of T Corp. in exchange for its own stock as well as stock of P Corp., its parent. If a (former) T shareholder sold the P stock, the shareholder would obtain cash from the transaction without substantially diluting his interest in A (and through A, in T). Were such transactions permitted, the efficacy of the "solely for voting stock" requirement of the B reorganization would be reduced. You may want to reconsider this point when you cover divisive reorganizations, because the effect of using stock of the acquiring corporation as well as stock of the acquiring corporation's parent could be to turn a B into something akin to a divisive reorganization.

(iii) "C" Reorganizations. Like an A reorganization, a C reorganization is an asset transfer, rather than a stock transfer like a B reorganization. In fact, a transaction that qualifies an A reorganization may also qualify as a C reorganization, and the C reorganization is sometimes referred to as a "de facto" (or practical) merger.

An asset acquisition meets the statutory requirements for a C reorganization if the following three requirements are met:

> (i) The acquiror acquires substantially all of the properties of the target corporation;

> (ii) The acquiror acquires the target assets using solely its voting stock or solely the voting stock of its parent (*i.e.*, a corporation that controls the acquiror); and

> (iii) The target liquidates.

---

[26] See *Groman v. Commissioner*, 302 U.S. 82 (1937); *Helvering v. Bashford*, 302 U.S. 454 (1938).

[27] See § 368(a)(1)(C); § 368(a)(2)(C)–(E).

[28] Regs. § 1.368–2(c).

§ 368(a)(1)(C) (for the first two requirements); § 368(a)(2)(G) (for the liquidation requirement).[29]

For example, suppose that Y Corp. transfers all of its assets to X Corp. in exchange for X voting stock. If Y Corp. liquidates immediately after the exchange, the exchange meets the statutory requirements for a C reorganization, because X Corp. acquired all Y assets (and thus at least "substantially all" of those assets), X Corp. used solely its voting stock in the acquisition, and Y Corp. liquidated.

Neither the statute nor regulations define what constitutes "substantially all" of a target's assets, although the Service has ruled that the transfer constituting 90 percent of the target's net assets and 70 percent of the target's gross assets will constitute "substantially all."[30] The D reorganization also includes a "substantially all" requirement, and in that context the courts have held that a transfer of all the operating assets satisfies the requirement even if the operating assets constitute less than 20 percent of the target's net assets. It is far from clear, however, that the same standards should apply for C reorganizations, and courts (or the Service) might define the "substantially all" requirement for C reorganizations to ensure that they are used to continue a corporate enterprise in modified form, rather than to divide and partially liquidate the company.[31]

As with a B reorganization, unless there are prohibited pre- or post-reorganization stock sales or redemptions, the continuity of interest doctrine must be satisfied in a C reorganization, because

---

[29] The Service may waive the liquidation requirement in cases of "substantial hardship." See § 368(a)(2)(G)(ii); Rev. Proc. 89-50, 1989-2 C.B. 631.

[30] Rev. Proc. 77–37, 1977–2 C.B. 568. For this purpose, 70% of gross assets are transferred if assets with a value equal to 70% of all target assets are transferred. In addition, 90% of net assets are transferred if net assets with a value equal 90% of all net assets are transferred. Net assets are gross assets less liabilities assumed (or taken subject to).

For example, suppose that a target corporation has assets worth $100,000 subject to $20,000 of debt. Its gross asset value is $100,000 and its net asset value is $80,000 ($100,000 gross asset value minus $20,000 of liabilities). Thus, 70% of the target's gross asset value is $70,000, and 90 percent of its net asset value is $72,000. Suppose that a corporation acquires exactly $75,000 worth of target assets but takes none of those assets subject to the debt. Then, the acquiror acquires target assets with a gross asset and net asset value of $75,000 meeting the "70/90" test.

This test is not met, however, if the acquired target assets are subject to a $10,000 liability. Although sufficient gross assets are acquired (their value is still $75,000), the value of the net assets acquired is less than the required $72,000. In fact, the net asset value is only $65,000 ($75,000, the value of the gross assets acquired, minus the $10,000 liability to which those assets are subject).

[31] Compare the partial liquidation provision of § 302(b)(4).

predominantly stock is used. However, the "solely for voting stock" requirement of the C reorganization lacks much of the bite of the B reorganization because of two provisions: § 368(a)(2)(B) and the final clause of § 368(a)(1)(C).

That final clause states that if the acquiring corporation assumes target liabilities, the assumption is disregarded. But for that final clause, if the acquiring corporation assumed target liabilities, it would be treated as acquiring target assets for consideration other than voting stock and the transaction might not qualify as a C reorganization. The final clause overturns the Supreme Court's decision in *United States v. Hendler,*[32] the case in which it was held that assumption of a liability, even in the context of a bulk transfer of corporate assets, should be treated as the equivalent of cash consideration. Because most companies are forced to mortgage their fixed or working assets to obtain commercial credit, a continuation of the *Hendler* doctrine would have made C reorganization commercially unavailable.

Congress further loosened the C reorganization's "solely for voting stock" requirement by enacting the boot relaxation rule of § 368(a)(2)(B). This provision permits the acquiring corporation to use cash or other boot as consideration in a C reorganization as long as at least 80 percent of the target's assets are acquired solely for voting stock. Thus, if the acquiring corporation acquires all of the target's assets, up to 20 percent of the consideration may be boot. On the other hand, if it acquires only 80 percent of the target assets, no boot at all is allowed. In between fall those transactions in which the target corporation transfers more than 80 percent but less than all of its assets. For example, if the target transfers 90 percent of its assets worth $900,000 to the acquiring corporation, the consideration must include at least $800,000 of voting stock of the acquiring corporation (or of its parent). Thus, up to $100,000 of the consideration could be boot.

One peculiar wrinkle tarnishes the boot relaxation rule. For purposes of the rule, boot includes any target liabilities assumed or taken subject to. Thus, if the acquiring corporation assumes target liabilities in the transaction and the liabilities exceed 20 percent of the gross value of target assets, the boot relaxation rule cannot apply, because the acquiror will then acquire less than 80 percent of the target assets for qualifying property. Because most targets have liabilities exceeding 20 percent of their gross asset value, the boot relaxation rule is therefore of limited practical importance.

---

[32] 303 U.S. 564 (1938).

Nevertheless, the boot relaxation rule occasionally applies, and the following example illustrates its application. Suppose that T Corp. has assets worth $100,000 subject to liabilities of $13,000. If A Corp. wants to acquire all of T's assets in a C reorganization, A Corp. must acquire at least $80,000 worth of T assets for voting stock. Because the net value of T's assets is $87,000, A Corp. presumably will provide an additional $7,000 of value. That additional value can be more voting stock, cash, or anything else pursuant to § 368(a)(2)(B). However, if A Corp. receives only 90 percent of T's assets, fully subject to the liability of $13,000, it can provide no boot if the acquisition is to qualify as a C reorganization. In fact, the maximum amount of boot that can be used under § 368(a)(2)(B) equals 20 percent of the value of the target corporation's assets *less* the value (if any) of the target's assets not transferred in the reorganization *and less* the target's liabilities (if any) assumed by the acquiring corporation.

Can the following transaction be a C reorganization? X Corp. owns 79 percent of the only class of Y stock. X Corp. exchanges its voting stock for the Y assets and Y liquidates, distributing 79 percent of the X stock back to X Corp. and the remaining 21 percent to the other Y shareholders. In form, X Corp. acquired the Y assets solely for its voting stock. In substance, however, its transfer and planned receipt of its voting stock could be disregarded under the step-transaction doctrine, and X Corp. could be treated as acquiring the Y assets in exchange, in part, for its Y stock.

Bausch & Lomb Optical Co. v. Commissioner[33] followed the substance of the transaction, concluding that the transaction failed to qualify as a C reorganization, because X Corp. obtained 79 percent of the Y assets for its Y stock and only 21 percent of the Y assets for X voting stock. As a result, the transaction was treated as a taxable liquidation rather than as a tax-free reorganization. While the court's holding follows the literal language of the statute, the "solely for voting stock" requirement seems intended to ensure that the target shareholders continue a proprietary interest in the continuing enterprise. The holding in *Bausch & Lomb* served to invalidate a transaction when the acquiring corporation is itself a substantial shareholder of the target corporation, a situation in which the continuity of interest is most evident.[34]

In fact, the taxpayer in *Bausch & Lomb* would have been better off if it had owned slightly more of the liquidating corporation's

---

[33] 267 F.2d 75 (2d Cir.1959).

[34] See Regs. § 1.368-1(e)(1)(i) (providing that a proprietary interest in the target corporation is preserved if it is exchanged "for a direct interest in the target corporation enterprise").

stock. If it had owned over 80 percent of that stock, the transaction would have been tax-free under the predecessor to § 332 as the liquidation of a controlled subsidiary. Further, if the subsidiary had merged into the taxpayer, the merger could have qualified as an A reorganization, as the court acknowledged. The court nevertheless concluded that the terms of the statute had to be read literally and it could not be tax-free.

By regulation, Treasury has overturned the result in *Bausch & Lomb*. Now, if the acquiring corporation has "old and cold" target stock, that stock is disregarded in determining whether the "solely for voting stock" requirement for a C reorganization has been met. Regs. § 1.368–2(d)(4). Of course, if the target stock is acquired in contemplation of the reorganization, the consideration furnished by the acquiring corporation for that stock (unless it consists exclusively of voting stock of the acquiring corporation) will have to fall within the boot relaxation rule of § 368(a)(2)(B). See Regs. § 1.368–2(d)(4) (example 2).

Because of parenthetical language in § 368(a)(1)(C), the C reorganization permits the acquiring corporation to use its voting stock or the voting stock of its parent, a reorganization sometimes referred to as a "parenthetical" or "triangular" C. Once again, voting stock of the acquiring corporation cannot be combined with voting stock of the parent,[35] although if 80 percent of the target's assets are exchanged for voting stock of the acquiring corporation or of its parent, use of the other's stock may be permissible under the boot relaxation rule of § 368(a)(2)(B).[36]

(iv) Acquisitive "D" Reorganizations. The statutory definition of a D reorganization incorporates two different kinds of transactions, an acquisitive or nondivisive D reorganization, in which two corporations combine and a divisive D reorganization, in which on corporation divides in two. Both types of D reorganizations involve a transfer of assets from one corporation to another followed by a distribution by the transferor corporation. If that distribution satisfies the requirements of § 354, the transaction may be an acquisitive D reorganization; if the distribution meets the requirements of § 355, the transaction may be a divisive D reorganization.[37] Divisive D reorganizations are discussed in section 10.04.

---

[35] Regs. § 1.368–2(d)(1).

[36] Note that the definition of "property" in § 317(a) applies by its terms only to part I of subchapter C; that is, to §§ 301–318. Accordingly, that definition of property is not applicable to the reorganization provisions in § 368(a).

[37] A D reorganization also can include a distribution meeting the requirements of § 356. Such a D reorganization will be one of the two basic

By the terms of § 368(a)(1)(D), an acquisitive D reorganization must satisfy the requirements of § 354, in particular § 354(b). Accordingly, the transferor-corporation must transfer "substantially all" of its assets to the transferee and then liquidate, distributing its remaining assets as well as anything received from the transferee to its shareholders. In addition, the terms of § 368(a)(1)(D) require that the transferor or its shareholders control the transferee immediately after the asset transfer. Thus, once the transferor corporation liquidates, some or all of its shareholders necessarily will control the transferee. As to these shareholders, the effect of the transaction is to combine the assets of the transferor and the transferee into a single corporation. If the transferee had no significant assets prior to the transaction, then the effect of the transaction is to substitute the transferee for the transferor.

An acquisitive D reorganization is much like a C reorganization. Both involve a transfer of "substantially all" of a corporation's assets, followed (always for a D, usually for a C) by a complete liquidation of the transferor. The two differ in how they implement the continuity of interest doctrine. In the C reorganization, continuity is ensured by the requirement that the transferee corporation obtain the assets in exchange for its voting stock or its parent's voting stock. In the acquisitive D reorganization, continuity is ensured by the requirement that the transferor or its shareholders *control* the transferee immediately after the exchange.[38]

Because the continuity requirement looks to control, can there be an "all-cash" acquisitive D reorganization? Consider the following transaction: B owns all stock of X Corp. and Y Corp., X Corp. sells all of its assets to Y Corp. for cash, and X Corp. liquidates, distributing the cash to B. Even though B receives no stock in the transaction, the transaction is a D reorganization. See Regs. § 1.368-2(l)(3) (example 1). Essentially, the continuity of interest requirement for acquisitive D reorganizations is met if all of the target and acquiror stock is owned by the same shareholders in identical proportions. Regs. § 1.368-2(l)(2)(i); *id.* at (l)(2)(ii) (determining ownership using the § 318 attribution rules, with modifications); *id.* at (l)(2)(iii) (disregarding *de minimis* variations in shareholder identity or ownership proportionality). See also *id.* at (l)(3) (example 2) (treating a mother and son as one individual for this

---

forms but with boot distributed in addition to stock and securities. Thus, a D reorganization qualifying with a distribution taxed under § 356 is either an acquisitive D reorganization with boot or a divisive reorganization with boot.

[38] Where a transaction qualifies as both a C and a D reorganization, it is treated as a D. § 368(a)(2)(A).

purpose). In the case of identical ownership, the issuance of stock would be a meaningless gesture.

However, if no stock or securities are actually distributed to B in the example, that result appears to violate the distribution requirement of §354(b)(1)(B), a requirement for an acquisitive D reorganization. Under the regulations, the requirement is deemed met, because the acquiror is deemed to issue a nominal share to the target, which the target is deemed to distribute to its shareholders. Regs. §1.368-2(l)(2)(i).

Note that the definition of "control" is expanded in the case of acquisitive D reorganizations from the usual 80-percent test down to the 50-percent vote or value test of § 304(c).[39] Since § 304 is an anti-abuse provision, you might suspect that the acquisitive D reorganization will on occasion be a tool of the Commissioner rather than of the taxpayer. In fact, the acquisitive D reorganization is the principal statutory provision by which the Commissioner attacks the *liquidation/reincorporation* problem; that is, the problem of taxpayers liquidating their corporations and then reincorporating some of the assets in an effort to obtain exchange treatment (including the possibility of loss) on what is tantamount to a dividend distribution.

For example, consider X Corp., which owns a building with a $1,000,000 adjusted basis and $650,000 fair market value. Assume that the corporation also has cash of $100,000, and that the X shareholders would like to have the cash distributed pro rata to them. If X simply declares a dividend, the shareholders will have ordinary dividend income equal to the full amount realized, assuming that X has earnings and profits of at least $100,000. A redemption will be no better, because none of the safe harbors of § 302(b) will protect the pro rata redemption from § 301 distribution treatment. However, if X liquidates and the building is reincorporated, a far different tax result obtains if form is followed.

First, X Corp. realizes and recognizes a $350,000 loss under § 336(a) (assuming the exceptions in § 336(d) do not apply). Second, the X shareholders apply the amount distributed against their stock bases, reporting any excess as capital gain or any deficit as capital loss. If the shareholders' aggregate basis exceeds $750,000, there will be no net tax at the shareholder level even though the shareholders receive $100,000 in cash. Regardless of the shareholders' taxation, X Corp. will have a $350,000 loss to offset its income. As a further tax benefit, X Corp. eliminates its earnings and profits ac-

---

[39] See § 368(a)(2)(H).

count as a result of the liquidation. The shareholders may then use § 351 to reincorporate the building without recognition of gain.

The Commissioner attacks such transactions under § 368(a)(1)(D), arguing that the liquidation and reincorporation should be treated, in substance, as a direct transfer to the continuing corporate entity. Because the X shareholders control the new corporation after the transaction, the terms of the acquisitive D reorganization will have been met. Accordingly, X Corp. will recognize no loss,[40] X Corp.'s earnings and profits account will not be eliminated,[41] and the shareholders will be prohibited from recognizing any loss on the transaction.[42] Moreover, the $100,000 removed from corporate solution may be taxable to the shareholders.[43]

Taxpayers have tried to avoid the D reorganization by reincorporating only a small portion of their assets. For example, in *Smothers v. United States,*[44] the taxpayers owned two corporations, TIL and IUS. Both corporations were engaged in the business of renting uniforms and cleaning equipment, and because IUS rented most of its heavy equipment, it owned few operating assets. IUS sold its operating assets and some rental property to TIL for $22,637.56 and then liquidated, distributing cash and property worth $149,162.35 to its shareholders. The taxpayers reported the transaction as a complete liquidation of IUS (producing capital gain to the shareholders under § 331) while the Commissioner argued that the transaction was an acquisitive D reorganization producing ordinary income pursuant to § 356(a)(2).[45]

At issue was whether IUS transferred "substantially all" of its assets to TIL.[46] The court in *Smothers* refused to define "substantially all" by reference to a fixed percentage of the corporation's assets. Instead, the court interpreted "substantially all" to mean most

---

[40] See § 361(a)–(b).

[41] In fact, the new corporation will succeed to that account. See § 381(a)(2), (c)(2).

[42] See § 354(a)(1); § 356(a).

[43] See § 356 discussed at Section 10.03(b) *infra*. Note that if the new corporation has no assets, the transaction may be characterized as a reorganization under § 368(a)(1)(F). Then the new corporation will essentially be treated as a continuation of X Corp., and the X shareholders will treat the $100,000 cash distribution as ordinary dividend income (assuming that X Corp. has adequate earnings and profits).

[44] 642 F.2d 894 (5th Cir.1981).

[45] Section 356 is discussed in more detail at Section 10.03(b) *infra*.

[46] The transaction formally did not meet the requirement imposed by § 354(b)(1)(A) that the transferee corporation (TIL) exchange its stock or securities for the assets received. Because the shareholders of IUS also owned TIL prior to the transaction, the receipt of stock by IUS would have added nothing to the exchange. See Regs. § 1.368-2(e)(2)(i).

of the corporation's operating assets. Its interpretation ensured that reorganization status would be given to any corporate rearrangement resulting in "a continuance of the proprietary interests in the continuing enterprise under modified corporate form." Because TIL acquired the operating assets of IUS and succeeded to its goodwill, reorganization status was appropriate.

The dissenting opinion in *Smothers* questioned the majority's conclusion that IUS *transferred* substantially all of its assets to TIL. The major operating asset of IUS was its goodwill and knowledgeable employees. Since the employees of IUS could have chosen not to join TIL, in what sense were they "transferred" by IUS? To be sure, the employees did join TIL and TIL did benefit from their experience. But that alone does not mean that they were "transferred" by IUS, at least without straining the meaning of "transfer."

The majority opinion recognized that the business enterprise of IUS was continued in TIL and that TIL was controlled by the IUS shareholders. Accordingly, the transaction met the spirit of the reorganization provisions. But did the court pay sufficient deference to the words chosen by Congress in defining the various forms of reorganization? Congress could have defined a D reorganization to include any transaction which continues the business of one corporation in a new corporate form. Instead, Congress spoke of a transfer of "substantially all" of the corporation's assets. For a capital-intensive business, presumably the business cannot be continued without substantially all of its operating assets. But for a service-intensive business such as was involved in *Smothers,* the assets used in the business may have little to do with the business itself. Was it proper for the court in *Smothers* to further the general policy behind reorganizations at the cost of ignoring the words of the statute?

(v) Transfers of Target Stock or Assets to a Subsidiary. In many circumstances, it may make sense for target assets to be held by a subsidiary but for the target shareholders to receive parent stock in the exchange. For example, if Big Corp. wants to acquire Little Corp. in a tax-free transaction, it may prefer to continue the business of Little Corp. in a separate corporation. This result could be accomplished through Big Corp. acquiring the Little Corp. stock in a B reorganization, but some of the shareholders may prefer consideration other than voting stock of Big Corp. If so, the transaction cannot fit within the B framework.

Could the target assets be transferred to Sub. Corp., a subsidiary of Big Corp.? Early on, the Supreme Court concluded that if the target assets were transferred to a subsidiary (directly or indirectly) but parent stock was used in the exchange, the transaction could not qualify as a tax-free reorganization.[47] Therefore, if Little Corp. transferred its assets directly to Sub Corp. but the Little Corp. shareholders received Big Corp. stock, the transaction historically could not qualify as a tax-free reorganization. Nor could it qualify if the Little Corp. transferred its assets directly to Big Corp., and Big Corp. dropped those assets down to Sub Corp. as part of the same plan. The statute and regulations now allow those triangular reorganizations and drop-downs if certain conditions are met.

Triangular Reorganizations. Congress first permitted triangular or parenthetical B and C reorganizations. The parenthetical C reorganization might be the answer for Big Corp. in the preceding example, but recall that if it pays boot, § 368(a)(2)(B) requires that at least 80 percent of all target assets be acquired for voting stock. If this restriction is not overly burdensome, the transaction can be structured as a parenthetical C reorganization, with voting stock of Big Corp. constituting the bulk of the consideration.

It may be, though, that the C form is too restrictive, and in that case the parties would prefer an A reorganization. In general, consideration in an A reorganization is limited only by the common law continuity of interest doctrine; that is, stock (not necessarily voting stock) of the transferee corporation must constitute a substantial and meaningful portion of the total consideration used in the transaction.

Merging Little Corp. with Sub Corp., the subsidiary of Big Corp., may be an ideal form for this transaction, offering significant non-tax advantages. For example, state law may well provide that a merger of two corporations requires the affirmative vote of both corporate parties. If so, merging Little Corp. with Big Corp. would require approval of the Big Corp. shareholders as well as those of Little Corp. If Big Corp. is publicly held, obtaining the approval of its shareholders may be prohibitively expensive.

On the other hand, if Little Corp. merges with Sub Corp., approval of the subsidiary's shareholders is easy to obtain, because it requires nothing more than approval by the directors of Big Corp. However, the shareholders of Little Corp. will likely not want to obtain Sub Corp. shares nor will Big Corp. likely want to dilute its equity interest in Sub Corp. Rather, both will likely prefer that stock in Big Corp. be used. That is, the ideal transaction may be a merger where the target shareholders receive parent, not subsidi-

---

[47] See *Groman v. Commissioner,* 302 U.S. 82 (1937); *Helvering v. Bashford,* 302 U.S. 454 (1938).

ary, stock as a consideration in the merger. These transactions can now qualify as tax-free reorganizations under § 368(a)(2)(D) and § 368(a)(2)(E), both of which supplement the general merger rule of § 368(a)(1)(A).

Under § 368(a)(2)(D), a transaction meets the statutory requirements of an A reorganization if the target corporation merges *into* a subsidiary corporation, but the target shareholders receive stock of the parent, a corporation that controls the subsidiary.[48] In the merger, no subsidiary stock may be used and the subsidiary must acquire substantially all of the target assets. §368(a)(2)(D)(i) and (ii).

For example, suppose that Big Corp. forms Sub Corp., contributing its own stock and other property to Sub Corp. in exchange for all of Sub Corp.'s stock.[49] The total value contributed to Sub Corp. should equal the value of Little Corp. Then, when Little Corp. is merged into Sub Corp., the shareholders of Little Corp. will give up their Little Corp. stock in exchange for the stock of Big Corp. held by Sub Corp. When the dust settles, the Little Corp. shareholders have become shareholders of Big Corp. and Big Corp. has become the parent of a subsidiary (*i.e.*, Sub Corp.) that owns the Little Corp. assets. Because of § 368(a)(2)(D), this merger, sometimes called a "forward subsidiary merger," will meet the statutory requirements of an A reorganization.[50]

---

[48] §368(a)(1)(A) and (a)(2)(D); Regs. § 1.368-2(b)(2). One corporation controls a second corporation if it owns at least 80 percent of the total combined voting power of the second corporation's stock plus at least 80 percent of the total number of shares of each other class of that corporation's stock. § 368(c); Rev. Rul. 59-259, 1959-1 C.B. 115.

As with all A reorganizations, the merger must meet the requirements of Regs. § 1.368-2(b)(1)(ii). Thus, it must occur pursuant to a statute or statutes, and as a result, the following two events must occur simultaneously: (i) All target assets and liabilities must become assets and liabilities of the surviving corporation; and (ii) the target must cease its separate legal existence.

[49] Even though the textual examples use newly formed subsidiaries, A reorganizations may be described in § 368(a)(2)(D) or § 368(a)(2)(E) if existing subsidiaries are used.

[50] It is also sometimes called a "forward triangular merger,' because it involves three corporate parties. This transaction is the analog to a triangular C reorganization. Generally in both types of reorganizations, a parent must control a subsidiary, the subsidiary must acquire substantially all target assets, and the target must liquidate. However, the reorganizations differ in amount and character of parent stock that must be received by target shareholders. With the triangular C reorganization, it must comprise at least 80% (if not more) of the total consideration transferred to the target shareholders and must be voting stock, while with the forward triangular merger, it may comprise just 40% (or perhaps less) of the total consideration and may be non-voting stock.

There may be business reasons for Little Corp. rather than Sub Corp. to survive the merger. For example, Little Corp. may own a favorable long-term lease, patents, a liquor license, or other assets that cannot be readily transferred. In those circumstances, the parties may prefer the following structure: As before, Big Corp. forms Sub Corp., transferring its voting stock to Sub Corp. Next, Sub Corp. merges into Little Corp., meaning that Little Corp. survives. As part of the merger, the Little Corp. shareholders exchange their Little Corp. shares for the Big Corp. shares held by Sub Corp. Also as part of the merger, Big Corp. exchanges its shares of Sub Corp. for all Little Corp. stock. In this way, Big Corp. controls Little Corp. after the transaction, and the former Little Corp. shareholders become shareholders of Big Corp. Although slightly more complicated than the forward subsidiary merger, this transaction allows the target corporation to survive the merger.

If certain requirements are met, this type of transaction, called a "reverse subsidiary merger," may be treated as an A reorganization.[51] In contradistinction to the forward subsidiary merger, Congress has added a statutory proprietary interest requirement to the requirements of a reverse subsidiary merger. Under § 368(a)(2)(E), only voting stock of the acquiring corporation (Big Corp. in the example above) may be used to acquire "control" of the target corporation. Thus, the consideration allowed in a reverse subsidiary merger is substantially less broad than that permitted in a forward subsidiary merger.

More precisely, § 368(a)(2)(E) requires that a subsidiary corporation, controlled by a parent corporation, must merge into a target corporation and—

> (i) In the transaction, former target shareholders must exchange, for parent voting stock, a controlling interest in the target stock; and

> (ii) After the transaction, the target must hold substantially all of its assets and substantially all of the merged subsidiary's assets.[52]

Although a reverse subsidiary merger is an analog to a B reorganization, its voting stock requirement differs significantly from that of a B reorganization. In a reverse subsidiary merger, boot can be used in a reverse subsidiary merger, and the target shareholders

---

[51] It is also sometimes called a "reverse triangular merger, because it involves three corporate parties.

[52] § 368(a)(2)(E); Regs. §1.368-2(j). Note that the merger must be described in Regs. § 1.368-2(b)(1)(ii) and control is defined in § 368(c).

must exchange a controlling interest in the target for parent voting stock.[53] Thus, the *Chapman* issue is resolved differently for reverse subsidiary mergers, allowing up to 20-percent boot. On the other hand, because the acquiring corporation must *acquire* control of the target in the transaction (and must acquire that control for its voting stock), the chance for a creeping reverse subsidiary merger is substantially restricted. For reasons known only to Congress (if to anyone), the reverse subsidiary merger is a strange creature, one part A, one part B, and one part like nothing else.

Technically, the statute requires that the target corporation in a reverse subsidiary merger hold substantially all of its own assets (and substantially all of the assets of the acquiring subsidiary that is merged out of existence, excluding stock of this corporation's parent) immediately after the transaction. Does this preclude the sale of a significant portion of the target's assets to third parties as part of the plan of reorganization? So long as the target retains (or reinvests) the sales proceeds and the sale does not cause the transaction to fail the continuity of business enterprise doctrine, it will not affect the tax-free status of the transaction.[54]

Drop-downs and Push-ups. Suppose that Little Corp. merges into Big Corp., the Little Corp. shareholders receive stock of Big Corp. but as part of the same plan, Big Corp. drops all or part of the Little Corp. assets down to its controlled subsidiary, Sub Corp. As noted above, historically the drop-down disqualified the transaction as a tax-free reorganization. The statute and regulations have since been amended to permit some drop-downs (and push-ups).

Under § 368(a)(2)(C), an A, B, C or G reorganization is not disqualified merely because the assets or stock acquired in a transaction are dropped down to a subsidiary controlled by the acquiring corporation. See § 368(c) (defining control). Thus, in the preceding example, if the merger of Little Corp. into Big Corp. otherwise qualifies as an A reorganization, it will not be disqualified by the drop-

---

[53] In the example above, if Little Corp. has one class of stock outstanding, the "controlling interest" requirement is met if the Little Corp. shareholders transfer their Little Corp. stock and receive 80% Big Corp. voting stock and 20% cash, but not if they receive 70% Big Corp. voting stock and 30% cash. Although in both cases, Big Corp. will end up with all Little Corp. stock (and thus control Little Corp.) only the first case meets the "controlling interest" requirement. In that case, the Little Corp. shareholders transfer 80% of (or a controlling interest in) the Little Corp. stock for Big Corp. voting stock and 20% of the Little Corp. stock for cash.

[54] Rev. Rul. 2001–25, 2001–22, I.R.B. 1291; Rev. Rul. 88-48, 1988-1 C.B. 117.

down of Little Corp. assets to Sub Corp., a corporation controlled by Big Corp.[55]

Regs. §1.368-2(k) interprets §368(a)(2)(C) to illustrate, rather than limit, permissible drop downs and other transfers of target assets or stock in a § 368(a) reorganization. For instance, in the example above, the Big Corp./Little Corp. merger could still be an A reorganization, if Sub Corp. also dropped the Little Corp. assets to Grandchild Corp., its controlled subsidiary, Grandchild Corp. then dropped those assets to Great Grandchild Corp., its controlled subsidiary, and so on.

This liberal interpretation of §368(a)(2)(C) is hard to square with the words of the statute. Under §368(a)(2)(C), authority to drop down assets appears confined to a single drop-down following A, B, C and G reorganizations, a list that notably excludes D reorganizations. Nonetheless, § 1.368-2(k) extends the benefit of §368(a)(2)(C) to multiple drop-downs and also to D reorganizations. See also Rev. Rul. 2002-85, 2002-2 C.B. 986 (extending that benefit on the theory that "§368(a)(2)(C) is permissive and not exclusive or restrictive"). To be sure, it is hard to see what's wrong with multiple drop-downs to controlled entities. It is also hard to see any principled reason why a post-reorganization transfer of assets to a controlled subsidiary ought to disqualify an otherwise valid D reorganization. But that disqualification appears to be exactly what Congress intended by excluding the D reorganization in §368(a)(2)(C). Indeed, in the parenthetical language in §368(a)(2)(A), Congress expressly provided that a transaction qualifying as both a C and a D reorganization could get the benefit of §368(a)(2)(C), language that would be unnecessary if D reorganizations qualified under §368(a)(2)(C) directly.

In any case, for *any* § 368 reorganization, Regs. § 1.368-2(k)(1)(ii) provides that drop-downs of assets or stock of the target or acquiring corporation do not disqualify the transaction as a reorganization (or cause it to be recharacterized) if the following requirements are met:

(i) The continuity of business enterprise requirement of § 1.368-1(d) continues to be satisfied after the drop-downs;

---

[55] Indeed, the Little Corp. assets can be divided between Big. Corp. and Sub Corp. as Big Corp. desires. See Rev. Rul. 64–73, 1964–1 C.B. 142. Do not confuse this ability to divide the target's assets between the acquiring corporation and its subsidiary with the *inability* in a B, C, or forward subsidiary reorganization to use voting stock of both corporations.

(ii) If stock of the target or acquiring corporation is dropped down, the corporation remains a member of the issuing corporation's qualified group; and

(iii) The target or acquiring corporation does not cease to exist for federal income tax purposes in connection with the drop-downs.[56]

Thus, in the example above, where Little Corp. merged into Big Corp., and the Little Corp. assets were transferred through Sub Corp. and Grandchild Corp. to Great Grandchild Corp., the three drop-downs would not disqualify the merger as an A reorganization. The two relevant conditions of Regs. § 1.368-2(k)(1)(ii) are met: First, the continuity of business enterprise requirement is met, since the Little Corp. assets are held by Great Grandchild Corp., a member of the Big Corp. qualified group.[57] Second, Big Corp. does not cease to exist in connection with the drop-downs. (Although Little Corp. ceases to exist, that cessation occurs in connection with the merger, not in connection with any drop-down.)

Note that if Regs. § 1.368-2(k)(1) applies, it prevents a recharacterization of the transaction because of the drop-downs. Without that rule, the Little Corp. assets could be deemed transferred directly to Great Grandchild Corp. under the step-transaction doctrine. If so recharacterized, the transaction that would not qualify as a tax-free reorganization. Because the drop-downs are described in Regs. § 1.368-2(k)(1)(ii), however, the merger is treated as a step independent of the drop-downs and the step-transaction doctrine does not apply.

Sometimes, a parent corporation may want a target corporation to merge into its controlled subsidiary to isolate the target liabilities in the subsidiary. Nevertheless, the parent may still want to acquire some of the target assets as part of the transaction. Could a

---

[56] Recall that in a forward subsidiary merger, the target corporation merges into a controlled subsidiary of a parent corporation, so that after the transaction the parent has not directly acquired target stock or assets. The parent might wish to rearrange its corporate structure by dropping the subsidiary stock to a lower tier. Despite the lack of statutory authority, this drop-down will not disqualify the merger as an A reorganization, because Regs. § 1.368-2(k)(1)(ii) applies to drop-downs of the acquiring corporation (*i.e.*, subsidiary) stock as long as the continuity of business enterprise requirement continues to be met. See also Rev. Rul. 2001–24, 2001–1 C.B. 1290 (reaching a consistent conclusion).

[57] The qualified group members include Big Corp., the issuing corporation, Sub. Corp., a corporation controlled by Big Corp., Grandchild Corp., a corporation controlled by a qualified group member (*i.e.*, Sub Corp.) and Great Grandchild, a corporation controlled by a qualified group member (*i.e.*, Grandchild Corp.). Regs. § 1.368-1(d)(4)(ii) (defining a qualified group).

distribution of target assets by the subsidiary to the parent affect the qualification of the merger as a forward subsidiary merger?

This issue is addressed by Regs. § 1.368-2(k)(1)(i). Under that provision, for any § 368 reorganization, a distribution of stock or assets (*i.e.*, a push-up) does not disqualify a transaction as a reorganization (or cause it to be recharacterized) if several requirements are met. First, the continuity of business enterprise requirement must continue to be met. Second, if target stock is distributed, the distribution must be of less than all target stock acquired in the transaction and the target must remain a member of the qualified group. If, instead, assets are distributed (or deemed distributed), the distribution cannot be deemed a liquidation, a determination made by disregarding all non-target assets of the distributing corporation.[58]

For example, suppose that Little Corp. merges into Sub Corp., a controlled subsidiary of Big Corp. in a merger that, standing alone, would qualify as a forward subsidiary merger. If Sub Corp. retains half of Little Corp.'s assets and distributes the other half to Big Corp., the distribution will not disqualify the merger as a forward subsidiary merger, because the relevant requirements of the drop-down rule are met. First, the continuity of business enterprise requirement continues to be met, because all Little Corp. assets are held by Big Corp. and Sub Corp., both members of the Big Corp. qualified group. Second, because Sub Corp. retains significant Little Corp. assets, no liquidation is deemed to occur. Regs. § 1.368-2(k)(2) (example 2) (for a comparable example).[59]

(vi) Multi–Step Reorganizations. Suppose that A Corp. makes a tender offer for the shares of T Corp. Under the terms of the offer, no T shares will be acquired unless a majority of the outstanding T shares are tendered, in which case A Corp. will acquire those shares in exchange for its own voting stock. If that first step is completed, A Corp. will acquire the remaining shares of T Corp. in a squeeze-out merger (i.e., where a newly formed subsidiary of A Corp. merges into T Corp.), using two-thirds of A voting stock and one-third cash as consideration. As a consequence, A Corp. will acquire the T stock

---

[58] If assets are both dropped down and pushed up, those transfers are tested under the push-up rule. Regs. § 1.368-2(k)(1)(ii)(A). Transfers are also tested under that rule if target assets are dropped into an entity and its ownership interests are distributed. *Id.* at (k)(1)(i)(A)(*1*). In the latter case, the distribution is treated as an indirect distribution of target assets, so that if all target assets are dropped into the entity, all target assets would be deemed distributed, resulting in a deemed liquidation. Then, Regs. § 1.368-2(k) would not apply. See *id.* at (k)(2) (example 3).

[59] Note as well that the transaction is not recharacterized as an acquisition of the Little Corp. assets by Big Corp. followed by a drop-down of half of those assets to Sub Corp.

in exchange for about 83% voting stock and 17% cash. Should this two-step acquisition be taxed as a single-step reverse subsidiary merger?

Several courts have been willing to treat such multi-step transactions as a unified, tax-free reorganization when the various steps are sufficiently interrelated to support application of the step-transaction doctrine under general tax principles.[60] In Revenue Ruling 2001–26,[61] the Service agreed with these cases. Note that the step-transaction doctrine will convert a multi-step acquisition into a tax-free reorganization only if the transaction, as stepped together, satisfies all of the statutory and judicial requirements of a tax-free reorganization, including the continuity of interest and continuity of business enterprise requirements.[62]

Suppose next that A Corp. acquires T Corp. in the following way: First, A Corp. creates a subsidiary corporation, X Corp., with cash and A Corp. voting stock. Second, X Corp. merges into T Corp., with T Corp. surviving. Under the terms of that merger, the T shareholders relinquish their T shares for the cash and A stock held by X Corp. while A Corp's X stock is cancelled in exchange for T common stock. Thus, after this step A Corp. owns all of the outstanding T stock and the former T shareholders own cash and A stock.

Third, T Corp. merges into A Corp. under applicable state law. (Note that when a controlled subsidiary merges into its parent, it is often called an "upstream merger"). Thus, after this transaction the former T assets are held by A Corp., and the former T shareholders, to the extent they were not cashed out, are A shareholders.

If each of these steps were treated as a distinct transaction (*i.e.*, if form were followed), then step 1 would be an incorporation under § 351, step 2 would be either a taxable stock purchase (a "qualified stock purchase" under § 338), or a reverse subsidiary merger under § 368(a)(2)(E) (depending on the relative proportion of stock and cash), and step 3 would be a subsidiary liquidation under § 332. But assuming these steps are all are parts of a single, integrated transaction, how should they be characterized? The Service has ruled that they will be treated as a merger of T Corp. into A Corp. which therefore will constitute a good A reorganization so

---

[60] *Seagram Corp. v. Commissioner*, 104 T.C. 75 (1995); *King Enterprises, Inc. v. United States*, 418 F.2d 511 (Ct.Cl.1969).

[61] 2001–1 C.B. 1297.

[62] For an excellent discussion of Revenue Ruling 2001–26, see Martin D. Ginsburg & Jack S. Levin, *Integrated Acquisitive Reorganizations*, 2001 Tax Notes 1909 (June 11, 2001).

long as the various judicial requirements of a reorganization are met.[63]

Reconsider this transaction but assume that A Corp. uses only cash to acquire T Corp. Now, the transaction cannot be recharacterized as an A reorganization because the continuity of interest requirement is not satisfied. Can the taxpayer nevertheless argue that the steps should be integrated to constitute a direct taxable purchase of T's assets, giving A Corp. a cost basis in those assets? The Service has ruled that such a recharacterization would be an impermissible end-run around the § 338,[64] a statutory provision intended by Congress to be the exclusive mechanism by which a taxpayer can purchase target stock but take a cost basis purchase in the target's assets.[65]

What happens if P Corp. acquires 80 percent of the only class of T Corp. stock for cash but, as part of the same plan, T Corp. merges into P Corp. and the remaining historic T shareholders receive P stock? If the stock purchase and merger are treated as an integrated transaction, the asset transfer will be taxable and P Corp. will take a cost basis in the T assets. Because the stock purchase was also a qualified stock purchase, however, that integrated treatment would act as an end-run around § 338: A § 338 election is intended to be the exclusive means for a purchasing corporation to acquire a cost basis in target assets following its qualified stock purchase of target stock.

As one way to prevent that end-run, suppose that the stock purchase and merger are treated as fully independent steps for tax purposes. Then, although the stock purchase would be taxable to the T shareholders selling their T stock for cash, the merger could qualify as an A reorganization, because P would be treated as an historic T shareholder in applying the continuity of interest requirement. If the merger is treated as an A reorganization, P would acquire T's assets at their historic asset bases, consistent with the policy underlying § 338. However, the remaining T shareholders

---

[63] See Rev. Rul. 2001-46, 2001-2 C.B. 321 (citing King Enterprises, Inc. v. United States, 418 F.2d 511 (Ct. Cl. 1969) and J.E. Seagram Corp. v. Commissioner, 104 T.C. 75 (1995)). But cf. Regs. §1.338(h)(10)-1(c)(2) (providing that if the first step in a two-step merger is a qualified stock purchase and a §338(h)(10) election is made for that first step, for all federal income tax purposes, the first step is treated as a qualified stock purchase independent of the second step, and not as part of a reorganization).

[64] See Rev. Rul. 2001-46, 2001-2 C.B. 321. For a more complete discussion of this transaction and ones like it, see Chapter 9.03(g) supra.

[65] Note that in the prior example when the steps were combined into a tax-free reorganization, the acquiring corporation ended up with a carryover basis in the acquired assets. Thus, that recharacterization was not inconsistent with the role of § 338.

would not recognize gain or loss on their exchange of T stock for P stock, a result inconsistent with the continuity of interest requirement. Overall, only 20 percent of the historic T shareholders received qualifying consideration, certainly too low a percentage to meet the continuity requirement

Thus, the transaction presents a conundrum: If its steps are fully integrated, it acts as an end-run around § 338, while if its steps are treated as being independent, the transaction acts as an end-run around the continuity of interest requirement. The regulations accommodate both policies by adopting a somewhat schizophrenic test. To determine the tax consequences of the potential reorganization to the target corporation, the corporation acquiring the target assets, and the purchasing corporation (*i.e.*, the corporation purchasing the target stock), the purchasing corporation is treated as an historic target shareholder.[66] However, to determine the consequences to the original target shareholders, the stock purchase and merger may be treated as part of one transaction (*i.e.*, integrated).[67] Thus, in our example, P Corp. takes a transferred basis in the T assets, but all original T shareholders, including those receiving P stock, recognize gain or loss.

As final example of the use of the step-transaction doctrine, assume that P Corp. owns all stock of two subsidiary corporations, S Corp. and T Corp. We know that a sale of all of the assets of T Corp. to S Corp., followed by a liquidation of T Corp., is treated as an acquisitive D reorganization. But what if P Corp. sells the T stock to S Corp. (making T Corp. a wholly owned subsidiary of S Corp.), followed by an immediate liquidation of T Corp? If the stock sale is treated separately, it will be taxed under § 304 as the sale of stock between related corporations. But when combined with the liquidation, the effect of the transaction as a whole is that of a D reorganization, and the Service has ruled that this is how the transaction should be characterized.[68] The Service examined the legislative history of § 304 and concluded that Congress did not intend § 304 to override the reorganization provisions.

(vii) "G" Reorganizations. Under prior law, a transfer of all or part of a corporation's assets to another corporation pursuant to a court-approved plan under the Bankruptcy Act could qualify for tax-

---

[66] See Regs. § 1.338-3(d)(2); *id.* at (d)(5), Ex. (i)-(iv). Note that in our example, P Corp. is both the corporation acquiring the T assets and the corporation purchasing the T stock. This regulatory regime would also apply if T Corp. merged into S Corp., a controlled P subsidiary. Then, S Corp. would be the corporation acquiring the T assets while P Corp. would be the corporation purchasing the T stock.

[67] See Regs. § 1.338-3(d)(1); *id.* at (d)(5), Ex. (v).

[68] Rev. Rul. 2004-83, 2004-2 C.B. 157.

free treatment under separate rules applicable to "insolvency reorganizations." The Bankruptcy Tax Act of 1980 ended the separate regime for debtor corporations in a title 11 (bankruptcy) case by adding a new category of tax-free corporate reorganization under section 368(a)(1): the G reorganization. Congress made this change to encourage and facilitate the rehabilitation of bankrupt debtor corporations. As a consequence, many prior law requirements for tax-free treatment were removed, parties were given additional flexibility in structuring the acquisition, and, most importantly, under § 381, the acquiring corporation succeeded to tax attributes of the acquired corporation, including its net operating loss carryovers.

The G reorganization is the most flexible of the acquisitive tax-free reorganization provisions, a hybrid provision that borrows characteristics from other acquisitive reorganization provisions. Like an A, C, or D reorganization, it involves an asset transfer by one corporation to another. Unlike the A reorganization, it does not require a merger. Unlike a C reorganization, it does not require an exchange of assets predominantly for voting stock. It is perhaps most like an acquisitive D reorganization, except a G reorganization does not require that the shareholders of the acquired corporation also be "in control" of the acquiring corporation.[69]

An acquisitive G reorganization must meet both statutory and judicial requirements. To meet the statutory requirements, (i) a target corporation must transfer substantially all of its assets to an acquiring corporation, (ii) that transfer must occur in a title 11 or similar case; and (iii) as part of the plan of reorganization, the target must distribute all of its property, including the qualified stock or securities and other property received in the transaction.[70]

Thus, a G reorganization requires a transfer by a corporation of all or a part of its assets to another corporation, provided one of the corporations is in a bankruptcy (or similar case) and provided the transfer occurs pursuant to a plan of reorganization approved by the bankruptcy court. § 368(a)(3)(B). Thus, the transfer of stock of

---

[69] If a transaction qualifies as both a G reorganization and another type of § 368(a)(1) reorganization (or qualifies under § 332 or § 351), the transaction is treated as qualifying only as a G reorganization. § 368(a)(3)(C) (applying this rule except for purposes of § 357(c)(1)).

[70] § 368(a)(1)(G) (also authorizing a divisive G reorganization if the distribution meets the requirements of § 355); § 354(b) (for the distribution and substantially all requirements). Thus, the target corporation must liquidate as a final step in the reorganization.

Qualified stock is stock of either the acquiring corporation or its parent, but not both. § 368(a)(2)(D) (authorizing use of parent stock in a G reorganization). The parent is a corporation that owns at least 80% of the total voting power of acquiror voting stock and at least 80% of each class of acquiror non-voting stock. § 368(c); Rev. Rul. 59-159, 1959-1 C.B. 115.

the debtor corporation to its creditors in satisfaction of their claims will not qualify as a G reorganization (although there may be no adverse tax consequences of such a transaction). Similarly, out-of-court transactions, Chapter 7 liquidating cases, and foreign reorganizations are ineligible.

For example, suppose that Loss Corp. is hopelessly insolvent. Immediately before it files a bankruptcy petition, Loss Corp. agrees to transfer all of its assets to Public Corp. in exchange for Public Corp. common stock and Loss Co. will then distribute the stock received to its creditors in satisfaction of their claims against Loss Corp. This acquisition will not qualify as a G reorganization because it did not occur within a title 11 or similar case. Accordingly, the transaction will be tax-free only if it meets the standards of one of the other acquisitive reorganization provisions such as the A, C, or D.

As a second example, suppose Loss Corp. is in a Chapter 11 bankruptcy case. Loss Corp.'s plan of reorganization provides for a transfer of cash and certain non-operating assets to secured creditors and of all newly authorized common stock to its unsecured creditors. Its previously authorized outstanding common stock is canceled. Loss Corp.'s plan will not qualify as a G reorganization, because Loss Corp. has not transferred its assets to another corporation. Although not qualifying as a G reorganization, this transaction likely qualifies for tax-free treatment as a E recapitalization, a form of tax-free reorganization below. See S. Rep. No. 96–1035, 96th Cong., 2d Sess. 36 (1980).

In addition, to meet the statutory requirements for a G reorganization, the target corporation must transfer substantially all of its assets. For "substantially all" target assets to be transferred in a C reorganization, the Service requires (for advanced rulings) that at least 90% of the net assets and 70% of the gross assets be transferred in the reorganization.[71] Congress has indicated that the "substantially all" requirement should be interpreted liberally in the context of the G reorganization in view of the underlying purpose of the provision to facilitate the rehabilitation of financially troubled corporations. Accordingly, "substantially all" of the assets of the debtor corporation should be acquired even if the debtor sells assets to pay creditors or to rearrange its business affairs in order to obtain creditor approval of its plan of reorganization. S. Rep. No. 96–1035, 96th Cong., 2d Sess. 36–36 (1980). Further, although it has issued no formal guidance, the Service has relaxed the requirement in its private rulings. For instance, the Service has ruled that this

---

[71] Rev. Proc. 77–37, 1977–2 C.B. 568.

requirement is met when more than 50 percent of the gross assets and 70 percent of all operating assets were acquired.[72]

As a final statutory requirement, as part of the plan of reorganization, the target must distribute its property, including the qualified stock or securities and other consideration received in the transaction.[73] To meet this requirement, at least one target security holder must receive qualified stock or securities (or at least one target shareholder must receive qualified stock) under the plan of reorganization.[74]

This distribution requirement should be met even if the value of the stock or securities received by shareholders and security holders represents a small percentage of the value of the total equity consideration paid out in the transaction. However, if (as is often the case in the typical corporate bankruptcy) all of the old stock of the debtor corporation is cancelled (because there is no equity left) and the acquiring corporation's stock is distributed to short-term creditors whose debt instruments do not rise to the dignity of a tax security, the threshold distribution requirement for an acquisitive G reorganization will not be met.

For example, suppose Loss Corp. is a party in a Chapter 11 bankruptcy case. Loss Corp.'s plan of reorganization provides for the transfer of "substantially all" of its assets to Public Corp. in exchange for $550 cash and Public Corp. common stock worth $450. The plan calls for the transfer of the cash and certain non-operating assets to secured creditors and the distribution of all Public Corp. common stock to Loss Corp.'s unsecured creditors. One of the unsecured creditors holds a 10–year bond, and assume that this bond is a "security" for tax purposes. Although the old Loss Corp. common stock is cancelled and the shareholders receive nothing under the plan, the statutory requirements for an acquisitive G reorganization should be met. First, Loss Corp. transferred substantially all of its assets to Public Corp. Second, that transfer occurred pursuant to a bankruptcy plan to which Loss Corp. was a party. Finally, as part of that plan, Loss Corp. distributed all of its assets, including the stock and securities received from Public Corp., and in the distribution at least one Loss Corp. security holder received Public Corp. stock.

---

[72] See Priv. Let. Rul. 201032009 (May 12, 2010); Priv. Let. Rul. 201025018 (July 8, 2010); Priv. Let. Rul. 9313020 (Dec. 30, 1992); Priv. Let. Rul. 8726055 (March 31, 1987); Priv. Let. Rul. 8521083 (Feb. 27, 1985); Priv. Let. Rul. 8503064 (Oct. 24, 1984). Operating assets, for this purpose excluded cash, accounts receivable, and investment assets *Id.*

[73] § 368(a)(1)(G); § 354(b).

[74] *See, e.g.,* Priv. Let. Rul. 9313020 (Dec. 30, 1990); Priv. Let. Rul. 9226064 (March 31, 1992); Priv. Let. Rul. 8503064 (Oct. 24, 1984).

The transaction in this example would not qualify as a G reorganization if all of Loss Corp.'s unsecured creditors held only short-term debt. One possible way to avoid this technical trap in the statute is to convert the claims of the creditors into stock of the acquired debtor corporation before the date that the G reorganization is consummated, relying on *Helvering v. Alabama Asphaltic Limestone Co.*, 315 U.S. 179 (1942). In that case, the Supreme Court held that creditors of an insolvent corporation who received stock of a reorganized corporation had a "continuing interest" because, under the full priority rule of bankruptcy proceedings, they had "effective command over the disposition of the properties" of the old corporation.

However, in *Neville Coke & Chemical Co. v. Commissioner*, 148 F.2d 599 (3d Cir.1945), it was held that note holders of a reorganized corporation who exchanged their notes for debentures and common stock could not claim non-recognition of their gain under what is now § 354. The court relied on *Pinellas Ice & Cold Storage Co. v. Commissioner*[75] and *Le Tulle v. Scofield*[76] as establishing that notes received on an exchange do not evidence a continuing interest in the enterprise and are not "securities." It then held that the notes are equally deficient if given up in the exchange. The debtor was in financial difficulties at the time of the exchange, but the court was unwilling to find that the creditors already owned the entire equity, and in fact the old stockholders did participate in the exchange. If, however, the creditors of a distressed corporation in reorganization received stock or securities evidencing a proprietary interest in the enterprise, is it not probable that the claims they gave up, whatever their form, already represented in economic reality a proprietary interest in the assets?

In addition to the statutory requirements, a G reorganization must meet additional judicial requirements imposed on all tax-free corporate reorganizations, that is, it must meet the "continuity of interest," "continuity of business enterprise" and "business purpose" requirements.

Unlike for a typical reorganization, in applying the continuity of interest requirement for a G reorganization, a creditor's interest may be treated as a proprietary interest. Recall that to satisfy this continuity requirement, holders of the target's proprietary interests must receive qualified stock as a significant part of their consideration in the transaction. This requirement should be met if those

---

[75] 287 U.S. 462 (1933).
[76] 308 U.S. 415 (1940).

holders receive qualified stock that in the aggregate comprises 40 percent of their total consideration.[77]

A creditor's claim against the target may be treated as a proprietary interest if the target is under the jurisdiction of the court in a title 11 or similar case.[78] In that case, the target's proprietary interest holders are divided into two groups: (i) the most senior class of target creditors that receives qualified stock in the transaction (the "senior creditors") and (ii) more junior target creditors and target shareholders.[79] Each claim of a junior creditor or target shareholder is treated in whole as a proprietary interest.[80]

The treatment of a senior creditor's claim depends on the consideration received by senior creditors as a group. If those creditors receive solely qualified stock in the transaction, each senior creditor's claim is treated in whole as a proprietary interest.[81] If, however, the senior creditors receive consideration in addition to qualified stock, a senior creditor's interest is bifurcated, treated in part as debt and in part as a proprietary interest. The part treated as a proprietary interest equals the percentage (by value) of the total consideration received by senior creditors that is qualified stock.[82]

For example, suppose that Public Corp. acquires all assets of Loss Corp. in a transaction that qualifies as a G reorganization as long as the continuity of interest requirement is met. Before the acquisition, Loss Corp. has $10 million of long-term debt and $20 million of trade debt, and the trade debt is junior to the long-term debt. As part of the bankruptcy plan, the long-term creditors receive $5 million of cash and $5 million worth of Public Corp. stock, while the trade creditors receive $5 million in cash. In measuring continuity, *one-half* of each long-term creditor's interest and *all* of each trade creditor's interest are treated as proprietary interests. Thus, the

---

[77] See Regs. § 1.368-1(e)(2)(v), *Ex. 1* (concluding that 40% continuity is sufficient).

[78] Regs. § 1.368-1(e)(6)(i) (also providing that treatment if the target is insolvent (*i.e.,* its liabilities exceed the value of its assets immediately before the potential reorganization)).

[79] See *id.* at (e)(6)(ii).

[80] *Id.* at (e)(6)(i).

[81] *Id. See also id.* at (e)(6)(ii). The value of each junior creditor interest and target stock interest equals the value of the interest holder's claim. *Id.* at (e)(6)(ii)(B). *See also id.* at (e)(6)(iii) (discussing the bifurcation of a claim between secured and unsecured components).

[82] *Id.* at (e)(6)(ii)(A) (also adding, however, that if there is only one class of creditors, the amount of stock received by that class cannot be de minimis when compared to the total consideration received in the transaction by the target, its shareholders, and its creditors). Thus, a G reorganization will have 100-percent continuity of interest if (i) each senior creditor receives solely stock (or the same ratio of stock to non-stock consideration) for its claim and (ii) no junior claim receives non-stock consideration.

total amount received for the Loss Corp. proprietary interests equals $10 million ($5 million for the long-term creditors' interests plus $5 million for the trade creditors' interests).

Suppose first that each long-term creditor receives (by value) one-half cash and one-half Public Corp. stock. In total, therefore, each long-term creditor is deemed to receive solely Public Corp. stock for its proprietary interest in Loss Corp. (*i.e.*, $5 million of Public Corp. stock in total). Thus, $5 million out of $10 million (or half) of the total consideration received for the Loss Corp. proprietary interests in Loss Corp. is Public Corp. stock, and the transaction meets the continuity of interest requirement.

Suppose, instead, that half of the long-term creditors receive solely cash for their interests while the other half receive solely Public Corp. stock. In total, therefore, half of the long-term creditors are deemed to receive cash for their Loss Corp. proprietary interests (worth $2.5 million), while half receive solely Public Corp. stock (also worth $2.5 million). Thus, only $2.5 million out of $10 million (or 25 percent) of total consideration received for the Loss Corp. proprietary interests is Public Corp. stock, too little to satisfy the continuity of interest requirement.[83]

(viii) The Status of Creditors in a Reorganization. Creditors of the target or transferee corporation will not necessarily participate in the reorganization exchange. For example, in a B reorganization, the target creditors may simply ride through the reorganization, preserving intact their claims against the target corporation.

Alternatively, the acquiring corporation may assume the liabilities of the transferee or take the properties subject to those liabilities, still without any formal exchange by the creditors. Ordinarily, this debt relief will not constitute "boot" to the transferee. § 357. Further, under the express language of § 368(a)(1)(C), the "solely for voting stock" requirement for a C reorganization is not violated merely because the acquiring corporation assumes target liabilities or takes target property subject to target liabilities.

Nor should an exchange of target debt for acquiror debt as part of a reorganization violate the solely for voting stock requirement for a B or C reorganization. See Rev. Rul. 98–10, 1998–1 C.B. 1 (exchange of debt securities of the acquired corporation for debt securities of the acquiring corporation incident to B reorganization not taxable).

---

[83] Regs. § 1.368-1(e)(2)(v) (example 2(ii) and 4) (concluding that 25% continuity is not sufficient).

Will the assumption of target liabilities by the acquiring corporation in connection with the reorganization be a taxable exchange to the target creditors? No, a target creditor will recognize no gain or loss if the acquiring corporation is merely substituted as the debtor as part of a reorganization to which § 381 applies. See Regs. § 1.1001-3(e)(4)(i)(B). Technically, the substitution is not deemed an exchange.

On the other hand, target creditors will frequently make an exchange. For example, the creditors may surrender bonds, debentures, or notes of one corporation and receive stock or securities of another corporation. However, an exchange of target securities for acquiror stock or securities qualifies for non-recognition under § 354 because it falls within the definition of that section: an exchange of stock or securities of a party to a reorganization for stock or securities of another party to the reorganization, all in pursuance of the plan of reorganization. One difficulty that may arise, however, is that short-term notes (whether given up or received) may not qualify as "securities."

Whenever creditors of a corporation swap old debt for new— whether in the context of a reorganization (often a bankruptcy reorganization) or not—it must be determined whether the exchange is taxable to the creditors (possibly producing gain or loss) as well as to the corporation (possibly producing cancellation of indebtedness income). Consider the situation in which a corporation replaces its outstanding debt with new debt having different terms. For example, short-term, low-interest notes might be replaced with long-term, higher interest bonds. What are the tax consequences of such a debt swap?

Under Regs. § 1.1001–3, "a significant modification of a debt instrument . . . is deemed to result in an exchange of the original instrument." Accordingly, gain or loss can be recognized by the debt holder. If, for example, the value of the debt received exceeds the holder's adjusted basis in the debt surrendered, gain will be recognized on the exchange. This might be the case when the corporation's distress has been reflected in the market price of its notes so that current holders of those notes may have paid significantly less than face value. What constitutes a "significant modification" is described in Regs. § 1.1001–3(e).

The transaction will also be taxable to the corporation, which raises the possibility of cancellation of indebtedness income to the corporation if it substitutes current low-value debt for outstanding obligations initially issued for face value. Thus, if a corporation transfers $800 face value bonds having current fair market value of

$800 in exchange for each $1,000 short-term note outstanding, the corporation will recognize $200 of cancellation of indebtedness income on each exchange. Unless the exchange occurs while the corporation is insolvent or in a bankruptcy proceeding, the cancellation of indebtedness income will be taxable immediately. See § 61(a)(12); § 108(a). And if the insolvency exception applies, it is limited to the extent of the debtor corporation's insolvency. § 108(a)(3).

A corporation might also swap stock for debt. To the extent that the issue price of the surrendered debt exceeds the stock's value, the corporation has cancellation of indebtedness income, included in gross income except to the extent provided in § 108. § 108(e)(8). And if application of § 108 to an insolvent or bankrupt corporation permits the corporation to exclude some or all of its cancellation of indebtedness income, the corporation will be forced to reduce its tax attributes (including its tax credits, NOL carryovers, and adjusted basis) as the tax "payment" for the exclusion. See § 108(b).

(ix) A Retrospective on the Rules of § 368. Having looked at the various definitions in § 368, what general conclusions can we draw? First, Congress seems to have agreed with the Supreme Court that the taxable sale of corporate stock or assets differs from a tax-free reorganization in the form of consideration received by shareholders of the transferor corporation. This notion, the continuity of interest doctrine, informs much of the case and statutory law in this area. Permissible consideration is broadest in regular A reorganizations and in forward subsidiary mergers, for in these situations the only limitation is that imposed by the common law. At the opposite end of the spectrum are B reorganizations, where the only allowable consideration is voting stock. In between lies C reorganizations and reverse subsidiary mergers, in which up to 20 percent boot may be allowable under § 368(a)(2)(B). The acquisitive D reorganization, because it requires that the shareholders of the transferor corporation either *have* or *acquire* control of the transferee corporation, does not easily fit anywhere into the pattern.

In addition, it should now be clear that the reorganization definitions are full of detail and complexity, detail and complexity that must be mastered by anyone involved in the transfer of corporate control. To be sure, two major principles run through the various forms of reorganization: continuity of interest and continuity of the business enterprise in modified corporate form. However, the implementation of these principles varies from provision to provision without rhyme or reason. The continuity of interest requirement, for example, is implemented differently in the A, B, C, D and reverse subsidiary reorganizations. Only the A and forward subsidiary reorganizations adopt the same approach to the continuing pro-prietary interest requirement, and what they adopt is the uncertainty and occasional irrationality of the common law in this area.

The American Law Institute adopted a series of proposals covering subchapter C. In particular, it proposed that any bulk transfer of assets from one corporation to another be treated as a tax-free reorganization if the corporate parties so elect. If not, gain or loss on the transfer is recognized and each party takes a fair market value basis in the property received. However, if the parties elect in favor of nonrecognition, then each party must use a transferred basis in the assets received. By making reorganization status formally elective, these proposals eliminate the various inconsistent definitions now comprising § 368.

These proposals also eliminate the continuity of interest requirement. Regardless of the corporate-level election, a shareholder who exchanges stock for stock as part of a bulk transfer of corporate assets is given nonrecognition on the exchange and an exchanged basis in the stock so acquired. Shareholders whose interests are cashed-out, on the other hand, are fully taxed. Thus the problems posed by *Kass*, *McDonald's* and *Paulsen* are eliminated. Of course, such an approach to corporate reorganizations will not eliminate all definitional questions. For example, the definition of a bulk transfer of assets necessarily will include some arbitrary lines. Nonetheless, such an approach would go a long way toward clearing the reorganization jungle.

10.03 Amalgamating Reorganizations: Taxation

Under § 1001, if a person sells or exchanges property, the person recognizes gain or loss, except as the Code provides. Thus, in the absence of special statutory provisions, the various stock-for-stock and stock-for-asset exchanges forming the reorganization transactions would be recognition events.[84] A host of special provisions apply when a transaction is described in § 368(a). Those provisions most notably include §§ 354, 356 and 358 at the shareholder level and §§ 357, 358, 361, 362, and 1032 at the corporate level.

In general under these provisions, gain or loss is not recognized and that basis remains unchanged. The acquiring corporation takes the acquired assets with a transferred basis and neither the target nor acquiring corporation generally recognizes gain or loss. If a target shareholder exchanges target stock solely for qualified acquiror (or parent) stock, the shareholder recognizes no gain or loss and takes the same basis in the stock received as the stock surrendered

---

[84] See *Marr v. United States,* 268 U.S. 536 (1925).

in the exchange. If the shareholder receives other property in addition to qualified stock (*i.e.*, receives boot), the shareholder may recognize gain, but not loss.

Many of the relevant rules refer to "parties" to a reorganization, a term defined in § 368(b). At the corporate level, the reorganization provisions apply only to corporations that are parties to the reorganization. See § 361. At the shareholder level, nonrecognition will apply only to exchanges of stock and securities of corporations that are, once again, parties to the reorganization. Parties to the reorganization include the target corporation, the acquiring corporation and, in a consolidation, the surviving corporation. § 368(b)(2). They also include the parent of the acquiring corporation in a parenthetical B, parenthetical C, and forward triangular merger and the parent of the merged corporation in a reverse subsidiary merger. § 368(b) (flush language).

(a) Corporate–Level Taxation.

In all reorganizations other than the B, there is a transfer of assets from one corporation to another and a distribution by the transferor corporation of the consideration received (and any remaining assets) to its shareholders. Section 361 governs the recognition of gain and loss by the transferor corporation. Section 361(a) and (b) deal with the transferor corporation's exchange of its assets with the acquiring corporation. Section 361(c) considers the transferor corporation's distribution of property to its shareholders or creditors.

Under § 361(a) and (b)(2), the transferor corporation recognizes no loss on its transfer of property, although it may recognize gain. It recognizes no gain, however, on its exchange of property *solely* for the stock and securities of another corporate party to the reorganization, such as the acquiring corporation. § 361(a). For this purpose, if the acquiring corporation assumes the transferor's liabilities, that assumption is generally disregarded. § 357(a). But see § 357(b) (providing that the assumption is treated as the payment of boot if a liability is assumed for a tax-avoidance purpose).

Even if the transferor corporation receives boot in the exchange, it recognizes no gain if the boot is distributed as part of the reorganization. § 361(b)(1)(A). Note that a distribution to a creditor satisfies this requirement. § 361(b)(3). Because the transferor corporation almost always liquidates as part of the reorganization (see § 368(a)(2)(G)(ii) for the possible exception for a C reorganization), gain recognition by the transferor corporation is unlikely. In the unusual case where the transferor fails to distribute any boot, it recognizes its realized gain up to the value of that undistributed boot. § 361(b)(1).

For example, suppose Target Corp. owns operating assets with a $950,000 adjusted basis and $1,000,000 fair market value. If Target Corp. transfers those assets to Acquiring Corp. in exchange for Acquiring stock in a C reorganization, Target recognizes none of the gain inherent in its assets. If instead Target receives $900,000 of stock and $100,000 cash, Target still will recognize none of its realized gain so long as it distributes the cash (including a distribution to one or more of its creditors) as part of the reorganization. However, if Target fails to distribute the cash,[85] it will recognize its realized gain up to the value of the undistributed boot (here $100,000). Thus, Target will recognize a $50,000 gain (*i.e.*, the smaller $50,000, its realized gain, or $100,000, the value of the undistributed boot).

When might the transferor corporation fail to distribute boot received in the reorganization? In a C reorganization, the transferor corporation is required to liquidate as part of the transaction absent special consent of the government. § 368(a)(2)(G). Similarly, a transferor corporation is required to liquidate as part of a non-divisive D reorganization. § 354(b)(1)(B). By operation of law, it must liquidate (or more precisely cease to exist) in an A reorganization. Thus, a transferor corporation rarely will fail to distribute boot received in the reorganization. However, the transferor corporation may be deemed to receive boot if the transferee corporation assumes the transferor's liabilities for a tax-avoidance purpose. See § 357(b). By its nature, of course, an assumed liability cannot be "distributed." Accordingly, a transferor corporation in that unusual circumstance will be forced to recognize gain if it transferred appreciated assets, because it cannot avoid the gain through a curative distribution.

The transferor corporation takes a basis in the qualified stock and securities received equal to (i) its basis in the property transferred, plus (ii) any gain it recognized on the exchange, minus (iii) the money and value of any non-cash boot received. § 358(a)(1). See also § 358(d) (treating assumed liabilities, other than those described in § 357(c)(3), as money for this purpose). That basis is allocated between the stock and securities in proportion to relative fair market values.[86] Noncash boot received takes a basis equal to its value. § 358(a)(2).

For example, reconsider the case in which Target Corp. transfers assets with a $950,000 adjusted basis and $1,000,000 fair mar-

---

[85] Recall that Target Corp. must liquidate as part of the reorganization unless consent of the government is obtained. § 368(a)(2)(G)(ii).

[86] See Regs. § 1.358–2.

ket value to Acquiring Corp. in a C reorganization. Assume now that Target receives $900,000 worth of Acquiring's stock, $60,000 cash, and Blackacre worth $40,000. Once again, if Target does not distribute the cash or Blackacre as part of the reorganization, Target will recognize a gain of $50,000 on the exchange. Under § 358(a)(1), Target will take a basis in the Acquiring stock of $900,000, equal to (i) $950,000, the basis of the transferred assets, plus (ii) $50,000, its recognized gain, minus (iii) $100,000 ($60,000 for the cash received plus $40,000 equal to Blackacre's value). Target takes a basis in Blackacre equal to its value, or $40,000. § 358(a)(2).

Reconsider this example but with the following variation: Target distributes the cash as part of the reorganization, retaining Blackacre and the Acquiring stock. Now, Target recognizes only a $40,000 gain on the exchange, equal to the smaller of (i) $50,000, its realized gain, and (ii) $40,000, the value of its undistributed boot (*i.e.*, Blackacre's value). Under § 358(a)(1), Target will take a basis in the Acquiring Corp. stock of $890,000, equal to (i) $950,000, the basis of the transferred assets, plus (ii) *$40,000*, its recognized gain, minus (iii) $100,000 ($60,000 for the cash received plus $40,000 equal to Blackacre's value). Thus, the $10,000 of Target's gain deferred on the exchange is preserved in Target's basis in the Acquiring stock. Note, though, that no gain will be recognized to Target if it distributes the Acquiring stock as part of the reorganization even though that stock has a basis below its fair market value. § 361(c). Target's basis in Blackacre again is equal to fair market value, or $40,000.

In most cases, the transferor corporation liquidates as part of the an acquisitive asset reorganization, but the usual rules applicable to corporate liquidations do not apply in this context.[87] Instead, § 361(c) governs the distribution. On the distribution, the transferor corporation recognizes no loss and recognizes gain, but only on its distribution of its appreciated property that it had not transferred to the acquiring corporation.[88]

The distribution may include three classes of property: (1) stock or securities of a party to the reorganization acquired from the ac-

---

[87] See § 361(c)(4).

[88] The usual rule is that loss can be recognized on a liquidating distribution but not on a non-liquidating distribution. See § 336(a) (liquidating distributions); § 311(a) (non-liquidating distributions). No loss can be recognized by the transferor-corporation on its liquidating distribution because, in the context of the overall reorganization, that distribution is best thought of as a nonliquidating distribution of the continuing entity. See § 311(b), discussed at Section 4.04 *supra* (no loss to distributing corporation allowed on nonliquidating distribution).

quiring corporation in the reorganization, (2) other property (*i.e.*, boot) acquired from the acquiring corporation, and (3) property held by the transferor corporation and not transferred to the acquiring corporation as part of the reorganization. The stock or securities described in class (1) are "qualified property" under § 361(c)(2)(B), and the transferor corporation recognizes no gain or loss on their distribution. § 361(c). The transferor corporation also recognizes no gain or loss on its distribution of the boot described in class (2), because its basis equals its fair market value (assuming that the distribution occurs just following the boot's receipt). § 358(a)(2) and (f). However, the transferor corporation recognizes gain but not loss on its distribution of any asset described in class (3), to the extent the asset has a fair market value in excess of its adjusted basis.[89]

In contradistinction to the transferor corporation, the transferee corporation often may recognize gain or loss on the reorganization. Under § 1032, a corporation recognizes no gain or loss on its acquisition of property for its stock or stock rights (whether or not in connection with a reorganization). That section does not literally apply when a subsidiary acquires assets using its parent's stock (or stock rights) in a parenthetical B or C reorganization or a forward subsidiary merger. However, Regs. § 1.1032-2(b) provides that the subsidiary recognizes no gain or loss on its use of parent stock (or stock rights) acquired from the parent as part of the plan of reorganization. See also Rev. Rul. 57-278, 1957-1 C.B. 124 (reaching the same conclusion).

If, however, the acquiring corporation uses non-cash boot to acquire assets in the reorganization, it generally recognizes gain *or* loss on that exchange. See § 1001. That gain or loss is not recognized, however, to the extent another non-recognition section applies to the exchange. See, e.g., § 1031.

For example, suppose that X Corp. transfers its voting stock worth $90,000 and Microsoft stock worth $10,000 to T Corp. in an A or C reorganization. No reorganization provision protects X from recognizing gain or loss on its transfer of the Microsoft stock. Accordingly, under the general rule of § 1001(a), X will recognize its realized gain or loss on its exchange of Microsoft stock for a portion of the T assets.

Suppose that X Corp. transfers its own debt to T Corp. or assumes T liabilities, instead of transferring Microsoft stock. Does X

---

[89] § 361(c)(2)(A). Note that if the transferor corporation distributes class (3) assets that have both built-in gain and built-in loss, it recognizes its gain on the built-in gain assets but does not recognize its loss on the built-in loss assets. Thus, the loss cannot offset the gain and simply disappears.

Corp. recognize gain or loss on the exchange? No Code provision exempts that part of the transaction from taxation. However, recall that the acquisition of property by a taxpayer in exchange for the taxpayer's promise to pay later is treated like a cash purchase.[90] Thus, under general principles, an acquiring corporation recognizes no gain or loss when it acquires assets for its newly issued debt or the assumption of liabilities.[91] Accordingly, X Corp. recognizes no gain or loss on its receipt of assets in exchange for X Corp.'s securities.

For example, suppose that in a C reorganization, X Corp. transfers its own stock worth $900,000 and Microsoft stock worth $100,000 to T Corp. in exchange for all of T's assets. If X Corp.'s basis in the Microsoft stock is $60,000, it will recognize a $40,000 gain on the exchange. T Corp. will take a fair market value $100,000 basis in the Microsoft stock. X Corp.'s basis in the property received, determined under § 362(b), is carried over from the transferee corporation (T Corp.), increased by any gain recognized by the transferee corporation (T Corp.) on the exchange. Consistent with treating the two corporations as a single entity after the reorganization, this basis rule ensures that asset appreciation will be taxed to the transferor corporation or to the transferee corporation but not to both.[92]

---

[90] See *Crane v. Commissioner,* 331 U.S. 1 (1947).

[91] The acquiring corporation does not escape tax by acquiring property for debt, since it will be taxed on the consideration (typically cash) that it uses to pay off the debt.

[92] In a triangular reorganization, the target shareholders receive parent stock even though the target stock or assets are acquired by the parent's subsidiary or, in a reverse subsidiary merger, the subsidiary merges into the target. Under Regs. § 1.358-6, the basis consequences of triangular reorganizations to the parent generally are as follows:

In a triangular "B" reorganization, the parent's basis in its subsidiary stock is increased by the target shareholders' aggregate adjusted basis in the acquired target stock. See Regs. § 1.358-6(c)(3). In a triangular "C" reorganization and a forward subsidiary merger, the parent increases its basis in the subsidiary stock by the net basis of the target assets. That net basis equals the excess, if any, of (i) the aggregate basis of the acquired target assets, over (ii) the amount of target liabilities assumed in the transaction (or to which acquired target assets were subject). *Id.* at (c)(1).

In a reverse subsidiary merger, the parent determines its basis in the target stock under one of two methods. Under the method that generally applies, its basis in the target stock equals (i) its basis in the subsidiary stock immediately before the transaction plus (ii) the net basis of the target assets. *Id.* at (c)(2)(i)(A). But see *id.* at (c)(2)(B) and (C) (for adjustments if less than all target stock is acquired or if the parent owned target stock before the transaction). If the transaction also qualifies as a § 351 transfer or a "B" reorganization, the parent can choose alternatively to determine its basis in the acquired target stock as if it acquired that stock in a "B" reorganization. *Id.* at (c)(2)(ii).

(b) Shareholder–Level Taxation.

(i) In general. Shareholder-level taxation is governed by §§ 354, 356 and 358. Under the general rule of § 354(a), a shareholder recognizes no gain or loss on the exchange of stock or of one party to the reorganization solely for stock of another party to the reorganization. If the shareholder receives other property ("boot") in addition to qualified stock, the shareholder still recognizes no loss but recognizes gain equal to the smaller of (i) the value of the boot received and (ii) the realized gain.[93] Note that if a target shareholder receives solely boot in exchange for target stock, the shareholder typically recognizes gain or loss under § 1001.[94]

The shareholder's basis in the qualified stock received equals (1) the shareholder's basis in the target stock surrendered in the exchange, plus (2) any gain recognized on the exchange (including as a dividend), minus (3) the value of any boot received.[95] The shareholder takes a fair market value basis in any boot received. § 358(a)(2).

As part of a tax-free reorganization, a shareholder might give up or receive "nonqualified preferred stock" as that term is defined in § 351(g)(2). Recall that such stock is both preferred and limited; in particular, that stock does not participate in corporate growth to any significant extent.[96] In addition, that stock must either include a redemption feature making it only a short-term investment in the corporate enterprise or have a dividend rate tied to interest rates or some equivalent index making the stock little more than subordinated debt.

If the parent supplies less than all consideration in the reorganization, the adjustments described above are reduced (but not below zero) by the fair market value of the other consideration exchanged in the reorganization but not provided by the parent. *Id.* at (d) (disregarding assumed liabilities for this purpose).

[93] § 356(a)(1). Cf. § 351(b); § 1031(b) (for comparable rules). The consequences to a target shareholder or security holder of the receipt of stock or securities of another party to the reorganization are described in § 10.03(c) infra.

[94] Rev. Rul. 74-515, 1974-2 C.B. 118, concludes that § 302 applies to a target shareholder receiving solely boot in an acquisitive asset reorganization. Thus, that target shareholder is deemed to receive the boot in redemption of his target stock, and typically the redemption should be described in § 302(b). Then, the shareholder would be deemed to sell or exchange his target stock, recognizing gain or loss under § 1001. See § 302(a).

[95] § 358(a)(1). For convenience, a reference to "qualified stock" in this subsection is a reference to stock of a party to the reorganization that the target shareholder can receive without the recognition of gain or loss under § 354 or § 356.

[96] See Chapter 2 supra.

In general, if a shareholder gives up such nonqualified preferred stock for new, nonqualified preferred stock or for any other
stock or securities of a party to the reorganization, the exchange is
tax-free under § 354. However, if a shareholder receives nonqualified preferred stock in exchange for stock (other than old nonqualified preferred stock), the stock received is treated as boot. Thus, if
solely nonqualified preferred stock is received, the exchange is typically fully taxable under § 1001(a). See § 354(a)(2)(C). In all events,
though, even nonqualified preferred stock is treated as "stock" to
determine whether the transaction qualifies as a reorganization,
and even nonqualified preferred stock is treated as stock rather
than as boot to determine the corporate-level tax consequences of
the transaction.[97]

(ii) Character of gain. If a target shareholder receives qualifying consideration plus boot in exchange for target stock in an acquisitive reorganization, two issues remain. First, if the shareholder
recognizes gain under § 356, what is the character of that gain? Second, how should the boot be allocated among the target stock surrendered in the exchange?

Consider first the character of the gain. Shareholder-level gain
can be ordinary dividend income or capital gain depending on the
effect of the distribution to the shareholder. With qualified dividend
income now taxed at the same rate as long-term capital gain, the
character of the shareholder's recognized gain becomes a relatively
minor issue. Note in particular that regardless of the character of
the income, it is the gain (rather than the gross amount received)
that is taxable in either event. Thus, even if the shareholder recognizes dividend income, that income arises only after basis recovery.

Under § 356(a)(2), if the effect is that of a dividend, the gain
will be recognized as dividend income up to each share's allocable
portion of accumulated earnings and profits. If not, the gain will be
capital if the stock transferred was a capital asset in the hands of
the shareholder. Even in a world in which dividends are taxed at
the same rate as capital gain, § 356(a)(2) remains relevant: capital
gain is better than dividend income because of the disabilities im-

---

[97] Thus, nonqualified preferred stock, if voting stock, may be used as
qualifying consideration in a B reorganization, possibly multiplying a single
stock loss. For example, suppose that D owns T common stock with a $150
basis and $100 value, and, as part of a B reorganization, P Corp. acquires
that stock in exchange for $100 worth of P nonqualified preferred stock. D
will recognize her $50 built-in loss in the T stock under § 1001(c), because
she treats the P stock entirely as boot. However, P Corp. will take a $150
basis in that stock, preserving the same loss. Its basis, determined under
§ 362(b), equals D's basis in that stock ($150) plus any gain that D recog-
nized ($0). No doubt as an oversight, § 362(b) does not require P Corp. to
reduce its basis in the T stock to account for D's recognized loss.

posed on the use of capital losses. An individual taxpayer can use a capital loss to offset capital gain without limitation yet can offset ordinary income only up to a maximum of $3,000 per year; a corporate taxpayer cannot use capital loss to offset ordinary income to any extent.[98] (Of course, a corporate taxpayer does not enjoy a preferential rate of taxation on capital gain or on qualified dividends but may enjoy a dividends received deduction on the receipt of dividend income.)

The courts have looked to the redemption rules of § 302 for guidance in determining the effect of receipt of boot under § 356. Although they agreed that the receipt of boot should have the effect of a dividend only if its receipt was *not* treated as a sale or exchange under the principles of § 302, they were divided over how those principles should be incorporated into the § 356 analysis. Some used a "before" test and some an "after" one, an issue finally resolved by the Supreme Court in *Commissioner v. Clark*[99] in favor of the "after" test.

The "before" test was created in *Shimberg v. United States.*[100] Under this test, § 302 was applied by treating the boot as if it had been distributed by the target corporation in a redemption of target stock before the reorganization. In this hypothetical redemption, each target shareholder was treated as exchanging target stock for the boot actually received in the reorganization. The rules of § 302 were then applied to this hypothetical redemption to determine the effect of the exchange on the shareholder.

The "after" test was fashioned in *Wright v. United States.*[101] As in *Shimberg,* the court in *Wright* was faced with shareholders of the target corporation who received boot in a reorganization. The court recharacterized the single reorganization as two transactions: (1) a reorganization in which each target shareholder received solely stock; and (2) a redemption of a portion of this stock in exchange for the boot actually received. The court applied the rules of § 302 to the hypothetical redemption.

The following example illustrates the *Wright* and *Shimberg* tests. Suppose that X Corp. merges into Y Corp. X Corp. has two shareholders, individuals P and Q. P and Q each owns half of the outstanding X stock with a $10,000 basis and a $100,000 fair market value. In the reorganization, P and Q each exchanges his X stock for Y stock worth $50,000 plus cash of $50,000. Assume that

---

[98] See § 165(f); § 1211; § 1212.

[99] 489 U.S. 726 (1989).

[100] 577 F.2d 283 (5th Cir.1978).

[101] 482 F.2d 600 (8th Cir.1973).

after the reorganization, P and Q each owns 1 percent of the outstanding Y stock.

Under the *Shimberg* test, the effect of the exchange on P and Q is that of a dividend: it is pro rata, and had it occurred prior to the reorganization, it would have been subject to the distribution rules of § 301. Yet, the effect of the transaction in its entirety is to reduce substantially P's and Q's interest in the corporate venture.

Under the *Wright* test, we act as if P and Q had received only Y stock in the reorganization. In this hypothetical redemption, P and Q would have received $100,000 in stock of Y, making them each almost 2-percent shareholders. Next, we assume that P and Q exchange the excess stock for the boot actually received. This exchange is a redemption in which P and Q go from 2-percent shareholders to 1-percent shareholders, and under the disproportionate distribution safe harbor of § 302(b)(2), the redemption would be taxed as an exchange. Accordingly, under the *Wright* test, the effect of the exchange is not that of a dividend, and P and Q will report their gain on the reorganization as capital gain.[102]

In *Commissioner v. Clark*,[103] the Supreme Court adopted the *Wright* test. The Supreme Court characterized the *Shimberg* "before" test as "sever[ing] the payment of boot from the context of the reorganization. . . . [Such an approach] is plainly inconsistent with the statute's direction that we look to the effect of the entire exchange." The Court also observed that the *Shimberg* test results in ordinary income treatment in most reorganizations, an improper effect of an "overly expansive reading of § 356(a)(2)."

While the Supreme Court was correct that the *Shimberg* "before" test usually is less advantageous to taxpayers than the *Wright* "after" test, there are situations in which it is not so. For example, suppose X Corp. merges into Y Corp. when each share of X and Y stock is worth $50, and each corporation is owned by individuals P, Q and R as follows:

---

[102] Perhaps it makes more sense to apply neither the *Wright* or *Shimberg* tests but instead to apply the principles of § 302 by comparing a target shareholder's ownership in the target corporation before the transaction with his ownership in the acquiring corporation (or its parent) after the transaction. See Michael L. Schler, *Rebooting Section 356: part I—The Statute*, 128 Tax Notes 285 (July 19, 2010) (for a compelling argument for using this approach).

[103] 489 U.S. 726 (1989).

Before Merger

	X Corp.	Y Corp.
P	50 (50%)	0 (0 %)
Q	50 50 (50%)	90 (90%)
R	0 (0%)	10 (10%)
Total	100	100

As a result of the merger, P receives $1,500 in cash and 20 shares of Y stock, while Q receives $2,000 in cash and 10 shares of Y stock. Thus, after the merger Y Corp. has 130 shares outstanding, of which P owns 20, Q owns 100, and R owns 10.

After Merger

	Y Corp.
P	20 (15.38%)
Q	100 (76.92%)
R	10 (7.69%)
Total shares	130

Under the *Shimberg* "before" test, P and Q are treated as if they receive the boot in a redemption before the merger. As a result of this hypothetical redemption, P's interest in X Corp. increases from 50 percent (50 of 100 shares) to 66.7 percent (20 of 30 shares[104]). Q's interest, on the other hand, drops from 50 percent (50 of 100 shares) to 33.3 percent (10 of 30 shares). Thus, although P will have dividend income on the $1,500 boot (assuming adequate earnings and profits), Q will obtain exchange treatment on the $2,000 of boot under the principles of § 302(b)(2).

A very different result obtains under the *Wright* "after" test. Following *Wright,* we act as if P and Q each received only Y stock in exchange for their shares of X Corp. (step 1), followed by a redemption of the shares hypothetically just received by P and Q (step 2). Because the shares of X Corp. and of Y Corp. are of equal value, P and Q would each receive 50 shares of Y Corp. stock in exchange for their 50 shares of X Corp. stock if each received only stock in the exchange. Thus, there would be 200 shares of Y Corp. outstanding, owned as follows:

After Hypothetical Exchange

	Y Corp.
P	50 (25%)
Q	140 (70%)
R	10 (5%)
Total shares	200

---

[104] Because each share of X Corp. stock is worth $50, the $1,500 boot corresponds to a redemption of 30 shares. Similarly, the $2,000 of boot received by Q corresponds to 40 shares of X Corp.

In step 2, we treat 30 of P's shares and 40 of Q's shares as redeemed by Y Corp. Accordingly, P's interest drops from 25 percent (50 of 200 shares) to 15.38 percent (20 of 130 shares). Q's interest, on the other hand, increases from 70 percent (140 of 200 shares) to 76.92 percent (100 of 130 shares). Thus, P now qualifies for exchange treatment under the principles of § 302 while Q has dividend income.

The Service's refusal to follow *Wright*[105] was based in part on some unfortunate dicta in that opinion. If a distribution has the effect of a dividend under § 356(a)(2), it must be determined whether there are sufficient earnings and profits to cover the distribution. The *Wright* court opined that the earnings and profits of only the acquiring corporation could be used to cover the distribution. The Service, unwilling to allow taxpayers to bail-out the earnings of the transferor corporation, refused to accept that dicta in *Wright*. Consistent with a "before" test, the court in *Shimberg* used the earnings and profits of the transferor corporation to characterize the distribution. One possibility, apparently overlooked by the *Wright* and *Shimberg* courts, is to use the earnings and profits of *both* corporations as is done in § 304.[106] The Supreme Court in *Clark* did not address this aspect of the § 356(a)(2) controversy. However, in deciding the *Clark* case the Tax Court[107] followed the *Wright* "after" approach and added:

> There is no reason why the redemption cannot be considered as having been made by one corporation with the consequences to be measured by the earnings and profits of another corporation.

Regardless of *how* the determination under § 356(a)(2) is made, note that the amount of income to a shareholder is limited to the shareholder's *gain* on the transaction. In general, corporate distributions not treated as exchanges are taxed as ordinary income to the full extent of the amount distributed without any basis recovery.[108] If an exchange incident to a reorganization has the effect of a dividend, one would expect that the entire distribution would be ordinary income. Nevertheless, Congress persists in limiting § 356(a)(2) to gain, making § 356 an easy loophole for high-basis taxpayers.

---

[105] Rev. Rul. 75–83, 1975–1 C.B. 112, revoked by Rev. Rul. 93–61, 1993–30 C.B. 10, in light of the decision in *Commissioner v. Clark*.

[106] See § 304(b)(2).

[107] *Clark v. Commissioner*, 86 T.C. 138 (1986).

[108] In other words, any dividend is limited to the shareholder's § 1001 gain on the exchange. This limitation, often criticized, is sometimes referred to as the "dividend within gain" rule.

For example, suppose that individual B owns all outstanding stock of X Corp. and Y Corp. Assume that Y Corp. has been quite profitable. How can B get his hands on Y Corp.'s income at a low tax cost? B will have ordinary dividend income under § 301 equal to any distribution from Y Corp. If B sells some X Corp. stock to Y Corp., § 304 will produce the same result. Suppose instead that the two corporations merge in an A reorganization, and B exchanges his X stock for Y stock plus cash. If B realizes no gain on the transaction (because the X stock was unappreciated in B's hands), the receipt of cash incident to the reorganization will be tax-free. Absent a reorganization or partial liquidation, there is no other way for a sole shareholder to remove funds from an on-going corporate venture without the imposition of tax.

(iii) Allocation of boot. Under § 356, a target shareholder recognizes realized gain in an acquisitive reorganization to the extent of boot received but recognizes no realized loss. Because the target shareholder computes his recognized gain share-by-share, he must allocate any boot received among the target shares surrendered. At least for closely held corporations, that allocation follows the terms of the exchange, if those terms are economically reasonable.[109] In the absence of such terms, the boot is allocated pro rata among the surrendered shares of target stock (i.e. in proportion to the shares' fair market values). *Id.* at (b). See also *id.* at (d) (example 3). Consistent rules apply to determine the shareholder's basis in the qualified stock received in the exchange. See Regs. § 1.358-2.

As the following example illustrates, this regime affords target shareholders considerable latitude to recognize gain. Suppose that B, the sole shareholder of T Corp., owns two T shares. Share 1 has a $1,000 basis and Share 2 has a $4,000 basis, and each share is worth $5,000. In an acquisitive reorganization, B exchanges those shares for one share of X stock worth $5,000 and $5,000 cash. If the terms of the exchange do not provide for an allocation of the boot, the boot is allocated equally to each share. Then, under § 356, B recognizes an overall $3,500 gain, a $2,500 gain on Share 1 (the smaller of B's $4,000 realized gain and the $2,500 cash received) plus a $1,000 gain on Share 2 (the smaller of B's $1,000 realized gain and the $2,500 cash received). If, however, the terms of the exchange specify that the boot is allocated entirely to Share 1, B recognizes a $4,000 gain (the smaller of B's $4,000 realized gain on Share 1 and the $5,000 cash received for that share). If the terms of the exchange instead specify that the boot is allocated entirely to

---

[109] Regs. § 1.356-1(b). See also *id.* at (d) (example 4). Proposed regulations would require a pro rata allocation of boot if the shareholder's exchange had the effect of a dividend. Prop. Regs. § 1.354-1(d).

Share 2, B recognizes a $1,000 gain (the smaller of B's $1,000 realized gain and the $5,000 cash received for that share).[110]

Thus, through a paper allocation in the acquisition agreement that has no effect on the consideration B receives, B can "elect" to recognize a $1,000 gain, $3,500 gain, or $4,000 gain. If well advised or sufficiently astute, B will make that election in his favor and to the detriment of the fisc.

As a word of caution, however, if B had a basis in Share 2 of $6,000, rather than $4,000, and the entire $5,000 boot was allocated to Share 2, he would recognize no loss. §356. More troubling, B's excess $1,000 basis would disappear, at least under the current position of the Service.

(c) A Note on "Securities".

To satisfy continuity of interest, stock (sometimes voting stock) of the acquiring corporation (or its parent) must be transferred to the shareholders of the acquired corporation. It is perhaps surprising then that the property that may be received tax-free in a reorganization includes not only stock but also securities, and this is true at both the corporate and shareholder levels. See § 361(a); § 354(a)(1). But what is a "security"? There are actually two types— debt and equity securities.

(i) Debt Securities. A debt security is a debt instrument of the issuing corporation, of course, but the term "security" does not encompass all debt instruments. In this context, a security is a debt instrument representing a continuing interest in the affairs of the issuing corporation. Other debt instruments—usually called notes rather than securities—more closely resemble the sale proceeds of the transferor's assets.

Until 1990, debt securities constituted qualified property (i.e., property that can be received tax-free) in an incorporation under § 351 as well as in a reorganization, and much of the judicial gloss on the term "security" developed in the § 351 context. Because courts treated a debt security equivalently in these two areas, the case law developed under § 351 should still be good law in defining a debt security for the reorganization provisions.

---

[110] In the latter two cases, A will also exchange one T share solely for one X share and because A receives no boot for that share, he will recognize no gain on that portion of the exchange. See § 356 (limiting gain to the value of the boot received).

A leading case on the definition of a debt security is *Camp Wolters Enterprises, Inc. v. Commissioner,*[111] where the Tax Court stated:

> The test as to whether notes are [debt] securities is not a mechanical determination of the time period of the note. Though time is an important factor, the controlling consideration is an over-all evaluation of the nature of the debt, degree of participation and continuing interest compared with similarity of the note to a cash payment.

As *Camp Wolters* suggests, a note's maturity is probably the most important factor distinguishing a note from a debt security. In general, debt instruments with a five-year term or less will seldom qualify as securities while obligations with a term of ten years or more are likely to qualify.[112] As *Camp Wolters* also points out, maturity is not the only factor. A demand note might be a debt security if repayment is contingent on the performance of the corporation and the notes are subordinated to other debt instruments.[113]

Suppose Target Corp. issued debt instruments in 2004 with stated maturity of 2016, and assume these debt instruments are "securities" within the meaning of § 354. In 2014, Target Corp. merges into Acquiring Corp, with Acquiring Corp. surviving. As part of the merger, Acquiring Corp. issues new debt instrument to the former holders of the Target Corp. debt instruments, and the new instruments have identical terms, including a stated maturity date of 2016, except that the interest rate is changed. While a debt instrument having a two-year term generally will not qualify as a debt security, the Service has ruled that on these facts the new debt instruments will be treated as "securities," because they "represent a continuation of the security holder's investment in the Target Corporation in substantially the same form." Rev. Rul. 2004-78, 2004-2 C.B. 108. While not directly relevant to the continuity of interest doctrine, this ruling might suggest a further willingness to rethink the law as developed in *Robeling v. Commissioner.*[114]

At the corporate level in a reorganization, the distinction between a debt security and a mere note is unlikely to be important because the transferor corporation receiving the debt instrument

---

[111] 22 T.C. 737, 751 (1954), aff'd, 230 F.2d 555 (5th Cir.1956).

[112] For typical cases, compare *Nye v. Commissioner,* 50 T.C. 203 (1968) (ten-year note is a security) *with Bradshaw v. United States,* 683 F.2d 365 (Ct.Cl.1982) (notes maturing annually for five years not securities).

[113] See, e.g., *D'Angelo Associates v. Commissioner,* 70 T.C. 121 (1978).

[114] 143 F.2d 810 (3d Cir. 1944); see *Paulson v. Commissioner,* 469 U.S. 131 (1985), discussed in Chapter 10.02 supra.

usually will distribute it, thereby precluding gain (or loss) recognition.[115] At the shareholder and creditor level the distinction can be more important because receipt of boot (and a note is boot while a debt security may not be) may force gain recognition. However, because gain from payment on a note can be reported on the installment method,[116] even here the distinction between a security and a note is largely irrelevant.[117]

However, if the shareholder's gain is treated as a dividend under § 356(a)(2), then installment reporting is not permitted and notes will be treated like cash boot:[118] gain on the exchange, to the extent of the fair market value of the boot, will be recognized immediately. Thus, the importance of the *Clark* decision becomes magnified when short-term notes are in the picture.

How should target shareholders and security holders generally treat the receipt of debt securities in a reorganization? Under the general rule of § 354(a)(1), a person recognizes no gain or loss on the exchange of stock or securities of a party to a reorganization for stock of securities of another party to the reorganization. The general rule appears to offer non-recognition to a person who exchanges target stock or securities for qualified stock, qualified securities, or some combination of both,[119] but the rule is subject to two signifi-

---

[115] See § 361(b)(1)(A).

[116] See § 453(f)(6) (final flush language); Prop. Regs. § 1.453–1(f)(3)(ii).

[117] One difference between receipt of a security and receipt of a note taxed on the installment method lies in the shareholder's allocation of basis to the debt instrument. In addition, recognition of income on an installment obligation can precede receipt of payment under some circumstances, see § 453(e), while a person who receives qualifying property in the form of a security will not recognize gain until principal payments received on the security exceed the shareholder's basis (or until the security is sold).

[118] Note the "is not treated as a dividend" language at the end of § 453(f)(6).

[119] Compare § 351 at Section 2.06(d) *supra* where securities do not constitute qualifying property. Note that qualified stock or securities are stock or securities of a party to the reorganization.

Note as well that a target shareholder may receive securities in exchange for target stock, particularly in an A reorganization, which tolerates a fair amount of non-stock consideration. Occasionally, a target shareholder may also receive securities in exchange for target stock in a C reorganization even though voting stock is the only qualified consideration: The securities may be received from the acquiror as boot (subject to the boot relaxation rule), or they may have been historically held by the target and distributed to the shareholder in liquidation (assuming that the C reorganization requirements are otherwise met).

Although target stock cannot be exchanged for securities in a B reorganization, target securities may be exchanged for securities and that exchange may qualify for non-recognition. For example, assume that P Corp. acquires all the outstanding stock of T Corp. in exchange for its own voting stock in a transaction that qualifies as a B reorganization. Also assume that as part of the transaction, P Corp. exchanges its own securities for the

cant exceptions. First, if a person surrenders no target securities in the exchange, any qualified securities received are treated entirely as boot. § 354(a)(2)(A)(ii); § 356(d)(1). Second, a person is treated as receiving boot to the extent the principal amount of the qualified securities received exceeds the principal amount of the target securities surrendered in the exchange. § 354(a)(2)(A)(i); § 356(d)(2)(B) (treating the value of that excess as boot).

Thus, if a target shareholder exchanges target stock for stock and debt of the acquiring corporation in an acquisitive reorganization, the debt is treated entirely as boot. Further, if the shareholder exchanges target stock solely for acquiror debt, the shareholder typically must recognize any realized gain or loss under § 1001(c). In either case, the result to the target shareholder is the same whether or not the acquiror debt is a debt security, because the shareholder surrenders no target securities in the exchange.

In contrast, if the holder of a target debt security exchanges that security solely for qualified stock in an acquisitive reorganization, the exchange is a non-recognition event under § 354(a)(1). In addition, that holder recognizes no gain or loss if he exchanges a target debt security solely for a qualified debt security of the same (or smaller) principal amount. §354(a) and (b)(1)(A). However, if the debt security holder receives more debt principal than he transfers in the reorganization, the value of that excess is treated as boot under § 356. §354(a)(2)(A)(i).

Consider example 4 of Regs. §1.356-3(b). Under a plan of reorganization, D exchanges a debt security with principal amount of $1,000 plus 100 shares of stock for a debt security with principal amount of $1,200 and fair market value of $1,100. The excess principal amount of the debt security received is $200, and its fair market value is $183.33 (*i.e.*, $200 time $1,100 divided by $1,200). Accordingly, D recognizes gain equal to the smaller of $183.33 or her realized gain on the exchange.

(ii) Equity Securities. Securities also include rights issued by a party to the reorganization to acquire its stock, and in applying § 354 and § 356(d)(2)(B), such an "equity" security is treated as having "no principal amount." Regs. § 1.354-1(e). Thus, in an acquisitive reorganization, if a person exchanges target stock for qualified stock and stock rights, the person recognizes no gain or loss. The result is the same if a person exchanges target stock rights solely

outstanding T securities. Because the exchange of the securities is pursuant to the plan of reorganization, it is also covered by § 354 even though the exchange of securities is not a part of the definition of a B reorganization. See, e.g., Rev. Rul. 98–10, 1998–1 C.B. 1.

for qualified stock, qualified stock rights, or a combination of qualified stock and stock rights. However, if a person exchanges target stock solely for qualified stock rights, the exchange is not described in § 354 or § 356, but may be one to which § 302 applies. See Rev. Rul. 74-515, 1974-2 C.B. 118.

10.04 Divisive Reorganizations

(a) Basic Requirements.

In a divisive reorganization, one corporate enterprise is divided into two or more. Specifically, one corporation distributes the stock of a second corporation that it controls immediately before the distribution. § 355(a)(1)(A). See also § 368(c) (defining control). The controlled corporation may be an existing corporation or it may be newly formed, with its assets contributed by the distributing corporation as part of the transaction.[120] Whether a divisive reorganization involves an existing or newly formed controlled corporation, § 355 defines its principal characteristics.

A divisive reorganization may be used, for example, to divide one corporation into two so that warring shareholders can go their separate ways. It may also be used for a host of other reasons, including to separate businesses that cannot, because of government regulations, be conducted by a single corporate entity.

A pro rata distribution by a parent corporation of the stock of a controlled subsidiary will effect a divisive reorganization in which parent shareholders end up owning a brother/sister pair. For example, if Sub Corp. is a wholly owned subsidiary of P Corp., a pro rata distribution of the Sub Corp. stock by P Corp. will change P Corp. and Sub Corp. from parent and subsidiary to two corporations owned by the same shareholders (*i.e.*, a brother/sister pair). The same transaction can be effected by distributing the stock of the subsidiary in a pro rata redemption, with the only change being the number of parent shares outstanding after the transaction. For historical reasons, the former transaction sometimes is called a "spin-off" while the latter is called a "split-off." A split-off often is not pro rata.[121] For example, if P Corp. distributes the Sub Corp. stock to some shareholders in exchange for their P Corp. stock, the result is

---

[120] Note that the asset contribution is described in § 368(a)(1)(D) and the asset contribution and stock distribution are sometimes referred to as a "divisive D" or "D/355" reorganization.

[121] In addition, a "splint-off" combines the characteristics of a spin-off and split-off. A splint-off occurs when some shareholders of the distributing corporation exchange their distributing stock solely for stock of the controlled corporation (like in a split-off) and other distributing shareholders receive a pro rata distribution of controlled stock without surrendering any of their distributing shares (like in a spin-off).

that some of the original P Corp. shareholders will continue to own P Corp. and some will own Sub Corp.

A divisive reorganization also might involve a § 351 incorporation as the first step. For example, if X Corp. owns two separate businesses, it might create a subsidiary corporation under § 351 by transferring one of the businesses to it. The subsidiary can then be spun-off (or split-off) as above. Alternatively, X Corp. could create two subsidiaries, Sub 1 and Sub 2. X would then transfer one business to Sub 1 and one to Sub 2, leaving X Corp. as a holding company. The complete liquidation of X would then result in a divisive reorganization, this time called a "split-up."

The different forms of a divisive reorganization share one common element: the potential for tax abuse. For example, consider X Corp. having substantial liquid assets (cash and marketable securities) as well as substantial earnings and profits. In order to bail out the cash and securities as capital gain, the shareholders of X might cause their corporation to spin off the liquid assets. If this divisive transaction were tax-free, the shareholders could then sell off the new corporation's stock and thereby obtain the economic value of the liquid assets while enjoying basis recovery and capital gain. The shareholders would continue to hold X and its business assets, and when the purchasers of the new corporation liquidated it, the bailout would be complete.[122]

To prevent this and similar abuses, the courts and Congress have limited tax-free divisive reorganizations to those meeting a variety of anti-abuse provisions. The statutory provisions are found in § 355, a section of the Code applicable to all divisive reorganizations. The Supreme Court has added to the statutory requirements the business purpose test, a test applicable to all reorganizations but having the most bite in the context of divisive reorganizations.[123] This test grew out of one of the most famous tax cases ever, *Gregory v. Helvering*.[124]

The taxpayer in *Gregory* owned all the shares of United Mortgage Corp. United Mortgage in turn owned 1,000 shares of Monitor Securities Corp. To bail out the Monitor shares as capital gain, the taxpayer caused United Mortgage to create a new corporation, the Averill Corp., by contributing the Monitor shares in exchange for Averill shares. United Mortgage then distributed the Averill shares

---

[122] Observe that this liquidation may be tax-free at both corporate- and shareholder-levels if the securities are unappreciated.

[123] Further, a continuity of interest requirement must be met for both the distributing and controlled corporations. Regs. § 1.355-2(c)(1).

[124] 293 U.S. 465 (1935).

to the taxpayer. Immediately thereafter, the Averill Corp. was liquidated, placing the Monitor shares in the taxpayers hands at capital gain rates.[125]

The relevant statute in force at that time provided that a reorganization included "a transfer by a corporation of all or a part of its assets if immediately after the transferor or its stockholders or both are in control of the corporation to which the assets are transferred." Accordingly, the transaction met the literal language of the then-applicable divisive reorganization provision. Nonetheless, the Supreme Court held that a tax-free reorganization did not occur because "[t]he whole undertaking . . . was in fact an elaborate and devious form of conveyance masquerading as a corporate reorganization, and nothing else." As subsequently interpreted by Judge Learned Hand, the Supreme Court's opinion in *Gregory* stands for the proposition that "in construing words of a tax statute which describes commercial or industrial transactions we are to understand them to refer to transactions entered upon for commercial or industrial purposes and not to include transactions entered upon for no other motive but to escape taxation."[126]

The Supreme Court's condemnation of the *Gregory* transaction seems sound, but its focus on the tax-avoidance motive of the taxpayer may be misplaced. To be sure, the transaction in *Gregory* was motivated by tax avoidance, but so is the purchase of municipal bonds, the formation of many corporations, and many investments in real estate. All in all, if given a choice, taxpayers prefer lower taxes to higher taxes. What was most peculiar about the *Gregory* transaction was the creation and immediate destruction of the Averill Corp. A narrower holding in *Gregory* might have focused on the effect of the transaction: a division of United Mortgage did *not* occur because the Averill Corp. was liquidated immediately after

---

[125] Under current law, any appreciation in the Monitor shares would be taxable to the Averill Corp. upon its liquidation. See § 336. At the time, though, the *General Utilities* doctrine allowed a distributing corporation to avoid recognizing gain on the distribution. Thus, the taxpayer in *Gregory* sought only a single, shareholder-level tax on the transaction even though the Monitor shares were appreciated.

[126] *Commissioner v. Transport Trading & Terminal Corp.,* 176 F.2d 570, 572 (2d Cir.1949). In Rev. Rul. 2003-52, 2003-1 C.B. 960, the stock of a farming corporation was owned equally by a father, mother, son, and daughter, but the two children managed the corporation. One child wanted the corporation to emphasize its livestock business while the other wanted the corporation to emphasize its grain business. The Service ruled that a § 355 distribution had a valid corporate purpose because the distribution eliminated the business disagreement between two owners of the company and allowed each sibling to devote full-time effort to the business in which he or she was most interested. Surprisingly, the Service was not troubled that the distribution also significantly furthered the estate planning objective of the parents of the corporation.

the transaction. Instead, under the step-transaction doctrine, United Mortgage Corp. could have been treated as simply distributing the Monitor Securities stock. Regardless of the taxpayer's motive, the transaction did not accomplish that which Congress intended in the divisive reorganization statute.[127]

As applied to divisive reorganizations, the business purpose test requires that the transaction be motivated by some non-federal income tax business purpose of the corporate enterprise.[128] Such purposes include compliance with an antitrust order, resolution of a shareholder stalemate, and facilitation of a public offering.[129] Note that in all cases these are purposes germane to the conduct of the *corporation's* business. A shareholder's purpose is, in general, irrelevant. However, a shareholder's purpose may overlap a corporate purpose—resolution of a shareholder stalemate being one example—without tainting the corporate purpose.[130]

The regulations use the business purpose test to impose a best-fit requirement on § 355 transactions: a distribution will fail to qualify under § 355 if the business purpose underlying the transaction could be accomplished in a tax-free manner not involving the distribution of stock, unless the alternative transactions are impractical or unduly expensive. Regs. § 1.355–2(b)(3); see also Regs. § 1.355–2(b)(5) (examples 4 and 5).

These regulations also provide that a valid corporate purpose does not include the attempt to reduce federal taxes even if that reduction does not involve a bailout or other abuse to which § 355 is directed. Regs. § 1.355–2(b)(2). For example, a distribution made to facilitate an election under subchapter S does not qualify under § 355 because the purpose is unacceptable. Regs. § 1.355–2(b)(5) (example 6).

---

[127] See *Chisholm v. Commissioner,* 79 F.2d 14, 15 (2d Cir.1935) ("Had [the taxpayers in *Gregory*] really meant to conduct a business by means of the two reorganized companies, they would have escaped whatever other aim they may have had, whether to avoid taxes, or to regenerate the world").

[128] A transaction motivated neither by legitimate business concerns nor by tax-avoidance will not qualify as a tax-free reorganization. *Commissioner v. Wilson,* 353 F.2d 184 (9th Cir.1965).

[129] See Regs. § 1.355–2(b)(5) (examples 1 and 2); Rev. Rul. 85–122, 1985–2 C.B. 118. See also Rev. Proc. 96-30, 1996-1 C.B. 696 (suggesting other business purposes, including distributions to (i) provide an equity interest to a key employee, (ii) facilitate borrowing, (iii) achieve significant cost savings, (iv) resolve management, systemic, or other problems caused by operating different businesses in one corporation or group (the "fit and focus" rationale), (v) facilitate an acquisition, and (vi) reduce risk).

[130] Regs. § 1.355–2(b)(2).

This aspect of the regulations may be subject to attack. Section 355 does not explicitly incorporate a business purpose test, so that the administrative or judicial imposition of such a test should be sustained only if the test furthers the underlying goal of the statute. Section 355 is an anti-bailout provision, not an anti-subchapter S provision. This aspect of the regulations demonstrates the extent to which the non-statutory business purpose test may have extended beyond its legitimate reach.

Having a business purpose will not guarantee tax-free treatment to the division, however, because § 355 imposes a series of additional hurdles.[131] The three statutory requirements imposed by § 355 are the "device" restriction of § 355(a)(1)(B), the "active business" limitation of § 355(a)(1)(C), and the "distribution" requirement of § 355(a)(1)(D). The "device" restriction is the most ambitious, denying tax-free treatment under § 355 to any transaction "used principally as a device for the distribution of the earnings and profits of the distributing corporation or the controlled corporation [i.e., the corporation whose stock is distributed], or both." As the language in § 355(a)(1)(B) suggests, the "device" restriction addresses transactions, such as the one in *Gregory,* in which the taxpayers intend to sell either the distributing or the controlled corporation after the transaction.

The regulations under § 355 list three factors which constitute evidence of a "device."[132] First, the regulations say that a distribution which is pro rata or substantially pro rata bears close resemblance to a dividend and therefore presents the greatest opportunity for abuse. While it is hard to fault this reasoning, Congress seemingly rejected it: in § 355(a)(2)(A), we are told that application of § 355(a) should be determined "without regard to . . . whether or not the distribution is pro rata." If a distribution being pro rata is treated as evidence of a "device," is § 355 being applied consistently with the mandate of § 355(a)(2)(A)?

The second factor treated as a "device" under the regulations is a post-distribution sale or exchange. The regulations further pro-

---

[131] It is § 355 and not § 368 that defines the outer boundaries of the divisive reorganization because not all divisive reorganizations will fall within the definition of the D (or any other) reorganization. For example, the distribution by a parent corporation of the stock of an existing subsidiary may qualify for tax-free treatment under § 355 despite not being a "reorganization" in the § 368(a) sense. On the other hand, if assets are spun off by a transfer to a controlled corporation whose stock is then distributed, the division will fall within the definition of a D reorganization. Note, though, that the definition of a divisive D reorganization references § 355, so that any corporate division—whether a D reorganization or not—must satisfy the requirements of § 355 to obtain tax-free treatment.

[132] Regs. § 1.355–2(d)(2).

vide that if such a sale or exchange is negotiated before the distribution, the sale or exchange is substantial evidence of a "device." Given the second parenthetical in § 355(a)(1)(B), it is surprising that a pre-arranged sale or exchange is not treated under the regulations as conclusive evidence of a "device."

The third factor under the regulations indicating that the distribution is a device for the distribution of earnings and profits is the "nature, kind, amount and use" of the assets of the distributing and controlled corporations. The regulations recognize that spinning off liquid assets or other assets not used in the distribution corporation's trade or business should not qualify for tax-free treatment. This aspect of the "device" limitation overlaps the active trade or business requirement, discussed below.

The regulations also list factors helping to show that a distribution is not a device for the distribution of earnings and profits[133] and, more strongly, describe distributions that ordinarily will not be treated as a "device."[134] For example, if neither the distributing corporation nor the controlled corporation has earnings and profits, the distribution will not be treated as a "device." This concession in the regulations certainly seems justified: no corporate distribution can bail out earnings and profits if there are no earnings and profits to begin with. More generally, a distribution will not be considered a "device" if, in the absence of § 355, the distribution would not be taxable as a dividend to the distributees because it would qualify as an exchange under § 302(a) or § 303. Do not forget, however, that avoiding the "device" restriction of § 355(a)(1)(B) does not guarantee qualification under § 355: one must still face the active trade or business hurdle of § 355(a)(1)(C) as well as the distribution limitation in § 355(a)(1)(D).

The "active business" limitation of § 355(a)(1)(C) in many ways mirrors and overlaps the role of the device restriction. Under § 355(a)(1)(C), a division will not be tax-free unless the distributing corporation and the controlled corporation actively conduct trades or businesses after the transaction. This limitation on the scope of § 355 ensures that a corporation cannot spin-off liquid assets or passive investments as a prelude to a bailout.

The "active business" provision of § 355(a)(1)(C) should remind you of the partial liquidation provision in § 302(b)(4).[135] You will recall that redemptions in partial liquidation of stock are given exchange treatment under § 302(b)(4) and § 302(a). The theory behind

---

[133] See Regs. § 1.355–2(d)(3).

[134] Regs. § 1.355–2(d)(5).

[135] See Section 5.02(d) *supra*.

preferential treatment for partial liquidations is that no bailout occurs when a shareholder is forced to give up equity participation in the corporate enterprise as part of the transaction. This is consistent with the tax treatment of the sale of stock to third parties: a shareholder can "bail out" the earnings and profits of a corporate business with impunity if the shareholder is willing to accept a reduced proprietary interest in the business.[136]

Consider the case of X Corp., a manufacturing corporation, which engages in the following transaction: First, X Corp. creates a new corporation, Y Corp., by transferring the land on which X Corp.'s manufacturing plant is located. Second, X Corp. leases that land from Y Corp. at fair rent of $100,000 per year for 25 years. Third, X Corp. distributes the Y stock to its shareholders pro rata. Should this distribution be tax-free under § 355?

In *Rafferty v. Commissioner,*[137] it was held that the holding of real estate for lease-back to the distributing corporation did not constitute an "active" trade or business. Accordingly, the distribution was not tax-free under § 355. Had the court held otherwise, the shareholders could receive the Y stock tax-free and then sell it, thereby recovering a substantial portion of their investment in X Corp. without diminishing their equity interests in the business.

A contrary result was reached in *King v. Commissioner.*[138] In that case, the court found significant that the real estate was fit for only a single use and was needed in the business conducted by the distributing corporation. That might have been relevant had not the real estate been leased back to the distributing corporation. In effect, what was spun-off was the right to receive lease payments. Lease payments often are a functional substitute for purchase payments made on an installment basis. Would the court in *King* have upheld the transaction if the distributing corporation had purchased the spun-off assets from the controlled corporation?

Leasing activities can constitute an "active" trade or business if the activity includes significant management or other services.[139] These services distinguish the activity from a mere passive investment. Note that the services must be conducted by employees of the corporation; hiring an independent contractor will not suffice.[140] If

---

[136] The definition of "common stock" applicable to § 305 and § 306 similarly reflects this interpretation of a bailout.

[137] 452 F.2d 767 (1st Cir.1971).

[138] 458 F.2d 245 (6th Cir.1972).

[139] Regs. § 1.355–3(b)(2)(iv)(B); see also Rev. Rul. 79–394, 1979–2 C.B. 141.

[140] Rev. Rul. 86–125, 1986–2 C.B. 57.

the services of an independent contractor could satisfy the active trade or business requirement, corporations could spin-off cash and then use the cash to pay independent contractors.

Cases like *Rafferty* and *King* can arise whenever an integrated business seeks to divide. For example, suppose X Corp. has engaged in the lumbering and milling business for several years. Can these two activities be separated tax-free under § 355? If all the lumbering output is sold to the mill, the answer is not obvious. Is an activity a "business" if there are no outside customers? Regs. § 1.355–3(c) (example 9) indicates such a horizontal division may be permissible.[141]

The active trade or business requirement plainly requires the conduct of two active trades or business after the division, but does it require two before as well? In *Coady v. Commissioner,*[142] a corporation engaged in heavy construction settled a dispute between its two shareholders by dividing itself in half. A subsidiary corporation was formed with part of the corporation's equipment, cash and a construction contract. The stock of the subsidiary was then distributed in complete redemption of one of the shareholder's stock. Although the Service challenged this division, it was sustained by the court. Such vertical divisions are now explicitly permitted by the regulations.[143]

The active business requirement will be satisfied only by businesses actively conducted for the prior five years. This rule ensures that a corporation will not be able to bail out earnings and profits by purchasing an active trade or business and then spinning it off. For example, just as X Corp. cannot spin off its liquid assets tax-free under § 355, so too X will fail to qualify under § 355 if it uses its liquid assets to purchase a business and then distributes this new business within 5 years.

On the other hand, a business may be acquired during the 5-year period in a tax-free transaction without violating the rule. Because tax-free transactions represent changes in form not significant enough to justify taxation, acquisition of a business in a tax-free transaction signifies that the corporation actually conducted the business prior to the acquisition, albeit in another form. Exam-

---

[141] But see Regs. § 1.355-2(d)(2)(iv)(C) (treating as evidence of a device the fact that the business of the distributing or controlled corporation is a secondary business (*i.e.*, a business whose principal function is to serve the business of the other corporation), if the secondary business can be sold without adversely affecting the business of the other corporation).

[142] 33 T.C. 771 (1960), aff'd, 289 F.2d 490 (6th Cir.1961); accord, *United States v. Marett,* 325 F.2d 28 (5th Cir.1963).

[143] Regs. § 1.355–3(c) (example 4).

ples of permissible tax-free transactions include incorporations under § 351, subsidiary liquidations under § 332 and § 337, and tax-free reorganizations as defined in § 368.

A corporation cannot use a newly created trade or business to satisfy the active trade or business requirement, but there is no prohibition on expanding an existing business during the five years before the § 355 distribution. See, for example, examples 7 and 8 of Regs. 1.355-3(c), in which expansions of existing business explicitly are permitted. But the line between the expansion of a business and the creation of a new business may be hard to discern. For example, exploiting newly discovered oil on land historically used for a ranching business is the creation of a new trade or business. Regs. § 1.355-2(c) (example 3). However, the expansion of a brick-and-mortar shoe store onto the web is a mere expansion of an existing trade or business rather than the creation of a new trade or business. Rev. Rul. 2003-38, 2003-1 C.B. 811.

The "active business" requirement applies to the distributing corporation as well as to the controlled corporation. Were the rule otherwise, the active business requirement could be avoided by transferring everything *other than* liquid assets or passive investment to the controlled corporation. Sale of the stock of the distributing corporation would then complete the bailout. There is thus a symmetry in § 355 as to the distributing corporation and the controlled corporation. You should not think of the distributing corporation as the original corporation or of the controlled corporation as the new corporation. Rather, both corporations should be considered as parts of the old corporate enterprise.

Note that to determine whether the distributing corporation is engaged in the active conduct of a trade or business, the activities of the corporation and all of its affiliated subsidiaries are aggregated.[144] This rule allows the activities constituting the trade or business to be divided among multiple corporations and still satisfy the active trade or business requirement. Indeed, there is no requirement that any part of the trade or business be conducted by the distributing corporation itself as long as it is conducted by its affiliated subsidiaries. Note that the same aggregation rule also applies to

---

[144] § 355(b)(3). Affiliation is determined under § 1504(a) by treating the distributing corporation as the common parent but disregarding § 1504(b). Thus, the affiliated subsidiaries of the distributing corporation include any subsidiary in which the distributing corporation owns stock that comprises at least 80% of the subsidiary's total voting power and at least 80% of its total value. They also include any other corporation in which the distributing corporation and other affiliated subsidiaries together own stock meeting those 80% thresholds. Note that in determining whether those thresholds are met, non-convertible, non-voting preferred stock is disregarded. § 1504(a)(4).

determine whether the controlled corporation is engaged in the active trade or business immediately after the distribution.

Suppose A Corp. acquires the assets of T Corp. in a taxable transaction, and assume that S Corp. is and has been a wholly owned subsidiary of T Corp. for more than 5 years. Will a distribution by A Corp. of the S Corp. stock qualify under § 355 if made within 5 years of the acquisition of T Corp. by A Corp.? No, because A Corp. acquired the T assets in a taxable transaction within five years of the distribution, it is irrelevant how long S Corp. has been actively conducting a trade or business. § 355(b)(2)(D)(i); § 355(b)(3)(C). See Rev. Rul. 89–37.[145] This rule ensures that A Corp. cannot spin off a business conducted in a subsidiary corporation more easily than it can spin off a business conducted internally.

Note that while the active trade or business requirement can be satisfied only if the distributing and controlled corporations are each considered to conduct an active trade or business, the requirement imposes no limitation on any other assets held by either corporation. So, for example, the controlled corporation might include a trade or business worth $100,000 as well as investment assets worth $1,000,000. If ownership of this controlled corporation is distributed in a § 355 distribution, a sale of the distributed stock by the shareholders will in effect bail out substantial investment assets at the minor cost of losing control of a small active business.

Congress determined that some cash-rich divisive reorganizations should not be tax-free and enacted § 355(g) to eliminate them. Under § 355(g)(1), a distribution will not qualify under § 355 if two-thirds or more of the assets of the distributing corporation or of the controlled corporation consist of investment assets as specified in § 355(g)(2)(B) *and* any person holds a 50% or greater interest in either corporation immediately after the distribution (an interest that was not held immediately prior to the distribution). The specific type of cash-rich division targeted by Congress was the situation where a minority shareholder of the distributing corporation essentially was redeemed out of the enterprise with investment assets. Such a distribution should be taxable to the distributing corporation and to the distributee, but (until § 355(g) was enacted) bundling a modest active trade or business and the investment assets into a new corporation could convert the distribution into a fully tax-free transaction.

Reconsider the "device" limitation of § 355(a)(1)(B) in light of the "active business" restriction. The "device" restriction speaks to pre-arranged sales. As we have seen, though, the active business

---

[145] 1989–1 C.B. 107.

limitation ensures that disposition of either corporation will result in a reduced interest of the corporate enterprise. Why should pre-arranged sales be condemned if the active business requirement has been met?

The regulations indicate that a "device" exists when the transaction has the potential for withdrawal of earnings and profits without implicating the usual distribution rule, namely § 301. They further provide that pro rata distributions, although allowable under § 355,[146] present the greatest opportunity for abuse. However, the factors cited by the regulations as relevant to the "device" inquiry—the nature and use of the assets transferred, whether either corporation ends up with a new trade or business or liquid assets—are adequately addressed by the active business limitation.

What role should the "device" language play? Consider the case of X Corp. which has conducted two distinct businesses for more than 5 years. The spin-off of one of X's businesses under § 355 ordinarily should present no problem, but what if the earnings of one of the businesses has been reinvested in the other business during the last 5 years? If the division is allowed, disposition of one business will effect a bailout of the earnings and profits of the other business. Such a transaction might be vulnerable to challenge under the active business limitation,[147] but the "device" language seems more appropriate.

The last restriction imposed by § 355 is the "distribution" requirement of § 355(a)(1)(D). That section requires the distributing corporation to distribute all of the stock of the controlled corporation that it owns or distribute control and establish that retention of the remainder "was not in pursuance of a plan having as one of its principal purposes the avoidance of Federal income tax." The concern to which § 355(a)(1)(D) speaks is illustrated by the following example.

X Corp. owns all the outstanding stock, both common and preferred, of Y Corp. X Corp. distributes all of the Y common stock but retains the Y preferred. If the shareholders subsequently dispose of their X stock, they will bail out some of the Y earnings and profits.[148] To prevent this bailout, the distribution requirement of

---

[146] See § 355(a)(2)(A).

[147] See, e.g., Rev. Rul. 59–400, 1959–2 C.B. 784.

[148] This is a "bailout" because the shareholders will receive a price for their X stock representing in part the value of the Y preferred stock owned by X. When that Y stock is subsequently redeemed, the bailout will be complete: funds will have come out of corporate solution and the shareholders will have been taxed at capital gains rates without surrendering a significant interest in X Corp. See Chapter 6 *supra*.

§ 355(a)(1)(D) mandates a complete division between the two corporations.

(b) Taxation of Successful and Failed Divisions.

If a corporate division meets all the tests of § 355, the distribution of stock and securities of the controlled corporation will be tax-free to both the shareholders and to the corporation. The corporation is protected from recognition of gain under § 355(c)(1) or § 361(c)(1). The shareholder is protected by § 355(a). Note, however, that a shareholder who receives securities with principal amount in excess of principal amount of any securities turned in will be taxed, just as under § 354. In addition, if a corporation distributes boot in addition to the stock and securities, gain (but not loss) can be recognized on the boot. § 355(c); § 361(c).

If a shareholder receives boot in a § 355 *distribution* (*i.e.*, a spin-off), whether excess securities or other property, the shareholder is taxed under § 356(b). This provision taxes the receipt of boot as a distribution of property under § 301. It is thus less favorable than § 356(a), which applies to boot received in amalgamating reorganizations and to § 355 *exchanges* (*i.e.*, split-offs or split-ups).[149] You will recall that recognition under § 356(a) is limited to a shareholder's realized gain on the transaction.

If a transaction fails to qualify under § 355, how will it be taxed?[150] If the transaction is a failed pro rata spin-off, presumably each shareholder will be taxed under § 301 on the stock received. However, if the transaction is structured as a split-off, then presumably the redemption rules of § 302 will be applied. Consider, though, the following split-up.

X Corp. operates two businesses. It transfers one of the businesses to newly formed Y Corp. and one to newly formed Z Corp., and then X Corp. completely liquidates. If this transaction fails to qualify under § 355, it should be taxed as a complete liquidation. Can it be taxed as a complete liquidation even if it does qualify under § 355? Note that if the distribution by X Corp. includes substantial boot, and if the X shareholders have a high basis in their X stock, then taxation as a complete liquidation may actually be pref-

---

[149] For this purpose, boot generally includes stock of the controlled corporation acquired in a taxable transaction within five years of the distribution. § 355(b)(3)(B). This general rule does not apply if (i) the controlled corporation is an affiliated subsidiary of the distributing corporation after the acquisition (but before the distribution), or (ii) the distributing corporation acquires the controlled stock from another member of an affiliated group that includes the distributing corporation. Regs. § 1.355-2(g).

[150] If the failed divisive reorganization contains within it a valid § 351 incorporation, that part of the transaction will remain tax-free under § 351.

erable to taxation under §§ 355 and 356(b).[151] Nevertheless, if taxation under § 355 is available, taxation as a complete liquidation is not, at least if the transaction is also described in § 368(a)(1)(D). See § 336(c).

(c) Divisive Reorganizations and Transfers of Control.

Congress has in two complex subsections of § 355 tried to ensure that tax-free divisions cannot be used to shield transactions that have the effect of a sale of a corporate business. These provisions, § 355(d) and § 355(e), each provide that what would otherwise be a tax-free distribution under § 355 becomes taxable to the distributing corporation. Neither provision, though, seeks to tax the distributee-shareholders. Thus, these provisions do not so much limit the reach of § 355 as limit its effect, and each provision is triggered (albeit in different ways) by a transfer of control of the distributing or of the controlled corporation.

(i) Pre–Distribution Transfers of Control. If one person holds "disqualified" stock that constitutes 50% or more (by vote or value) of the stock of the distributing corporation or of the controlled corporation immediately after the distribution, then gain on the distribution is taxable to the distributing corporation. § 355(d)(1) and (2). Disqualified stock includes (i) stock of the distributing or controlled corporation acquired by purchase within five years of the distribution, and (ii) stock of the controlled corporation received in the distribution and attributable to stock or securities of the distributing corporation acquired by purchase within five years of the distribution. § 355(d)(3). For purposes of this section, special attribution rules apply, see § 355(d)(7), and "purchase" is defined to include any taxable acquisition as well as some tax-free incorporations, see § 355(d)(5).

Consider the following example. P Corp. owns operating assets with a $300,000 fair market value and all of the stock of Sub Corp. with a $100,000 adjusted basis and $150,000 fair market value. Acquiring Corp. wishes to purchase the business operated by Sub Corp., and to do so it purchases one-third of the outstanding P stock for $150,000 (the stock's value). The stock purchased by Acquiring Corp. is then redeemed by P Corp. in exchange for all stock of Sub Corp., and if this redemption were tax-free to P Corp. under § 355(c), it would in effect have permitted the sale of Sub Corp. to Acquiring Corp. without the imposition of a corporate-level tax.

---

[151] Of course, if the corporation's assets have substantially appreciated, taxation as a complete liquidation will entail recognition of gain at the corporate level under § 336(a).

However, because of § 355(d), the distribution is taxable to P Corp., forcing P Corp. to recognize $50,000 of gain. This taxation is imposed because Acquiring Corp. ends up owning 50% or more of Sub Corp., and that stock interest either was purchased directly (here, it was not) or was received as a distribution on stock that was itself purchased (as was the case here). Accordingly, the stock of Sub Corp. is a "disqualified distribution" under § 355(d)(1), the distributed shares of Sub Corp. therefore no longer are treated as "qualified property" and so the distribution of those appreciated shares is taxable to P Corp. under § 355(c)(2).

It is worth observing that there is no obvious tax abuse to which § 355(d) speaks because transactions described in § 355(d) represent a mere change in corporate ownership without any change in corporate asset basis. That is, distributions taxed under § 355(d) consist only of financial assets (stock and securities of the controlled corporation), and so never remove appreciated real assets from corporate solution nor increase the basis of real assets remaining within corporate solution. Since one corporation can purchase the stock of another corporation without the imposition of a tax to the purchased corporation (and, of course, without a corporate-level step-up in basis), it is unclear why the same result should not hold true when the purchaser wishes to buy only a single division within a corporate structure. But the operation of § 355(d) clearly prevents it.

Of course, if the acquiror had directly purchased the stock of the controlled corporation, the seller would have recognized a corporate-level gain. Perhaps, § 355(d) may be viewed as merely assuring that the same result occurs if that stock is purchased indirectly.

(ii) Post–Distribution Loss of Control. Recall that the "device" language of § 355(a)(1)(B) condemns distributions otherwise described in § 355(a) if there is a pre-arranged transfer of stock following the distribution. While this "device" language seems absolute on its face,[152] lawyers argued that some pre-arranged stock transfers might nevertheless pass muster. The *Morris Trust*[153] case involved a divisive reorganization followed by an A (amalgamating) reorganization. In *Morris Trust*, a state bank spun-off its insurance business prior to merging with a national bank. Because a national bank may not, in general, conduct an insurance business, the division was a necessary condition to the merger. After the merger, share-

---

[152] However, note that while the distributing corporation must distribute at least 80% control of the controlled corporation, the shareholders need end up with only 50% control, see § 368(a)(2)(H), so that the shareholders can, as part of the overall transaction, transfer a significant portion of the distributed stock to others.

[153] *Commissioner v. Morris Trust,* 367 F.2d 794 (4th Cir.1966).

holders of the state bank owned the insurance business but only a minority interest in the merged national bank—control of assets formerly used by the state bank, in other words, was transferred to the shareholders of the acquiring national bank.

The Commissioner attacked the tax-free status of the spin-off as a device. The thrust of the challenge was that the shareholders did not have "control" of the distributing corporation immediately after the transaction. The court, however, found nothing in the statute requiring the shareholders to control the distributing corporation immediately after the transaction. Such a requirement, the court held, applied only to the controlled corporation (i.e., to the corporation whose stock is distributed as part of the transaction).

The court's analysis of the statute, at least in one regard, was deficient. The statute requires that shareholders of the distributing corporation be "in control" of the controlled corporation immediately after the distribution. While there is no statement that they must also be in control of the distributing corporation, this absence of statutory language is easy to explain: the shareholders of the distributing corporation, as a group, are *always* "in control" of the distributing corporation immediately after the transaction. After all, they are the shareholders.

What caused the problem in *Morris Trust* was that the shareholders relinquished control of the distributing corporation immediately after the transaction. In other words, they "sold or exchanged" some of their stock immediately afterward, precisely the conduct condemned by the device language of § 355(a)(1)(B). The court in *Morris Trust* completely overlooked the symmetries of § 355, thinking that a bailout could occur only by disposition of stock of the controlled corporation. Yet, as we have seen, the distributing corporation and the controlled corporation play equal roles in § 355.

The issue posed by *Morris Trust* that the court should have focused on was whether a pre-arranged disposition is condemned by the device language of § 355(a)(1)(B) when the disposition occurs as part of a *tax-free* transaction. Such a disposition does not bail out any earnings and profits, because the shareholders continue to hold stock, though stock of a new corporation. On the other hand, the transaction in *Morris Trust* does seem to have failed the literal language of the "device" requirement because there was a pre-arranged disposition of shares of the distributing corporation.

The effect of the transaction in *Morris Trust* was to give control of part of the corporate enterprise to new shareholders. Does the statute permit such a result? The transaction in *Morris Trust* could have been accomplished an alternate way: the state bank/insurance company could have transferred its banking business to the national bank in exchange for a minority interest in the national bank, and then that stock could have been distributed to the state bank's shareholders. However, had this route been taken the transaction would have been taxable at two levels: (1) at the corporate level because the transfer by the state bank/insurance company fails the control test applicable to § 351 transactions; and (2) at the shareholder level because the distribution fails the control test applicable to § 355 distributions.

Consider first the corporate level taxation. While the transfer from one corporation to another corporation of appreciated assets does not represent a bailout of earnings and profits (because the transferred assets remain in corporate solution), such a transfer generally is a taxable event under the general rule of § 1001(a): when appreciated assets are sold or exchanged by a corporate or noncorporate taxpayer, gain is realized and usually recognized.

To be sure, the various acquisitive reorganization provisions permit the transfer of assets between corporations without the imposition of a corporate-level tax, but Congress has limited those provisions to the transfer of substantially all of the transferor corporation's assets. In *Morris Trust*, the banking business was transferred but the insurance business was retained, and assuming the insurance business was not insubstantial, the transaction should therefore fail to qualify for tax-free reorganization treatment at the corporate level.[154]

Consider next the shareholder-level tax. Some of the pre-transaction value in the state bank/insurance company shares was converted into shares of the national bank. In general, the realization doctrine subjects to taxation appreciation in assets when converted into a new form, and from that perspective the transaction should also have been taxable at the shareholder level. However, the change in form was not considerable: stock has been converted into other stock, and the new stock continues ownership in a previously owned business (the state banking business). Thus, Congress might well postpone the shareholder-level tax until disposition of the new shares.

In the actual *Morris Trust* case, the court held for the taxpayer, and that holding was codified and expanded in the current regulations. Now, regulations permit a pre-arranged disposition of shares of the distributing or the controlled corporation without triggering the "device" language of § 355(a)(1)(B) so long as this disposition is

---

[154] See *Helvering v. Elkhorn Coal Co.*, 95 F.2d 732 (4th Cir.1937).

part of a tax-free reorganization.[155] In addition, even taxable dispositions will not necessarily be treated as a bailout: taxable dispositions of less than 20 percent of the corporation's stock are, under these regulations, substantial but not conclusive evidence of a "device." However, Congress ultimately determined that the *Morris Trust* case represents an abuse of § 355, and in § 355(e) that perceived abuse is attacked in a peculiar and complex way.

Section 355(e) was enacted in 1997 for two principal reasons: first, because Congress believed "[i]n cases in which it is intended that new shareholders will acquire ownership of a business in connection with a spin off, the transaction more closely resembles a corporate level disposition of the portion of the business that is acquired." H.R. Rep. No. 105-148, at 542 (1997). Second, rejecting the asymmetries in *Morris Trust*, Congress "believe[d] that the differences in treatment of certain transactions following a spin-off, depending upon whether the distributing or controlled corporation engages in the transaction, should be minimized." *Id.*

Consider the following: B Corp., a state-chartered bank, has owned for many years all the stock of I Corp., an insurance company. The stock of I Corp. is distributed to the shareholders of B Corp., and then B Corp. changes its charter to that of a national bank and raises new funds through a public offering. Assume that the spin-off of I Corp. was a necessary first step in the public offering because national banks cannot own insurance companies.

Assuming the active trade or business requirement of § 355(a)(1)(C) is met, the distribution by B Corp. of the I Corp. stock should satisfy all the requirements of § 355(a)(1). Indeed, the device language of § 355(a)(1)(C) should not be implicated because no stock of the distributing corporation (i.e., B Corp.) and no stock of the controlled corporation (i.e., I) is sold or exchanged as part of the transaction. However, if the post-distribution public offering is sufficiently large, the distribution by B Corp. of the I Corp. stock will be taxable at the corporate level (though it will remain tax-free at the shareholder level) under § 355(e).

Section 355(e) is triggered if an otherwise tax-free spin-off under § 355 is part of a plan for one or more persons to acquire 50% or

---

[155] Regs. § 1.355–2(d)(iii)(E); see also Rev. Rul. 2003-79, 2003-2 C.B. 80, in which the Service ruled that a § 355 distribution could be followed by a C reorganization in which the assets of the controlled corporation are acquired by an unrelated corporation and the controlled corporation then liquidates. Sadly, in that ruling the Service reaffirmed that if the assets of the distributing corporation (rather than the assets of the controlled corporation) had been acquired, the post-distribution acquisition would not have qualified as a C reorganization under *Elkhorn Coal.*

more control (by vote or value) of the distributing corporation or of the controlled corporation.[156] In the example above, if the public offering results in new shareholders acquiring 50% or more of the vote or value of B Corp. (see § 355(e)(4)(A) incorporating § 355(d)(4)), gain (but not loss) will be recognized to B Corp. on the spin-off as if B Corp. sold the I Corp. stock for its fair market value. And note that the same taxation would result if new shareholders acquired 50% or more control of I Corp. rather than of B Corp.

The legislative history of § 355(e) makes clear that no adjustment should be made to the basis of any corporate assets as a result of this taxation, a result that makes little sense and imposes a triple tax on corporate earnings: once under § 355(e) on the distribution by the distributing corporation of the stock of the controlled corporation, a second time at the corporate level when the controlled corporation sells the appreciated assets or otherwise earns income from them, and a third time when the shareholders sell or exchange the distributed stock of the controlled corporation. One would expect that the controlled corporation would get a step-up in the basis of its assets if the distributing corporation is taxed under § 355(e), just as would occur if the assets had simply been sold in a taxable transaction. Indeed, such a basis step-up is mandated by statute in a similar context under § 338.[157] Nonetheless, the effect of § 355(e) apparently is to demand an eventual extra corporate level tax as the price for obtaining shareholder level deferral (under § 355(a)) on the transaction.

Not all transfers of control will trigger taxation under § 355(e). If the new shareholders acquiring control of the distributing or controlled corporation already had control of the other corporation, taxation under § 355(e) is avoided. See § 355(e)(3)(A)(iv). And, of

---

[156] Although § 355(e)(2)(B) presumes that any transfer of control occurring less than two years before or after the spin-off is part of such a plan, the regulations are more forgiving. They contain nine safe harbors under which a distribution and acquisition do not trigger § 355(e). See Regs. §1.355-7(d). For example, a distribution and later acquisition will not be considered part of a plan if—

   (i) The distribution is motivated in whole or substantial part by a business purpose other than the acquisition of the acquired corporation; and

   (ii) The acquisition occurs more than six months after the distribution and there is no prohibited activity during the period that begins one year before, and ends six months after, the distribution.

Id. at (d)(1) (Safe Harbor I). Further, a distribution and later acquisition will not be considered part of a plan if there is no prohibited activity at the time of, and within one year after, the distribution. *Id.* at (d)(3) (Safe Harbor III). For these purposes, prohibited activities include an agreement, understanding, arrangement, or substantial negotiations concerning the acquisition or a similar acquisition.

[157] See § 338(e)(1).

course, the actual distribution under § 355(a) works a transfer of control (from the distributing corporation to its shareholders), but that inevitable transfer of control is irrelevant under § 355(e)(3)(A)(ii).

While § 355(e) is triggered by the transfer of corporate control, certain asset acquisitions are treated as control transfers. Under § 355(e)(3)(B), tax-free asset acquisitions (such as a tax-free merger or C reorganization) are equated to stock transfers for purposes of § 355(e). Note that both taxable and tax-free stock transfers can trigger § 355(e) but only tax-free asset transfers can have that effect. This rule makes sense because § 355(e) imposes a corporate-level tax on the transaction, and if the assets were transferred in a taxable transaction, the corporate-level tax has already been incurred.

This discussion should make clear that § 355(e) is both more and less than a congressional rejection of the *Morris Trust* case. *Morris Trust* held that a tax-free transfer of control of the distributing corporation is not a "device" within the meaning of § 355(a)(1)(C), and that holding remains good law. On the other hand, taxation at the corporate level under § 355(e) is triggered if post-distribution control of the distributing corporation or of the controlled corporation is transferred in any manner. Thus, this rule applies to tax-free acquisitions (including tax-free asset transfers as occurred in *Morris Trust*) and to taxable transactions. Note, though, that nothing in § 355(e) limits the device language in § 355(a)(1)(C) so that a pre-arranged taxable transfer of control might invalidate the entire transaction under § 355(a)(1)(C), thereby subjecting the transaction to taxation at both the corporate and shareholder levels.

Because § 355(e) subjects the distributing corporation to taxation on any appreciation in the stock of the controlled corporation, at least one asymmetry remains. Suppose P Corp. owns two businesses, a toy business with assets having adjusted basis of $500,000 and fair market value of $900,000 and a software business with assets having adjusted basis and fair market value of $900,000. If P Corp. wishes to divide these two business under § 355 and then transfer control of one of the two to new investors, it can do so without paying any toll charge under § 355(e) by transferring the assets of the software business to a newly formed corporation and then distributing the stock of the newly formed corporation to its shareholders under § 355. To be sure, when control of either business is relinquished, § 355(e) will be implicated, but because the software assets were unappreciated (so the controlled stock was as well), no taxation results. Had P Corp. instead dropped the assets of the toy business to the controlled corporation, the controlled corporation stock would have had a $400,000 built-in gain and § 355(e) would have forced P Corp. to recognize a $400,000 gain on the spin-off.

(d) Alternatives to § 355.

Congress has tried to ensure that all divisive transactions run the gauntlet of § 355 if they are to be tax-free. For example, the transferor-corporation in a C or a non-divisive D reorganization must liquidate as part of the transaction, thereby guaranteeing that only the transferee corporation will survive the reorganization and carry on the corporate business. Taxpayers, though, have sought to avoid the restrictions of § 355 by shoe-horning divisive transactions into other Code sections. For example, suppose that Subco is the wholly owned subsidiary of P Corp. If Subco distributes shares of its own stock to the P shareholders for some of the P Corp. stock, the effect of the transaction is to convert the parent/subsidiary pair into a brother/sister pair (albeit with cross-ownership between brother and sister). How should the exchange of Subco stock for P Corp. stock be taxed?

Formally, the transaction looks to be an exchange at the shareholder-level, taxable under § 1001(a). To Subco on the other hand, it is simply a distribution of its own stock for property, a tax-free event under § 1032(a). Accordingly, the transaction will produce little or no tax liability if the P Corp. shareholders have a high stock basis in their P Corp. shares.

Because Subco is distributing its own stock, the transaction does not fall under § 355 even though the transaction does have a divisive impact. The Commissioner has sought to tax such transactions under § 304(a)(2), and under that provision the distribution of property can be taxed as ordinary income to the distributees.

However, § 304(a)(2) only applies to the distribution of "property," and "property" for purposes of § 304 does not include stock of the distributing corporation. § 317(a). The Service takes the position that P Corp. should be treated as the distributing corporation in the transaction, but the courts have refused to read § 304(a)(2) that way.[158] Yet, if Subco (or P Corp.) owns only liquid assets, the distribution opens the door for a possible bailout.

For example, suppose P Corp. has substantial earnings and profits as well as considerable cash. P Corp. creates Subco by contributing the cash to Subco in exchange for Subco common stock. This transaction is tax-free to P under § 351 and to Subco under

---

[158] *Bhada v. Commissioner,* 89 T.C. 959 (1987), aff'd sub nom. *Caamano v. Commissioner,* 879 F.2d 156 (5th Cir.1989).

§ 1032. Subsequently, the P shareholders transfer some of their P Corp. common stock to Subco in exchange for Subco preferred stock of equal value. To maximize the bailout, the P Corp. stock given up should be worth exactly as much as the cash now held by Subco. Since the Subco stock is not "property" for § 304(a)(2), this exchange is taxable to the P shareholders under § 1001(a), giving them a recovery of basis and then capital gain. In addition, because the issuance of the Subco preferred stock is fully taxable to the P shareholders (albeit as capital gain), this preferred stock is not § 306 stock.

The P shareholders can then sell the newly acquired Subco preferred shares to outside investors who will then have those shares redeemed, or the P shareholders can have those shares redeemed directly from them. Once the Subco preferred stock is redeemed, the bailout is complete: no gain will be recognized on the redemption (or on the pre-redemption sale to outside investors) because the P shareholders' bases in the preferred stock are equal to their fair market value. Thus, the value of the cash will be removed from corporate solution at a tax cost of only capital gain.

10.05 One–Party Reorganizations

In § 368(a)(1)(E) and (F), Congress has defined two different one-party reorganizations. An E reorganization is a recapitalization in which a single corporation rearranges its financial structure. For example, as part of a recapitalization, a corporation might create a new class of stock, replace outstanding debt instruments with preferred stock, or alter the relationship between common and preferred stockholders. In each case, some or all of the shareholders or creditors will turn in their old stock or securities and receive in exchange new stock or securities. If the transaction qualifies as an E reorganization, the transaction may be tax-free.

The second type of one-party reorganization is an F reincorporation. As the language of § 368(a)(1)(F) indicates, reincorporations involve the change of a single corporation's state of incorporation or similar attribute. Although the reincorporation provision once played a substantial role in the reorganization drama, recent statutory changes to § 368(a)(1)(F) have reduced its importance.

The most important use of the recapitalization technique is to allow older management of a closely held corporation to make room for the next generation. Consider the case of X Corp, which has a single class of common stock outstanding, held equally by three sisters. The sisters formed the company many years ago and watched it prosper. They would like to pass control of X Corp. on to their daughters while preserving a steady income stream for life. The daughters are eager to run the company, but they lack sufficient assets to buy it outright.

In those circumstances, a preferred-stock recapitalization will accomplish the goals of both generations. X Corp. will recapitalize, issuing preferred stock to the founding sisters with aggregate par value equal to the current value of the company. As part of the recapitalization, the daughters will contribute a small amount of cash in exchange for common stock.

Because the par value of the preferred stock equals the total value of the company, the fair market value of the common stock is almost nil. Thus, the founders of the company have not lost any part of their investment. However, if the preferred stock is limited to par value on liquidation, then all future growth will inure to the benefit of the new generation. In addition, the preferred stock can provide a stable form of income for the founding sisters in the form of annual dividends.

Just as not all statutory mergers qualify as A reorganizations, so too not all rearrangements of a corporation's capital structure qualify as recapitalizations. In *Bazley v. Commissioner,*[159] a corporation recapitalized by causing each shareholder to turn in his shares and receive in exchange five new shares plus some securities. The taxpayer characterized the exchange as a tax-free reorganization while the Commissioner characterized it as a taxable distribution of the securities, resulting in dividend income.

The Supreme Court had no difficulty in agreeing with the Commissioner. This case had considerably more impact before the enactment of § 354(a)(2) because that section treats excess securities received in a reorganization as boot. Had § 354(a)(2) been in force at the time of *Bazley,* the taxpayer would have been required to recognize gain on the transaction even if it had qualified as an E reorganization. Nonetheless, treating the securities as boot under § 354(a)(2) and § 356 is not the same as the transaction failing to qualify as a statutory reorganization, especially in light of section § 453(f)(6).[160]

Under § 453(f)(6), securities received in a reorganization and taxed as boot qualify, in some circumstances, for recognition under the installment method. Under the installment method, gain is recognized only as proceeds on the obligations are received or if the

---

[159] 331 U.S. 737 (1947).

[160] Under § 356 as well, any dividend amount is limited to the taxpayer's realized gain, even if the gain is less than the securities' value. If the receipt of the securities is treated as a dividend, however, the full value of the securities may be treated as dividend income.

installment obligation is sold. In the case of securities received in a reorganization, this allows a taxpayer to defer recognition of gain until the securities are sold or called by the corporation.

The benefit of § 453(f)(6) is unavailable to readily tradable securities.[161] In addition, it cannot apply to securities received in a reorganization unless any gain recognized is taxable under § 356(a)(1), that is, if the exchange does not have the effect of a dividend. Whether boot received in a reorganization has the effect of a dividend is determined by application of the "after" test under *Commissioner v. Clark*.

The continuing importance of *Bazley* is that securities received under § 301 never qualify for the installment method. Thus, if the transaction fails to qualify as a recapitalization or other statutory reorganization, securities received in the transaction will be taxable when received. Stock exchanged as part of the transaction, on the other hand, under some circumstances will still be received tax-free.[162]

The taxation of securities received thus can be (1) tax-free under § 354(a)(1) to the extent of securities turned in, (2) taxable (not in an amount in excess of gain realized) and reported on the installment method, or (3) taxable immediately.[163] All three methods will produce different tax results for the recipient shareholder. In particular, the basis consequences to the shareholder are different under § 354 and § 453(f).[164]

Recall that "nonqualified preferred stock" as defined in § 351(g)(2) generally is not treated as stock if received by a shareholder as part of a corporate reorganization. However, this taint for preferred, nonparticipating stock is removed in the case of recapitalizations of family-owned corporations, see § 354(a)(2)(C)(ii), an important exception for elderly taxpayers hoping to pass on control of

---

[161] See § 453(f)(4).

[162] See § 1036 (tax-free exchange of common for common or preferred for preferred).

[163] If, as in *Bazley*, the transaction fails to qualify for reorganization treatment, then receipt of the securities may be taxed under § 301 and, if there are sufficient earnings and profits, will be taxed as ordinary income equal to the fair market value of the securities received.

[164] Under § 358, basis is divided between the stock and securities received tax-free in proportion to relative fair market values. § 358(b). Under § 356 and § 453(f), the boot securities are allocated a fair market value basis, see § 358(a)(2), with a consequent reduction in the shareholder's stock basis, see § 358(a)(1)(A)(i). Of course, the shareholder's basis in the securities will not equal fair market value until the installment gain is recognized. See generally Prop. Regs. § 1.453–1(f)(2).

a family business without the imposition of substantial estate and gift tax.

Reincorporations under § 368(a)(1)(F) once included the amalgamation of several corporations owned by the same shareholders.[165] However, the Tax Equity and Fiscal Responsibility Act of 1982 added the words "of one corporation" to § 368(a)(1)(F), thereby ending the use of the F reorganization to join multiple corporations.

The legislative history for this amendment to § 368(a)(1)(F) makes clear that Congress did not intend to remove the following kinds of transactions from the scope of the F reorganization. X Corp. desires to reincorporate in a new state. Accordingly, New X Corp. is formed in the new state. X then transfers all of its assets to New X in exchange for all New X's stock, and then X completely liquidates. This simple reincorporation technically involves two corporations (X and New X), but only one *active* corporation (or at least only one corporation with any tax history). The legislative history of the 1982 act indicates that F reorganizations can involve multiple corporations so long as only one is active.

Because the A, B, C and nondivisive D reorganizations specifically cover multi-party amalgamating reorganizations, you might wonder why taxpayers have tried so hard to fall within the confines of the F reorganization. The answer is that the rules historically governing the carryover of tax attributes such as net operating losses were much more favorable to the single party reorganizations (recapitalizations and reincorporations) than to the multi-party reorganizations. The carryover of tax attributes incidental to corporate reorganization is discussed in the next Chapter.[166]

A multi-step transaction, if it results in the assets of one corporation remaining in corporate solution in the hands of a nominally different corporation, may qualify as an F reorganization. For example, suppose X Corp. conducts two businesses and wishes to separate each business from the liabilities of the other. This can be accomplished in a variety of ways. For example, one business could be dropped into a wholly owned subsidiary or disregarded entity. Similarly, X Corp. could become a holding company by dropping each business into a new subsidiary.

---

[165] See, e.g., *Reef Corp. v. Commissioner,* 368 F.2d 125 (5th Cir.1966); *Davant v. Commissioner,* 366 F.2d 874 (5th Cir.1966).

[166] In addition, if a corporation engages in an F reorganization, its tax year does not end, unlike when the corporation is the target in an acquisitive asset reorganization. See § 381(b). Thus, if the corporation has a soon-to-expire net operating loss carryover, it may prefer an F to an acquisitive asset reorganization to better preserve that carryover.

But what if one of the businesses includes real estate subject to potential environmental clean-up costs that can be imposed on the owner of the property *or on a prior owner*? Now, transferring the real estate to a subsidiary will not shield X Corp's other assets from the remediation liability because that liability can be imposed directly on X Corp. as a prior owner of the real estate.[167] A divisive reorganization will do the trick but satisfaction of the various § 355 requirements might be impossible.

Consider the following transaction. X Corp. creates NewCo as a wholly owned subsidiary and transfers its non-real estate business to NewCo. NewCo then forms Y LLC, a wholly-owned limited liability company that is treated as a disregarded entity for tax purposes. X Corp. then merges into Y LLC under applicable state law, with Y LLC surviving. After these steps, NewCo owns the non-real estate assets directly and owns the real estate assets indirectly through its ownership of Y LLC. Further, because Y LLC, rather than NewCo, succeeded to the X Corp. liabilities, the transaction shields NewCo from the remediation liability. Finally, since Y LLC is a disregarded entity for federal income tax purposes, its assets and liabilities are deemed NewCo's assets and liabilities. Thus, NewCo succeeds to all X Corp. assets and liabilities for federal income tax purposes, and the multi-step transaction should qualify as an F reorganization.

---

[167] Note that retaining the real estate in X Corp. and dropping the other business in a subsidiary entity will not work, because the subsidiary interest will be owned by X Corp. and so potentially subject to the liabilities of X Corp., including its remediation liability.

Chapter 11

COMBINING TAX ATTRIBUTES

11.01 Introduction

In transactions covered by §§ 332, 351, 355, and 368, the Code has specific provisions that generally preserve built-in gain or loss through a carryover of basis in assets transferred of a substitution of basis in stock received in exchange. For example, § 358 provides, generally speaking, for a transfer of the adjusted basis of exchanging shareholders to the new stock or securities acquired by them. Similarly, § 362 provides that property acquired by a corporation in connection with a § 351 transaction or in connection with a reorganization typically will have the same basis as the property had in the hands of the transferor. See also § 1223 relating to the holding period of property received in connection with such transactions and § 168(i)(7) for a step-in-the-shoes rule applicable to depreciation.

However, corporations have a great many more tax attributes than basis and holding periods of assets. Different corporations may have different accounting methods, methods of depreciation with respect to property, earnings and profits accounts, foreign tax credits, and net operating loss ("NOL") carryovers. Consistent with the philosophy of the non-recognition provisions such as § 351, § 355, and the operative provisions for § 368 reorganizations, those tax attributes should remain undisturbed after such transactions. One would also expect similar rules to apply for liquidations of controlled subsidiaries into their parents to which §§ 332, 337, and 334(b) apply.

For example, if two corporations merge, one would expect that after the merger, in calculating whether distributions were made out of earnings and profits, one would look to the combined earnings and profits of the two corporations. Generally speaking, § 381 (providing for carryover of tax attributes in certain tax-free exchanges) and other provisions of the Code carry out such expected results.

On the other hand, it should also be noted that where a corporation sells all of its assets, the purchaser does not succeed to the selling corporation's tax attributes, because the selling corporation remains in existence. If a selling corporation liquidates and § 332 does not apply to the liquidation, the selling corporation's tax attributes disappear. Similarly, when a corporation makes an election under § 338 to be treated as if it sold its assets to itself, the corporation's tax attributes disappear (at least if a regular § 338 election is made).[1]

This simplified discussion ignores the problems created over many decades by what some call the "trafficking" in corporations having substantial NOL carryovers and other desirable tax attributes (for example, high-basis low-value assets). Individuals having business deductions in excess of income can carry those losses back or forward as prescribed by § 172 but cannot readily sell these tax benefits to others. When NOL carryovers are lodged in a corporate entity, however, sale of the loss is no more difficult than the sale of the stock of the corporation—provided that the tax attributes are not reduced or eliminated by the transfer of the stock. As described below, Congress and the Treasury have actively resisted perceived "trafficking" in loss corporations.

11.02 Section 381

Section 381 provides for the carryover of tax attributes from a transferor corporation to an acquiring corporation in certain transactions. The transactions covered are (1) a liquidation of a controlled subsidiary and (2) type A, C, or F tax-free reorganizations as well as acquisitive D or G reorganizations. Note that in a § 368(a)(1)(B) stock-for-stock reorganization, there is no need for the rules of § 381 since the corporate existence of the acquired company continues even though there is an exchange at the shareholder level. The same holds true for § 368(a)(1)(E) recapitalizations. In other words, § 381 deals, as its opening sentence states, with "the acquisition of assets of a corporation by another corporation."

The inherited attributes in a qualified transaction are subject to the operating rules of § 381(b). Section 381(b)(3) provides that the acquiring corporation may not carry back a post-acquisition NOL or net capital loss to a pre-acquisition year of the transferor. Here the rules impinge not on the carryover of the transferor's attributes to the transferee but instead block the use by the transferee of its own losses against income of a transferor corporation for a year before the merger.

Section 381(c) lists numerous tax attributes of the transferor that the transferee inherits. Of these, the most prominent one that will be discussed in greater detail below is the NOL carryover of § 381(c)(1). Note that while loss carryovers are transferred to the acquiring company, they can be used only against future income of the transferee. Other important inherited attributes include the transferor's earnings and profits. § 381(c)(2). Under § 381(c)(2)(A)

---

[1] For a discussion of § 338, see Section 9.03 *supra.*

the earnings and profits or deficit in earnings and profits of the transferor carry over to the transferee, but under § 381(c)(2)(B) an inherited deficit in earnings and profits may be applied only against the transferee's post-transfer earnings and profits and not against the transferee's accumulated earnings and profits.

11.03 Section 382

Suppose in year 1 of its existence, X Corp. operates at a $100 loss (i.e., deductions exceed income by $100). In year 2, X Corp. produces $100 of income. Over the two year, X Corp. has $0 of net income, which its tax consequences should reflect. Strict adherence to the annual accounting concept would prevent X Corp. from offsetting income in year 2 with the loss from year 1. In fact, X Corp. is permitted to carry forward the year 1 loss to offset the income earned in year 2. § 172. Similarly, if X Corp. had earned $100 of income in year 1 and had suffered a $100 loss in year 2, the year 2 loss could be carried back to offset the year 1 income (i.e., X Corp. would file an amended return for year 1). Under § 172(b), a corporation can generally carry a loss back 2 years and forward 20 years, using up the loss in the earliest year or years in which there is sufficient income to absorb the loss.

Now suppose that X Corp. has a $100 loss in year 1 and that Y Corp. has $100 of income in year 1. If, at the end of the year, X Corp. merges into Y Corp. with the X shareholders receiving Y stock, should Y Corp. be able to use X's $100 loss to offset its $100 of income? After all, if X Corp. could carry its losses back and forward, why should it not be permitted to carry its losses sideways to offset Y Corp.'s income? However, if Y Corp. could use X's loss, there may be some concern that the X-Y merger is solely (or primarily) motivated by the presence of the NOL. For example, suppose that X Corp.'s assets at the time of the merger are worth $0. Even so, Y Corp., if it pays taxes at a 35-percent rate, may be willing to exchange up to $35 of Y Corp. stock for the X stock in the merger, because the use of the X NOL will save $35 in taxes that Y Corp. would otherwise pay on its $100 of income.

While it is by no means clear that such a tax-motivated purchase is economically inefficient, Congress has since 1954 wrestled with the perceived problem of "trafficking" in NOLs. On one hand, the carryover provisions perform an averaging function that allows corporations to overcome the limits of our annual accounting system. On the other hand, where NOLs are used to offset totally unrelated income (such as the acquisition of a corporation solely to obtain its NOLs), no legitimate averaging function seems to be performed.

The main tool to fight this loss trafficking is § 382, a section intended to remove the tax incentive for a buyer to acquire a corporation because of its tax losses. Under § 382, after a substantial ownership change, the earnings which can be offset by a pre-change NOL are limited, although the amount of the NOL that may be used is not directly limited. The limitation-on-earnings approach is intended to approximate the results that would occur if a loss corporation's assets were combined with those of a profitable corporation in a partnership. In that case, only the loss corporation's share of the partnership's income could be offset by the corporation's NOL carryforward.[2] Generally, the loss corporation's share of the partnership's income reflects the value of the assets contributed by the loss corporation. Section 382(f) prescribes an objective rate of return (the federal long-term tax-exempt rate) on the value of the corporation's net equity. The annual limitation, then, equals that the prescribed rate multiplied by the value of the loss corporation's equity immediately before a specified ownership change. § 382(b).

For example, suppose that X Corp., a calendar-year taxpayer, has $1 million of NOL carryforwards. On January 1 of year 1, all X stock is sold in a transaction that triggers § 382. On that date, the X stock has a $500,000 value and the applicable rate of return is 10 percent. In year 1 (and for each year thereafter), X Corp. can offset $50,000 (10 percent of $500,000) of income with the NOL carryforward. The same limitation would apply if X Corp. were merged into another corporation if the merger resulted in an ownership change of X Corp., as defined in § 382(g). To the extent that X Corp. does not earn enough in year 1 to absorb the $50,000 amount, the excess loss is carried forward to year 2 and is added to the $50,000 NOL limitation allowed in that year. § 382(b)(2).

It may seem peculiar that the limitation of § 382 applies to the sale of stock of a loss corporation if the only post-sale income sheltered by the corporation's losses is generated by the loss corporation itself. There is no obvious trafficking from a stock sale, even one that results in a transfer of control. There are two reasons, however, why Congress likely applied § 382 to these stock sales. First, the loss corporation may join the consolidated group of the purchaser (if the purchaser is a corporation), and its losses may otherwise offset post-change income of the group. Second, the purchaser may contribute assets that may generate income that could be absorbed by the pre-change losses.

The § 382 limitation, although somewhat artificially determined, applies notwithstanding the actual performance of a loss

---

[2] See § 704(b).

company. For example, suppose that all of the stock of L Corp., a loss corporation, is sold by B to P in a transaction that triggers § 382. After the acquisition, the amount of income that can be offset by the pre-acquisition NOLs is determined under § 382 (*i.e.*, the value of L Corp. multiplied by the federal long-term tax-exempt tax rate). This limitation applies even if L Corp.'s income for a year exceeds the § 382 limitation. Conversely, if L Corp. is merged into P Corp. in a transaction that triggers § 382, P Corp. can offset income up to the § 382 limitation even if the former L assets in fact produce less than that amount of income. Thus, using the federal long-term tax-exempt rate as a proxy for the actual return on the assets may produce too large or too small a deduction. However, once the § 382 limitation is determined, it is used every year until the pre-change NOLs are used up (or those losses expire unused).

(a) Ownership Changes.

Section 382 is triggered by an "ownership change." An ownership change occurs if, as the result of an "owner shift" or "equity structure shift," the percentage of the stock of a loss corporation owned by one or more 5-percent shareholders has increased by more than 50 percentage points[3] over the lowest percentage owned by each such shareholder during the testing period. The testing period is three years or, if shorter, the period since the last ownership change. § 382(i) (also providing that the period does not begin until the first day of the first year for which there is a carryforward of losses). Note that an ownership change may be triggered by a series of unrelated transactions occurring over the testing period.

Keys to applying § 382 include identifying a loss corporation's 5-percent shareholders, its owner shifts, and its equity structure shifts. Generally, a 5-percent shareholder is any individual who owns (actually and constructively) 5 percent or more in value of corporate stock at any time during the testing period.[4] For this purpose, "stock" excludes stock described in § 1504(a)(4). *Id.* at (k)(6)(A). Section 1504(a)(4) is stock that is nonvoting, is limited and preferred as to dividends, is not convertible, does not participate in corporate growth to any significant extent, and has redemption and

---

[3] An ownership change occurs when there is a 50-percentage point change, not a 50-percent change. For example, if X owns 30 percent of Y Corp., X must end up with more than 80 percent, not more than 45 percent of Y Corp. to trigger § 382.

[4] § 382(k)(7). *See also id.* at (l)(3) (adopting the constructive ownership rules of § 318 with modifications). Thus, stock owned by entities is deemed owned by the shareholders, partners, or beneficiaries of those entities in proportion to their interests.

liquidation rights not exceeding the issue price (except for a reasonable redemption or liquidation premium).[5]

As one source of real complexity, 5-percent shareholders may also include public groups of non-5 percent shareholders. Generally, all non-5 percent shareholders of the loss corporation are grouped together to from one "public" group. See Regs. § 1.382-2T(j). However, separate public groups of these shareholders may be formed if, for example, the loss corporation participates in an acquisitive reorganization (as the target or acquiring corporation) or if it issues its stock in a public or private offering.

Consider how those 5-percent shareholder rules apply to an owner shift, which occurs when there is a greater than 50-percentage point change in stock ownership by 5-percent shareholders. § 382(g)(2). Assume that Y Corp. is publicly traded and held by shareholders, none of whom own at least 5 percent of the Y stock. Y Corp. therefore has one 5-percent shareholder, the public group of its non-5 percent shareholders (*i.e.*, all of its shareholders). Random trading among Y's less than 5-percent shareholders is essentially disregarded, because before and after this trading, Y's single public group owns all Y stock. Thus, that trading has no impact on the application of § 382. However, if B and C each buy one half of the Y stock from those "public" shareholders, an owner shift occurs, because there has been a more than 50 percentage point change in the ownership of Y stock by 5-percent shareholders: B and C, each 5-percent shareholders, have gone from holding 0 percent to 100 percent of the that stock, resulting in Y Corp.'s ownership change.

Similarly, if Y Corp. were a closely held corporation owned by B and C, and Y Corp. made a public offering of 51 percent of its stock, an ownership change would occur. Those who bought the stock in the public offering would constitute a public group treated as one 5-percent shareholder. Because the public group would go from holding 0 percent to 51 percent of Y Corp., the group would increase its percentage interest in Y Corp. by 51 percentage points, resulting in an ownership change.

An "equity structure shift" generally includes any tax-free reorganization except a divisive D, an F, or a divisive G reorganization. § 382(g)(3). An equity shift results in an ownership change when after the reorganization, the percentage of stock held by one or more of the new loss corporation's 5-percent shareholders is more

---

[5] The label of the stock (common or preferred) is not determinative, and the Secretary has broad discretion in deciding which stock is counted.

than 50 percentage points higher than the percentage of the old loss corporation's stock held by them during the testing period.[6]

Suppose that X Corp., a loss corporation, merges into Y Corp. in a tax-free acquisition reorganization. Thus, under § 381, Y Corp. succeeds to X Corp.'s NOL carryovers. Assume that neither corporation has any individual 5-percent shareholders and in the merger, the former X shareholders receive 49 percent of the Y stock. An ownership change has occurred. The former X and Y shareholders constitute separate public groups of Y Corp., the new loss corporation, after the merger. An ownership change has occurred, because the Y shareholder's group increased its percentage interest by 51 percent: It has a 51-percent interest in Y Corp. after the merger but had a 0-percent interest in X Corp. before the merger.[7]

(b) Options.

Generally in determining whether an ownership change has occurred, a stock option is deemed exercised only if it was issued or transferred for an "abusive" principal purpose. See generally Regs. § 1.382-4(d)(1) and (2). An option may be deemed exercised if it has that abusive purpose and satisfies an ownership, control or income test. Regs. § 1.382-4(d)(2)(i). However, those tests generally do not apply to many commercially reasonable stock purchase agreements, security arrangements in typical lending transactions, typical compensatory stock options, and options exercisable only upon a shareholder's death, disability, or retirement. *Id.* at (d)(7)(i)-(v).

(c) Continuity of Business.

Following an ownership change, the section 382 limitation for a loss corporation is zero unless during the two-year period following the ownership change the new loss corporation either (1) continues the old loss corporation's historic business or (2) uses a significant portion of the old loss corporation's assets in a business. §382(c) (increasing the limitation, however, by recognized built-in gains). This continuity requirement is designed to distinguish acquisitions motivated principally by loss trafficking from those motivated by a desire to obtain assets or a business.[8]

---

[6] The old loss corporation is the one with NOLs before the reorganization; the new loss corporation is the one entitled to use the NOLs after the reorganization. § 382(k).

[7] If X Corp. shareholders received at least 50 percent of the Y Corp. stock, there would have been no ownership change triggered by the merger.

[8] See *Alprosa Watch Corp. v. Commissioner,* 11 T.C. 240 (1948) (shareholder purchased stock of loss corporation, sold assets to original shareholders, and infused corporation with new business).

(d) Corporate Value.

Recall that the § 382 limitation is computed by multiplying the value of the loss corporation's assets by the federal long-term tax-exempt rate. The value of the corporation generally is the value of its stock, including any § 1504(a)(4) stock, immediately before the ownership change. § 382(e)(1). This value may be reduced, however, if the loss corporation (i) has substantial non-business assets, (ii) redeems its stock in connection with the ownership change, or (iii) receives a capital contribution in contemplation of the ownership change.

Section 312(l)(1), an "anti-stuffing" rule, addresses the last point. The loss corporation's value is reduced by any capital contribution made "as part of a plan, a principal purpose of which is to avoid or increase" the § 382 limitation. § 382(l)(1)(A) Although a finding of principal purpose is based on the facts and circumstances, this anti-stuffing rule does not apply to contributions made (i) on formation of the corporation (if the incorporated assets did not have a net unrealized built-in loss), (ii) before its first loss year, or (iii) in exchange for stock issued for services.[9] Section § 312(l)(1) curbs the incentive that shareholders of the loss corporation otherwise may have to inflate the loss corporation's value by making capital contributions to the corporation in anticipation of its sale.

Congress was also concerned that the value of a loss corporation might be inflated because of investment assets held by the loss corporation, assets that could generate income to be offset by the corporation's business NOLs. Under § 382(l)(4), if at least one-third of a loss corporation's assets are "nonbusiness" assets (*i.e.*, assets held for investment), the value of the loss corporation is reduced by the net value of those assets. § 382(l)(4)(A)-(D). In applying this one-third test, if the loss corporation owns at least 50 percent of the vote and value of a subsidiary's stock, a "look-through" rule applies. § 382(l)(5)(E). Under the look-through rule, the loss corporation determines its "non-business" assets by taking into account a ratable share of the subsidiary's assets and disregarding the subsidiary stock and securities. *Id.*

The anti-stuffing and non-business asset rules both attack steps taken to inflate the value of a loss corporation *before* an ownership change. In contrast, the redemption rule considers *post-change* redemptions of a loss corporation's stock that diminish its

---

[9] See H.R. Rep. No. 841, at Sess. II-189; Notice 2008-78, 2008-2 C.B. 851 (also excluding many contributions made more than six months before the ownership change if those contributions were also made before there was an agreement, understanding, arrangement, or substantial negotiations regarding the transaction that resulted in the ownership change).

value. Under the redemption rule, the value of the loss corporation is reduced to account for any redemption or other corporate contraction that occurs "in connection with" an ownership change. § 382(e)(2).

(e) Special Rule for Bankrupt Corporations.

A bankrupt corporation may have a value of $0 immediately before its ownership change, and under § 382"s general rule, the corporation's § 382 limitation would be zero (so that it could use no pre-change losses) after the ownership change. Section 382(*l*)(5) provides a decidedly more favorable rule for corporations involved in bankruptcy or similar proceedings if at least 50 percent of the loss corporation's stock immediately after the ownership change is owned by former shareholders and certain long-term creditors. Under § 382(*l*)(5), the ownership change does not limit use of the bankrupt corporation's pre-change losses, subject to two caveats. First, § 382(*l*)(5) may require a significant reduction in the pre-change losses and excess credits that can be carried forward to post-change years.[10] In addition, if a second ownership change occurs within two years of the initial change, the § 382 limitation is reduced to zero.

Section 382(*l*)(6) applies to the ownership change of a bankrupt corporation if § 382(*l*)(5) does not apply (by election or otherwise). If § 382(*l*)(6) applies, the bankrupt corporation's pre-change loss is subject to a § 382 limitation, but in computing that limitation, the corporation's value is specially determined. That value equals the smaller of (i) the value of the corporation's stock immediately *after* the ownership change, or (ii) the gross value of its pre-change assets immediately *before* the ownership change. Regs. § 1.382-9(j).

In valuing the loss corporation's pre-change assets, the redemption rule does not apply but that value is reduced by the value of any capital contributions or non-business assets to which the anti-stuffing and non-business asset rules apply.[11] In valuing the stock, the redemption and non-business asset rules apply, but the anti-stuffing rule does not. Regs. § 1.382-9(k)(1)-(5). Because the anti-stuffing rule does not apply to determine the value of the loss corporation's stock, a new investor can purchase stock as part of the bankruptcy plan and increase the post-change value of the corporation's stock (and possibly its § 382 limitation).

---

[10] § 382(*l*)(5)(B) (requiring the carryfoward amounts to be reduced by certain interest accrued on debt converted to stock as part of the bankruptcy). Because of this interest "haircut," § 382(*l*)(5) may be disadvantageous, and § 382(*l*)(5)(G) allows a taxpayer to elect *not* to have the provision apply.

[11] § 1.382-9(l)(1) (adding that their value is determined without regard to liabilities); *id*. at (l)(2) and (4)-(5). Those anti-stuffing, redemption, and non-business asset rules are described in the preceding subsection.

(f) Built-in Gain and Built-in Losses.

The income that can be offset by NOLs includes expected future income from operations and gain inherent in the loss corporation's appreciated assets. Under § 382(h)(1)(A) a loss corporation with "unrealized net built-in gain" may increase its § 382 limitation by the "recognized built-in" gain for any taxable year within the recognition period, which is the five-year period beginning on the change date. § 382(h)(7)(A) (defining recognition period). A "net unrealized built-in gain" is the amount by which the value of the corporation's assets exceeds their aggregate basis immediately before an ownership change.[12] A "recognized built-in gain" is any gain recognized on disposition of an asset during the recognition period to the extent that the taxpayer establishes that the asset was held by the loss corporation before the change date and the gain accrued before the change date. § 382(h)(2)(A). Recognized built-in gain cannot exceed the net unrealized built-in gain reduced by the recognized built-in gains for prior years in the recognition period. § 382(h)(1)(A)(ii).

Section 382 limits the deductibility of pre-change loss, which includes (i) NOL carryforwards arising before the change year, (ii) the allocable portion of a corporation's NOLs for the year in which the change occurs, and (iii) certain built-in losses and deductions. §§ 382(d), (h)(1)(B). Just as a corporation with NOLs may be attractive, acquisition of a corporation with built-in losses may be equally desirable. Under § 382(h)(1)(B), if a loss corporation has net unrealized built-in loss, any recognized built-in loss during the five-year recognition period is deemed a pre-change loss, and is subject to the § 382 limitation.[13] Recognized built-in loss cannot exceed the net unrealized built-in loss reduced by the recognized built-in losses for prior years in the recognition period. § 382(h)(1)(A)(ii). Note that to the extent the § 382 limitation restricts the use of a recognized built-in loss in a recognition year, the loss is treated as a loss

---

[12] The net unrealized built-in gain is deemed to be zero if it is not greater than a threshold amount, which is the smaller of (i) 15 percent of the value of the corporation's assets immediately before the ownership change or (ii) $10 million. § 382(h)(3)(B)(i); *id.* at (h)(3)(B)(ii) (computing the threshold amount by disregarding cash, any cash item, and any marketable security that has an adjusted basis not substantially different from its value).

[13] A "net realized built-in loss" is the amount by which the aggregate basis of the corporation's assets exceed their value immediately before an ownership change, but that amount is deemed to be zero if it is not greater than the threshold amount (as defined in the preceding footnote). § 382(h)(3). A "recognized built-in loss" is any loss recognized on disposition of an asset during the recognition period, except to the extent that the taxpayer establishes that the asset was not held by the loss corporation before the ownership change or the loss exceeds the built-in loss in the asset on the change date. § 382(h)(2)(B).

carryforward to subsequent years, still subject to the § 382 limitation. § 382(h)(4).

11.04 Section 383

If an ownership change occurs, § 383 may limit the use of capital loss carryforwards under § 1212 to the portion of the loss corporation's taxable income not exceeding the § 382 limitation. Any capital loss carryforward used in a post-change year will reduce the § 382 limitation that is applied to pre-change losses. § 383(b); Regs. § 1.383-1(d)(2). Similar rules apply to excess credits (e.g., the alternative minimum tax credit under § 53 and the foreign tax credit under § 901) and passive activities losses.

11.05 Section 384

With only § 382 and § 383, a loss corporation might indirectly "traffic" in its losses as follows: It might acquire a corporation with built-in gain assets and use its losses to offset the built-in gain, sharing the tax benefit of that offset with the shareholders of the gain corporation. Suppose that L Corp., a loss corporation owned by B, acquires P Corp., a profitable corporation owned by C, for cash, and that L Corp. and P Corp. report tax liability on a consolidated return. The ability of L Corp. to use its pre-acquisition NOLs to offset P Corp.'s post-acquisition income is not inhibited by § 382 (or § 383). The same is true if P Corp. merged into L Corp., as long as no ownership change in L Corp. takes place.

But suppose C owns all stock of P Corp., and P Corp. is a "burnt-out" tax shelter—an entity that has produced depreciation deductions for its owners and which now has a large built-in gain because the bases of its assets have been adjusted downwards under § 1016 while the property's fair market value has not decreased correspondingly. For example, suppose that after generating depreciation deductions, P Corp. has depreciable assets with a $100,000 aggregate basis and $900,000 fair market value, subject to an $800,000 mortgage liability. Assume as well that if P Corp. sells the assets, the taxes on the $800,000 gain will far exceed the $100,000 of cash that P Corp. can expect to net on an arm's-length sale.

Suppose that the stock of P Corp. is acquired by L Corp. and they file a consolidated return or that P Corp. merges into L Corp. In the absence of a remedial provision, L Corp.'s pre-existing NOLs can be used to offset gain generated by the post-acquisition sale of the acquired assets. L Corp. may be happy to pay some amount of cash (but likely less than $100,000) to acquire the appreciated assets. C, the ultimate seller of the tax shelter, may be happy to receive that cash for her interest in the burnt-out shelter. But

Congress was unhappy with this technique of "laundering" the built-in gain from the sale of assets with pre-existing NOLs.

Section 384 applies if one corporation acquires control of another corporation and either corporation is a gain corporation (i.e., a corporation with net unrealized built-in gain at the time of acquisition). Control is defined as stock representing at least 80 percent of vote and value of the acquired corporation's stock. § 384(c)(5) (disregarding for this purpose § 1504(a)(4) stock). Section 384 also applies to an asset acquisition if the acquisition qualifies as an A, C or acquisitive D reorganization. If both the acquiring and the acquired corporations were part of the same control group under § 1563 (using a 50-percent ownership test) at all times during the previous 5–year period (or the term of a corporation's existence if shorter), § 384 will not apply. § 384(b).

If § 384 is applicable, the provision denies the use of any "pre-acquisition loss" of a loss corporation (but not the gain corporation) to offset any "recognized built-in gain" of the gain corporation during the 5–year recognition period. § 384(a). In the examples above, L Corp.'s NOLs cannot be used to offset gain recognized on the sale of P Corp.'s appreciated assets. The term "pre-acquisition loss" includes NOLs and net unrealized built-in losses that are recognized during a 5-year recognition period. § 384(c)(3)(A). The term "recognized built-in gain" refers to any gain on the disposition of an asset during a 5-year recognition period, except to the extent that it can be established that the asset was not held by the gain corporation on the acquisition date or the gain exceeds the built-in gain in the asset on the acquisition date. § 384(c)(1)(A).

There is overlap between §§ 382 and 384 in some cases, while in other cases one or neither of the provisions will apply. Suppose that B owns all of the stock of L Corp., a corporation with NOLs, and C owns all of the stock of P Corp., a corporation with built-in gains. If L Corp. purchases all of the P stock and they file a consolidated return, § 382 will not prevent the use of L Corp.'s losses against P Corp.'s future income because there is no ownership change for L Corp. However, § 384 will prevent the use of the NOLs to offset any built-in gains recognized by P Corp. during the 5–year recognition period.

If instead, L Corp. merges into P Corp. and C ends up with more than 50 percent of the P stock, § 382 will limit the use of L Corp.'s NOLs and § 384 will also apply to limit any NOLs allowable under § 382 which would otherwise be used to offset any of P Corp.'s recognized built-in gains. If P Corp. had no built-in gains prior to the merger, then only § 382 would apply to limit the use of the NOLs.

Suppose L Corp. and P Corp., which are unrelated, form a joint venture partnership, LP, which attempts to allocate income under the partnership agreement disproportionately to L Corp. As a technical matter, there has been no triggering event for purposes of § 382 or § 384. Nevertheless, Congress has given the Service authority to apply these loss limitation principles in abuse situations. § 382(m)(3); § 384(f)(1).

11.06 Section 269

Enacted in 1943, § 269 is one of the longest standing anti-abuse rules in the Code. It provides for the disallowance of tax benefits when the "evasion or avoidance of Federal income tax" is the principal purpose for—

(i) A person or persons acquiring control of a corporation; or

(ii) A corporation acquiring property of another corporation, not controlled by the acquiror or its shareholders, in a transferred-basis acquisition (*i.e.*, a tax-free asset acquisition).

For this purpose, a person or persons control a corporation if they own at least 50 percent of either the total combined voting power or total value of its shares.

The term "evasion or avoidance of tax," although not defined, is not restricted to behavior that would precipitate criminal or civil fraud penalties. Regs. § 1.269-1(b). Despite the potential breadth of § 269, its standard often seems a difficult one to meet. To become operative, it requires more than just "a" principal purpose of tax avoidance.[14] Instead, the tax avoidance purpose must be "the" principal purpose of the transaction (*i.e.*, the predominant purpose), an often demanding factual standard. Regs. § 1.269-3(b).

Note that § 382 is triggered by objective criteria, § 269 by a subjective tax avoidance purpose. Because of its scope, § 269 may

---

[14] See § 1.269-3(a) (stating that the tax avoidance purpose must exceed in importance any other purpose). See also U.S. Shelter Corp. v. United States, 13 Cl. Ct. 606 (1987) (allowing a corporation to combine non-tax motives, concluding that the combination exceeded any tax avoidance purpose in importance).

disallow an NOL carryover, even though its use is not limited under § 382.[15]

Today, § 269 may have its greatest impact when a corporation purchases the stock of another corporation and liquidates that corporation within two years of the purchase. Under § 381(a)(1), a parent also succeeds to the tax attributes of its liquidated subsidiary. Under § 269(b)(1) deductions and other tax attributes that would otherwise be acquired may be disallowed if: (1) there is a qualified stock purchase; (2) a § 338 election is not made; (3) the acquired corporation is liquidated pursuant to a plan adopted within two years of acquisition; and (4) the principal purpose of the liquidation is tax avoidance.

11.07 Consolidated Groups

In principle, every corporation reports its income and deductions separately from other corporations. But see §482 (authorizing the Service to allocate tax items among related taxpayers to prevent tax evasion or clearly reflect income). The consolidated return provisions offer an exception to this principle, allowing several corporations to combine their income and loss.

The use of multiple corporations might result from internal growth (*i.e.*, new corporations formed via § 351), purchase or reorganization (i.e., a subsidiary acquisition through a B reorganization). Why might individuals choose to operate a business or businesses through multiple corporations rather than through a single corporation? There may be a host of reasons—including both tax and non-tax reasons. Some of the non-tax reasons include: (1) minimizing potential tort liability; (2) avoiding regulatory restraints on combining businesses within a single corporation; (3) avoiding state law complications; (4) preserving favorable, nontransferable contractual arrangements; (5) alleviating labor problems; and (6) maintaining corporate goodwill.

Some of the tax advantages associated with multiple corporations include: (1) the availability of differing accounting methods, taxable years, and other elections; (2) reallocation of income to avoid progressive tax rates; (3) the availability of multiple tax benefits, such as the accumulated earnings tax credit; (4) more favorable disposition of unwanted assets (*e.g.*, through a tax-free spin-off); and

---

[15] Regs.§ 1.269-7. Indeed, if a taxpayer structures a transaction deliberately to avoid § 382(a), that planning may show that use of NOL carryovers was the principal purpose for the acquisition. Luke v. Commissioner, 351 F.2d 568 (7th Cir. 1965).

(5) greater flexibility with regard to earnings and profits and share-holder distributions.[16]

Despite these tax advantages, an affiliated group of corporations often elects to file a single return that combines the income, deductions, gain, and loss of its members. See §§ 1501–1504. A group that makes this election is called a "consolidated group." Note that only corporations controlled by a common parent corporation may make this election. Thus, if B, an individual, owns all stock of X Corp. and Y Corp., the two corporations may not file a consolidated return. If, though, B owns the stock of H Corp. which owns the stock of X Corp. and Y Corp. and the corporations are otherwise eligible to do so, they may file a consolidated return.

Once the election is made for a taxable year, the corporations must continue to file on a consolidated basis, unless the Commissioner consents to a discontinuance or the group terminates. Regs. § 1.1502-75(a)(2). Under a broad statutory grant (§ 1502), the Treasury has promulgated detailed regulations that describe how a consolidated group applies the Code. As the Code has become more complex, so have these consolidated return regulations. These regulations constitute the "law" of consolidated returns, and by electing to file consolidated returns, a group consents to the regulations. See §1501.

(a) Eligibility for Filing.

A consolidated return may be filed only by an "affiliated group" of corporations. Under § 1504, all members of an affiliated group must be "includible" corporations and those corporations must be linked through specified stock ownership requirements. If a consolidated return election is made by an affiliated group, all includible corporations in the group must join in filing the consolidated return.

Most corporations are "includible," corporations. There are exceptions for tax-exempt corporations, certain life insurance companies, foreign corporations, regulated investment companies, and S corporations. § 1504(b). But see § 1504(c) (for circumstances when life insurance companies may be includible corporations).

An affiliated group includes its common parent and subsidiaries, and a subsidiary is (a) any corporation in which the common parent owns an affiliated interest, and (b) any other corporation in which other members collectively own an affiliated interest.

---

[16] Note that the benefits listed in (3) and (4) may be substantially restricted under § 1561, which applies many corporate dollar limitations to members of a controlled group as a whole and requires a controlled group to share one set of graduated rates.

§1504(a)(1). For this purpose, an affiliated interest in a corporation is at least 80 percent of the total voting power of its stock plus at least 80 percent of the total value of its stock. §1504(a)(2). See Alumax, Inc. v. Commissioner, 109 T.C. 133 (1997) (interpreting the 80-percent voting control requirement of §1502(a)). Thus, a corporation owned by individuals cannot be the member of an affiliated group unless it is the common parent.

In measuring whether the group owns an affiliated interest in subsidiary stock, the subsidiary's "plain vanilla" preferred stock is disregarded. "Plain vanilla" preferred stock is nonvoting, nonconvertible stock that, is limited and preferred as to dividends, does not participate in corporate growth to any significant extent, and has redemption and liquidation rights not exceeding the issue price (except for a reasonable redemption or liquidation premium). § 1504(a)(4). Under § 1504(a)(5), options are generally ignored in determining eligibility unless not treating the option as exercised would result in substantial federal tax savings and it is reasonably certain that the option will be exercised. Regs. § 1.1504–4.

(b) Election to File a Consolidated Return and Other Accounting Considerations.

A consolidated return may be filed only if all affiliated corporations consent on the first consolidated return. Regs. § 1.1502–75(b). Once an election is made, the affiliated group must continue to file on a consolidated basis unless the Commissioner grants permission to discontinue for "good cause." Regs. § 1.1502–75(c)(1). The taxable year for a consolidated return is based on the common parent's annual accounting period. In general, the subsidiaries must adopt the parent's period. Regs. § 1.1502–76(a)(1) (with an exception for a subsidiary using the 52-53 week year). Subject to an anti-abuse rule, however, the subsidiaries are not required to adopt the accounting method (or methods) of the common parent. Instead, each member of the group employs the method that would be used if it were filing a separate return. Regs. § 1.1502–17(a). Finally, if a corporation is a member of a consolidated group for any part of a taxable year, it is severally liable any tax for that year computed in accordance with the consolidated return regulations. Regs. § 1.1502–6.

(c) Computing Consolidated Taxable Income: In General.

A consolidated group combines the tax items of its members in computing its overall federal income tax. Through this combination, one member's loss may offset another member's income, the main benefit of filing consolidated returns. In this significant way, the group is treated like a single entity for federal income tax purposes.

A consolidated group's tax liability is based on its consolidated taxable income ("CTI"). Using CTI, the group computes its gross consolidated tax liability in accordance with §§ 11, 541, 531, 1201, and so on. Finally, it subtracts any available consolidated credits, including the investment credit or foreign tax credit. Regs. § 1.1502-2.

A group's CTI for any taxable year includes the common parent's tax items for the whole year and each subsidiary's tax items for the portion of that year for which it was a member. Regs. § 1.1502-76(b). Thus, if a subsidiary leaves or enters a consolidated group during the group's year, the subsidiary's items must be allocated between its separate and consolidated periods. Id.

A group's CTI is the sum of each member's separate taxable income ("STI") plus a number of consolidated items. Regs. § 1.1502-11(a). Broadly speaking, a member's STI includes all of its tax items except for those computed on a consolidated basis. Regs. § 1.1502-12. Tax items computed on a consolidated basis include the group's net operating loss, capital gain and loss, § 1231 gain and loss, any charitable contribution deduction, and any dividends received deduction. Id.

A member computes its STI under the Code as a separate corporation but with several modifications. In addition to excluding any items computed on a consolidated basis, it takes into account other rules in the consolidated return regulations that affect income (and loss) computations. For example, STI is computing by considering rules relating to intercompany transactions, excess loss accounts, investment basis adjustments, earnings and profits, and various consolidated loss limitations. Id.

(d) Computing Consolidated Taxable Income: Intercompany Transactions.

A consolidated group accounts for intercompany transactions using two main rules, the "matching" and "acceleration" rules. See Regs. § 1.1502-13(c) and (d). Under the matching rule, the timing, holding period, and attributes of tax items related to an intercompany transaction are accounted for using a single-entity approach. However, the location and amount of those items are determined by treating the members as separate corporations. Regs. § 1.1502-13(a)(2). These rules often defer income, gain, or loss on an intercompany transaction.

An intercompany transaction is a transaction between corporations that are members immediately after the transaction. Id. at (b)(1)(i). Note that Regs. § 1.1502-13 refers to the member transferring property (*e.g.*, by sale, lease, or loan) or providing services in an intercompany transaction as "S" and the member receiving the property or services as "B." See Regs. § 1.1502-13(b)(1). For convenience, this description does as well.

Broadly stated, the matching rule is intended to assure that the overall income or loss of the group is unaffected by an intercompany transaction until S or B deals with an outsider. Under the matching rule, S takes its income, gain, or loss on the intercompany transaction into account as B takes its "corresponding" items into account under its separate accounting method. Regs. § 1.1502-13(c)(2)(i). See also id. at (b)(3) (defining B's corresponding items as its income, gain, deduction or loss from the intercompany transaction or from the property acquired in that transaction). The amount that S takes into account reflects the difference for the year between B's actual tax items and what whose items would have been if S and B had been divisions of a single corporation and the intercompany transaction had occurred between those divisions. See Regs. § 1.1502-13(b)(4).

For example, assume that S holds land with an $8,000 basis and $10,000 value and sells the land to B for $10,000. Under § 1001(c), S recognizes a $2,000 gain and under § 1012, B takes a $10,000 basis in that land. Under the matching rule, however, S's $2,000 gain is deferred (*i.e.*, not then reported on the group's consolidated return). If B sells the land to another member, S's gain continues to be deferred. Regs. § 1.1502-13(j)(4). Suppose, however, that B sells the land to an unrelated non-member, X, for $11,000. On the sale, B recognizes a $1,000 gain, S also takes its $2,000 gain into account, and both gains are reported on the group's return. S takes its $2,000 gain into account, because it fully reflects the difference between B's actual gain ($1,000), and what B's gain would have been if S and B had been divisions of a single corporation ($3,000). If they had been divisions, B would have acquired the land with an $8,000 basis[17] and therefore recognized a $3,000 gain on the sale.

Suppose that B had sold the land to X on the installment basis and could report its $1,000 gain using the installment method. See § 453. The matching principle also requires that S takes its gain into account on the installment method as B reports its gain on the installment sale. Regs. § 1502–13(c)(7)(ii) (example 5).[18]

---

[17] A corporation cannot take a cost basis of property (or recognize gain or loss) by transferring property from one division to another.

[18] Suppose that S is a dealer in real property and that if S and B were divisions of a single corporation, B's gain from the sale would be ordinary

Suppose that instead of S's selling land to B, S sold B a depreciable asset, still recognizing a $2,000 gain. Assume that for the first year after the sale, B actual depreciation deduction on the asset is $500, but if S and B had been divisions of a single corporation, its depreciation deduction would have been only $400. In that first year, S must take into account $100 of its $2,000 gain, reflecting the difference between B's actual depreciation deduction ($500) and what its deduction would have been if S and B had been divisions ($400). Regs. § 1.1502–13(c)(7)(ii) (example 4). Further, because B's depreciation deductions can offset ordinary income, the matching principle requires that S's income must also be ordinary. See Regs. § 1.1502–13(c)(4)(i).

Note that the matching rule does not always defer S's tax items. For example, assume that at the beginning of year 1, S loans B $100, with B obligated to pay S $5 interest at the end of each year for ten years, when the principal amount of the loan must be repaid. Assume that each year, B deducts the $5 interest payment. S also takes $5 of interest income into account each year, reflecting the $5 difference between B's actual interest deduction ($5) and what its deduction would have been if S and B had been divisions of a single corporation ($0) (because there can be no loan between divisions for tax purposes). Thus, in this example, S and B account for the items on the loan under Regs. § 1.1502-13 just as they would have if they were not members of the same consolidated group.

Consider again the example where S sells land with an $8,000 basis to B for $10,000, and S defers its $2,000 gain under the matching rule. Would S be able to continue deferring its gain if either S or B left the consolidated group but B retained the land? The answer is no, because of the acceleration rule, a kind of "last clear chance" rule. Under that rule, S must take its intercompany items into account immediately before it first becomes impossible to treat S and B as divisions of a single corporation. Regs. § 1.1502-13(d)(1)(i)(A). Stated differently, S must take its intercompany items into account once the matching rule can no longer apply. Thus, if either S or B left the group, it would no longer be possible to treat S and B as divisions of a single corporation, and S's $2,000 deferred gain would be "triggered."

Because the consolidated return regulations provide their own timing rules for intercompany transactions, they also provide that many of the Code's more general provisions do not apply in the consolidated context. Thus, there are no § 1031 exchanges between

income because of S's activities. Then, installment reporting would not be available for either S or B. See Regs. § 1.1502-13(c)(7)(ii) (examples 3).

members of a consolidated group, Regs. § 1.1502-80(f), and section 304 does not apply to sales between consolidated corporations, § 1.1502-80(b). On the other hand, many anti-abuse provisions continue to apply to intercompany transactions including §§ 269. 482, and 1091. Regs. § 1.1502-13(a)(4).

(e) Computing Consolidated Taxable Income: Intercompany Distributions.

An intercompany distribution is an intercompany transaction to which § 301 applies. Regs. § 1.1502-13(f)(2)(i). Typically, the shareholder member excludes the entire intercompany distribution from gross income, no matter how the distribution is treated under § 301(c). Id. at (f)(2)(ii) (excluding the distribution to the extent it results in a negative adjustment under the investment adjustment rules, described below). The shareholder member also takes a basis in any distributed property equal to its fair market value. § 301(d).

The distributing member recognizes any gain or loss on an intercompany distribution, since the regulations provide that the principles of § 311(b) apply to loss as well as gain. Regs. § 1.1502-13(f)(2)(iii). The member accounts for that recognized gain or loss under the matching and acceleration rules described in the preceding section. Note that § 311(a) continues to apply to a member's § 301 distribution to a non-member, so that a distributing member does not recognize loss on that distribution.

Most intercompany liquidations of solvent subsidiaries are described in § 332.[19] Under that section, a shareholder member recognizes no gain or loss on its receipt of a liquidating distribution. Note that for § 332 to apply to a shareholder, the shareholder must own an affiliated interest in the liquidating corporation, and for this purpose, a consolidated group member is deemed to own all stock owned by the group. Regs. § 1.1502-34. For example, if two members each own half of the stock in a third member, which liquidates, § 332 can apply to each distributee member, because under Regs. § 1.1502-34, each member is treated as owning all stock of the liquidating corporation.

In a § 332 intercompany liquidation, the liquidating corporation recognizes no gain or loss on any liquidating distributions to which § 337 applies and recognizes gain and may recognize loss on its other liquidating distributions. § 337(a); § 336(a). But see § 336(d)(3); § 336(d)(1). For § 337 to apply to an intercompany liquidating distribution, the shareholder member must *actually* own an affiliated interest in the liquidating subsidiary, since the special

---

[19] See Chapter 8 *supra*.

consolidated ownership rule in Regs. § 1.1502-34 does not apply. See § 337(c) (second sentence). Thus, the liquidating subsidiary recognizes gain and perhaps loss on an intercompany distribution *other than* to an actual "80-percent" shareholder. That recognized amount will be deferred and taken into account by the shareholder members under the matching rule. See Regs. § 1.1502-13(j)(2) (describing successors). To the extent that the liquidating corporation does not recognize gain or loss on a § 332 intercompany liquidating distribution of property, the distributee member takes a transferred basis in the property, preserving that gain or loss. § 334(b)(1).

Note that if one member has sold subsidiary stock to another member at a gain, that gain is deferred under the matching rule. Regs. § 1.1502-13(c). If the subsidiary then liquidates under § 332, the selling member must take the deferred gain into account, even though the stock never left the group. Regs. § 1.1502-13(f)(4). However, this harsh result may be mitigated under several regulatory provisions. *Id*. at (f)(5); *id*. at (c)(6)(ii).

(f) Investment Basis Adjustments and Excess Loss Accounts.

A consolidated group adjusts its basis in subsidiary stock to reflect the subsidiary's tax items. Cf. § 705(a) (for similar adjustments to a partner's basis in a partnership interest); § 1366(a) (for similar adjustments to the basis of S corporation stock). These basis or "investment" adjustments are intended to prevent the subsidiary's tax items from being taken into account a second time when the group sells its subsidiary stock. See Regs. § 1.1502-32(a)(1).

Under the investment adjustment system, a shareholder member increases its basis in subsidiary stock for positive adjustments and decreases that basis for negative adjustments. *Id*. at (b)(2). The subsidiary's taxable income and tax-exempt income result in positive adjustments and its absorbed losses, noncapital, nondeductible expenses (including for expiring NOL carryovers), and distributions (measured by the value of the distributed property) result in negative adjustments. See *id*. at (b)(3).

Each year, those adjustments are allocated among the subsidiary's shares, including shares owned by non-members. *Id*. at (c)(1). (An amount allocated to a share owned by a non-member has no effect on that share's basis, however. *Id*.) Broadly speaking, the allocations are made among subsidiary shares in a manner intended to reflect changes in value of the shares. See generally *id*. at (c)(2) and (3).

To treat a consolidated group more like a single entity, the consolidated return regulations allow a member to have a *negative basis* in subsidiary stock, called an excess loss account or ELA.[20] Because of this ELA device, a group can take into account all of a subsidiary's losses in, and exclude all subsidiary distributions from, CTI, even if the losses and distributions exceed the group's positive basis in subsidiary stock. However, the group must include the ELA in income if, for example, it sells the subsidiary stock to a nonmember. § 1.1502-19(b)(1)(i) and (c)(1).

For instance, assume that P buys all S stock for $30, taking a $30 cost basis in that stock, and that P and S join in filing a consolidated return. If S suffers a $50 loss that the P group absorbs, P's S stock will have a $20 ELA ($30 starting basis minus $50 absorbed loss). If P later sells the S stock for $25, it must recognize a $45 gain—the $25 sales proceeds plus the $20 ELA. The group's overall $5 tax loss related to S ($50 of losses less $45 stock gain) matches P's $5 economic loss on its S stock investment—$30 paid for the stock less $25 received on the sale.

(g) Subsidiary Stock Loss.

After the *General Utilities* doctrine was repealed, some consolidated groups used the investment adjustment rules to create non-economic loss in subsidiary stock. They also structured transactions to enjoy both a subsidiary stock loss and a duplicate subsidiary asset loss. Concerned with both non-economic and duplicated losses, Treasury responded with the subsidiary loss disallowance rules.

Under Regs. § 1.1502-20, first issued in 1990, a group's loss on subsidiary stock was generally disallowed to the extent it exceeded the sum of three factors. Regs. § 1.1502-20(c) (2001) (laying out those factors). Although the three factors were intended to allow the group to recognize its economic loss when it sold the subsidiary stock, in practice, they proved less than perfect.

Regs. § 1.1502-20 was invalidated, at least in part, by *Rite Aid Corp. v. United States*, 255 F.3d 1359 (Fed. Cir. 2001), *rev'g* 46 Fed. Cl. 500 (Ct. Cl. 2000), *reh'g denied*. Treasury quickly withdrew the regulation and after several intervening steps and a lot of spilled ink, it has replaced the invalidated regulation with Regs. § 1.1502-36.

Regs. § 1.1502-36 addresses both non-economic loss and loss duplication with three main rules that may apply on the group's

---

[20] See generally Regs. § 1.1502-19. In other contexts, we have encountered basis adjustments, see, e.g., § 301(c)(2) and § 1367, but in these contexts basis cannot be reduced below zero.

transfer of subsidiary stock at a loss, rules that are technically masterful but extraordinarily complex. First, under Regs. § 1.1502-36(b), the group may redetermine its basis in transferred and nontransferred subsidiary stock, a rule that complements the investment adjustment rules of Regs. § 1.1502-32 and is an analog to § 704(c).[21] Second, the group's loss on subsidiary stock may be disallowed, in whole or in part, under a basis-reduction rule found in Regs. § 1.1502-36(c). Technically under that rule, the group reduces its basis of subsidiary stock, with the reduction intended to avoid non-economic loss.[22] Even with the basis-redetermination and basis-reduction rules, a group could dispose of subsidiary stock at a loss but the loss could be duplicated in subsidiary tax attributes (like basis). To the extent of that duplication, the attribute-reduction rule, found in Regs. § 1.1502-36, requires the subsidiary (and perhaps lower-tier corporations) to reduce tax attributes, including NOL carryovers and basis.

(h) Limitations on Consolidated Reporting.

Congress and the Treasury have perceived a danger of consolidated reporting when a loss corporation is acquired in order to apply its net operating loss deductions (or other favorable tax attributes) against income of profitable affiliated group members. The problem here is the same as that raised in a reorganization or purchase context under §§ 381 and 382. Indeed, where applicable, those provisions govern the treatment of consolidated group members.

If a loss consolidated group has an ownership change, it generally applies § 382 like a single corporation. See Regs. § 1.1502-91(a)(1); see generally Regs. § 1.1502–91 to Regs. § 1.1502–99. To compute its consolidated § 382 limitation, the group determines its value as the aggregate value of each member's stock, other than

---

[21] Under § 704(c), if a partner contributes built-in gain or loss property to a partnership, the built-in gain or loss may be specially allocated back to the contributing partner, an allocation taken into account in determining the partners' bases in their partnership interests. See § 705(a). Regs. § 1.1502-32 does not have a corresponding rule for built-in gain or loss property contributed by a member to a subsidiary in a § 351 exchange. In a sense, the basis-redetermination rule of Regs. § 1.1502-36(b) acts as the corresponding rule.

[22] That rule targets non-economic stock loss that may arise, for example, in a "son-of-mirrors" transaction. As one variation of that transaction, a consolidated group purchases the stock of a target corporation, and when purchased, the target holds some assets with built-in gain. The target sells those assets at a gain, the group increases its target stock basis to reflect the gain (see Regs. § 1.1502-32), and the group then sells the target stock at a loss. Because the stock loss corresponds to the recognized built-in asset gain, if the loss were allowed, the group could eliminate (or at least substantially reduce) the effective tax on the gain, inconsistent with the repeal of the *General Utilities* doctrine. The basis-reduction rule generally disallows that stock loss.

stock owned directly or indirectly by any member.[23] The group's consolidated § 382 limitation equals the group's value multiplied by the applicable long-term tax exempt rate. Regs. § 1.1502-93(a)(1).

A loss group has an ownership change if its common parent has an ownership change, and as a general rule, this determination is made by considering only changes in the ownership of common parent stock. Regs. § 1.1502-92(b)(1)(i). (This general rule is referred to as the "parent change" method.) In determining whether the common parent has an ownership change, the group's loss attributes are treated as NOLs (or built-in losses) of the common parent, and the common parent determines the testing period by reference to those attributes.[24]

For example, suppose that B owns all of the stock of P. which files a consolidated return with its 80-percent owned subsidiary, S. Individual C owns the other 20 percent of the S stock. During year 1, the P group incurs a $200 consolidated NOL, attributable entirely to S. In year 2, B sells 60 percent of the P stock to D, an unrelated individual. C retains her 20-percent minority interest in S. Because the consolidated group is treated as a single entity for purposes of § 382, the sale of stock from B to D triggers § 382 (*i.e.*, D's ownership in the P group has gone from 0 percent to 60 percent) even though D's constructive ownership of S would not trigger § 382 (*i.e.*, after the purchase D constructively owns only 48 percent of the S stock (60 percent of 80 percent)). Under § 382, the P group's use of S's NOL will be limited.

The P group's consolidated § 382 limitation equals (i) the value of the stock of each member of the group (other than stock owned directly or indirectly by another member) multiplied by (ii) the federal long-term tax-exempt rate. Suppose that when B sold the 60-percent interest in P to D, the P stock was worth $1,000, the S stock was worth $500, and C's S stock was therefore worth $100 (*i.e.*, one-fifth of $500). Thus, the P group's value equaled $1,100, $1,000 (the P stock value) plus $100 (the value of C's S stock) If the federal long-term tax exempt rate was then 10 percent, the P group's consolidated § 382 limitation was $110, equal to $1,100 (its value) multiplied by 10 percent (the applicable rate). Accordingly, the P group

---

[23] Regs. § 1.1502-93(b). The group's value includes the value of the stock held by non-members, presumably because the group includes all subsidiary tax items in consolidated taxable income even for subsidiaries with non-member shareholders.

[24] *Id.* If a consolidated group sells a subgroup that joins another consolidated group, similar rules apply to account for the subgroup's loss. See *id.* at (b)(1)(ii). The regulations also provide special rules applicable to new members entering a loss group and leaving the loss group. Regs. § 1.1502–94 (entering members); Regs. § 1.1502–95 (departing members).

could offset up to $110 of consolidated taxable income each year with S's NOL.

The other rules that apply under § 382 generally apply in the consolidated group context to the entire group. For example, the ability to use an NOL is increased if a loss group has a net unrealized built-in gain that is recognized during the five-year recognition period. Regs. § 1.1502–93(c). Also, the business continuity requirement of § 382 is applied to the group as a whole. Regs. § 1.1502–93(d).

While § 382 applies to consolidated groups, the regulations also impose an additional limitation on the ability of the a group to use pre-acquisition NOLs of an acquired member. This limitation is known as the "separate return limitation year" or "SRLY" limitation. Regs. § 1.1502–1(f). Generally, pre-affiliation losses of a new member cannot be utilized to offset post-affiliation CTI, except to the extent that the new member of the group contributes to the consolidated taxable income. Regs. § 1.1502–21(c). The new member's contribution is determined on a cumulative basis over the period during which it is a member of the consolidated group. Also, with some twists and turns, the SRLY limitation can be applied on a subgroup basis to members who were previously affiliated in another group and who continue to be affiliated in the new group. Similar rules exist for other tax attributes. See Regs. § 1.1502–4(f) (foreign tax credit carryovers); Regs. § 1.1502–22(c) (capital loss carryovers).

The SRLY rule in some ways may appear to duplicate the § 382 limitation, but there are situations where § 382 does not apply but the SRLY rule does. In addition, the reach of the SRLY rule is substantially limited by the overlap rule. See Regs. § 1.1502–15(g); Regs. § 1.1502–21(g). Under the overlap rule, the SRLY limitations generally do not apply if a member joins the group in a transaction that causes § 382 to apply or within six months of such a transaction.

For example, suppose that B, an individual, and P, a corporation that is the common parent of a consolidated group, each owns 50 percent of L stock and L has NOLs. If P purchases an additional 30 percent of the L stock from B, no ownership change has occurred under § 382 because L shareholders have not increased their ownership in L by more than 50 percentage points.[25] Although § 382 does not apply, the SRLY rule limits the use of L's pre-affiliation NOL by the P group. Under Regs. § 1.1502–21(c), the deduction of that NOL (a SRLY loss) by the P group is limited to the

---

[25] P has increased its stock ownership in L by only 30 percentage points.

cumulative contribution by L to the group's CTI. In some cases where the acquired corporation with a SRLY loss is part of an acquired subgroup of corporations, the cumulative contribution is determined on a subgroup basis. Regs. § 1.1502–21(c)(2).

Suppose finally that a profitable corporation acquires another corporation, not because it has any net operating losses, but rather because it has a large debt that is about to become worthless. Or perhaps the corporation to be acquired has assets that it is about to sell at a loss. Section 382 discourages the acquisition of a corporation with such "built-in" losses. While the SRLY rules can apply to the acquisition of a corporation having such built-in losses, see Regs. § 1.1502–15, those rules generally will not be triggered if those built-in losses are limited under § 382. See § 382(h); Treas. Reg. § 1.1502-15(g) (for the overlap rule for built-in losses).

Chapter 12

PENALTY PROVISIONS

12.01 Introduction

The organizing feature of Subchapter C is that corporate earnings from operations be taxed twice—once when the corporation earns them and once again when they are distributed. Historically, it has been Congress's intention that both taxes should be at ordinary income rates. Whether these guiding principles are sound is explored in Chapter 1. In this Chapter, the focus is on two sets of Code provisions enacted to safeguard this double-tax regime.

It is not true that Congress intended that all corporate earnings be taxed twice at ordinary income rates. For example, a corporation might earn income that is taxed at ordinary income rates, but rather than distributing those earnings as a dividend to its shareholders, the corporation might accumulate the income, thereby increasing the fair market value of its stock. The shareholders could then turn that appreciation into cash by selling this stock, having the corporation redeem the stock, or liquidating the corporation. All three of these possibilities might allow the shareholders effectively to receive the corporate earnings at capital gains rate. Avoiding or deferring the shareholder-level tax or turning ordinary income into capital gain is a strategy taxpayers have historically pursued.

Suppose instead that the corporation has not yet recognized a gain because it has not yet sold its appreciated inventory. If it sells the inventory and distributes the proceeds, the corporation will be taxed at ordinary income rates on the sale, and the shareholders will have ordinary income on the distribution (perhaps taxed at preferential rates). If instead a shareholder sells the stock of the corporation which has appreciated in value to reflect the corporation's appreciated inventory, the shareholder would normally recognize a capital gain in the absence of any remedial provisions.

Having envisioned that Subchapter C permits circumvention of the double-tax system, Congress has enacted two sets of penalty provisions intended to prod corporations into making taxable dividend distributions. These provisions are the accumulated earnings tax and personal holding company tax, taxes that may be levied on the corporation in addition to normal corporate taxes (e.g., under §§ 11 and 55).

371

12.02 Accumulated Earnings Tax: Overview

Historically, corporate tax rates have been lower than individual rates. This differential led some high-bracket individuals to incorporate their businesses and accumulate earnings at the corporate-level until such time as the individual was in a lower tax bracket. Even when the top individual rates are lower than the top corporate rates, accumulation remains a useful strategy. Once a corporation has earned income and paid the appropriate taxes, the decision whether to distribute or accumulate is not based solely on any differential between the corporate and individual rates. Instead, the decision is based partly on the differential between the tax rate on ordinary income and the rate on capital gains and partly on the advantages gained from deferral.

If a corporation earns $100 after its taxes, the decision whether to distribute is influenced in part by the potential for deferral. By not distributing, the corporation can invest the $100 earning a return that will be taxed once at the corporate level. While it is true that there may be a shareholder-level tax on the eventual distribution, meanwhile the corporation is earning income on dollars that would otherwise have been paid in taxes. If instead the corporation distributes the $100, the shareholders will have $100 minus the shareholder-level tax to invest.

Historically what has made this deferral troublesome is the ability of shareholders to defer distributions until the shareholders are in lower tax brackets. Or shareholders might be able to convert ordinary income into capital gain. Moreover, as long as our tax system allows a step-up in basis of assets at death under § 1014, taxpayers will have an incentive to defer taxes with a consequent loss to the Treasury. Suppose a taxpayer holds stock with a $30 basis and $100 fair market value due to $70 of corporate earnings. Upon death, the taxpayer's estate or beneficiary can either sell the stock or have the corporation redeem the stock without recognizing gain since both the basis and fair market value of the stock will be $100.

The accumulated earnings tax is a penalty intended to encourage distributions to shareholders. The tax is triggered by an accumulation of earnings beyond the reasonable needs of the business. If there are excess earnings, the base of the accumulated earnings tax is the corporation's "accumulated taxable income" for the year. Notice that *accumulated* earnings provide an evidentiary foundation for imposition of the tax. But once it is determined that the tax applies, the tax base is *current* earnings available for distribution—accumulated taxable income.

Section 535 defines "accumulated taxable income" as taxable income minus a dividends-paid deduction and a specified accumulated earnings credit. Taxable income is modified to reflect more accurately dividend-paying capacity. Once the tax base is determined, § 531 imposes a tax at 20 percent (*i.e.,* the highest rate for qualified dividend income).

Historically, many tax observers (but not the Service) believed that the accumulated earnings tax could not apply to publicly held corporations since there would be difficulty in ascertaining the tax-avoidance motive where no individual or group had effective control. However, Congress sided with the Service by enacting § 532(c) which provides for application of the accumulated earnings tax regardless of the number of shareholders.[1]

12.03 Accumulated Earnings Tax: Unreasonable Accumulations

Section 532(a) imposes the accumulated earnings tax on corporations that accumulate income with a subjective tax-avoidance motive. Section 533 presumes the improper motive if there is an accumulation "beyond the reasonable needs of the business"—a more objective standard. Theoretically, it would be possible for a corporation with an improper motive to be subject to the accumulated earnings tax even though in fact the corporation did not accumulate earnings in excess of the reasonable needs of the business. Conversely, a corporation that accumulates beyond the reasonable needs of the business should not be subject to the tax if there is no improper motive for the accumulation.

The regulations contain a list of factors to be considered in determining whether the tax-avoidance motive is present, including: (a) dealings between the corporation and its shareholders, including loans or expenditures for the shareholders' personal benefit; (b) investments in assets not connected to the corporation's business; and (c) the corporation's dividend history. Regs. § 1.532-1(b). Because proof of a tax-avoidance motive requires weighing all relevant facts and circumstance, a corporation might not be subject to § 531 even though it has a poor dividend record.

If a tax-avoidance motive is present, how strong must it be to activate the accumulated earnings tax provisions? In *United States v. Donruss Co.*,[2] the government argued that the taxpayer must es-

---

[1] See *Technalysis Corp. v. Commissioner*, 101 T.C. 397 (1993) (court noted that widely held corporations can be subject to accumulated earnings tax if tax-avoidance purpose exists; Technalysis had 1,500 shareholders but 30 percent of its stock was held by five members of the board of directors).

[2] 393 U.S. 297 (1969).

tablish that tax avoidance was not "one of the purposes" for accumulating earnings. The taxpayer argued that it must prevail if tax avoidance was not the "dominant, controlling, or impelling" reason for the accumulation. The Court resolved the case in favor of the government. *Donruss* does not address how much of a prohibited purpose is enough, though. Do the accumulated earnings tax provisions apply if the taxpayer has a 1 percent tax-avoidance motive and a 99 percent business motive?

Notwithstanding the subjective standard contained in § 532, it is the more objective "reasonable needs of the business" test in § 533 that is generally dispositive. While no statutory definition exists, § 537(a)(1) provides that reasonable needs includes the "reasonably anticipated needs of the business." The regulations identify five nonexclusive grounds that may justify an accumulation.[3]

The first two grounds embrace a bona fide expansion of the business or the acquisition of a new business. Either of these reasons is a common justification for accumulation. The two major concerns pertaining to this justification are the relationship between the accumulation and the expansion, and the definition of what constitutes "the business." The more attenuated the relationship between the accumulation and the expansion, the more likely it is that the Service will charge an unreasonable accumulation. Concrete plans for expansion are helpful but not controlling. If the accumulations were reasonable when made, a subsequent abandonment of plans will not result in liability.

Determining what is the business of the corporation is no easy matter. The regulations provide that the business includes "any line of business which [the corporation] may undertake."[4] The "any line of business" language appears to support even a radical change in the nature of a corporation's business. Suppose a corporation engaged in manufacturing designer clothes in Beverly Hills accumulates earnings to acquire a meatpacking plant in Chicago? So long as the corporation is accumulating earnings to expand "the business" rather than to make "an investment," the regulation should protect the taxpayer.

A third ground justifying accumulation is the retirement of bona fide business indebtedness. The tension here is between debt held by non-shareholders and debt held by shareholders. Accumulating earnings to retire the former is a reasonable business need. Debt held by shareholders—particularly if held pro rata—is more suspect. Generally, accumulation of earnings for the purpose of lat-

[3] Regs. § 1.537–2(b).
[4] Regs. § 1.537–3(a).

er redeeming shareholders' stock is not permitted.[5] To allow accumulation for debt retirement but not for stock redemption is a factor favoring capitalization with debt rather than equity.

The fourth ground listed in the regulations is assuring a fund of liquid assets to finance operations of a business during its typical operating cycle. In *Bardahl Manufacturing Corp. v. Commissioner,*[6] the court created a statistical formula for determining the anticipated working capital needs of a business during an operating cycle. The formula serves as a guideline only. The operating cycle is the period of time required to convert cash into inventory, inventory into accounts receivable, and accounts receivable into cash. For example, if the period from purchase of inventory to receipt of cash for the goods sold is three months, the working capital needs are 25 percent of total annual operating costs and costs of goods sold.

The fifth ground is accumulation for investments or loans to suppliers or customers to maintain the business of the corporation. These types of investments are considered by the regulations to be integral to the taxpayer's trade or business.[7]

In addition to the listed reasons for accumulations, accumulations can be justified for a host of other business reasons, including the need to fund a pension plan, reasonable self-insurance against casualties or litigation liability and reserves to meet a threatened strike.

Even if a taxpayer can establish reasonable needs of the business, one might argue that accumulated earnings could be distributed to shareholders and then reinvested in the corporation. The Supreme Court in *Helvering v. Chicago Stock Yards Co.,*[8] considered a corporation, owned by a single shareholder, that accumulated earnings to pay off certain obligations of its subsidiaries. The Court suggested that the taxpayer could distribute the earnings to the shareholder who would either reinvest the earnings or discharge the liabilities directly. Applied rigorously, this reasoning would make virtually all accumulations unreasonable if the shareholders' after-tax proceeds would be sufficient to meet corporate needs.

---

[5] If a corporation can show that the redemption will further the corporation's business, the accumulation may be justifiable. Thus, accumulation to redeem the stock of a dissenting minority shareholder may be reasonable. See also *Hughes, Inc. v. Commissioner,* 90 T.C. 1 (1988) (accumulation to redeem stock to prevent a takeover was reasonable).

[6] 24 T.C.M. 1030 (1965) and 25 T.C.M. 935 (1966).

[7] See *Corn Products Refining Co. v. Commissioner*, 350 U.S. 46 (1955). But see *Arkansas Best Corp. v. Commissioner*, 485 U.S. 212 (1988).

[8] 318 U.S. 693 (1943).

12.04 Accumulated Earnings Tax: Matching Earnings and Reasonable Needs

Even if the reasonable needs of a business can be accurately quantified, determining what corporate assets are available to meet those needs is not always clear. That determination must be made to determine if for the year or years in question the taxpayer is unreasonably accumulating earnings. Suppose X Corp. has accumulated earnings and profits of $1 million, its reasonable needs for the year in question require $600,000, and its current earnings and profits, which are not distributed, are $500,000. Just because the accumulated earnings exceed the needs of the business does not mean that the current earnings are being unreasonably accumulated. For example, if the accumulated earnings have all been reinvested in productive corporate assets, there may be no earnings available other than the current earnings to meet the reasonable needs of the business.[9]

On the other hand, if the accumulated earnings have been retained or reinvested in assets unrelated to the corporation's business, then the current accumulation might be unreasonable. Thus, if X Corp. invested the $1 million of accumulated earnings and profits in marketable securities, those securities would serve as evidence that current accumulations were unnecessary. Suppose instead that X Corp. invested $900,000 of its accumulated earnings in needed machinery and equipment and $100,000 in marketable securities which have appreciated in value to $600,000. In evaluating whether the current $500,000 accumulation is reasonable, should the securities be valued at cost or fair market value? If the former, then the current accumulation would be reasonable to meet the corporation's $600,000 needs. If the latter, then the current accumulation would be unreasonable since the securities could be sold to meet the corporation's needs. In *Ivan Allen Co. v. United States*,[10] the Supreme Court held that the fair market value was the appropriate measure despite the taxpayer's argument that the realization doctrine mandated valuation of the securities at cost.[11]

12.05 Accumulated Earnings Tax: Burden of Proof

Initially the burden of proof is on the taxpayer to prove that earnings have not been accumulated with a tax-avoidance motive.

---

[9] It is important to keep in mind that the earnings and profits account is not the equivalent of cash-on-hand.

[10] 422 U.S. 617 (1975).

[11] The Court did not force the taxpayer to be taxed on unrealized gain, but instead used the unrealized gain as evidence of an unreasonable accumulation.

See generally § 533; § 534. Section 534 allows the taxpayer to shift the burden of proof to the government in proceedings before the Tax Court.[12] Summarily stated, the provision places the burden of proof on the government, unless it notifies the corporation about the proposed imposition of an accumulated earnings tax before the notice of deficiency is sent. Even then, the burden shifts back to the government if the taxpayer submits a statement setting forth with specificity the grounds on which it will rely.[13]

12.06 Accumulated Earnings Tax: Computation of the Accumulated Earnings Tax

The accumulated earnings tax is imposed on accumulated taxable income which is defined in § 535 to be taxable income with specified adjustments minus a dividends-paid deduction and an accumulated earnings credit. The adjustments to taxable income are intended to measure more accurately dividend-paying capacity. Many of the adjustments are similar to or the same as those made in computing earnings and profits. Thus, taxable income is reduced by nondeductible expenses that nevertheless diminish dividend paying capacity such as accrued corporate income taxes, disallowed charitable deductions, and disallowed capital losses under § 1211. Conversely, some items that are deductible in computing taxable income are added back in determining accumulated taxable income, since the items do not diminish the ability to pay dividends. These items include the net operating loss deduction, capital loss carryovers and the dividends-received deduction.

Once the adjustments have been made, § 535 allows the taxpayer to take a dividends-paid deduction since the tax base is aimed at *undistributed* corporate earnings. The dividends-paid deduction is permitted for dividends actually paid during the taxable year and for consent dividends. §§ 561–565. A consent dividend is a dividend that is not actually distributed. Instead the shareholders agree to treat a portion of the corporation's earnings as if they were distributed and then contributed by the shareholders back to the corporation. The consent dividend procedure allows a corporation to avoid the accumulated earnings tax without actually making a distribution (as long as the shareholders report dividend income). § 565.

The final step in computing accumulated taxable income is the determination of the accumulated earnings credit. Congress created the credit to permit a small corporation to accumulate some earn-

---

[12] Why should the shift in burden only apply in Tax Court proceedings?

[13] The Tax Court will rule in advance on the sufficiency of the taxpayer's response.

ings and profits without subjecting itself to accumulated earnings tax liability. Under § 535(c)(2) a corporation may accumulate up to $250,000 of earnings and profits without risk of the accumulated earnings tax.[14] The $250,000 amount is a cumulative and not a yearly amount. Amounts accumulated in excess of $250,000 are still permitted if the corporation can show that the accumulation is necessary to meet the reasonable needs of the business.

Once the accumulated taxable income is determined § 531 applies a tax on that income at a 20-percent rate. § 531. The accumulated earnings tax is not a self-assessing tax. A taxpayer becomes liable for the tax only after notification by the Service rather than when the taxpayer's return is filed. In light of this fact, interest has historically been charged only from the date the Service demands payment rather than the date the return was originally due to be filed. Since 1986, interest accrues from the date the return was originally due to be filed. § 6601. It seems odd, somehow, that interest can accrue before a liability arises.

12.07 Personal Holding Company Tax: Overview

Enacted in 1934, the personal holding company provisions were aimed at corporations controlled by a limited number of shareholders who use the corporate form to avoid higher individual tax rates. Congress felt that the accumulated earnings tax provisions were inadequate to address the problem, in part because it is often difficult to show the subjective forbidden purpose. The personal holding company provisions apply more objectively.

For example, the perceived misuse of the corporate form may arise with incorporated portfolios, personal service corporations and incorporated personal assets. If corporate rates are lower than individual rates, there is an incentive for an individual to organize a corporation to hold investment assets so that the interest, dividends and other portfolio income would be taxed at the lower rates.[15] The same shifting of income can apply to personal services. An actor, athlete or any other worker might organize a corporation and agree to work for it at a modest salary. The corporation would then hire itself out to those desiring the service, charging a fair market value rate for the services. The difference between the fair market value

---

[14] For corporations whose "principal function . . . is the performance of services in the field of health, law, engineering, architecture, accounting, actuarial science, performing arts, or consulting" the credit is restricted to $150,000. § 532(c)(2)(B). It is not clear why these service corporations should receive a smaller credit than a corporation with investment income that has virtually no business activities.

[15] The individual could cause the corporation to distribute the income at a time when the individual is in a lower bracket.

amount received and salary paid would be taxed at the lower corporate rates. The third device involved the transfer of a personal asset such as a yacht or country estate to a corporation, which would then rent the asset back to the shareholder. The intention here is that the corporation could use the depreciation and other related deductions to offset not only the rental income but other corporate income.

To be a personal holding company income, a corporation must meet a stock ownership test and an income test. Under the stock ownership test, the tax applies to closely held corporations if more than 50 percent in value of the stock is owned directly or indirectly through attribution by five or fewer individuals. The income test is satisfied if at least 60 percent of "adjusted ordinary gross income" is "personal holding company income." § 542.

If the personal holding company provisions apply to a corporation, its "undistributed personal holding company income" is taxed at a 20-percent rate. § 541. Since the purpose of the provision is designed to force distributions, a corporation can avoid the tax through a deficiency dividend mechanism. § 547.

12.08 Personal Holding Company Tax: Stock Ownership Test

The purpose of the stock ownership test is to ensure that the personal holding company tax falls only on those corporations most likely to be manipulated by their shareholders for nonbusiness purposes. The behavior that concerned Congress is more likely to occur in closely held corporations where a handful of shareholders determine corporate behavior. The test is satisfied if at any time during the last half of the taxable year, more than 50 percent in value of the corporation's stock is owned directly or indirectly by or for not more than 5 individuals. § 542(a)(2). Note that if there are fewer than 10 shareholders, the stock ownership test must be satisfied.

Attribution rules found in § 544 apply in determining stock ownership. But note that the rules under § 544 differ somewhat from those in § 318. For example, there is attribution among siblings under § 544. These attribution rules prevent a holding company from escaping the personal holding company tax by interposing an operating company between the holding company and the individual owner or by spreading ownership among many family members.

12.09 Personal Holding Company Tax: Income Test

Since almost all closely held corporations will satisfy the stock ownership test, it is the income test that has taken on the most importance in the personal holding company area. Congress did not intend for the personal holding company tax to apply to every corporation with the "tainted" personal holding company income. It is only where the personal holding company income is a significant part of the corporation's operating income that the tax might apply. The income test is satisfied if at least 60 percent of the corporation's "adjusted ordinary gross income" for the year is personal holding company income.

(a) Adjusted Ordinary Gross Income

In computing adjusted ordinary gross income, ordinary gross income is first determined by excluding from gross income gains from the sale or disposition of capital assets and § 1231 assets.[16] These items are excluded to provide a better picture of the corporation's "every day" operating income. Further adjustments are made to reflect some high-gross/low-net income activities. Since the personal holding company tax applies only if personal holding company income (the numerator) equals or exceeds 60 percent of adjusted ordinary gross income (the denominator), there is an incentive for taxpayers to increase the denominator (adjusted ordinary gross income) of the fraction. Operating high gross income activities that produce little or no net income is a means of increasing the denominator.

For example, rental and royalty activities can produce high gross income but low net income once depreciation, interest and property taxes are taken into account. Accordingly, only the net income from rents and mineral royalties enters the adjusted ordinary gross income calculation.

Note that a corporation can still swell the denominator by operating a high-gross/low-net business. Suppose X Corp. has $60,000 of personal holding company income and adjusted ordinary gross income of $80,000. By adding a business that produces $21,000 of

---

[16] § 543(b)(1). Section 1231 assets predominantly include real or depreciable property used in a trade or business and held for more than one year. § 1231(b)(1) (but excluding property held for sale in the ordinary course of business).

ordinary income but has $21,000 of deductions, the corporation will avoid satisfying the income test.[17]

Note also that a corporation with a high cost of goods sold might find itself unwittingly a candidate for personal holding company taxation if it has even a small quantity of personal holding company income since its gross income and hence its adjusted ordinary gross income will be quite small.[18]

(b) Personal Holding Company Income.

Section 543(a) attempts to distinguish the "tainted" personal holding company income from "legitimate" operating income. The provision is aimed at income from passive sources. Accordingly the following items may qualify as personal holding company income: dividends, interest, royalties, annuities and rents. In keeping with the original intention to discourage personal service corporations, amounts received under personal service contracts may be personal holding company income. To discourage the incorporation of personal assets, amounts received from certain shareholders for the use of corporate property are personal holding company income.

Of all the passive income sources, perhaps the most troubling are royalties and rents. Royalties generally include periodic receipts from licenses to use various kinds of intangible property such as patents, trademarks and franchises.[19] Sometimes it is difficult to distinguish a license which generates a royalty from an outright sale on the installment method which is not classified as personal holding company income or from rental payments which are subject to the special requirements of § 543(a)(2).[20] A second problem is that some royalties may be generated by active business operations. For example, a corporation that actively developed and licensed computer software prior to 1986 was subject to the personal holding company provisions on the royalty income. The Tax Reform Act of 1986 added § 543(a)(1)(C) and § 543(d) to provide that such royalties do not constitute personal holding company income if earned by an active business. To qualify, the recipient must: (1) be actively engaged in the trade or business of developing software; (2) derive at least 50 percent of its income from such software; (3) incur substantial trade or business expenses; and (4) distribute to its shareholders most of its passive income other than the royalties.

---

[17] The corporation will have personal holding company income of $60,000 and adjusted ordinary gross income of $101,000.

[18] See Regs. § 1.61–3(a) which defines gross income from a manufacturing business as total sales less the cost of goods sold.

[19] Mineral, oil and gas royalties are addressed separately. § 543(a)(3).

[20] See, e.g., *Dothan Coca–Cola Bottling Co. v. United States,* 745 F.2d 1400 (11th Cir.1984).

Rental income like royalty income can be generated both passively and actively. Section 543(a)(2) makes the distinction with a bright-line test based on the percentage of adjusted ordinary gross income that is from rental income. If adjusted income from rents[21] constitutes 50 percent or more of a corporation's adjusted ordinary gross income, the rental income is not personal holding company income.[22] Therefore, a corporation engaged primarily in rental activities can escape personal holding company status. Note that the provision makes no effort to determine the amount of corporate involvement in the rental activities. A corporation with rental income that comprises 40 percent of its adjusted ordinary gross income must treat the rental income as personal holding company income to be added to any other personal holding company income even though the corporation, through its employees, actively participated in the rental activity.[23] Even if the 50 percent test is satisfied, rental income will constitute personal holding company income if a corporation having substantial nonrent personal holding company income fails to distribute it to its shareholders.[24]

Not all rents are addressed by § 543(a)(2). Compensation for the use of corporate property by a shareholder owning 25 percent or more stock is automatically personal holding company income. § 543(a)(6). This provision reaches payments for incorporated personal assets such as yachts and summer estates. Moreover, any deductions in excess of the rent cannot be used to offset other personal holding company income in determining undistributed personal holding company income, the base on which the tax is applied.[25]

Note also that if § 543(a)(6) applies, it applies to all assets rented by 25-percent shareholders—even nonpersonal, business assets. For example, if a 25-percent shareholder rents a hotel from a corporation that satisfies the stock ownership test and the shareholder operates that asset, the rent received by the corporation will constitute personal holding company income.[26] Section 543(a)(6) sof-

---

[21] Defined in § 543(b)(3), the term essentially means net rental income.

[22] A similar test is applied to royalties from copyrights as well as mineral, oil, and gas royalties. § 543(a)(4) (copyrights), § 543(a)(3) (mineral, oil and gas royalties).

[23] See, e.g., *Eller v. Commissioner,* 77 T.C. 934 (1981) (income from operation of commercial shopping center and mobile home park was personal holding company income despite level of services).

[24] Section 543(a)(2)(B) provides that dividends paid (or deemed paid) must equal or exceed the amount (if any) by which the nonrent personal holding company income exceeds 10 percent of adjusted ordinary gross income.

[25] Section 545(b)(6) will not limit the deductions if the rent paid by the shareholder is reasonable and other conditions are met.

[26] See, e.g., *Hatfried, Inc. v. Commissioner,* 162 F.2d 628 (3d Cir.1947).

tens this result by applying only if the corporation has personal holding company income—other than rent—in excess of 10 percent of its adjusted ordinary gross income.[27] Note then that it may still be possible to incorporate personal assets without personal holding company tax implications if a corporation does not exceed the 10-percent threshold.

Finally, § 543(a)(7) along with § 269A were enacted in part to discourage the use of the corporate form by entertainers and other providers of services. Section 269A allows the Commissioner in appropriate cases to reallocate income from a corporation to the individual actually performing the services. Section 543(a)(7) respects the corporation as an entity but treats the personal services income as personal holding company income if the individual who is to perform the services is designated or can be designated by some person other than the corporation and the service provider owns directly or indirectly 25 percent or more by value of the corporation's stock. If there is merely an expectation on the part of the payor that a particular shareholder will perform the services but no designation, the income is not personal holding company income.[28]

12.10 Personal Holding Company Tax: Computation

If a corporation satisfies both the stock ownership and income tests, § 541 imposes a tax at a 205-percent rate on undistributed personal holding company income. Section 545 defines undistributed personal holding company income as taxable income adjusted to reflect the corporation's net economic gain for the year. The adjustments are similar to those made in determining accumulated taxable income for purposes of the accumulated earnings tax. Thus, federal taxes are deducted, the dividends-received deduction is eliminated, and charitable deduction restrictions are eased. Net capital gains are deducted thereby allowing corporations to accumulate long-term capital gains. § 545(b).

Once these adjustments are made, the corporation is permitted a dividends-paid deduction in accordance with § 561. The deduction is the sum of actual dividends paid during the year,[29] consent dividends, and the dividend carryover. The consent dividend mechanism in § 565 allows shareholders to agree to treat a specified por-

---

[27] Amounts received from 25 percent or greater shareholders are excluded from this calculation.

[28] See, e.g., Rev. Rul. 75–67, 1975–1 C.B. 169 (no personal holding company income for doctor's personal service corporation).

[29] Dividends paid within the first two and one-half months of the following year also can be deducted to a limited extent. § 563(c).

tion of the corporation's earnings and profits as a dividend even in the absence of an actual distribution. The procedure enables a corporation wishing to avoid the personal holding company tax to do so without making an actual distribution. The amount of the consent dividend is treated as though the corporation made a distribution followed by a contribution to capital by receiving shareholders. The dividend carryover under § 564 is the excess of dividends paid during the two preceding years over the corporation's taxable income for those years.

Dividends paid in property will qualify for a deduction. Under Regs. § 1.562–1(a), the deduction is limited to the property's adjusted basis at the time of distribution. In *Fulman v. United States*,[30] the regulation was upheld, but in light of the substantial repeal of *General Utilities*[31] in § 311(b), the regulation would cause strange results. A corporation might make a distribution of appreciated property that would increase its taxable income (and therefore its undistributed personal holding company income) by the difference between the property's fair market value and its adjusted basis. Yet, the undistributed personal holding company income would be decreased only by the property's adjusted basis. It would be bizarre if a distribution of property could increase personal holding company liability.

Once the corporation's personal holding company tax liability has been determined, it can mitigate or eliminate the liability through the dividend deficiency procedure. § 547. This procedure allows a corporation to make a dividend distribution to shareholders once the Service has determined that there is personal holding company liability. However, the deficiency dividend procedure does not diminish the liability for interest or penalties.

---

[30] 434 U.S. 528 (1978).

[31] See discussion at Section 4.04 *supra*.

Chapter 13

S CORPORATIONS—AN OVERVIEW

13.01 Introduction

We have already looked at C corporations, corporations that are treated as taxpayers independent of their shareholders. Some corporations, though, called S corporations, file an informational return but do not (with some exceptions) pay income taxes.[1] Instead, an S corporation's items of income and deduction are passed-thru to its shareholders who report these items directly on their individual income tax returns.

Subchapter C of the Internal Revenue Code,[2] §§ 301–385, provides most of the provisions governing the taxation of *all* corporations, C corporations and S corporations alike. Subchapter S, §§ 1361–1379, adds those provisions specially applicable to S corporations. One important aspect of the taxation of S corporations is the coordination of the rules in these two subchapters. Indeed, § 1371(a)(1) provides: "Except as otherwise provided in this title, and except to the extent inconsistent with this subchapter, subchapter C shall apply to an S corporation and its shareholders." Accordingly, in this Chapter we will examine sections in both subchapters C and S, but when examining a provision in subchapter C, our emphasis will be on its application to S corporations.

There are two basic models upon which pass-thru taxation can be designed: the entity model and the aggregate model. Under a pure entity model, the entity computes its taxable income without reference to any tax attributes of its beneficial owners. That is, the entity's basis in its assets is independent of any asset basis of its shareholders or partners, the entity has a taxable year and method of accounting independent of the taxable years and accounting methods of its owners, and so on. Once the entity's taxable income or loss is computed, it is passed thru to its owners.

Under a pure aggregate model, the entity has no tax attributes of its own and does not compute a taxable income. Instead, the entity is treated as no more than an aggregate of its owners, so that, for example, it has no independent basis in its assets but instead uses

---

[1] The terms C corporation and S corporation are defined in § 1361(a).

[2] More accurately, that reference is to subchapter C (corporate distributions and adjustments) of Chapter 1 (normal taxes and surtaxes) of Subtitle A (income taxes) of the Internal Revenue Code of 1986, as amended.

385

the aggregate of its owners' bases. Thus, a separate depreciation schedule must be maintained for each owner's interest in each entity asset, each owner may have a distinct holding period for each asset, etc. While a pure aggregate approach to pass-thru taxation is possible, in practice it would be very cumbersome to implement.[3]

The remainder of this chapter presents an overview of the taxation of S corporations, but before that overview begins, one more detail should be mentioned. A corporation can be a C corporation at some times and an S corporation at other times. To be sure, most corporations begin and end as one type or the other without any mid-life changes. But a C corporation is permitted to file an S corporation election and an S corporation's election may terminate, and in either event transition issues arise. This chapter as well as the next consider only S corporations wholly lacking all C corporation history. Chapter 15 looks at transition issues faced by the corporation and its shareholders after a C corporation files an S election and after an S election terminates.

13.02 Qualification and Election

An entity can be an S corporation only if it is treated as a corporation for federal income tax purposes and qualifies for and elects S corporation status. For federal income tax purposes, corporations include all entities organized under federal or state law as corporations. Regs. § 301.7702-2(b)(1). Thus, federal- or state-law corporations and certain specialty corporations (such as insurance companies) must be treated as tax corporations. Other entities include general partnerships, limited partnerships, business trusts, limited liability companies, and limited liability partnerships. Such an entity is treated as a corporation if it so elects. See Regs. § 301.7701-3(b)(1). If an entity is treated as a corporation for federal income tax purposes and qualifies as a "small business corporation," it may elect to be treated as an S corporation.

---

[3] The taxation of S corporations is close to a pure entity model. For those familiar with the taxation of partnerships, this means: (1) there is no corporate analog to § 752; (2) distributions of appreciated property from a corporation to a shareholder result in recognized gain to the entity (and through it, to its shareholders), and contributions to a corporation can be taxable depending on the ownership interests of the contributing shareholders; (3) there are no optional basis adjustments akin to §§ 734(b) and 743(b); (4) there is no provision equivalent to § 704(c); and (5) the flexibility for which partnership taxation is most noted is absent from subchapter S because there are no special allocations of corporate-level income and deductions. Thus, subchapter S is very different from subchapter K.

(a) Small Business Corporation.

Despite the name, the definition of a small business corporation is not based in any way on the size of the corporation's business. "Small" in this context refers to the number of shareholders. A "small business corporation" under § 1361(b) cannot have more than 100 shareholders, and a husband and wife (and their estates) are treated as a single shareholder, as are all family members (and their estates). § 1361(c)(1). Family members include any common ancestor, lineal descendants of that ancestor, and their spouses or former spouses. § 1361(c)(1)(B)(i). *See also id.* at (c)(1)(C) (treating the following as children by blood: adopted children, certain individuals lawfully placed for adoption with an individual, and certain foster children). However, to be a common ancestor of a family, a person can be no more than *six* generations removed from the youngest generation of shareholders to be included in the family. *Id.* at (c)(1)(B)(ii) and (iii). In other words, a family includes all persons who have a common ancestor (even if dead) in the preceding six generations.[4]

In addition to the 100-shareholder requirement, a "small business corporation" has the following requirements: (1) It must be a domestic corporation;[5] (2) all of its shareholders must be individuals, decedents' or individual bankrupts' estates, certain trusts, pension, profit-sharing or stock bonus plans qualifying under § 401, or § 501(c)(3) organizations;[6] (3) no nonresident alien may be a shareholder; and (4) the corporation must have only one class of stock outstanding.[7] In addition, a small business corporation cannot be an ineligible corporation (*i.e.*, not an insurance company, financial institution that uses the reserve method for accounting for bad debts, § 936 corporation, or DISC or former DISC). *See* § 1361(b)(2).

---

[4] Although all members of a family are treated as one shareholder for purposes of the 100-shareholder limit, each member must still qualify as an S corporation shareholder. Thus, no family member can be a non-resident alien and, when appropriate, each must file a Subchapter S election.

[5] A domestic corporation is a corporation organized in (or under the laws of) the United States. § 7701(a)(5). In certain cases, a foreign corporation may be deemed a domestic corporation (*e.g.*, a "stapled" foreign corporation).

[6] See § 1361(c)(2) (describing permitted trusts as including grantor trusts, voting trusts, and electing small business trusts); *id.* at (d) (treating a qualified subchapter S trust or "QSST" as a grantor trust for this purpose; a QSST is a trust that must distribute (or be required to distribute) all income currently to a citizen or resident of the United States and that, at any time, has only one income beneficiary, the beneficiary must be entitled during her life to all trust distributions (including upon trust termination), and her income interest must terminate at death (or, if earlier, the trust termination)); *id.* at (e) (defining an electing small business trust).

[7] § 1361(b).

(b) Election.

If a corporation satisfies these requirements, it may elect to be treated as an S corporation. Every shareholder must consent to this election, although once made, the election need not be ratified by shareholders who acquire stock after the election is filed. § 1362(a)(2). Because the effect of an S corporation election is to pass thru and tax shareholders on the corporation's income, requiring unanimous shareholder consent eliminates any possible argument that taxing a shareholder on the corporation's income violates the Constitution.

If an S corporation election is filed during the first 2½ months of the corporation's taxable year, the election may be effective for the current year or for the subsequent year, whichever the corporation prefers.[8] If the election is filed more than 2½ months into a taxable year, it automatically becomes effective for the subsequent year.[9] Once filed, an election continues until it is revoked or the corporation ceases to be a "small business corporation." *See* § 1362(c). However, once an S corporation's Subchapter S election terminates, the corporation is prohibited from filing a new election for 5 taxable years, unless the Service consents to the new election. § 1362(g).

(c) Revocation and Termination.

An S corporation may file a revocation of its election so long as shareholders holding more than one-half of its shares agree. § 1362(d)(1). Note that this does *not* require consent by a majority of the shareholders. If, for example, one shareholder owns more than half of the shares of a corporation's stock, that shareholder alone has the ability to terminate the S corporation election and the remaining shareholders have no say in the matter. The revocation may specify a prospective date, although like the election itself, a revocation can be effective for the current taxable year if filed within the first 2½ months of the year. § 1362(d)(1)(C).

An S corporation election will also be terminated if the corporation ceases to qualify as a small business corporation. § 1362(d)(2)

---

[8] § 1362(b)(2). The election is treated as made for the subsequent taxable year if (i) the corporation did not qualify as a small business corporation during the taxable year before the election is made or (ii) one or more persons who were shareholders during the taxable year but before the election date did not consent to the election. *Id.*

[9] § 1362(b)(3). If an eligible corporation makes a late election or makes no election at all for the current year, the corporation may nevertheless be treated as an S corporation if the Secretary of the Treasury determines that the failure to make a timely election was due to reasonable cause. § 1362(b)(5). The Service has adopted a surprisingly generous interpretation of its authority under this provision. *See* Rev. Proc. 2003-43, 2003-1 C.B. 998, supplemented by Rev. Proc. 2007-62, I.R.B. 786.

(also providing that the termination is effective on and after the date of cessation). For example, if one shareholder sells her shares to several others, the total number of shareholders may exceed 100, immediately terminating the S corporation election. Similarly, a shareholder could sell her stock to an impermissible trust, a nonresident alien, a corporation, or a partnership, and again the S corporation election would be terminated.

It may be that the corporation accidentally terminates its S corporation election under § 1362(d)(2). If the corporation takes steps within a reasonable period after discovering the termination to remedy the problem and convinces the Service that the termination was inadvertent, S corporation status can be restored without legal interruption. § 1362(f) (also applying to a failure to obtain necessary shareholder consents). However, the Service may require the corporation and its shareholders to make any adjustments (*e.g.*, income inclusion and basis adjustments) that the Service deems appropriate.

Note that the provisions governing the S corporation election plainly contemplate that a corporation may spend part of its time as a C corporation and part as an S corporation. In this and the next Chapter, we will consider only those corporations electing to be taxed as S corporations throughout their entire existence; the taxation of an S corporation having a C corporation history is substantially more complex. For example, such S corporations can terminate their S corporation election by having too much passive income, § 1362(d)(3), an issue considered briefly in Chapter 15.

13.03 Formation

Because no special rules govern the formation of an S corporation, the general rules of Subchapter C apply. For example, under § 351, a person may recognize no gain or loss on the transfer of property to a corporation in exchange for the corporation's stock. The application of § 351 is described in detail in Chapter 2 *supra*.

In brief summary, § 351 applies when a person or persons transfer property to a corporation, receive stock of the corporation in the exchange, and control the corporation immediately after the exchange. See § 351(a) and (b); § 368 (for a definition of control). If § 351 applies to a person's exchange, relevant tax consequences include the following: If the person receives solely stock of the controlled corporation, she recognizes none of her realized gain or loss on the exchange. § 351(a). If, however, she receives property in addition to stock ("boot"), she recognizes none of her realized loss but recognizes any realized gain up to the value of the boot received. § 351(b). Further, generally, the person's basis in the stock received equals (i) the aggregate basis of the property transferred, plus (ii) any gain recognized, and minus (ii) the value of any boot received. § 358(a). Finally, the controlled corporation generally takes a basis in a transferred asset equal to the shareholder's adjusted basis in the asset plus any gain recognized by the shareholder on the transfer. § 362(a).

However, those basis consequences change if, under § 362(a), the controlled corporation would take an aggregate basis in property transferred by the shareholder that exceeded its aggregate value. Then, as a general rule under § 362(e)(2), that built-in loss is eliminated at the corporate level, but preserved at the shareholder level. The shareholder and corporation may elect, instead, to preserve the built-in loss at the corporate level, but eliminate it at the shareholder level. § 362(e)(2)(C). That election could be unwise for an S corporation, however, because if the corporation recognized the built-in loss, its shareholders would reduce their stock bases by the same amount. See § 1367(a)(2)(B). Then, their sale of that stock would then eliminate any overall benefit from the loss.

For example, assume that individual B forms an S corporation, S Corp., transferring an asset with a $1,000 basis and $600 value to S Corp. in a § 351 exchange for all S stock. Under § 362(a), S Corp. would take a $1,000 basis in the transferred asset, a basis exceeding its value. Thus, § 362(e)(2) applies, and unless B and S Corp. make the § 362(e)(2)(C) election, S Corp. must reduce its basis in the asset to $600, while B retains his $1,000 basis in the S stock. See § 358(a)(1). If S Corp. sells the asset for $600 and B then sells his stock for $600, S Corp. will recognize no gain or loss, while B will recognize a $400 loss. § 1001(c).

Suppose, instead, that B and S Corp. make the § 362(e)(2)(C) election. Then, S Corp. takes a $1,000 basis in the transferred asset, while B reduces his basis in the S stock to $600, its fair market value. That election may prove shortsighted if S Corp. sells the asset and B then sells his S stock. If S Corp. sells the asset for $1,000, it will recognize a $400 loss, which will pass thru to B. Although B can report that loss on his tax return, he must reduce his basis in his S stock by $400, from $600 to $200. See § 1366 (for the pass-thru); § 1367 (for the basis adjustment). If B then sells the S stock for $600, he will recognize a $400 offsetting gain. Particularly if the gain and loss are of the same character, B may enjoy a tax savings from the loss but suffer an offsetting tax cost on the gain and receive only a time-value benefit if the loss arises in a year before the gain. If B takes the gain and loss into account in the same year, he may enjoy no benefit at all from the loss.

Still, a § 362(e)(2)(C) election may makes sense in certain circumstances. First, if B's stock sale occurs years after the asset sale, the time-value benefit noted in the preceding paragraph may exceed the time-value benefit that B would enjoy if the election were not made and B recognized a loss on the stock sale. Further, if B held the S stock until his death, the basis in that stock may be stepped up under § 1014, eliminating any built-in gain in the stock that could be traced to the election. Finally, the loss on the asset sale may be ordinary while any gain on the stock sale should be capital, and that difference in character may benefit B, even if the asset and stock sales occur in the same year.[10] Thus, although a § 362(e)(2)(C) election may at times be improvident, its effect may vary significantly depending on the facts.

13.04 Pass-Thru of Corporate Income and Deduction

An S corporation is generally not a taxpayer.[11] Like a partnership, an S corporation computes its income, loss, deductions and other tax items and then passes those items through to its owners.[12] Its owners are its shareholders, and each shareholder reports a proportion of the corporation's income, loss, and deductions based on the shareholder's relative ownership of the corporation's outstanding shares. For example, if shareholder X owns 15 of the 100 outstanding shares of S Corp.'s outstanding stock, X reports 15% of S Corp.'s taxable income or loss. If a shareholder's percentage of stock

---

[10] The benefit of the election in this case depends, among other things, on applicable tax rates and the extent to which any stock loss would offset long- or short-term capital gain. Suppose that S Corp. and B make the § 362(e)(2)(C) election. Assume that S Corp. recognizes a $400 ordinary loss on the asset sale, which passes thru to B, and offsets ordinary income otherwise taxed at a 35% rate. Assume as well that B recognizes a $400 long-term capital gain on his S stock sale taxed at a 15% rate. If the asset and stock sales occur in the same year, B enjoys an overall $80 benefit, the excess of the $140 benefit (35% of $400) from the loss minus the $60 cost (15% of $400) of the gain.

In contrast, if the § 362(e)(2)(C) election had not been made, S Corp. would recognize no gain or loss on the asset sale, while B would recognize a $400 long-term capital loss on the stock sale. If that loss offset long-term capital gain otherwise taxed at a 15% rate, B would enjoy only a $60 benefit (15% of $400). If, however, the loss offset short-term capital gain otherwise taxed at a 35% rate, B would enjoy a $140 benefit (35% of $400). Thus, in this example, the election would make sense if the stock loss that B would enjoy (without the election) would offset short-term capital gain but not if it would offset long-term capital gain.

[11] An S corporation with a C corporation history may sometimes be a taxpayer, however.

[12] *See* § 1363(b) (providing that an S corporation generally determines its taxable income in the same manner as an individual). An S corporation is treated as a corporation, however, in applying § 311, § 354-§ 356, § 361, § 362, § 368, and § 1032. *See* § 1371(a)(2) (providing that Subchapter C applies to an S corporation to the extent not inconsistent with Subchapter S).

ownership changes during the year, the corporation's income is allocated ratably to each day of the year and then passed thru to each shareholder in proportion to the shareholder's ownership interest on each day. § 1377(a)(1). *But see id.* at (a)(2) (for an election to close the books if a shareholder terminates her interest in the corporation); Regs. § 1.1368-1(g) (for a similar, but broader election).

As in the partnership context, the character of items of income and deduction recognized by the corporation and passed thru to its shareholders is preserved. § 1366(b). For example, capital gain recognized by the corporation will be reported as capital gain by the shareholders, and charitable contributions made by the corporation will be treated as charitable deductions of the shareholders. § 1366(a)-(b); *cf.* § 702(a)-(b).

An S corporation must allocate its tax items among its shareholders in proportion to their stock ownership. § 1366(a)(1). In contrast, a partnership has much more flexibility to allocate its tax items among its partners, limited only by the requirement that allocations have "substantial economic effect." *See* Treas. Reg. § 1.704-1(b)(2). This flexibility is wholly missing from Subchapter S. In fact, corporate income must be apportioned according to stock interests, even in the face of assignment of income concerns.

For example, suppose individuals X and Y form S Corp., with X contributing $10,000 cash and Y contributing inventory with $6,000 adjusted basis and $10,000 fair market value. Each receives 50 shares of S Corp. stock, so that when the inventory is sold, each is allocated and reports half of the $4,000 gain realized on the sale. In the partnership arena and consonant with assignment of income concerns, pre-contribution appreciation in the contributed assets must be allocated to the contributing partner under § 704(c). Thus, if X and Y instead formed a partnership, Y would be allocated the entire $4,000 gain on the inventory. Under Subchapter S, however, the gain is allocated between X and Y in proportion to relative stock ownership.

A shareholder increases her stock basis for her allocable share of income and decreases her stock basis for her allocable share of losses and deductions. *See* § 1367(a). These adjustments prevent a shareholder from taking her allocable share of S corporation income and loss into account again when she sells her stock. The adjustments under § 1367(a) parallel those under § 705. Both provisions require a basis increase for taxable income and tax-exempt income and a basis decrease for losses, deductions, and non-deductible, non-capitalizable expenses like illegal bribes and kickbacks. § 1367(a).

Of course, realized but unrecognized corporate-level income should not pass-thru to an S corporation's shareholders. Rather, that income should be taken into account only when it ultimately is recognized by the corporation.[13] For example, if an S corporation exchanges Blackacre for Whiteacre in a transaction qualifying for non-recognition under § 1031 as a like-kind exchange, the shareholders should not increase their stock bases by any unrealized appreciation in Blackacre. Because that unrealized appreciation is carried over at the corporate level into Whiteacre, no shareholder-level basis adjustment is yet appropriate.

An S corporation's items of income and deduction are passed thru to its shareholders on the last day of the corporation's taxable year, and the shareholders generally must report those items on their tax returns and pay any resulting tax.[14] Accordingly, shareholders whose taxable years do not coincide with that of the corporation will enjoy some deferral, with the greatest deferral enjoyed by those shareholders whose taxable years end just prior to the close of the corporation's taxable year.

Under § 1378, however, an S corporation cannot freely choose its taxable year. Unless the S corporation can convince the Service

---

[13] In *Gitlitz v. Commissioner*, 531 U.S. 206 (2001), the Supreme Court in dicta appeared to reach the opposite conclusion. In that case, the Court attempted to apply in a consistent way a number of complex (and arguably inconsistent) statutory provisions, including § 108. The case is most notable for its emphasis on a plain reading of the statute in lieu of a detailed examination of the purposes underlying a particular code section and the legislative history behind it. But as part of its analysis, the Court asserted that the shareholders of an S Corporation must increase their stock basis for their share of taxable, tax-exempt, *and tax-deferred* corporate level income. As to taxable and tax-exempt income, the Court plainly is correct. But as to tax-deferred income (such as the realized but unrecognized gain in a tax-free like-kind exchange), the Court's statement makes no sense and simply cannot be right, since it could result in multiple basis increases for essentially the same gain. Presumably, this *Gitlitz* dicta about tax-deferred income will be ignored by future courts.

Note that the *Gitlitz* court concluded that S corporation shareholders enjoy a basis step-up for their share of the corporation's cancellation of indebtedness ("COD") income excluded by § 108, a result quickly reversed by Congress in § 108(d)(7)(A). Under that provision, if an S corporation excludes COD income, the excluded amount into is not taken into account under § 1366(a) (and therefore also not taken into account to increase basis under § 1367).

[14] § 1366(a)(1). A tax-exempt shareholder other than an employee stock ownership plan ("ESOP") treats stock in an S corporation as an interest in an unrelated trade or business and must take into account its allocable share of the S corporation's tax items in computing its unrelated business taxable income. § 512(e)(1). Consequently, those shareholders may be taxed on income (*e.g.*, their allocable share of passive income) that would have been non-taxable if directly received. Note, however, that these unfavorable rules do not apply to employee securities held by ESOPs and income allocations to an ESOP escape current federal income tax. § 512(e)(3) (for the ESOP exception).

that it has a sufficient business purpose to justify some other taxable year, an S corporation must use the calendar year as its taxable year. While this rule eliminates deferral opportunities for calendar-year taxpayers, it mandates deferral for fiscal-year taxpayers beyond that enjoyed by most taxpayers. Of course, because most shareholders of S corporations must be individuals and individuals almost always are calendar-year taxpayers, restricting S corporation's use of fiscal years should present little real opportunity for deferral.

As a final note, pass-thru of corporate loss is limited to a shareholder's outside basis. § 1366(d). For this purpose, outside basis includes not only the shareholder's stock basis but also her basis in certain corporate debt. While the limitation of § 1366(d) operates much like § 704(d) limiting the pass-thru of partnership loss to the partner's outside basis, the § 1366(d) concept of debt basis makes the S corporation limitation considerably more complex. This complexity is deferred until the next chapter.

13.05 Non-liquidating Distributions

When an S corporation makes a non-liquidating distribution of property to a shareholder with respect to the shareholder's stock, the corporation recognizes gain but not loss, determining gain or loss separately for each distributed asset. § 311(a)-(b)(1). Thus, if the corporation distributes an appreciated asset, it recognizes gain as if it sold the asset to the distributee for its fair market value, recognizing the asset appreciation at the time of distribution. This gain, like all corporate income, is passed thru to the corporation's shareholders at the close of the taxable year

Note again that a corporation does not recognize loss on a non-liquidating distribution of loss property. § 311(a). Because the distributee shareholder takes a fair market value basis in the distributed property, if a corporation (foolishly) distributes loss property, the built-in loss disappears.

The distribution can also result in gain to the distributee shareholder, but only to the extent the value of the property distributed exceeds the shareholder's stock basis.[15] The result is com-

---

[15] § 1368(b). The gain is gain from the "sale or exchange of property," presumably the shareholder's S corporation stock. § 1368(b)(2). *Cf.* § 301(c)(3)(A) (for a similar characterization).

Although this determination is made on a share-by-share basis, if the amount attributable to a share exceeds its basis, it appears that the excess is applied to reduce the remaining bases of all other shares owned by the shareholder, in proportion to those remaining bases. Regs. § 1.1367-1(c)(3) (providing that result). *See also* P.L.R. 9607003 (Nov. 3, 1995) (citing to the

parable for a C corporation shareholder who receives a distribution
from a C corporation with no earnings and profits. See § 301(c)(2)
and (3). Cf. § 731(a)(1) (requiring a partner to recognize gain on a
distribution, but only to the extent that *cash* distributed (or deemed
distributed) exceeds her outside basis). To account for the distribution, the distributee must reduce her stock basis (but not below zero) by the value of the property distributed. § 1367(a)(2).[16] The
shareholder takes a fair market value basis in any property distributed. See § 301(d).

Because a distribution of appreciated property produces gain
that passes thru to the shareholders, including the distributee, one
may ask whether the distributee may use the stock basis increase
for that allocated gain to reduce any gain that she otherwise would
recognize on the distribution. For example, suppose individual B
owns 50% of the outstanding stock of S Corp. with an adjusted basis
of $10,000 in that stock. What are the tax consequences to B if S
Corp. distributes Blackacre to B when Blackacre is worth $12,000
and has an adjusted basis to S Corp. of $8,000?

A possible (unpleasant) result might be that (i) B recognizes a
$2,000 gain on the distribution, because Blackacre's value ($12,000)
exceeds B's $10,000 stock basis by $2,000; and (ii) B is also taxed on
an additional $2,000 of corporate-level income, his 50% share of S
Corp.'s $4,000 recognized gain on Blackacre. Could B, instead, *first*
adjust his S Corp. stock basis to account for his $2,000 allocable
share of S Corp.'s gain on Blackacre, and *then* account for the distribution? With this ordering, B's stock basis would increase by
$2,000, from $10,000 to $12,000, and he would recognize no gain on
the distribution of Blackacre, worth $12,000.

The more favorable ordering is supported by § 1368(d)(1). Under that provision, a distributee-shareholder takes into account any
stock basis adjustments under § 1367(a)(1) for a taxable year before
accounting for distributions made during the year. See also Regs.
§ 1.1368-1(e) (repeating this rule). Section 1367(a)(1) provides that a
shareholder increases her stock basis for her allocable share of the S
corporation's income for a taxable year, including for any gain recognized on a distribution. Because that income passes through to

---

regulation with approval). Cf. Regs. § 1.1368-3 (examples 1 and 2) (determining the consequences of a distribution on a share-by-share basis).

Note that if the S Corporation has subchapter C earnings and profits
(*e.g.*, from a previous year in which it was not an S corporation), the shareholder-level treatment of the distribution is more complex. A discussion of
that complexity is deferred until chapter 15.

[16] More precisely, the shareholder reduces her stock basis by the portion of the distribution not included in income. § 1367(a)(2)(A).

the shareholder on last day of the corporation's taxable year (§ 1366(a)(1)), the shareholder also increases her stock basis on the last day of the year. Thus, § 1368(d)(1) implies that a shareholder cannot determine the consequences of a distribution until the close of the corporation's taxable year.[17]

Regulations make clear that the shareholder-level tax consequences of a distribution cannot be determined until the close of the corporation's tax year. As a consequence, later activities of the corporation can affect the shareholder's tax treatment of a mid-year distribution. Consider the following example taken from the Regs. § 1.1368-3 (example 2):

A, an individual, owns all 10 outstanding shares of S Corp. with adjusted basis of $1 per share. S Corp. is a calendar-year S corporation. On March 1, S makes a distribution of $38 in cash to A. For the entire year, A's pro rata share of items described in § 1367(a)(1) is $50, and A increases basis in each share of S stock by $5 ($50/10) to $6. Thus, A recognizes no gain on the distribution, because A's basis in each share ($6) at the end of the year exceeds the distribution on that share ($3.80 or $38/10). A reduces each share's basis by $3.80, from $6 to $2.20 to account for the distribution. The regulatory example also illustrates that after A accounts for the distribution, she next accounts for any share of non-capitalizable, non-deductible expenses and finally accounts for any share of losses and deductions.

This treatment is similar to how an advance is treated under Subchapter K but different from how a "regular" partnership distribution is treated. Under § 731(a), a "regular" distribution of cash to a partner is taxable to the partner to the extent the amount of cash distributed exceeds the partner's *pre-distribution* outside basis.[18] In Subchapter S, we use the shareholder's *year-end* outside (i.e., stock) basis adjusted first for the shareholder's pass-through items of income.

Reconsider the example above but assume that the distribution consists of property having an adjusted basis to the corporation of $10 and a fair market value of $38 and that S Corp.'s only income

---

[17] That timing may present a quandary for a calendar-year shareholder of a fiscal-year corporation, because the shareholder may be unable to determine the tax consequences of a distribution before the associated federal income tax return is due.

[18] However, if the distribution is made on the last day of the partnership's taxable year, the partner's outside basis is increased by her allocable share of income before accounting for the distribution. *See* Regs. § 1.704-1(d)(2) and Rev. Rul. 66-94, 1966-1 C.B. 166. An advance, unless repaid, is treated as a distribution made on the last day of the partnership's taxable year. See Regs. § 1.731-1(a)(ii).

for the year results from the distribution. The distribution will not result in any recognition to A, because A's year-end stock basis, after adjusting for pass-through income, is $38,[19] and that amount is sufficient to absorb the entire $38 value of the distribution. A's stock basis will end up at $0, reflecting an increase of $28 for pass-thru income and a decrease of $38 for the distribution. See § 1367(a)(1)(A) and (2)(A).

In summary, under the ordering rule of § 1368(d)(1), a shareholder first makes positive stock basis adjustments for the year, next reduces stock basis to account for distributions, and finally takes into account other negative stock basis adjustments. This ordering rule makes it less likely that a shareholder will recognize gain on a distribution, even in a year in which the S corporation loses money.

For example, suppose that B owns one share of stock in an S corporation with an adjusted basis of $10 as of the beginning of the taxable year. The corporation distributes $9 to B during the year but has a net loss, of which $3 is allocable to B. B has no income on the distribution, because the § 1367(a)(2) negative stock basis adjustment is made only after determining the tax consequences of the distribution. Immediately before accounting for the distribution, B has a stock basis of $10, an amount that exceeds the cash distributed. Under § 1367(a)(2)(A) and § 1368(b)(1), B reduces his stock basis by $9, from $10 to $1, and recognizes no gain. Under § 1367(b)(2), B then reduces his stock basis to $0 to account for the $3 loss. Matching the $1 basis reduction for the loss, B can report only $1 of the $3 loss, deferring the remaining $2 under § 1366(d), subject to the debt rule of § 1366(d)(1)(B). § 1366(d)(1); § 1367(b)(2).

Does the ordering rule of § 1368(d)(1) apply *item-by-item* or only on a *net* basis. For example, suppose an S corporation has $100 of income and $150 of loss for a taxable year in which it makes a distribution to a shareholder. Does the shareholder first increase her basis by $100, then determine the tax consequences of the distribution, and only thereafter reduce basis for the $150 of loss, or is the income and loss netted to a single loss of $50 so that the shareholder never increases basis but only determines the tax consequences of the distribution and then reduces basis for the net loss of $50? The answer turns on whether the items of income and deduction are "nonseparately computed" items within the meaning of § 1366(a)(2). An S corporation's nonseparately computed items of income and deduction are netted together to form a single item of income or deduction; if that net figure is income, then it increases the distribu-

---

[19] The $38 amount equals A's original stock basis ($10) plus A's allocable share of the gain ($28).

tee's basis immediately before the distribution while if it is a net deduction it is taken into account immediately after the distribution. Separately stated items are passed through without any netting so that separately stated income items increase stock basis immediately before the distribution while separately stated deductions are taken into account immediately after the distribution. See Regs. § 1.1368-3 (example 2). Thus, the ordering rule of § 1368(d)(1) applies on both a net basis (as to nonseparately computed items) and on an item-by-item basis (as to separately stated items). In general, separately stated items are those having a distinct character (such as long-term capital gains) that must be preserved as they pass through the corporation to the shareholders' individual tax returns. See Regs. § 1.1366-1(a)(2) (for the computation of separately stated items, which may themselves be net amounts (*e.g.,* net long-term capital gain)).

As a final note, if the shareholders' aggregate basis in their S corporation stock equals the S Corporation's net basis in its assets, that equality will be broken if the S corporation distributes property to a shareholder with a value exceeding the shareholder's stock basis.[20] In Subchapter K, this equality also may be broken by a distribution (but only of cash), though it is reestablished if the partnership has a § 754 election in effect. Because an S corporation's distribution of property as well as of cash can break the equality, and because there is no Subchapter S equivalent to § 754, inside/outside bases conformity is more likely to disappear for S corporations than it is for partnerships.

13.06 Dispositions of Shares and Liquidating Distributions

(a) Dispositions of Stock Not in Redemption.

If a shareholder sells or exchanges stock in an S corporation, the shareholder recognizes gain or loss on each share, equal to the difference between the amount realized and her adjusted basis in the share, just as a C corporation shareholder would. *See* § 1001. Nevertheless, disposition of stock in an S corporation is more complex, because the disposition (i) affects the pass-thru of corporate-

---

[20] For example, assume that B is the sole shareholder of Corp. S, an S corporation, and that he has a $50 basis in his S stock. S Corp. owns two assets, Asset 1 with a $60 basis and $60 value and Asset 2 with a $90 basis and $150 value. Because S Corp. has a $100 liability, B's stock basis ($50) equals S Corp.'s net inside basis ($50, or its $150 aggregate asset basis minus its $100 liability). In a taxable year when S Corp. has no income or loss, it distributes Asset 1 to B. Under § 1368(b), B reduces his S stock basis by $50, from $50 to $0, and recognizes a $10 gain. After the distribution, B's stock basis ($0) differs from S Corp's net inside basis (-$10 or $90 asset basis minus $100 liability).

level items to the selling shareholder and (ii) may affect how that shareholder treats distributions. Because distributions and pass-thru of corporate-level tax items affect stock basis, a shareholder who sells stock of an S corporation cannot determine gain or loss on the sale until the close of the corporation's taxable year.

If a person disposes of shares in an S corporation, the disposition affects the allocation of the corporate-level items to the shareholder. As a general rule under § 1377(a)(1), a corporate-level item for a year is apportioned equally to each day of the year and then allocated pro rata among the shares outstanding on that day. For example, suppose individual A owns 50 of the 100 outstanding shares of S Corp., an S corporation using the calendar year as its taxable year. On June 30, A sells 25 of those shares to individual B. If the corporation has net taxable income for the year of $2,000, A must report $750 on her individual return: $500 for six months ownership of 50% of S Corp. and $250 for six months ownership of 25% of S Corp.[21]

Suppose that A had sold all 50 of her shares in S Corp. on June 30. Now, A reports only $500 of S Corp.'s income, equal to half of the income for half the year. Note that it does not matter *when* S Corp. earned the income. Under the ratable allocation method, A reports the same $500 whether S Corp. earned $1,000 in each half year or S Corp. lost $1,000 in the first six months and then earned $3,000 in the last six months. Because corporate tax items are ratably allocated to each day of the corporation's taxable year, it is irrelevant when during the year the corporation accrued or received any particular item.

A shareholder who sells her entire interest in an S corporation during the corporation's taxable year might prefer that her share of the corporation's tax items not be affected by post-sale corporate activities. If the corporation, the seller and all buyers agree, they may elect to treat the corporation's taxable year as ending on the date of sale as to those shareholders, with a new taxable year beginning on the following day.[22] If such an election is filed, the outgoing shareholder will be taxable on her share of corporate activities occurring only on or before the day she terminates her interest

---

[21] For ease of computation, June 30 is treated as the midpoint of the year.

[22] § 1377(a)(2) (adding that if the stock is transferred to the S corporation, the affected shareholders are "all persons who [were] shareholders during the taxable year"). Note that this election applies only to the seller and buyers and essentially creates a closing of the books. The election does not otherwise affect the S corporation or other S corporation shareholders. Thus, it does not affect when the S corporation must file its tax return or the taxable year when an affected shareholder takes the S corporation items into account. Regs. § 1.1377-1(b)(3)(ii) and (iii).

in the S corporation. Similarly, the incoming shareholder will be taxable on her share of corporate activities occurring after the sale.[23]

A disposition of some or all of a shareholder's stock in an S corporation also affects the taxation of distributions made to the selling shareholder before the sale of the stock. Recall that distributions of cash or property are tax-free to the distributee-shareholder to the extent that the amount of the distribution does not exceed the distributee-shareholder's stock basis. § 1368(b)(1). Recall also that this comparison is made by looking to the shareholder's stock basis as of the close of the corporation's taxable year, so that the shareholder's stock basis is also adjusted for pass-thru items of income and deduction.

If a shareholder sells some or all of her shares during the taxable year, § 1367(a) adjustments to the basis of the transferred shares for pass-thru items of income and deduction as well as the downward basis adjustments for all prior distributions are effective immediately before the stock transfer. Regs. § 1.1367-1(d)(1). For example, assume that individual A owns 40 of the 100 outstanding shares of S Corp., an S corporation using the calendar year as its taxable year. As of January 1, A's 40 shares have an adjusted basis of $10 per share. On June 30, A sells 15 of her 40 shares to individual C for $15 per share. During the entire calendar year, S Corp. earns $200.

To compute A's gain (or loss) on the sale of the 15 shares, we must know A's adjusted basis in those shares. We begin with A's adjusted basis of $10 per share as of the beginning of the calendar year. We then increase that adjusted basis for A's share of the corporation's income. Treating June 30 as the mid-point of the year,

---

[23] Regs. § 1.1368-1(g) offers a broader closing of the books election. Under that provision, an S corporation may elect to close its books if (i) a shareholder disposes of at least 20% of the corporation's outstanding stock over a 30-day period during the corporation's taxable year; (ii) the corporation redeems from a shareholder at least 20% of the corporation's outstanding stock over a 30-day period during the corporation's taxable year and § 302(a) or § 303 applies to the redemption (or redemptions); or (iii) the corporation issues an amount of stock equal to at least 25% of its previously outstanding stock to one or more new shareholders over a 30-day period during its taxable year. Regs. § 1.1368-1(g)(2) (labeling these events "qualifying dispositions"); *id.* at 1(g)(2)(iv) (providing that this election cannot be made if the election under § 1377(a)(2) may be made). This election applies to all of the S corporation's shareholders. If made, the pre- and post-disposition periods are treated as separate taxable years for purposes of allocating the S corporation's tax items, making adjustments to stock basis, and determining the tax treatment of distributions. *Id.* at (g)(2)(ii). *See also id.* at (g)(1) (providing that the first of the separate taxable years is deemed to end at the close of the day on which there is a qualifying disposition of stock).

$100 of the corporation's gain is allocated to the period from January 1 through June 30 and the remaining $100 is allocated to July 1 through December 31. Accordingly, each of the 100 outstanding shares is allocated $1 for the first half of the year, so that A's stock basis as of June 30 is increased to $11 per share. Thus, the sale of 15 shares for $15 per share yields a recognized gain of $4 per share, or $60 in total. In addition, A must report $65 of pass-thru income for the year ($40 for the first half plus $25 for the second half).

Assume in addition that A received a distribution of $80 sometime during the first half of the year. Now, we must adjust the basis of the transferred shares not only for the pass-thru income allocable to the pre-transfer period but also for the distribution. The tax effect of the $80 distribution is to reduce A's stock basis by $80 total, or $2 per share. Accordingly, A's adjusted basis in the shares as of the date of sale is now $9,[24] producing a recognized gain of $6 per share or $90 in total. Individual A still reports pass-thru income of $65 on her individual return.

To make this example even more complicated, assume that A uses a fiscal year ending August 31 as her taxable year. This wrinkle means that A must report her gain from the sale of the 15 shares in one taxable year and her share of the pass-thru income in the next taxable year. Further, A cannot compute her gain from the stock sale until the close of the corporation's taxable year (i.e., until sometime after December 31), which is after A's individual tax return is due! A must estimate her stock gain and pay her taxes based on that estimate. If (as is likely) her estimate is not perfect, she should file an amended return showing additional income or seeking a refund.

(b) Redemptions of Stock.

The characterization of redemptions (i.e., as sales or distributions) is governed by § 302 and § 303. If the redemption of a shareholder's stock is described in § 302(b) or § 303, the shareholder is treated as selling the redeemed stock for the redemption proceeds.[25] § 302(a). Thus, the shareholder recognizes gain or loss equal to the difference between the amount realized and her adjusted basis in the redeemed shares.

If the transaction does *not* fall within § 302(b) or § 303, the shareholder is taxed as if the redemption proceeds had been received in a simple distribution. Thus, as long as the shareholder's

---

[24] This $9 per share adjusted basis is computed as follows: initial basis of $10 plus pass-thru income of $1 less distribution of $2 equals $9.

[25] The application of § 302(b) and 303 is described in detail in Chapter 5 *supra*.

stock basis equals or exceeds the amount of the distribution, the shareholder recognizes no gain.[26] However, if the amount of the distribution exceeds the shareholder's stock basis, the shareholder recognizes gain equal to that excess. The shareholder reduces her stock basis (but not below zero) by the amount of the distribution. *See* § 1367(a)(2)(A). Note that any unused basis in the redeemed shares flows into the shareholder's remaining shares. Regs. § 1.302-2(c).

S corporation shareholders often have different stakes in a redemption than individual C corporation shareholders. An individual C corporation shareholder may prefer sale treatment, which allows basis recovery and may result in long-term capital gain taxed at preferential rates, instead of non-sale treatment, where the entire distribution may be taxed as a dividend. Cf. § 1(h)(11) (taxing qualified dividend income at the same rate as long-term capital gain). However, an S corporation shareholder may prefer non-sale treatment, because it may allow basis recovery without gain.[27]

For example, suppose individual B owns 40 of the 100 outstanding shares of X Corp., an S corporation. If X Corp. redeems 20 of B's shares for $100 per share when B has an adjusted basis of $80 per share, exchange treatment will cause B to recognize a gain of $20 per share or $400 in total (20 times $20). On the other hand, if the redemption is taxed as a distribution, the entire $2,000 distributed can be absorbed by B's stock basis of $3,200, so B will recognize no gain on the distribution. Of course, B's adjusted basis in his remaining 20 shares will be only $1,200 or $60 per share. In contrast, if the transaction had been taxed to B as an exchange, his adjusted basis in the remaining shares would be $1,600 or $80 per share. Thus, distribution treatment reduces the gain that B must recognize currently but at the cost of a corresponding reduction in stock basis.

The effect of a redemption on the redeeming corporation does not turn on application of § 302—that section governs only the shareholder's taxation. To the corporation, a distribution in redemption of stock is simply a distribution, so that the corporation recognizes any gain (but not loss) in the distributed property. § 311(a) and (b). Of course, any gain so recognized is passed thru to the shareholders, generally in proportion to their stock interests on a day-by-day basis.

---

[26] This determination apparently takes into account the basis of all of the redeemed shareholder's stock. Regs. § 1.1367-1(c)(3).

[27] Because of the dividends-received deduction available to corporate shareholders, see § 243, the stakes for a corporate shareholder of a C corporation in a redemption are in some ways like those of an S corporation shareholder.

(c) Liquidating Distributions.

When a corporation liquidates—that is, when it distributes all of its assets to its shareholders in exchange for all of its outstanding shares—the transaction technically is a distribution in redemption of stock. However, liquidating distributions are not taxed to the shareholders under § 302 or to the distributing corporation under § 311; rather, the special provisions of §§ 331, 334(a), and 336 apply.[28]

Consider first the corporation. Recall that non-liquidating distributions of appreciated property produce recognition of income to the distributing corporation as if the property had been sold to a third party. This taxation continues for liquidating distributions, but now loss generally can be recognized as well. § 336(a). However, corporate-level recognition loss is limited by the rules of § 336(d), discussed more fully in the context of C corporations.[29] As always, corporate-level recognition of gain or loss will be includible by the shareholders, § 1366, and will increase or decrease their stock basis, § 1367(a).

At the shareholder level, the transaction is treated as an exchange of the stock for the distributed assets. § 331(a). As a result, gain or loss (generally capital gain or loss) can be recognized on the transaction. Often, though, the basis adjustment rules of § 1367(a) will work so that each shareholder's stock basis precisely equals the value of assets received in the distribution. In any event, the shareholder takes a fair market value basis in the distributed assets. § 334(a).

(d) Acquisitive and Divisive Reorganizations.

S corporations may engage in acquisitive reorganizations as the acquiring or target corporation and may also engage in divisive reorganizations, distributing the stock of controlled corporations. See generally § 355; § 368. These transactions are described in Chapter 10 *supra*.

---

[28] These provisions are described in more detail in Section 8.02 *supra*.
[29] See Section 8.02(b) *supra*.

Chapter 14

S CORPORATIONS—SELECTED TOPICS

This chapter first examines the "one class of stock" requirement, in particular considering how shareholder agreements and debt affect that requirement. It next surveys rules relating to qualified subchapter S subsidiaries, discussing how they are treated, some consequences of their formation and termination, and their use in planning. The chapter then considers limitations on the use of an S corporation's allocable losses under § 1366(d), § 465, and § 469. Next, it explores how § 1366(e) addresses a possible assignment of income between family members. The chapter then describes how § 338(h)(10) applies to S corporation targets. It concludes by briefly reviewing how S corporations compute employment taxes for their shareholder-employees, a computation that may sometimes favor choosing an S corporation over a partnership.

14.01 One Class of Stock

Every system of pass-thru taxation needs a mechanism for allocating the entity's income and loss among its owners. For partnerships, that mechanism is § 704. Most partnership income can be allocated among the partners as they see fit, subject only to the "substantial economic effect" test of § 704(b). However, to address concerns with assignment of income, under § 704(c), the partnership must specially allocate gain or loss on contributed property if the property, when contributed, had a basis-value disparity. Much of the flexibility and complexity of Subchapter K can be traced to those two provisions.

Because an S corporation must have "one class of stock" (§ 1361(b)(1)(D)), its income and loss must be allocated in proportion to stock ownership. Thus, this "one class of stock" rule avoids the complexity of § 704(b)-(c) but lacks its flexibility.

An S corporation is treated as having one class of stock if "all outstanding shares of stock [of the corporation] confer identical rights to distribution and liquidation proceeds." Regs. § 1.1361-1(l)(1). In particular, different shares may have different voting rights without violating the one class of stock requirement. § 1361(c)(4).

(a) Shareholder Agreements.

Especially in closely held corporations, shareholders often sign agreements restricting their rights to transfer their stock. For example, an employee may be required to sell her stock to another shareholder or back to the corporation if she terminates her employment. Sale and redemption agreements triggered by death, bankruptcy and divorce also are common. If a shareholder signs such an agreement, do the restrictions transform the shareholder's stock into a second, impermissible class of stock?

In general, the answer is no. Under the regulations, "[t]he determination of whether all outstanding shares of stock confer identical rights to distribution and liquidation proceeds is made based on the corporate charter, ... applicable state law, and binding agreements relating to distribution and liquidation proceeds." Regs. § 1.1361-1(*l*)(2)(i). The regulations specify that these "governing instruments" do not include buy-sell agreements, agreements restricting the transferability of shares, and similar arrangements unless (1) a principal purpose of the agreement is to circumvent the one class of stock requirement and (2) the agreement establishes a purchase price that, at the time the agreement is entered into, is significantly in excess of or significantly below the fair market value of the stock. Regs. § 1.1361-1(*l*)(2)(iii)(A).[1] Further, bona fide agreements to redeem or purchase shares at death, divorce, disability or termination of employment are disregarded in determining whether a corporation's shares confer identical rights. Regs. § 1.1361-1(*l*)(2)(iii)(B).

The regulations offer several examples applying these rules. For example, suppose an S corporation enters into an agreement providing that distributions to its shareholders will be made in such proportions as to ensure that each shareholder will receive the same amount after taking into account state tax burdens. Thus, shareholders residing in a state that imposes no state income tax will receive $100 per share, while shareholders in state that imposes a state income tax, say at 6%, will receive $106.38 per share.[2]

In this example, the corporation will be treated as having *more than* one class of stock outstanding because a binding agreement relating to distribution proceeds is a "governing instrument" and this governing instrument alters distribution rights such that those

---

[1] These regulations also state that agreements that provide for the purchase or redemption of stock at book value or at a price between book value and fair market value will not be considered as establishing a price significantly in excess of or below the fair market value of the stock. *Id.*

[2] A 6% tax imposed on $106.38 equals $6.38, so that the after-tax amount equals $100.00.

rights are not identical among all outstanding shares. An opposite result would be reached if the corporation declared equal distributions but then withheld differing amounts in accordance with differing state withholding laws: In this latter circumstance, the amounts withheld would constitute constructive distributions so that the total distribution (including any constructive amount) would be equal for all shareholders. Compare examples (6) and (7) of Regs. § 1.1361-1(*l*)(2)(v).

As a second example, suppose an S corporation distributes 50% of its taxable income within 3 months of the close of its taxable year, and suppose further that this distribution must be made in the same proportion as the corporation's taxable income is reported. If individual A owned all 100 outstanding shares of the corporation at the beginning of the corporation's taxable year and sold 50 of those shares half way through the year to individual B, the distribution would be made 75% to A and 25% to B.

Does this arrangement create a second class of stock? Note that the corporate distribution is *not* made in proportion to stock ownership *as of the date of the distribution*. Although one might think that the outstanding shares do not have identical rights with respect to distributions and therefore constitute more than a single class of stock, the regulations specifically permit distributions to be made in proportion to varying stock ownership during the year. Regs. § 1.1361-1(*l*)(2)(iv) (noting that if the distributions are not made "within a reasonable time after the close of the taxable year," the distributions may be recharacterized but will not create a second class of stock).

(b) Corporate debt as a second class of stock. A shareholder investment in the form of debt often offers tax advantages over investment in the form of equity. For example, periodic returns on debt (*i.e.*, interest) are deductible by the corporation while periodic returns on equity (*i.e.*, dividends) are not. Similarly, payments in retirement of corporate debt qualify for exchange treatment (*i.e.*, recovery of basis followed by capital gain) while payments in retirement of corporate equity must pass the hurdles of § 302(b) to garner exchange treatment.

Ever vigilant in protecting the federal fisc, the Commissioner often asserts that shareholder debt should be reclassified (and taxed) as equity. For an S corporation and its shareholders, the usual advantages of debt over equity disappear, because the corporation generally does not pay tax. Nonetheless, the Commissioner might seek to reclassify nominal debt as equity to challenge the very validity of the corporation's Subchapter S election: Critically, if nominal debt is reclassified as equity, it could be treated as a second class of stock which then terminates the S corporation election.

Importantly, the regulations provide that a corporate instrument not nominally classified as equity (*i.e.*, debt, call options, and other financial instruments) will not violate the one class of stock requirement unless (i) the instrument is reclassified as equity under general principles of tax law, and (ii) a principal purpose of issuing the instrument is to circumvent the rights to distribution or liquidation conferred on the corporation's outstanding shares by the governing instruments or to circumvent the limitation on eligible shareholders.[3] Further, debt instruments owned only by the corporation's shareholders and in proportion to their stock holdings (and for that reason more likely to be reclassified as equity) are not treated as a second class of stock under these regulations.[4] As a corollary, no debt held by the sole owner of an S corporation can violate the one class of stock rule.[5]

Even corporate debt failing these standards can still avoid being classified as a second class of stock if it is a written unconditional promise to pay a sum certain on demand or on a specific due date and if (i) the interest due and interest payment dates on the debt are not contingent on the corporation's profits, the payment of dividends, the borrower's discretion, or similar factors; (ii) the debt is not convertible into corporate equity; and (iii) the debt is held only by an individual (other than a nonresident alien) or a trust or estate allowed to be a shareholder of an S corporation under § 1361(c)(2).[6] This safe harbor for "straight debt" is available even to debt subordinated to other debt of the corporation. Regs. § 1.1361-1(*l*)(5)(ii).[7] This safe harbor is also available for indebtedness held by "a person which is actively and regularly engaged in the business of lending money;" that is, "straight debt"

---

[3] Regs. § 1.1361-1(*l*)(4)(ii)(A).

[4] Note that in this case, a shareholder's allocable share of the S corporation's interest expense on the debt is matched by offsetting interest income on the debt.

[5] *Id.* at (*l*)(4)(ii)(B)(*2*). *See also id.* at (*l*)(4)(ii)(B)(*1*) (treating as debt unwritten advances from shareholders that do not exceed $10,000 in the aggregate at any time during the corporation's taxable year if they (i) are treated as debt by the parties and (ii) are expected to be repaid within a reasonable time). See also *id.* at (*l*)(4)(iii)(A) (for rules relating to a call option, warrant, or similar instrument).

[6] § 1361(c)(5); Regs. § 1.1361-1(*l*)(5)(i).

[7] This safe harbor no longer applies if the debt is materially modified so that it no longer satisfies the safe harbor or it is transferred to an ineligible person. *See id.* at (*l*)(5)(3). *See also id.* at (*l*)(5)(iv) (generally treating an instrument that meets the safe harbor as debt for federal income tax purposes).

can be held by financial institutions even though financial institutions are not eligible shareholders of an S corporation.[8]

14.02 Qualified Subchapter S Subsidiaries

A subsidiary of an S corporation may be treated for income tax purposes like a division of its S corporation parent if (i) the parent holds all of the subsidiary's stock; (ii) the subsidiary is a domestic corporation; (iii) the subsidiary is not an ineligible corporation (*i.e.*, not an insurance company, financial institution that uses the reserve method of accounting for bad debts, § 936 corporation, DISC, or former DISC); and (iv) the parent makes an appropriate election.[9] A subsidiary that meets these requirements is called a "qualified subchapter S subsidiary" or "QSub." Because a QSub is not treated as a corporation separate from its parent, its assets, liabilities, and tax items are treated as assets, liabilities, and tax items of its parent. § 1361(b)(3)(A). *See also* Regs. § 1.1361-4(a). For this reason, a QSub is sometimes called a "disregarded entity" or "tax nothing."

Note the difference in the stock ownership of an S corporation and a Q–Sub: while the shareholders of an S corporation generally must consist exclusively of individuals, the only permissible shareholder of a Q–Sub is an S Corporation. However, if the actual shareholder of a Q–Sub is a disregarded entity, we look through that entity to its parent for tax purposes. Thus, S Corp., an S corporation, can own 100% of the outstanding shares each of Daughter Corp. and Son Corp., two Q–Subs, and then Daughter and Son can each own one-half of the outstanding shares of GrandChild Corp., yet another Q–Sub. In this way, Q–Subs can be used to form complex corporate structures.

QSubs offer a liability shield to S corporations and their shareholders without imposing a second level of tax. For example, suppose that an S corporation has an active but risky business as well as substantial investment assets. If the business and investment assets are held by a single corporation, the investment assets are exposed to creditors of the risky business. If, instead, the risky business is placed in a QSub, the QSub may shield the investment assets from that liability exposure.[10] However, the S Corporation

---

[8] See § 1361(c)(5)(B)(iii).

[9] § 1361(b)(3)(B). Note, however, that a QSub is not disregarded to determine its tax liability (or tax refunds) for any periods when it was treated as a separate corporation. Regs. § 1.1361-4(a)(6). It is also treated as a separate corporation for purposes of employment taxes and certain excise taxes. *Id.* at (a)(7) and (8).

[10] Placing the *investment assets* in the QSub would not eliminate that exposure, because the QSub stock, as an asset of the S corporation parent, could be used satisfy creditors' claims arising out of the risky business.

parent is treated as holding the assets of the risky business for federal income tax purposes. As this example demonstrates, the QSub's dual nature—transparent for income tax purposes but respected for state law purposes—provides a fertile field for planning.[11]

(a) Election.

The S corporation parent may make a QSub election for an eligible subsidiary at any time during the taxable year. Regs. § 1.1361-3(a)(3). The election may be effective no more than 2½ months before, or 12 months after, the date of filing. *Id.* at (a)(4). If no effective date is specified on the election form, the election is effective on the date the form is filed. *Id.* Thus, an S corporation may acquire a C corporation in the middle of the year, and if the C corporation is otherwise eligible, elect to treat it as a QSub immediately. *Id.* at (a)(5) (example). Of course, if the S corporation is formed solely for this purpose, the Commissioner might challenge the transaction under § 269 or the general business purpose doctrine. See Regs. § 1.1361–4(a)(2).

(b) Effect of the Election.

If an S corporation makes a valid QSub election for a subsidiary, the subsidiary is deemed to liquidate into the S corporation.[12] However, "[t]he tax treatment of the liquidation or of a larger transaction that includes the liquidation will be determined under the Internal Revenue Code and general principles of tax law, including the step-transaction doctrine."[13]

For example, if an S corporation forms a subsidiary and makes a valid QSub election for the subsidiary effective on the date of formation, the transfer of assets to the subsidiary and its deemed liq-

---

[11] An S corporation could hold its assets through disregarded entities other than QSubs. For example, it could form a wholly owned limited liability company ("LLC") that would be disregarded as entity separate from the S corporation, absent an election to treat it as a corporation for federal income tax purposes. *See* Regs. § 301.7701-3(b)(1)(ii). There may be non-tax advantages, however, to holding assets through a corporation, rather than an LLC, and therefore choosing to use a corporate subsidiary that qualifies as QSub.

[12] Regs. § 1.1361-4(a)(2)(i).

[13] *Id. See also id.* at (a)(2)(iii) (providing that the making of the QSub election may be deemed the adoption of the plan of liquidation); *id.* at (a)(2)(v) (determining stock ownership by disregarding options, debt instruments, and other arrangements that are not considered stock for purposes of § 1361). *Cf. id.* at (a)(5) (for some transition relief).

uidation are disregarded.[14] Instead, the subsidiary is deemed to be a QSub from its inception.[15]

As another example, suppose that an S corporation acquires all stock of a solvent C corporation in a qualified stock purchase, does not make a § 338 election for the purchase, but, as of the date of the purchase, elects to treat the target as a QSub. The stock purchase and deemed liquidation are treated as separate steps for tax purposes. Regs. § 1.1361-4(a)(2)(ii) (example 1) (illustrating a case where the acquiring corporation is a C corporation that elects to be an S corporation as of the purchase date); see also Rev. Rul. 90-95, 1990-2 C.B. 67. The target C corporation is treated as distributing all of its assets to its S corporation parent in a liquidating distribution to which § 332 and § 337 generally should apply.[16]

Suppose, finally, that the target is a solvent S corporation, instead of a C corporation, the S corporation acquiror does not make a § 338 election for the purchase and, as of the date of the purchase, elects to treat the target as a QSub. The stock purchase and deemed liquidation still should be treated as separate steps for tax purposes, and the target corporation still should be treated as distributing all of its assets to its S corporation parent in a liquidating distribution to which § 332 and § 337 generally should apply. Importantly, however, because the target's liquidation is deemed to occur at the beginning of the acquisition date immediately following the termination of the target's S election, there is no time during which the target is deemed to be a C corporation.[17]

If, however, a § 338 election is made for the target, the target (as a new corporation) is deemed to acquire its assets on the day after the acquisition date and the liquidation triggered by the QSub election is deemed to follow immediately after the deemed pur-

---

[14] *Id.* at (a)(2)(i)

[15] Thus, there is no moment in time when the newly formed subsidiary is treated as a C corporation and the formation and deemed liquidation of the subsidiary will not cause § 1374 to apply. Section 1374 is discussed in the next Chapter.

[16] *Id. See also id.* at (a)(2)(ii) (example 2) (illustrating that if an S corporation acquires the stock of a target for its voting stock and makes a QSub election for the target, the transaction may be treated in substance as a C reorganization); *id.* at (a)(2)(ii) (example 3) (illustrating that if an individual contributes stock of a wholly owned corporation to her wholly owned S corporation and the S corporation makes a QSub election for the subsidiary effective immediately upon the contribution, the contribution and deemed liquidation may be treated in substance as a D reorganization).

[17] Because § 332 and § 337 apply to the deemed liquidation, the acquiring S corporation succeeds to the target's historic bases and other tax attributes. *See* § 381. Further, because there is no moment in time when the target is treated as a C corporation because of the acquisition, § 1374 should not apply because of the acquisition and deemed liquidation.

chase.[18] Thus, at least for a moment in time, the new target appears to be treated as a C corporation subsidiary of the acquiring S corporation, a treatment that may have unpleasant (and perhaps unintended) consequences under § 1374 following the deemed liquidation, particularly if the stock purchase was a bargain purchase.

Note that if QSub elections for tiered subsidiaries are effective on the same date, the S corporation may specify the order of their liquidations.[19] If no order is specified, the liquidations are deemed to occur from the bottom up.[20]

(c) Revocation and Termination.

An S corporation parent may revoke a QSub election for its subsidiary at any time. Regs. § 1.1361-3(b)(1). The revocation can be effective up to 2½ months before, or 12 months after, the revocation is filed. *Id.* at (b)(2). This retroactive revocation has no counterpart for the S corporation parent.

A QSub election is also terminated if the corporation ceases to be an eligible entity, its parent ceases to own all of its stock, or its parent ceases to be an S corporation. § 1361(b)(3)(C); Regs. § 1.1361-5(a). There is a parallel rule for the S corporation parent. § 1362(d)(2) (for similar circumstances where a corporation's S corporation status terminates). Indeed, if the parent ceases to be an S corporation, the subsidiary will immediately loses its status as a QSub. See § 1361(b)(3)(B)(i). Perhaps more importantly, the subsidiary will lose its status as a QSub if a single share of its stock is transferred by the parent to any person or entity, including a transfer of less than all of the QSub stock to another S corporation.[21]

---

[18] Regs. § 1.1361-4(b)(4); *id.* at (d), (example 3) (illustrating this case).

[19] Regs. § 1.1361-4(b)(2).

[20] *Id.* With the default order, it is more likely that there will be only one § 1374 pool for the tiered subsidiaries. Further, if the acquired subsidiaries formed a consolidated group immediately before the acquisition, it is more likely that no excess loss accounts will be triggered. *See* Regs. § 1.1502-19(b)(2)(1).

[21] *Id.* Following the termination of a QSub election, by revocation or otherwise, a new QSub or S election generally cannot be made, broadly speaking, for five years, unless the Service waives this five-year requirement. § 1361(b)(3)(D) (more precisely prohibiting an election before the fifth taxable year that begins after the first taxable year for which the termination was effective). See also Regs. § 1.1361-3(b)(4) (not imposing this five-year requirement if a revocation is effective on the first day that the QSub election was to be effective)

As an exception, following the termination of a QSub election, an S or QSub election may be made for the corporation without the Service's consent if (i) immediately following the termination, but for the five-year rule, the relevant election can be made for the corporation (or its successor); and (ii) the relevant election is made immediately following the termination of

When a QSub election terminates, the former QSub generally is treated as a new corporation that acquires its assets from the S corporation parent in exchange for its stock and the assumption of its liabilities. § 1361(b)(3)(C). Regs. § 1.1361-5(b)(1)(i). However, the tax treatment of this exchange (or any larger transaction that includes the exchange) is determined under the Code and general principles of tax law. *Id.* The following examples illustrate those points. In each example, assume that X, an S corporation, owns all stock of Y, a QSub and that Y has only one class of stock outstanding.

First, assume that Z, unrelated to X, transfers property to Y in exchange for 21 percent of the Y stock. Because Z acquires Y stock, Y ceases to be a QSub. Consequently, Y is treated as a new corporation, acquiring its assets in exchange for its stock. Because X and Z are co-transferors, transfer property to Y in deemed or actual exchange for Y stock, and control Y immediately after the exchange, § 351 applies to their exchanges. *Id.* at (b)(3) (example 3).

Changing the facts slightly, assume that X sells 21 percent of the Y stock to Z. Because of the sale, Y ceases to be a QSub and is treated as a new corporation, acquiring all of its assets in exchange for its stock. X is treated as selling an undivided 21-percent interest in each of the Y assets to Z, recognizing gain or loss. X and Z are then deemed to contribute the Y assets to a new corporation in a § 351 exchange.[22]

Suppose instead that X merges into Y. Y's QSub election terminates, but the merger is treated as an F reorganization. Regs. § 1.1361-5(b)(3) (example 8).

---

the QSub election. Regs. § 1.1361-5(c)(2). *Id.* at (c)(3) (example 1) (following the distribution of a all QSub stock, allowing an S election without consent effective on the distribution date); *id.* at (c)(3) (example 2) (following the sale of all QSub stock from one S corporation to an unrelated S corporation, allowing a QSub election without consent effective on the date of purchase).

[22] § 1361(b)(3)(C)(ii) (providing for this result). Note that an example in the regulations has a contrary conclusion, but was published before § 1361(b)(3)(C)(ii) was enacted. *See* Regs. § 1.1361-5(b)(3) (example 1).

As another example, suppose that X also owns all interests in L, a limited liability company that is disregarded as entity separate from X. Y merges into L. Although Y's QSub election terminates because of the merger, under step-transaction principles, the deemed transfer of Y's assets to a new corporation and the corporation's immediate deemed liquidation are disregarded, and X is simply treated as retaining Y's assets. *Id.* at (b)(3) (example 2). If X then sells Z a 21% interest in L, it is deemed to sell an undivided 21% interest in L's assets and X and Z are deemed to contribute L's asset to a partnership in exchange for partnership interests. *Id.*

Finally, assume that X sells all of the Y stock to Z, a C corporation. X is treated as selling the Y assets to Z, and Z is treated as transferring those assets to Y in exchange for the Y stock. *Id.* at (b)(3) (example 9). Cf. Rev. Rul. 70-140, 1970-1 C.B. 73 (adopting a recharacterization of this sort for a similar transaction). The result would be the same if Z was an S corporation, unless Z elected to treat Y as a QSub immediately after the purchase. If Z made that election, the deemed formation and liquidation of Y would be disregarded and Z would be treated simply as acquiring the Y assets. See Regs. § 1.1361-5(b)(3) (example 9); Rev. Rul. 2004-85, 2004-2 C.B. 189.

(d) Avoiding Risk.

A QSub has many of the non-tax, business advantages of other disregarded entities.[23] Its principal advantage is that it offers liability protection at no potential additional tax cost. Suppose that Old Corp., an S Corporation, runs two businesses, a risky business and a secure business. The Old Corp. shareholders want to insulate the assets of the secure business from the liabilities of the risky business. However, because of loan restrictions, the assets of risky business cannot be transferred until the loans are fully repaid. How can the Old Corp. shareholders achieve their goal?

If Old Corp. simply transfers the assets of the secure business to a QSub, the transfer will not achieve the intended purpose, since the assets of secure business will still be at risk (indirectly through the QSub stock). That purpose could be achieved if Old Corp. transferred the assets of the risky business to a QSub, but loan restrictions block that transfer.

Consider, however, the following three-step transaction: First, the shareholders of Old Corp. form a new S corporation (New Corp.) and transfer their Old Corp. stock to New Corp., so that Old Corp. becomes New Corp.'s wholly owned subsidiary. Second, New Corp. makes a QSub election for Old Corp. that is effective upon the transfer. Third, Old Corp. distributes the assets of the secure business to New Corp. in a state-law dividend. Both the stock transfer and asset distribution should avoid federal income tax. Because of the QSub election, the stock transfer should be characterized as a

---

[23] A QSub, as a corporation, also offers some potential tax advantages. *See* Regs. § 1.1361-5(b)(3) (example 4) (illustrating that a distribution of all QSub stock may be a non-taxable § 355 distribution, rather than a taxable distribution of assets); *id.* at (d)(3) (example 8) (illustrating that the merger of the parent S corporation into its QSub may be treated as an F reorganization). Note that an S corporation parent may effectively "convert" a QSub into another type of disregarded entity by forming the entity and merging the QSub into it. *Id.* at (d)(3) (example 2) (illustrating that such a merger is disregarded for federal tax purposes).

non-taxable F reorganization. See *id.* at (d)(3) (example 8). The asset distribution is a non-transaction for federal income tax purposes, because Old Corp.'s assets are treated as owned by New Corp. Overall, therefore, these steps help to protect the assets of secure business from the risks associated with risky business at little or no tax cost.

14.03 Loss Limitations—§ 1366(d)

If an S corporation allocates losses to a shareholder, the amount of those losses that the shareholder can take into account is limited to the shareholder's basis in the corporation.[24] Any loss limited by § 1366(d) is suspended and treated as incurred by the S corporation in the succeeding year with respect to that shareholder.[25] Although pass thru of an S corporation loss is limited to a shareholder's outside basis, the shareholder may use both her equity and debt basis in her corporate investment to absorb those losses. To better understand this loss limitation rule, we must first look closely at the basis consequences of a loan.

Suppose Debtor borrows $100 from Lender. To Lender, the loan is an asset. As with any asset, we can sensibly ask what the owner's basis in the asset is. Basis, of course, is the amount of cash the asset holder can receive in exchange for the asset without recognizing gain. See § 1001(a). Here, Lender can receive the $100 principal amount of the debt back from Debtor without recognizing gain. Accordingly, Lender's basis in the debt must be $100. Indeed, if Lender receives less than $100 back from Debtor, Lender will be entitled

---

[24] § 1366(d). If the limitation applies, a proportionate amount of each allocated loss for the year is limited. Regs. § 1.1366-2(a)(4). Note that a reference in Section 14.03 to a "loss" includes a reference to a deduction.

[25] § 1366(d)(2); Regs. § 1.1366- 2(a)(2) (also providing that the loss retains its character). If a shareholder dies or transfers all of her S corporation stock, the shareholder's suspended loss, if any, generally disappears. *Id.* at (a)(5)(i).; *id.* at (a)(5)(ii) (providing for an allocation of the suspended loss between the transferor and transferee following a transfer described in § 1041(a) (*i.e.*, certain transfers between spouses or former spouses)). If, however, the shareholder transfers some, but not all, of her stock, the entire suspended loss generally remains with the shareholder. *Id.* at (a)(5)(i). Further, if the S corporation is a target in an acquisitive § 368 reorganization with an S corporation acquiror and the shareholder owns stock in the acquiror, the loss will be treated as incurred by the acquiror with respect to the shareholder's acquiror stock. Regs. § 1.1366-2(c)(1) (adding a rule that applies to the post-termination transition period if the acquiror is a C corporation). Finally, if the S corporation engages in a divisive § 368(a)(1)(D) reorganization (or § 355 distribution), the shareholder's suspended loss is allocated between the distributing and controlled corporations. See *id.* at 2(c)(2) (making the allocation using any "reasonable" method, including one based on the relative fair market values of the stock of the distributing and controlled corporations, one based on the aggregate asset bases of those corporations, or one attributing loss to the corporation to which it is "clearly attributable").

to claim a deduction for a bad debt, see § 166(a)(2), a result fully consistent with ascribing a $100 basis to Lender's debt.

When Debtor uses the borrowed proceeds to purchase property, Debtor will take a cost basis in the property acquired. Thus, the effect of the loan is to give $100 of basis to both Lender and to Debtor; for Lender, basis is in the right to repayment; for Debtor, basis is in the borrowed proceeds or in property acquired with those proceeds. A borrowing transaction thus produces a doubling of total basis.[26]

To determine the extent to which pass-thru losses may be claimed on an S corporation shareholder's individual return, the shareholder may use both her equity and debt basis to absorb such losses. Equity basis is just stock basis.[27] Debt basis is shareholder's basis, if any, in loans she has made to the S corporation. That is, debt basis refers to basis enjoyed by the shareholder not in her capacity as shareholder but rather in her capacity as lender. Of course, if the shareholder has made no loans to the corporation, debt basis is zero.[28]

Losses allocated to a shareholder first reduce equity basis before reducing debt basis. § 1366(b)(2)(A). Because of the basis reduction for debt, an S corporation shareholder may recognize gain on the sale of that debt to a third party even if the third party pays less than face value for the debt. That is, the rule of § 1366(d) does not create additional basis for the lender-shareholder but only permits the lender-shareholder to shift basis from the note to the shareholder's equity interest in the venture.

Note that debt basis is available only for absorbing pass-thru loss and not for absorbing distributions. An S corporation shareholder who receives a distribution of cash or property in excess of stock basis must report the excess as gain, and in this context only true stock basis is counted. Debt basis is simply irrelevant in computing a shareholder's gain from a distribution.

---

[26] More accurately, no doubling of basis occurs because Debtor has a negative basis in the debt itself. That is, Debtor will have to repay the principal amount of the debt without receiving a deduction for the expenditure. Debtor sometimes is said to have a $100 "sisab" (backward basis) in the repayment obligation to make clear that Debtor's tax relationship to the loan transaction is the inverse of Lender's relationship. For the remainder of this discussion, we will ignore Debtor's inverse basis (sisab) in the loan.

[27] The shareholder determines her stock basis for this purpose by taking into account any basis adjustments under § 1367(a) other than for losses and deductions described in § 1367(a)(2)(B) and (C). Regs. § 1.1366-2(a)(3)(i).

[28] The treatment of S shareholders is in clear contrast to the treatment of partners. A partner is allocated a share of all partnership debt, whether or not the partner is the creditor on that debt. *See* § 752.

Income allocated to an S corporation shareholder increases the shareholder's outside basis. § 1367(a)(1). How is this income allocated if the shareholder has both debt and stock basis? Subchapter S provides a simple ordering rule: If pass-thru losses have reduced a shareholder's debt basis, subsequent pass-thru income first increases debt basis to the extent of the reduction, and the balance, if any, is allocated to stock basis. § 1367(b)(2)(B).

For example, suppose individual A forms S Corp., an S corporation, by contributing $10,000 in exchange for 100 shares of S Corp. stock. In addition, A loans $40,000 to S Corp., and assume that the loan is respected for tax purposes (i.e., the loan is not treated as equity). If the corporation distributes $15,000 to A, A must report $5,000 of gain because the amount of the distribution exceeds A's stock basis by that amount. § 1368(b). A reduces her stock basis to zero. § 1367(a)(2).

Suppose that the corporation invests its remaining cash of $35,000 in some activity, and suppose further that this activity produces a loss of $5,000 the following year. Although A's stock basis is zero, the $5,000 loss may pass-thru to A because it can be absorbed by A's debt basis. That is, A reports the $5,000 loss on her individual return and reduces her debt basis by $5,000, from $40,000 to $35,000.

If the corporation recognizes $8,000 of income the following year, that income will pass-thru to A and will increase outside basis. Because debt basis is restored before equity basis, the first $5,000 of pass-thru income restores A's debt basis to $40,000. § 1367(b)(2)(B). The balance, or $3,000, increases A's stock basis from zero to $3,000. Any future pass-thru of income will increase A's stock basis only (unless A's debt basis subsequently is reduced): Debt basis is not increased under § 1367(b)(2)(B) above its original amount.

As this example makes clear, debt basis is important despite the absence of a provision like § 752. Shareholders, then, will fight for debt or equity basis, even in circumstances when it is less than clear that the statute authorizes it.

Equity or debt basis can be increased by contributing additional amounts to the corporation. Amounts that are contributed to capital, exchanged for additional stock or loaned to the corporation will increase a shareholder's basis in the stock or, in the case of a loan, the basis in corporate debt. There may be a risk though in contributing money to a corporation experiencing losses in order to pass-thru the losses. It may not be wise to contribute $50,000 in order to pass-through $50,000 of losses (which will save less than $50,000 in actual taxes) if the shareholder stands to lose the investment because the corporation performs poorly.

Instead of buying additional stock for cash, suppose that a shareholder exchanges her $50,000 note for the stock as part of a § 351 exchange. Does the shareholder take a $50,000 basis in the stock, which would permit the shareholder an additional $50,000 of pass-thru loss, or is the basis $0? Some courts have upheld[29] the Service's position that the shareholder's basis in the stock does not reflect the note.[30] This position seems directly contrary to the Supreme Court's decision in *Crane* that the cost of property includes borrowed proceeds.[31] When a taxpayer acquires real estate with a purchase money mortgage, the fair market value of the note given to the seller is included in basis.[32] Why should the purchase of stock be treated any differently?[33]

While the Tax Court has upheld the Service's "$0 basis" position when a shareholder contributes his own note to the corporation, two Courts of Appeal have disagreed.[34] Although differing in their reasoning, each court concluded that a shareholder should be given basis for the fair market value of the shareholder's own note contributed to the corporation, at least when the note bears fair interest and the note represents a bona fide indebtedness of the contributing shareholder. However, one court made clear that its conclusion did not extend to the contribution of a shareholder's note to an S corporation,[35] a peculiar reservation given that the same provisions—§§ 351, 357, and 358—apply in the C and S contexts.

Suppose that instead of lending money directly to the corporation, a shareholder guarantees a $50,000 loan obtained by the corporation. Can the shareholder claim a debt basis of $50,000, basis which can then be used to absorb the S corporation's losses? It is often the case that lenders will insist that shareholders co-sign notes on loans made to closely held corporations. Allowing each shareholder to claim a debt basis for the full amount of the loan or even a pro rata portion of the loan might allow shareholders loss deductions for amounts they might never have to lose if the lender looks to the principal-corporation for payment or if the guarantor-

---

[29] See *Alderman v. Commissioner*, 55 T.C. 662 (1971).

[30] See Rev. Rul. 81–187, 1981–2 C.B. 167.

[31] *Crane v. Commissioner*, 331 U.S. 1 (1947).

[32] See, e.g., *Mayerson v. Commissioner*, 47 T.C. 340 (1966).

[33] For a discussion of the Service's possible concern, see Chapter 2.04 *supra*.

[34] *Peracchi v. Commissioner*, 143 F.3d 487 (9th Cir.1998); *Lessinger v. Commissioner*, 872 F.2d 519 (2d Cir.1989).

[35] *Peracchi*, 143 F.3d at 494 n.16.

shareholder has a right of indemnification against the principal-corporation. On the other hand, if the shareholder is in substance the principal or a principal debtor, then it might be appropriate to claim a debt basis as if the lender had loaned the money to the shareholder who re-loaned it to the S corporation.

Typically, courts will use a two-step process to resolve these surety/principal debtor situations.[36] First, under applicable state law, a court will determine if the shareholder is a principal debtor. To the extent the debtor has a right of indemnification, it is not a principal. If the shareholder is a principal debtor, then the shareholder can claim a basis in the debt for purposes of absorbing losses incurred by the S corporation. If the shareholder is determined not to be a principal on the note, then the second step of the process gives the shareholder a debt basis only to the extent a shareholder actually makes payments on the note.

However, some courts have focused more on the economic reality surrounding the loan. If in fact the lender looks to the shareholder as the principal and the borrowing S corporation is thinly capitalized, perhaps the principal's right of indemnification against the corporation is virtually worthless.[37] In such a case, perhaps it is appropriate to allow the shareholder a basis in the debt which can be used to offset S corporation losses.[38] Or should the shareholder be bound by the legal ramifications of signing the note as a guarantor rather than a principal?

In *Estate of Leavitt v. Commissioner,*[39] a bank made a loan to an S corporation that was guaranteed by the shareholders. At the time of the loan, the corporation's liabilities exceeded its assets and the corporation was unable to meet its cash flow requirements. The loan was issued by the bank only because of the financial strength of the shareholders. When the S corporation experienced further losses, each shareholder sought to deduct his proportionate share of the loss to the extent of his basis in the stock and debt of the corporation, increased by the amount of the loan.[40] The shareholders ar-

---

[36] See, e.g., *Harrington v. United States,* 605 F.Supp. 53 (D.Del.1985).

[37] Similarly, if a corporation is wholly owned, should the sole shareholder's right of indemnification deprive her of a basis in the debtor? Or is it a meaningless right since the shareholder will bear the burden of repayment by decreasing the worth of her corporation? Perhaps the indemnification right does have significance where it might allow the shareholder to recover corporate assets that might otherwise be used to satisfy the claims of others against the corporation.

[38] See, e.g., *Selfe v. United States,* 778 F.2d 769 (11th Cir.1985).

[39] 875 F.2d 420 (4th Cir.1989).

[40] It is not clear whether each shareholder increased basis by the full amount of the loan because the guarantees were unlimited or by a pro rata portion of amount loaned.

gued that they should be viewed as borrowing the money and advancing it to the corporation (either as a debt or stock investment). The court rejected the shareholders' position, emphasizing the shareholders' inconsistent behavior in claiming to be the principal debtor but at the same time not reporting interest and principal payments made by the corporation as constructive distributions.[41]

There is much to the argument that a guarantor should receive debt basis as if the bank made a loan to the shareholder followed by a loan to the S corporation. Ultimately, a guarantor is "on the line" for payment to the lender if the corporation fails to pay. That is, the test used to justify a debt basis when a shareholder makes an actual loan to the corporation could be: if the corporation defaults, will the shareholder bear the risk of loss. Should the result be different where the shareholder has made the same promise to a bank but has not advanced the proceeds? Under *Crane v. Commissioner,*[42] the Supreme Court established that basis consequences are the same to a taxpayer whether property is acquired with borrowed funds or through an actual cash outlay. Arguably, it should be irrelevant that the S corporation shareholder has not made an immediate economic outlay. Whether the corporation is thinly capitalized should also be irrelevant. The central question is who bears the economic risk in the event of the corporation's default. To the extent a shareholder bears the risk of loss (*i.e.*, the bank will look to the shareholder-guarantor), a shareholder should have a basis that will allow the shareholder to claim a pro rata portion of the S corporation's loss deductions.[43]

On the other hand, when a shareholder actually makes a loan to an S corporation, there is an asset—the corporation's note—that has basis in the hands of a shareholder. When a shareholder is just a guarantor, there is no note to which basis can attach. Further, the shareholder-guarantor may never be called on to pay off the debt. Accordingly, in the absence of a major revision of subchapter S, it may be appropriate to deny a guarantor a basis for purposes of using loss deductions unless she makes an actual payment on the note. And in any event that is where the law now is.[44]

---

[41] *Old Colony Trust Co. v. Commissioner,* 279 U.S. 716 (1929). The court assumed that a constructive distribution would be taxable to the shareholders. However, a shareholder of an S corporation receiving a constructive dividend would reduce stock basis before reporting any income. § 1368.

[42] 331 U.S. 1 (1947).

[43] To the extent a shareholder reduces her debt basis in taking corporate-level loss deductions, the shareholder should recognize income when the corporation pays off the loan.

[44] See also Prop. Reg. § 1.1366-2(a)(2)(ii) (effectively confirming that result). Of course, a shareholder-guarantor has a simple way to avoid this

14.04 Loss Limitations—the At-Risk and Passive Loss Rules

Concerned that taxpayers sometimes generate "artificial" deductions, Congress has enacted an arsenal of provisions to impose "better" accounting for tax purposes. Two of the more important provisions are the at-risk rules and the passive loss rules, both of which apply to taxpayers in their capacity as S shareholders.

Shareholders of an S corporation are subject to the at-risk rules of § 465 which limit losses from specified activities passed thru from the corporation to the amount that a shareholder has at risk in the activity. A shareholder's amount at risk equals the amount of personal funds plus the adjusted basis of unencumbered property committed to the enterprise.[45] If a shareholder borrows funds and provides them for use by the corporation in an activity, the shareholder is at risk only to the extent the shareholder is personally liable for repayment. If a shareholder contributes encumbered property to the S corporation, the shareholder is considered at risk for an amount equal to the basis of the asset minus any encumbrance for which the shareholder is not personally liable.[46] If the S corporation borrows money for an activity, the shareholders cannot increase their personal at-risk amount unless they are personally liable without any right of indemnification.

In addition, in an effort to discourage tax-motivated investments, Congress has attempted to limit losses from passive business activities to offsetting income from those activities, not income from active businesses or portfolio income (e.g., interest, dividends). This layer of loss limitations applies after other limitations specified in the Code (including the at-risk rules).

For example, suppose S Corp. is engaged in a publishing business, but shareholder B does not "materially participate" in the business.[47] B has a $7,000 stock basis and a $5,000 debt basis. In year 1, S Corp. suffers a $10,000 loss. Under the subchapter S provisions, B can offset other income with the loss to the extent of B's investment in the corporation—her stock and debt bases. Accordingly, B would reduce the stock basis from $7,000 to $0 and the basis in the debt from $5,000 to $2,000. Having jumped the loss-limitation

---

issue. If the creditor, in substance, will look to a shareholder to pay off the debt, it may make sense to just make the shareholder the named debtor, so that the shareholder can more fully utilize § 1366(d).

[45] See § 465(b)(1).

[46] Prop. Regs. § 1.465–24.

[47] See § 469(h) and especially Regs. § 1.469–5T.

hurdle of § 1366(d), B must then confront the passive loss limitation of § 469. The $10,000 loss can only be deducted to the extent B has at least $10,000 of income from passive activities. B will not be able to offset earned income or portfolio income with the loss. If B has insufficient passive income to offset, the deduction will be suspended. § 469(b). Note that the bases of B's investment in S Corp. decrease regardless of whether § 469 permits the deduction.

Note as well that § 469(c)(2) defines rental activity as passive notwithstanding the level of a shareholder's participation in the activity. An S corporation engaged in renting thus will be subject to the passive loss limitation. But if a taxpayer "actively participates"—a standard less stringent than material participation—in a rental real estate activity, losses from the activity can be used to offset up to $25,000 of non-passive income.[48] Active participation might include activities such as approving new tenants, deciding on rental terms and approving expenditures.

14.05 Assignment of Income Concerns

(a) Pre-contribution Appreciation and Related Problems.

While the one class of stock rule ensures that an S corporation's income and loss will be allocated among its shareholder's in proportion to ownership interests, it plays havoc with assignment of income concerns. For example, suppose individuals X and Y form XY Corp., an S corporation, with X contributing cash of $10,000 and Y contributing Blackacre with a $6,000 adjusted basis and $10,000 fair market value. If each shareholder receives 10 shares of XY stock in exchange for the contribution, they will each report one-half of the corporation's income, gain, loss, and deductions. Accordingly, if the corporation sells Blackacre for its current value of $10,000 (its only activity), each shareholder will be allocated $2,000 of the resulting $4,000 gain, will report $2,000 of gain on her individual return, and will increase outside basis by the same amount. Thus, by contributing Blackacre to the corporation in anticipation of sale, Y is able to shift half of the gain and tax on Blackacre to X.[49]

Assume that the corporation invests its $20,000 in Whiteacre, and that when Whiteacre increases in value to $30,000, Y sells her shares of stock to Z. Z is acquiring one-half of a corporation now worth $30,000, and assume that Z will pay $15,000 for those shares.

---

[48] See § 469(i). However, the $25,000 amount is reduced by 50 percent of the amount by which the taxpayer's adjusted gross income exceeds $100,000. § 469(i)(3).

[49] In the partnership context, Y would be taxable on the full $4,000 gain under § 704(c).

If Whiteacre is subsequently sold for $30,000, half of the $10,000 gain will be allocated to, and reported by, Z even though no corporate asset has appreciated since Z bought in to the enterprise. The sale of shares from Y to Z did not so much work a shift of income as a doubling: Y was taxed implicitly on her share of the increase in value of Whiteacre when she sold her stock to Z, and Z is taxed again on that increase in value when Whiteacre is sold to a third party and the gain is passed-thru to the shareholders. Of course, this income will adjust Z's stock basis upward from $15,000 to $20,000, so that Z will enjoy an offsetting loss should she sell her stock. But because Y's share of gain from Whiteacre is taxed to Z upon disposition of the property by the corporation and the offsetting loss is deferred until Z sells her shares, Z may suffer a present-value cost: The tax on the gain precedes the tax benefit from the loss.[50]

(b) Family Ownership and § 1366(e).

Suppose Mother forms S Corp., an S corporation, by contributing cash of $10,000 in exchange for 100 shares. As the corporation begins to turn a profit, Mother gives some or all of the shares to her children. Because the corporation's income is taxed to its shareholders, the stock transfer shifts some or all of the corporation's income from Mother to her children. Does this shift run afoul of the assignment of income doctrine?

In general, the answer is no, because income from property can be shifted by a transfer of an undivided interest in the income-producing property.[51] The corporation's profit is just one form of income from property, and transfer of the stock is the transfer of the income-producing property. A transfer of the corporation's stock is, in general, no more abusive than a transfer of the initial $10,000 cash.

But what if the corporation's profit is derived in part from Mother's labor? For example, suppose that S Corp. is in the business of accounting, and it provides accounting services to its customer by hiring Mother, a public accountant. If Mother is paid less for her efforts than a reasonable salary, much of the value of Mother's services will be reported as corporate profit and will be passed thru and taxed to the children. In those circumstances, the Service may reallocate some of the corporation's income back to Mother to more accurately reflect her contribution to the enterprise. § 1366(e).

---

[50] In the partnership context, this timing problem could be avoided by the partnership filing an election under § 754 so that Z's purchase of Y's interest in the venture would trigger an optional basis adjustment under § 743(b).

[51] See, e.g., *Blair v. Commissioner*, 300 U.S. 579 (1941).

Indeed, if Mother has transferred all of her shares so that she is no longer a shareholder, the Service may still allocate some of the corporation's profit directly to Mother to approximate a fair salary for her services.

Under § 1366(e) and its associated regulations, the Service may reallocate income from an S corporation to an individual (or a pass-through entity in which the individual owns an interest) if (i) the individual or entity provides services or capital to the S corporation, (ii) the individual is a member of the family of one or more S corporation shareholders and (iii) the individual or entity fails to receive reasonable compensation for the services or capital provided.[52] In making this reallocation, the Service takes into account all facts and circumstances, including the arms-length price for the capital or services. *Id.* Section 1366(e) is similar to, but broader than, § 704(e)(2), a section targeted at family partnerships.[53]

14.06 Section 338(h)(10)

Suppose that P Corp., a C corporation, is interested in acquiring the business conducted by T Corp., an S corporation. Among other alternatives, the acquisition can be structured as a purchase of the T assets, followed by a liquidation of T Corp., or as a purchase of the T stock. Will these two similar transactions produce identical tax results?

If P Corp. purchases the assets directly, P Corp. will take a cost basis in the assets. T Corp. will recognize gain and loss on the sale, with the character and amount of the gain and loss dependent on T Corp.'s adjusted basis in each asset and the character of each asset in its hands. This gain and loss will pass thru to the T shareholders, and they will adjust their T stock basis accordingly. § 1366; § 1367. If T Corp. then distributes the cash proceeds to the shareholders in a complete liquidation, a shareholder will recognize gain or loss to the extent that the cash distributed is greater or less than her stock basis, as adjusted for the sale of assets. § 331.

If P Corp. purchases the T stock from the shareholders, each the shareholder' will recognize gain or loss on the stock sale, which will equal her net gain or loss in the prior transaction (*i.e.*, the pass-thru gain or loss from the asset sale and the gain or loss recognized

---

[52] Although § 1366(e) refers only to allocations to family members, the regulations extend the application of the statute to cover a pass-thru entity in which the individual holds an interest. Regs. § 1.1366-3(a) (adding that a shareholder's family includes only her spouse, ancestors, lineal descendants, and any trust for the primary benefit of any of those persons).

[53] For example, § 1366(e) does not depend on whether shares were transferred between family members, and it allows allocations of income to non-shareholders, including certain passthrough entities.

on the liquidation). Indeed, the only difference should be in the character of that gain or loss because, in the first transaction some of the gain or loss arises from disposition of the corporation's assets, while in the second transaction all of the gain or loss arises from the sale of the stock.

While the shareholder-level taxation of the two transactions is similar, the corporate-level tax consequences differ greatly: If P Corp. purchases the T stock, T Corp. retains its historic asset bases.[54] To be sure, P Corp. can take a cost basis in the T assets by purchasing them directly, but for a variety of business reasons, a stock acquisition may be more advantageous. For example, the T assets might include favorable leases that cannot be transferred or the assets might be encumbered by indebtedness that includes a due-on-sale provision.

Regulations promulgated under § 338(h)(10) respond to this problem by permitting the shareholders of an S corporation to elect to treat the sale of their stock as the sale of the corporation's assets followed by a liquidation of the corporation.[55] That is, the regulations permit a transaction cast in the second form described above to be taxed like it had been cast in the first form. This characterization offers significant tax advantages to the corporate purchaser, and presumably such a purchaser will be willing to pay more for the stock if such an election is made.

A § 338(h)(10) election is filed jointly by the purchaser and selling shareholders and can be made only if the purchaser is a corporation that makes a "qualified stock purchase" of the S corporation's stock. Broadly speaking, a "qualified stock purchase" is the acquisition of 80% or more of both the total voting power and value of the S corporation's stock in a transaction fully taxable to the selling shareholders.[56] Further, for this acquisition to qualify for a § 338(h)(10) election, that 80-percent interest in target stock must be acquired all on one day and on the immediately preceding day, the target must have been an S corporation.[57]

---

[54] In addition, T Corp.'s election to be treated as an S corporation terminates because the corporation now has an impermissible shareholder. See § 1361(b)(1)(B); § 1362(d)(2). As a result, the former S corporation becomes a C corporation; the consequences of such a transition are discussed more fully in Chapter 15.

[55] See Regs. § 1.338(h)(10)–1, especially Regs. § 1.338(h)(10)–1(e) (example 10).

[56] See § 338(d)(3); § 338(h)(3).

[57] Regs. § 1.338(h)(10)-1(b)(4) and (5) (providing in relevant part that the target must be an S corporation immediately before the acquisition date).

If a valid § 338(h)(10) election is made, the target S corporation is deemed to sell its assets, recognizing gain or loss, and it then takes a cost basis in those assets.[58] Note that if the S corporation was once a C corporation, the deemed sale can trigger the tax on built-in gains under § 1374.[59] The deemed sale gain or loss is allocated to each target shareholder, who adjusts her stock basis to account for the gain or loss.[60] Then, on the deemed liquidation, the shareholder recognizes gain or loss, measured by the difference between the sales proceeds received and her adjusted basis in the S corporation stock.[61] If an S shareholder does not sell her target stock, she is still deemed to receive a liquidating distribution, recognizing gain or loss, and then deemed to buy back that stock on the day after the acquisition date for its fair market value.[62]

14.07 Employment Taxes

Wages paid to an S corporation shareholder are subject to withholding Social Security, and unemployment taxes.[63] However, income that passes thru to a shareholder, unless recharacterized, is not subject to withholding and those taxes. In contrast, a general partner is subject to self-employment tax on her distributive share of a partnership's trade or business income.[64]

---

[58] See generally § 338(a) and (b). See also Regs. § 1.338-4; Regs. § 1.338-5; Regs. § 1.338-6. Note that § 338 elections are discussed in more detail in Chapter 9 *supra*.

[59] See Chapter 15.01(b) *infra*.

[60] § 1367. See also Regs. § 1.338(h)(10)-1(d)(3)(i).

[61] § 331. See also Regs. § 1.338(h)(10)-1(d)(5)(i). Note that a shareholder may report this gain on the installment method if she sold her stock for an installment obligation of the purchasing corporation. Regs. § 1.338(h)(10)–1(d)(8). Note as well that the shareholder does not recognize gain or loss on the sale of target stock in the qualified stock purchase, since all relevant gain or loss is accounted for in the deemed liquidation. *Id.* at (d)(5)(iii).

[62] *Id.* at (d)(5)(i); *id.* at (d)(5)(ii) (providing that the price deemed paid is pegged to the price paid for the purchased stock).

[63] Rev. Rul. 73-361, 1973-2 C.B. 331.

[64] See § 1401(a). Cf. § 1401(a)(13) (excepting limited partners from this rule except for guaranteed payments for services to or on behalf of the partnership). See also Prop. Regs. § 1.1402-2(h)(2) (excluding as a limited partner, among others, a person who participates in the partnership's trade or business for more than 500 hours during the partnership's taxable year).

Chapter 15

S CORPORATIONS—TRANSITION ISSUES

15.01 From C Corporation to S Corporation

An existing C corporation may elect S corporation status so long as it is a small business corporation (*i.e.*, it satisfies the requirements set forth in § 1361(b) relating to the maximum number of shareholders (100), maximum number of classes of shares outstanding (one), and so on). That election will be effective for the corporation's next taxable year, except that the election will be effective for the current taxable year if it is filed within the first 2½ months of the year.[1] Once the election is effective, the corporation is subject to Subchapter S and is taxed as described previously. However, because the corporation has a C corporation history, it is also subject to some special Subchapter S rules to transition from C corporation to S corporation status.

(a) Shareholder Taxation of Distributions.

In general, profits earned by a C corporation are taxed twice, once when earned by the corporation and a second time when distributed to the corporation's shareholders. However, not all distributions from a C corporation to its shareholders are taxable dividends: Distributions exceeding the corporation's earnings and profits are treated as a non-taxable recovery of the shareholder's stock basis, with any excess taxed as gain from the sale or exchange of shares of stock. § 301(c). Every C corporation must maintain an "earnings and profits" account, and distributions are taxed as dividends only to the extent of this account.

In contrast, the earnings of an S corporation are typically taxed only once. If the S corporation has no accumulated earnings and profits (even if it was previously a C corporation), its distributions are taxed to its shareholders under § 1368(b). Under this provision, the distribution is first a tax-free recovery of the shareholder's stock basis, with any excess treated as gain from the sale or exchange of stock.

---

[1] § 1362(b)(2). The election is treated as made for the subsequent taxable year if (i) the corporation did not qualify as a small business corporation during the taxable year before the election is made or (ii) one or more persons who were shareholders during the taxable year but before the election date did not consent to the election. *Id.*

When an existing C corporation with a positive earnings and profits account elects S corporation status, the following seems intuitive: Distributions of post-election earnings should be passed thru tax-free to the shareholders, while distributions out of pre-election earnings and profits should be treated as dividends under the Subchapter C regime. What is less than intuitive, however, is when a distribution should be treated as paid out of pre- or post-election earnings.

Section 1368(c) adopts a pro-taxpayer rule: In general, distributions are assumed to be paid out of post-election earnings to the extent of such earnings; only after all post-election earnings have been exhausted are distributions treated as coming from pre-election earnings and profits. To keep track of the corporation's post-election earnings, the statute defines an "accumulated adjustments" account (often called the "AA" account or simply the "AAA"), an account that must be maintained by each S corporation with accumulated earnings and profits (*i.e.*, positive C corporation earnings and profits). See § 1368(e)(1). This AA account reflects, with one modification, the corporation's post-election undistributed earnings.

More precisely, if an S corporation has accumulated earnings and profits, distributions are taxed to its shareholder under § 1368(c), and that section divides distributions into three tiers:

Tier 1. First, distributions are taxed under § 1368(b) to the extent paid out of the corporation's accumulated adjustments account; that is, the distributions are taxed like distributions made by S corporations without accumulated earnings and profits.[2]

Tier 2. Second, distributions in excess of a corporation's accumulated adjustments account are taxed as dividends to the extent of the corporation's accumulated earnings and profits account.[3]

---

[2] § 1368(c)(1). If the distributions for a year exceed the accumulated adjustments account, the account is allocated proportionately by value among the distributions. Regs. § 1.1368-2(b)(2) (determining distributions by excluding those treated as paid out of earnings and profits under a § 1368(e)(3) election). See also *id.* at (c) (for a special rule if loss property is distributed and the corporation has earnings and profits).

[3] § 1368(c)(2). The S corporation reduces its accumulated earnings and profits to the extent any distribution is considered paid out of that account. See § 312(a); § 1371(c)(3). The S corporation also makes appropriate adjustments to accumulated earnings and profits to account for redemptions, liquidations, reorganizations, and divisions. See § 1371(c)(2); Regs. § 1.1368-2(d)(1)(iii); § 312(n)(7). Otherwise, the S corporation does not adjust its accumulated earnings and profits. § 1371(c)(1).

Tier 3. Third, to the extent distributions exceed *both* the corporation's accumulated adjustments account *and* the corporation's earnings and profits account, distributions are taxed under § 1368(b) (*i.e.*, the same as tier 1 distributions). § 1368(c)(3).

Consider the following example: X Corp. files an S corporation election effective January 1 of year 1. As of that date, X Corp. has accumulated earnings and profits of $10,000. All outstanding shares of X Corp. are owned by J with aggregate stock basis of $12,000. During year 1, X Corp. recognizes $6,000 of taxable income and makes distributions totaling $30,000.

First, the $6,000 of post-election earnings pass thru to shareholder J and increase her stock basis to $18,000. § 1367(a)(1). X Corp. also increases its accumulated adjustments account by $6,000, from $0 to $6,000. Second, of the $30,000 distributed to J, $6,000 is received tax-free under § 1368(c)(1) and § 1368(b) (*i.e.*, under tier 1), reducing her stock basis back to $12,000. Of the remaining $24,000 distributed to J, $10,000 is taxed as a dividend under § 1368(c)(2) (*i.e.*, under tier 2), reducing X Corp.'s earnings and profits to $0 and leaving J's stock basis at $12,000. What's left, $14,000, is taxed under § 1368(c)(3) and § 1368(b) (*i.e.*, under tier 3), so that $12,000 (equal to J's remaining stock basis) is received tax-free and $2,000 is treated as gain from the sale or exchange of her stock. J reduces her stock basis to $0. § 1367(a)(2)(A).

Because of the distribution, X Corp.'s accumulated earnings and profits are $0. Thus, as long as the corporation does not succeed to the accumulated earnings and profits of another C corporation, its shareholders will take subsequent distributions into account under § 1368(b).[4] For example, suppose that X Corp. has $2,000 of taxable income in year 2. That taxable income increases its accumulated adjustments account from $0 to $2,000 (and increases J's basis in her X stock by the same amount). Thus, X Corp. can distribute up to $2,000 to J tax-free.

The accumulated adjustment account is determined in a manner similar to the stock basis adjustments under § 1367 with two exceptions. First, unlike stock basis, the account may be reduced

---

[4] Even though an S corporation has no accumulated earnings and profits, it may still maintain an accumulated adjustments account, because it may succeed to earnings and profits, for example, in a § 381 transaction, such as a tax-free reorganization.

below $0. Second, the account is not adjusted for tax-exempt income (and related expenses).[5]

More specifically, an S corporation's accumulated adjustments account may be reduced below zero because of losses.[6] For example, suppose Y Corp. has earnings and profits of $10,000 and accumulated adjustments of $7,000. If the corporation distributes $5,000 and during the same taxable year has a $6,000 taxable loss, Y Corp. adjusts its accumulated adjustments account for the distribution before the loss. Thus, the distribution is considered in full as a distribution under § 1368(c)(1) (and § 1368(b)), reducing Y Corp.'s accumulated adjustment account by $5,000, from $7,000 to $2,000. Next, to account for the $6,000 loss, the accumulated adjustments account is reduced by the same amount, from $2,000 to negative $4,000. If Y Corp. earns only $3,000 in the following year, the accumulated adjustments account remains negative (*i.e.*, negative $1,000), so again tier 1 is unavailable to shelter distributions. Thus, if Y Corp. distributes $1,000 during that year, its shareholders treat the full $1,000 as a dividend (*i.e.*, a tier 2 distribution out of earnings and profits), even though Y Corp. distributes less than it earns during the year.

Recall that an S corporation's tax-exempt income increases its shareholders' stock bases. § 1367(a)(1). Otherwise, that income would be taxed indirectly when distributed or when its shareholders sold their stock. However, tax-exempt income does not increase an S corporation's accumulated adjustments account. To understand the impact of this rule, consider the following example.

Z Corp. files an S corporation election effective January 1 of year 1. As of that date, Z Corp. has earnings and profits of $5,000. All of the outstanding shares of Z Corp. are owned by individual M with aggregate adjusted basis of $12,000. During year 1, Z Corp. recognizes no taxable income or loss but receives tax-exempt income of $1,000. In addition, Z Corp. distributes $500 to M.

Under § 1367(a)(1)(A), the tax-exempt income increases M's stock basis by $1,000, from $12,000 to $13,000. However, the tax-exempt income does not increase Z Corp.'s accumulated adjustments account, so that account remains at $0. Thus, the entire distribution is taxed under § 1368(c)(2) (*i.e.*, under tier 2) as a

---

[5] § 1368(e)(1)(A); Regs. § 1.1368-2(a)(2) and (3). See also *id.* at (d)(2) (and (3) (for rules that apply when two S corporations combine in an acquisitive reorganization or an S corporation engages in a divisive reorganization); § 1368(e)(1)(C) (for the order in which income, losses, and distributions are taken into account).

[6] Regs. § 1.1368-2(a)(3)(ii).

dividend to M and reduces Z Corp.'s earnings and profits account to $4,500. M's stock basis remains at $13,000.

Do not conclude from this example that the tax-exempt income received by the corporation will be taxed as a dividend when distributed to M. Because of a shareholders stock basis is increased to account for tax-exempt income, that income may be distributed tax-free to the shareholder. See § 1367(a)(2)(A); § 1368(b)(1). However, because the accumulated adjustment account is not increased for tax-exempt income, distributions are considered paid out of the pre- or post-election accounts before being paid out of the tax-exempt income "fund." In other words, the exclusion of tax-exempt income from the accumulated adjustments account essentially provides an ordering rule.

Recall that the effect of the three tiers in § 1368(c) is to provide that distributions are assumed to come first out of the accumulated adjustments account and, once that account is exhausted, out of pre-election earnings and profits. Because post-election tax-exempt income does not increase the corporation's accumulated adjustments account, distributions will be deemed to come out of pre-election earnings and profits before they are assumed to come out of post-election tax-exempt income. Distributions out of post-election tax-exempt income still come out tax-free to the shareholders but under tier 3, rather than under tier 1 as does a distribution of post-election taxable income. That is, distributions out of post-election tax-exempt income get the same treatment to the shareholders as does post-election taxable income, but such distributions are deemed to be made last, after the accumulated adjustments account and the earnings and profits account are depleted. Because post-election tax-exempt income does not increase the corporation's earnings and profits account, its distribution will not result in additional dividend income.

If the shareholders of an S corporation having accumulated earnings and profits so elect, the ordering rule of § 1368(c)(1)-(2) can be reversed, so that distributions are treated as paid out of earnings and profits before the accumulated adjustments account.[7] This election is made on an annual basis and requires the consent of all shareholders receiving a distribution during the year. § 1368(e)(3). Because the effect of such an election is to accelerate dividend income to the shareholders, it rarely is made. However, certain disabilities sometimes are imposed on an S corporation that has accumulated earnings and profits, and these disabilities may be avoided

---

[7] With this election, a shareholder would treat a distribution first as a dividend and then as a non-taxable recovery of the stock basis, with any excess taxed as gain from the sale or exchange of stock. Cf. § 301(c).

by depleting the corporation's earnings and profits, something that the election may accelerate. These disabilities are discussed below.

(b) Corporate-Level Tax on Built-In Gains.

Suppose a C corporation owns substantially appreciated property. If this corporation sells the property, it will recognize gain, and if it distributes the proceeds, the shareholders will have dividend income. Thus, two taxes may be owed: one on the corporate-level gain and a second on the shareholder-level dividend income, a double tax that is an essential feature of the C corporation regime. If the corporation sells the property and then files an S corporation election, both taxes still may be incurred: the first as a C corporation and the second upon eventual distribution because of § 1368(c)(2). But suppose the corporation files an S corporation election before selling the property. As long as the election is effective *before* the sale of the property, the corporation's gain will not increase its accumulated earnings and profits account because the gain will be recognized *after* the corporation's earnings and profits account is closed by the election.

To inhibit corporations from electing S corporation status to avoid the double tax on appreciated property, Congress enacted § 1374.[8] This section, which applies each year during the "recognition period," imposes an annual tax equal to the corporation's "net recognized built-in gain" for the year times the highest corporate income tax rate (currently 35%).[9] This tax can be understood only by working though the definitions in § 1374(d).

---

[8] Note, however, that § 1374 may treat the shareholders of a corporation that converts to S status more severely than shareholders of a similar C corporation. If § 1374 applies to an S corporation's built-in gain, that gain is subject to a corporate-level and an immediate shareholder-level tax. In contrast, a C corporation's gain is subject to a corporate-level tax but may be subject to a shareholder-level tax only when an amount reflecting the gain is distributed (or the shareholder sells her stock). Thus, the C corporation shareholders may defer their direct tax on the corporation's gain.

[9] The "recognition period' is generally the 10-year period beginning with the first day of the corporation's existence as an S corporation. § 1374(d)(7)(A). That period is shortened to five years, however, if that first day occurs in a taxable year beginning in 2012 or 2013..*Id.* at (d)(7)(C); see *id.* at (d)(7)(B) (possibly limiting this tax on net recognized built-in gain for an S corporation for any taxable year of the S corporation beginning in 2009, 2010, or 2011). See also § 1374(d)(8)(A) (providing that if an S corporation acquires an asset and determines its basis in the asset by reference to a C corporation's basis in that asset (or any other property), applying § 1374 to net recognized built-in gain attributable to any such assets); Regs. § 1.1374-8(e) (example 1) (illustrating a case where a C corporation merges into an S corporation in an A reorganization); § 1374(d)(8)(B)(i) (providing that the recognition period for a "§ 1374(d)(8)" asset begins when the asset is acquired).

A corporation has recognized built-in gain only if it has net unrealized built-in gain. Its "net unrealized built-in gain" equals the excess, if any, of the fair market value of its assets over their aggregate adjusted basis, determined as of the effective date of the S election.[10] "Net unrealized built-in gain" is fixed in amount once the election becomes effective and need not be recomputed each year.

If the corporation sells or exchanges an asset that it held when its S corporation election became effective, it may realize and recognize unrealized built-in gain or loss. During each year of the recognition period, the corporation computes the excess, if any, of its recognized built-in gains for the year over its recognized built-in losses, and this excess is called its "net recognized built-in gain." As you might expect, post-election appreciation does not contribute to the computation of "built-in gain,"[11] and post-election reduction in value does not add to "built-in loss."[12] These amounts, adjusted for certain items of income and deduction, are then netted to form the corporation's "net recognized built-in gain" for the year. As a limitation, however, net recognized built-in gain for a year cannot exceed the excess of the net unrealized built-in gain over the net recognized built-in gain taken into account in prior years.[13]

The § 1374 tax is then imposed on the net recognized built-in gain or, if less, the corporation's total taxable income for the year.[14] The taxable income limitation should come into play only if the corporation recognizes a net loss for the year, excluding recognized built-in gains and losses.[15] Note that if the taxable income limitation applies, any amount that escapes the § 1374 tax because of the limitation is treated as recognized built-in gain the next year.[16] Thus, all of the corporation's net unrealized built-in gain

---

[10] § 1374(d)(1).

[11] See § 1374(d)(3).

[12] See § 1374(d)(4).

[13] See also Regs. § 1.1374-4(h) (providing special rules to take installment gain into account); *id.* at (i) (providing special rules to account for partnership interests).

[14] For this purpose, a corporation's taxable income is computed under § 63(a) but without allowance for any net operating loss deduction in § 172 and without taking into account the deductions in § 241-§ 249 (other than § 248, the deduction for organizational expenditures). § 1374(d)(2)(A)(ii) (incorporating the definition of taxable income found in § 1375(b)(1)(B)). Note in computing this tax, the S corporation may use unexpired loss and credit carryovers from C years. § 1374(b)(2) and (3). Note as well that the tax on net recognized built-in gain may be limited for any taxable year of the S corporation beginning in 2009, 2010, or 2011. § 1374(d)(7)(B).

[15] Thus, a corporation may reduce its taxable income by paying additional "reasonable" salary and bonuses. See § 162(a)(1).

[16] See § 1374(d)(2)(B).

should eventually be subject to the § 1374 tax, unless the corporation holds the "built-in gain" property for more than 10 years after its S corporation election becomes effective.

If an S corporation is subject to the § 1374 tax on built-in gains, the tax is treated as a loss of the corporation for the year in which the tax is imposed. § 1366(f)(2). As a result, the amount of the tax is passed thru to the corporation's shareholders like any other corporate loss, with the character of the loss determined by reference to the built-in gains upon which the § 1374 tax was imposed. *Id.*

(c) Recapture of LIFO Benefits.

Many taxpayers find it advantageous to account for inventory on a last-in, first-out ("LIFO") basis, an accounting convention generally permitted by the Code. See generally § 472. However, upon the conversion of a C corporation using LIFO status to an S corporation, an immediate tax is imposed on the net benefit obtained by using LIFO accounting as compared with the more conservative first-in, first out accounting. § 1363(d)(1). While this additional tax can be paid over four years, § 1363(d)(2), the tax burden it imposes can be so large as to eliminate the conversion as a viable option.

(d) Disabilities Associated with Passive Investment Income.

Consider a C corporation with substantial earnings and profits when its S corporation election becomes effective. Under the general ordering rule of § 1368(c), the shareholder-level tax on those earnings will be deferred until all post-election taxable income has been distributed. Congress apparently feels that this deferral is inappropriate if the corporation amounts to no more than an incorporated pocketbook. Stated more directly, if the corporation has too much passive investment income, it will be subject to a special corporate-level tax and can even lose its status as an S corporation. However, because these penalties apply only to S corporations having accumulated earnings and profits, they can be avoided by distributing out the earnings and profits before or after the S election is effective.

Of course, if an S corporation retains earnings and profits, the penalties may apply until those earnings and profits are fully distributed. To expedite distributions of its earnings and profits, an S corporation may elect under § 1368(e)(3) to treat its distributions as coming first out of its earnings and profits, rather than its accumulated adjustments account.

(i) Corporate tax on excessive passive income. Section 1375 imposes a tax on an S corporation with accumulated earnings and profits if its "net passive income" exceeds 25% of its gross receipts for the year. That tax equals the highest corporate tax rate (currently 35%) multiplied by the following fraction (an amount the Code labels "excess net passive income"):

$$\frac{\text{excess passive investment income} \ \times \ \text{net passive income}}{\text{passive investment income}}$$

§ 1375(a); Regs. § 1.1375-1(a). See also *id.* at (c) (providing that this tax generally cannot be offset by credits).[17] Any § 1375 tax reduces the amount of the corporation's passive investment income passed thru to the corporation's shareholders. § 1366(f)(3).

For this purpose, a corporation's *excess passive investment income* equals the excess of its *passive investment income* over 25% of its *gross receipts* for the year. Generally, *passive investment income* includes rents, royalties, dividends, interest, and annuities.[18] Further, *gross receipts* generally include the total amount that the corporation receives or accrues under its method of accounting, unreduced by returns, costs of goods sold, and deductions.[19] Finally, *net passive income* is *passive investment income* less deductions directly connected with the production of that income.[20]

Consider the following example: Z Corp. is an S corporation with accumulated earnings and profits. During the current taxable year, the corporation has passive investment income of $50,000, deductions directly connected with the production of that income of $10,000, and total gross receipts of $80,000.[21]

---

[17] Note, however, that the corporation's excess net passive income under § 1375 cannot exceed the corporation's taxable income. For this purpose, the corporation's taxable income is computed under § 63(a) but without allowance for any net operating loss deduction under § 172 and without taking into account the deductions in § 241-§ 249 (other than § 248, the deduction for organizational expenditures). § 1375(b)(1)(B).

[18] See generally § 1362(d)(2)(3)(C); Regs. § 1.1362-2(c)(5). Note that passive investment income excludes any recognized built-in gain or loss taken into account by the S corporation under § 1374 for any taxable year during the recognition period. § 1375(b)(4).

[19] Regs. § 1.1362-2(c)(4)(i). However, gross receipts include only capital gain net income from the disposition of capital assets (other than stocks and securities) and only gains (not losses) from sales or exchanges of stocks or securities. § 1362(d)(3)(B).

[20] A deduction item is directly connected with the production of income if it has a "proximate and primary relationship" to the income. Regs. § 1.1375-1(b)(3)(i).

[21] Assume that the corporation has no other deductions. Thus, its taxable income equals $70,000.

Section 1375 imposes a tax on the S corporation, because it has accumulated earnings and profits and its passive investment income ($50,000) exceeds 25% of its gross receipts ($20,000 or $25% of $80,000). Z Corp.'s excess passive investment income equals that excess, or $30,000. Its net passive income equals $40,000, the excess of its passive investment income ($50,000) over the expenses directly connected with the production of that income ($10,000).

Thus, Z Corp.'s excess net passive income equals $24,000, determined as follows: (i) $30,000, its excess passive investment income, multiplied by (ii) $40,000, its net passive income, divided by (iii) $50,000, its passive investment income.[22] Stated as a formula, that amount is—

$$\frac{\$30,000 \ \times \ \$40,000}{\$50,000}$$

The tax under § 1375 is then imposed on this amount at the highest corporate income tax rate (currently 35%) for a total tax of $8,400.

Unlike the § 1374 tax on built-in gains, this tax is not imposed unless the corporation has accumulated earnings and profits. Suppose that the shareholders of an S corporation believe that their corporation lacks accumulated earnings and profits and they allow the corporation to invest most or all of its funds in passive-income producing assets. If the Service then audits the corporation for a C corporation year and the audit yields even one dollar of accumulated earnings and profits, the corporation may now be subject to the § 1375 tax. To be sure, had the corporation known of the additional accumulated earnings and profits, it would have distributed them, but without that knowledge, it now appears trapped.

Section 1375(d) offers a possible remedy. The Service may waive the § 1375 tax if the following two conditions are met. First, the S corporation must have determined in good faith that it had no accumulated earnings and profits. Second, it must distribute the unanticipated accumulated earnings and profits within a "reasonable" time after they are discovered. § 1375(d); Regs. § 1.1375-1(d). Of course, if the corporation has a positive accumulated adjustments account, an election under § 1368(e)(3) may also be necessary.

---

[22] Because the corporation's taxable income is $70,000, the excess net passive income of $30,000 is not limited by the taxable income limitation of § 1375(b)(1)(B).

(ii) Forced termination of S Corporation status. While § 1375 imposes a corporate-level tax on excessive passive investment income received by an S corporation with accumulated earnings and profits, the tax should encourage such a corporation to distribute out its earnings and profits or reduce its passive investment income. However, any corporation willing to pay the § 1375 tax faces possibly an even greater problem. Under § 1362(d)(3), if an S corporation with accumulated earnings and profits has passive investment income exceeding 25% of its gross receipts for three consecutive taxable years, the corporation's election as an S corporation terminates. As with § 1375, "passive investment income" is gross receipts from "royalties,   rents,   dividends,   interest,   and   annuities," § 1362(d)(3)(D)(i), with some exceptions, see § 1362(d)(3)(D)(ii)-(v).

Because the forced termination in § 1362(d)(3) is so easy to avoid, it rarely applies. However, since its impact is so severe, one should be certain to avoid it. As with the corporate-level tax in § 1375, the forced termination under § 1362(d)(3) applies only to corporations with accumulated earnings and profits. Accordingly, S corporations without accumulated earnings and profits may simply ignore § 1362(d)(3), and any other S corporation can make § 1362(d)(3) less likely to apply by electing under § 1368(e)(3) to treat its distributions as coming first out of its accumulated earnings and profits.

(e) No Carryover from C Year to S Year.

If a C corporation incurs capital losses in excess of its capital gains, the excess may not be deducted but instead is carried back or forward to a taxable year or years in which excess capital gains are recognized. § 1211(a); § 1212(a). Similarly, if a C corporation incurs operating deductions in excess of taxable income, the excess is carried backward or forward as a net operating loss deduction. *See* § 172. However, in no event may an excess capital loss, a net operating loss, or any other carryover be carried from a year in which a corporation is a C corporation to a year in which the corporation is an S corporation to reduce income allocable to a shareholder. § 1371(b)(1). Cf. § 1374(b)(2) (allowing net operating loss and capital loss carryovers from C corporation years to offset net recognized built-in gain for purposes of § 1374). Note that no carryover of any kind can originate in any year in which the corporation is an S corporation. § 1371(b)(2). As a result, there are no carryovers from S years to C years or from S years to other S years. However, losses allocated to a shareholder but limited by § 1366(d) may be available for the shareholder's use for a short time after the corporation's Subchapter S election terminates. See § 1366(d)(3).

15.02 From S Corporation to C Corporation

A corporation's status as an S corporation can terminate by revocation under § 1362(d)(1), by the corporation failing to meet the standards of § 1361(b), see § 1362(d)(2), or by receipt of excessive passive investment income if the corporation has accumulated earnings and profits, see § 1362(d)(3). Regardless of the method of termination, the results are the same. If the termination is effective on a date other than the last day of the corporation's taxable year, the taxable year is divided into two short taxable years.[23] The first short taxable year ends on the day preceding the date of termination of the S corporation's election, § 1362(e)(1)(A), and the second short taxable year begins on the termination date, § 1362(e)(1)(B). By this mechanism there is no taxable year during which the corporation is sometimes an S corporation and sometimes a C corporation. The two short years together are sometimes referred to as the "S termination year. § 1362(e)(4).

Recall that when a corporation with accumulated earnings and profits becomes an S corporation, distributions out of pre-S corporation earnings and profits are taxed as dividends while distributions out of S corporation earnings are taxed as a return of basis. See § 1368(c). When an S election terminates, a similar issue arises because distribution of pre-termination earnings should be taxed as basis recovery while post-termination distributions should be taxed as dividends. Unfortunately, the rule is not so simple.

Under § 1371(e)(1), a post-termination distribution on a shareholder's stock may be tax-free up to the smaller of the corporation's accumulated adjustments account and the shareholder's stock basis. However, to qualify for this treatment, the distribution must be paid in cash during the post-termination transition period.[24] Further, the shareholder must reduce her stock

---

[23] § 1361(e)(1). If a corporation's status as an S corporation terminates because it has excessive passive investment income, the termination is necessarily effective on the first day of the corporation's taxable year. § 1362(d)(3)(A)(ii). If termination occurs because the corporation's shareholders revoke its S status or because the corporation ceases to be a small business corporation, the termination need not be effective on the first day of the corporation's taxable year. § 1362(d)(1)(D); § 1362(d)(2)(B).

[24] § 1371(e)(1). The "post-termination transition period" begins on the first day that the corporation is no longer an S corporation and ends at the later of (i) one year after that date or (ii) the due date for the federal income tax return (including extensions) for the corporation's final taxable year as an S corporation. § 1377(b)(1). See also *id.* at (b)(1)(B) (including in the post-termination transition period the 120-day period beginning on the date of any audit determination that follows the termination but adjusts an item of income, loss, or deduction for the corporation while it had S status); *id.* at (b)(1)(C) (also including the 120-day period beginning on the date of a determination that the corporation's S election had terminated for a previous taxable year). See also *id.* at (b)(2) (defining termination).

basis by the amount of this tax-free distribution. *Id.* See also § 1371(e)(2) (for an election to not apply § 1371(e)(1)). All other distributions are taxed under § 301, the section generally applicable to distributions from C corporations. Thus, distributions made after the close of the post-termination transition period are subject to § 301 even if the corporation's accumulated adjustments account has not been fully depleted.

Note that post-termination gains and losses will not affect the corporation's accumulated adjustments account. In addition, post-termination distributions of non-cash property are taxed under § 301 even if the property was acquired or appreciated while the corporation was an S corporation. § 1371(e)(1). Accordingly, if a corporation is contemplating changing from an S corporation to a C corporation, it may make sense to distribute the property before the change if that property is likely to be sold in the near future.

Finally, recall that tax-exempt income of an S corporation does not add to its accumulated adjustments account. § 1368(e)(1)(A). When a C corporation transitions to an S corporation, this peculiarity affects the order in which corporate distributions are deemed to paid be out of accumulated earnings and profits or out of S corporation earnings. When the transition is the other way around, though, the exclusion of tax-exempt income from the corporation's accumulated adjustments account has a more dramatic impact. A post-termination distribution of the tax-exempt income will always be taxed under Subchapter C's § 301. This result occurs because the relief offered by § 1371(e)(1) to post-termination distributions of S earnings extends only to the extent of the corporation's accumulated adjustments account. Because tax-exempt income does not enter the accumulated adjustments account, distributions related to the tax-exempt income are unprotected by § 1371(e)(1).[25]

While the transition from S to C status brings little tax relief, there is one positive aspect. If the corporation had a prior C history, and if there is a surviving net operating loss carryover from that earlier C period, it can be used by the corporation in its reincarnation as a C corporation. While § 1371(b)(1) prohibits carryovers from C years to S years, there is no prohibition on carryovers from C years to C years, even if several S years are sandwiched in between.

---

[25] It may be more precise to say that distributions of earnings and profits occur before any distribution of the tax-exempt income. Because S shareholders increased their S stock bases to account for the tax-exempt income, the distribution of amounts related to that income may result in a non-taxable recovery of basis. See § 1367(a)(1)(A) (for the basis increase); § 301(c)(2) (for the non-taxable basis recovery).

However, those S years count to determine whether the carryover period has expired. § 1371(b)(3).

While S corporation losses generally pass thru to the shareholders, § 1366(d)(1) limits the pass-thru to the extent of a shareholder's stock and debt basis. If a corporation's status as an S corporation terminates, any losses suspended by application of § 1366(d)(1) can be claimed by the affected shareholders in the post-termination transition period, subject to the limitation that such losses cannot exceed their stock basis at that time. § 1366(d)(3). Of course, any losses so claimed must reduce stock basis, § 1366(d)(3)(C), just as they would were Subchapter S applicable in full, see § 1367(a)(2)(B).

TABLE OF CASES

441

INDEX